POETRY
for Students

Advisors

Jayne M. Burton is a teacher of secondary English and an adjunct professor for Northwest Vista College in San Antonio, TX.

Klaudia Janek is the school librarian at the International Academy in Bloomfield Hills, Michigan. She holds an MLIS degree from Wayne State University, a teaching degree from Rio Salado College, and a bachelor of arts degree in international relations from Saint Joseph's College. She is the IB Extended Essay Coordinator and NCA AdvancEd co-chair at her school. She is an IB workshop leader for International Baccalaureate North America, leading teacher training for IB school librarians and extended essay coordinators. She has been happy to serve the Michigan Association for Media in Education as a board member and past president at the regional level, advocating for libraries in Michigan schools.

Greg Bartley is an English teacher in Virginia. He holds an M.A.Ed. in English Education from Wake Forest University and a B.S. in Integrated Language Arts Education from Miami University.

Sarah Clancy teaches IB English at the International Academy in Bloomfield Hills, Michigan. She is a member of the National Council of Teachers of English and Michigan Speech Coaches, Inc. Sarah earned her undergraduate degree from Kalamazoo College and her Master's of Education from Florida Southern College. She coaches the high-ranking forensics team and is the staff adviser of the school newspaper, *Overachiever*.

Karen Dobson is a teen/adult librarian at Plymouth District Library in Plymouth, Michigan. She holds a Bachelor of Science degree from Oakland University and an MLIS from Wayne State University and has served on many committees through the Michigan Library Association.

Tom Shilts is the youth librarian at the Okemos branch of Capital Area District Library in Okemos, Michigan. He holds an MSLS degree from Clarion University of Pennsylvania and an MA in U.S. History from the University of North Dakota.

POETRY
for Students

Presenting Analysis, Context, and Criticism on Commonly Studied Poetry

VOLUME 53

Sara Constantakis, Project Editor

Foreword by David J. Kelly

GALE
CENGAGE Learning·

Farmington Hills, Mich • San Francisco • New York • Waterville, Maine
Meriden, Conn • Mason, Ohio • Chicago

Poetry for Students, Volume 53

Project Editor: Sara Constantakis

Rights Acquisition and Management: Ashley Maynard, Carissa Poweleit

Composition: Evi Abou-El-Seoud

Manufacturing: Rhonda Dover

Imaging: John Watkins

For product information and technology assistance, contact us at
Gale Customer Support, 1-800-877-4253.
For permission to use material from this text or product,
submit all requests online at **www.cengage.com/permissions.**
Further permissions questions can be emailed to
permissionrequest@cengage.com

Gale
27500 Drake Rd.
Farmington Hills, MI, 48331-3535

ISBN-13: 978-1-4103-1449-9
ISSN 1094-7019

This title is also available as an e-book.
ISBN-13: 978-1-4103-1452-9
Contact your Gale, a part of Cengage Learning sales representative for ordering information.

Printed in Mexico
1 2 3 4 5 6 7 20 19 18 17 16

Table of Contents

Just a Few Lines on a Page

I have often thought that poets have the easiest job in the world. A poem, after all, is just a few lines on a page, usually not even extending margin to margin—how long would that take to write, about five minutes? Maybe ten at the most, if you wanted it to rhyme or have a repeating meter. Why, I could start in the morning and produce a book of poetry by dinnertime. But we all know that it isn't that easy. Anyone can come up with enough words, but the poet's job is about writing the *right* ones. The right words will change lives, making people see the world somewhat differently than they saw it just a few minutes earlier. The right words can make a reader who relies on the dictionary for meanings take a greater responsibility for his or her own personal understanding. A poem that is put on the page correctly can bear any amount of analysis, probing, defining, explaining, and interrogating, and something about it will still feel new the next time you read it.

It would be fine with me if I could talk about poetry without using the word "magical," because that word is overused these days to imply "a really good time," often with a certain sweetness about it, and a lot of poetry is neither of these. But if you stop and think about magic—whether it brings to mind sorcery, witchcraft, or bunnies pulled from top hats—it always seems to involve stretching reality to produce a result greater than the sum of its parts and pulling unexpected results out of thin air. This book provides ample cases where a few simple words conjure up whole worlds. We do not actually travel to different times and different cultures, but the poems get into our minds, they find what little we know about the places they are talking about, and then they make that little bit blossom into a bouquet of someone else's life. Poets make us think we are following simple, specific events, but then they leave ideas in our heads that cannot be found on the printed page. Abracadabra.

Sometimes when you finish a poem it doesn't feel as if it has left any supernatural effect on you, like it did not have any more to say beyond the actual words that it used. This happens to everybody, but most often to inexperienced readers: regardless of what is often said about young people's infinite capacity to be amazed, you have to understand what usually does happen, and what could have happened instead, if you are going to be moved by what someone has accomplished. In those cases in which you finish a poem with a "So what?" attitude, the information provided in *Poetry for Students* comes in handy. Readers can feel assured that the poems included here actually are potent magic, not just because a few (or a hundred or ten thousand) professors of literature say they are: they're significant because they can withstand close inspection and still amaze the very same people who have just finished taking them apart and seeing how they work. Turn them inside out, and they will still be able to come alive, again and again. *Poetry for Students* gives readers of any age good practice in feeling the ways poems relate to both the reality of the time and place the poet lived in and the reality of our emotions. Practice is just another word for being a student. The information given here helps you understand the way to read poetry; what to look for, what to expect.

With all of this in mind, I really don't think I would actually like to have a poet's job at all. There are too many skills involved, including precision, honesty, taste, courage, linguistics, passion, compassion, and the ability to keep all sorts of people entertained at once. And that is just what they do with one hand, while the other hand pulls some sort of trick that most of us will never fully understand. I can't even pack all that I need for a weekend into one suitcase, so what would be my chances of stuffing so much life into a few lines? With all that *Poetry for Students* tells us about each poem, I am impressed that any poet can finish three or four poems a year. Read the inside stories of these poems, and you won't be able to approach any poem in the same way you did before.

David J. Kelly
College of Lake County

Introduction

Purpose of the Book

The purpose of *Poetry for Students* (*PfS*) is to provide readers with a guide to understanding, enjoying, and studying poems by giving them easy access to information about the work. Part of Gale's "For Students" Literature line, *PfS* is specifically designed to meet the curricular needs of high school and undergraduate college students and their teachers, as well as the interests of general readers and researchers considering specific poems. While each volume contains entries on "classic" poems frequently studied in classrooms, there are also entries containing hard-to-find information on contemporary poems, including works by multicultural, international, and women poets.

The information covered in each entry includes an introduction to the poem and the poem's author; the actual poem text (if possible); a poem summary, to help readers unravel and understand the meaning of the poem; analysis of important themes in the poem; and an explanation of important literary techniques and movements as they are demonstrated in the poem.

In addition to this material, which helps the readers analyze the poem itself, students are also provided with important information on the literary and historical background informing each work. This includes a historical context essay, a box comparing the time or place the poem was written to modern Western culture, a critical overview essay, and excerpts from critical essays on the poem. A unique feature of *PfS* is a specially commissioned critical essay on each poem, targeted toward the student reader.

To further help today's student in studying and enjoying each poem, information on audio recordings and other media adaptations is provided (if available), as well as reading suggestions for works of fiction and nonfiction on similar themes and topics. Classroom aids include ideas for research papers and lists of critical and reference sources that provide additional material on the poem.

Selection Criteria

The titles for each volume of *PfS* are selected by surveying numerous sources on notable literary works and analyzing course curricula for various schools, school districts, and states. Some of the sources surveyed include: high school and undergraduate literature anthologies and textbooks; lists of award-winners, and recommended titles, including the Young Adult Library Services Association (YALSA) list of best books for young adults.

Input solicited from our expert advisory board—consisting of educators and librarians—guides us to maintain a mix of "classic" and contemporary literary works, a mix of challenging and engaging works (including genre titles that are commonly studied) appropriate for different age levels, and a mix of international, multicultural and women authors. These advisors also consult on each volume's entry list, advising on which titles are most studied, most appropriate, and meet the broadest interests across secondary (grades 7–12) curricula and undergraduate literature studies.

How Each Entry Is Organized

Each entry, or chapter, in *PfS* focuses on one poem. Each entry heading lists the full name of the poem, the author's name, and the date of the poem's publication. The following elements are contained in each entry:

Introduction: a brief overview of the poem which provides information about its first appearance, its literary standing, any controversies surrounding the work, and major conflicts or themes within the work.

Author Biography: this section includes basic facts about the poet's life, and focuses on events and times in the author's life that inspired the poem in question.

Poem Text: when permission has been granted, the poem is reprinted, allowing for quick reference when reading the explication of the following section.

Poem Summary: a description of the major events in the poem. Summaries are broken down with subheads that indicate the lines being discussed.

Themes: a thorough overview of how the major topics, themes, and issues are addressed within the poem. Each theme discussed appears in a separate subhead.

Style: this section addresses important style elements of the poem, such as form, meter, and rhyme scheme; important literary devices used, such as imagery, foreshadowing, and symbolism; and, if applicable, genres to which the work might have belonged, such as Gothicism or Romanticism. Literary terms are explained within the entry, but can also be found in the Glossary.

Historical Context: this section outlines the social, political, and cultural climate in which the author lived and the poem was created. This section may include descriptions of related historical events, pertinent aspects of daily life in the culture, and the artistic and literary sensibilities of the time in which the work was written. If the poem is a historical work, information regarding the time in which the poem

is set is also included. Each section is broken down with helpful subheads.

Critical Overview: this section provides background on the critical reputation of the poem, including bannings or any other public controversies surrounding the work. For older works, this section includes a history of how the poem was first received and how perceptions of it may have changed over the years; for more recent poems, direct quotes from early reviews may also be included.

Criticism: an essay commissioned by *PfS* which specifically deals with the poem and is written specifically for the student audience, as well as excerpts from previously published criticism on the work (if available).

Sources: an alphabetical list of critical material quoted in the entry, with full bibliographical information.

Further Reading: an alphabetical list of other critical sources which may prove useful for the student. Includes full bibliographical information and a brief annotation.

Suggested Search Terms: a list of search terms and phrases to jumpstart students' further information seeking. Terms include not just titles and author names but also terms and topics related to the historical and literary context of the works.

In addition, each entry contains the following highlighted sections, set apart from the main text as sidebars:

Media Adaptations: if available, a list of audio recordings as well as any film or television adaptations of the poem, including source information.

Topics for Further Study: a list of potential study questions or research topics dealing with the poem. This section includes questions related to other disciplines the student may be studying, such as American history, world history, science, math, government, business, geography, economics, psychology, etc.

Compare & Contrast: an "at-a-glance" comparison of the cultural and historical differences between the author's time and culture and late twentieth century or early twenty-first century Western culture. This box includes pertinent parallels between the major scientific, political, and cultural movements of the time or place the poem was written, the time or place the poem was set (if a historical work), and modern Western culture. Works written after 1990 may not have this box.

What Do I Read Next?: a list of works that might give a reader points of entry into a classic work (e.g., YA or multicultural titles) and/or complement the featured poem or serve as a contrast to it. This includes works by the same author and others, works from various genres, YA works, and works from various cultures and eras.

Other Features

PfS includes "Just a Few Lines on a Page," a foreword by David J. Kelly, an adjunct professor of English, College of Lake County, Illinois. This essay provides a straightforward, unpretentious explanation of why poetry should be marveled at and how *PfS* can help teachers show students how to enrich their own reading experiences.

A Cumulative Author/Title Index lists the authors and titles covered in each volume of the *PfS* series.

A Cumulative Nationality/Ethnicity Index breaks down the authors and titles covered in each volume of the *PfS* series by nationality and ethnicity.

A Subject/Theme Index, specific to each volume, provides easy reference for users who may be studying a particular subject or theme rather than a single work. Significant subjects from events to broad themes are included.

A Cumulative Index of First Lines (beginning in Vol. 10) provides easy reference for users who may be familiar with the first line of a poem but may not remember the actual title.

A Cumulative Index of Last Lines (beginning in Vol. 10) provides easy reference for users who may be familiar with the last line of a poem but may not remember the actual title.

Each entry may include illustrations, including photo of the author and other graphics related to the poem.

Citing Poetry for Students

When writing papers, students who quote directly from any volume of *PfS* may use the following general forms. These examples are based on MLA style; teachers may request that students adhere to a different style, so the following examples may be adapted as needed.

When citing text from *PfS* that is not attributed to a particular author (i.e., the Themes, Style, Historical Context sections, etc.), the following format should be used in the bibliography section:

> "Grace." *Poetry for Students*. Ed. Sara Constantakis. Vol. 44. Detroit: Gale, Cengage Learning, 2013. 66–86. Print.

When quoting the specially commissioned essay from *PfS* (usually the first piece under the "Criticism" subhead), the following format should be used:

> Andersen, Susan. Critical Essay on "Grace." *Poetry for Students*. Ed. Sara Constantakis. Vol. 44. Detroit: Gale, Cengage Learning, 2013. 77–80. Print.

When quoting a journal or newspaper essay that is reprinted in a volume of *PfS,* the following form may be used:

> Molesworth, Charles. "Proving Irony by Compassion: The Poetry of Robert Pinsky." *Hollins Critic* 21.5 (1984): 1–18. Rpt. in *Poetry for Students*. Ed. Sara Constantakis. Vol. 44. Detroit: Gale, Cengage Learning, 2013. 189–92. Print.

When quoting material reprinted from a book that appears in a volume of *PfS,* the following form may be used:

> Flora, Joseph M. "W. E. Henley, Poet." *William Ernest Henley*. New York: Twayne, 1970. 119–41. Rpt. in *Poetry for Students*. Ed. Sara Constantakis. Vol. 43. Detroit: Gale, 213. 150–52. Print.

We Welcome Your Suggestions

The editorial staff of *Poetry for Students* welcomes your comments and ideas. Readers who wish to suggest poems to appear in future volumes, or who have other suggestions, are cordially invited to contact the editor. You may contact the editor via E-mail at: **ForStudentsEditors @cengage.com.** Or write to the editor at:

Editor, *Poetry for Students*

Gale

27500 Drake Road

Farmington Hills, MI 48331-3535

Literary Chronology

1572: John Donne is born in London, England.

1631: John Donne dies of cancer on March 31 in London, England.

1633: John Donne's "Love's Growth" is published in *Poems*.

1830: Emily Dickinson is born on December 10 in Amherst, Massachusetts.

1886: Emily Dickinson dies of Bright's Disease on May 15 in Amherst, Massachusetts.

1891: Emily Dickinson's "I like to see it lap the Miles" is published as "The Railway Train" in *Poems by Emily Dickinson: Second Series*.

1917: Gwendolyn Brooks is born on June 7 in Topeka, Kansas.

1919: Lawrence Ferlinghetti is born on March 24 in Bronxville, New York.

1924: Lisel Mueller is born on February 8 in Hamburg, Germany.

1927: W .S. Merwin is born on September 27 in New York, New York.

1928: Maya Angelou is born on April 4 St. Louis, Missouri.

1930: Gary Snyder is born on May 8 in San Francisco, California.

1934: N. Scott Momaday is born on February 27 in Lawton, Oklahoma.

1934: Kamala Das is born on March 31 in Punnayurkulam, India.

1939: Margaret Atwood is born on November 18 in Ottawa, Ontario.

1945: Gwendolyn Brooks's "Sadie and Maud" is published in *A Street in Bronzeville*.

1950: Gwendolyn Brooks is awarded the Pulitzer Prize for Poetry for *Annie Allen*.

1951: Lesley Choyce is born on March 21 in New Jersey.

1952: Alberto Ríos is born on September 18 in Nogales, Arizona.

1965: Kamala Das's "Punishment in Kindergarten" is published in *Summer in Calcutta*.

1965: Deborah Garrison is born on February 12 in Ann Arbor, Michigan.

1966: Margaret Atwood's "Speeches for Dr Frankenstein" is published in *The Animals in That Country*.

1968: Major Jackson is born on September 9 in Philadelphia, Pennsylvania.

1969: N. Scott Momaday is awarded the Pulitzer Prize for Fiction for *House Made of Dawn*.

1971: W. S. Merwin is awarded the Pulitzer Prize for Poetry for *The Carrier of Ladders*.

1975: Maya Angelou's "Alone" is published in *Oh Pray My Wings Are Gonna Fit Me Well*.

1975: Lisel Mueller's "Alive Together" is published in *The Private Life*.

1975: Gary Snyder is awarded the Pulitzer Prize for Poetry for *Turtle Island*.

1980: Tarfia Faizullah is born in Brooklyn, New York.

1981: Lisel Mueller is awarded the National Book Award for Poetry for The Need to Hold Still.

1983: W. S. Merwin's "Yesterday" is published in *Opening the Hand*.

1983: Gary Snyder's "Axe Handles;rdquo; is published in *Axe Handles*.

1992: N. Scott Momaday's "The Delight Song of Tsoai-talee" is published in *In the Presence of the Sun: Stories and Poems, 1961–1991*.

1997: Lisel Mueller is awarded the Pulitzer Prize for Poetry for Alive Together: New and Selected Poems.

1998: Lesley Choyce's "I'm Alive, I Believe in Everything" is published in *Beautiful Sadness*.

1998: Deborah Garrison's "Please Fire Me" is published in *A Working Girl Can't Win and Other Poems*.

2000: Margaret Atwood is awarded the Booker Prize for *The Blind Assassin*.

2000: Gwendolyn Brooks dies of cancer on December 3 in Chicago, Illinois.

2001: Lawrence Ferlinghetti's "The Changing Light" is published in *How To Paint Sunlight: Lyric Poems & Others, 1997–2000*.

2005: Major Jackson's "Urban Renewal: XVIII" is published in *TriQuarterly*. It is published in *Hoops* in 2006.

2005: Alberto Ríos's "The Pomegranate and the Big Crowd" is published in *The Theater of Night*.

2009: Kamala Das dies on May 31 in Pune, India.

2009: W. S. Merwin is awarded the Pulitzer Prize for Poetry for *The Shadow of Sirius*.

2010: Tarfia Faizullah's "En Route to Bangladesh, Another Crisis of Faith" is published in *Missouri Review*. It is published in *Seam* in 2014.

2014: Maya Angelou dies of natural causes on May 28 Winston-Salem, North Carolina.

Acknowledgements

The editors wish to thank the copyright holders of the excerpted criticism included in this volume and the permission managers of many book and magazine publishing companies for assisting us in securing reproduction rights. We are also grateful to the staffs of the Detroit Public Library, the Library of Congress, the University of Detroit Mercy Library, Wayne State University Purdy/Kresge Library Complex, and the University of Michigan Libraries for making their resources available to us. Following is a list of the copyright holders who have granted us permission to reproduce material in this volume of *PfS*. Every effort has been made to trace copyright, but if omissions have been made, please let us know.

COPYRIGHTED EXCERPTS IN *PfS*, VOLUME 53, WERE REPRODUCED FROM THE FOLLOWING PERIODICALS:

America, April 25, 1998. © 1998 Edward J. Ingebretsen.— *Booklist*, October 15, 1996. ©1996 *Booklist.*— *British Journal of Canadian Studies*, 2004. ©2004 *British Journal of Canadian Studies.*— *Canadian Literature*, No. 187, 2005. ©2005 *Canadian Literature.*— *Canadian Literature*, No. 208, 2011. ©2011 *Canadian Literature.*— *Canadian Literature*, No. 213, 2012. ©2012 *Canadian Literature.*— *Christian Century*, Vol. 119, No. 13, June 19, 2002. ©2002 Christian Century Foundation.— *Contemporary Literature 11.1*, 1970. ©1970 The University of Wisconsin Press.— *ForeWord*, October 20, 2011. ©2011 Nancy E. Walker.— *The*

Hollins Critic, February 2015. ©2015 *The Hollins Critic.*— *The Hudson Review*, 2011. ©2011 *The Hudson Review.*— *Knot Magazine*, 2015. ©2015 *Knot Magazine.*— *Library Journal*, Vol. 132, No. 8, May 1, 2007. ©2007 American Library Association.— *MELUS*, Vol. 35 Issue 2, 2010. ©2010 Oxford University Press.— *Ploughshares*, Issue 120, 2013. ©2013 *Ploughshares.*— *Poetry Nation Review*, 1998. ©1998 *Poetry Nation Review.*— *Poetry Nation Review*, July/August 2008. ©2008 *Poetry Nation Review.*— *Prairie Schooner*, Vol. 88, No. 3, 2014. ©2014 *Prairie Schooner.*— *Publishers Weekly*, Vol. 243, No. 44, October, 28, 1996. ©1996 *Publishers Weekly.*— *Publishers Weekly*, Vol. 248, No. 11, March 12, 2001. ©2001 *Publishers Weekly.*— *Publishers Weekly*, Vol. 249, No. 17, April, 29, 2002. ©2002 *Publishers Weekly .*— *Publishers Weekly*, Vol. 252, No. 19, May 9, 2005. ©2005 *Publishers Weekly.*— *World Literature Today*, Vol. 77, No. 2, 2003. ©2003 *World Literature Today.*— *YA Hotline*, 2011. ©2011 *YA Hotline.*

COPYRIGHTED EXCERPTS IN *PfS*, VOLUME 53, WERE REPRODUCED FROM THE FOLLOWING BOOKS:

Gwendolyn Brooks. From *Sadie and Maud*, Brooks Permissions. ©Brooks Permissions. Reprinted by Consent of Brooks Permissions.— Laura Coltelli. From *Winged Words: American Indian Writers Speak*, University of Nebraska Press, 1990. ©1990 University of Nebraska

Press.— Cheri Davis. From ***W.S. Merwin***, Twayne Publishers, 1981. ©1981 Twayne Publishers.— John Donne. From ***The Songs and Sonnets of John Donne***, Harvard University Press, 2009. ©2009 Harvard University Press.— Tafia Faizullah. From ***Seam***, Southern Illinois University Press, 2014. ©2014 Southern Illinois University Press.— Lawrence Ferlinghetti. From ***How to Paint Sunlight***, 2001. ©2001 New Directions Publishing Corporation.— Francis X. Gillen. From ***Margaret Atwood: Vision and Forms***, Southern Illinois University Press, 1988. ©1988 Southern Illinois University Press.— Barbara Hardy. From ***The Advantage of Lyric: Essays on Feeling in Poetry***, The Athlone Press, an imprint of Bloomsbury Publishing Plc., 1977. ©1977 Bloomsbury Publishing Plc.— H.L. Hix. From ***Understanding W.S. Merwin***, University of South Carolina Press, 1997. ©1997 University of South Carolina.— Shirley Geok-lin Lim. From ***De/Colonizing the Subject: The Politics of Gender in Women's Autobiography***, University of Minnesota Press, Oregon State University Press, 1992.

©1992 University of Minnesota.— Eli Mandel. From ***Critical Essays on Margaret Atwood***, G.K. Hall, 1988. ©1988 G.K. Hall.— Patrick D. Murphy. From ***A Place for Wayfaring: The Poetry and Prose of Gary Snyder***, 2000. ©2000 Oregon State University Press.— Anisur Rahman. From ***Marginalized: Indian Poetry in English***, Brill Academic Publishers, 2014. ©2014 Brill Academic Publishers.— David Robertson. From ***Critical Essays on Gary Snyder***, G.K. Hall, 1990. ©1990 G.K. Hall.— Stan Sanvel Rubin. From ***The Post-Confessionals: Conversations with American Poets of the Eighties***, Fairleigh Dickinson University Press, 1989. ©1989 Fairleigh Dickinson University Press.— Donald E. Thackery. From ***Emily Dickinson: A Collection of Critical Essays***, University of Nebraska Press, 1963. ©1963 University of Nebraska Press.— Sharon R. Wilson. From ***Margaret Atwood: Works and Impact***, Camden House, 2000. ©2002 Camden House.— Allistair Wiske. From ***The Beat Generation Writers***, Pluto Press, 1996. ©1998 Pluto Press.

Contributors

Cynthia A. Bily: Bily is an English professor at Macomb Community College in Michigan. Entry on "I like to see it lap the Miles." Original essay on "I like to see it lap the Miles."

Rita M. Brown: Brown is an English professor. Entries on "Sadie and Maud" and "Speeches for Dr Frankenstein." Original essays on "Sadie and Maud" and "Speeches for Dr Frankenstein."

Klay Dyer: Dyer is a freelance writer specializing in topics relating to literature, popular culture, and the relationship between creativity and technology. Entries on "Axe Handles" and "The Changing Light." Original essays on "Axe Handles" and "The Changing Light."

Kristen Sarlin Greenberg: Greenberg is a freelance writer and editor with a background in literature and philosophy. Entries on "The Delight Song of Tsoai-talee" and "Please Fire Me." Original essays on "The Delight Song of Tsoai-talee" and "Please Fire Me."

Michael Allen Holmes: Holmes is a writer with existential interests. Entries on "En Route to Bangladesh, Another Crisis of Faith," "The Pomegranate and the Big Crowd," and "Urban Renewal: XVIII." Original essays on "En Route to Bangladesh, Another Crisis of Faith," "The Pomegranate and the Big Crowd," and "Urban Renewal: XVIII."

David Kelly: Kelly is a college professor in creative writing and literature. Entry on "Yesterday." Original essay on "Yesterday."

Amy L. Miller: Miller is a graduate of the University of Cincinnati, and she currently resides in New Orleans, Louisiana. Entries on "I'm Alive, I Believe in Everything" and "Punishment in Kindergarten." Original essays on "I'm Alive, I Believe in Everything" and "Punishment in Kindergarten."

Jeffrey Eugene Palmer: Palmer is a freelance writer, scholar, and high-school English teacher. Entry on "Alive Together." Original essay on "Alive Together."

April Paris: Paris is a freelance writer with a degree in classical literature and a background in academic writing. Entry on "Alone." Original essay on "Alone."

Bradley Skeen: Skeen is a classicist. Entry on "Love's Growth." Original essay on "Love's Growth."

Alive Together

LISEL MUELLER

1975

"Alive Together" is a poem published in 1975 by the German-born poet Lisel Mueller as part of a collection titled *The Private Life*. In 1996, she selected the poem for inclusion in the Pulitzer Prize–winning volume *Alive Together*, which Mueller claimed was her farewell to the world of poetry.

The single-stanza poem is consistent with the early twentieth-century conception of lyric poetry that emerged with modernist poets like Ezra Pound and T. S. Eliot, favoring simplicity and gravity over constraints of rhyme and elevated language. In a style Mueller attributed equally to her midwestern sensibilities and early exposure to clipped, powerful Germanic words, "Alive Together" is characterized by accessible language and simple sentiments of gratitude, wonder, and love. The relatability of the emotions the poem evokes, however, is balanced by the obscure nature of many of its historical and mythological references. This feature of Mueller's poetry reflects not only her formal education in literature and folklore but also her fascination with the flux of time and the inherent irrationality of chance.

Thematically, the poem is in the tradition of American confessional poets of the preceding decades, who relied heavily upon themes of domesticity and human relationships, as well as Beat poets. "Alive Together" is above all else a poem reflecting Mueller's adoration of her husband, Paul, and the unknowable providence that brought them together against all odds.

Mueller describes the struggles of women throughout history. *(© Oleg Golovnev | Shutterstock.com)*

AUTHOR BIOGRAPHY

Mueller was born on February 8, 1924, into a middle-class Jewish household in Hamburg, Germany, where she spent the first decade of her life in relative comfort with her mother and father, Ilse and Fritz Neumann, and her older sister, Inge. By the middle of the 1930s, however, the Neumanns were prompted by the growing persecution of Jews in Germany to abandon their ancestral home and seek refuge in various locales across southern Europe, such as Italy and France. In 1939, just before the outbreak of the Second World War, the fifteen-year-old Lisel along with her mother and sister joined Fritz in Evansville, Indiana, where he had acquired a professorship at the local university. Although her immediate family was able to escape further persecution at the hands of the Nazis, many of the future poet's relatives, including her grandparents, perished in the death camps.

A transplanted teenager, Mueller wasted no time adapting to the customs of her adopted home and mastering English. After her graduation from high school, Mueller attended the University of Evansville, where her father still held a professorship, before completing her graduate studies in folklore and mythology at Indiana University. Although she had a facility with language and an enduring love of words from an early age, Mueller was a relative latecomer to the poetic craft, initially working as a secretary, social worker, and librarian. It was only with her mother's death in the summer of 1953 that Mueller began her official career as a poet in an attempt to articulate her overwhelming sensations of grief and loss.

Among many honors, Mueller went on to receive the National Book Award for Poetry (1981), the Carl Sandburg Award (1990), a National Endowment for the Arts fellowship (1990), the Pulitzer Prize for Poetry (1997), and the Ruth Lilly Prize (2002). She published twelve volumes and several celebrated larger collections, including the award-winning *The Private Life*

(1975), in which "Alive Together" was initially published. In addition to her poetic endeavors, Mueller also earned recognition as an essayist and translator and brought countless students to poetry while an instructor at Elmhurst College in Illinois and Goddard College in Vermont. Two decades after the release of her first book of poems, Mueller was named Illinois poet laureate for 1987.

Mueller met her husband, Paul, during her undergraduate years at the University of Evansville, and the couple was married for more than fifty years, building a house in Illinois and raising two daughters. Paul died in 2001. Mueller retired from poetry writing after she accepted the 1997 Pulitzer Prize. She experienced rapidly worsening loss of vision, which made writing difficult, and moved from her house in rural Illinois to a retirement community in Chicago.

POEM SUMMARY

The text used for this summary is from *Alive Together: New and Selected Poems*, Louisiana State University Press, 1996, pp. 84–85. Versions of the poem can be found on the following web pages: http://www.poemhunter.com/poem/alive-together/ and http://www.illinois.gov/poetlaureate/Pages/lisel_alive.aspx.

Lines 1–8
"Alive Together" begins with an invocation of providence and its marvelous implications for the life of the poet in particular. The speaker's assertion that she might have lived during any other era with anyone else echoes Ecclesiastes 1:9 with its specific turn of phrase, one of the most often quoted passages in the Bible, and imbues the verse with a sense of divinely ordained timelessness and immutability, the inability to change.

The poetic *I* of the poem imagines herself first as the enigmatic Héloïse d'Argenteuil, a medieval French scholar who was seduced by the renaissance man Peter Abelard and bore him an illegitimate son. Although he later married Heloise in secret, a misunderstanding resulted in Abelard's castration at the vengeful hands of his lover's family. After the traumatic incident, both Abelard and Heloise took religious vows and retreated into lives of celibacy and study. Although she eventually rose to the position of a revered and well-loved abbess, Heloise was initially resistant to her

new way of life and was pressured into the decision by both her family and her former lover.

This evocative example is swiftly followed by another in which the speaker assumes the identity of an unnamed, illicit mistress of a pope in the Renaissance. In an era infamous for its excesses and perversion of religious ideals, it was not uncommon for popes to bear arms into battle, engage in all manner of monetary corruption, and father illegitimate children. This line suggests the boundless hypocrisy of certain men and their age-old mistreatment of their female counterparts.

In the third tragic scenario of this segment, the speaker of the poem becomes a peasant wife deprived of both simple affection and the food necessary to survive. Her one link to a brighter future, her offspring, have died of plague and sealed the fate of her blood line forever.

Lines 8–13
The scene changes halfway through line 8, as the speaker envisions herself as the wife of Tyco Brahe, the famed Danish astronomer who took to wearing a prosthetic nose after he was mutilated in a duel. She sleeps in a comfortless alcove while her husband, consumed by scientific endeavors, peers into the heavens and hungers after knowledge.

The celestial imagery is transferred to the star-spangled American flag, which was first sewn, somewhat apocryphally, by the thrice-married Betsy Ross after a visit from General George Washington, who was prompted by vanity to wear false, wooden teeth.

In both instances, the women, although not blatantly mistreated, are made to seem almost incidental next to the ambitions of their male counterparts. They are mere placeholders in a history written and perpetuated by men.

Lines 14–22
The exemplary persona of Pocahontas, held by popular tradition to be a figure embodying selfless love and the reconciliation of two peoples, is juxtaposed with a nameless woman, presumably a slave, confined against her will to the bed of her master. Her true husband and daughter are lost to what seem arbitrary and drunken transactions. This jarring disparity juxtaposes the idyllic myth of select women through the ages with the tragic realities that countless others face.

The next two scenarios break from the ecclesiastic framework established by the opening lines of the poem to embody elements of older, pre-Christian sacrifice. In the first of these, the speaker imagines herself an offering to some nameless deity demanding human tribute. In the second, she is left to exposure on a desolate cliff, a girl child whose value is outweighed by the expense of maintaining her existence, suggesting the patriarchal culture of China or India. The detail of the child's gender indicates that the sacrifice is practical as well as ritualistic in nature and that a son likely would not have been abandoned to the same cruel fate.

Lines 22–25

The following sentiments, beginning at the bisection of line 22, set themselves apart with one of the first glimmers of optimism and female agency in the poem. Here the speaker is no longer a completely passive victim of fate but proudly envisions herself as Mary Shelley, the famous gothic novelist and purported beauty. As possible love interests, Mueller includes two allusions of dubious origin. The first of these takes the form of a wayward angel and may refer to Shelley's most celebrated literary character, Frankenstein's monster, who is referred to as a demon and calls himself a fallen angel but seems as much confused and emotionally damaged as he does truly evil. Likewise, the friend mentioned in relation to Mary Shelley may refer tongue-in-cheek to the famous indiscretion between the novelist and the poet Percy Bysshe Shelley who was, at their time of their first meeting, married to another woman.

To conclude her long and intriguing list of possible personas, the speaker makes the striking decision to bring the verse full circle to its opening lines and use apostrophe by directly addressing her husband. In so doing she shifts the entire tenor of the poem and directly suggests, for the first time, that she might have been someone other than a woman defined only by her relationship to a man. This departure from the subject matter of the first half of the poem signals a broadening of the significance of chance that is realized fully with the speaker's concluding statements.

Lines 26–32

The poem switches tracks in its concluding lines to address the irrationality of chance, which leads to the speaker's present circumstances with her husband and the endless permutations of what might have been instead. She alludes to the irony of being alive in an age that many believe to be humanity's last. Mueller references both religious beliefs of eschatology, the study of the end of the world, and more academic discussions of impending natural disaster. By reconciling the beliefs of religious sects like the Jehovah's Witnesses and the deductions of university-trained academics, she brings together and aligns elements of religion and rationality previously at odds in the poem. In so doing, Mueller also elevates the potency of chance over any powers of human speculation or faith.

Lines 33–41

This segment begins with mention of the two young daughters shared by the speaker and her husband and the countless combinations of chance that have allowed them to be born at all and partake of life's wonders. This mention is succeeded by an almost overwhelming list of some of the short-lived triumphs and tribulations that characterize fleeting human existence. Pleasant and painful associations are equally balanced with virtues and frailties to create an impression of the totality of experience.

The final word of the poem refers back to chance and seems startlingly out of place in the list of human experiences and emotions that the speaker attributes to her children. It at once serves to underscore a thematic current within the verse, connecting the poem's conclusion back to its beginning, and reminds the reader that there are no certainties in life. Just as the reader is lulled into a false sense of comfort by the familiar associations evoked by the speaker's list of everyday occurrences, the reintroduction of chance reveals the enormity of what is taken for granted and what, in an instant, can be taken away.

THEMES

Chance

Although the word itself occurs only intermittently throughout the poem, *chance* constitutes a thematic undercurrent that informs every historical scenario and personal anecdote Mueller commits to the page. The almost unfathomable dictates of circumstance are consistently weighed against humanity's feeble attempts to predict the future and exercise personal control over a world governed largely by chance. The speaker praises her lot in life, in particular her relationship with her husband, as a wonder but also acknowledges the possibility of far less pleasant scenarios.

TOPICS FOR FURTHER STUDY

- The final lines of "Alive Together" take the form of a list of poignant emotions and experiences that the speaker feels represent a small swath of all-encompassing human existence. With the help of a partner, brainstorm some of your own words that you agree embody the most essential aspects of day-to-day life. These words can be complicated or simple, rooted in emotion or concrete reality, and can carry either pleasant or unpleasant associations. Next, through use of the computer program Wordle, design a visual using your selections, and share your creation and the concepts behind its making with the larger group. Pay special attention to both the similarities and differences between your selections and discuss how this activity is consistent with the poet's preoccupation with interconnectivity.

- Anne Frank was born in Germany at around the same time as Mueller. Frank's story poses a sobering alternative to Mueller's escape from Nazi persecution and subsequent adulthood in the United States. Read Frank's *The Diary of a Young Girl*, and using your own poetic voice but from the perspective of Frank, compose a stanza of verse beginning "I might have been" for insertion into Mueller's poem.

- Keeping your own unique cultural background in mind, identify and research a figure from either folklore or history who you believe represents an archetype of romantic devotion or civic or familial responsibility. Locate an illustration or draw your own rendering of this person, and in a presentation share the reasons behind your selection with the larger group.

- In line 23 of "Alive Together," the speaker transitions from describing the victimhood of various women through the ages to choosing her own identity, that of Mary Shelley. Who would you want to be if an alternative existence were made available to you? Using the poet's introduction to this portion of the poem, write a short essay based on an identity of your choosing. Start with "I would like to think I might have been _____."

- The age-old practice of divination figures largely in Mueller's poem and represents humanity's overwhelming desire to predict and prepare for an unknowable future. In this spirit, concoct a prediction of your own that takes the form of a mystical utterance, scientific thesis, or deeply held conviction. Design a brief presentation using a tool such as PowerPoint that describes your prediction and lays out your source and means of divination.

Toward the middle of the poem, chance assumes an almost antagonistic role characterized by the language of extreme improbability but is redeemed by mention of the speaker's children and all they owe to providence. A mention of chance concludes the poem and allows for ambiguity of interpretation. The placement of the word at the end of a long list of familiar aspects of existence suggests that chance is equally capable of lavishing blessings on individuals and depriving them of all they hold dear.

Poverty

The most striking alternative historical scenarios that the speaker provides in place of her own life are characterized by degrees of poverty and squalor. This is evidenced by such substituted personas as the peasant wife and her tragic existence, the nameless slave woman, the papal whore, and the abandoned girl child. Inherent in these shocking examples is the grim understanding that poverty, then as now, runs rampant and largely unchecked throughout the world.

Mueller references the separation of slave families on the whims of their white masters. *(© Culture Club / Getty Images)*

Instead of sharing a comparatively idyllic existence with her husband and children, the speaker acknowledges, she might just as easily have been one of the countless millions who live and die in obscurity having never known the meaning of luxury or even comfort.

History

Obscure historical references are rife in "Alive Together" and lend the poem a gravity afforded by precedence. The comparison between the speaker's life and the lives of her historically modeled alter egos provides the reader with intriguing exemplars of the complexity of human relationships and their myriad variables. Furthermore, the juxtaposition of the past with the present allows for a cyclical, recurring progression that manages to defy the linear progression of most narratives. Mueller suggests that the element of fate inherent in the poem is not fixed in time but is eternal and that all history is the product of endless permutations of chance. The poet anchors her verse in concrete past events to better illustrate the wonder and strangeness of an ongoing existence that defies all attempts at human understanding.

Love

The uniquely human concept of love acts as a compelling counterbalance to the heedlessness of chance that saturates the poem from its opening to its concluding lines. Through her depiction of various relationships through the ages, the poet suggests that love, imperfect and frequently devastating as it may be, remains one of the few constants in an otherwise uncertain world. By the end of the poem, Mueller's own love for her family emerges as the main impetus behind her musings on the nature of existence and the role of chance in shaping human lives. Her boundless gratitude for those she holds dear, tempered with her wonder at the ultimate improbability of coexistence, anchors the terror of being cast adrift by random circumstance to the bedrock of human emotion.

Misogyny

An element of sexual inequality is quickly revealed in analysis of the poem and acts as a sobering reminder of the unenviable condition of countless women throughout history and their mistreatment at the hands of men. This thematic undercurrent exists in the description of various historical relationships, both specific and broadly generalized, and in Mueller's inclusion of ancient sacrificial rites. Many of Mueller's unfortunate alter egos are distastefully objectified through such descriptions as the *mistress* of Abelard and the pope's *whore*, denied names, individual identity, and any degree of personal agency. This is evidenced especially by the horrifically commodified slave woman without a name whose true family is bought and sold away from her at the will of heedless masters.

Sacrifice

The subservience implicit in Mueller's descriptions of objectified, commodified women subject to abusive relationships is deepened by the poem's parallel theme of sacrifice. Although killed at the behest of a cruel god or a biased culture rather than a man, the two sacrificial victims present in "Alive Together" are equal victims of societies encouraging such rites and practices. The use of the descriptor *useless* implies that women and girls have been deemed of less importance than their male counterparts in many cultures of the ancient and modern worlds. Sacrifice, Mueller suggests, is sometimes merely the enshrinement of human ignorance in purported spiritual validity.

STYLE

Apostrophe

Mueller uses the poetic technique of *apostrophe*, the direct address of an abstraction, inanimate entity, or offstage presence, at several points throughout the poem. She does so through her use of the second-person pronoun *you* to denote her husband. Within the context of "Alive Together," this device serves various functions, including personalizing the poem, allowing readers to better align themselves with the perspective of the speaker, and providing further insight into an implied but absent presence.

Archetype

The poet makes ample use of archetypes, widely recognized embodiments of certain virtues or realities, to model alternative examples of relationships compared with her own happy marriage. The inclusion of famous names like Pocahontas and Mary Shelley offsets the equally numerous nameless personas that exist within the poem. This device also brings into question the divide between the factual and fictional elements that make up human history.

Folklore

The numerous historical references in "Alive Together" are offset by a pervasive element of strangeness, unreality, and folklore. Mentions of astronomy, eschatology, blood sacrifice, and national myth contribute to the ultimate improbability of human existence. This harmonious coexistence of fact and fiction pays homage to the unfathomable nature of chance on the stylistic and thematic levels.

Motif

Although the poet uses a colorful array of historical and mythical anecdotes to illustrate the complexity and wonder of chance, certain *motifs*, that is, distinctive literary themes or symbols, predominate in "Alive Together." Perhaps the most prevalent and striking of these is the image of the suffering woman who is neglected or commodified by an abusive male partner or even sacrificed, as in the case of the unwanted girl child, to appease the will of an unequal society. A close second to the motif of the suffering woman may be examples of human attempts at divination that run the gamut from rational to religious to mystical. Whether taking the form of a pronouncement from a university academic or fervent Jehovah's Witness or a celestial prediction made by an early astrologer, the motif of attempts to see beyond present circumstances reinforces humanity's blindness in the face of chance.

Tone

The tone Mueller adopts in her crafting of "Alive Together" provides valuable insight into the poet's own relationship with chance and its heedless, often cruel dictates. The awe and almost inexpressible gratitude permeating the verse are tempered by a corresponding emotion of relief at having avoided the tragedies suffered by so many other women through the ages. "Alive Together" is at once a modern-day hymn of thanksgiving, a warning against the human tendency to take the world for granted, and an attempt to apply rationality to an unknowable, universal will.

COMPARE & CONTRAST

- **1970s:** Prevailing millennial and pre-millennial ideology begins to take shape in the shadow of despair and disillusionment following the Vietnam War and in anticipation of the looming twenty-first century. Many Christian denominations look forward to the reappearance of the Messiah, the final judgment of mankind, and the end of the world as we know it.

  Today: Eschatological beliefs persist even after the uneventful turn of the millennium, most notably in the anticipated 2012 phenomenon foretold by the ancient Mayan calendar and the apocalyptic prediction of the Russian mystic Grigori Rasputin.

- **1970s:** The ideas of second-wave feminism begin to take root and gain momentum around the world. As opposed to first-wave feminism, which focused on establishing voting privileges and basic human rights for women, this new movement seeks to extend the discussion into the domestic and legal spheres. Among other pressing issues, proponents champion increased reproductive rights for women, so egregiously denied to many of the suffering personas in "Alive Together," and equality in the workplace.

  Today: President Obama lends his full support to the establishment of the nascent White House Council on Women and Girls, which is aimed at facilitating the fulfillment of many of the progressive reforms begun in the 1990s through third-wave feminism.

- **1970s:** In the regional unrest following the Vietnam War, Communist factions under the banner of the Khmer Rouge perpetrate a campaign of terror and genocide across Cambodia, which claims the lives of an estimated three million civilians. This shocking figure nevertheless pales when compared with the roughly six million Jews who perished in the Holocaust of Mueller's youth and informs much of her poetry.

  Today: Racial tensions persist across the world. In an avalanche following the so-called Arab Spring and revolutions that convulse the Middle East, the Syrian civil war intensifies, claiming an ever increasing number of lives and resulting in the flight of hundreds of thousands to ports across Europe and the United States. At the heart of the complex reasons behind the conflict remains the age-old antagonism between ethnic Sunni and Shia Muslims.

HISTORICAL CONTEXT

Less than a decade after Mueller's birth in Hamburg, in 1933, Adolf Hitler rose to the position of German chancellor. He immediately encouraged the persecution of Jews through widespread propaganda and boycotting and in isolated outbreaks of vandalism and violence. By 1935, the growing inequality had gained official political recognition, and the Nuremberg laws were passed, depriving Jews of citizenship and prohibiting their familial mingling with German gentiles. With the *Anschluss* of 1938, the official joining of Germany and Austria, racial violence reached new heights, and the so-called undesirables of German society were forced to wear marks of identification and were often segregated from the rest of society to be confined in cramped, guarded ghettos. In 1939, a year that marked both the official outbreak of war in Europe and the settling of the Neumann household in their adopted home of Indiana, infamous Nazi concentration camps such as Auschwitz were in full operation.

By the end of the Second World War in 1945 and the liberation of the survivors of the camps, an estimated six million Jews, including the older generation of the Neumann household, had been erased from human history.

The poem offers the historical figure of Pocahontas as "exemplary." *(© Joseph Sohm / Shutterstock.com)*

Mueller was a relative latecomer to poetry who penned her first publishable verses at age thirty. The deprivations and tragic near-misses of her earliest recollections in Nazi Germany were never far from her poetic sentiments. The persecution and murder of countless millions of her countrymen at the hands of Hitler and his infamous Third Reich proved unforgettable to the poet and imbued her work, whether through direct reference or subtle allusion, with themes of isolation, dark disbelief, and senseless misfortune and cruelty.

A less traumatic, though no less significant influence of Mueller's childhood on her subsequent work stems from her bilingualism and relatively late adoption of the English language. The poet stated that the clipped gravity of her first tongue contributes to the staccato simplicity of her verse, and that the necessity of universalizing sentiments of experience across two distinct national identities aids her in piercing to the

heart of poetic insight. The English of her young adulthood and poetry is, for Mueller, a language of healing and reconciliation that helps to ease the associations of a language forever tainted by the events of the Holocaust.

As a more mature poem that Mueller wrote when well into middle age, "Alive Together" is stylistically consistent with the poet's larger body of work but seems a thematic departure from her earliest poetic experiments. Expressing both awe and gratitude and a sense of interconnectivity, this later composition is colored less by the troubled history of the 1930s than by the self-acknowledged shift in consciousness that resulted in Mueller's relocation to bucolic Lake County, Illinois, many decades after the upheavals of her childhood.

CRITICAL OVERVIEW

Although "Alive Together" was not initially released as part of the Pulitzer Prize–winning collection of the same name, it was widely recognized by critics, and by Mueller herself, as a defining achievement embodying her mature poetic sensibilities. Alison Townsend of the *Women's Review of Books* considered the composition singularly representative of a central theme of Mueller's work, the interconnectivity of the individual within a web of human history and hope for the future. Townsend writes, "In these quiet, luminous poems Mueller explores what it really means to be 'alive together' when there are so many other histories or lives one might have lived."

Echoing this sentiment, the poetry critic John Taylor remarked on the role of the present in achievements such as "Alive Together" in countering the horrors of the past and the vagaries of the future. In addition, he remarked that Mueller's insistence on the elevating and persistent power of love marks her as one of the rare artists who can render simultaneously all that is best and worst about humanity without ever losing sight of optimism. Taylor writes,

> Her poetry constantly turns us back to the living, to the vibrant existences in our midst.... Mueller indeed nurtures the hope that we can cure solitude by seeking out unifying or reconciling moments in the here and now.

Rohan B. Preston, writing for the *Chicago Tribune*, admired Mueller above all else for her dedication to delivering relevant and unaffected poetry that does not pull its punches and speaks, first and foremost, from the authority of personal experience. In a profile of Mueller, the translator and scholar Nell Casey discusses the poet's bilingualism and how it contributed to the precision and simplicity of language especially apparent in compositions like "Alive Together." This reconciling and balancing of emotional equivalents between the words of her native and adopted tongues forced Mueller to distill expressions of pure meaning in her work rather than rely on overwrought language or complex metaphors.

More thematically driven critics such as Linda Nemec Foster have focused on the commonplace existence of elements of folklore and fairy tale in the works of Mueller. In "Transformation of the World: The Metaphor of Fairy Tale in the Poetry of Lisel Mueller," Foster contends that these recurring motifs imbue poems like "Alive Together" with a degree of universality and human interconnectivity and more believably render the theme of transformative potential so central to the poet. Foster writes,

> Her sense of the universality of the fairy tale to explore the human psyche gives her poems a metaphoric brilliance. And in the center of this brilliance is the power of the fairy tale—and indeed, of the poem—to transform.

Janet Ruth Heller, another critic, argues that interconnectivity does not always represent a positive reality in Mueller's poems but is more closely linked to interdependency and the corresponding, if unachievable, desire for isolation. As hard as people try to distance themselves from the plight of their neighbors, Mueller suggests, the problems confronting the individual belong to everyone.

CRITICISM

Jeffrey Eugene Palmer

Palmer is a freelance writer, scholar, and high-school English teacher. In the following essay, he examines Mueller's treatment of time and the painful past in "Alive Together."

One of the compelling observations central to the critic John Taylor's assessment of Mueller's craft is that she seeks to slip the phantoms of her past through the proposed antidote of depicting the present. Even the poet's reliance on her adopted language of English rather than her

> AS A POEM ROOTED IN SUCH A WEALTH OF IMAGES DERIVED FROM THE FOLKLORE AND HISTORY OF EARLIER AGES, 'ALIVE TOGETHER' IS A COMPOSITION ALMOST OBSESSIVELY IN TOUCH WITH WHAT HAS COME BEFORE."

native tongue of German in crafting her work, he contends, speaks to this tendency toward skillful evasion of time's cruel constraints. Although characterized by an undeniable sadness and backward-looking melancholy, Mueller's poetry should be seen to seek to dwell in the present and thereby preserve what must, necessarily, one day be lost.

According to Taylor in his review of "Alive Together," this brand of poetic cowardice, as he calls it, stems from a rather grim understanding that a true appreciation of value can only result from loss and that life's fleeting existence serves only as the necessary counterpart to the true master of this world: death. As Taylor writes,

> This remark in fact defines the challenge that Mueller sets for herself. She seeks to determine whether we can become aware—through poetry—of the precious gifts of the present before they are lost. Her poetry constantly turns back to living, to the vibrant existences in our midst.

"Alive Together," with its emphasis on the miraculous existence of the here and now, conforms in many respects to the model Taylor proposes. In other ways, however, with its introduction of chance and the doubt posed by an uncertain future, this singular poem qualifies and complicates the otherwise cozy assertion that the poet prefers to dwell in the present. Taylor pays brief homage to the notion that love and human connection help to bridge the abyss separating the past and the present; it is the rendering of time as unreliable and even impotent, however, as alluded to by the reviewer Alison Townsend in "Naming the Unnamable," that best characterizes Mueller's stance about the relentless march of the years. In her critical analysis, Townsend states,

WHAT DO I READ NEXT?

- W. H. Auden's *Collected Poems*, published in 1991, is a decisive, updated collection of the works of a prolific American poet. It provides insight into one of the formative influences on Mueller's own poetry from the perspective of another artist of divided nationality.

- Published in 1918 as the final installment of Willa Cather's Great Plains trilogy, *My Ántonia* is the emotionally charged tale of an unlikely relationship between a Nebraska native and a young girl recently immigrated from Bohemia, half a world away.

- Published in 2007 as the sequel to Khaled Hosseini's literary debut, the award-winning novel *The Kite Runner*, *A Thousand Splendid Suns* portrays the hardships endured by women and girls in war-torn Afghanistan.

- *Main Street*, by Sinclair Lewis, published in 1920, endures as one of the preeminent descriptions of small-town life in the American Midwest.

- Published in 1980, Mueller's *The Need to Hold Still* was awarded the National Book Award for the following year and is especially representative of her reliance on folklore in crafting her poetry.

- *Sarah's Key* (2006), the international best-selling novel by Tatiana de Rosnay, tells the compelling story of a modern-day American journalist whose research leads her to uncover horrific Holocaust events that transpired in wartime France. Unable and unwilling to forget, she attempts to reconcile the wrongdoings of the past with the small degree of justice she can help to bring about in the present.

- Although the extent of the contributions of famous women to world history would prove impossible to incorporate into a single volume, the 2001 reference guide *Encyclopedia of Women in the Ancient World*, edited by Joyce E. Salisbury, provides formidable background on the study of women's achievements in the ancient world and sheds light on many of the references Mueller includes in her poem.

- Published by the Australian author Markus Zusak to widespread acclaim in 2006, *The Book Thief* depicts the deprivations of Nazi Germany from the perspective of a young girl just before the outbreak of World War II, in the same year that Mueller immigrated to the United States.

The journey defined by this kind of witness is established early on in Mueller's work. To some extent it is inspired by roads not taken.... But it also means embracing memory and the insubstantial nature of time.

As a poem rooted in such a wealth of images derived from the folklore and history of earlier ages, "Alive Together" is a composition almost obsessively in touch with what has come before. The verse makes no attempt to run from or disavow the weight of tradition but rather embraces historical precedent in all its colorful, and often unseemly, manifestations. Through such sobering descriptions as that of the whore, slave girl, and devastated peasant wife, the universal current of human relations is seen not so much as an affirmation and a comfort, as Taylor proposes, but as a multigenerational plague afflicting countless archetypal and unnamed women.

The poem is equally anchored in the here and now of Mueller's present idyllic existence with her husband in rural Illinois. The awe and gratitude she expresses at being alive to enjoy such pleasant circumstances lends credence to Taylor's assertion of the role of the present as a safe haven in Mueller's poems.

The present of Mueller's poem, however, is no less overshadowed by the threat of trauma than is its past. For the first time in the verse, humanity's spiritual and intellectual instincts are aligned in their consensus on the imminent destruction of the race to coincide with the coming millennia. Against the edicts of scholars and sermonizers foretelling doom, the speaker and her family express awe and thanksgiving for the small slice of existence they are privy to. This suggests that the poet believes no generation or season of life to be fully shielded from misfortune. Faith and the fearlessness that it engenders are the only antidotes to the inevitable rise and fall of human fortune.

The analysis Taylor poses further breaks apart in the final lines of the poem, when it becomes clear that the present is not the final destination of the verse but merely the midway point of a much grander trajectory that includes the future generations of the speaker's household. The poem's initial fixation with the relationship between a man and a woman is suddenly marginalized, and all the hopes, dreams, and frustrations of the couple are transferred to their two young daughters, who, despite the innumerable odds against their existence, will continue to live out the expectations inherited from their parents. It is the as-yet unshaped destiny of these children, characterized by a string of vague and universal nouns, that bears the brunt of the poem's emotional power and sweeps away concerns of both the past and the present.

Contrary to Taylor's initial assertion, in "Alive Together" the poet places value not on that which has ceased to exist but on that which has yet to be fully realized. In this way the anxieties of the past, far from being forgotten, are transferred to future lives dictated by the caprices of chance.

In lieu of evasion of the relentless march of time, Mueller seeks an altogether different form of refuge in poems like "Alive Together." By diffusing her own essence across an array of alternative personas, the poet makes the statement that although individual existences may be subject to misery and even eradication, humanity, as a collective manifestation of experience, will endure. In "Naming the Unnamable," Townsend alludes to this characteristic of Mueller's work and to the power of the individual to attain immortality only through the larger web of human existence past, present, and future. Townsend contends,

The trajectory of the individual life journey, and how it interacts with both history and the journeys of others, lies at the heart of Mueller's aesthetic, and makes for a poetry of interconnectedness that reaches out, seeking to illuminate even the saddest moments.

By juxtaposing historical archetypes of loyalty and patriotism like Betsy Ross and Pocahontas with the falsified myths surrounding their personas, Mueller reveals history as yet another human construction superimposed on an elemental force of nature. In "On Reading an Anthology of Postwar German Poetry," also in *Alive Together*, Mueller suggests that history played her false. This notion seems representative of her understanding that time, like chance, lies utterly beyond comprehension or human conceptions of rationality. History and folklore are two sides of the same coin, "Alive Together" suggests, and both deal as much in invention as they do in reality.

The thematic ambiguity between what people claim as fact and fiction acts as another weapon in Mueller's arsenal against the steady advance of time in her work. In her scholarly analysis of the importance of folklore and fairy tale in shaping the poet's sentiments, "Transformation of the World," Linda Nemec Foster asserts that this intentional untruth not only reinforces the interconnectivity of all human life but also acts as a vehicle for the theme of transformation so central to Mueller's outlook:

> Mueller's poems that resonate with the emblems of the fairy tale are indeed mythical because they represent emotional states and progressions in our psyche that function as metaphoric language, a language of images for the wordless soul. Myth may not provide us with all the answers to our lives, but it can be the connection between our past and our present, our present and our future.

The myriad projected personas of "Alive Together" render time, and the perceived end it necessitates, utterly non-menacing. Time is not the great destroyer for Mueller but is merely the natural progression of a ceaseless string of transformations and renewed opportunities. Only through rebirth into new circumstances can the soul endure.

Mueller's response to the archenemy, time, is neither naive nor cowardly, as Taylor suggests. It turns toward the future in preference to running from the past. Mueller does not disavow

The poem is celebrating that the speaker is alive now and happy with her partner and not experiencing the suffering of the past. *(© Rock and Wasp | Shutterstock.com)*

the current of relentless change that underlies painful human history but suggests our flawed perceptions regarding altered circumstances and destruction itself. To live, to age, to die is to experience the greatest marvel the universe has to offer, and to surrender completely to the miracle that is chance. One's triumphs, tribulations, and tragedies are immaterial compared to the ultimate unlikelihood of having lived at all.

Source: Jeffrey Eugene Palmer, Critical Essay on "Alive Together," in *Poetry for Students*, Gale, Cengage Learning, 2016.

Patricia Monaghan

In the following review, Monaghan praises Mueller's "marvelous, lyric talent."

Mueller's work possesses such power and authority that this collection that includes poems from her previous five books and a significant set of new poems is cause for celebration. Her major theme is announced in the title poem. It is the miracle of human love, despite all odds: "Speaking of marvels," the poem begins, "I am alive / together with you, when I might have been / alive with anyone under the sun...This poem is endless, the odds against us are endless." Yet such love, being alive together, exists and sustains itself amid wars and other losses. A constantly recurring trope for Mueller is Lot's wife, turned into a pillar of salt for looking back at burning Sodom. Mueller turns that salt tower into a witness who lives and speaks and never ceases to love. There is more genuine joy in this book than in any dozen other recent poetry collections—genuine in that it does not retreat from pain but persists while acknowledging it. Mueller's marvelous, lyric talent deserves much wider acclaim.

Source: Patricia Monaghan, Review of *Alive Together: New and Selected Poems*, in *Booklist*, Vol. 93, No. 4, October 15, 1996, p. 400.

Publishers Weekly

In the following review, an anonymous reviewer marvels at Mueller's consistently strong work over a long career.

"When I am asked / how I began writing poems, / I talk about the indifference of nature," Mueller writes in "When I Am Asked." Many of the new and previously published poems here seem intent upon correcting that indifference. With images of flowers, trees, birds, snow and sun, Mueller is ruminating and philosophical without being doctrinaire; she inhabits a world the Romantics might recognize and offers poems with such titles as "Joy" "Immortality" and "Tears." The next line in "When I Am Asked," however, is "It was soon after my mother died," indicating another central concern. Often using her exodus from Hitler's Europe as a quiet backdrop, she probes family relationships, as in "Happy and Unhappy Families II," which references Electra: "In the play, we know what must happen / long before it happens, / and we call it tragedy. / Here at home, this winter, / we have no name for it." Tapping the resources of narrative, she revisits tales, ancient and modern, always insightful in her revisions and extensions of the originals. Mueller's *The Need To Hold Still* won the 1981 National Book Award. Readers will be struck by the poet's steadfast ability to sustain the same focus and techniques over six volumes spanning 35 years.

Source: Review of *Alive Together*, in *Publishers Weekly*, Vol. 243, No. 44, October 28, 1996, p. 77.

Stan Sanvel Rubin, William Heyen, and Lisel Mueller

In the following interview excerpt, Mueller talks about her writing process.

> TRANSLATING FROM GERMAN INTO ENGLISH OR READING GERMAN IS NO PROBLEM FOR ME AT ALL. BUT THE KIND OF FLUENCY IN SPEAKING THAT YOU HAVE TO HAVE IN CONVERSATIONAL GERMAN OR IN WRITING LETTERS REALLY DRIED UP FOR ME, AND TRANSLATING HELPED TO BRING IT BACK."

. . . Rubin: I'd like to ask you about the poem you just read, "After Whistler." You've said it took twenty drafts. Does it normally take that kind of effort to complete a poem, and if not, what was it about this one that made it more difficult?

Mueller: This was an extreme case. I don't usually go that long without giving up; I was being stubborn. It took me so long because it was a poem written with nothing to start on. I usually don't force myself to write poems but wait until I get some kind of language fragment going through my mind that will start the poem and generate more language. In this case, I didn't have anything, but since I hadn't written a poem for a long time, I decided I simply had to write something. I let my mind go blank and used the first image that came. That's very unusual for me.

Rubin: Could I ask how you chose the title?

Mueller: Originally it had nothing to do with Whistler. It was a poem about white mist, because the first image that came when I decided to let my mind go blank was one of whiteness, probably since I was sitting outside and it was a very bright day. About halfway through the process of writing, the poem wasn't getting anywhere very fast and I decided I had to hang it on some sort of frame. I thought of James McNeill Whistler's famous painting *The Little White Girl*, the one in which a girl who is dressed all in white is standing in front of a mirror; she is holding a Japanese fan, and there are flowers next to her on the floor. She's a very fragile-looking creature. I felt that in order to make a poem about whiteness stick I had to give it that title and connect it to even a small extent with that Whistler painting.

Heyen: I like the poem very much, right from its beginning, "There are girls who should have been swans." I'm reminded of a William Stafford poem that begins, "My father owned a star." It's a beautiful beginning.

Did you say that you thought, in general, that poems that came more easily were your best ones? Why do you think that's true?

Mueller: I don't know. It probably has to do with spontaneously generated language being less labored, and the connections are more easily made.

Heyen: And maybe your subconscious works on what will be the poem for a long time.

Mueller: I don't know. There are certain times when I seem to be open to the possibility of seeing in a new way. I can walk along for weeks and look at all kinds of interesting objects that suggest nothing to me, and there are other times when all of a sudden I make some kind of connection. I see something or hear about something, and it connects with something else in my mind; therefore, it becomes metaphor, or at least contains the possibility of metaphor. And I don't know why that only happens at certain times and not at others.

Rubin: When you're in such a state, do you feel a desperate need to do something about it, or do you wait until something comes?

Mueller: I've learned to be pretty patient most of the time. At first I used to be frightened— you've heard it a million times and maybe you've even heard yourself say, "I'll never be able to write another poem; I've dried up"—but it's happened so many times that by now I'm pretty confident that the juices will start flowing again.

Heyen: And maybe now that you have three good-sized collections behind you, you can relax about that kind of thing. Could you tell us how you started writing poetry?

Mueller: I didn't think about becoming a writer for a long time. I did write some poems while I was in college—some very bad poems. They were overly romantic, very flowery. But it was a natural way for me at the time to release tension or express emotion. A lot of people who never become writers do that when they're adolescents. After I left college, I really didn't think about writing very much; I just assumed that it was the kind of thing one does when one is young. I was twenty-nine when my mother died. I felt a great need to express my grief in a poem; it seemed the only way to get some relief. It was at that moment that I really wanted to be a poet.

Rubin: In the poem, "After Whistler," you have the phrase "steady interior hum." That's the kind of thing I imagine a writer always to have going. You must have heard that "hum" before you took poetry seriously.

Mueller: It must be true that I did have that steady interior hum and that need to use a rhythmic language which is very important to me. My poetry is very rhythmic, and it's probably a rhythmic drive that really gets me going. It must have been there all along, but I didn't know it. I did read quite a bit of poetry during those intervening years, and that perhaps allowed me to use language in a way that became publishable.

Rubin: You were in a bilingual environment, weren't you?

Mueller: Not really. When I came over here, I was fifteen, and, of course, I lived with my mother, father, and sister; so as long as I lived at home I was in a bilingual environment. I graduated from college very young, at twenty, and I was already married at that time to the man who is still my husband. He is a native American, so I spoke very little German after that.

Rubin: But you're still fluent in German.

Mueller: Translating from German into English or reading German is no problem for me at all. But the kind of fluency in speaking that you have to have in conversational German or in writing letters really dried up for me, and translating helped to bring it back. Strangely enough, I found when I became deeply involved in German again—and in English too, since you go very deeply into both languages in translating—that I had not forgotten German to the extent that I thought I had. Perhaps it's like swimming or riding a bicycle—if you once learn it, it's always there.

Heyen: Probably about ten or fifteen years of poems went into Dependencies, *I assume. I see that your title is from Wallace Stevens's "Sunday Morning." I noticed other echoes of Stevens. Was he the most important poet for you of that generation? I hate to ask these questions about influences, because I know they're tough to answer.*

Mueller: I don't think I write at all like Stevens. I can't recognize any influence of him in my work, but I would love to write like him. He's my favorite poet of that generation.

Heyen: When you look back on your own first book now—it goes back to 1965—how do you like it? What do you think of your first poems?

Mueller: A lot of it I don't like anymore. Many of the poems seem overly decorated, too metaphorical. Some are sentimental. I've come to write barer poems. But I'm still fond of a few poems in *Dependencies*. Maybe about ten poems in that collection I'm happy to have written.

Heyen: I care for many of them. Somehow, though, it's a more "literary" book than your others: more poems are based on other writers, and on paintings or music.

Mueller: That's true.

Heyen: What change did you sense in your-self, then, toward the next book eleven years later? Was there some other emotional complex that went into The Private Life?

Mueller: The Private Life has two main springs. One was domestic, the experience of family: my husband, my two daughters as they were growing up. There's a lot of material in the book that has to do with recognizing human growth through the examples of my children and the relationship between parents and children. The other was the Vietnam War, which affected me deeply. It made me think about the interdependency, certainly in our age, of the private and the public life. There's no way anymore for the individual to escape from History, the public life we all share. Being European-born, I felt this very strongly. That is the story of my parents, who were born shortly before World War I, and their whole life was determined by History. Everything was imposed on them from the outside, because the twentieth century in Germany was catastrophic. We came over here as a result of the Nazis in Germany, since my father was political. It's reinforced in my next book, *The Need to Hold Still*—that sense that came to me as a result of the war in Vietnam.

Heyen: There's a beautiful poem in The Private Life *called "My Grandmother's Gold Pin," which ties many of these things together. Would you read it?*

Mueller: This pin was sent to me after my grandmother had died. It was the only piece of hers I had because all her other things were lost during the war. I'm talking in the poem about all the objects that I remember my grandparents having when I was a child. They lived in the same city, and I was with them a lot and fingered these objects from the Edwardian period. In fact, they were very poor when I was a child, but they had at one time been better-off. So the objects are really metaphors for an historical period that is gone . . . .

Rubin: It does catch up all the things you were speaking of.

Mueller: One of my daughters asked me why I wore the pin so much when she was small. The poem is my answer to her.

Heyen: In another poem, you say, "I know enough to refuse to say that life is good, but I act as though it were." I sense in poem after poem the same struggle to believe in something, but with the knowledge of a terrible history behind you. Even in that poem, when you speak of their "death in an animal shed," you want to say what you don't want to say. That holding back leaves a lot to our imagination. It's a very personal poem, but at the same time it's a poem within its own language.

Mueller: Simone de Beauvoir said, "In language I transcend my particular case."

Rubin: Your mentioning Beauvoir reminds me that there are poems in the book that deal with being a woman and a poet in America. Would you say something about that in your work?

Mueller: It's not something that I'm ever conscious of when I write poems. I naturally write in a feminine voice, and the experience I know best has to do with being a woman. When I write a dramatic monologue, which I do frequently, I assume the voice of a woman more often than that of a man. Other than that, I'm not really conscious of being a "woman poet" as opposed to being a poet who happens to be a woman.

Rubin: Do you speak your poems aloud while composing? Do you feel that energizes your sense of language or interest in drama?

Mueller: I like to assume someone else's voice. When I was young, I would have loved to be an actress. Maybe it stems from that, that possibility of being in someone else's shoes and imagining how the person feels. I find it boring to be constantly writing about myself. There are so many other more interesting people in the world, or have been. At the same time, I have the satisfaction of taking the liberty of trying to be that other person and imagining how I would feel had I been that person. So there is a double satisfaction in being someone else and still being myself. . . .

Source: Stan Sanvel Rubin, William Heyen, and Lisel Mueller, "'The Steady Interior Hum': A Conversation with Lisel Mueller," in *The Post-Confessionals: Conversations with American Poets of the Eighties*, edited by Earl G. Ingersoll, Judith Kitchen, and Stan Sanvel Rubin, Fairleigh Dickinson University Press, 1989, pp. 66–71.

SOURCES

"Cambodian Genocide Program," Yale University website, http://www.yale.edu/cgp/ (accessed November 4, 2015).

Casey, Nell, "Slightly Larger Than Life Size," Poetry Foundation website, May 8, 2008, http://www.poetryfoundation.org/article/178148 (accessed September 22, 2015).

Foster, Linda Nemec, "Transformation of the World: The Metaphor of Fairy Tale in the Poetry of Lisel Mueller," in *Midamerica*, Vol. 33, 2006, pp. 111–20.

Heller, Janet Ruth, "The Theme of Isolation in Recent Poems by Lisel Mueller," in *Midwestern Miscellany*, Vol. 33, 2005, pp. 43–54.

Landes, Richard, "Millennialism from the Renaissance to the Modern World," in *Encyclopædia Britannica*, http://www.britannica.com/topic/millennialism/Millennialism-from-the-Renaissance-to-the-modern-world (accessed November 4, 2015).

"Lisel Mueller," Poetry Foundation website, http://www.poetryfoundation.org/bio/lisel-mueller (accessed September 22, 2015).

Mueller, Lisel, "Alive Together," in *Alive Together: New and Selected Poems*, Louisiana State University Press, 1996, pp. 84–85.

———, "On Reading an Anthology of Postwar German Poetry," in *Alive Together: New and Selected Poems*, Louisiana State University Press, 1996, p. 88.

Orihill, Jackie, "Lisel Mueller," in *Encyclopædia Britannica*, 2015, http://www.britannica.com/print/article/396053 (accessed September 22, 2015).

Preston, Rohan B., "Everything Is Autobiography," in *Chicago Tribune*, April 11, 1997, http://articles.chicagotribune.com/1997-04-11/features/9704110298_1_gwendolyn-brooks-pulitzer-prize-poetry-center (accessed September 22, 2015).

Rampton, Martha, "The Three Waves of Feminism: Now a Fourth?," Pacific University of Oregon website, October 25, 2015, http://www.pacificu.edu/about-us/news-events/three-waves-feminism (accessed November 4, 2015).

"Syria Country Profile," BBC News website, June 25, 2015, http://www.bbc.com/news/world-middle-east-14703856 (accessed November 4, 2015).

Taylor, John, Review of *Alive Together: New and Selected Poems*, in *Poetry*, Vol. 171, No. 3, 1998, pp. 219–21.

Townsend, Alison, "Naming the Unnamable," in *Women's Review of Books*, Vol. 15, No. 4, January 1998, pp. 18–19.

FURTHER READING

Eliot, T. S., *On Poetry and Poets*, Faber and Faber, 1957.
    The poetic genius responsible for such monumental works as *The Waste Land* and "The Love Song of J. Alfred Prufrock," T. S. Eliot also crafted many of the essays that would later influence Mueller's achievements in verse. Originally published in 1957, *On Poetry and Poets* remains one of the seminal criticisms regarding the craft to this day.

Grimm, Jacob, and Wilhelm Grimm, *The Complete Grimms' Fairy Tales*, Pantheon, 1972.
    This comprehensive collection of some of the world's best-loved fairy tales provides valuable insight, especially in combination with Mueller's earlier collections of verse, into the poet's reliance on folklore and human wonder in crafting her poems.

Kaschnitz, Marie Louise, *Circe's Mountain*, translated by Lisel Mueller, Milkweed Editions, 1990.
    Translated by Mueller and published in English in 1990, *Circe's Mountain* is a collection of short stories from one of Germany's most beloved authors and reflects both the joys and anxieties the poet experienced in reconciling her native and adopted tongues.

Mueller, Lisel, *Learning to Play by Ear: Essays and Early Poems*, Juniper Press, 1990.
    While *Alive Together* represents Mueller's swan song in the world of poetry, this collection contains many of her first poetic attempts along with rare interviews and essays that informed the trajectory of her brilliant career.

SUGGESTED SEARCH TERMS

Lisel Mueller

Lisel Neumann

Alive Together AND Mueller

The Private Life

Illinois poet laureate

midwestern poets

bilingual poets

German-born poets

modern American poets

American confessional poets

Alone

MAYA ANGELOU

1975

"Alone," by Maya Angelou, is a lyric poem that explores the themes of suffering, isolation, and community. Published in 1975, "Alone" addresses the economic misery and negativity felt by many during the decade. In this brief poem, Angelou attempts to share her personal experience and observations in hopes of bringing understanding to her audience and connecting with them on a personal level. Like many of Angelou's poems, "Alone" relies heavily on repetition to consistently keep specific words and phrases in the minds of the readers. First published in *Oh Pray My Wings Are Gonna Fit Me Well*, "Alone" is also available in *Maya Angelou: The Complete Poetry*, published in 2015.

AUTHOR BIOGRAPHY

Angelou was born Marguerite Johnson in St. Louis, Missouri, on April 4, 1928. After her parents were divorced, three-year-old Angelou and her brother, Bailey, were sent to live with their paternal grandmother, Annie Henderson, in Stamps, Arkansas. When Angelou was seven, her mother's boyfriend assaulted her. After the murder of her attacker, Angelou ceased to speak for five years, according to Mary Jane Lupton's *Maya Angelou: A Critical Companion*. She gained her love of literature and found her voice again with the help of a Mrs. Flowers, who later appeared in Angelou's children's story *Mrs. Flowers: A Moment of Friendship*.

Maya Angelou (© *Brian Doben | Contour by Getty Images*)

Angelou earned a scholarship to study dance and drama in San Francisco after graduating from the eighth grade. When she was fourteen, she was the first female African American to work as a cable car conductor. After graduating from high school, Angelou gave birth to her son, Guy. She worked different jobs to support her son, and in 1950 she married a Greek sailor named Anastasios Angelopulos (also known as Tosh Angelos). The marriage was short-lived. According to the Academy of Achievement, "When she began her career as a nightclub singer, she took the professional name Maya Angelou, combining her childhood nickname with a form of her husband's name." Angelou had a successful career as a performer, and she toured Europe in the musical *Porgy and Bess* between 1954 and 1955. She also appeared on television and in recorded albums.

Angelou joined the Harlem Writers Guild, where she met her lifelong friend James Baldwin and became involved in the civil rights movement and Dr. Martin Luther King Jr.'s Southern Christian Leadership Conference. In 1960,

Angelou and her son moved to Cairo, Egypt, with the activist Vusumzi Make, where she worked at the *Arab Observer*. Angelou moved to Ghana in 1962 and worked for both the *Ghanaian Times* and the *African Review*.

She returned to the United States in 1964 and began working on her first autobiography, *I Know Why the Caged Bird Sings*, which was first published in 1969 and was nominated for a National Book Award. Five autobiographies followed, the last being *A Song Flung up to Heaven*, released in 2002. The poetry collection *Just Give Me a Cool Drink of Water 'fore I Diiie* was published in 1971 and nominated for a Pulitzer Prize. Her screenplay *Georgia, Georgia*, the first produced screenplay written by an African American woman, was performed. Angelou was also nominated for an Emmy for her work in the miniseries *Roots. Oh Pray My Wings Are Gonna Fit Me Well*, which includes "Alone," was published in 1975.

Angelou was awarded over sixty honorary doctorates and served as the Reynolds Professor of American Studies at Wake Forest University from 1982 till her death. In 1993, she read her poem "On the Pulse of the Morning" at President Clinton's inauguration. Angelou continued writing poetry, autobiographies, essays, screenplays, cookbooks, and children's books throughout her life. She died on May 28, 2014, in Winston-Salem, North Carolina.

POEM SUMMARY

The text used for this summary is from *Maya Angelou: The Complete Poetry*, Random House, 2015, pp. 73–74. Versions of the poem can be found on the following web pages: http://www.poets.org/poetsorg/poem/alone and http://www.poemhunter.com/poem/alone-6/.

"Alone" has thirty-seven lines separated into six different stanzas. The poem does not follow a traditional rhyme or metrical pattern. The meter is the rhythm of the poem, which is created with stressed and unstressed syllables. It also employs a refrain in the even-numbered stanzas that is reminiscent of church services that encourage congregant participation.

Lines 1–13

Stanza 1 has ten lines. Lines 1 and 2 serve to identify the setting, and enjambment links them together in a single phrase in the mind of the

MEDIA ADAPTATIONS

- In 2001, Random House Audio released the CD *Maya Angelou Poetry Collection*, which includes "Alone." Angelou performs the collection, which lasts for one hour and fifty-five minutes.

reader. *Enjambment* occurs when a sentence or idea continues from one line to the next without any pause or break from punctuation. Here, the speaker identifies the place of epiphany. The speaker is presumably in bed and lost in thought. Lines 3–5 identify the question that the speaker asks, which is where her spirit can find its homeland. The descriptions in lines 4 and 5 are biblical references concerning the water of life and Christ's temptation to turn stones into food. The last word of line 3 is an example of assonance with a long *o* sound that continues through the stanza in lines 5, 8, 9, and 10. *Assonance* occurs when vowels or diphthongs are repeated in multiple words or syllables. The assonance carries into the refrain and throughout the poem.

In lines 6 and 7, the speaker introduces the truth she discovered after personal reflection. The truth is revealed in lines 8–10. The truth is that no one can survive without other people. The comma that ends line 8 is the first line-ending punctuation in the poem, creating an emphatic pause before continuing to line 9. The final words of lines 8 and 9 are the same, which provides repetition along with rhyme. Additionally, the last word of line 10 rhymes with the last word of line 5. A period ends line 10 and completes the stanza. The words in line 10 are repeated at the end of every stanza in the poem.

Stanza 2 is the first refrain of the poem. Lines 11–13 repeat the same idea from the previous three lines. The first word of line 11 is the same as the final word in line 10. This line provides an example of repetition that draws the stanzas together. The comma that follows the first word in line 11 creates another pause with the word that gives a sense of isolation. The idea of isolation is further emphasized by the repetition of

the same word at the end of the line. Line 12 uses a comma and repetition to remind readers that no one is exempt from the truth that the speaker imparts. Line 13 is a reminder that no one can go through life without other people. It repeats line 10 exactly. The repetition of the word ending lines 11 and 13 also creates a rhyme. The stanza concludes with a period, creating a stop to introduce stanza 3.

Lines 14–25

Stanza 3 moves from the speaker's idea to the observation of people. Line 14 introduces wealthy individuals. Line 15 reveals that the wealthy have more than they could use in a lifetime. The spouses described in line 16 are compared to creatures from mythology known for their terrifying screams. Their screams are specifically associated with death. Line 17 introduces the offspring of the wealthy. They live in unhappiness and depression, which is evident from the slang used in the final three words of the line. There is a rhyme between the end of lines 15 and 17.

Line 18 introduces the physicians the wealthy hire to help them overcome their problems caused by their isolation from each other. The physicians work to help them with their hardened hearts, which are described in line 19. The final word of line 19, used to describe the wealthy family members, is a repetition of the last word of line 5. The repetition connects the speaker's guiding idea with the wealthy in this scenario. The period at the end of line 19 ends the description of the rich.

Lines 20–22 repeat lines 8–10 closely. The conjunction that begins line 20 introduces the cure for the isolation of the wealthy and their family members. The negative interjection that begins line 21 is set off with a comma that serves to remind the reader that no one is exempt from the universal truth that the poet shares. As the speaker reiterates, the wealthy, like everyone else, need the support of other people to thrive. The final words of lines 19 and 22 rhyme, as do lines 20 and 21.

Stanza 4 repeats stanza 2 exactly. The repetition reinforces the speaker's main idea and applies the point made to the wealthy of the previous stanza.

Lines 26–37

Like stanza 3, stanza 5 has nine lines. Line 26 is a call to action that encourages the reader to pay close attention to what the poet has to say. The adverb that begins the line requires the attention to be immediate. In line 27, the speaker explains that she has important information to share, revealing her authority on the subject. In lines 28–31, the speaker shares her knowledge of humanity. The speaker states that there is a tempest coming in line 28, and line 29 reveals that the tempest is windy. In line 30, the speaker mentions human misery specifically. The stormy weather is a metaphor for human anguish, and the speaker listens to the cries of pain in line 31. Line 27 rhymes with line 29, and line 28 rhymes with line 30. The comma at the end of line 31 creates a pause before introducing the final three lines of the stanza.

Lines 32–34 is another rephrasing of the final three lines of stanzas 1 and 3. The colloquial word that begins line 32 enhances the conversational tone. The comma that ends line 32 and the conjunction that begins line 33 reinforce the speaker's assertion that everyone needs the help of other people. Line 31 rhymes with line 34, and the repetition in lines 32 and 33 creates another rhyme. A period in line 34 completes the stanza.

The three lines of stanza 6 repeat stanzas 2 and 4 exactly. The speaker completes the poem this way to leave the refrain in the minds of the readers.

THEMES

Isolation

Angelou addresses the dangers of isolation in the poem "Alone." The feeling of isolation begins in the title of the poem and continues throughout the verse. The speaker is by herself in the first stanza, and her heart longs for a place of its own in line 3. In this stanza, she hints at her personal sense of isolation. Stanza 3 moves to the isolation of the wealthy. Individual family members are separate from each other and unhappy. The effects of loneliness and isolation are evident from the unnatural wails of the spouses in line 16 and the term for depression that appears in line 17. The speaker does not see their connection with each other or any other people, and she reminds the readers that even the wealthy cannot thrive in isolation.

Fortunately, the poet has a cure for the wealthy family members as well as herself. She recognizes that individuals cannot only rely on themselves. Everyone needs the support of other people and community. Without human connection, individuals become hard-hearted like the wealthy family members described in line 19 of the poem.

TOPICS FOR FURTHER STUDY

- Read *The Absolutely True Diary of a Part-Time Indian*, by Sherman Alexie. This young-adult novel blends storytelling with drawings. The main character, Junior, grapples with isolation and community in the story. Create your own illustrated story in which Maya Angelou and Junior meet. What would they say to each other? What advice would be given? The images may be hand drawn, or you can use a computer program.

- Research the history of African American literature. Pay attention to prevalent themes and changes in style over the years. Create a web site that provides an overview of influential authors and their works. Be sure to include a link for Angelou.

- Read the young-adult volume *Poetry Speaks Who I Am: Poems of Discovery, Inspiration, Independence, and Everything Else*, edited by Elise Paschen and Dominique Raccah. Choose a poem to compare and contrast with "Alone." Write an essay that examines the differences and similarities between the poems. Pay attention to the themes and style of each poem and include discussion of them in your paper. Post the paper on a blog or present it to the class.

- Research and read different examples of lyric poems. Create your own poem using one or more themes found in "Alone." Place the poem on a blog, and use music, images, or other art to help improve reader understanding.

- Research the history of the United States in the 1970s. Pay close attention to civil rights, as well as the economic changes in society. How do they relate to each other, and how are they reflected in "Alone"? Use easel.ly to create graphics that organize your information, and present your findings to the class.

Community

The need for community is made clear in the poem "Alone." It is echoed in the refrain that claims individuals cannot succeed without the help of others. The speaker understands this fundamental

"Alone" captures the isolation and loneliness of modern society. *(© Karuka | Shutterstock.com)*

need when she is alone with her thoughts, specifically in line 6. The wealthy of stanza 3 are examples of lives lived without community. The spouses act out in their isolation, and the younger members of the family are described as blue or depressed. Without any support from their families, they live in misery. Their ability to fully feel and enjoy life is damaged by the loneliness that consumes them. As the refrain promises, the lonely can find their redemption in a community.

The speaker shifts from the need for a familial community to society's need for community in stanza 5. The speaker directly states in line 30 that all of humanity is in pain, and in line 31, she can hear the cries of pain of those around her. Again, she reminds the readers of the need for community in the following lines of the stanza, as well as the last refrain. By reminding the readers that all people need human connection, the speaker provides a way out of human misery. By working together to build a community, humans will find the support that they need to move forward.

Suffering

Suffering is a central theme in the poem "Alone." The speaker examines suffering at the individual,

family, and social levels. In stanza 1, the speaker reveals her personal longing and the suffering of a soul that longs for a place of its own in lines 3–5. While contemplating her sorrow, the speaker has an epiphany. She realizes that every person needs human companionship in order to succeed in life. The speaker goes on to apply this lesson to people she has observed.

In stanza 3, the speaker describes the wealthy. While it is easy to assume that money can remove suffering, the truth is very different. Their offspring are clearly suffering from depression in line 17, and their spouses live lives that are not fulfilling. Although they are part of family units, they suffer alone. Separated from each other, they suffer from hardened hearts that prevent them from living full and happy lives.

The speaker then shifts to the suffering of humanity in stanza 5. The trouble that life can bring is shown in the storm metaphor of lines 28 and 29. The pain that all people feel is heard in the cries of line 31.

After each description of suffering, the speaker returns to her revelation. She shows that pain is inevitable for everyone, but she also

COMPARE
&
CONTRAST

- **1970s:** The Civil Rights Act of 1964 encourages the feminist movement, which addresses issues of equality for women in society and in the workplace. In 1972, Congress passes the Equal Rights Amendment.

  Today: The Equal Rights Amendment is not yet ratified. While different states have amendments that provide equal rights regardless of gender, politicians are still working for federal protection.

- **1970s:** The economy of the United States is volatile. Poverty increases because of high inflation and oil prices, as well as high unemployment rates. By 1975, the unemployment rate is 9 percent.

Today: The economy is a topic of political debate after the recession of 2008. The unemployment rate has lowered from the 10 percent high in 2009 to below 6 percent in 2015.

- **1970s:** The economy does not affect all Americans equally. A loss of blue-collar jobs has a greater impact on African Americans and other minority communities. The rates of poverty and unemployment are higher for African Americans than white Americans.

  Today: Race is still a factor in economic inequality despite political progress. Unemployment and poverty rates remain higher for African Americans and other minority groups than for white Americans.

---

understands that moving forward is possible with the help of other people. The line that ends each stanza reinforces the idea that no individual is capable of finding success and happiness without the support of other people.

STYLE

Repetition

Angelou employs repetition throughout "Alone." According to William Harmon and Hugh Holman's *A Handbook to Literature*, repetition is the "reiteration of a word, sound, phrase, or idea." The refrain of stanzas 2, 4, and 6 is a perfect example of repetition. Additionally, the refrain repeats the same idea and many of the words from lines 8–10. In fact, the last line of each stanza is completely identical. The poem's repetition serves to reinforce the themes and ideas in the poem to the audience.

Lyric

M. H. Abrams, in *A Glossary of Literary Terms*, defines a lyric as a "fairly short poem, consisting of the utterance by a single speaker, who expresses a

state of mind or a process of perception, thought, and feeling." "Alone" follows this description. For example, the use of the first person provides insight into the mind of the speaker, including her personal thoughts and observations. Also, lines 1 and 2 indicate that the speaker is lying in bed when she discovers a fundamental truth that applies to everyone. Her own desire is to find a place of refuge for her spirit, according to line 3.

Stanzas 3 and 5 are examples of the speaker's observations. She sees in stanza 3 that the wealthy are not exempt from the need for human companionship. In stanza 5, she can sense the changing weather and hear the sounds of pain throughout humanity. Each desire and observation can be addressed through the speaker's personal understanding that people need each other.

HISTORICAL CONTEXT

Civil Rights in the Late 1960s and Early 1970s

Angelou was active in the American civil rights movement, knowing and working with both

The poem captures how important it is for an individual to have the support of others. (© Jacob Lund / Shutterstock.com)

Malcolm X and Dr. Martin Luther King Jr. The fight for equality led to the passing of the Civil Rights Act of 1964. The Civil Rights Act was landmark legislation that helped push racial equality and integration forward, but backlash followed. Civil rights leaders saw the bill as incomplete, and opponents objected to changing the status quo. According to *America in Revolt during the 1960s and 1970s*, "riots occurred in virtually every major American city" in 1966. Martin Luther King was assassinated in 1968, striking a blow to the civil rights movement. Because of the unrest, President Nixon chose to "de-emphasize desegregation" in 1970. The violence of the 1960s and 1970s is echoed in the weather metaphor in "Alone."

Other minority groups began to follow the lead of African American civil rights leaders in the fight for equality. For example, the feminist movement started to gain momentum, and "by the early 1970s, television news, magazines, and newspapers all carried stories about sex discrimination in employment and women's struggles against it, as well as the wider reports of the

women's movement," according to Nancy MacLean's "The Hidden History of Affirmative Action: Working Women's Struggles in the 1970s and the Gender of Class." The Equal Rights Amendment (ERA), guaranteeing equal pay for equal work, was passed in 1972 but never ratified. As with the Civil Rights Act, there was a political pressure to return to tradition. As *UShistory.org* explains, opponents of feminism "suggested that ratification of the ERA would lead to the complete unraveling of traditional American society."

American Economy in the 1970s

The American economy suffered in the 1970s. In 1969, the United States saw a decline in the gross domestic product and an increase in unemployment rates across the nation. These factors, coupled with rising inflation, negatively affected the cost of living for most Americans. The oil crisis recession of 1973 did little to boost the American economy. According to *Investopedia*, "This long, deep recession was brought on by the quadrupling of oil prices and high government spending on the Vietnam War." Unemployment rose, and by 1975, when "Alone" was published, the unemployment rate was 9 percent. Additionally, the opening of the international markets and changes in technology saw a decrease in positions requiring manual labor.

The high unemployment rate was not equal across race and gender lines. The loss of traditional, blue-collar jobs was particularly damaging to African Americans who did not have the same access to educational opportunities. High unemployment served to increase the number of people living in poverty and created a sense of hopelessness regarding the future of the United States. According to Yanek Mieczkowski's *Gerald Ford and the Challenges of the 1970s*, "Economic problems, Vietnam, creeping isolationism, and the crumbling of the cold war consensus led to the perceptions of U.S. decline throughout the world." The negative perception of the nation is reflected in Angelou's poem, specifically line 30, where the speaker says that everyone is in pain.

CRITICAL OVERVIEW

Angelou enjoyed a long and successful literary career. She was best known for her six autobiographies. The first volume, *I Know Why the Caged Bird Sings*, was published in 1969 and praised by critics. Ward Just's review in the *Washington Post* says, "There isn't any easy, which is to say false line in the book. The distance, which is everything, is as true as a plumb line." The critical praise for her memoirs continued throughout her life, although the reviews became more mixed over time. While her later autobiographies did not have the same acclaim as the first, many critics continued to view her work favorably. For example, Margaret Busby calls the 2001 installment *A Song Flung up to Heaven* "the culmination of a unique autobiographical achievement, a glorious celebration of indomitable spirit," in her review "I Am Headed for Higher Ground."

Angelou's poems are beloved by readers, but they did not always gain the same critical reception as her prose. On the one hand, Angelou's 1971 volume of poetry, *Just Give Me a Cool Drink of Water 'fore I Diiie*, was nominated for a Pulitzer Prize. *Kirkus Reviews*, on the other hand, says that her poetry is not "a match for Miss Angelou's prose, where her real poetry flows without restraint." *Oh Pray My Wings Are Gonna Fit Me Well*, which includes "Alone," was given similarly weak praise. For example, Katherine Gibbs Harris of *Library Journal* says that the volume contains "good heritage ballads and excellent lyrics." Stefanie K. Dunning points out in her entry for *The Oxford Encyclopedia of American Literature*, "Critics have long discounted her poetry as simplistic." Still, Angelou was selected to write and perform the presidential inauguration poem "On the Pulse of the Morning" in 1993. Throughout her life, Angelou created respected plays, films, children's books, essays, and poems that gained the love of her readers even when her critics did not always agree.

CRITICISM

April Paris

Paris is a freelance writer with a degree in classical literature and a background in academic writing. In the following essay, she examines how in "Alone," Angelou uses oratory traditions from sermons and spirituals to share her personal understanding of isolation and community with her readers.

Maya Angelou has been referred to as the people's poet because of the way her work reaches readers on an emotional level. Angelou's use of the oral tradition is part of her appeal to readers. Vicki Cox explains the effect that the oral tradition has on Angelou's work when she quotes the poet's editor, Robert Loomis, in *Maya Angelou: Poet*. In a letter to critic Lynman Hage, Loomis wrote, "What she is writing is poetry that . . . can be read aloud and even acted. When her words are spoken, they are extremely effective and moving." "Alone" draws from Angelou's experience as a performer along with the oral traditions of the church. Part song and part sermon, "Alone" communicates the poet's wisdom while borrowing from familiar and effective oratory techniques.

As Rachael Groner explains in *Contemporary American Ethnic Poets: Lives, Works, Sources*, "Angelou's poetry often recalls the style of black spirituals and the cadence of black preachers, using repetition, alliteration, and rhythm to create poems that are much like songs or speeches." The linguistic elements of spirituals and sermons speak to readers individually, allowing the speaker to share important themes and lessons. Angelou's use of this style is clear from the beginning of "Alone," specifically the title. The title obviously introduces the theme of loneliness with the simple

WHAT DO I READ NEXT?

- Published in 2013, the Poetry for Young People series volume *Maya Angelou* is an anthology of Angelou's poems compiled for young readers. The anthology includes definitions and illustrations to improve understanding.

- *The 1970s: A New Global History from Civil Rights to Economic Inequality*, by Thomas Borstelman, examines the decade in which Angelou published "Alone." This nonfiction book was published in 2011 and is a useful tool that provides historical perspective on civil rights, women's rights, and the economy, along with changes in popular culture.

- *My Own True Name: New and Selected Poems for Young Adults* (2000), by Pat Mora, is a collection selected for a young audience. The collection examines universal themes from a Latina point of view.

- *Maya Angelou: A Creative and Courageous Voice*, by Jill Egan, is part of the Life Portraits series, created for young adults. The biography was published in 2009 and provides an overview of Angelou's life, work, and influence on American culture.

- Edited by Joanne M. Braxton and published in 1993, *The Collected Poetry of Paul Laurence Dunbar* is a nearly complete collection of Dunbar's poetry. Dunbar heavily influenced Angelou's work, and her first autobiography takes its name from Dunbar's poetry.

- *We Were Here*, by Matt de la Peña, is a work of young-adult fiction. Published in 2011, the book explores the themes of isolation and community as the main character, Miguel, attempts to find himself.

definition of the word. The long *o* sound in the title, however, appears throughout the poem in an example of assonance. The assonance slows the rhythm of the verse while creating a somber and contemplative tone. This sound regularly appears in "Alone," helping the poet create continuity while targeting the emotion of her audience as she introduces themes and ideas.

The continued use of the title in the poem does more than sustain the assonance. It also provides repetition, which Groner identifies as another characteristic of spirituals and sermons. The repetition of the word is a constant reminder of the theme of isolation that the poem explores. The title is not the only word that undergoes repetition in "Alone." Angelou also repeats the second word of line 8, *nobody*, numerous times. The word also contains the same long *o* sound as the title, which continues the assonance and somber tone.

As in most sermons, in "Alone," the poet is attempting to share wisdom and experience with her audience. She does so by following a pattern. The speaker begins by presenting personal problems or observations. She then reveals a fundamental truth that can help guide readers through their times of difficulty. The solution that the author provides follows the call-and-response pattern found in many church services. Call and response, according to Anne H. Charity Hudley in "The Language of Maya Angelou," "creates verbal and nonverbal interaction between speaker and listener by punctuating statements or 'calls' from the speaker with responses from the listener." The call found in lines 8–10 is a declaration, not a question like some examples. The statement, however, does require a response from her readers. They either believe her, or they do not.

Angelou introduces problems in the first few lines of stanzas 1, 3, and 5. After identifying each obstacle in life, the speaker provides a call where she asks the readers to learn from her experience and wisdom. In lines 8–10, the call is an epiphany. She sees there is only one way through her personal difficulty, and she shares it with her readers. It is also a call to action for the audience, because the readers must accept or reject the solution that the speaker provides. The refrain in lines 11–13 is the response. The response repeats the idea of the call, using the same words in a slightly different order. Repeating the call signals the acceptance of the poet's authority, as well as the acceptance of the speaker's solution. The call and response benefits readers by guiding them away from the problem of isolation and toward the solution of relationship and community. The difficulties that the

" ANGELOU UNDERSTANDS THAT PERSONAL

BONDS ARE MORE IMPORTANT THAN

LOCATION, WEALTH, OR SOCIAL STATUS. IT IS

THROUGH CONNECTING WITH OTHERS THAT

PEOPLE FIND THEIR TRUE DESIRES."

poet observes shift from personal problems to familial problems and end on global issues.

Stanza 1 is confessional and introduces the first problem, which is the personal disconnect that the poet experiences. The speaker is contemplating her own life in lines 1 and 2 of the poem. Her solitary thoughts reveal the desire to address her personal sense of isolation in line 3. It is clear from lines 3–5 that she does not feel connected to the world around her. She is looking for a place where her heart will be free. Again, Angelou borrows from the tradition of the church, because the descriptive language she uses in lines 4 and 5 refers to biblical passages and lessons. The description in line 4 is reminiscent of the water of life that quenches spiritual thirst, which is outlined in John 4:14. Line 5 can refer to both the temptation of Christ and the promise of God's provision. In the biblical story of Christ's temptation, Satan tells a fasting and hungry Jesus to turn stones into bread. In Matthew 7:9, Christ reminds listeners of God's provision by asking them if they would give a stone to their hungry children and reminding them that God gives abundantly to those who ask. By borrowing biblical language, the speaker makes clear that the problem she faces has a spiritual element to it. The isolation she feels is simply a condition of her physical surroundings.

By contemplating her isolation, the speaker discovers the solution to overcoming her predicament in lines 6 and 7. Developing relationships and a supportive community can combat the problem of isolation and assist the speaker in her quest to live a life that allows her soul to connect with the world around her. The solution that the speaker discovers is universal, which is evident from the second word of line 8. Everyone needs to connect with other people to find

personal happiness. As the poem continues, the speaker shifts from her personal experience to observations as she addresses the problem of seclusion on different levels.

The third stanza begins with a problem. It shows the readers the dangers of living in isolation. In this stanza, the poet moves on to the loneliness that exists within family units. The family members described in this stanza all suffer on their own. Simply being part of a family is not enough to give them the support that they need to find their place in the world, and the individual disconnect takes a dangerous toll. The spouses are compared to shrieking mythological creatures in line 16, creatures that are also harbingers of death. Their offspring are obviously suffering from depression based on the last three words of line 17. The family members are so isolated that they have become petrified and unfeeling. They hope that money and medical intervention will make them happy again.

The family members in this stanza are unique because they are rich. In fact, they are so wealthy that they have more than any person needs. Money, however, cannot provide the answers that the suffering family members seek. It cannot save them from suffering caused by isolation or remove their fundamental need for close human connection. The call and response that follows the speaker's observation reinforces the poet's solution, which is the understanding that people need to be involved in a community to move forward and live meaningful lives. The call also reminds readers that the advice applies to everyone, regardless of individual wealth or power.

After making clear that the poet's call resonates with all people, regardless of socioeconomic status, the speaker shifts to the general problem of human misery in stanza 5. The metaphor of harsh weather that the speaker sees in line 28 is a reminder that life often brings unhappiness and sorrow beyond our control. Even though the poet is addressing the general idea of human suffering, the poem implies that loneliness and isolation are still elements that affect how people respond to the hardships that life brings. Regardless of the type of pain someone endures or its cause, the poet is sure that connecting with others is the answer to help everyone move beyond sorrow. She provides the same call and response in this stanza as she does in the stanzas describing personal and familial isolation. Human misery on a global scale can be

Angelou uses the image of gathering storm clouds to represent trouble coming. (© Krivosheev Vitaly / Shutterstock.com)

addressed by remembering that all people require close, supportive relationships. Becoming part of a community can provide the path through suffering that isolation never will.

With each call and response, the poet shifts from the themes of isolation and loneliness to the themes of relationship and community. Angelou understands that personal bonds are more important than location, wealth, or social status. It is through connecting with others that people find their true desires. Line 3 explains that the poet wants a place for her soul. Cox explains that Angelou discovered a way to attain her heart's desire when she "realized that 'home' was not in a geographical location, but in the heart. For her, 'home' was centered in her love of her son, Guy." "Alone" is the vehicle through which the poet shares this wisdom. This poetic sermon allows her to share a lesson in hopes that her audience will take steps to build community and continue moving forward.

Source: April Paris, Critical Essay on "Alone," in *Poetry for Students*, Gale, Cengage Learning, 2016.

Nancy E. Walker

In the following review, Walker calls one of Angelou's poetry collections a "glorious book."

Readers expect superlative performances from celebrated writers and artists when they present new works to the public. The most recent publication in Welcome Books' Art & Poetry series, *Love's Exquisite Freedom*, a love poem by Maya Angelou paired with artwork by Pre-Raphaelite artist Edward Burke-Jones, exceeds these high expectations. It is a treasure, a feast for eye and ear.

In one hundred words, Angelou takes us on the emotive journey called love—from living "coiled in shells of loneliness" to the aftermath of love's arrival, including "ecstasies / old memories of pleasure / ancient histories of pain." Through these experiences, she reminds us, "In the flush of love's light / we dare to be brave." And so, "it is only love / which sets us free."

Renaissance woman Maya Angelou, Reynolds Professor of American Studies at Wake Forest University, has published more than thirty bestselling titles. She has distinguished herself as poet and memoirist, novelist and dramatist, producer and actress, educator and historian, and as a civil rights activist. In 2000, she was awarded the Presidential Medal of Arts and, in 2008, the Lincoln Medal. She has earned three Grammy Awards and more than thirty honorary degrees, and has served on two presidential committees.

In a world filled with terror and hatred, Angelou's message of the redemptive power of love is welcome relief. We can live our lives guided by fear or guided by love, so the saying goes. Maya Angelou exhorts us to take the latter path and, in so doing, to become truly free.

Each line of Angelou's lyrical poem is accompanied by the glorious artwork of nineteenth-century British artist Edward Burne-Jones (1833–1898), who portrays love using an impressive variety of media: tapestry, oil on canvas, watercolor, stained and painted glass, graphite, and tempera. His evocative scenes, rich use of color, and exquisite compositions delight and inspire, giving credence to his own words: "Only this is true, that beauty ... softens and comforts, and inspires, and rouses, and lifts up and never fails."

Love's Exquisite Freedom is a glorious book, one destined to lift readers' spirits each time they revisit it.

Source: Nancy E. Walker, Review of *Love's Exquisite Freedom*, in *ForeWord*, October 20, 2011.

Rochelle Ratner

In the following audiobook review, Ratner describes some of Angelou's work as more political than poetic.

Whether it's President Clinton's inauguration or Oprah's birthday, you can count on Angelou to pen a poem in commemoration that is perfectly balanced between appreciation and struggle. There are also the lesser occasions—a bar mitzvah tribute to her nephew, memorials to friends or family (including one of her strongest poems, on her lifelong difficulties with her mother). While she's written much else (most significantly the widely translated novel *I Know Why the Caged Bird Sings*), these politically motivated poems,

rooted in African American feminism, have become her trademark. While one applauds the sentiments and background here, the fact remains that these works are more polemic than lyric. And, if looked at closely, all the cliches stand out. Then, too, there is her reading style. Angelou was hailed 20 years ago as an extremely strong reader, but compared with recent poets who have gained strength from poetry slams and a more oral tradition of writing, her rendering seems almost placid. All said, this would be the perfect audio to give the activists in your life, but it's not recommended for lovers of poetry. Still, considering Angelou's popularity, libraries might want to purchase more than one copy.

Source: Rochelle Ratner, Review of *Celebrations: Rituals of Peace and Prayer*, in *Library Journal*, Vol. 132, No. 8, May 1, 2007, p. 112.

Wayne A. Holst

In the following review, Holst praises Angelou's ongoing autobiographical work.

"Rise and be prepared to move on and ever on," is the continuing theme of Maya Angelou's autobiographical cycle, and the phrase succinctly sums up the story of her life. The first of this series of six splendid testaments, *I Know Why the Caged Bird Sings*, published in 1970, accounted for her first 17 years. That memoir met with much acclaim and popular success. Succeeding volumes included *The Heart of a Woman* (1981) and *Wouldn't Take Nothing for My Journey Now* (1993). Angelou writes autobiography as literature, telling a story of tragedy and triumph, well stated and clearly stamped by her own unique blend of Afro-Americanism.

In *A Song Flung Up to Heaven*, an account of her activities during the '60s, a certain resignation replaces the contentiousness found in at least some of the books in the series. "At that point in the '60s," she writes, "American blacks were acting as if they believed 'A man lived. A man loved. A man tried and a man died and that was all there was to that.' Sometimes, it is hard to believe, in retrospect, that much has really changed. And yet ... "

Those born before that tumultuous decade when civil rights activists Martin Luther King Jr. and Malcolm X were assassinated while still in their prime will treasure the author's personal assessments of the times and her commitment to the dreams of both men. Angelou returned from four years in Africa to work for Malcolm X, only to learn soon after her arrival that he had been killed. King also died just a few weeks after she had agreed to help him organize his poor people's march. She supported what she believed both men ultimately sought to accomplish and did not see their goals at odds.

Those born in the wake of those times, seeing them only through the eyes of history, are offered a unique perspective into the causes of the devastating riots that broke out in many American cities in the late '60s. Angelou writes about her 1965 discoveries as a door-to-door consumer surveyor in Watts a few years before everything came unstuck. It was not hard for her to understand why people burned their own homes and looted community stores. The poignant beauty of Angelou's writing enhances rather than masks the candor with which she addresses the racial crisis through which America was passing.

The book is more of a summing up than a breaking of new ground. Much of Angelou's wisdom has already appeared earlier in the series. For example, she repeats here—using slightly different wording and context—the advice her grandmother gave her as a child, earlier reported in *Nothing for My Journey*: "Sister, change everything you don't like about your life. But when you come to a thing you can't change, then change the way you think about it."

"You'll see it new, and maybe a new way to change it."

On the whole, Angelou's book is a worthy addition to what she originally set out to accomplish: to examine that quality in the human spirit that makes it continue to rise despite the slings and arrows of outrageous fortune. What has served Angelou well is now bestowed upon us. Her autobiographies are statements of profound faith and hope.

Source: Wayne A. Holst, Review of *A Song Flung up to Heaven*, in *Christian Century*, Vol. 119, No. 13, June 19, 2002, pp. 35–36.

SOURCES

Abrams, M. H., "Lyric," in *A Glossary of Literary Terms*, 7th ed., Cornell University Press, 1999, p. 146.

Angelou, Maya, "Alone," in *Maya Angelou: The Complete Poetry*, Random House, 2015, pp. 73–74.

Barufaldi, Dan, "A Review of Past Recessions," *Investopedia*, http://www.investopedia.com/articles/economics/08/past-recessions.asp (accessed September 13, 2015).

"Biography," Caged Bird Legacy website, http://www.mayaangelou.com/biography (accessed September 13, 2015).

Busby, Margaret, "I Am Headed for Higher Ground," in *Guardian* (London, England), June 14, 2002, http://www.theguardian.com/books/2002/jun/15/biography.highereducation (accessed September 12, 2015).

Carlisle, Rodney P., and J. Geoffrey Golson, eds., *America in Revolt during the 1960s and 1970s*, ABC-CLIO, 2008, p. 9.

Cox, Vicki, *Maya Angelou: Poet*, Infobase Publishing, 2006, p. 80.

Dunning, Stefanie K., "Maya Angelou," in *The Oxford Encyclopedia of American Literature*, edited by Jay Parini, Oxford University Press, 2003, pp. 60–62.

"The Equal Rights Amendment," in *UShistory.org*, http://www.ushistory.org/us/57c.asp (accessed September 13, 2015).

Gibbs Harris, Kathryn, Review of *Oh Pray My Wings Are Gonna Fit Me Well*, in *Library Journal*, October 1, 1975, p. 1829.

Groner, Rachael, "Maya Angelou," in *Contemporary American Ethnic Poets: Lives, Works, Sources*, edited by Linda Cullum, Greenwood Press, 2004, pp. 25, 28.

Harmon, William, and Hugh Holman, "Repetition," in *A Handbook to Literature*, 9th ed., Prentice Hall, 2003, p. 431.

Hudley, Anne H. Charity, "The Language of Maya Angelou," in *Slate*, May 29, 2014, http://www.slate.com/blogs/lexicon_valley/2014/05/29/maya_angelou_language_how_the_poet_s_words_reflect_both_african_american.html (accessed September 13, 2015).

Just, Ward, Review of *I Know Why the Caged Bird Sings*, in *Washington Post*, April 3, 1970.

Lupton, Mary Jane, *Maya Angelou: A Critical Companion*, Greenwood Press, p. 5.

MacLean, Nancy, "The Hidden History of Affirmative Action: Working Women's Struggles in the 1970s and the Gender of Class," in *Feminist Studies*, Vol. 25, No. 1, Spring 1999, p. 51.

"Maya Angelou Biography," Academy of Achievement website, http://www.achievement.org/autodoc/page/ang0bio-1 (accessed September 12, 2015).

Mieczkowski, Yanek, *Gerald Ford and the Challenges of the 1970s*, University Press of Kentucky, 2005, p. 289.

Review of *Just Give Me a Cool Drink of Water 'fore I Diiie*, in *Kirkus Reviews*, September 1, 1971, https://www.kirkusreviews.com/book-reviews/maya-angelou/just-give-me-a-cool-drink-of-water-fore-i-diiie/ (accessed September 13, 2015).

FURTHER READING

Angelou, Maya, *I Know Why the Caged Bird Sings*, Turtleback, 1991.

Angelou's first and most popular autobiography, *I Know Why the Caged Bird Sings*, was originally published in 1969. The book was released again by Turtleback in 1991.

Bailey, Beth, and David Farber, eds., *America in the Seventies*, University Press of Kansas, 2004.

This nonfiction text is a collection of essays that address the history and culture of the 1970s. From the economy to Vietnam and civil rights, the book provides valuable information about the decade.

Bloom, Harold, ed., *Maya Angelou*, Chelsea House Publishers, 2009.

This collection of critical essays provides useful insight into Angelou's work. The book is suitable for readers with different levels of understanding and includes a literary chronology.

Jarrett, Gene Andrew, *The Wiley Blackwell Anthology of African American Literature*, Vol. 2, *1920 to the Present*, Wiley Blackwell, 2014.

This collection of short stories, poems, plays, essays, novellas, and autobiographies dating back to the early twentieth century shows the development of African American literature over the years. The text includes Angelou and many of the writers who influenced her.

Schulman, Bruce J., *The Seventies: The Great Shift in American Culture, Society, and Politics*, Free Press, 2001.

Schulman examines the political and social changes that occurred in the 1970s. The text offers a general overview of the years that provided the background for Angelou's poem "Alone."

SUGGESTED SEARCH TERMS

Maya Angelou

Maya Angelou AND biography

Maya Angelou AND Alone

Maya Angelou AND poetry

1970s AND United States

Maya Angelou AND criticism

African American literature

1970s AND civil rights

African American literature AND Maya Angelou

Axe Handles

GARY SNYDER

1983

Winner of the American Book Award, Gary Snyder's collection *Axe Handles* (1983) contains a poem by the same name that is a quiet yet profound exploration of the power of art and creativity in the transmission of wisdom across generations. An example of the ecological poetics that shaped the life and writing of one of the most influential American poets of a generation, the poem "Axe Handles" shows how a single idea—how to make an axe handle—can travel across centuries, language barriers, and diverse cultures while retaining its power to inspire new ideas and new understandings of the world. This poem is a wonderful introduction to the poet who brought readers the Pulitzer Prize–winning *Turtle Island* (1974).

AUTHOR BIOGRAPHY

Gary Snyder was born in San Francisco, California, on May 8, 1930, to Harold and Lois Hennessy (née Wilkey) Snyder. The family struggled terribly through the Great Depression, and when Gary was two years old they moved to King County, Washington, in order to tend a small subsistence farm. The family moved again to Portland, Oregon, when Gary was twelve. Following his parents' divorce in 1942, Gary lived with his mother and younger sister, Anthea.

Graduating from Lincoln High School, Snyder enrolled in Reed College, where he published his

Gary Snyder *(© Getty | Chris Felver)*

first poems in a student journal before graduating with a double major in anthropology and literature in 1951. During his college years, Snyder married Alison Gass; the couple separated seven months later before divorcing in 1952. Following graduation, Snyder worked in a logging camp before heading to Indiana University to continue his studies in anthropology. He left Indiana after one term and moved to San Francisco to dedicate himself to honing his poetry while working variously as a fire lookout and logger.

It was in San Francisco that Snyder became interested in Zen Buddhism as well as Asian culture and language. From 1956 through 1968, Snyder lived extensively in Japan, where he met Masa Uehara. The two married in 1967 and had two sons, Kai (1968) and Gen (1969). The couple divorced in 1989. Snyder was married a third time to Carole Lynn Koda, who passed away from cancer in 2006.

Beginning his career as part of the so-called Beat generation, Snyder is more well-recognized as a dedicated and poetic spokesperson for the preservation of the natural world and what he saw as the earthy consciousness of indigenous cultures. Although distinct from such Beats as

Allen Ginsberg and Jack Kerouac, Snyder was an influential member of his generation. Kerouac, for instance, modeled his character Japhy Ryder in *The Dharma Bums* (1958) on Snyder.

Many of Snyder's poems aim directly at instilling an ecological consciousness, from his earliest *Riprap* (1959) and *Myths & Texts* (1960) through his most acclaimed collection, *Turtle Island* (1974), which won the Pulitzer Prize in 1975. His 1983 collection *Axe Handles*, which includes the poem of the same name, won the American Book Award in 1984. In these poems, Snyder layers his familiar ecological themes with reflections on a life lived as a husband, father, and devoted steward of the land. He wrote of similar ideas as well in his prose, most notably *The Practice of Wild* (1990) and *A Place in Space: Ethics, Aesthetics, and Watersheds* (1995). His long poem *Mountains and Rivers without End* (1996) was almost universally acclaimed by critics for its conscious effort to resurrect the social impacts of the classic epic. He followed this success eight years later with an entirely new collection of verse, *Danger on Peaks: Poems*, in 2004.

Snyder has been recognized with a variety of awards throughout his career, including the Bess Hokin Prize (1964), an American Academy of Arts and Letters award (1966), a Guggenheim Foundation fellowship (1968), and the Bollingen Prize (1997).

POEM SUMMARY

The text used for this summary is from *Axe Handles*, North Point Press, 1983, pp. 5–6. Versions of the poem can be found on the following web pages: http://www.poetryfoundation.org/poem/248068, http://www.americanpoems.com/poets/Gary-Snyder/7860, and http://www.best-poems.net/gary_snyder/axe_handles.html.

"Axe Handles" comprises thirty-six free-verse lines that range from three to ten syllables each. Most of the sentences carry across line breaks, in most instances without an encumbering terminal punctuation.

The opening line sets the poem on an afternoon at the end of April. It is a poem of late spring, and the speaker is showing a young man named Kai how to throw a hatchet so that it sticks in a stump. The flight of the hatchet through the air is at once precise (half a turn only) and graceful, with the result being a perfect landing in the stump. Given that Kai is the name of Snyder's son, it is fair to read the writer/speaker of the poem as Snyder himself.

The act of watching his father throw the hatchet triggers a memory for Kai of another axe head, this one in the nearby workshop. Finding a broken axe handle behind the shop door, father and son set themselves to converting one type of handle (axe) to another (hatchet) so that the newly found axe head will become functional again in the present world of these two generations of woodsmen.

Cutting the axe handle the appropriate length for a hatchet, they take the pieces of the puzzle (new handle, axe head, and complete hatchet) to the wood block, where the poet/speaker begins to work the wood into its new shape as his son watches closely. As he begins to work the wood, the speaker recalls a phrase from another poet, the American Ezra Pound (1885–1972), which he rehearses in his own mind as he prepares for the task at hand.

Turning to Kai, the speaker paraphrases Pound's poetry into more common language, telling his son that they will make a new handle by copying the one they have. As Kai acknowledges his understanding of this creative process, the poet remembers a second piece of literature that refers to the building of an axe handle. This second remembered piece, by a fourth-century Chinese writer, was the source of Pound's phrase. Like an archaeologist, the poet uncovers another layer of memory of this phrase as he recalls his own teacher, Shih-hsiang Chen, translating and explaining the importance of the same fourth-century phrase years earlier.

Reflecting on this transmission of language and wisdom across generations and cultures, the poet arrives at two levels of understanding of the moment in which he is living. The first is that he, like Pound and a fourth-century Chinese writer, is a metaphoric axe bringing knowledge to his own son/student. As the student/son learns the craft of making, as well as the importance of models, he too begins the journey toward maturation, which will see him one day become an axe for his own child or student. In this sense, the poem examines the power of cultural transmission of values and insights across generations.

The poet/speaker also takes this moment to reflect on his role as a writer/creator. In this sense, he is again the creative force of the axe,

with his handles as the poems that he produces and sends into the world as part of the craft that sustains a culture across generations.

THEMES

Ecology

Although Snyder is very often positioned as an environmental or nature poet, he is more accurately described as an *ecological* poet. The formal study of the interactions between living organisms and their environment, ecology is a deeply interdisciplinary field. It expands in Snyder's case to include the expected (biology and geography) as well as the unexpected (poetry, culture, and craftsmanship). Topics of interest within this broad theme include diversity, cooperation, competition, and also, as in "Axe Handles," the power of succession.

Although related, *ecology* is not synonymous with such terms as *environment* and *environmentalism*. An important focus of ecologists that Snyder picks up on is improving the general understanding of how diversity impacts the functioning of an environment or culture. Accordingly, in "Axe Handles" Snyder aligns both past (fourth century), present (the poet/speaker), and future (Kai) with a geocultural diversity that extends from fourth-century China through twentieth-century America.

Unlike many writers with an ecological or environmental focus, Snyder is not prone to doomsday scenarios. On the contrary, as he explains in the *Paris Review*, he believes that

> the environmental movement in the last twenty years has never done well when it threw out excessive doom scenarios. Doom scenarios, even though they might be true, are not politically or psychologically effective. The first step, I think...is to make us love the world rather than to make us fear for the end of the world. Make us love the world, which means the non-human as well as the human, and then begin to take better care of it.

Key to an ecological perspective, too, is a focus on holism, or the idea that the organization of life (and culture) into a whole system that functions according to higher-order patterns cannot be understood as a simple summation of the individual parts. New ideas and concepts emerge because of how the components interact rather than how they combine through mere addition. In "Axe Handles," for

TOPICS FOR FURTHER STUDY

- The term *community*, Snyder says in an interview in the *Paris Review*, applies to a group of "diverse people who live in the same place and who are tied together by their inevitable association with each other, and their willingness to engage in that over a long period of time." In a *Western American Literature* interview, he refers to the collection *Axe Handles* as "a description, an account in many ways, of coming into the community and coming into the place in subtle ways." In a well-written and thoughtful essay, discuss how the poem "Axe Handles" relates to Snyder's understanding of the complexities of community.

- "We think before language, and thought-images come into language at a certain point. We have fundamental thought processes that are prelinguistic. Some of my poetry reaches back to that," Snyder says in the *Paris Review* interview. Taking Snyder's own thoughts on language as an invitation and cue, create a graphic, multimedia, or digital representation of "Axe Handles" in an attempt to paraphrase its meaning in a prelinguistic fashion. Be prepared to display your final creation as part of a class exhibit dedicated to the work of Snyder.

- Performance is an essential part of Snyder's poetry, and he is famous for delivering powerful readings of his poems. Create a video performance of "Axe Handles." Feel free to use multiple voices, sound effects, and whatever else you feel will help your video convey the complexities and subtleties of Snyder's poem while at the same time respecting its key message.

- Select a poem by the poet Shel Silverstein, whose work is aimed at young readers as well as adults. In an essay, compare and contrast your Silverstein selection with Snyder's "Axe Handles," which is a poem about an adult using words to shape the understanding of a younger person. Be sure to draw on details of each poem as often as possible in your essay.

instance, the poet produces a new poem in his decision to paraphrase his own wisdom in his instructions to Kai rather than repeating the words of Pound, for instance. His common-sense rendering of the poetic phrase does, of course, add to the catalogue of commentaries on the act of axe handling. However, it also emerges as a new way of talking about the act of making a handle, one that is more conducive to a contemporary audience that might be inclined to turn away from the traditional craft method of fixing the broken tool, in favor of simply buying a new one.

In this sense, "Axe Handles" is opposed to any reductionist approach to the problem of the broken axe handle. The poet focuses not solely on the basic and functional act of replacing the handle, but on the life and artistic lessons that can be learned from the building process. Every small moment, the poem suggests, contains the possibility of such learning if the participants are open to the opportunities to see the world in a different way.

Romanticism

An artistic and intellectual movement that originated in Europe near the end of the eighteenth century, romanticism was a reaction, in part, to the Industrial Revolution and to the scientific, rational approach to the natural world. In contrast to the detached rationalism of the day, the romantics emphasized emotion as the most authentic response to an experience, especially when confronting new opportunities for the first time. Like Snyder, the romantics considered folk, ancient, or even primitive cultures to be more directly engaged with the emotional and creative powers of nature and, accordingly,

The axe handle of the title is a literal object in the poem but also a metaphor. *(© TTstudio | Shutterstock.com)*

more resistant to the increasing pressures of industrialization, population growth, and urban sprawl.

Influenced heavily by the events and ideas of the French Revolution, romanticism assigned a high value, too, to artists who would serve as role models for the rest of society. Similarly, in "Axe Handles," the poet traces the genealogy of his own understanding of craft and creativity to artists who influenced his life. In turn, the poet comes to understand his own position (and with that the responsibilities) as a role model for Kai.

Simplicity

Simplicity is the quality of something that is easy to understand, compared to something that is complicated. Simplicity can be used to describe scenery, beauty, and even poetry, as when the speaker in "Axe Handles" paraphrases a line written by Ezra Pound in a language that the much younger Kai can (and does) understand. Through this and other poems, Snyder foregrounds, as Allan Williamson explains in the *New Republic*, "a somewhat Thoreauvian poetic treatment of the psychic value of simplification" that foregrounds the cultural and personal benefits of decluttering as a means of connecting with a more primitive sense of belonging in the world. In "Axe Handles," the focal activity itself (the carving of a handle) is appealing in its unmediated interaction between man, wood, and a previous model.

STYLE

Metaphor

Drawn loosely from the Greek term *metaphora* (to transfer or carry across), metaphor is a type of figurative language that effectively carries a meaning associated with one subject across a point of comparison to connect with another, typically unrelated object. More simply, a metaphor compares two very unlike objects with each other (as in, "love is open rose light"). Most theories of metaphor suggest that all language contains within it a kind of metaphoric energy, most of which is overlooked or ignored in everyday use, in which the connection between ideas and words is much more direct than in poetry. Nonetheless, metaphor, even when left dormant, is central to how individuals think about and perceive the world.

In poetry, however, the use of metaphor (linking writing to a game of catch, for instance) opens language and perception outwards, effectively cracking the edges of language so that possibilities of meaning cascade to previously unimagined opportunities. As William Pratt underscores in his review of *Axe Handles*, the title poem is one in which Snyder extends the metaphor of axe handles in a number of directions simultaneously. Most obviously, the act of creating an axe handle is a metaphor for the transmission of culture from father to son, or more generally from one generation to the next. Seen from another angle, the axe is a metaphor for the creative individual (woodworker or poet) who has the handle standing in as the product of that creativity (the handle or the poem).

Repetition

Given that "Axe Handles" is a poem that explores how culture is learned and inherited across generations and cultures, it is appropriate that Snyder uses repetition. The word *axe*, for instance, appears seven times throughout the poem, but also in three different contexts: as part of the speaker's present moment with Kai, as part of Ezra Pound's poetic phrase, and as part of the fourth-century Chinese essay on literacy (which itself has been translated). The word has been passed across time and, with each passing, adds layers of meaning for each new generation to engage in as a platform for its own understanding and creativity.

The poem is also held together by the repetition of the conjunction *and*, which appears more than a dozen times, often more than once in a single line. As a conjunction, this word provides a logical connection between the parts of a sentence, establishing a building of detail that implies a certain equality of value of the items connected. By using some of these repetitions to begin a sentence, Snyder underscores the transitional properties of the axe and the handle. These are not items (nor a creative process) that are sealed off from other times and cultures; instead the items serve as engaged transitions between generations.

Rhymes

As Allan Williamson celebrates in his discussion of Snyder's poetry as a body of work, one of the distinguishing characteristics of his writing is an "unexpected persistence of rhyming" that moves beyond traditional end rhymes with lines establishing a clear pattern toward what Williamson calls a strategic use of "syncopated rhyming," or rhyming that seems to set the poem off beat rather than pulling it into an easy, almost natural rhythm. He accomplishes this, for instance, by "the odder habit of rhyming the ends and beginnings of nearby lines."

HISTORICAL CONTEXT

Advancing Technology

"Axe Handles" appeared originally in 1983, the year that is usually seen as both the official beginning of public accessibility to the Internet and the first mobile cellular telephone call. It was, in short, a year in which two of the technologies that would change the world in dramatic ways rose to prominence. Technological announcements defined this year in many ways. In January, for instance, IRAS was launched from Vanenberg Air Force Base in California in order to conduct the world's first all-sky infrared survey from space. The same month saw the transformational software program Lotus 1-2-3 released for IBM PC-compatible computers.

The year 1983 also reminds the world of many of the dangers associated with industrialization and more specifically with the increasing role of advanced technologies in business and personal lives. In February, the US Environmental Protection Agency announced its intention to purchase the community of Times Beach, Missouri, in order to evacuate its residents from a landscape that had become toxic from dioxin contamination. Later that month, the Salem Nuclear Power Plant in New Jersey hit the news when an automatic shutdown failed. The year 1983 was, in fact, one of many such nuclear-related events, including at the Kursk Nuclear Power Plant in Russia and the Embalese Nuclear Power Station in Argentina.

Snyder's poem, in contrast, seems to step back from this surging technology to remind

COMPARE
&
CONTRAST

- **1983:** The speaker of Snyder's poem refers to carving the new axe handle as he and Kai look to repair a broken axe they discover in the shop. In 1983, the act of wood carving is part of a trades community that was still relevant but waning as a skill that was valued in a world increasingly shaped by new technologies and methods of production. Like many such skills, wood carving is seen as an artisanal practice, that is, one that requires an unusually heavy reliance on human (as distinct from mechanical) skill, patience, attention to detail, and overall craftsmanship.

  Today: Instead of carving the axe handle out of wood, the poet and Kai might visit a local maker space and create a perfect replica of the original axe handle using 3D printing technology. 3D printers are foundational tools in what has come to be known as additive manufacturing, which make three-dimensional objects by the use of a computer. The printer uses repeating layers of material to create a three-dimensional effect. In this sense, a 3D printer is a type of "industrial robot" that replicates the craftsmanship of previous generations at a fraction of the time required.

- **1983:** The poet/speaker refers to a Chinese passage that he was taught years earlier and that he knows through another poem, which he acquired in his diverse reading.

The 1980s continued the legacy of the 1960s emphasis on a liberal education based on broad readings from across a range of disciplines.

Today: The Chinese passage might be reworked into English via a digital translator, and later retrieved from a digital database of online poetry using the search term "axe." The context and focus of education has shifted in recent decades towards applied and career-based learning, which has made some learned skills (including, arguably, the reading of poetry) to be considered of lesser value than other, more practical skills.

- **1983:** The poet is teaching Kai how to throw an axe at a stump. The activity would be seen in this era as a bonding experience, and even a right of passage as the older man demonstrates how to plan, aim, and use a certain speed and dexterity when throwing the axe.

  Today: All US states now have laws in place that hold parents accountable for the actions and activities of their children. The act of axe throwing, for instance, could be seen as irresponsible parenting, creating if not a legal questioning of the parent involved, then a moral one given the tone of today's culture.

---

audiences of the other side of the cultural dialogue, the one focused on preservationist and conservationist issues. The early 1980s saw a notable rise in membership in such organizations as the Sierra Club, the National Audubon Society, and the National Wildlife Federation. Snyder's poem does not resist technology directly but instead offers a quiet and gentle alternative to a discourse increasingly shaped by advances in technology.

The natural world made the headlines in 1983 almost by way of underscoring the importance of Snyder's ecological message. In May, a powerful earthquake and tsunami in northern Japan killed over a hundred and injured hundreds more. Hurricane Alicia hit the Texas coast in 1983, killing twenty-two and causing almost four billion dollars in damage. Elsewhere, heavy rain triggered flooding in areas of Spain, killing dozens and causing millions in damages.

As the speaker shapes the wood of the axe handle, so will he shape his son, teaching him how to make his way through life. *(© Carlos andre Santos | Shutterstock.com)*

CRITICAL OVERVIEW

Writing in the *Paris Review*, Eliot Weinberger describes Snyder as "America's primary poet-celebrant of the wilderness, poet-exponent of environmentalism and Zen Buddhism, and poet-citizen of the Pacific Rim," pointing out in particular that Snyder was "the first American poet to gaze almost exclusively west toward the East, rather than east toward Western civilization." His style, Weinberger continues, is "an idiosyncratic combination of the plain speech of [William Carlos] Williams, the free-floating, intensely visual images of [Ezra] Pound, and the documentary information of both."

Such praise of Snyder and his poetry is not uncommon in the critical assessment of a lifetime of writing. Allan Williamson, in a profile for the *New Republic*, describes Snyder as

> an inheritor of the Poundian clarity, the sharp-edged seeing and thinking in which the whole mind seems to quicken; and because he conceives of his task as a poet so widely, as an

inclusive meditation—political, psychological, religious—on the human situation.

In his essay "Gary Snyder and the Curve of Return," Robert Schultz describes *Axe Handles* as a collection in which Snyder "celebrates the whim and wisdom of middle age" and more specifically "gives special emphasis to the loops of cultural transmission." These are poems, Schultz continues, that explore how "our most fundamental knowledge is discovered in moments of experience which stand out of time." In this poem and collection, he concludes, there is a strong "sense of continuity and cultural transmission which Snyder has acquired as a husband, father, and homesteader, a sense which has changed him over the course of his career from *dharma* hitch-hiker to domestic visionary."

Placing *Axe Handles* in the context of Snyder's achievement up to 1984, *World Literature Today*'s William Pratt argues that the collection "adds nothing especially new to his achievement, but it provides further examples of his latter-day imagism." "Much of the force of Snyder's work,"

Pratt continues, "lies in the audacity of his choice of subjects, and he seems to take as much delight in producing poems out of trivial circumstances as a child might in making toys out of kitchen gadgets." This said, Pratt is hesitant to align Snyder with the pantheon of American poets to which he is often compared. "Snyder seems more exceptional than he really is," he concludes,

> because he has an eye for original subjects and a protective instinct toward the natural world. So, though his poetry may be minor, it echoes major voices, and he is the bearer of a tradition of poetic realism which, however faint, it is good to know is still alive.

Poetry reviewer Bruce Bawer sees in *Axe Handles* a clear signal of "Snyder's heightened interest in tradition, culture, and family." It is, Bawer concludes, "Snyder's finest book" to date and one in which the poet "quietly, gently . . . conveys a luminous, poignant vision of a life afforded joy and strength by recognition of the essential things which give it meaning." Snyder is, as John P. O'Grady observes, "one of our culture's venerable teachers."

CRITICISM

Klay Dyer

Dyer is a freelance writer specializing in topics relating to literature, popular culture, and the relationship between creativity and technology. In the following essay, he explores how Gary Snyder's "Axe Handles" reimagines work as part of a metaphysical awakening to an individual's connection to the natural world.

Gary Snyder is best known as a poet of landscape and the environment, as well as a poet who introduced Zen Buddhism both to the writers of the Beat generation and to mainstream audiences who enjoyed his poetry in print and in performance. Snyder has always maintained that his sensibilities arose from his youthful interest in Native American cultures and their involvement with a holistic vision of the natural world. Throughout his life, he has sought to align these early inclinations with his adult interest in Buddhist practices, Yamabushi initiation, and other similar experiences. In other words, he is a poet: a man whose writing (and life) provides a profound synthesis of biology, mysticism, anthropology, and an ecological poetics that

> TOOLS PROVIDE A MEANS FOR INTERACTING WITH THE ENVIRONMENT AND FOR NEGOTIATING A HUMAN PRESENCE. THEY ARE A MEANS, IN OTHER WORDS, OF INTEGRATING PHYSICAL LABOR INTO SNYDER'S REFLECTIONS OF THE EXCHANGE OF ENERGIES BETWEEN INDIVIDUALS AND THE NATURAL WORLD IN WHICH THEY LIVE."

allows readers to probe the interface connecting culture, nature, and the world in its complexity.

Sitting down to an extended interview with Snyder, the critic John O'Grady asked a question that reflects the eclectic and multidisciplinary nature of Snyder's interests: What might a Buddhist landscape look and feel like? Snyder paused, acknowledged the insightfulness of the question, and answered,

> A Buddhist landscape would be a living landscape. It would not just be rocks and minerals and plants, etc. It wouldn't be an assemblage of things. It would be a spiritual ecosystem, an energy-flow model. It would be like a Chinese painter trying to present landscape—it would be matter in process.

A recurring theme in Snyder's poetry is his love for tools as functional extensions of the landscapes he imagines. Tools provide a means for interacting with the environment and for negotiating a human presence. They are a means, in other words, of integrating physical labor into Snyder's reflections of the exchange of energies between individuals and the natural world in which they live. The axe represents Kai's introduction to a kind of work that allows for an emotional, intellectual, and physical immersion in the world. By teaching Kai to master the design and creation of a new handle (getting a handle on the making of a handle), Snyder's speaker introduces the young man to a sense of competence in a new creative task.

Work is not something to be avoided in Snyder's world, nor is it a burden. "The goal of living is not to consider work work," Snyder explains, "but to consider it your life and your play." In this sense, "work per se does not bring

WHAT DO I READ NEXT?

- Snyder's *Turtle Island* (1974) is considered by many critics to be his most accomplished and complete collection of poetry. In it, he sets out to reclaim through poetry a sense of understanding of contemporary culture as a holistic balancing of language, philosophy, and spiritual vision.

- As an example of his fine work in prose, Snyder's *The Practice of the Wild* (1990) is a captivating collection of nine essays in which he explores his thoughts on wilderness, nature, culture, and Zen philosophy.

- Jack Kerouac's *The Dharma Bums* (1958) features the character of Japhy Ryder, who Dana Goodyear of the *New Yorker* describes as "a sprightly, cocksure poet with a background and set of interests striking similar to Snyder's, [who] introduces the narrator, Ray Smith, to Zen Buddhism and mountaineering." One of the definitive novels of the Beat generation, *The Dharma Bums* "incited a 'Rucksack Revolution' and fed a craze for Zen. It made Snyder famous."

- Aldo Leopold's *A Sand County Almanac* (1949) is foundational reading for anyone interested in the roots of ecological thought in the twentieth century. Widely cited as one of the most influential nature books ever published, it is based on Leopold's experience in a summer shack along the banks of the Wisconsin River. Part memoir, part essay, and part environmental call to arms, it remains a compelling read.

- Canadian Sharon Butala's *Coyote's Morning Cry: Meditations and Dreams from a Life in Nature* (1996) reveals a deep kinship with Snyder's body of work while at the same time being geographically specific to another part of North America.

- Ursula K. Le Guin's *The Word for World Is Forest* (1972) is a young-adult novel set centuries in the future. It is a world in which the Terrans have established a logging colony and military base named "New Tahiti" on a tree-covered planet whose small, green-furred, big-eyed inhabitants have a culture centered on lucid dreaming. Terran greed spirals around native innocence and wisdom, overturning the ancient society.

- Caribbean poet Derek Walcott's *White Egrets* (2010) echoes many of Snyder's themes with poems that focus on the wisdom that comes through the passing of time and traditions, as well as the lessons that can be learned from the sometimes terrifying beauty of the natural world.

---

about salvation, nor is it automatically virtuous. It has more the quality of acknowledgment and recognition and making necessity charming." As James I. McClintock argues in *The American Biology Teacher*, work in "Axe Handles" and more explicitly "the carving of the boy's axe handle with his father's axe comes to represent . . . the passing on of knowledge and skills from one generation to the next."

Work is part of what McClintock suggests is Snyder's interest in the "generally known and fundamental ecological principle" of succession. Very generally, succession refers to the fact "that in any ecosystem over time there exists a pattern of change from initial instability and simplicity to a mature 'climax state' of optimum stability and maximum diversity." As the handle is carved, the poet discovers a stability in the fact that this present moment of creation is linked intimately and organically with similar moments from other times and other places. Work, in this sense, allows the poet to imagine and appreciate a "stable ecosystem in later stages of succession [that] has 'learned' about changes in the environment and can accept new information with less change and energy." Kai understands quickly the language of the speaker, who is changing the language of his past teachers (both Pound and Shih-hsiang Chen) without diminishing the energy of the message. The change of culture is negotiated seamlessly, creating what ecological theory calls a loop.

As McClintock observes, Snyder's poetry is rich with such loops, which serve in "Axe Handles," for instance, as a clearly established conduit "between past and present, direct experience and thought, ordinary experience and extraordinary, so that energy pathways are maintained for personal and cultural sustenance." This loop of work combined with creativity and a deep sense of connectedness to a shared past shows readers a way out of finding the past a burden to bear. Instead Kai, like the poet/speaker before him, opens his ears and imagination in order to hear the words spoken down from generation to generation. Again, stability of the ecosystem comes from an embeddedness in the past, not in spite of it. It is reassuring that axe handles continue to exist and to break and that there is a need for them to be recreated by each generation. The relationship between Kai and the poet is a continuation of a long series of relationships between students and teachers and between readers and the poems that have made lasting impressions on their lives.

In "Axe Handles," the handle itself is of metaphorical importance, representing the poet's tools of the trade. The poet is passing down not only a set of woodworking skills but a set of word-working ones as well. His paraphrase of Ezra Pound's translation of a fourth-century Chinese saying is a passing down of not only a new (common-language) poetry but a poetics (philosophy of creating poetry). The poet/speaker is both describing and demonstrating the act of creation to Kai, showing him how the tools (the axe and language) are always both an artifact (something created) and a model for creating more axe handles, more poems, and more culture. As McClintock explains, in ecological terms "the poem itself is, therefore, a special kind of recycled energy that carries information (or intelligence and wisdom) through the network." Driving the network, too, is the work of the poet to rework the languages of fourth-century China and Ezra Pound into more common speech patterns that capture the attention of Kai without ever diminishing the message or lesson. The reworking of language "takes an enormous amount of cultural shaping, too, at some point," as Snyder explained to O'Grady.

What this cultural rework also underscores is that language (and the language of work) has the qualities of what ecologists call *wild systems.* Snyder pointed out to O'Grady that these systems, which are critical to all broad relational moments (human to nature, human to work), "are highly complex [and] cannot be intellectually mastered—that is to say they're too complex to master simply in intellectual or mathematical terms—and they are self-managing and self-organizing." The language of "Axe Handles" is such a wild system. With complex ties to other places and times, it is a language of work that cannot be contained but must be expressed in a way that is at once different from and aligned with other systems of expression. To build an axe handle is to engage with fourth-century China, the intellect of a translator, and the interpretations of a poet. It is also to engage in the physical acts of cutting and shaping, of measuring and sizing, and of forcing the handle into the head. A seemingly simple act (creating an axe handle) expands in this poem to become both a physical and metaphysical experience for Kai and for the poet/speaker with whom he works.

As stated previously, Snyder does not see work as labor or as toil. His view is much more aligned with an understanding of work as an expression of one's vocation or calling in the world. Therefore, what "Axe Handles" reveals through its intricate layering is that one's calling is rarely stable or intractable. Snyder sees work as based on the opportunities that come into an individual's life, and work offers to each individual a moment in which emotion, creativity, and physical skills can merge. Work is not an easy task but a process of personal exploration of how work aligns with such life-affirming activities as creativity and living as one with the natural world.

Gone from "Axe Handles" is the traditional Western call to use work as a means of subduing or controlling the natural world. Snyder reimagines the language and the practice of work to be a good thing and a cornerstone of a life lived well and in harmony with the wild systems that track across each lifetime. The axe handle, like the poem, is an extension of its creator and an expression of the personal values that give it shape. Work is, as this poem underscores, not so much about production as it is about the process of learning, of creating a culture of craft and humility, and of becoming one with traditions both human and natural. Work is both the physical

Snyder highlights the sense of history in the father-son relationship, as well as the responsibility.
(© Jack Frog / Shutterstock.com)

and metaphysical engine of Snyder's poem, allowing both teacher and student to bow respectfully to the past while moving forward into a future of new tasks, new words, and new visions.

Source: Klay Dyer, Critical Essay on "Axe Handles," in *Poetry for Students*, Gale, Cengage Learning, 2016.

Patrick D. Murphy

In the following excerpt, Murphy offers a close study of the first section of the collection Axe Handles.

...Part One of *Axe Handles* is titled "Loops" and comprises twenty-five poems, with the title poem placed first. As Julia Martin notes, "Snyder has frequently used the idea of 'looping back' to indicate a recursive sense of history and tradition. The metaphor implies at many levels a reconnection with origins, 'the old ways,' and a recognition of continuity with ancient tradition." Martin's claims are certainly implied in the epigraph to the volume and restated without ambiguity in the poem "Axe

Handles." But to understand this poem, one needs first to consider its epigraph.

If the dedication, "This book is for San Juan Ridge," can be said to emphasize place, then the epigraph can be said to emphasize time, specifically the transmission of culture down through generations. Snyder identifies his epigraph as "a folk song from the Pin area [of China], 5th c.b.c." Rather than "high" literature, he draws on popular tradition, orally transmitted. The opening two lines indicate that the new is crafted on the basis of the old and that such transmission of knowledge requires models. This lesson is then applied to marriage, so that craft and culture, as well as the older generation, the present generation, and the one yet to come are all implicated in custom and ritual. The "go-between" is literally a marriage broker. In a broader cultural sense, however, one could say it is also the artist or poet who, through his or her role as a communicator, brings different people together and educates them about each other. Snyder has explained that "*Axe Handles* goes back to being very close to the functional origins of poetry in

CLEARLY, MANY OF THESE POEMS CAN BE

UNDERSTOOD IN TERMS OF 'LOOPS,' HISTORICAL,

GENERATIONAL, CULTURAL, AND REGIONAL."

terms of folksong and folklore. It's not for nothing that the whole poem, the whole book, the
title and the lead poem is out of the Book of
Song, the Odes. I am looking back to the Book
of Odes as a model for that book of verse, to its
simple poems about planting fields and getting
together for feasts—real early agricultural community poetry."

Robert Schultz and David Wyatt comment
that "instruction is at the heart of this book,
emphasized in its beginning and returned to frequently." In essence, "Axe Handles" (5–6) provides a contemporary version of the epigraph's
lesson, emphasizing generational communication.
The "hatchet-head" lies dormant, awaiting a handle, until the poet's son Kai remembers it and
wants to own a hatchet in imitation of his father.
We could think of Kai as also being a hatchet-
head, full of potential for useful labor but lacking
the vehicle for translating that promise into practice. As Snyder shapes the hatchet handle, he is
serving as a handle of knowledge that Kai can
grab in order to use the hatchet properly when it
comes his turn to labor. Snyder makes this point
through his own recollection of Pound and the
saying that Pound derived from the ancient Chinese, that when making an axe the model is close
at hand. Snyder, in his youth, served as a hatchet-
head in need of a handle and found his handle in
the poet Ezra Pound, the essayist Lu Ji, and the
college professor Shih-hsiang Chen, as the poem
indicates. At the same time, Snyder is shaping Kai
so that he will also become a handle, as indicated
near the end of the poem.

Snyder does not call Pound or Chen either a
hatchet-head or a handle but calls each an "axe,"
because in their lives they joined together the
potential of the head and the knowledge of the
handle in poetic and educational practice. Snyder
in his fifties has also become an "axe," complete in
both functions as a "model" and as an instrument
in the service of the "craft of culture," and he
appears confident that Kai will become an "axe"

as well. As Katsunori Yamazato succinctly
explains it, "Snyder's commitment to the wild
territory and the subsequent inhabitory life leads
him to understand a cycle of culture—flowing
from Pound, Chen, the poet himself, and to his
son Kai—in which one is both 'shaped' and
'shaping,' a cycle preserving and transmitting
'craft of culture.'" The end of the poem emphasizes a positive sense of the continuity of culture
that includes internal change, rather than the cultural rupture emphasized in some of the *Turtle
Island* poems. There a monolithic national culture
needed to be criticized and challenged. Here,
Snyder has moved beyond national culture to a
larger sense of culture as the multigenerational
force of positive human shaping that works
simultaneously on entire societies and on one
person at a time across nations and across
centuries.

The next poem in "Loops," "For/From Lew,"
continues the emphasis on serving as a teacher.
The poem depicts a dream vision in which
Snyder's dead friend Lew Welch speaks to him.
The first two lines echo the song "Joe Hill," about
a hero of the American Left. Snyder implies by
this allusion that Welch should also be seen as a
working-class kind of hero, one who serves in this
poem as a "go-between" attempting to marry the
worlds of the living and the dead. Welch instructs
Snyder in his responsibilities as a poet in the 1980s:
"teach the children about the cycles"; i.e., the
cycles of all entities on the planet, which would
necessarily include teaching them about death as
well as life.

"River in the Valley" embodies the practicing
of this task in Snyder's role as a teacher to his
sons. The poem also shows the fine attention to
specific details that recurs throughout *Axe Handles*. The first stanza establishes a set of relationships: through numerical difference, between the
human "we" and the "thousands of swallows"; by
means of an abandoned "overhead/roadway,"
between the humans who have created but cannot utilize it and the swallows who are able to
adapt it to their own purposes; and through the
solid-fluid dichotomy, between the river/creek of
flowing water and the road/bridge of seemingly
static concrete. The next section treats the behavior of the three humans in the presence of the
nesting swallows. Gen imitates the flock's swirl-
ing flight, while Kai focuses on tracking a single
bird. Their games mimic the two simultaneous
forms of energy: wave and particle, as well as

two different types of hunting. Meanwhile, the swallows' flight mimics the action of fish, as they flow in and out under the bridge. And as for Snyder? He is busy removing grass seeds that have stuck to his socks. As the swallows engage in a pattern replicated elsewhere in nature, so too the humans participate in such patterns, linking animal and human together. Even Snyder unwittingly finds himself participating in wild seed dispersal, since the plant has used his socks to give its seeds a free ride to another location. This action duplicates his function as father and provides him with the same role as numerous other animals, such as bears and birds, who contribute to the flourishing of plant life by moving seeds as part of their eating patterns.

As the three of them move on, from the abandoned causeway through the town of Colusa and out toward the mountains, "One boy asks, 'where do rivers start?'" Snyder provides a factual answer that quickly becomes metaphysical in its implications. The cycles of planetary life are treated as "One" cycle, just as it is "One boy" who speaks rather than a named individual. Snyder moves out from the particular to the universal, and a qualitative change occurs at the point at which "threads" of water coalesce to form a river; and the river itself comprises a whole more than the volume of individual molecules, more than the sum of its parts. Like the river, the world does not consist of isolated locations, independent atoms, but is "all flowing at once."

The sophistication of this poem arises not just from the philosophical complexity of its conclusion but also from its form, which is structured to replicate the phases of that final stanza. The beginning of "River in the Valley" consists of details and questions, perception without understanding. The second section depicts a deepening of perception through identification of humanity and nature. The third enlarges the context of the poem in terms of both land and community. The fourth fills out the rest of the watershed and provides the people with the vision necessary to encompass the entire land of which they comprise an integral part. As Yamazato observes in regard to the poem's conclusion: "this is the kind of answer that comes from an inhabitory poet who has deeply meditated on 'the whole network,' or 'Gaia,' always focusing his attention on 'the Whole Self.' He rejects the prevalent dissecting mode of knowledge, and instead teaches the sons (and the readers) to see the interpenetrating whole all one place.'"

Several other poems in "Loops" need to be discussed briefly before turning to the next section of *Axe Handles*. "Among," for instance, seems at first to be a descriptive poem. It tells of "a Douglas fir" growing amidst a stand of "Ponderosa Pine." While "River in the Valley," can be read metaphysically, "Among" can be read as a political allegory, embodying the old Wobbly slogan about the new society forming within the shell of the old. That slogan, however, is based on the idea that the old society will eventually be overthrown and replaced by the new. In contrast, Snyder seems to be speaking not of *succession* in this poem but rather coexistence. The kind of inhabitory life-styles that Snyder embraces and practices can individually survive and flourish while being surrounded by the dominant society. If social succession, like arboreal succession, is to take place, it will be more evolutionary than revolutionary according to this allegory.

"Berry Territory" results from Snyder's friendship with Wendell Berry, another ecologically focused writer. Unlike Snyder, Berry makes his home in Kentucky and writes out of a Southern Protestant agrarian background and ethics. Snyder, in effect, pays tribute to the differences between them and their territories and to the ways in which Berry has sought to integrate himself with his particular place, much like the tortoise of the first stanza. "Berry Territory" comments on the importance of continent-wide networks and sharing mutual concerns while retaining differences appropriate to one's own locale—a fundamental premise of bioregional politics.

"Painting the North San Juan School" turns back to the kind of teaching called for in "For/From Lew," while at the same time having obvious connections with "Among." "Painting" focuses on community while maintaining attention on generational responsibility for handing down the culture. Even as Snyder describes the painting of the school house, he manages to engage in teaching the readers about the knowledge the Ridge community has and shares. This knowledge the adult members of the community intend to teach their children in the face of the opposing values found in mainstream American culture. This conflict of values is first expressed through the juxtaposition of the logging trucks that shake the school in the first stanza and the local practices of grafting, planting, and growing trees in the next one. Snyder then expresses the conflict through the contradictions, between a bioregional sense of history that includes the original inhabitants of the area and one based exclusively on the practices of the ruling culture of only the past three centuries. The fragility of what the Ridge community is attempting to do is suggested by the poem's closing image: "Ladders resting on the shaky porch."

Clearly, many of these poems can be understood in terms of "loops," historical, generational, cultural, and regional. Woody Rehanek suggests that "Soy Sauce" addresses another type: "man identifying with, representing, and finally becoming a totem animal. This experience transcends intellectual rapport and becomes a total affinity with the nonhuman. . . . A vital aspect of shamanism is this ability to become one with the animal." While "Soy Sauce," then, focuses on the human-animal relationship, it also includes Snyder's looping back to Japan, invoking a strong memory of his life there even after his years away. "Delicate Criss-crossing Beetle Trails Left in the Sand" is written from the experience of his family's visit there in 1981. Here the loop is completely literal rather than metaphoric in that the village where Masa takes her husband is a place he has visited once before. While his "trails" do indeed crisscross, the question remains as to their purpose. But as Yamazato suggests, means and ends, experiences and purposes, are equally interpenetrating and impermanent: "From a Buddhist-ecologist view, all that is endowed with life is engaged in impermanent activities, traveling, as it were, on a dusty road to the final dispersal into the permanent cycles of things in this universe." . . .

Source: Patrick D. Murphy, "Handing Down the Practice," in *A Place for Wayfaring: The Poetry and Prose of Gary Snyder*, Oregon State University Press, 2000, pp. 124–28.

David Robertson and Gary Snyder

In the following interview excerpt, Snyder discusses the environmentalism and politics that feature heavily in his work.

David Robertson: Let's begin by talking about the writing projects you have planned for the winter.

Gary Snyder: For the past three years most of my writing has been in prose, researching, thinking out, and now, since last winter, the writing of a series of essays that I am going to call *The Practice of the Wild.* This is the first extended prose

> I DON'T REALLY HAVE A HISTORICAL THEORY THAT I WORK FROM, OR, IF I DO, IT IS INFORMED MORE BY ANTHROPOLOGY THAN ANYTHING ELSE."

undertaking I've done for some time. It grew out of the workshops I've given during the last ten or twelve years dealing with ecology, environmental problems, native peoples, as well as spiritual, cultural, and literary interrelationships. I thought I should bring together a whole lot of territories that I've worked in, such as bioregionism, Native American spirituality, the Buddhist quest for environmental values, deep ecology, my own rising interest in Occidental literature—for example, my rereading in the last few years, since I've been at Davis, of Emerson and Thoreau. I have found a lot of pleasure in learning how to write prose better; it's been very interesting and challenging. I also have a number of other writing projects.

DR: For the moment let's continue with The Practice of the Wild. *Have you projected the subject matter of the various chapters?*

GS: I have quite a clear picture of the book now. You saw the first four chapters, which were circulated in the graduate class I taught this spring. In addition, there is the essay already out called "Good, Wild, Sacred." Another essay that fits in is called "On the Path, Off the Trail." And about three or four more essays that are in the works right now. I would say that the book is two-thirds finished. I have blocked out most of the fall to complete it.

DR: Why don't you go back and describe in more detail the first four chapters. The initial chapter is entitled "The Etiquette of Freedom."

GS: Yes. It deals with some basic definitions, of such words as *nature*, *wild*, and *wilderness*. Then, having defined *wild* in terms of natural order and self-maintaining systems, I take another look at human beings not just as animals, but wild animals. Also I take some phenomena that are commonly taken as cultural, such as language, and consider them as wild systems. That's in the first chapter. The second chapter is about how we place ourselves. I start with the most immediate context of our existence, our localness, our childhood sense of place, and consider how that expands as we grow. Not to have been rooted in place is to have missed a fundamental aspect of human education. That leads into a discussion of regionalism and bioregionalism. The third chapter is called "Tawny Grammar." It grows out of conversations I've had with Alaskan natives about problems of culture and teaching in the modern age. There is also more exploration of the wild side of language, borrowing Thoreau's phrase, "tawny grammar." The fourth chapter is a retelling of the story of the girl who married a bear from the bear's point of view. Then will come "Good, Wild, Sacred" and "On the Path, Off the Trail," followed by "Fear of Bears," which I've already written, but it will have to be integrated into the book.

DR: And you expect to finish . . .

GS: My target date is winter solstice; that's to get it to the publisher, North Point Press.

DR: One of the things I like so much about your prose writing is your ability to lay out a vision of life as it ought to be, at the same time recognizing very hardheadedly that actual life is rooted in ambiguity and frustration over uncompleted goals. This quality is quite evident in the chapters of the book I've already read. I feel encouraged to strive and simultaneously helped to deal with my own inadequacies. Not only that, but taught that daily routine, which I so often see as getting in the way, is part of my "real" work. What about your other writing projects?

GS: After I complete *The Practice of the Wild*, I'm going to finish "Mountains and Rivers without End," my long poem project. Also, either sequentially or simultaneously, I'm projecting a volume of essays on Zen, poetry, and love. I've written about a third of it already. Another project I have about sixty percent completed is a history of Chinese environmentalism. So there are two books of prose and one of poetry after *Practice of the Wild*.

DR: Where does "Mountains and Rivers without End" stand at this point?

GS: It is not easy to say where it stands. I have written some new sections for it in the past few years, like the New York and Los Angeles city poems, but I don't know what shape it will take until I lay it all out again. I have a lot of notes, and semiwritten stuff, as well as finished stuff. I want to mull over where I want it to go and what it will take to finish it. I shouldn't make any predictions. I feel that it is going to take a

new shape, it's going to show me some new things when I really look at it again, when I hold it all in mind at once.

DR: I take it you don't plan to finish it anytime soon, that is, in the near future?

GS: Oh, I expect to finish it within a year or two from the time I start back to work on it. I will go at it hammer and tongs until it is done. Probably I will work on it that way instead of doing several projects parallel. I feel that it is ready to be finished. I've had a lot of fun with it because it is so weird. I've given myself so much freedom. It is rather different from a lot of my other poetry, which is rather minimal, stripped down, pointed in rather careful, intense directions. This is a poem where I allow myself to use much more information and a lot more mythological and symbolic material. It is a different order of poetic, and it is nice to do that kind of writing also.

DR: And there are the two other projects. One is the history of the environment in China.

GS: Yes, that is going to be called *The Great Clod*. One of the questions is why Buddhist and Taoist worldviews are inadequate to halt environmental degradation in China and Japan. It is a study of the relationship between the effects of a society and that society's own value system, how, for example, the Japanese can continue to call themselves great lovers of nature and at the same time do such horrendous things to the land. My conclusion is, basically, that religious and philosophical value systems are small potatoes in the dynamics and thrust of a civilization, where the real power lies in the mercantile sector. Ideologies are never much more than window dressing.

DR: Are you taking a Marxist point of view here?

GS: No, not really. My use of Marxism is really my own use of it. Any historical analysis can benefit from an application of Marxist ideas. The class struggle is not the only reality of history, but it certainly is one of the bigger ones. I'm far from being any kind of orthodox Marxist. I don't really have a historical theory that I work from, or, if I do, it is informed more by anthropology than anything else. Two real flaws in Marxist thought are its neglect of the environment and its failure to grasp the importance of ethnic minorities and primitive peoples. I am also interested in the question of how civilization arises.

DR: And you mean by civilization?

GS: Class structure, centralization, metal-working, a military class, and a priesthood. That cluster of phenomena. I take the Chinese state as a reference point. Some really interesting work has been done by a Chinese scholar named Kwang-chih Chang. Independently, we have arrived at the conclusion that the Chinese state served no useful function and that it comes into existence as an extortion racket, as a device to siphon wealth off from a large number of people and concentrate it in the hands of a few, with no benefits whatsoever accruing to the masses. Apparently civilization arises in China without any major technological advances. Tools used by the peasants were the same before and after. It is not as if a new mode of production called into being a new institution. The state seems to be a function of the discovery that with the right kind of organization and a few weapons you can enforce your will on others. It's raiding, essentially. The institution of raiding becomes the Chinese state.

DR: At the present time does the Neolithic play a crucial role in your thinking? How do you characterize the Neolithic anyway?

GS: The Neolithic is characterized by localism, village-level self-government, virtually no specialized military, and a much more vernacular and unspecialized religious system. It is stable and self-governing, with a modest amount of wealth and comfort. The way to understand the Neolithic is to realize that self-sufficient, autonomous villages for the last twelve to fifteen thousand years have been the life of the world, that the governments of China and Japan up until recently were just that. On the local level the Chinese and Japanese have been essentially self-governing, and that self-governing capacity is a transmission directly from the Neolithic. In Southeast Asia even today what is government is the village council. In India village life goes on uninterrupted from the Neolithic.

DR: Our modern conceptions of the Neolithic seem to play a very large role in your notions about how human groups ideally ought to be organized.

GS: Actually, the Paleolithic, and especially the upper Paleolithic, is in a sense more critical to me.

DR: What is the difference between the Paleolithic and the Neolithic as it figures in your present thinking?

GS: The Paleolithic, blending into the Mesolithic, is economically nonagricultural, that is, hunting and gathering. It is a very viable lifestyle. A number of scholars, including Marshall Sahlins, have argued rather convincingly that agriculture is a step down in terms of the ratio of the energy put out to the energy coming in. It is an era of greater mobility and independence in comparison with the Neolithic, and possibly more and better food, not to speak of a more intimate relationship with the natural region. The distinction between cultivated and wild lands is not made. There is a much broader territory of interaction with wild animals and plants, a very broad species consciousness. With the development of agriculture gradually people's knowledge of plants and animals is narrowed down to a very small spectrum.

DR: In terms of your work in the immediate future, how do you see your association with the University here at Davis fitting in?

GS: On a very concrete level, it puts me back in touch with students, who are able to give me feedback in both realms of writing, poetry and prose. Access to a library, that's basically it, along with the possibility of working ideas through consistently with people over a period of time. In the last decade and a half I have done a lot of teaching, but it was usually one-weekend workshops, or at the most two or three days on a campus. There is a real collaborative effect that happens when you are a member of a faculty. The longer commitment and engagement with people is very stimulating.

We are entering into a really critical age. Things are bad, and they are going to get worse. The territory to address problems we face is not the purely scientific. All the scientific information in the world will not do any good unless it is applied, and for it to be applied you have to have people who have a broad cultural and political understanding of how societies work. The people who take the type of classes I and others here at Davis are beginning to teach will be prepared to go into areas of environmental policy-making and enlighten legislators and the like about how we have come to the present crisis. Several points need to be made clear. One is the interlocking nature of all systems. Another is the area of how we get good information about these systems. Still another is the disparity between the needs of natural systems and public policy, the discrepancy between what is taken as common wisdom by people who run counties, cities, and states, by developers and planners, on the one hand, and the facts of the planetary situation, on the other.

DR: One area that we might cover briefly is politics. Do you contemplate any new moves in the political arena?

GS: I plan to continue my involvement on the local level, with matters on the San Juan Ridge, but actually, because of my writing, I am not doing much at present. It is a pleasure and an obligation to keep in touch with local activists, but the forestry issue leads right into world deforestation, and that leads into questions about the World Bank and multinational corporations. As the Soviet Union and China, each in their own way, seem to be going in some sort of reformist direction, people are saying that socialism has failed and free-market economies are more practical. People are saying that the world is moving toward democratic capitalism. So far so good. But if so, then thinkers of the capitalist world had better get their act together and figure out how it can be restrained. How do you set limits? How do you shape it? Can capitalism put its own house in order, and not be simply driven by the market and by profits? If it is driven by nothing but the market, then the defeat of socialism will not be much of a victory, for capitalism will go on to wreck the whole world and its resources. Here is a new direction and a new challenge. The challenge that comes from below is the rise of the green movements all over the planet. We seem to be on the edge of an era when the green movements will be the counter party to that of democratic capitalism, or at least the ecological and social conscience of democratic capitalism. So I expect that I will be engaged in the international green movement.

What shape a green movement in the United States will take is hard to guess. It is not likely that it will become a viable third party. It might be something more like Common Cause, a powerful caucus of a special territory of interests that would cut across the right and left of traditional American politics. You might have Democratic green people and Republican green people who would unite on green-related issues.

DR: If a green movement of some viability came into existence, it might embody what you mean by the "practice of the wild."

GS: To some extent. I hope that the book I am now writing will be stimulating to a broad range of people and provide them with historical, ecological, and personal vision all at the same time. I would like to see the book be political in the sense of helping people shape the way they want to live and act in the world.

Source: David Robertson and Gary Snyder, "Practicing the Wild—Present and Future Plans: An Interview with Gary Snyder," in *Critical Essays on Gary Snyder*, edited by Patrick D. Murphy, G. K. Hall, 1990, pp. 257–62.

SOURCES

Bawer, Bruce, Review of *Axe Handles*, in *Poetry*, Vol. 144, No. 6, September 1984, pp. 346–48.

Goodyear, Dana, "Zen Master: Gary Snyder and the Art of Life," in *New Yorker*, October 20, 2008, http://www.newyorker.com/magazine/2008/10/20/zen-master (accessed September 1, 2015).

McClintock, James I., "Gary Snyder's Poetry and Ecological Science," in *The American Biology Teacher*, Vol. 54, No. 2, February 1992, pp. 80–83.

O'Grady, John, "Living Landscape: An Interview with Gary Snyder," in *Western American Literature*, Vol. 33, No. 3, Fall 1998, pp. 275–91.

Pratt, William, "Review of *Axe Handles*," in *World Literature Today*, Vol. 58, No. 3, Summer 1984, pp. 417–18.

Schultz, Robert, "Gary Snyder and the Curve of Return," in *VQR: A National Journal of Literature and Discussion*, Fall 1986, http://www.vqronline.org/essay/gary-snyder-and-curve-return (accessed September 1, 2015).

Snyder, Gary, "Axe Handles," in *Axe Handles*, Shoemaker Hoard, 2005, pp. 5–6.

Weinberger, Eliot, "Gary Snyder: The Art of Poetry No. 74," in *Paris Review*, http://www.theparisreview.org/interviews/1323/the-art-of-poetry-no-74-gary-snyder (accessed September 1, 2015).

Williamson, Allan, "Gary Snyder: An Appreciation," in *New Republic*, Vol. 173, No. 18, November 1975, pp. 28–30.

FURTHER READING

Buell, Lawrence, *The Environmental Imagination: Thoreau, Nature Writing, and the Formation of American Culture*, Belknap Press, 1996.

    This book remains a seminal discussion about how contemporary American writers, including Snyder, have been deeply influenced by the ideas of Henry David Thoreau (1817–1862).

Glotfelty, Cheryl, and Harold Fromm, eds., *The Ecocriticism Reader: Landmarks in Literary Ecology*, University of Georgia Press, 1996.

    A wide-ranging and engaging collection of essays from the historical frontlines of ecocriticism, this remains an influential text in understanding the place of Snyder as a poet whose vision extends beyond environmental concerns.

Mickey, Sam, *Whole Earth Thinking and Planetary Coexistence: Ecological Wisdom at the Intersection of Religion, Ecology, and Philosophy*, Routledge, 2015.
    Simultaneously accessible and deeply considered, this discussion of some of the most problematic issues facing our world today is a wonderful guide for students looking to understand Snyder's poetry in a broader ecological context.

Murphy, Patrick, *A Place for Wayfaring: The Poetry and Prose of Gary Snyder*, Oregon State University Press, 2000.
    A series of close readings of selected poems and prose pieces, this book gives some interesting insights into the complexities underlying seemingly simple common-language poems.

SUGGESTED SEARCH TERMS

Gary Snyder

Gary Snyder AND Axe Handles

Axe Handles AND poem

American poetry

poetry AND Chinese influence

poetry AND Ezra Pound

poetry AND ecology

poetry AND nature

poetry AND land

poetry AND work

The Changing Light

LAWRENCE FERLINGHETTI

2001

One of Lawrence Ferlinghetti's later poems, "The Changing Light" first appeared in his 2001 collection *How to Paint Sunlight: Lyric Poems & Others (1997–2000)*. Blending his familiar use of simple language and deeply textured rhythms, the poem pays homage to his longtime home, San Francisco. It is a city that has seen much change during Ferlinghetti's life, from its time as the founding grounds for the Beat generation through the Summer of Love (1967) and Haight-Ashbury through to its current reimagining as the technical capital of the United States and home of the legendary Silicon Valley. Part lament, part celebration, and part creative call to action, "The Changing Light" evokes a San Francisco that Ferlinghetti remembers and knows, in his heart, will always be perched on the edge of the Pacific regardless of the changes that it might endure.

AUTHOR BIOGRAPHY

Lawrence Monsanto Ferlinghetti was born on March 24, 1919, in Bronxville, New York. His mother, Albertine Mendes-Monsanto, was of French and Portuguese heritage, and his father, Carlo Ferlinghetti, was Italian. At some point after emigrating from Italy, Lawrence's father shortened the family name to Ferling, which is the name the poet used until learning of the fuller, original version in 1942. Ferlinghetti's father died

Lawrence Ferlinghetti (© *Chris Felver* / *Getty Images*)

six months before the birth of his son, and his mother was institutionalized for psychological issues soon after his birth. He was raised by his French aunt, Emily, who moved the family to Strasbourg, France, for the first five years of his life.

Upon returning to the United States, Ferlinghetti was placed in an orphanage in Chappaqua, New York, while his aunt looked to reestablish herself. Eventually she found employment as a governess for the family of Presley Eugene Bisland and his wife, Anna Lawrence, who took over care of Ferlinghetti in 1926. Ferlinghetti attended a series of schools in his formative years, before attending the University of North Carolina in Chapel Hill, where he earned a degree in journalism.

Spending his summers working along the Maine coast, Ferlinghetti enrolled in midshipmen's college following the attack on Pearl Harbor in 1941. He worked aboard numerous military vessels throughout World War II, including a visit to Nagasaki six weeks after the atomic bomb devastated the site. This experience moved him profoundly, and he became a staunch pacifist.

After the war, Ferlinghetti continued his education, first at Columbia University, where he earned a master's degree in English literature in 1947, and then in France, where he received a Doctorat de l'Université de Paris in 1951. It was during his years in France that he met Selden Kirby-Smith, whom he married in 1951. When the couple returned to the United States, they settled in San Francisco, where Ferlinghetti and a friend, Peter D. Martin, opened City Lights Bookstore. Two years later, when Martin left the business, Ferlinghetti opened a publishing wing of the business, which soon became the primary publisher of Beat generation writers (both poetry and prose), as well as prominent political books and important books in translation. Ferlinghetti was arrested in 1956 on obscenity charges after the bookstore sold copies of Allen Ginsberg's *Howl*. The subsequent trial drew national attention. Ferlinghetti was acquitted in October 1957.

Unlike the Beat poets, Ferlinghetti is grounded in a lyric and narrative tradition that sees his influences as T. S. Eliot (1888–1965), Ezra Pound (1885–1972), and E. E. Cummings (1894–1962). His first book of poems, *Pictures of the Gone World*, appeared in 1955. He accredited himself as a skilled poet and painter as well as a political activist throughout his life, most notably in such books as *Two Scavengers in a Truck, Two Beautiful People in a Mercedes* (1968), and *Open Eye, Open Heart* (1973). His poem "The Changing Light" first appeared in *How to Paint Sunlight: Lyric Poems & Others (1997–2000)* (2001).

Ferlinghetti has won numerous awards during his career, including the Robert Kirsch Award, the National Book Critics Circle Award for Contribution to American Arts and Letters, and the Robert Frost Memorial Award (2003), to name but a few. As of 2015, he continued to operate his bookstore in San Francisco.

POEM SUMMARY

The text used for this summary is from *How to Paint Sunlight: Lyric Poems & Others (1997–2000)*, New Directions, 2001, p. 8. Versions of the poem can be found on the following web pages: https://www.poets.org/poetsorg/poem/changing-light, http://www.poemhunter.com/poem/the-changing-light/, and http://writersalmanac.publicradio.org/index.php?date=2008/03/24.

"The Changing Light" is an excellent example of colloquial free verse, which means that Ferlinghetti avoids such formal elements as regular meter and rhyme. *Meter* refers to the basic rhythmic structure of a poem, which is described through the arrangement of stressed and unstressed syllables in a line. An iamb, for instance, is a poetic unit, or foot, that has an unstressed syllable followed by a stressed syllable. Five (*penta* in Greek) iambs collected in a single line means that the line is written in iambic pentameter. Rather than staying with a regular pattern of stressed followed by unstressed syllables, Ferlinghetti varies the lengths of his lines and engages irregular rhythms.

"The Changing Light" opens by establishing the focal point of the poem on the city of San Francisco and more specifically on the light of the city as it changes from daylight to dusk to night. The speaker of the poem then defines this city light through a series of negations. San Francisco light is not the light of an East Coast city (like New York), nor is it the light of Paris, which he compares to the color of a pearl. What the light of San Francisco is, the poet continues, is a light inspired and determined by the sea, which dominates the city's geography, and by things that only a coastal city can boast; it is much like the light on an island.

The conjunction that begins line 9 gives depth to the description by adding the image of fog covering the hills and drifting in under the famous Golden Gate bridge at night, to be found lying on the city as a blanket when the sun rises at dawn. Building again through a conjunction in line 14, the speaker talks about the late morning, when the fog burns off, revealing an idyllic, peaceful kind of light. Moving to the imagery of another great sea, the Mediterranean, the speaker suggests that the light of San Francisco is comparable to the light of Greece, which reflects off the water to create sharp shadows and gives a painting-like quality to the landscape.

Line 21 starts with another conjunction that twists the direction of the poem. The speaker shifts focus from the quiet movement of fog and light to the more aggressive (and potentially destructive) movement of the wind, which does not blanket or caress the landscape but sweeps across the hills of the city. As the day clock continues to track the unfolding of the poem, the speaker watches the evening light settle like a piece of fine material worn to protect or conceal the face. The light of the city, which can

provide highlights and depth to the speaker's vision, can also conceal elements of the city from view. Morning fog is replaced by night fog, which balances the poem as the city seems to be lifted away from the land as the fog and light combine to make it appear to be floating.

THEMES

Activism

Many of the issues and themes that caught the attention of the so-called Beat generation of writers would go on to shape the more well-known counterculture of the 1960s. Predominant among these was the backlash against status quo politics, capitalism (which is linked to the expansion of the military-industrial complex in the United States), and the rise of suburban living and middle-class consumerism. Many of the original Beat poets were staunch supporters and activists in the antiwar movement, for instance, and were engaged in the civil rights movement throughout the 1960s.

The Beats as a loosely acknowledged group supported spiritual liberation, sexual liberation, civil rights, and counterculture activism. They worked towards an ecological consciousness, most notably through the writings of such authors as Gary Snyder (b. 1930) and Michael McClure (b. 1932). Along with their openly political and sexual agenda, the Beats had a respect for the land and indigenous peoples and cultures, which they proclaimed often in their prose writings.

Ferlinghetti's career has been spent urging artists to engage in the political and cultural life of their country. With Ginsberg and other like-minded writers, he was a frequent participant in public readings that focused on such issues as the Cuban revolution, the nuclear arms race, the Vietnam War, and the Sandinistas in Nicaragua.

Fueled by his ongoing travels in France, Italy, Cuba, and Mexico and throughout South America, Ferlinghetti's vision was a mix of local and global concerns. In 2012, for instance, he added his voice to a San Francisco movement to save a historic bar. That same year, he generated controversy when he refused to accept the inaugural Janus Pannonius Poetry Prize upon learning that it was sponsored in part by what he saw as a right-wing Hungarian government.

TOPICS FOR FURTHER STUDY

- Like many of the Beats, Ferlinghetti recognized the responsibility "of non-political writers and thinkers and poets and artists to make a statement on the state of the world," as he explained in an interview with Paul Wilkes. Embrace the spirit of the Beats by creating a work of art (poem, prose, painting, sketch, etc.) that makes a statement on a current issue. Be prepared to share your creation with your classmates as part of an exhibit.

- City Lights, the bookstore that Ferlinghetti founded in 1953 with his friend Richard D. Martin, was named for the 1931 Charlie Chaplin movie of the same title. Watch Chaplin's original film, and in a thoughtful and well-structured essay, explain what aspects of the film align with the ideas and beliefs of what would become the Beat generation. In other words, what about *City Lights* inspired Ferlinghetti and Martin to name their bookstore after it?

- Janet Nichols Lynch's young-adult novel *My Beautiful Hippie* (2013) explores a young girl's reaction to a San Francisco neighborhood during the 1967 Summer of Love, a time that saw Ferlinghetti's influence continue to grow across the city. Read Lynch's novel and compare her physical and cultural descriptions of San Francisco with those of Ferlinghetti in "The Changing Light." What role does fog play, for instance? The geography of the hills? The sea and islands? Share your comparison in either essay, poster, or some combined form, keeping in mind that interdisciplinary expression (poetry and art, song and art, etc.) was a hallmark of both the Beats and hippies.

- Ferlinghetti was a skilled and respected visual artist as well as poet. By hand or using a digital drawing program (ArtRage, for example), represent visually your interpretation of the powerfully visual poem "The Changing Light." Feel free to incorporate words or symbols into your final product, and be prepared to show your work as part of a class exhibition.

Language and the freedom to write openly about a full range of topics was also a fundamental focus of the Beats, who were often the target of censors. Ferlinghetti was at the center of much of this controversy following his arrest and trial for selling Allen Ginsberg's *Howl* in 1956, which had been deemed lewd and indecent material by the local authorities. He engaged the American Civil Liberties Union for his defense and openly welcomed his court case as a test of freedom of speech and thought. He was acquitted of all charges in October 1957, and *Howl* went on to become one of the most widely read poems of the century.

Beat Movement

The *Beat movement* is a term used to describe a group of writers that emerged in the post–World War II era whose philosophies and politics directly challenged many of the norms and mores that had come to define American culture. Openly engaged in experimentation with psychedelic drugs, the group were anti-industry, anti-war, open about their sexual orientations (often bisexuality), and generally nonconformist in all aspects of their lives. Having met initially at Columbia University in New York City, the group wandered the country but came to be associated most directly with San Francisco.

Although the majority of the Beats' best-known works were published in the 1950s, they continued to be active well into the sixties. Creatively, they privileged a number of common themes and concerns: a concentrated opposition to standard narrative values; the belief in writing (especially of poetry) as a spiritual quest; the benefits of exploring Native American and Eastern spiritualities; and the power of the first-person point of view to undertake a direct and unwavering examination of the human condition.

As one of the founders of City Lights Bookstore and the publishing house affiliated with it, Ferlinghetti was instrumental in forwarding the work of the Beat generation. (© nito / Shutterstock.com)

Like most of the Beat writers, Ferlinghetti felt strongly that art should be made for all people and should not be limited to the appreciation of critics and intellectuals. Not surprisingly, his poetry challenges the idea of an elite cultural class, engages readers with its elegance and simplicity, and reflects clearly the patterns and rhythms of American idiom. Interestingly, Ferlinghetti never aligned himself with the Beat movement, favoring instead the term "wide-open" to describe his poetry.

STYLE

Language

Despite the fact that he saw himself as of a different era and poetic philosophy than the Beat writers, Ferlinghetti shares their concerns with the limitations of traditional language to convey the depth of subjective experience in a world that includes transcendent opportunities through meditation, Buddhism, and even consciousness-altering drugs. In

"The Changing Light," for instance, he consciously moves to simple language that is juxtaposed by the sporadic introduction of less common words (*pearly*, instance) that imbue the localness of San Francisco with another layer of meaning. In this sense, language is used in the poem to layer the natural world (fog, wind, waves) with both the world of common language and the world of uncommon, or artistic language. Just as the fog floats freely across the poem, the meaning of the city to the speaker of the poem is created through the layering of language across and within the individual lines.

Musicality

Ferlinghetti's writing style, in both prose and verse, was heavily influenced by many of the cultural changes taking place in the fifties and sixties, most notably the appreciation of jazz music as part of mainstream culture. He translated this musicality to a poem like "The Changing Light" through his almost improvisational style, or what he called "wide-open" poetry. Nearing a kind of stream-of-consciousness writing, Ferlinghetti's "The Changing

COMPARE & CONTRAST

- **2001:** In the decade prior to 2001, San Francisco saw an economy shaped by what came to be known as the dot-com boom, driven by companies associated with the Internet industry. Both established and start-up companies flocked to the San Francisco Bay Area, with the southern part of the region gaining the now-familiar nickname of Silicon Valley. Large numbers of entrepreneurs and computer application developers moved into the city, followed by marketing, design, and sales professionals. This influx altered the texture of all parts of the city as demand for housing and office space ignited a firestorm of new development. All of this changes in 2001, when the dot-com bubble bursts, stock values plummet, and companies either collapse or lay off large numbers of employees.

  Today: By the mid-2000s, a second wave of economic boom had begun. Now the focus is on a combination of Internet and social media companies such as Google and Yahoo that redefine the cultural landscape of the city.

- **2001:** Climate change and global warming are at the forefront of public concerns, especially given that most countries of the developed world have signed the resolutions of the United Nations Framework Convention on Climate Change (UNFCCC). The ultimate objective is to prevent dangerous human interference with the global climate system, with a particular emphasis on the stabilization of greenhouse gas concentrations. Given that San Francisco is positioned somewhat precariously on the Pacific coast, concerns with climate change and the attendant predictions of sea-level changes are of particular interest in the Bay Area.

  Today: Gallup polls show that a relatively small number of people (10 percent or less) are convinced of the seriousness of global warming. There are increasingly polarized opinions on whether climate change is something to be concerned about or not.

- **2001:** City Lights Bookstore is a cornerstone of San Francisco culture, both as a bookstore where people can browse and read without pressure of sales and as a dynamic cultural meeting space.

  Today: As traditional in-store sales continue to decline, bookstores turn to online platforms and to expanding merchandise options (from tea to T-shirts) in order to continue to evolve the experience for customers.

Light" generates a strong rhythm through his use of short lines (often only three or four words), strong repetitions of words and sounds, dramatic spacing, an absence of terminal punctuation (period or comma), and his use of constructed words and symbols to convey meaning.

HISTORICAL CONTEXT

A Time of Chaos and Pessimism

It is not surprising, in many ways, that at the turn of the twenty-first century there appeared a poem about quietness and the seductive powers of light and natural shifts in perspective, given that the world was increasingly defined by a darkening lens of chaos and violence. A couple of years before the appearance of "The Changing Light," in 1999, a sitting president (Bill Clinton) was acquitted in an impeachment hearing, and tensions were on the rise following a series of high-profile and intensely violent incidents: the shooting of Amadou Diallo in New York City, the murder of James Byrd Jr. by white supremacist John William King, and the Columbine High School massacre, to name only three.

The speaker describes the way the fog of San Francisco affects the light. *(© Francesco Carucci | Shutterstock.com)*

The new decade did not ring in with a resoundingly more positive tone, with both natural and man-made tragedies stunning the world. In the latter category, Dr. Harold Shipman was found guilty of murdering fifteen patients between 1995 and 1998, while flooding in Mozambique killed over eight hundred people, and significant earthquakes jolted many parts of the world throughout the year. Considered collectively, these events created a world that felt more than a little out of control and chaotic, all of which was underscored tragically on September 11, 2001, when four coordinated terrorist attacks forever rocked the consciousness of the United States and the world.

The attacks, which quickly came to be referred to as 9/11, saw four passenger airliners hijacked by nineteen al-Qaeda terrorists who had boarded the planes at a number of East Coast airports. Two of the planes were redirected into New York City, where they crashed into the North and South Towers of the World Trade Center. Within two hours, both massive towers had collapsed in piles of rubble, dust, smoke, and

fire. The collapse was so destructive that it caused significant and devastating damage to dozens of surrounding structures.

A third plane crashed into the Pentagon in Arlington County, Virginia. The crash culminated in a partial collapse in the western wing of the complex that houses the US Department of Defense. The fourth plane was initially steered toward Washington, DC, but crashed prematurely in a field near Shanksville, Pennsylvania. In total, the attacks claimed the lives of over three thousand people and caused billions of dollars of damage.

The movie industry of that time was dominated by films that imagine other places and times and in which the powers of good overcome the darkness of evil: *Harry Potter and the Philosopher's Stone, The Lord of the Rings: The Fellowship of the Ring*, and even *Shrek*, to name but a few. Even films that might be considered realistic or possible in the real world were relatively black-and-white in their depictions of humankind, as in *Ocean's Eleven* and *Pearl Harbor*, or clearly lamented the degradation that could

WHAT DO I READ NEXT?

- Ferlinghetti's collection *Time of Consciousness* (2012) takes its title from an aeronautical term used to denote the time between when a person loses oxygen and the moment when he or she loses consciousness—a brief time when lifesaving is still a possibility. The book is an eclectic and highly allusive collection of poems that provides an excellent sampling from an exemplar of stream-of-consciousness poetry that echoes of William Carlos Williams, Charles Olson, and Allen Ginsberg.

- Ferlinghetti's novel *Love in the Days of Rage* (1988) is widely acclaimed and considered one of his best prose works. The chronicle of a love affair between an expatriate American painter and a Parisian banker of Portuguese heritage, the novel is set against the backdrop of the student revolutions of 1968.

- Jack Kerouac's *On the Road* (1957) is a true must-read for students and fans of the Beat generation and its influence on American counterculture from the 1950s onward. Based loosely on the travels of Kerouac and his friends across the United States, it is a story of friendship and creativity set against a vivid backdrop of jazz, poetry, and drug use.

- A young-adult title, *The Beats: A Graphic History* (2010) combines cultural history with graphic storytelling techniques in an accessible primer on the art and ideas of the Beat writers.

- John Tytell's *Naked Angels: The Lives and Literature of the Beat Generation* (2006) remains a seminal and imminently readable sociocultural study of Kerouac and his fellow Beat writers in the context of 1950s conservatism, as well as the backlash of 1960s counterculture.

- Robert Pirsig's *Zen and the Art of Motorcycle Maintenance* (1974) ranks as one of the great road books of all times, and is relevant to "The Changing Light" in that it attempts to articulate the spirituality and spiritual awareness that can come from an act as prosaic as maintaining a motorcycle. Pirsig finds in this mechanical work the same depth of experience that Ferlinghetti's speaker finds in his experiences of the changing light as it caresses the landscape and the city.

- Shel Silverstein's poetry, including the collection *Falling Up* (1996), is in many ways a tame but nonetheless relevant contemporary homage to the open creativity of the Beat writers through his blending of sketch and verse.

- Spanish poet Pablo Neruda's "The First Sea" is, like Ferlinghetti's "The Changing Light," a poem about a speaker's discovery of the sensuality and aesthetic of the physical world around him, in this case the discovery of the sea. "The First Sea" appeared originally in English in *On the Blue Shore of Silence*, which was published in 2003.

---

overtake individuals or communities, as in such obvious examples as Christopher Nolan's *Memento*, Ridley Scott's *Hannibal*, or Jonathan Glazer's *Sexy Beast*.

Overall, the year 2001 was one of pessimism and disruption. It was a context that saw the need for some sense of lyric quietness, such as that offered by "The Changing Light," that might counteract the noise that threatened to overwhelm hope and creativity.

CRITICAL OVERVIEW

Perhaps it is a reflection of a changing *zeitgeist* (spirit of the age) that no longer places poetry in high esteem or because it is the collection of a poet late in his career, but *How to Paint Sunlight* slipped well under the radar of reviewers. *Publishers Weekly* labels the volume "late-career miscellany" that "draws some of life's great polarities... into the quotidian whorl" of a "beloved West Coast–transplant poet." Defined by "a familiar blend of direct talk and belief in poetic enlightenment," the poems, the review argues, are hindered somewhat by "intentionally over-simple rhymes" and, at times, "long-winded poetic preaching." Nonetheless, they conclude, the overwhelming sense of a "loss of youth and life" comes across clearly.

This dearth of attention, albeit somewhat surprising, does little to diminish Ferlinghetti's legacy. He remains widely recognized as an essential figure in the establishment of the Beat movement, and his City Lights bookstore was a cultural gathering place that inspired and nurtured an entire city. Scanning the panorama of Ferlinghetti's career underscores his influence across a generation and as a creative force dedicated to social engagement, literary experimentation, and engaged social activism.

CRITICISM

Klay Dyer

Dyer is a freelance writer specializing in topics relating to literature, popular culture, and the relationship between creativity and technology. In the following essay, he explores how Lawrence Ferlinghetti's "The Changing Light" pays homage to the natural rhythms of the city of San Francisco.

As an influential poet, visual artist, and political activist of the Beat generation, Lawrence Ferlinghetti was part of a community of writers and thinkers who believed deeply that part of the problem facing the human race was the attempt to separate culture from nature, to distance the citizens of the world from the natural environment. According to the Beat thinkers, civilization was in an existential crisis, having created a self-exile from nature through any number of methods, most notably the increasing prominence of technology.

It is not surprising, then, to find Ferlinghetti's "The Changing Light" focusing on the natural elements of an area that has come to be known as Silicon Valley, the hub of technological advances in a wired world. This is a fitting focal point from an eclectic writer as deeply immersed in nature and the tradition of deep connectedness as Ferlinghetti has always been. What is a bit surprising, however, is the fact that he goes on to emphasize the almost dream-like quality of the city by the sea. It is in this city of technological dreams that

> NIGHTFALL (THE SPACE BETWEEN NIGHT AND DAY) ALLOWS FOR LIGHT BLOSSOMS TO BURST FORTH. THE VIEW OF THE CITY (NEITHER WHOLLY NATURAL NOR WHOLLY ARTIFICIAL IN THE NOON LIGHT) APPEARS RECONFIGURED IN SHADOWS, MANUFACTURED PLACES OF COLOR AND INSPIRATION THAT ARE DESIGNATED CLEARLY (EDGES AND BORDERS) BUT NOT PRACTICALLY."

Ferlinghetti sees, too, a struggle for people to find a sense of how each of us relates not only to each other (as in a community) but to the expansive universe as a whole. Though biologically unable to disconnect from nature, we are increasingly unable (or unwilling) to recognize the power of the natural rhythms—of fog, wind, and tides, for instance. This lost sense of connectedness, combined with an increasingly untenable dependence on our technology, leaves us in an apparently spirit-numbing double bind: if nature is no longer a source of spiritual connectedness, and if technology is unable to fill this space in a meaningful way, where do we turn as humans for those profoundly transcendent moments we so deeply desire?

Ferlinghetti's answer is neither simple nor singular but is to be found in the small spaces between the lines of the poem, in the natural rhythms and energies that separate the world of nature from the overbearing pressures of ever-present technology. It is in these spaces that Ferlinghetti locates the possibility of a transcendent experience, of a spiritual connectivity, and of a future that can (and does) acknowledge simultaneously the traditional rhythms of nature and the emerging rhythms of technology. As the opening line of the poem suggests, the city of San Francisco is one that can be understood as suspended between two seas: one natural and the other technological. Navigation in this cityscape is challenging, to be sure, but it is possible if one is open to the horizons of collective dreams and the grace of collective wisdoms.

Read carefully, "The Changing Light" becomes two poems. The first describes a firmly established and bifurcated world that is shaped by easy binaries (night and day, dark and light), as well as by a plethora of negations (statements focused on the word *none*, for instance). It is a slow world, a methodical world, and a world rich with color and texture that can inspire a receptive imagination. It is a world that is far removed from the natural cycles of an agrarian life (this is the world of Silicon Valley now) but with the natural rhythms of that lifestyle still firmly in place. Seasons continue to change. Winds come in as though scheduled by a celestial clock, and tides ebb and flow as scheduled.

As one of Ferlinghetti's favorite artists, Charlie Chaplin, reminded audiences in such films as *City Lights* (1931) and the much darker *Modern Times* (1936), these natural rhythms are all too quickly being replaced by the numbing and even tragic desperation that accompanies an industrial schedule. In this reading, "The Changing Light" is at once illusory and intensely ironic, a place of failed dreams and desperation rather than of hope and joyfulness. It is a divided world in which nature and technology work never coexist and in which the future is one that appears anchorless and without a sense of meaning.

Read another way, though, Ferlinghetti's poem can be reimagined as one of challenge. The gaps that are captured and celebrated in this poem offer readers evidence of the possibility of change and of a future that finds the balance that Ferlinghetti hopes for in the technological wilderness of the ever-advancing San Francisco. In this second poem, a breeze blowing in off the ocean or a wisp of fog caressing the curves of the hills resonates as a symbol of rebirth, resiliency, and opportunity.

Spaces between the lines or words of "The Changing Light" accumulate subtly in this second reading of Ferlinghetti's poem. Nightfall (the space between night and day) allows for light blossoms to burst forth. The view of the city (neither wholly natural nor wholly artificial in the noon light) appears reconfigured in shadows, manufactured places of color and inspiration that are designated clearly (edges and borders) but not practically. Just as the scent of a garden flower can catch on a breeze and be transported across hills and through windows, the changing light of a day moves fluidly across the cityscape, catching the attention of those within range of its glow.

As these gaps appear and accumulate across the lines of the poem, control of time and space are increasingly muddled. How does one manage a time that is neither night nor day but is both at the same time? How does one regulate a light that is neither brightness nor darkness but serves both needs equally well? And how does one function in a city of perpetually changing light, in which the traditional notions of shape and shadow give way to a transparent sharpness that edges metaphorically towards spiritual openness and communal imagining?

Ferlinghetti's answer is to encourage denizens of this technological city to embrace the gaps and spaces and to inhale the changing light as a sign of hope. For in the gaps, he suggests, one can find remnants of other times and other places rich with cultural opportunities for meaningful connections. The "spaces between" allow individuals to reconnect physically and imaginatively with the invisible powers of the tides and the guiding pull of the stars. These natural discoveries, Ferlinghetti suggests, are themselves intimately and inexorably intertwined with cultural traditions that can also help forge a sense of community and connection. The key, he implies, is knowing how to look for them and, more importantly, how to feel them when they are rediscovered.

It is this level of knowing that ultimately guides readers to a richer understanding of "The Changing Light." This type of knowing comes from a willingness to look beyond the obvious in search of a deeper meaning to the city and one's place in it. Seeing the city only with one's eyes is not the best way to know it, the poem suggests. Seeing the city is to recognize it for its steepness and sharp edges, its Monday mornings, and its failures. The key to knowing is to feel the city, to open oneself to the full network of senses and experiences that this city presents. By opening oneself up to this all-encompassing experience, an individual realizes a truly inclusive, synthesized understanding of the whole of the city, not just its surfaces. Shadows and fog are understood as related parts of a whole rather than as existing in opposition to a fully enclosed, fully completed reality. Interiors and exteriors are seen as complementary rather than in competition. Finally, the physical (visible, tangible) and metaphysical (unseen, spiritual) worlds coexist, thereby allowing all moments and all things to be imbued with the potential for spiritual connection and community building.

After the fog clears, the light is changed again, becoming clear and fresh. *(© ventdusud | Shutterstock.com)*

The ability to see and to know Ferlinghetti's city is ultimately connected to the ability to dream of possibilities that extend beyond the realm of the merely physical and knowable, as the title of the poem suggests in its emphasis on the changing perceptions brought about by the shift of light from dawn to daylight, or from dusk to full night. As the later reference to *halcyon* times (and the myth of Alcyone) underscores, this is a poem that explores metamorphosis as a view or understanding shifts over the duration of the day. Dreaming allows for boundaries to be renegotiated and for attitudes, assumptions, and fears to be revised. The future city, in the end, is limited not by the weight of the machinery or the grime underfoot but by the power of its citizens to dream a different future than the one that seems determined to unfold. Looking to the spaces between allows the city to be reconnected to the universe, and that connection releases the past from its amber prison to carry forward its wealth of wisdom, knowledge, and grace. Past and future collide in the spaces between the bricks and the cracks in the sidewalks. Past and future explode into a celebration of grace, and the wonders of twilight blossom.

Source: Klay Dyer, Critical Essay on "The Changing Light," in *Poetry for Students*, Gale, Cengage Learning, 2016.

Publishers Weekly

In the following review, an anonymous reviewer faults Ferlinghetti's "long-winded poetic preaching."

"All I ever wanted was to paint light on the walls of life," Ferlinghetti writes in a foreword— "these poems are another attempt to do it." A late-career miscellany divided into four sections, this eighth collection draws some of life's great polarities—light and dark, tragedy and comedy, ecstasy and despair—into the quotidian whorl of this beloved West Coast–transplant poet. In the eponymous first section, Ferlinghetti combines a familiar blend of direct talk and belief in poetic enlightenment to give voice to the "Big Sur Light" ("The moon / After much reflection says / Sun is God") and "White Dreams," and to give "Instructions to Painters and Poets": "stand back astonished." The "New York, New York" section features a "Manhattan Mama" and "Overheard Conversations," and makes stops in Europe and China before heading "Into the Interior," the last and best section. There, a series of three poems dealing with Allen Ginsberg's death takes us from the deflectively wry news of his imminent departure ("Death the dark lover / is going down on him") to a bedside visitation by the poet's released spirit and beyond: "Allen died 49 nights ago, and in Bixby Canyon now the white misshapen moon sailed listing through the sky. . . ." The intentionally oversimple rhymes ("What is light What is air What is life so passing fair?"), puns (as when he addresses his work to "the good burghers eating burgers") and long-winded poetic preaching of the earlier sections may not quite come off, but loss of youth and life and their attendant nostalgias come through, "made of love and light and dung / some great immortal song."

Forecast: Fans of *A Coney Island of the Mind* and *A Far Rockaway of the Heart* will find this book repetitive and diffuse, but Ferlinghetti has earned it. And since he does not over publish, fans old and new will pick it up if it is placed in a demographically strategic spot.

Source: Review of *How to Paint Sunlight*, in *Publishers Weekly*, Vol. 248, No. 11, March 12, 2001, p. 85.

Edward J. Ingebretsen

In the following review, Ingebretsen characterizes Ferlinghetti's work as a "significant feature of American literary life."

New Directions Press is itself a press of historical interest in the study of American poetry. Many of the "canonical" poets of the 20th century (now heralded as such, at least) found their beginnings with this press. Lawrence Ferlinghetti's *A Coney Island of the Mind*—of which *A Far Rockaway of the Heart* (New Directions, 134p., $21.95) is something of a companion volume—is one of the founding documents in the Beat Movement, while his City Lights Press has the distinction of having published Allen Ginsberg's *Howl*. As the title of this volume suggests, Ferlinghetti writes today with 1958 in mind. Unfortunately, 40 years does make a difference in poetic as well as political sensibility. What was revolutionary in the Eisenhower era is not so fresh today. The poet will use the word "postmodern," for example, in three separate instances, almost as if to suggest that he is supposed to be, in some way, articulating a postmodern poetic vision. However, what results is not always remarkable: "Where is that little fish / I caught and left on the line / still swimming in the still water / under that little bridge / by Bronx

River Parkway / when I was a boy of nine / meaning to return? Swept away! / And I with it / in a flood of time." One of the pleasures of this book, however, is the vivid reminder of a generation (or two) of American poets; Ferlinghetti cites, echoes and quotes with ease a range of poets—William Carlos Williams, Ezra Pound, e.e. cummings, Walt Whitman, T. S. Eliot and Samuel Beckett.

Pound's confused economics and the post-World War II socialist critique of American culture, however, do not wear well in post-Reagan America: "'Only connect!' / cried Columbus / staring through his telescope / And he scoped it out all right / the 'new world' as he saw it / And he saw it plain / made of gold / bullion and bloody Marys." Actually, "Only connect!" derives from William Carlos Williams, whose dispassionate eye was critical for reading "against the American grain," and for making possible the poetry of the Beats. Yet missing from this volume are precisely the connections that Williams espoused: "No ideas / but in things." Reading these poems jointly with *A Coney Island* one would have to conclude that nothing has happened—either in this country or its poetry—in 40 years. In "Number 11" the poet addresses Pound as mentor, and critiques his "Cantos" as "At worst an old man's mumbled jumble / of erudicities and profundities / by turns noble and incoherent." One could say that about these poems, too, but again, listen to Ferlinghetti quoting Pound on himself: "[T]he modern world / needs such a rag-bag / to stuff its thoughts in." And that, too, is true enough. Ferlinghetti is one of the poets who made such rag-bags a significant feature of American literary life.

Source: Edward J. Ingebretsen, Review of *A Far Rockaway of the Heart*, in *America*, Vol. 178, No. 14, April 25, 1998, p. 29.

Alistair Wisker

In the following excerpt, Wisker explains how Ferlinghetti opened City Lights book shop and began publishing.

Ferlinghetti returned to the United States and, after an unsuccessful stay in New York, which he said was just too tough and avaricious for him, he went to San Francisco early in 1951. The city which was to become his home and a central factor in his inspiration "had a Mediterranean feeling about it. I felt it was a little like Dublin when Joyce was there. You could walk down Sackville Street and see everyone of any

> **"** IT IS PRECISELY AS A RESULT OF THE
> CONTAINMENT, QUALIFICATIONS AND
> INTERROGATION OF SPECIFIC CHARACTERISTICS OF
> ROMANTICISM BY SPECIFIC CHARACTERISTICS OF
> MODERNISM THAT THE ENERGY, TENSIONS, AND
> VOLATILITY OF THE BEST BEAT WRITING ARISES."

importance on one walk." Early in 1953, Ferlinghetti and his wife, Kirby, moved into an apartment in a hillside house with a view of the Bay. Here the poet began the poems which were to form the centre of *Pictures Of The Gone World.* These poems make reference to Brancusi, Picasso, Dada and Sarolla and the Spanish Impressionists amongst the painters and art movements, and Dante, Yeats and Rimbaud amongst the writers. But the collection is most remarkable for the painterly treatment of Ferlinghetti's immediate subject matter. Characteristic of this is his first completely San Francisco poem, as he described the piece which opens the collection:

> Away above a harborful
> of caulkless houses
> among the charley noble chimneypots
> of a rooftop rigged with clotheslines
> a woman pastes up sails
> upon the wind
> hanging out her morning sheets

Ferlinghetti believes that style is a feeling for the weight and arrangement of words on a page. In "Away above a harborful," it is clear that he is using the page as a canvas, as he develops his style in which the page is analogous to the open form of the abstract expressionist painters. Meanwhile he was also sending off his Prévert translations and it was through this activity that he came across Peter Martin's *City Lights* which has been named after a Charlie Chaplin film:

> The hero of the film...was the perennial outsider—dispossessed, alienated, victimized by the immense mechanism of the modern world. It was a figure with whom Ferlinghetti instinctively sympathized. Though he didn't see himself as a victim like Charlie, he clearly felt himself one of the "common men," threatened by the massed forces of the bureaucratic, materialist, conformist world.

Pete Martin and Ferlinghetti met and, in June 1953, they opened the immediately successful City Lights Pocket Book Shop. The following year Martin sold his share in the store to Ferlinghetti and went back to his native New York to open a bookstore in Manhattan. Straightaway Ferlinghetti set about realising one of his plans, which was to base a publishing venture in the bookstore. He got together the 27 poems which became *Pictures Of The Gone World*—number one in the pocketbook series, published by City Lights Press on 10 August 1955. City Lights very soon became one of the major imprints in the history of American literature, and Ferlinghetti began to publish William Carlos Williams, Allen Ginsberg, Kenneth Patchen, Kenneth Rexroth, Denise Levertov, Gregory Corso, Neal Cassady, Jack Kerouac and many others—most of the writers needed for a course in the new American literature, postwar, have appeared from City Lights. The press was one of the major catalysts for the arrival and output of the Beat generation. Around 1955, poetry went public in San Francisco, based on the bringing together of the East Coast Beat writers—Ginsberg, Kerouac and Corso—with the West Coast writers—Rexroth, Ferlinghetti himself, Snyder, McClure, Whalen, Lamantia and others. One of the most inspiring outcomes of this meeting was a reading which Ginsberg organised at the Six Gallery in San Francisco, to which he invited McClure, Snyder, Whalen and Lamantia—with Rexroth as master of ceremonies. The Six Poets at the Six Gallery reading was given in October 1955. It was on this occasion that Ginsberg gave the first reading of his long poem *Howl*, which launched his career as a poet at the same time as it celebrated the inauguration of the San Francisco poetry renaissance; the event brought a new awareness to the audience of the large group of talented poets in the city; it also brought to the poets themselves a new sense of belonging to a community. What was emerging was something more than the "New York poets" or the "San Francisco poets." The sum of the parts was a literary movement that was to become a national and international phenomenon.

This phenomenon turned out to be enigmatic, simultaneously a celebration and a condemnation of the postwar world, a rich compound of nihilistic, committed, romantic, modernist and existentialist impulses. Getting Ferlinghetti, Ginsberg, Kerouac, Corso, Burroughs and Cassady grouped together under an umbrella labelled "Beat" has always been difficult; there is always a stray philosophy, an infectious idea, a broken ideal, an individuality and a commitment which has defied any such attempt. The label "Beat" has often been used but seldom defined; indeed, one of its characteristics is that it is an embattled position which is resistant to definition. The contradictory, dialectical, tendentious character of the Beat generation has been its critical downfall; it has often seemed confused because there has been an obsession with the lifestyle rather than the works of the generation. The characteristic preoccupations of the Beats have to do with art, and particularly abstract expressionism, popular music, particularly some forms of jazz, drugs, sex, community and communal living, travel, anarchistic politics, religious experimentation, a fascination with criminality, being on the offensive against society whilst at the same time acknowledging alternative kinds of society. These characteristics, which are not intended to be exhaustive, are exhibited in different measure and different combinations by the different writers who were fashioning their particular literary aesthetics in the culturally repressive America of the Cold War era. They sought to oppose its philistine and repressive mores by exploring and exploiting the extreme potential of the individual self. Not surprisingly, these characteristics become the subject of the art produced, and hence the focus on lifestyle in the contemporary critical response. It is not surprising, either, that the Beats professed close allegiances with some of the great figures of the romantic movement, and particularly with the Romantic ideology expressed by Blake, Shelley, Whitman and Lawrence. However great the debt to European Romantic ideology and indigenous American Transcendentalism, it is without doubt mediated by post-Romantic thought:

> It is hardly possible to read a classic Beat text without being aware of the way in which its Romanticism is continued, qualified and interrogated by the Modernism of Stein, Pound, Eliot, Williams (who wrote the introduction to *Howl*), Faulkner, Hart Crane, Thomas Wolfe and Henry Miller (who wrote the preface to *The Subterraneans*); the Surrealism of Apollinaire, Prévert (whose *Paroles* Ferlinghetti has excellently Englished), Eluard, Reverdy and Lorca; and the Existentialism of Hemingway, Céline, Artaud (whose *In Order to have finished with the judgement of God* Ginsberg has proclaimed a major influence on his early works), Sartre and Camus (whose *The Myth of Sisyphus* has been a touchstone for Ferlinghetti).

It is precisely as a result of the containment, qualifications and interrogation of specific characteristics of Romanticism by specific characteristics of Modernism that the energy, tensions, and volatility of the best Beat writing arises. Ferlinghetti is in no way a disengaged writer; in fact, a powerful sense of commitment is evidenced in a great deal of his writing. He was incensed, whilst writing about his "Tentative Description of a Dinner Given to Promote the Impeachment of President Eisenhower," by those he described as Beat natives who said he could not be both Beat and committed at the same time:

> all the tall droopy corn about the Beat Generation and its being "existentialist" is as phoney as a four-dollar piece of lettuce. Jean-Paul Sartre...would give the horse laugh to the idea of Disengagement and the Art of The Beat Generation. Me too. And that Abominable Snowman of modern poetry, Allen Ginsberg, would probably say the same. Only the dead are disengaged. And the wiggy nihilism of the Beat hipster, if carried to its natural conclusion, actually means the death of the creative artist himself. While the "non-commitment" of the artists is itself a suicidal and deluded variation of this same nihilism.

Ferlinghetti's sense of commitment became very clear after the Six Poets at the Six Gallery reading when he sent a telegram to Ginsberg offering to bring out *Howl* as a City Lights publication. He used the words which Emerson had used in writing to Whitman about his *Leaves of Grass*—"I greet you at the beginning of a great career." He added, "When do I get the manuscript?" Ferlinghetti and Ginsberg worked together, supplementing *Howl* with some other poems, including "A Supermarket in California," which wonderfully realises a dream encounter with Walt Whitman. Ferlinghetti sent the manuscript to William Carlos Williams, who wrote an introduction to the volume describing Ginsberg as a poet who "sees through and all around the horrors he partakes of in the very intimate details of his poem. He avoids nothing, but experiences it to the hilt." In September 1956, City Lights took delivery of the first fifteen hundred copies, but it was when the second printing arrived the following March that the trouble started.

On 25 March 1957, the Collector of Customs, Chester MacPhee, ordered the second printing to be seized. This was reported in the *San Francisco Chronicle*:

> collector of Customs Chester MacPhee continued his campaign yesterday to keep what he considers obscene literature away from the children of the Bay Area. He confiscated 520 copies of a paperbound volume of poetry entitled *Howl and Other Poems* ... "The words and the sense of the writing is obscene," MacPhee declared. "You wouldn't want your children to come across it."

Ferlinghetti was prepared for this. He demonstrated a real grasp of literary, social and political affairs over the following months. On 3 April, the American Civil Liberties Union (to which he had submitted the manuscript of *Howl* before it went to the printers) informed MacPhee that it would contest the legality of the seizure. The first printing had been done by Villiers in Great Britain, chosen by Ferlinghetti because they were both experienced and reasonable. Now he announced an entirely new edition to be printed within the United States, and thus removed from the jurisdiction of the customs. This photo-offset edition was for sale at the City Lights bookstore, while the customs held on to the few copies from Britain.

The ensuing events did much to bring together and advertise the work of the Beats. Both the customs and the police, albeit unintentionally, did much to aid this development:

> I recommended a medal be made for Collector MacPhee, since his action was already rendering the book famous. But the police were soon to take over this advertising account and do a much better job—10,000 copies of *Howl* were in print by the time they finished with it.

On 19 May 1957, the book editor of the *San Francisco Chronicle*, William Hogan, gave his Sunday column over to an article by Ferlinghetti who viewed *Howl* as without doubt the most significant long poem to be published since the Second World War, and perhaps since Eliot's *Four Quartets*. As Ferlinghetti himself says, many added "Alas" to this:

> Fair enough, considering the barren, polished poetry and well-mannered verse which has dominated many of the major poetry publications during the past decade or so, not to mention some of the "fashionable incoherence" which has passed for poetry in many of the smaller, avant-garde magazines and little presses. *Howl* commits many poetic sins; but it was time.

The unswerving commitment which Ferlinghetti revealed throughout the trial of *Howl* is characteristic. He challenged critics to identify another single long poem which was as resonant of its time and place and generation....

Source: Alistair Wisker, "An Anarchist among the Floorwalkers: The Poetry of Lawrence Ferlinghetti," in *The Beat Generation Writers*, edited by A. Robert Lee, Pluto Press, 1996, pp. 82–86.

SOURCES

Ferlinghetti, Lawrence, "The Changing Light," in *How to Paint Sunlight: Lyric Poems & Others (1997–2000)*, New Directions, 2001, p. 8.

Morgan, Bill, *The Typewriter Is Holy: The Complete, Uncensored History of the Beat Generation*, Free Press, 2010.

Watson, Steven, *The Birth of the Beat Generation: Visionaries, Rebels, and Hipsters, 1944–1960*, Pantheon Books, 1995.

Wilkes, Paul, "Interview with Lawrence Ferlinghetti," in *Library Journal*, Vol. 115, No. 5, September 1990, pp. 220–26.

Review of *How to Paint Sunlight*, in *Publishers Weekly*, Vol. 248, No. 11, March 12, 2001, p. 85.

FURTHER READING

Felver, Christopher, *Ferlinghetti: A Rebirth of Wonder*, First Run Features, 2012.
> This well-made documentary considers Ferlinghetti as a poet, an artist, and an engaged citizen activist. Rich with interviews and first-person reflections by many of the key figures of the Beat generation, this piece gives valuable insight into a man and a mind at the forefront of a cultural revolution.

Ferlinghetti, Lawrence, and Frederic Amat, *What Is Poetry?*, Zare Books, 2010.
> This collection of Ferlinghetti's aphorisms (an *aphorism* is a very brief saying that attempts to convey a universal truth) combined with Amat's art makes for fascinating reading. Although many of these sayings have appeared in other books, they are given new relevance and crispness when paired with Amat's paintings.

Morgan, Bill, *I Greet You at the Beginning of a Great Career: The Selected Correspondence of Lawrence Ferlinghetti and Allen Ginsberg, 1955–1997*, City Lights, 2015.

Comprising primarily previously unpublished letters, this impressive volume is a rich collection of gossip, travelogue, and thoughts on everything from writing to politics. It is also the story of a lifelong friendship between two of the finest writers America has ever produced, both of whom were incomparable craftsmen. It is indispensable for anyone interested in the Beat generation, American cultural history, or poetry in general.

Smith, Larry, *Lawrence Ferlinghetti: Poet-at-Large*, Southern Illinois University Press, 1983.

This volume is the first detailed critical study that focuses on the writing of Ferlinghetti and is still an important addition to any reading about the man and his art. Setting out to explain Ferlinghetti's vision and method, Smith notes that, in the end, Ferlinghetti remains a man easily defined by simple categories. He is part poet, part painter, part visionary, and part political activist, to name but a few.

SUGGESTED SEARCH TERMS

Lawrence Ferlinghetti

Lawrence Ferlinghetti AND The Changing Light

The Changing Light AND poem

How to Paint Sunlight AND book

stream of consciousness

Beat generation

American lyric poetry

poetry AND painting

poetry AND art

poetry AND landscape

poetry AND San Francisco

The Delight Song of Tsoai-talee

N. SCOTT MOMADAY

1976

Within his genre-breaking literary work *The Way to Rainy Mountain* (1969), Native American writer N. Scott Momaday tells the story of the formation of Devils Tower, which the Kiowa people call Tsoai. A group of children are playing: a boy and his seven sisters. The boy is magically transformed into a bear, and his terrified sisters flee. As they run, they come to the stump of a huge tree, which they climb in their desperation to escape. The girls rise into the sky to become the seven stars of the Big Dipper, and as the bear tries to reach up to them, his claws score the distinctive vertical grooves in the surface of Tsoai, the great rock tree. The story is about loss but also about the connections between humans and the living things around them.

In an interview with Charles L. Woodard (quoted by Jim Charles in *Reading, Learning, Teaching: N. Scott Momaday*), Momaday explains: "My Kiowa name, *Tsoai-talee*, means 'Rock Tree Boy,' and it is, of course, associated immediately with the rock tree, which is now called Devils Tower." The place is therefore of deep personal significance to Momaday, and he celebrates his people's relationship with the larger world in "The Delight Song of Tsoai-talee." This poem—indeed like many of the poems in his collection *The Gourd Dancer* (1976) and the vast majority of his other work—reflects Momaday's Kiowa heritage and his interest in the Native American oral traditions of song and storytelling.

N. Scott Momaday (© Chris Felver / Getty Images)

AUTHOR BIOGRAPHY

Navarre Scott Momaday was born in Lawton, Oklahoma, on February 27, 1934. His family was of Kiowa Native American heritage, and he grew up in the southwestern United States, mostly on reservations, where his parents were teachers. Momaday was an excellent student, and when the reservation high school proved to be not challenging enough, he went to military school in Virginia for a year. He then enrolled at the University of New Mexico and, in 1958, earned a bachelor's degree in political science.

It was while Momaday was in college that he published his first poem, "Earth and I Gave You Turquoise" (1959). He also submitted a few poems to a verse contest sponsored by Stanford University. The competition would influence the rest of Momaday's career, because his work was noted by influential poet and critic Yvor Winters, a judge for the contest, who awarded Momaday a scholarship and became a mentor. Momaday earned both a master's degree and a doctorate at Stanford and honed his writing skills under the guidance of Winters.

Momaday's best-known work is his Pulitzer Prize–winning first novel, *House Made of Dawn* (1968), which describes the struggles of a young soldier returning to his home in a Kiowa pueblo. He did not publish a second work of fiction until 1989, when *The Ancient Child* was released. Momaday's early poems, including those in *Angle of Geese and Other Poems* (1974) and *The Gourd Dancer* (1976), which includes "The Delight Song of Tsoai-talee," are collected in *In the Presence of the Sun: Stories and Poems, 1961–1991* (1992). In 1999, he released the poetry collection *In the Bear's House*. He has also written widely in other genres. *The Way to Rainy Mountain* (1969) is a blending of traditional Kiowa folklore, modern Kiowa history, and personal reflections. He also authored the memoir *The Names* (1976), the children's book *Circle of Wonder* (1994), and the play *The Indolent Boys* (2002) and has edited several anthologies and collections. Momaday's poetry, prose, drama, and essays all reflect his Native American heritage, his respect for nature, and his interest in the oral tradition.

In addition to his Pulitzer, Momaday has been awarded numerous honors for his work, including the Academy of American Poets Prize in 1962, a Guggenheim Fellowship in 1966, a National Institute of Arts and Letters grant in 1970, and the National Medal of Arts in 2007. He has received a dozen honorary degrees from colleges and universities across America. Momaday has taught English, comparative literature, and creative writing at the University of California both in Santa Barbara and in Berkeley, Stanford University, and the University of Arizona and has been a visiting professor at Columbia, at Princeton, and in Moscow. As of 2015, he is still writing and is a Regents Professor of the Humanities at the University of Arizona.

POEM SUMMARY

The text used for this summary is from *In the Presence of the Sun: Stories and Poems, 1961–1991*, St. Martin's Press, 1992, p. 16. Versions of the poem can be found on the following web pages: http://www.poetryfoundation.org/poem/175895 and http://www.poemhunter.com/poem/the-delight-song-of-tsoai-talee/.

The title of "The Delight Song of Tsoai-talee" is significant. Momaday is of the Kiowa

MEDIA ADAPTATIONS

- Momaday read some of his poems and related stories about his experiences in a lecture at the University of California at San Diego, which was recorded and is available on YouTube (https://www.youtube.com/watch?v = rbqzm6x7Noo).

tribe, and *Tsoai* is the Kiowa name for Devils Tower, a rock formation that is over eight hundred feet tall and approximately a mile in circumference at its base. Although Devils Tower is now under the management of the National Park Service, it has been a sacred site to local Native American tribes for countless generations. It is also a personally meaningful place for Momaday, whose Kiowa name is *Tsoai-talee*, which means "Rock Tree Boy." Momaday's choice of words in the title—*delight* and *song*—have joyful connotations, providing a clue to readers that the poem will have a positive tone.

The poem is divided into two stanzas, with the first much longer than the second. The line breaks occur at natural pauses, where punctuation would appear at the end of sentences, rather than the phrases being enjambed. (An *enjambed* phrase runs from one line to the next rather than stopping at a line break.) The poem has no regular rhyme or meter.

Stanza 1
In the first stanza, all of the lines have the same structure, with the first two words repeating. The speaker expressly identifies himself with a series of images from nature. The most common type of image is of an animal. Lines 2, 3, 6, 14, 16, and 17 all describe an individual animal, and many of these lines also give a hint of the animal's habitat, which stresses the connections between living things and the earth on which they live. Most of the remaining images, though not alive, are elements of the natural world, such as various kinds of weather and celestial bodies. Lines 1 and 7 mention a feather and beads, objects associated with the symbolic decorations in

traditional Native American art and clothing. The final line of the stanza draws all of the images together as a whole, reinforcing the idea of the unity of the natural world, which includes the speaker.

Stanza 2
The first and last lines of stanza 2 are identical, and the lines between all start with the same phrase, repeating the first six words. In this stanza, the speaker asserts his living existence, which he believes is properly tied to everything around him. The speaker also directly addresses the reader or listener, inviting him or her to serve as a witness. In lines 20 and 21, the speaker reiterates his connection to the earth and its deities, and line 22 notes the beauty of the world. The penultimate line makes specific reference to Momaday's Kiowa heritage: Tsen-tainte is the daring Kiowa chief White Horse, who died in 1892.

THEMES

Nature
In "The Delight Song of Tsoai-talee," Momaday presents a vivid image in almost every line of the first stanza, and most of them are from nature. The images include animals (deer, fish, geese, and so on), elements of the weather (snow, rain, and wind), and celestial bodies (a star, the moon, and the rising sun). The images of nature reflect its central importance in Native American culture and oral tradition, to which Momaday feels very connected. Specific traditions vary from tribe to tribe, of course, but a reverence for nature is common to all.

For some tribes, the connection to nature takes on a religious significance. Some believe each person has a particular animal to which he is spiritually connected. Others worship animal spirits or natural elements like the wind as gods. Even in practical matters, a profound respect for nature runs throughout Native American culture. Though tribes take from the land and kill animals to feed themselves, it is done with humility and a sense of gratitude, and nothing is wasted. For example, if a deer is killed, the meat is eaten, the hide is used for fabric, and the bones and antlers are used for tools.

Belonging
"The Delight Song of Tsoai-talee" could be read as a deeply contemplative poem. The lines could be read as a somber chant, creating a dramatic, thoughtful meditation on the beauty of nature

TOPICS FOR FURTHER STUDY

- Read some of the poems in *Walking on Earth and Touching the Sky: Poetry and Prose by Lakota Youth at Red Cloud Indian School* (2012) and then read a selection of the poems in *Paint Me like I Am: Teen Poems from WritersCorps* (2003). Compare the poems in terms of themes and content. Do you think the Native American students tend to write on different subjects than do the teen poets in *Paint Me like I Am*? Write an essay highlighting the similarities and differences between the poems you find most interesting in each volume.

- Momaday uses numerous natural images in "The Delight Song of Tsoai-talee." Make a digital audiovisual presentation of your interpretation of the poem to share with your class. Record yourself reading the poem aloud and add appropriate, meaningful music as a soundtrack. Also include pictures that reflect the poem's themes and imagery.

- Using online and traditional print resources, research Native American oral tradition and songs. Make a presentation to your class in which you explain some of the differences between the music of various Native American groups, playing selections. Alternatively, if you have musical talent, write a song using the lines of "The Delight Song of Tsoai-talee" as lyrics, mimicking a particular tribe's traditional style of music.

- Write a poem that uses numerous images that are significant to you personally and to your heritage. You may either imitate Momaday's free verse or opt for a traditional poetic form.

- Although Devils Tower is a sacred place for several Native American groups, it is also a national monument, under the auspices of the National Park Service, and its unique geological features make it a popular site for rock climbing. Because there are many traditional ceremonies that take place in June, the National Park Service has called for voluntary closure of the tower in June: though they do not absolutely forbid climbing, they strongly urge visitors to be respectful and schedule recreational climbing at other times of year. Uluru (Ayers Rock) in Australia has a similar history. It is of huge cultural importance to the Aboriginal people and has been for thousands of years, but it is also part of the Australian national park system. Since 1985, the Australian park service has shared management of the site together with the Aboriginal elders. Do you think the US National Park Service should share responsibility for Devils Rock with the local tribes? Do you believe that climbing on such sacred sites should be made illegal, either during particularly significant times or year-round? Or do you believe no one group should be allowed to monopolize the site? Write a letter to the park service explaining your views. Research Devils Rock, Ayers Rock, and other sites significant to native peoples and use what you learn to support your opinions.

---

and humankind's connection with it. However, the title of the poem includes the word *delight*, which denotes a joyful feeling. Momaday also purposefully opted to use the word *song* as part of the title, bringing to mind the idea that the speaker is so happy he bursts into song. The title therefore sparks a question for the reader: Why is the speaker feeling delight?

The repetition in the poem offers a possible source for the speaker's happiness. The entire first stanza is devoted to a list of beautiful scenes from nature, and as the speaker thinks about each image, he is reminded of how he is connected to, and indeed identifies with, every other living and natural thing. With each line of his song, the speaker celebrates these connections. The second stanza then allows the speaker to assert his own existence. He seems to truly understand his place in the world. His relationship to all of the creatures and people around him gives

Momaday's word choice adds interest to the poem, such as the eagle who "plays" with the wind. (© teekaygee | Shutterstock.com)

him a feeling of certainty and security—a sense of belonging that is delightful to him.

Native American Culture

Although he is thoroughly educated in English literature, Momaday is well aware that the Native American literary tradition is no less valuable than the Western canon. Part of what makes Momaday's work so interesting is his ability to blend various elements from Native American and mainstream culture to create unique work. He might compose a poem that uses the structure of a traditional Western poetic form, but the content will particularly relate to his heritage. "The Delight Song of Tsoai-talee" is a free-verse poem, with a two-stanza structure and standard typography (referring to how the text appears on the page, including punctuation, line length, and the arrangement of words), and as such it would not look out of place in any collection of modern poetry. However, Momaday introduces elements in his "song" that reflect his heritage. For example, the animals mentioned in the poem are all of particular significance in Native American folklore. The style of the poem also channels Native American culture, reflecting the repetitive structure of some traditional storytelling.

STYLE

Free Verse

Free verse is poetry without a consistent arrangement of meter (the pattern of stressed and unstressed syllables in poetry) or rhyme. "The Delight Song of Tsoai-talee" is a free-verse poem. It does not have a rhyme scheme, and though there is a rhythm to the poem, it does not form a regular pattern. The lines have different numbers of syllables, and if one were to read the poem aloud, one would stress different numbers of words or syllables in different phrases. This poem is an example of how free verse may lack regular rhyme and meter but not be completely without form. The poet simply uses other devices to create the structure. Instead of rhyme at the end of each line, Momaday uses the repetition of phrases at the start of each line to give the poem a feeling of order.

Repetition

The repetition of words and phrases appears commonly in the Native American oral tradition. Before European influences led to traditional narratives being written down, tribal culture, stories, and history were passed from generation to generation orally. To some degree, as is explained by the Winged Messenger Nations website, repetition is used simply to help make the words easier to remember, which is important when relating lengthy texts such as the Navajo Nightway Ceremony, which "includes about four hundred songs that are sung over nine days and eight nights." However, the repetition is not just a mnemonic device. In his essay "Native American Oral Narrative," Andrew Wiget explains that "these repetitions have an aesthetic function: they create a sense of expectation, and when one arrives at the full number of repetitions, a sense of completeness, satisfaction, and fulfillment."

Momaday borrows this practice of repetition from the oral tradition, and repeated phrases give his poems resonance, creating the feel of a song or chant. In "The Delight Song of Tsoai-talee," Momaday starts every line of the first stanza with the same two words. In the Western tradition, such line-beginning repetition is called *anaphora*. In the second stanza, the first and last lines are repeated word for word, and the remaining lines all begin with the same six words. This repetition serves to reinforce the theme of the poem, stressing over and over the speaker's connection with the natural world.

COMPARE
&
CONTRAST

- **1970s:** Since World War II, the Native American community has been divided between those believing it best to assimilate into mainstream culture and those hoping to maintain tribal independence in all matters from government to culture. With the Indian Self-Determination and Education Assistance Act of 1975, the US government allows tribal governments to take charge of local programs and decreases the powers of the Bureau of Indian Affairs. The 1978 federal Acknowledgement Project recognizes almost three hundred Native American groups, making them eligible to receive grants and other federal benefits, but almost two hundred tribes remain unrecognized. Native American groups seek to reclaim their land, language, and culture, but other than through gambling establishments and the sale of natural resources from tribal land, they struggle to achieve success in the mainstream American economy.

  Today: Native American governments still struggle to maintain autonomy in the face of federal policies that encourage assimilation and integration over independence. Tribal leaders look for new ways to foster economic success to fight the chronic poverty on reservations, focusing on community projects, where all tribe members share responsibility and assets, rather than the efforts of independent entrepreneurs.

- **1970s:** The Education Amendments Act of 1978 gives control of local schools to tribal governments. The Indian Child Welfare Act (1978) gives parents the legal right to refuse the placement of their children in off-reservation schools, a practice started long before, largely in the hope of assimilating Native American youth into mainstream culture.

  Today: Native American students as a whole are struggling to compete with their contemporaries. Standardized test scores and graduation rates are low, even when compared with other historically disadvantaged minorities. "It's been almost 12 years since No Child Left Behind was implemented, and we essentially have no appreciable results to show for it," explains David Beaulieu in *Education Week*. Beaulieu, a member of the Minnesota Chippewa Tribe–White Earth and former director of the Office of Indian Education in the US Department of Education, continues: "What we see are declines not only in measures of achievement, but declines in the overall quality of educational programs."

- **1970s:** After decades of depicting Native Americans on television and in film as untrustworthy, violent, and primitive, if sometimes noble, popular culture latches on to the overly idealized image of tribes living in an almost utopian communion with nature that is spoiled by the interference of the white man. Cultural and political groups—from hippies wanting to experience the spiritual side of Native American religion to environmentalists hoping to channel the connection with nature—adopt elements of Native culture, though without always doing sufficient research to get the details correct.

  Today: Native Americans are still underrepresented in popular culture. Though Native American characters are appearing in surprising ways, such as in the *Assassin's Creed* video game, some members of the community object to the continued violent associations. Native American filmmakers are meeting with some success, but negative stereotypes are plentiful, such as with the mascots of sports teams like the Washington Redskins and the Cleveland Indians. There is progress, however: the Florida State University Seminoles have consulted with tribe members to create an image that is realistic and positive rather than a caricature. Tribal elder Louise Gopher explains to the *Washington Post*: "FSU in earlier times was showing the Seminoles in feathers and war bonnets, which they never wore, and with caricature faces. We were being stereotyped with what was seen on the movies and television. Now Florida State University makes sure that the Seminoles are not depicted in a disrespectful manner in any way."

Many of the poem's images are from nature, and include fish, deer, and geese. *(© oceanfishing | Shutterstock.com)*

HISTORICAL CONTEXT

Native American Literature

Many critics mark the beginning of the Native American literary renaissance with Momaday's 1969 Pulitzer Prize for *House Made of Dawn*. However, Momaday draws from a long tradition in Native American culture. The oral tradition is particularly important in Native American communities. Through storytelling, older members of the tribe preserved history and shared personal experiences. The stories were also entertaining. In the oral tradition, nature and animals often play central roles. Also common is a trickster character, who serves to teach moral lessons; the younger members of the community see that lies and tricks often lead to problems. The trickster appears in the stories of various tribes as Coyote, Raven, Skeleton Man, and Spider. In addition to myths and legends, "the sources and forms of oral tradition are very diverse," explains an essay on the subject at the Winged Messenger Nations website. Apart from storytelling, the forms or oral tradition include

> eyewitness accounts, poems, songs, choreography, speeches, and instances of spoken word that have contributed to the development of rituals and ceremonies. Each type of oral

tradition varies a bit from the next, although all contribute to the collective identity of a particular tribe.

The arrival of white Europeans in America led some Native American authors to set their stories in print. These writers were usually writing in English, however, because they had been forced to attend schools run by the government or the church. At such schools, Native American children were not allowed to speak in their native tongues.

In the eighteenth and nineteenth centuries, Native American literature was heavily influenced by European American culture. Although the oral tradition remained important within the tribal community, Native writers adopted such genres as the autobiography and the novel, adding elements from Native American myths. While many authors hoped to use their writing to fight stereotyping and prejudice, that very prejudice made it difficult for Native American authors to get their work published. Other literary figures supported assimilation into mainstream culture; in the *Cherokee Phoenix*, the first Native American newspaper, editor Elias Boudinot (ca. 1804–1839), a member of the Cherokee Nation, encouraged assimilation because he believed it was necessary for survival.

For a long time, writing by early Native American writers was not treated as literature. Instead, it was examined by anthropologists for its significance within Indian culture. In the 1960s and 1970s, this began to change. Although many authors wrote about the suffering of the Native American people and the prejudice and oppression they faced, authors like Momaday "helped redefine the American Indian voice from one of victim to one of survivor," according to Elizabeth Archuleta. Other influential writers include Leslie Marmon Silko, James Welch, Louise Erdrich, Simon Ortiz, Joy Harjo, Ray Young Bear, Duane Niatum, Roberta Hill, Wendy Rose, Paula Gunn Allen, Gerald Vizenor, and Barney Bush. Some critics fear this generation of authors paints a grim picture by presenting the realities of drinking, drugs, poverty, and a lack of educational opportunities, but during the literary renaissance, there also was a shift to focus on celebrating the unique aspects of the Native American culture and community rather than describing the pressures to conform.

CRITICAL OVERVIEW

Momaday holds an honored place in the history of modern Native American literature. Many critics date the start of the Native American Renaissance to 1968 and the publication of Momaday's first novel, *House Made of Dawn*. As Elizabeth Archuleta explains in *American Indian Quarterly*, the book "introduced a mainstream audience to American Indian literature." Because of this, Archuleta describes Momaday as "one of the most important American Indian writers in American literary history." Archuleta also asserts that it was how he brought contemporary Native Americans to life that made his contribution significant. "Many American Indian writers previous to Momaday spoke about Indians in the past tense, as if their culture was dead and dying or already gone," Archuleta writes, whereas Momaday's "voice helped redefine the American Indian voice from one of victim to one of survivor." In *Reading, Learning, Teaching: N. Scott Momaday*, Jim Charles agrees that Momaday's talent for portraying Native American culture is what makes his work great:

> Like all great writers, Momaday provides readers entrée into a unique world. His happens to be a world made unique on the basis of race, culture, history, and experience. Momaday's

world is one shaped by his experiences as a Kiowa who grew up among the Pueblo peoples and Navajo.

Critics also point out Momaday's knack for effectively adapting style elements from traditional Native American sources. Alan R. Velie, in his essay "Post-Symbolism and Prose Poems: Momaday's Poetry," writes that as of 1982, Momaday "continues to write poems in his conservative Wintersian mode" (by which Velie refers to the influence of Momaday's mentor Yvor Winters). However, Velie points out that Momaday "has also begun to experiment with a more fluid form, the prose poem," which seems a "radical departure" from his more traditional poems. However, not all appreciate Momaday's more experimental poetry: Velie writes that "Momaday is a fine poet, but in my opinion he is at his best in prose."

In *N. Scott Momaday*, Martha Scott Trimble highlights Momaday's "control of language, a control which develops from a deep respect for the word." Perhaps this respect stems from his long-lived appreciation for the Native American oral tradition of storytelling and song. Many critics note how Momaday's heritage influences his work. Velie points out that many of Momaday's poems "resemble the oral tradition of the Indian tale," and Archuleta writes that although *In the Presence of the Sun* "includes a voice that is more formal and Western, it also contains the feel of the oral tradition." Some critics feel that Momaday's blend of Native American and Western elements is not completely successful. A *Publishers Weekly* review of *In the Presence of the Sun* points out that while Momaday's "attraction to forms, whether that of the folk tale, the rhyming couplet or the song" is an "interesting aspect of his work," in many of the poems, this "formality belongs to the tradition of English poetry, which can seem jarringly rhetorical" in contrast to less formal works. The *Publishers Weekly* reviewer believes this contrast gives the collection a certain "unevenness."

CRITICISM

Kristen Sarlin Greenberg
Greenberg is a freelance writer and editor with a background in literature and philosophy. In the following essay, she examines how the seemingly straightforward images in Momaday's "The Delight

WHAT DO I READ NEXT?

- In the traditional Japanese poetic form of haiku, nature is often the focus. Translator Robert Hass collects the haiku of three classic Japanese poets in *The Essential Haiku: Versions of Basho, Buson & Issa* (1994).

- Sherman Alexie's young-adult novel *The Absolutely True Diary of a Part-Time Indian* (2007) captures the difficulties of blending one's heritage with mainstream society. Every day, high-school student Junior leaves the Spokane reservation where he has grown up to attend an all-white school in a nearby town. He feels out of place there, but the troubled reservation school does not challenge him, and he is determined to be a success.

- Momaday won a Pulitzer Prize for his first novel, *House Made of Dawn* (1968), which many critics still credit as his best work. The book's protagonist is a young Kiowa man struggling to return to his old life in the pueblo where he grew up after serving in the army in World War II.

- Lawrence Sullivan's nonfiction volume *Native Religions and Cultures of North America: Anthropology of the Sacred* (2003) provides a broad background on Native American spiritual traditions and beliefs.

- The poems in Momaday's *The Gourd Dancer* (1976) illustrate his belief, influenced by Native American tradition, that people must live with close ties to the land.

- Maurice Boyd fills the two volumes of *Kiowa Voices* (1983) with the traditional stories of Momaday's tribe.

Song of Tsoai-talee" hint at a wealth of history and culture, drawing on his Native American heritage.

In "The Delight Song of Tsoai-talee," Momaday presents the reader with a flood of images. Many of these images are from nature—sun and rain and stars and animals—and with each repetition throughout the poem, the poet reasserts his connections to the world around him. The animal images often provide contexts, a hint of each animal's habitat, which also stresses the interconnectedness of all living creatures and their relationships with their environment. The horse roams the plains, the fish swims through the water, and the eagle soars on the breeze. Each image reinforces the speaker's deep feeling of belonging and his security regarding his place in the world. Delving into this theme would be enough to make Momaday's poem worthy of appreciation. However, the particular images Momaday includes have deeper significance.

The symbols Momaday uses—each one only a small part of the litany of natural images spanning the first stanza of the poem—all have a much more complicated meaning than just the literal object. Animals have symbolic importance in Native American culture. The specific interpretations of these symbols vary from tribe to tribe, of course, but there are many common threads. For example, the wolf frequently represents loyalty, courage, strength, and skill in hunting, whereas the deer often represents creation and fertility; deer are seen as the caretakers of the world.

The symbolic importance of animals is likely no surprise to anyone who has ever considered Native American art, and the few images of man-made objects that appear in the poem are perhaps not any more unexpected: the stereotypical idea of a Native American often includes clothing decorated with beads and feathers. However, these elements are not merely decorative in Native American culture. Feathers, for example, are used as symbols of strength and courage in many tribes. A feather might be given as a reward for a particularly brave or honorable deed. Feathers are used to denote wisdom, power, and freedom, so the image of a wise chief with a feathered headdress, though still a stereotype and not a practice shared by all Native American groups, is not altogether incorrect.

Beads have an even more interesting history than feathers. Archaeologists have found beads thousands of years old that reveal a lot about Native American culture, such as the fact that beads were likely used as trade items in prehistoric times in addition to being used decoratively. Some tribes create necklaces with carved beads and specific patterns to tell stories. Because beads are so significant, for some groups working with beads can be a sacred task or a religious experience. Today, beads are still used in the old ways,

> THE SYMBOLS MOMADAY USES—EACH ONE ONLY A SMALL PART OF THE LITANY OF NATURAL IMAGES SPANNING THE FIRST STANZA OF THE POEM—ALL HAVE A MUCH MORE COMPLICATED MEANING THAN JUST THE LITERAL OBJECT."

preserving tradition. Over the years, people have also moved forward to modernize traditional beadwork and jewelry making, with beads made of glass or metals like silver and copper. Also, some Native American artists earn their living selling their traditional handmade beaded wares to tourists or on the Internet. With the simple image of the bead, Momaday recalls elements of Indian culture from prehistory to the present day.

Even more interesting than the man-made ornaments in the poem are the plants listed. Sumac, which was used as a source for food and medicine, is mentioned, and then Momaday includes the *pomme blanche*, which translates in English to "white apple." The name dates from 1805, when French-speaking members of Lewis and Clark's expedition saw Native Americans in the plains digging up a tuber much like a potato. It goes by many names: prairie turnip, prairie potato, Indian breadroot, breadroot scurf pea, tipsin, tipsinna, timpsula, and pomme de terre. Kay Fleming, writing for the Manataka American Indian Council, describes the prairie turnip as "probably the most important wild food gathered by Native Americans who lived on the prairies." It can be eaten raw but is more often boiled in a stew, fried, or ground into fine flour, which can be used to make fry bread (dough flattened and fried in a pan rather than baked in an oven). By mentioning the prairie turnip, Momaday highlights the significance of this important and versatile staple and also subtly raises the issue of a negative aspect of white European American settlers on Native lands: prairie turnips are still found plentifully in the plains but not in areas that have been heavily farmed.

The richness of Momaday's imagery is particularly well illustrated by explaining the meanings behind the poem's second line. While the image of the horse fits well into the poem's nature imagery, it also makes not one but two significant references that enhance the poem's overall meaning. The first is the traditional legend of a blue horse—the first horse brought to America by Europeans. In the old story, the horse was ridden by a Spanish soldier. The soldier's armor frightens a young Native American man, who shoots the Spaniard with an arrow but spares him because he promises he can explain how to talk to horses. When the Native American man later dies, the other members of his tribe, not knowing how to speak to the horse, set it free to roam the prairie, still wearing the sky-blue silk ornaments of his first master. With the young Native American man's fear of the Spaniard and the tribe's fear of the horse, this story reflects the understandable caution that met the arrival of white settlers. However, horses also became a vital part of Native American life and culture, showing that with the negative consequences of contact with European Americans also came benefits.

In addition to this legend, Momaday surely means to bring to his readers' minds the Lakota leader Blue Horse (1822–1908). Though he was a brave warrior, fighting to preserve sacred tribal lands and protect his people and their way of life, he was also a statesman, working with white settlers in an attempt to keep the peace. He was one of the early US Army Indian Scouts and, on behalf of his people, signed the Treaty of Fort Laramie in 1868. This clearly shows Momaday's subtle touch. All of this—the brave warrior as well as the ancient story about how horses were introduced to the land—is suggested by a single line of the poem.

Just as the second line of the poem references one great Native American leader, the penultimate line mirrors it. Near the poem's close, Momaday mentions Tsen-tainte, which is the Indian name of White Horse, a Kiowa chief who died in 1892. Unlike Blue Horse, White Horse rarely attempted diplomacy to maintain peaceful relations with white settlers. He was known for his fierce, daring fighting. There is historical proof that he several times participated in raids on US cavalry forts that led to the murder or kidnapping not only of soldiers and officers but also of their wives and children.

Although the interest of White Horse's story again shows the wealth of detail Momaday hints at in his poem for the well-informed reader, referring to a leader whose life was filled with violence and revenge might seem like a jarring

Momaday's Native American name, Tsoai-talee, comes from Devils Tower, a site sacred to the Kiowa people. (© *Rruntsch / Shutterstock.com*)

lecture when a student asked Momaday "why he had 'chosen the white man's way'" because he taught English literature and sometimes wrote using traditional poetic forms. Momaday answered, "Don't kid yourself.... I don't think I have." Trimble explains why the student's puzzlement is interesting:

> Implicit in the question was an image of "the Indian" as someone totally different from other men. Dr. Momaday's answer reveals his fundamental philosophy of life: he sees no contradiction in being both an American Indian who participates in tribal dances and a college professor.

Momaday's poetry is a reflection of this philosophy: it includes images from his culture and the rhythms of the oral tradition but is also influenced by his formal education and the influence of his mentor, Yvor Winters. "The Delight Song of Tsoai-talee" is ideal for introducing readers to Momaday's work, because the poem, taken at face value, seems like a simple reflection on man's relationship with nature but, when looked at more closely, offers so much more. It is an example of what Momaday is best at—infusing a seemingly mainstream poem with elements of his Native American heritage.

Source: Kristen Sarlin Greenberg, Critical Essay on "The Delight Song of Tsoai-talee," in *Poetry for Students*, Gale, Cengage Learning, 2016.

end to a poem about the speaker's unity with nature. However, Momaday softens the reference by declaring his relationship to the "daughter" of White Horse rather than the warrior himself. The distance of a generation might be intended to draw attention away from the warrior: rather than having a tie with White Horse, the poem actually highlights the speaker's connection to the family that White Horse fought to protect. Alternately, perhaps Momaday means the term *daughter* to be taken less literally and include the following generations, which changes the meaning of the penultimate line to indicate that the speaker has a positive relationship with all of the women of his people. Regardless of how this line is interpreted, it draws attention to the troubled relations between tribal leaders and white settlers, which is an undeniable part of Native American history.

Martha Scott Trimble, in her 1973 monograph on Momaday, relates an anecdote concerning a

SOURCES

Anderson, H. Allen, "White Horse," in *Handbook of Texas Online*, June 15, 2010, http://www.tshaonline.org/handbook/online/articles/fwh81 (accessed September 14, 2015).

Archuleta, Elizabeth, Review of *In the Presence of the Sun*, in *American Indian Quarterly*, Vol. 35, No. 2, 2011, pp. 258–60.

"Beads," Indians.org, http://www.indians.org/articles/beads.html (accessed September 14, 2015).

"Blue Horse," American-Tribes.com, http://www.american-tribes.com/Lakota/BIO/BlueHorse.htm (accessed September 14, 2015).

Brookeman, Christopher, "The Native American Peoples of the United States," AR Net, http://www.americansc.org.uk/Online/brookman.htm (accessed September 13, 2015).

"The Bureau of Indian Education," Bureau of Indian Affairs website, http://www.bia.gov/WhatWeDo/ServiceOverview/IndianEducation/ (accessed September 13, 2015).

Champagne, Duane, "Termination and Indian Sovereignty (1945 to 2000)," in *History and the Headlines*, ABC-CLIO website, http://www.historyandtheheadlines. abc-clio.com/ContentPages/ContentPage.aspx?entryId = 1171628&currentSection = 1161468 (accessed September 13, 2015).

Charles, Jim, *Reading, Learning, Teaching: N. Scott Momaday*, Peter Lang, 2007, pp. 8, 24–25.

Culpepper, Chuck, "Florida State's Unusual Bond with Seminole Tribe Puts Mascot Debate in a Different Light," in *Washington Post*, December 29, 2014, https:// www.washingtonpost.com/sports/colleges/florida-states-unusual-bond-with-seminole-tribe-puts-mascot-debate-in-a-different-light/2014/12/29/5386841a-8eea-11e4-ba53-a477d66580ed_story.html (accessed September 13, 2015).

"Devils Tower: Frequently Asked Questions," National Park Service website, http://www.nps.gov/deto/faqs.htm (accessed September 14, 2015).

"Early Native American Literature," in *Native American Writers*, http://nativeamericanwriters.com/ (accessed September 13, 2015).

"Elias Boudinot (ca. 1804–1839)," in *New Georgia Encyclopedia*, http://www.georgiaencyclopedia.org/articles/ history-archaeology/elias-boudinot-ca-1804-1839 (accessed September 13, 2015).

Fleming, Kay, "Timpsula, Turnip of the Prairie," Manataka American Indian Council website, http://www.manataka. org/page827.html (accessed September 14, 2015).

Martin, Michael, "Has Pop Culture Moved beyond Cowboys and Indians?," NPR website, http://www.npr.org/ 2012/11/14/165121081/has-pop-culture-moved-beyond-cowboys-and-indians (accessed September 13, 2015).

Maxwell, Lesli A., "Education in Indian Country: Running in Place," in *Education Week*, December 4, 2013, http://www. edweek.org/ew/projects/2013/native-american-education/ running-in-place.html (accessed September 13, 2015).

Momaday, N. Scott, "The Delight Song of Tsoai-talee," in *In the Presence of the Sun: Stories and Poems, 1961–1991*, St. Martin's Press, 1992, p. 16.

—————, *The Way to Rainy Mountain*, University of New Mexico Press, 1976.

"Native American Authors: N. Scott Momaday, 1934–," ipl2, http://www.ipl.org/div/natam/bin/browse.pl/A50 (accessed September 11, 2015).

"Native American Culture," Native Net, http://www. native-net.org/na/native-american-culture.html (accessed September 14, 2015).

"Native American Deer Mythology," Native Languages of the Americas website, http://www.native-languages. org/legends-wolf.htm (accessed September 14, 2015).

"Native American Feathers," Native Net website, http:// www.native-net.org/na/native-american-feathers.html (accessed September 14, 2015).

"Native American Wolf Mythology," Native Languages of the Americas website, http://www.native-languages. org/legends-deer.htm (accessed September 14, 2015).

"N. Scott Momaday," Poets.org, http://www.poets.org/ poetsorg/poet/n-scott-momaday (accessed September 11, 2015).

"N. Scott Momaday: American Author," in *Encyclopædia Britannica*, http://www.britannica.com/biography/N-Scott-Momaday (accessed September 11, 2015).

"Oral Tradition in Native America," Winged Messenger Nations: Birds in American Indian Oral Tradition, http:// nativeede.wix.com/wingedmessenger#!oral-tradition-in-native-america/c1kv6 (accessed September 15, 2015).

"An Overview of Post-1960 Native American Literature," Writers of the Native American Renaissance website, in http://nativeamericanlit.com/ (accessed September 13, 2015).

Review of *In the Presence of the Sun*, in *Publishers Weekly*, http://www.publishersweekly.com/978-0-312-08222-2 (accessed September 13, 2015).

Shanley, Kathryn W., "Native American Literature," in *Encyclopedia of the Great Plains*, edited by David J. Wishart, http://plainshumanities.unl.edu/encyclopedia/ doc/egp.lt.050 (accessed September 13, 2015).

Stratton, Florence, "The Swift Blue One," in *When the Storm God Rides: Tejas and Other Indian Legends*, collected by Bessie M. Reid, 1936, http://www.sacred-texts.com/ nam/se/wsgr/wsgr15.htm (accessed September 14, 2015).

Trimble, Martha Scott, *N. Scott Momaday*, Caxton Printers, 1973, pp. 5, 41, 42.

Velie, Alan R., "Post-Symbolism and Prose Poems: Momaday's Poetry," in *Four Literary Masters: N. Scott Momaday, James Welch, Leslie Marmon Silko, and Gerald Vizenor*, University of Oklahoma Press, 1982, pp. 48–49.

Wiget, Andrew, "Native American Oral Narrative," Georgetown University website, http://faculty.georgetown.edu/ bassr/heath/syllabuild/iguide/nativeon.html (accessed September 14, 2015).

FURTHER READING

Charles, Jim, *Reading, Learning, Teaching: N. Scott Momaday*, Peter Lang, 2007.

> Charles offers an introduction to Momaday's work, including an analysis of how his heritage and cultural experiences have influenced his writing. Though Charles's target audience is teachers, students can also use the advice offered for independent study.

Merrill, Christopher, ed., *The Forgotten Language: Contemporary Poets and Nature*, Peregrine Smith Books, 1991.

> Merrill collects over one hundred nature poems by such well-known writers as William Stafford, James Dickey, and Margaret Atwood. The volume is suitable for young adults, and it includes

an introduction that analyzes some common themes of the selected works.

Momaday, N. Scott, *Angle of Geese and Other Poems*, D. R. Godine, 1974.

This early collection of Momaday's poetry, like most of his work, reflects his Native American heritage and his focus on people's relationship with nature.

Velie, Alan R., and A. Robert Lee, eds., *The Native American Renaissance: Literary Imagination and Achievement*, University of Oklahoma Press, 2013.

This nonfiction volume offers a broad selection of literary criticism touching on all genres of literature by Native American writers from the late 1960s into the twenty-first century.

SUGGESTED SEARCH TERMS

N. Scott Momaday AND Delight Song of Tsoai-talee

N. Scott Momaday AND In the Presence of the Sun

N. Scott Momaday AND Pulitzer Prize

N. Scott Momaday AND Kiowa

N. Scott Momaday AND Native American oral tradition

Native American symbols

Native American folklore

Native American Renaissance

En Route to Bangladesh, Another Crisis of Faith

TARFIA FAIZULLAH

2010

Included in Tarfia Faizullah's multiple-award-winning debut collection *Seam* (2014) is a forty-line poem entitled "En Route to Bangladesh, Another Crisis of Faith." The poem begins to speak to Faizullah's broader concerns in the volume, which is organized around a series of interviews that she conducted with women in Bangladesh known as *birangona*, which means "brave women" or "war heroines." These women were victims, during the nation's 1971 Liberation War, of mass rape at the hands of Pakistani soldiers, who used it as a military tactic. In a conflict lasting some eight months, between two hundred thousand and four hundred thousand women were raped or made to serve as sexual slaves.

Appearing as the second poem in *Seam*, "En Route to Bangladesh, Another Crisis of Faith" helps set the stage for the collection by offering a narrative self-portrait of a Bangladeshi American woman making her way through Dubai International Airport and reflecting on her identity and perhaps on the virtue of her project. *Seam* in fact contains two poems with the aforementioned title, which does lend itself to repetition. The one treated here first appeared in the *Missouri Review*, Vol. 33, No. 4, Winter 2010, and is more widely known for also appearing on the Poetry Foundation website. The second poem of the same title, which is the penultimate poem of *Seam*, was first published in the *Massachusetts Review*, Vol. 52, No. 1, Spring 2011, and can also

Although the speaker looks like the people around her, she feels set apart because she is American. *(© Rob Byron | Shutterstock.com)*

be found in the *Ploughshares* blog post "Hearing Voices: Women Versing Life Presents Tarfia Faizullah and the Unpublished Manuscript."

AUTHOR BIOGRAPHY

Tarfia Faizullah was born in Brooklyn, New York, in 1980 as part of a Muslim family formed through an arranged marriage; her parents had immigrated two years earlier, and her mother was eighteen when Faizullah was born. She grew up in Midland, Texas, in a region marked by billboards condemning to hell all nonbelievers in Jesus. Her father had a clinic (of some kind) situated between fast-food restaurants on a long road leading out to the oil fields. One profound interest of her youth was the Slinky, which she would recall spending many hours with; she realized as an adult that the toy approximated the curl of her hair (and she would use it as a key metaphor in

one of her better-known poems). There was a substantial South Asian community in the area, and Faizullah grew up speaking Bengali at home in addition to learning English; she still sometimes dreams in Bengali. She attended religious services at a mosque situated in an office building, where she would cover her head and learn to read Arabic—though during breaks with friends she would eat Western junk food and gossip about boys. She did read the entirety of the Qur'an by age seven. Meanwhile, she attended an Episcopal private school, Trinity, where she attended chapel and sang hymns, conducting Muslim prayers with her family upon returning home. As an adult, she would come to recognize ways that Islam confined her identity as a woman, and she no longer prays or considers herself religious. Tragically, when Faizullah was twelve, her family was in a car accident, and her sister, seven-year-old Tangia, died from her injuries.

As she told an online *Best New Poets* interviewer, Faizullah considered herself as having been "shy, overweight, and nerdy" as a youth—a lamented self-perception that encouraged her to appreciate the release and escape offered by the creation of poetry. The loss of her sister, too, led her to take solace in writing verse. Her engagement with words was reflected more academically in her advancing as far as the national spelling bee in eighth grade. Having graduated from high school and attended college, Faizullah had a formative experience in attending a 2006 poetry panel at the University of Texas, Austin, featuring Bangladeshi writer Mahmud Rahman, who had translated a portion of a novel about a woman who endured rape during the 1971 Liberation War. Faizullah had never heard of this part of the history of her family's home country, which resonated with her in part because she endured such a sexual assault herself shortly after high school. It was around this time that Faizullah entered graduate school at Virginia Commonwealth University, where she earned an MFA and served as an associate editor of *Blackbird*.

Having sometimes visited Bangladesh with her family from 2007 onward, Faizullah began the project that would become her first volume of poems with imaginative engagement. She wrote a poem about a young woman not unlike herself returning from Bangladesh after interviewing some of the women who were raped during the war—now known as *birangona*, acknowledging their brave endurance of the wartime horrors— and transcribing those interviews. From there Faizullah wrote poems imagining the interviews themselves, and she won the Cohen Award from *Ploughshares* in 2009 for an excerpt from her poem "Interview with a Birangona." By then she had already realized that in order to truly honor the *birangona* and their experiences, she would need to actually travel to Bangladesh and interview them. She applied for a Fulbright, winning a fellowship that allowed her to go to Bangladesh and stay for a year in 2010–2011.

Faizullah's life since returning from Bangladesh has been peppered with fellowships, honors, and awards. The submission of her manuscript for her debut collection won the 2012 Crab Orchard Series in Poetry First Book Award, entailing two thousand dollars and the publication of the manuscript by Southern Illinois University Press. *Seam*, which proceeded to win the 2015 New Writers Award in Poetry from the Great Lakes Colleges Association, includes two different poems titled "En Route to Bangladesh, Another Crisis of Faith." Meanwhile, Faizullah joined Kundiman, an Asian American poetry collective, as a fellow, and she also participates in a writing group called the Grind. She moved to Washington, DC, where she taught creative writing. She has served as an editor for several publications, including the *Asian American Literary Review*, and for Organic Weapon Arts Chapbook Press, which she coedits with poet Jamaal May, her partner. May's identity as a non-Muslim black led to a lapse in communication between Faizullah and her parents. Faizullah staged a reading of her verse at the Library of Congress in May 2014. Moving to Detroit, she served as a writer in residence for InsideOut Literary Arts, and in the fall of 2014, she began serving as the Nicholas Delbanco Visiting Professor of Creative Writing in the Helen Zell Writers' Program at the University of Michigan.

POEM TEXT

—at Dubai International Airport and ending with a line by César Vallejo

Because I must walk
through the eye-shaped
shadows cast by these
curved gold leaves thick   5
atop each constructed
palm tree, past displays
of silk scarves, lit
silhouettes of blue-bottled
perfume—because   10
I grip, as though for the first
time, a paper bag
of french fries from McDonald's,

MEDIA ADAPTATIONS

- Faizullah can be heard reading "En Route to Bangladesh, Another Crisis of Faith" on the One Pause Poetry website, at http://www.onepausepoetry.org/explore/poets/profile/tarfia_faizullah.

and lick, from each fingertip,
the fat and salt as I stand alone   15
to the side of this moving
walkway gliding me past dark-
eyed men who do not look
away when I stare squarely
back—because standing   20
in line to the restroom I want
only to pluck from her
black sweater this one shimmering
blond hair clinging fast—
because I must rest the Coke, cold   25
in my hand, beside this
toilet seat warmed by her thighs,
her thighs, and hers.
Here, at the narrow mouth
of this long, humid   30
corridor leading to the plane,
I take my place among
this damp, dark horde of men
and women who look like me—
because I look like them—   35
because I am ashamed
of their bodies that reek so
unabashedly of body—
because I can—because I am
an American, *a star*   40
of blood on the surface of muscle.

POEM SUMMARY

The text used for this summary is from *Seam*, Southern Illinois University Press/*Crab Orchard Review*, 2014, pp. 11–12. A version of the poem can be found on the following web page: http://www.poetryfoundation.org/poem/247528.

Beyond the title, where a dedication might appear, Faizullah notes that the poem takes place at the Dubai airport, in the United Arab Emirates, and includes a line borrowed from Peruvian poet César Vallejo (as translated from the Spanish).

Lines 1–27

"En Route to Bangladesh, Another Crisis of Faith" begins with a dependent clause indicating that what follows is the cause of something; through the first several lines, that something remains undetermined. The cause in question is the fact that the poet is obliged to walk through shadows that are shaped like eyes; between lines 2 and 3, the reader may imagine that the narrator is physically walking *through* something, but of course the shadows do not have any tangible physical existence; the gap between what is at first imagined and what proves to be the reality may evoke in the reader a sense of dislocation that befits the poem's general sense of psychic dislocation (the crisis of faith). The shadows are noted to be those of the golden fronds of a series of artificial palm trees. The poet also walks past silk scarves on display and perfume in blue bottles that are somehow lit up—perhaps by sunshine coming in through a window or, more likely, by a display stand designed to attract people's attention with light and color.

In line 9, a dash concludes the long clause and introduces the beginning of a parallel clause: again the poet is describing a cause of something, while the something remains unstated. This second cause is the fact that the poet clutches, in a way suggesting a novelty of experience, a paper bag that contains fast-food French fries, from a McDonald's restaurant evidently located somewhere within the Dubai airport. She may be clutching the bag tightly because she feels enthralled with the experience of eating the fries; this is further suggested by her licking each one of her fingertips to collect the grease and salt deposited there.

While the poet eats, as she relates beginning in the middle of line 14, she is now standing by herself on a moving walkway, off to the side (to allow room for people to walk past). The walkway steadily propels her past something dark, as the end of line 16 notes; line 17 specifies that what are dark are the eyes of men—presumably on the opposite walkway or off on the adjacent unmoving floors—who regard her and continue to regard her even when she declines to avert her own eyes. While

Faizullah's identity as a woman does not guarantee that her narrator is a woman, this passage strongly suggests that, as an object of men's interest, she is female.

In line 19, another dash concludes this second cause of the unstated something, and another *because* introduces a third cause. By this point the reader may feel a need to jump to a conclusion as to what is the result of all of these causes; a logical conclusion is that the result is the very crisis of faith referred to in the title. Still unstated, if that is the case, is the type of faith— whether in a religion or in something else—with regard to which there is a crisis.

The third cause is the fact that, while waiting to take her turn in the ladies' restroom, the poet feels a desire to reach out and remove a single, shining blond hair from the black sweater worn by another woman, presumably the one lined up in front of her. Line 23 brings another cause, the fourth: the fact that the poet is obliged to set her cup of Coke (likely meaning Coca-Cola, though perhaps just generically meaning *soda pop*, as the word is sometimes used), which is cold to the touch, beside the seat of the toilet she is using— presumably on a raised shelf or perhaps atop the toilet-paper dispenser. The toilet seat, she notes, has been warmed by the thighs of several women referred to only as *her*, though it might be hard to say exactly which women happened to have used that particular seat. Line 27 ends with the poem's first of two periods.

Lines 28–40

Taking up a new idea in line 28, the poet begins a sentence declaring that in this particular place, at the opening or entrance or exit of the extended, damp-aired hall leading to the airplane (the one the poet must be boarding for Bangladesh), she can situate herself in the midst of the crowd of men. With the use in line 32 of the word *horde*, along with the description of the men themselves (not just their eyes) as dark and also as damp, as if from sweat, the men are lent an overwhelming, even threatening presence. There are also women, however, as line 33 goes on to note, without describing them anymore than to say that their appearance resembles that of the poet herself. In that she is traveling to Bangladesh, presumably alongside many who are returning home or visiting family there, one readily imagines that the skin of the men, of a South Asian hue, is what earns them the label *dark*, while the women and the poet must also have dark skin.

Line 34 reintroduces the word *because*, apparently to suggest the circular formulation that the women look like her because she looks like the women. This line ends with another dash, followed again by the word *because*, though now again the something being caused is unclear. In fact, three more dashes and *because* clauses follow, which seem to suggest neither causes for why the women look like her nor causes for why she is able to take her place among all of these people. The (ambiguous) cause stated in lines 35–37 is the fact that the poet feels shame over the extent to which the body odor of the surrounding people permeates the air, indicating that they have taken no trouble to mask their natural scent with deodorant; it is possible that some of them have not bathed as recently as the poet might wish they had, as suggested by her impression that they do not care in the least about whether or not they are publicly sharing their natural scent.

The first three words of line 38 introduce a very brief cause: the fact that the poet is, quite simply, able—presumably meaning able to do the very something being "caused." Considering again here the crisis of faith of the title, she may be suggesting that she is having the crisis in question simply because she is able to have it. A last cause is stated through lines 38–40—the fact that the poet is an American, one who might be characterized (the italics indicating that this is the line from Vallejo) as blood in the shape of a star that can be found on the surface of a muscle.

THEMES

Travel

That the narrator of Faizullah's poem is in a state of travel is made apparent by the title, with the phrase *en route* meaning "on the way" somewhere. Moreover, the state of travel seems to be a central aspect of the fact that the poet is having her crisis of faith, given that these two circumstances share the title, side by side. This accords with reason, since the perspectives brought about by travel— especially to locales that drastically differ from what one is used to in terms of the texture of existence—can lead a person to rethink what one has long believed, such as with regard to culturally weighted truths and one's own identity. Of course,

such a crisis of faith, vaguely defined, would be most likely to come about if one were traveling somewhere for the first time or perhaps more likely returning from that somewhere to one's once-familiar world. Many a Peace Corps volunteer, along with other Westerners who take equivalent journeys of prolonged engagement with a developing-world culture, can vividly recount that first trip back from whatever foreign locale they were stationed in. Specifically, at least for those returning home to the United States, the senses of materialism, consumerism, and consumption can be overwhelming—and that comes merely from exposure to the surface of things. American attitudes, as well, are likely to make a traveler quite explicitly rethink one's faith in one's own culture.

Interestingly, though, the fact that the poet is having *another* faith crisis, as well as the nonchalant manner in which she endures the experience of travel—munching fries while letting a moving walkway get her quickly enough to wherever she needs to go—suggests that this is not her first trip to Bangladesh. Comments by Faizullah have confirmed that she visited her ancestral home nation multiple times prior to the occasion of this poem. The sense of repetition invoked by the word *another* might seem to diminish the import of this particular faith crisis; on the other hand, that it has happened more than once, indeed likely happens again and again, can be seen to heighten the significance of the crisis—much like how the significance of a dream is strengthened if it is a recurring dream. Thus does the narrator go through the motions of traversing the airport and, as if despite her intent to be unruffled by the experience, nevertheless experience a crisis of faith, for a series of closely related reasons.

American Culture

While the poet's identity as an American is not revealed until the penultimate line, the reader likely gets the feeling well before that she bears a US passport, given the way she seems to be infused with aspects of American culture—the link connecting a majority of the reasons for her crisis, though at times one has to look for it. The poem's first cause, for example, is not at all clear. It is possible that the poet is saying here only that the crisis occurs because she *must* walk a portion of the way from point A, somewhere in America, to point B, Bangladesh—that the travel itself causes the crisis, and no more. Beyond line 1, the objects described seem to speak largely of non-American culture, as the golden palm

TOPICS FOR FURTHER STUDY

- Write a poem in which the narrator relates his or her actions at some point in the process of traveling from one place to another, with the nature of the actions somehow reflecting the difference or distance between the destination and the place departed from as well as the purpose of the journey. Where Faizullah has the context of *Seam* to amplify the meaning of her poem, you may wish to either simply make your poem more expansive or write a brief contextual prose piece to set the scene for the poem.

- Faizullah's other "En Route to Bangladesh, Another Crisis of Faith," the second-to-last poem in *Seam*, has a feel far different from its predecessor. Read that poem and write an essay in which you analyze it independently and also contrast it either with the first poem of the same title or with the Emily Dickinson poem "There's a certain Slant of light," which Faizullah has said made an impression on her as a youth.

- Read the Dickinson poem "There is no Frigate like a Book," which can be found in the Poetry for Young People series collection *Emily Dickinson* (1994), edited by Frances Schoonmaker Bolin, and online. In an essay, analyze this poem in terms of theme as well as style—meter, rhyme, and so on—and then discuss how it relates to the journey the poet is making in "En Route to Bangladesh, Another Crisis of Faith" in two different ways, drawing on the sense of the real-life journey Faizullah took in 2010.

- Produce an artistically hyperlinked version of "En Route to Bangladesh, Another Crisis of Faith" which—mimicking, in a sense, Faizullah's "link" to Vallejo's poem—provides links to other poems, articles, photos, or websites to enhance the reader's experience with the poem. Use your series of links to bring out the meaning of the poem as you see it; to accompany your version, write a brief statement indicating your artistic intents.

---

trees, silk scarves, and perfumes in and of themselves call Arabian culture to mind. However, considered as merely Arabian, these items hardly help explain a crisis of faith; they might instead be considered as representing the infusion of American cultural values overseas, the Dubai airport being the glittering capitalist, materialist jewel of the Middle East. Here, the palm trees are golden and fake, the scarves are on sale by the dozen, and the perfume's blue bottles are lit up not simply to ensure that they are visible but also to accentuate the style and color of the bottle, in a brazen marketing ploy.

The poem's next cause, that of lines 9–19, more directly speaks of American culture, with the McDonald's bag and the fries that apparently make the narrator feel covetous taking center stage. That the poet has been influenced by American-style feminism, as it is considered in

certain parts of the world, is suggested by her refusal to avert her eyes from the gazes of men, as women in some traditional cultures are expected to do, as a sign of deference. In the cause of lines 19–23, there is a concern for superficial appearance—the removal of the stray hair—even on the sweater of someone other than herself, and a blond (non-Bangladeshi) someone at that. In lines 24–28, there is the Coke, another aspect of the McDonald's meal, not to mention the fact that she feels compelled to take it into the stall with her, perhaps out of the (legitimate) fear that her drink might be tampered with were she to leave it, say, on the counter at the sinks. She also thinks of the thighs of other women who have sat on the same toilet, as if overly conscious of the germs she might find there. All of these attitudes that seem to underlie the causes of her crisis of faith can be regarded as characteristically American.

The poem is set in the airport near the wealthy city of Dubai, United Arab Emirates. (© Alexander Tolstykh / Shutterstock.com)

Identity

One gathers by now that the poet's crisis of faith might indeed be thought of as, at bottom, an identity crisis. She is—or at least she must be for the poem to make sense—an American, whether by birth or by immigration and assimilation. Her identity as American is apparent to her, as it becomes to the reader, in the way she prizes her fast-food fries, the way she stares back at men, the way she wants to help another woman keep her appearance pristine, the way she worries about potential assailants, whether humans or germs. But the utmost significance is attached to the way she feels shame over the smell of the fellow bodies with whom she is boarding the plane. If the crisis of faith has been building as a result of the preceding moments, however small, which together are communicated in a single sentence, then the moment of shame over the others' scents must be the climax of the crisis, the point at which her identity as American is evinced not merely by her behavior, or even by her inclinations, but by her very feelings, which perhaps run counter to the way she would prefer

to feel—as suggested by the fact that this feeling is the pinnacle of the crisis. Looking like those likewise heading to Bangladesh, the poet is presumably Bangladeshi American (as is Faizullah), and she would perhaps prefer to feel unabashed affiliation with the people of her ancestral country—and yet instead she is embarrassed by them, and she is inclined to dissociate herself from them. In that moment, it seems, she is not Bangladeshi but simply American, whether she wants to be or not.

Faith

Yet the poem is not called "En Route to Bangladesh, Another Crisis of Identity." The poet may well have a firm understanding of who she is— sometimes more Bangladeshi, sometimes more American—and be at peace with her identity, regardless of how it shows itself. She may feel, in the end, that if people can afford to travel by air, presumably they have some chance to wash their bodies, if not perfume them, before embarking on that travel. Regardless of how she feels about the surrounding scented bodies in the end, the narrator's crisis is decidedly one of *faith*—and so, of course, the reader must determine, faith in *what*. A few related possibilities suggest themselves, as may or may not be revealed within the poem—faith, indeed, in her identity; faith in American values; or perhaps faith in the purpose of her trip, about which the reader of this poem alone knows nothing.

The poet may leave the repository of the faith over which she is having a crisis unspecified precisely because it is not specifiable. She may experience, in traveling to Bangladesh, a weakening within herself, a sense of collapsing, or impending collapse, that could be pinpointed only as a weakening of her faith in humanity or the universe in general. Wherever the poet's faith might be located, the reader, too, is left to linger in the uncertainty brought about by the ruminations of the poem.

STYLE

Indentation

The poems in Faizullah's volume *Seam* cycle through a number of different forms, especially couplets and tercets, alongside more unique presentations marked by differentiated spacing or indentation. Indentation is in fact the only stylistic strategy used in "En Route to Bangladesh," with every even-numbered line indented about as much as an ordinary paragraph indentation and without any stanza breaks in the forty lines. As the lines are fairly short, the indentation seems significant by comparison, tending to group every two lines as a sort of internal couplet, since the reading flows much more smoothly from the end of line 1 to the indented beginning of line 2 than from the distant end of line 2 to the beginning of line 3 way back at the margin. However, Faizullah does not seem to draw on these perceptible internal couplets to amplify the poem's meaning. Rather, her interest may lie more in the way the progress through the series of indented and nonindented lines lends a pendulum-like, back-and-forth feel to the verse, as if the poet, like the poem, is being swayed in two different directions. Such a circumstance is indeed suggested by the fact of the crisis of faith. The indentation might thus be seen to connote the pendulum of the poet's identity, if she is ethnically and ancestrally Bangladeshi but

culturally and psychologically American, going regularly back and forth between the two sides.

Anaphora and Fragmentation

Faizullah challenges her reader in presenting a poem whose syntactical structure is not easily broken down for logical interpretation. Even if the crisis of faith is known to be central to the poem based on its mention in the title, the reader may well proceed through the entire poem without understanding just what is being caused by all the stated circumstances. The repeated use of the word *because* at the beginning of clauses, eight in all, constitutes the poetic technique of *anaphora*. Anaphora is more readily recognized when the repeated introductory word or phrase appears at the beginning of the lines themselves.

Naturally, if a reader encounters a sentence begun, one expects it to be logically concluded, but as it happens, the entire sentence of lines 1–28 is only a fragment, consisting of four dependent *because* clauses unanchored to any independent clause. This structure, while not easily analyzed, does help the reader make sense of the remaining twelve lines, which actually do make up a complete sentence. But if these lines are to be understood as a self-contained complete sentence, the four additional *because* clauses would have to be attached to some part of that sentence. Only line 34 is readily attached to what precedes it, to line 33. Since lines 1–28 do not constitute a legitimate sentence, perhaps the reader should not expect one here; thus one more readily realizes that the final three *because* clauses, which defy attachment to what precedes them, appear to be dependent clauses that are, in the end, independent—like the first four, attached only to the title, as it seems.

HISTORICAL CONTEXT

The Bangladesh Liberation War

While the implied circumstance of "En Route to Bangladesh, Another Crisis of Faith" is the trip that Faizullah took in 2010, the significance of that trip lies further back in history, in the region's war and genocide of 1971. Modern-day Bangladesh was created as East Pakistan when Great Britain, finally vacating its Indian colony in 1947, decided (for its own reasons) that the region would be broken up into a Hindu nation, India, and a Muslim nation, Pakistan. This event alone brought about widespread social instability, refugee populations, and deaths, and it also set the stage for future bloodshed by leaving half the region of Bengal, now called East Pakistan, under the rule of the ethnic majority in West Pakistan, from which it was geographically divided by Indian territory. With West Pakistan refusing to grant East Pakistan full autonomy or official status for the Bangla language, a nationalist movement inevitably developed. This movement came to a head in 1970, when the Awami League, favoring independence, swept into power, and Bangladesh's independence was declared on March 26, 1971.

The military government of Pakistan immediately embarked on a campaign specifically designed to exterminate vast swaths of the Bangladesh population, which was then seventy-five million. As recorded in the Bangladesh Genocide Archive, Pakistani president Yahya Khan had told his generals in February 1971, "Kill three million of them,...and the rest will eat out of our hands." Retrospective estimates of the number murdered—by the thousands in cities, at universities, and among Hindus—range from one million to as many as three million. The atrocities committed were not unlike those committed during World War II by the Germans against the Jews—except that the Pakistani military also made a point of raping women, often repeatedly, whether they ultimately killed them or not. They went so far as to establish locales referred to as "rape camps"; as many as four hundred thousand women, or more, are estimated to have been victims. Many women who endured these horrendous trials and survived were actually shamed upon returning to their families and communities. Some were murdered by their husbands, some killed themselves, and some killed the half-Pakistani children they bore.

Because of the societal shame, the stories of these women—who were given the honorific appellation of *birangona* by the Bangladesh government—long went untold, especially in the English language. Among others who have seen fit to tell the *birangona*'s stories to a global audience, as a means of better honoring them, is Faizullah, who thus traveled to Bangladesh in 2010. But being an extensively conscientious person, she could not do so without seriously interrogating her role and her integrity in the process. The poems in *Seam* offer evidence that she closely considered such matters as the morality

The speaker notes that when she catches the eyes of passersby, they steadfastly meet her gaze. (© *Warren Goldswain / Shutterstock.com*)

of asking the *birangona* to share and thus relive their horrific experiences; of depicting what they endured without sensationalizing it; and of intending, however honorably, to profit from their experiences with the book of poetry she had already conceived as revolving around her journey—the book she had won a Fulbright Fellowship to create. Faizullah spoke directly to this concern in an interview with the *Lantern Review*: "*Seam*, in the end, is a deeply problematic and troubled book. It must be, because it attempts the impossible: to plumb the very thin line between witnessing and voyeurism." Although one cannot know it in reading "En Route to Bangladesh, Another Crisis of Faith" in isolation from the rest of *Seam*, it is likely, based on Faizullah's broader purpose, that the poet's crisis concerns precisely her faith in her project, in everything that the journey to Bangladesh will entail for her as a woman, as a poet, as an American, and as a human being.

CRITICAL OVERVIEW

Reviewers of *Seam* have been highly complimentary. *Ploughshares* interviewer Patricia Caspers, writing two years before *Seam* was published, found one of Faizullah's poems, "Dhaka Nocturne," to be "an eerie, beautiful mingling of the sensual and the grief-stricken," while the other poems she could find online were "all stunning." Adam DePollo, in his article "Tarfia Faizullah and the Illumination of Poetry," calls the verse in *Seam* "formally diverse and devastatingly immediate."

Robin LaMer Rahija, reviewing *Seam* for *Hollins Critic*, characterizes the volume as "an intimate piece of journalism in verse." She adds, "Touching on personal and political traumas, both recent and culturally historical, *Seam* is an exploration on how to live through a complex and troubling past." Rahija concludes, "Despite the horrendous acts she brings to the page, this book is ultimately one of hope and connection. A seam marks a divide, but only in its ability to connect." In *Slate*, Jonathan Farmer states,

> *Seam* feels unusually honest and exceptionally rich. Its self-critiques are not veiled attempts at absolution through awareness, nor do they give Faizullah an excuse to stop looking. Instead, they feel like the quickened presence of a flawed person (flawed as we are all flawed) who has committed to making as much as she can of the horrors she feels compelled to see.

In the *Blue Lyra Review*, Paul David Adkins declares that *Seam* is best suited not to the faint of heart but to readers who are "galvanized by compassion and empathy." In its treatment of women's experiences during the genocide in Bangladesh, Faizullah's verse is found to be "unsparing in detail, unrelenting in intensity, and breathtaking in scope and vision." Adkins affirms that "Faizullah brilliantly navigates the horrors" of the *birangona*'s experiences.

Susan Cohen, in *Prairie Schooner*, calls *Seam* a "singular, eloquent collection" showing that Faizullah is "a poet who feels tremendous empathy and who takes risks to express it." In Cohen's estimation, "Faizullah succeeds because, while her language is beautiful, she never prettifies the urgent story these poems tell.... Also, she acknowledges the question that hangs over her enterprise: what justifies making art from horror." Cohen concludes that the volume justifies its own existence and the profound consideration that Faizullah put into it:

Seam demonstrates both that fine art can be fashioned from history's atrocities, and that art is necessary—not to make sense of them—but to recognize them in their full horror. Shock and pity are both emotions safe at a distance. But empathy... for that, you must come close. You must enter bodies and minds as Faizullah does, and the reader with her.

CRITICISM

Michael Allen Holmes

Holmes is a writer with existential interests. In the following essay, he weighs the significance of the final lines of "En Route to Bangladesh, Another Crisis of Faith."

In what is already a poem that challenges the reader—to make grammatical sense of what is being said, to identify what all of the poem's causes have brought about, to understand the collective significance of those causes—the last nine words of "En Route to Bangladesh, Another Crisis of Faith" throw down one last gauntlet in the path of comprehension. The reader may well long consider this italicized line and a half, borrowed from César Vallejo (as the heading promises), without settling upon any satisfactory significance for the image presented. Tarfia Faizullah, like any good modernist, favors a certain degree of intertextuality throughout her debut collection, *Seam*, demonstrating both the advantages and drawbacks of loaded allusion to other writers and their works. Several of the volume's poems situate the narrator as reading a particular author—in turn, Willa Cather, Tomas Tranströmer, and Paul Celan—whose literary presence is inflected in the experience of the poem. Even a passing familiarity with these authors thus enhances the sense of Faizullah's verse. Cather's *The Song of the Lark*, from which Faizullah uses several lines, is about a woman claiming her identity as an artist; Paul Celan is a Holocaust survivor known for his memorial poetry. On the other hand, more than passing familiarity with Swedish Nobel Prize winner Tranströmer may be needed to grasp his relevance to the poem citing him. Regarding the Peruvian poet Vallejo, cited in "En Route to Bangladesh, Another Crisis of Faith"—that is, the first of the two poems of that title—while his verse in general is evoked by the sense of shared humanity represented by the earthy Bangladeshis, the use of his line remains quite obscure. It seems that the matter

WHAT DO I READ NEXT?

- Faizullah's planned second collection, like her first, will delve into a serious social issue, this time ethnic atrocities committed against the Kurds, an Asian people whose homeland has been divided up into parts of several countries, including Iraq and Turkey. The collection is tentatively titled "Register of Eliminated Villages" and is slated for publication in 2017.

- Kazi Nazrul Islam (1899–1976), a Bengali writer as well as a musician and revolutionary who participated in India's independence movement, is recognized as the national poet of Bangladesh. A recent collection sharing his verse with the Western world is *Selected Nazrul: In English* (2014), translated and edited by Giasuddin Dalal.

- Sarmila Bose has composed a history, *Dead Reckoning: Memories of the 1971 War* (2012), drawing on interviews, news reports, unpublished documents, and other sources to explore the contemporary and persisting impact of the Bangladesh Liberation War.

- The Bangladeshi writer who introduced Faizullah to the atrocities of the 1971 war through a work of translation, Mahmud Rahman, has published a collection of his own short fiction in English, titled *Killing the Water: Stories* (2010).

- The Bengali novel *Black Ice* (2012), written by Mahmudul Haque and translated by Rahman, is a semiautobiographical work based on Haque's experiences during and after the partition of 1947, when he was ten, which left him to travel back and forth between West Bengal, in India, and East Bengal, which became East Pakistan and is now Bangladesh.

- *Masala: Poems from India, Bangladesh, Pakistan and Sri Lanka* (2005), edited by Debjani Chatterjee, is a poetry collection aimed at juvenile and young-adult audiences that includes notes elaborating the cultural and historical references found in the poems, all of which are by South Asian writers.

- Faizullah has said that Lynda Hull is one of her favorite lesser-known poets of the past. After running away from home at sixteen, Hull went through heroin addiction. She had become a college instructor and editor for *Crazyhorse* by the time she died in a car crash at the age of thirty-nine; her third and final collection, *The Only World* (1995), was published posthumously.

- Faizullah has expressed her conviction that Jamaal May, her partner, is her soul mate, and, like Faizullah's, his debut collection has been honored several times over. A native of Detroit, May is a former public school teacher and audio engineer. His collection is titled *Hum* (2013).

---

needs to be plumbed further for sense to be made of everything.

Naturally, one first goes back to the source, which is Vallejo's poem "Imperial Nostalgias," published in his breakthrough volume *The Black Heralds* (1919) and also found in *Selected Writings of César Vallejo* (2015). The poem itself is highly imagistic, lyrical, and abstract all at once, making it problematic to pinpoint the sense of any given line—especially in the absence of more intimate knowledge of Vallejo's life and verse. But one at least gathers that the sense of the title is not nostalgia for a time of imperialism, but nostalgia that is itself *imperial*, which demands that the subject—the one feeling the nostalgia—heed it and allow it to flourish. The first two lines of the poem indicate, straightforwardly enough, that the Peruvian landscape at twilight creates the nostalgia. The third line, less clearly, indicates that

THE ENTIRE PROCESS NEEDED TO REACH THIS DEEPER UNDERSTANDING—WHICH ARGUABLY CANNOT BE FULLY ATTAINED WITHOUT THE INPUT OFFERED BY THE POET HERSELF IN A VENUE SEPARATE FROM THE POEM—DEMONSTRATES THE DIFFICULTY OF ALLUSIVE, MODERNIST-STYLE POETRY IN GENERAL."

the poet's word allows *the race* to take shape. The fourth line comprises the nine words cited by Faizullah.

Advancing from the first two lines to the third, one gathers that, perhaps, the poet's nostalgia for the landscape entails a nostalgia for the humanity of the landscape, that is, the native people—Vallejo himself was part Peruvian Indian. As such, poetic thoughts of the landscape lead to the possibility of his giving shape to the people of the landscape, the race, through his poetry. This represents a powerful commentary on the significance of the poetic act of representing a people collectively in verse—essentially enshrining a perspective on them. One proceeds then to the fourth line, and an approximate significance emerges: perhaps the sense is that where the people of the poet's race are the muscle itself, accomplishing the labor and acts of strength that sustain the race, the poet's words are like an emblem etched out in blood on the surface of that muscle, like a tattoo. That tattoo represents both the exposure of what is internal and essential (blood) to the external world (surface) and the permanence of the shape of the exposure, as fashioned by the poet.

One returns, then, to Faizullah's poem, and the application of the meaning in Vallejo's poem to the meaning here is not too incongruous—and yet it is problematic. There is a relation between the poet and the earthy Bangladeshi people, as signified by her poetic representation of them. Yet at the moment of the poem, the narrator can hardly be said to be allied with them. The title of the poem indicates a crack in the poet's faith, a fault line—a seam where the stitches have frayed. In the course of the poem, the narrator depicts herself in a way that consistently differentiates her from the common people of Bangladesh, as culminating in the moment when she is appalled by their odor—at which point precisely she is an *American*, as different from the native Bangladeshi as can be. It is true that she remains tied to them by ethnic heritage, indeed by blood, and so she might be seen as refiguring Vallejo's line to suggest perhaps a discrepancy between the substance of the muscle and the superficial appearance of the star of blood. And yet again, these people are only passing figures in both the poem and the greater collection; she may have a sort of blood-muscle link worth pondering, but that link will be with the women whom she interviews, who have not yet appeared at this point in the volume. If she is prefiguring that relationship, she is doing so ambiguously, and perhaps not fruitfully.

The issue of the problematic use of Vallejo's line becomes clearer if one finally turns to Faizullah's own comments on the matter, as presented in an online post for the *Kenyon Review* about that very line. One thing she makes clear is the circumstance of the writing of the poem, which might well have been called—in accordance with "Reading Willa Cather in Bangladesh" and "Reading Celan at the Liberation War Museum"—"Reading Vallejo at the Dubai International Airport." In the post Faizullah rhetorically asks, "Is it a coincidence . . . that Vallejo's *Collected Poems* was the only book I had with me on my long layover in Dubai? Is it a coincidence that I opened the book to 'Imperial Nostalgias'?" It may have been; her own poem citing Vallejo cannot really be said to be about nostalgia. In the post, she further relates that the people boarding the plane who have not masked their scents are a class of people whom she encounters regularly in traveling to Bangladesh—"migrant workers shoving their way to the front of the line." While they may feel compelled to do so to get the best seats, whether this actually helps them or not, Faizullah suggests that she need have no such concerns in traveling as an "upper class Bangladeshi American." She regards the migrant workers, then, and feels both a connection and a disconnect—a discrepancy that she consciously wants to resolve. This discrepancy, she notes, "is why Vallejo, visionary poet of his people, is who I had to seek guidance from." This makes clearer why Faizullah grasped at a line signifying connection where such a connection was not necessarily felt.

In the *Kenyon Review* post, Faizullah further makes clear that nostalgia is a notion near and dear to her heart. She quotes a friend as stating the conviction—one she apparently shares—that "nostalgia... is what makes us Bangalis." This may be the sort of nostalgia that virtually all immigrant groups feel from generation to generation, as some traditions are lost while others are maintained, but all remain represented in the distant homeland, which may well be "remembered" only through the stories of parents and grandparents. Or it may be a special sort of nostalgia that accords with a Bengali or Bangladeshi worldview. Either way, Faizullah has affirmed her own special affiliation with the emotion, remarking in a *Southeast Review* interview, "I am obsessed with nostalgia." She related this after noting that a mentor once suggested that "we must write from and through our obsessions because our obsessions choose us, not the other way around." In the *Kenyon Review* post, Faizullah comments further on the significance of nostalgia and of Vallejo's poem in her writing of "En Route to Bangladesh, Another Crisis of Faith":

> What I love about Vallejo's poem is what I love about nostalgia: the way the present of what is is always on its way to becoming a longing for the landscape of what was. Similarly, what I love about the line "a star of blood on the surface of muscle" is the line before: "and the race takes shape in my word."

Finally, Faizullah's use of the line seems to become crystal clear. She has been not necessarily feeling, but rather reaching for a feeling of nostalgia with regard to the people of Bangladesh, especially those from whom she has regularly "flinched away" (citing the post), despite the shame she felt afterward. Vallejo's poem is seen to represent such a nostalgia, such a sentimental connection; the use of the fourth line to, in effect, summon the meaning of the third line is itself an embodiment of nostalgia, a reaching back for something past. The reader who digs this far into the genealogy of her poem may feel greatly rewarded for reaching a deeper understanding of the significance of the line.

Yet the entire process needed to reach this deeper understanding—which arguably cannot be fully attained without the input offered by the poet herself in a venue separate from the poem—demonstrates the difficulty of allusive, modernist-style poetry in general: it is not accessible. Consulting Vallejo's poem takes the reader only so far in grasping the image borrowed

from him. Even from reading the *Kenyon Review* post, one does not necessarily come away with an understanding, whether clear or vague, about what the blood star on the muscle is supposed to mean. As for those who assess "En Route to Bangladesh, Another Crisis of Faith" without consulting any outside source, readers able to conjure some meaning from the closing image may be few and far between.

Finally, then, one may be inclined to posit something fairly insolent, from a humble reader to a poet who may have published only a single (groundbreaking) volume but has won numerous scholarships, fellowships, and awards and heaps of praise in the process of doing so. Faizullah certainly offers the grounds for positing this insolent something, in that she has, first of all, felt compelled to write about the genesis of her use of Vallejo's line in her poem and yet, second of all, gets through that entire post not only without attributing any sensible significance to that borrowed line but without indicating that she herself *can* directly attribute any significance to it. Rather, as she herself states, the line behind that one—the third line of Vallejo's poem, not the fourth—is where her interest really lies. If one deposits that line, rather, at the end of her poem, the result is this: *because I am an American, and the race takes shape in my word.* This line, as placed there, indeed has multiple evident meanings. America's status as a culturally hegemonic superpower that engulfs other nations in its brands of individualism and materialism—which has been demonstrated in the images of the poem—is evoked in the suggestion that as an American, she is able to *shape a race*, whether hers or anyone else's. It also directly suggests, in a way that can be immediately understood, the sense from Vallejo's poem that she can be allied with the race she represents, the very earthy Bangladeshis who trouble her. It further connotes the great responsibility borne by the writer who attempts to represent a race, or a subgroup of a race, which is what she is about to do in visiting and writing about the *birangona* of Bangladesh. The line thus concisely evokes both sides of the push and pull of the poem, the American and the Bangladeshi sides, in a way that the actual closing line of the poem cannot, because the meaning of that line is founded in the one she actually favored but declined to use. In Vallejo, the *star of blood* appears to be the poet's *word*, not the poet himself, making the meaning much clearer.

As the speaker passes through the airport, she shops and eats fast food. *(© Daniel M. Nagy / Shutterstock.com)*

Faizullah may have inadvertently indicated, in the *Kenyon Review* post, that she made the decision to include the Vallejo line she included without adequate consideration, in that it was "reinscribed hastily on the airplane before the flight attendant sternly commanded me to put my tray table up for takeoff." She has acknowledged that as a poet, she can trust only her own voice, which is undoubtedly what all successful poets do. But one may hazard here that circumstances conspired to push her voice in the wrong direction—to put not quite the right words of someone else's in her mouth—and had she included the line she did not include, she would have capped what is undeniably an intriguing and memorable poem with a figurative exclamation point, rather than a question mark.

Source: Michael Allen Holmes, Critical Essay on "En Route to Bangladesh, Another Crisis of Faith," in *Poetry for Students*, Gale, Cengage Learning, 2016.

Robin LaMer Rahija

In the following review, Rahija points out the hopeful note of Faizullah's collection in spite of the sadness and violence depicted.

Seam is an intimate piece of journalism in verse centering on the author's trip to Bangladesh to research the 1971 Pakistani Civil War. Faizullah speaks in the voices of women raped during the conflict, whom the government deemed "birangonas (war heroines)," though they were frequently ostracized by their families." Touching on personal and political traumas, both recent and culturally historical, *Seam* is an exploration on how to live through a complex and troubling past.

Theses traumas create seams across the landscape of the book: Faizullah's inability to break into the violent history of her own cultural background ("I am ashamed / of their bodies that reek so / unabashedly of body— / because I can—because I am / an American"); the fragile layers of skin and clothes that separate two bodies from each other ("How thin / the seam between / the world and the world / a few layers of muscle / and fat, a sheet wrapped / around a corpse"); and the political line dividing Pakistan and Bangladesh ("Each map I have seen / of this country obscures / . . . these / long porous seams between / us still irrepressible—").

Faizullah attempts to maintain an emotional distance while exploring these seams despite the use of first person when telling the stories of the birangonas. She does so through obsessive analysis of her role as an interviewer in poems that always occur in second or third person. She vituperatively criticizes her own role in the manipulation of these women for her book:

> But wasn't it the neat narrative you wanted? The outline of the rape victim standing against a many-winged darkening sky, shadow flurrying across shadow?—from "Interviewer's Note (v.)"

Faizullah is further distanced from her subjects by her American citizenship. Born and raised in Texas, her first act when she arrives at the Dubai International Airport is to "grip, as though for the first / time, a paper bag / of french fries from McDonald's." Under the humor of these lines is a comment on the spread of American consumerism and Faizullah's own fear of cultural inclusion. At one point, she pauses amid sari fittings (an outward symbol of her culture) to acknowledge her outsider status:

> . . . smell after pungent smell
> rising from gutter to rooftop:
> fruit: rot: spice: body. It is the sea
> itself. It belongs and does
> not belong to me . . .
> —from "Reading Willa Cather in Bangladesh"

The death of Faizullah's own sister in childhood continually presses itself into her present experiences. The journey to Bangladesh is being narrated to her sister in poems such as "The Interviewer Acknowledges Grief": "Sister, I waste time. I play / and replay the voices of these / hurt women flowering / like marigolds or thistles." The responsibility to provide living experiences, both the marigolds and thistles of life, to her sister is a tangible tension in the poems.

Faizullah's own vulnerability and self-awareness negate the potential voyeurism of retelling the graphic and sad stories of the birangonas. Her grief over her sister is the bridge to understanding the grief of these women. The will to survive, to leave behind the violence of a previous life to enter a new one, is present in all the women Faizullah interviews and in Faizullah herself. Despite the horrendous acts she brings to the page, this book is ultimately one of hope and connection. A seam marks a divide, but only in its ability to connect.

Source: Robin LaMer Rahija, Review of *Seam*, in *Hollins Critic*, Vol. 52, No. 1, February 2015, p. 17.

Susan Cohen

In the following review, Cohen praises Faizullah's understanding of the delicate "ethical complexity" of her work.

From the opening lines of Tarfia Faizullah's singular, eloquent collection *Seam*, chosen by Chad Davidson for the Crab Orchard Series in Poetry First Book Award, it is apparent she's a poet who feels tremendous empathy and who takes risks to express it. "In West Texas, oil froths / luxurious from hard ground / while across Bangladesh, // bayoneted women stain / pond water blossom," Faizullah begins, immediately letting readers know she dares to confront a horrific history in a lush and lyric voice.

Faizullah succeeds because, while her language is beautiful, she never prettifies the urgent story these poems tell about the mass rape of Bengali women during East Pakistan's 1971 War of Independence. Also, she acknowledges the question that hangs over her enterprise: what justifies making art from horror. *Seam* begins with an epigraph by Paul Celan: "Everything is near and unforgotten." Survivor of Nazi labor camps, Celan famously distanced himself from his best-known mournful and intensely musical poem "Death Fugue," fearing he had poeticized the Holocaust. That Faizullah invokes Celan, both in the epigraph and again in a crown of sonnets called "Reading Celan at the Liberation War Museum," demonstrates how well she understands the ethical complexity of her work. She probes the lines between witness, appropriation, and exploitation.

Seam revolves around the campaign West Pakistan waged against civilians in East Pakistan, which seceded and fought to become Bangladesh. More than three million people were killed in this war according to Bangladeshi sources, Faizullah tells us, and two hundred thousand women raped. Two hundred thousand! After liberation, the government of Bangladesh proclaimed the women war heroines, or *birangonas*. Still, many remain stigmatized and ostracized, even by their families. These events occurred before Faizullah was born in Brooklyn and then raised in West Texas. Her parents emigrated from Bangladesh in 1978, and she portrays herself as an unobservant Muslim. Yet, the underreported story compelled her to travel to Dhaka to interview some of the *birangonas* and to make poetry from her experience and from theirs.

Eight poems, all of them titled "Interview with a Birangona," form the central portion of the book, each a persona poem in which the woman speaks, each rendered in deceptively gentle couplets as if to slow them down and not overwhelm with their brutality.

... Braided in and around these devastating poems are others in the voice of the interviewer, who also asks difficult questions of herself, including whether she's morally justified when she urges the victims to relive their rapes. In "The Interviewer Acknowledges Grief," Faizullah puts it directly: "Because you / can't reassure me I have / the right to ask anything / of women whose bodies won't / ever again be their own." In a masterful poem titled "The Interviewer Acknowledges Shame," she describes how the interviewer—back in a hotel room after videotaping women "unlocking the desiccated coffins of their grief—touches and sexually satisfies herself."

... What might be voyeurism in another context instead becomes an intimate expression of empathy: The speaker moving closer to women she now understands have been robbed of their sexual lives. The poet exposing herself, as she has requested from the survivors.

Faizullah never directly compares her shame and grief with that of the "war-raped" women, of course, but she bookends the Dhaka poems with some about the deaths of her grandmother and a sister. These explicitly autobiographical poems also come across as steps toward emotional identification with the torn women whose experiences most readers can barely approach. In the end, Faizullah indicates with characteristic subtlety that she returns home changed, not leaving Bangladesh behind. Though at this point you might expect to hear her slipping back into her American life, in the next-to-last poem she is just setting forth, "En Route to Bangladesh, Another Crisis of Faith." On the airplane flying to Asia (in retrospect? again? still?) over the ocean, she contemplates "everything—blue on blue on blue—like the one // seam of light left always on the airplane ceiling / that the pale, plastic shades cannot shut away— // until that narrow vein of light is the only / belief left, a cream-thick ribbon across our eyes." The word *seam*, used in several poems in different ways, by now evokes Faizullah's two worlds, and her ongoing exploration of how those worlds conjoin within her body.

At the last Association of Writers & Writing Programs Conference, a panel in defense of narrative poetry noted that some began dismissing narrative as passé and the "lyric I" as self-indulgent about the time new groups began finding their voices and telling their stories. So it seems significant that Faizullah is a young poet—she was born in 1980—who chooses to bear witness with her important first book. She mentions in poems that she took Cesar Vallejo, Tomas Transtromer, and the novelist Willa Cather, as well as Paul Celan, to read on her journey. But surely the spirit of Adrienne Rich also hovers here, her belief in the personal as political, and her insistence that poetry reach out to history.

Seam demonstrates both that fine art can be fashioned from history's atrocities, and that art is necessary—not to make sense of them—but to recognize them in their full horror. Shock and pity are both emotions safe at a distance. But empathy ... for that, you must come close. You must enter bodies and minds as Faizullah does, and the reader with her. For that, isn't narrative poetry one of the finest arts?

Source: Susan Cohen, Review of *Seam*, in *Prairie Schooner*, Vol. 88, No. 3, Fall 2014, p. 167.

SOURCES

Adkins, Paul David, "A Cleansing and Breaking Water: Tarfia Faizullah, *Seam*, and the Genocide of Bangladesh," in *Blue Lyra Review*, Vol. 3, No. 6, October 30, 2014, http://bluelyrareview.com/tarfia-faizullah/ (accessed August 17, 2015).

Bangladesh Genocide Archive, http://www.genocidebangladesh.org/ (accessed August 17, 2015).

Bigos, Justin, "An Interview with Tarfia Faizullah," in *Waxwing*, No. 3, Summer 2014, http://waxwingmag.org/archive/03/writing.php?item = 125 (accessed August 16, 2015).

Carman, Sean, "Everything Is Near and Unforgotten: An Interview with Tarfia Faizullah," in *Paris Review*, February 10, 2014, http://www.theparisreview.org/blog/2014/02/10/everything-is-near-and-unforgotten-an-interview-with-tarfia-faizullah/ (accessed August 17, 2015).

Caspers, Patricia, "Hearing Voices: Women Versing Life Presents Tarfia Faizullah and the Unpublished Manuscript," in *Ploughshares*, June 26, 2012, http://blog.pshares.org/index.php/hearing-voices-women-versing-life-presents-tarfia-faizullah-and-the-unpublished-manuscript/ (accessed August 17, 2015).

Cohen, Susan, Review of *Seam*, in *Prairie Schooner*, Vol. 88, No. 3, Fall 2014, pp. 167–70.

"A Conversation with Tarfia Faizullah," in *Lantern Review*, March 1, 2013, http://www.lanternreview.com/blog/2013/03/01/a-conversation-with-tarfia-faizullah/ (accessed August 17, 2015).

Danziger, Jazzy, "Interview with Tarfia Faizullah," in *Best New Poets*, November 6, 2013, http://bestnewpoets.org/blog/2013/11/6/interview-with-tarfia-faizullah (accessed August 16, 2015).

DePollo, Adam, "Tarfia Faizullah and the Illumination of Poetry," in *UWIRE Text*, February 18, 2015, p. 1.

Faizullah, Tarfia, "En Route to Bangladesh, Another Crisis of Faith," in *Seam*, Southern Illinois University Press/*Crab Orchard Review*, 2014, pp. 11–12.

Farmer, Jonathan, "The Book of Injustice," in *Slate*, August 6, 2014, http://www.slate.com/articles/arts/books/2014/08/tarfia_faizullah_s_book_of_poems_seam_reviewed.html (accessed August 17, 2015).

Hodge, Anna Claire, "Tarfia Faizullah," in *Southeast Review*, http://southeastreview.org/tarfia-faizullah/ (accessed August 17, 2015).

Hossain, Anushay, "1971 Rapes: Bangladesh Cannot Hide History," in *Forbes*, May 21, 2012, http://www.forbes.com/sites/worldviews/2012/05/21/1971-rapes-bangladesh-cannot-hide-history/ (accessed August 17, 2015).

"Independence War," Bangla2000, http://www.bangla2000.com/bangladesh/war.shtm (accessed August 17, 2015).

Mulligan, Joseph, ed., Introduction to *Selected Writings of César Vallejo*, Wesleyan University Press, 2015, pp. xvii–xxv.

Nandini, Tanwi, "Dust Settles in Different Patterns: A Conversation with Poet Tarfia Faizullah," in *Hi Wildflower*, April 10, 2014, http://hiwildflowermag.com/dust-settles-different-patterns-conversation-tarfia-faizullah/ (accessed August 16, 2015).

Rahija, Robin LaMer, Review of *Seam*, in *Hollins Critic*, Vol. 52, No. 1, February 2015, p. 17.

"Tarfia Faizullah," One Pause Poetry, http://www.onepausepoetry.org/explore/poets/profile/tarfia_faizullah (accessed August 16, 2015).

Vallejo, César, "Imperial Nostalgias," in *Selected Writings of César Vallejo*, edited by Joseph Mulligan, Wesleyan University Press, 2015, p. 19.

Yalamanchili, Pavani, "Poet Tarfia Faizullah on Her Upcoming Book, the 1971 Liberation War, and 'Our Complicated Histories,'" in *Aerogram*, June 20, 2013, http://theaerogram.com/tarfia-faizullah-talks-to-the-aerogram-about-her-poetry/ (accessed August 16, 2015).

York, Jake Adam, and Tarfia Faizullah, "Craft Note: Duet—Part Two (Ending with a Post by Tarfia Faizullah Ending with a Line by Vallejo)," in *Kenyon Review*, April 20, 2012, http://www.kenyonreview.org/2012/04/craft-note-duet-part-two-ending-with-a-post-by-tarfia-faizullah-ending-with-a-line-by-vallejo/ (accessed August 17, 2015).

FURTHER READING

Akthar, Shaheen, Suraiya Begum, Meghna Guhathakurata, Hameeda Hossain, and Sultana Kamal, *Rising from the Ashes: Women's Narratives of 1971*, translated by Niaz Zaman, University Press, 2013.

> Akhtar is the writer whose novel *Talaash*, as partly translated by Mahmud Rahman, drew Faizullah's attention to the atrocities of the Bangladesh Liberation War. This volume, for which Akhtar served on the editorial board, collects stories of women who survived their ordeal.

Gordon, Alastair, *Naked Airport: A Cultural History of the World's Most Revolutionary Structure*, University of Chicago Press, 2008.

> In this volume Gordon explores virtually every aspect of the airport, from history to architecture to politics to functionality to how air travel has changed the way people think and behave.

Sontag, Susan, *Regarding the Pain of Others*, Farrar, Straus and Giroux, 2003.

> Sontag wrote four novels, several plays, and a short-story collection but is best known as one of the most important social theorists of the modern era. In this volume, which Faizullah has praised, Sontag focuses on the ways people are exposed to and come to empathize with—or fail to empathize with—other people's traumatic experiences.

Tagore, Rabindranath, *The Home and the World*, translated by Surendranath Tagore, Penguin Books, 2005.

> Easily the best-known Bengali writer, Tagore won the Nobel Prize in Literature in 1913. This novel dramatizes the attractions and repulsions of Western culture for two conscientious Bengali men. First published in 1916 and translated into English in 1919 by his son, it has been republished in the original translation with an introduction by Anita Desai.

SUGGESTED SEARCH TERMS

Tarfia Faizullah AND En Route to Bangladesh, Another Crisis of Faith

Tarfia Faizullah AND Seam

Tarfia Faizullah AND interview

Bangladesh Liberation War 1971

Bangladesh AND Pakistan

Bangladesh AND genocide

Bangladesh AND birangona

Bengal AND history

Bengal OR Bangladesh AND literature

Tarfia Faizullah AND Slinky

I like to see it lap the Miles

EMILY DICKINSON

1891

"I like to see it lap the Miles" is a four-stanza rhyming poem written by Emily Dickinson in 1862. The poem describes a train rolling through the countryside, in valleys, and over mountains and finally arriving back home. It uses vivid imagery and a clever trick: the poem plays off the familiar phrase *iron horse* as reference to a train, comparing the machine to a running horse without ever actually using the words *train* or *horse*.

Like nearly all of Dickinson's poems, this one was not given a title by the poet, and it is commonly referred to by its first line. (This is why the working title is given in quotation marks but without the capitalization of all the key words that titles generally have.) It was found among Dickinson's papers after she died and first published after her death in the 1891 collection *Poems by Emily Dickinson, Second Series*. In this collection, the poem was given a title, "The Railway Train," and the poet's unusual capitalization, spelling, and punctuation were "corrected" by the editors. It was not until the twentieth century that scholars were able to examine Dickinson's manuscripts and publish versions of her poems as she wrote them herself. "I like to see it lap the Miles" appears as poem number 383 in what is now the standard edition, *The Poems of Emily Dickinson* (1999), edited by R. W. Franklin, but it can also be found with the title "The Railway Train" in many collections of best-loved poems.

Emily Dickinson (© *Library of Congress*)

AUTHOR BIOGRAPHY

Emily Elizabeth Dickinson was born into a wealthy family in Amherst, Massachusetts, on December 10, 1830. Her father was treasurer of Amherst College and later served in state and national government. For some years, he was director of the Amherst and Belchertown Railroad.

Dickinson had a brother, Austin, and a sister, Lavinia. All three siblings were encouraged by their father to take their education seriously. Their mother seems to have been unable to show much interest in or affection for her children. Dickinson attended a nearby elementary school, and at the age of ten she entered the Amherst Academy, a girls' school offering a rigorous but ladylike curriculum of English, Latin, French, German, science, history, mathematics, and philosophy. She enrolled in Mount Holyoke Female Seminary at sixteen but stayed only a year. She enjoyed learning, but she missed weeks of school at a time because of illness.

Dickinson returned to the family home and lived nearly the rest of her life in the house her grandfather had built on Main Street in Amherst. She liked gardening and was friendly with neighborhood children, but she missed the intellectual stimulation she had had at school. Her mother was often ill, and Dickinson and her sister took care of her until her death in 1882. Dickinson occasionally made short visits to Philadelphia or Boston in the first half of her life, but after 1865 she mostly stayed in touch with friends by exchanging long letters with them. Some of her letters included original poems. She was close to her brother's wife, Susan, who lived next door, and over time she shared more than three hundred poems with her sister-in-law.

For the most part, though, Dickinson lived a quiet and reclusive life, battling emotional and physical illness. She had friends who sent her books of poetry and encouraged her to write. The details of the last forty years of her life come mainly from writing she left behind in letters, in hand-sewn books, and on scraps of paper. Dozens of biographies, novels, plays, and articles have been written by scholars believing they have discovered why she never left her home after around 1869, or why she wore white every day, or who her mysterious lover may have been, or what caused her to doubt the Christian faith she was raised with.

Dickinson was a prolific but mostly private poet. In 1862 she wrote "I like to see it lap the Miles" and over 350 more poems. She copied out many of her poems neatly by hand, sewed them into small books, and hid them in a drawer. During her lifetime fewer than a dozen of her poems were published. Most of them appeared in newspapers (which used to regularly publish poetry), printed without her name on them, without her permission, and with titles that she had not given the poems herself. Dickinson's final illness struck her in 1884, and she lingered until May 15, 1886, finally dying in the bed she had been confined to for months. When Lavinia went through her sister's things, having been instructed by Dickinson to burn all her papers, she found hundreds of letters and more than fifteen hundred unpublished poems. Lavinia burned most of the letters but could not bring herself to destroy the poems. Hundreds of them were finally published in book form—with standardized spelling and punctuation and with added titles—beginning in 1890.

POEM SUMMARY

The text used for this summary is from *The Poems of Emily Dickinson*, edited by R. W. Franklin, Harvard University Press, 1999, p. 176. A version

MEDIA ADAPTATIONS

- *Essential Dickinson*, a collection of poems read by the actress Julie Harris, was recorded by Caedmon in 1960. It was reissued as a CD in 2006 and runs sixty minutes.

- *Classic American Poetry: 65 Favourite Poems* is a set of two audio CDs. The set, which runs for two and a half hours, contains poems by important American poets including Dickinson, arranged in chronological order. It was published by Naxos Audio-Books in 2000.

- In 1986, composer Gordon Getty set some of Dickinson's poetry to music in *The White Election: A Song Cycle*. The cycle is available on CD from PentaTone Classics, published in 2007. It features Lisa Delan, soprano, accompanied by Fritz Steinegger on the piano. The run time is seventy minutes and thirty seconds. The audio for "I like to see it lap the Miles" is available on YouTube at https://www.youtube.com/watch?v=aSaeA WqZa58

- Another sung version of the poem is on the CD *Songs by George Perle: 13 Dickinson Songs/2 Rilke Songs*. Musicians Bethany Beardslee and Morey Ritt recorded the songs in 1978 for New World Records; the CD was issued in 2011.

---

of the poem with the text as Dickinson wrote it can be found on the following web page: http://www.poetryfoundation.org/poem/245176. Other versions, with spelling and punctuation standardized by other editors, can be found at the following web pages: http://www.poets.org/poetsorg/poem/i-see-it-lap-miles-43 and http://www.poem hunter.com/poem/i-like-to-see-it-lap-the-miles/.

The versions in Franklin's volume *The Poems of Emily Dickinson* are considered to be the authoritative versions of the poems. Because Dickinson did not give titles to most of her poems, this one is frequently identified by the number assigned to it by Franklin, or F383. The

poem's seventeen lines and four stanzas make up only one long sentence. The clause that is typically thought of as the title ("I like to see it lap the Miles") is actually just the poem's first line. Dickinson did not tend to title her poems, and she followed her own rules for capitalizing nouns. This is why when scholars attempt to refer to the poem by a working title they do not capitalize the major words and why throughout the rest of the poem many of the nouns are capitalized, wherever they may fall in the sentence.

In the first stanza, an unnamed narrator speaks in the first person, introducing a mysterious and also unnamed creature that she or he admires. The narrator describes this creature or thing moving speedily through the landscape, occasionally stopping for food or water and continuing on. In these first four lines, Dickinson's characteristic use of dashes at the ends and in the middle of lines is obvious; the stanza employs four dashes that create a somewhat breathless tone, though the poet's precise intention behind the many dashes remains something for scholars to puzzle and argue over. In the second stanza, the landscape changes from low ground to higher altitudes. Whatever this creature is, it looks at the shacks it passes with a *supercilious* or haughty, perhaps even sneering look. For many readers, this image of sneering at the shabbiness of poor people's homes has been problematic. They have wondered whether Dickinson was demonstrating her own privilege with this line, looking with condescension at folks who were less well-off.

As the second stanza ends and the third begins, the creature is shown to slice or *pare* through rock or between rocks. This passage through a tunnel or passageway is not as easy as crossing valleys and mountains, and the mysterious creature makes terrible noises as it goes along. Also noticeable in this stanza is the poet's misspelling of the word *its* in line 9 (it is misspelled again in the poem's last line). This misspelling is one of the items that Dickinson's editors corrected when the poem was first published, and the poem is frequently published today with this error corrected. In the last line of the third stanza, the noises end, and the creature begins to descend again.

The fourth and final stanza is the hardest to understand. In the stanza's first line, the narrator gives the strongest clue to the creature's identity when she describes the creature's noises as a "neigh." Suddenly it seems clear that she has been describing a horse. The imagery makes sense: the way the poem describes the motion across the landscape, the manner of taking on food from a tank. This vague idea is snapped into focus in the poem's last line, when the creature arrives at a barn, where horses live. Still, the stanza contains difficult imagery that shows that this is not just a poem about a horse. In the first line, the narrator compares the creature to "Boanerges," a nickname that the Christian Jesus gives to two of his followers in a story in the New Testament Gospel of Mark. The name "Boanerges" is commonly understood to mean "son of thunder," which is certainly a colorful name to give to a horse. What is more, a horse could not go as many miles as the creature in this poem covers, nor could it run easily between rocks. The poem is a riddle. Using horse imagery and playing with the common nickname *iron horse*, the poem actually describes an important new piece of technology in Dickinson's world: a train. Even this understanding of the poem's central metaphor does not explain line 15 in the fourth stanza. In what way can a star—or a horse, or a train—be considered prompt? Perhaps the narrator is referring to the way that stars and planets appear in the sky on a regular schedule. If this is the intent, it may be that the narrator is pointing to the fact that trains run on schedules, just as stars do. They are not free to go where and when they please. In the first three stanzas, the train has run through the countryside, seemingly in charge of its destination and its speed, but in fact it is only a machine and can do only what people make it do.

THEMES

Technology

"I like to see it lap the Miles" was written during a time when technology was rapidly advancing and machines were doing work that people had previously been doing—a time reminiscent of the twenty-first century. Factory machines had been spreading for decades, but the railroads, particularly in North America, were relatively new. The poem, in playing with the metaphorical nickname *iron horse*, emphasizes the power of the machine, the train. For example, there are five verbs describing the train's actions in the first stanza. The opening of the poem expresses the narrator's admiration for the train before the rest of the stanza shows the train in motion,

racing across the landscape, pausing for food, and then starting up again. Most of the verbs suggest active eating or consumption; the train is not just crossing the ground but devouring it. There is no mention of an engineer or conductor or other human agent; the train seems to be acting on its own. The train even seems to take on a bit of personality in the second stanza, when it is said to look condescendingly through the windows of the shacks alongside its tracks. The narrator does not describe the train's purpose, how many cars it has, or whether it carries passengers or freight. As the poem describes the train's motion and sounds, the stress is always on how big, how fast, how loud, how powerful it is.

In the last stanza, the tone changes. When the train reaches its station (or when the horse reaches its barn), it makes one last cry and then falls silent. Now the powerful creature becomes tame, submissive. It is still strong, but it is not under its own power now. The horse has a master; the train is a machine created and operated by humans. Technology is powerful, and big machinery leads to important and lasting change, but in the end an engine is only a tool.

Nature and Civilization

An important conflict in the poem is between the natural world and human control or development of it. The first two stanzas call to mind imagery of a vast landscape, full of mountains and valleys, but this is no wilderness landscape. The train finds stations to stop at for fuel and water and shacks to raise its eyebrow at as it runs over the tracks. As it passes, the train seems to consume the valleys, and the mountains are being cut down or cut into as rock is quarried and cut through to provide passageways for the train. For every natural image in the first two stanzas, there is also an image that reminds the reader that humans have made their mark on nature. In the final, difficult stanza, there is the suggestion that even the heavens ultimately become tame under the hand of human civilization. (Dickinson could hardly have guessed that around a hundred years after she wrote this poem, a man would walk on the moon.) Interestingly, though, there are no humans present in the poem, other than the narrator. The damage—if it is damage—has already been done. This is not a poem about how humans are leaving their tracks on the natural world, but simply a description of what those tracks look like now.

TOPICS FOR
FURTHER
STUDY

- Write a poem of your own about a piece of modern transportation technology: a gas-powered or electric car, an airplane or space shuttle, a superfast train, or maybe your bicycle. Try to capture the essential qualities of the vehicle or device without naming it in your poem, as Dickinson describes a train without ever using the word *train*.

- Although Dickinson's poem appears to celebrate the iron horse, the railroad was not a strong benefit to everyone who encountered it in the nineteenth century. Research how the coming of the railroad brought negative consequences to some groups, including Native Americans and Chinese laborers. You may want to read *Death of the Iron Horse* (1987), by Paul Goble; *The Building of the First Transcontinental Railroad* (1950), by Adele Gutman Nathan; or other sources. Write a poem, a speech, or a letter to an editor in the voice of someone who had good reason to fear or resent the railroads.

- Find two copies of "I like to see it lap the Miles": one with Dickinson's original spelling, punctuation, and capitalization and one in which these features have been regularized. The two versions will be easy to find in various places. For example, the Poetry Foundation presents the poem as Dickinson originally wrote it at http://www.poetry foundation.org/poem/245176, while the organization Poets.org presents the standardized version at http://www.poets.org/poet sorg/poem/i-see-it-lap-miles-43. In a formal contrast essay, describe the differences between the two versions and explain why one would be better than the other for classroom use.

- Make a video presentation of the poem. The audio will probably include the poem itself read aloud, but the visuals should be whatever you believe will capture something important about the poem and make the poem understandable to viewers. For inspiration, look at two video versions of William Wordsworth's poem "Daffodils": a straight dramatic reading at https://www.youtube.com/watch?v=crGftnW8y9s and the hip-hop version at https://www.youtube.com/watch?v=VXbrSALG684.

- Research the connections between the building of the railroads in nineteenth-century America and the construction of shanties and shanty towns in the same period. Prepare a presentation in which you educate classmates about the literal meaning of stanza 2 of the poem and persuade them that the poet is—or is not—making a political or social comment in this poem.

- Read Robert Louis Stevenson's famous poem "From a Railway Carriage," from his collection *A Child's Garden of Verses* (1885). His poem and "I like to see it lap the Miles" have many images in common, but they are very different poems. Make a chart or other representation showing which differences come from the two being written for readers of different ages and which come from the fact that Stevenson's narrator is aboard the train while Dickinson's is watching the train from far away. Then write a poem or an essay showing how Dickinson's poem might be different if she had written it for children or if her narrator were aboard the train.

Humor

Although many of her poems deal with death and faith in rather somber or even grim tones, Dickinson also wrote several poems that show her sense of humor. "I like to see it lap the Miles" is built around a central metaphor that is, in the end, a riddle: The poem describes the iron horse in language that is suitable for both a horse and a

Dickinson playfully describes the path of a locomotive, sometimes called an "iron horse." (© Peter Gudella / *Shutterstock.com*)

train. Most readers will begin the poem wondering what the narrator is describing. What is "it"? A few lines in, however, it becomes clear that the creature is a horse, and the reader settles in to enjoy the imagery of running up and down hill, eating and drinking, whinnying and showing some personality. But in the third and fourth stanzas, the reader is puzzled again, as the language seems to suggest something other than a horse. Aha! It is a train engine. The riddle has won over the reader, who can now be expected to go back up to the top of the poem and see all of the imagery in a new light.

STYLE

Ballad Stanza

"I like to see it lap the Miles" is written in four stanzas—or groups of lines separated by line spaces—commonly called ballad stanzas. The ballad stanza is a quatrain, or a stanza with four lines, and its pattern of stressed and unstressed syllables is often called "common meter." The first and third lines of the ballad stanza have four stressed beats or accented syllables, while the second and fourth lines have only three. Often, the longer, four-beat lines have exactly eight syllables, as can be seen in this poem in lines 1, 3, 7, and 16. The first two lines of the third stanza, lines 9 and 10, are short lines of two beats apiece and actually could be read together as one line, comprising exactly eight syllables and four beats. (Frequently, in modernized or standardized versions of this poem, these two shorter lines are simply combined into one, making four neat four-line stanzas. But the manuscript copy of the poem clearly divides the lines into two.) Another feature of the ballad stanza is the pattern of rhyming words. Typically, the second and fourth lines—the shorter lines—rhyme with each other or come close to rhyming. Dickinson is known as a poet who often used near rhymes, also called "slant rhymes," as she does here in each stanza. The words at the ends of the second and fourth lines in each stanza clearly echo the sounds of each other, yet they are not exact rhymes. Most commonly, the longer lines of ballad stanzas do not rhyme, as they do not in this poem.

In many poems written in ballad stanzas, each stanza forms a single sentence or a complete thought. Here, however, the entire poem is just one long sentence, and ideas and images run past the ends of stanzas. For example, the image of the horse or train moving through mountains begins with the last line of the first stanza and continues through the first line of the second; the image of squeezing through a narrow passageway or tunnel begins with the last line of the second stanza and continues into the third. Only the fourth stanza—the last one—holds a complete thought and image in its four lines.

Lyrical Poetry

A lyrical poem, or lyric, is usually a short poem spoken by a narrator. Although the narrator will use the first-person *I*, it should not be assumed that the narrator is necessarily speaking the feelings or thoughts of the poet. Lyric poetry originated with the ancient Greeks, who set such poems to music and accompanied them with the stringed instrument known as a lyre. This is why the word *lyrics* is still used for the words to a song. Over the centuries, other kinds of poetry came in and out of prominence: plays in verse, for example, or long narrative poems including epic poems like the *Iliad* or the *Odyssey*. The nineteenth century in the English-speaking world still loved long narrative poems, including John Greenleaf Whittier's immensely popular book-length poem *Snow-Bound* (1866), but for the most part lyric poetry had taken over as the dominant form. "I like to see it lap the Miles" is typical of lyric poetry. It is short, at seventeen lines. It has a first-person narrator who shares a simple idea and strong imagery spanning a brief period of time. Also, the poem has musicality—strong meter and rhyme—that makes it possible to imagine the poem as the words to a song. Indeed, it has been set to music more than once.

Alliteration

In addition to a fairly standard meter and rhyme scheme, Dickinson uses the repetition of consonant sounds at the beginnings of words, or alliteration, to add to the musicality of the poem and to strengthen the connections between images. In the first two lines, for example, the poet uses three one-syllable accented words that begin with the letter *l*. These stressed words with common consonant sounds gain extra emphasis because of the repetition of the sound, and this in turn emphasizes that the creature is an active

force, since two of the the three words are active verbs. Stanzas 2 and 4 contain several words that begin with the letter *s* (the words in stanza 4 begin with a two-letter sound, *st*), and the last two lines of stanza 3 contain three words beginning with the letter *h*. In each case, the alliteration draws attention to the words that begin with the common letter, create a pleasing sound, and emphasize the rhythm of the lines.

Metaphor

The central idea that holds the entire poem together is that a train is like a horse. The term *iron horse*, as used to refer to a train engine, made a good deal of sense in the middle of the nineteenth century, when the horses that provided the energy for machines and carriages were gradually being replaced with iron engines. Much of the imagery in the beginning of "I like to see it lap the Miles" seems to describe a horse moving through the landscape; as the reader gets further into the poem it becomes clear that the narrator is actually describing a train. This type of comparison between two things that at first seem to be very different is called a *metaphor*. When a poet keeps a single metaphor going through an entire poem or long passage, it is called an *extended metaphor* or *conceit*.

In this poem, Dickinson uses language that could apply to either the horse or the train, such as her reference to the tanks where her unnamed creature eats or drinks. Horses drink from water tanks, and trains get water and fuel from tanks. Some of the language applies better to the horse, as when the poet talks about movement and sounds in a way that suggests the creature is active and willful, rather than a nonliving machine. Still, most of the verbs in the poem are active—the creature does things, rather than being made to do them by human engineers. Some of the imagery fits a train better than a horse; in fact, no horse could cover all of the ground that the poem's unnamed being covers. By sustaining the comparison throughout the extended metaphor and by moving back and forth between language that favors one part of the comparison and then the other, Dickinson shows the ways that the horse and train are alike, both literally and figuratively.

Punctuation and Spelling

Because Dickinson wrote her poems by hand, with little thought of publishing them, her work did not go through what is now a standard cleanup process of word processing, copyediting, and proofreading. That is to say, her handwritten poems demonstrate an individual sense of punctuation and capitalization and occasional uncaught mistakes in spelling. In "I like to see it lap the Miles," Dickinson uses twelve dashes at the ends and in the middle of lines, where another writer might have used commas or periods. The editors of the earliest book-length collections of her poetry changed the dashes to more common punctuation, probably thinking that she would have preferred to see her work in print that way if she had had the chance to edit them for publication or perhaps thinking that a more regular appearance would make her poems more acceptable to readers. The poems are still frequently published without Dickinson's dashes. Scholars who prefer to examine Dickinson's handwritten manuscripts, on the other hand, have gone so far as to consider whether Dickinson intentionally made some dashes longer than others, or whether the variation in length is just the by-product of writing rapidly. Dickinson is known to have had poor eyesight and to have frequently written late at night, and she was often ill. It is possible that some of her variations are simply mistakes or the result of caring less about handwriting than about what she was saying.

Dickinson also has a tendency to capitalize most nouns, as seen in lines 1, 2, 3, 5, 7, 8, 13, and 15 of this poem. Finally, she made what would today be considered a spelling or usage error, substituting the word *it's* for *its* twice in the poem. "I like to see it lap the Miles" frequently appears with these quirks silently changed or corrected.

HISTORICAL CONTEXT

The Railroads

In 1830, the year Dickinson was born, the first successful steam locomotive in North America, nicknamed *Tom Thumb*, traveled a distance of about thirteen miles, beginning the age of railroad trains in the United States. In England, railroad tracks had been laid and put to use in many parts of the country, often for the purpose of moving goods from mines and ports to cities. But, as George H. Douglas explains in *All*

Aboard! The Railroad in American Life, while these railroad tracks provided smooth paths for heavy loads to be wheeled along, the carts on the tracks were pulled by horses. Goods in the United States were carried by animal-driven coaches or by water, and the opening of the Erie Canal in 1825 made it possible for the first time to move freight to the Great Lakes region (which was then the western part of the country) relatively cheaply and quickly. The Erie Canal, and the pressures it put on manufacturers and shippers, increased the demand for better transportation. Following the work of British inventors and engineers, the United States began to develop steam engines that could do the pulling work that horses had been doing, which explains the new term *iron horse*.

It took longer for trains to become vehicles for passengers. Americans were at first skeptical about the idea of riding on trains pulled by the new steam locomotives—for good reason. The new machines were huge. They were loud, dirty, expensive, and sometimes dangerous, and many people feared that the trains would leave their tracks and chase people down the street. Editorials and cartoons suggested that the engines were the work of the devil. Through the 1830s and 1840s the trains became safer and faster, more track was laid, and people increasingly saw the benefits of the new transportation system. It became clear that being on the railroad line was going to be important for economic development. In time, the arrival of the first train in town became an event for community celebration.

Still, Douglas points out, train transportation then did not resemble the large integrated systems that would come much later. In the 1850s, he writes, one could travel from Boston to most of the important cities in New England as well as to New York and Montreal. One could not necessarily travel between these cities; each trip involved a separate line, often owned by a separate company and often with a separate size of track and engine. For example, Boston was served by the Boston and Albany Railroad, the Boston and Maine Railroad, the Boston and Providence Railroad, and the Boston and Worcester Railroad, among others. To go from one large city to another often meant changing trains—and even time zones—several times,

COMPARE
&
CONTRAST

- **1860s:** The first Pacific Railroad Act is passed in 1862, providing federal money for the construction of a transcontinental railroad.

  Today: Passenger and freight rail service is largely privately funded, though the federal government subsidizes passenger service. Federal funding comes through the Highway Trust Fund, and its renewal by Congress is always controversial.

- **1860s:** Most poetry published in the United States has regular rhyme, meter, and stanza structure. However, Walt Whitman's *Leaves of Grass* (1855) has demonstrated that American readers will accept and even admire poetry that breaks this mold.

  Today: Poetry is experiencing a renaissance of sorts, with a wide variety of poetic forms available on a wide variety of platforms, including poetry slams, public readings, videos and vlogs, as well as publication in books, chapbooks, and magazines.

- **1860s:** Women are a strong presence in the world of poetry. Their works appear in popular magazines and newspapers, and their books of poems sell well. Many of the best-selling poets of the nineteenth century, including Ella Wheeler Wilcox, Emma Lazarus, and Julia Ward Howe, write poems that remain popular through the twentieth and into the twenty-first centuries.

  Today: After a long period of dominance by men, the world of establishment poetry again includes many women. Natasha Trethewey served as US Poet Laureate for 2012–2014; women poets won the Pulitzer Prize for Poetry in 2010, 2011, 2012, and 2013; and Elizabeth Alexander was asked to write and read a special poem at the 2009 inauguration of President Barack Obama. These and other women poets are important figures in American poetry.

and the different companies running the lines did not coordinate their schedules. It took decades for the railroads to become a normal part of American life.

Dickinson's father, Edward Dickinson, tried for years to get a branch line run to Amherst, Massachusetts, where the family lived. With other prominent men in town, he formed the Amherst and Belchertown Railroad in 1850 and began raising the necessary funds to bring a line from Palmer, Massachusetts, through Belchertown and Amherst and on to Montague. In his biography *My Wars Are Laid Away in Books: The Life of Emily Dickinson*, Alfred Habegger describes the scene when hundreds of people gathered in Amherst in 1852 to celebrate the start of the new line's construction with speeches, cannons, and cheers. When the first train arrived in 1853, he observes, the reclusive poet did not

attend the festivities at the station a few blocks from her home, even though her father was a prominent part of the ceremonies. Instead, she watched alone from a quiet place in the woods as the train chugged away. Over the years, even as she spent more and more time at home, the train was a central feature of her family's business dealings and her town's economic and community life.

In 1862, the year Dickinson wrote "I like to see it lap the Miles," President Abraham Lincoln signed the first Pacific Railroad Act, calling for an integrated railroad line running nearly two thousand miles, all the way from the Atlantic to the Pacific Ocean. The line, which opened in 1869, became known as the transcontinental railroad. Until they began to be replaced by cars in the 1920s, railroads would be an important part of American life, and of American literary imagination.

The train weaves around obstacles like mountains and quarries. (© *Vadym Zaitsev | Shutterstock.com*)

CRITICAL OVERVIEW

Dickinson is generally considered one of the greatest of the American poets, and "I like to see it lap the Miles" is one of the most popular of her poems, in large part because it is one of the easiest to understand. Unlike Dickinson's many poems filled with difficult imagery and mysterious pondering about death and faith, "I like to see it lap the Miles" can be enjoyed as a clever and vivid riddle, a celebration of the power and joy of language. The poem is featured in collections of favorite poems for general readers as well as in anthologies for students. Although it is a popular poem with readers, it has not drawn a great deal of attention from critics.

The poem, not published during the poet's lifetime, was included in the second published collection of Dickinson's work, *Poems by Emily Dickinson, Second Series* (1891). Her poems sold well and were widely read and discussed in the nineteenth century. In fact, a study by Willis J. Buckingham, *Emily Dickinson's Reception in the 1890s* (1989), lists more than six hundred reviews and articles about the poetry from that first decade alone. Wendy Martin, in her *Cambridge Introduction to Emily Dickinson* (2007), reports that while "nineteenth-century British critics saw [Dickinson] as a rebel, . . . American respondents used this criticism as a means of developing greater national pride." In more than a century since her work was first published in book form, Dickinson's poetry has never gone out of print.

Even so, her work was not universally admired when it first reached readers. The poet Thomas Bailey Aldrich, reviewing Dickinson's poetry in the *Atlantic Monthly* in 1892, writes, "I fail to detect in her work any of that profound thought which her editor professes to discover in it." He concludes that interest in her work would prove to be only a passing fad. In 1938, the poet and critic Yvor Winters commented that "probably no poet of comparable reputation has been guilty of so much unpardonable writing." Finding fault with her meter and her diction, he singles out "I like to see it lap the Miles" as an example to "illustrate the defects in perfection." Famously, he sums up the poem this way: "The poem is abominable."

Serious study of individual poems did not really begin until 1951, when Thomas Johnson published a three-volume collection based on his careful study of Dickinson's original manuscripts. Scholars now had definitive versions of the poems and could confidently analyze her lines closely. While most modern scholars have enjoyed "I like to see it lap the Miles," they tend to bring the poem into their discussions primarily as an insight into the poet herself rather than as a piece of literature to analyze. The biographer Alfred Habegger is an example. He mentions the poem in *My Wars Are Laid Away in Books* (2002) only to illustrate a point he is making about the poet's way of fitting into her community. He writes, "The poem evokes two opposing aspects of Dickinson's life: her sympathy with her father's invincible push for a rail link, and her dependence on the bucolic shelter he provided." The poet's relationship with her father and his railroad, as revealed through the poem, is also the subject of a more extended discussion in a 1998 article titled "The Train, the Father, His Daughter, and Her Poem," by

Domhnall Mitchell, published in the *Emily Dickinson Journal.*

Some critics have discussed this poem as an example of Dickinson's humorous side. In *Emily Dickinson's Poetry: Stairway of Surprise* (1960), Charles R. Anderson calls the poem "a bright piece of wit." He notes that her imagery describing the train is lively and fabulous but observes that she does not actually praise the train. "This is her ironic tribute to modern science," he writes, "which invents machines of monstrous power yet firmly controlled, here serving no purpose but her own amusement." John B. Pickard briefly comments on the poem in *Emily Dickinson: An Introduction and Interpretation* (1967), seeing it as evidence of the poet's engagement with current events. Comparing the poem to a tall tale with its "elaborated and exaggerated" imagery, he finds Dickinson to be "wryly amused" at "the whole idea of the fabulous 'iron horse.'" But Patrick F. O'Connell disagrees with these assessments. In a 1980 article in *American Literature*, he argues that "beneath [the poem's] undoubtedly humorous surface, Dickinson is making a serious and pointed comment about nineteenth-century technological achievement." The poem, he writes, is actually "an ironic warning of impending technological catastrophe," and the train is "an ecological monster."

CRITICISM

Cynthia A. Bily

Bily is an English professor at Macomb Community College in Michigan. In the following essay, she examines the connections between Dickinson's train and the world of imagination in "I like to see it lap the Miles."

When people talk about the "romance of train travel," they are not thinking about couples in love. Instead, they are thinking about the way a train trip draws people to think about distant places, gliding through strange lands, gentle rocking and sleep, and chance encounters with strangers who become important and then disappear. In the nineteenth century, train lines opened up the world for travelers and explorers, who discovered over a span of just a few decades that a trip across a city, or a state, or a country, or even a continent was suddenly possible. One hundred fifty or more years ago, the idea of such long-distant travel seemed impossible and wondrous, and in literature

> IF THE SPEAKER AND THE POET ARE ONE, DICKINSON IS SAYING THAT WHAT SHE LIKES IS THE POWER OF DREAMS AND IMAGINATION."

train rides became linked with travel into magical worlds and dream states. Even though train travel itself is now not quite the high-tech marvel that it was, this image has stayed with us, and trains still appear in literature to carry innocent and unsuspecting characters to surprising and mystical destinations. Thus, Miss Pym and her students ride the Rocky Mountain Unlimited back to prehistoric time in Paul Fleischman's *Time Train* (1991); Harry Potter rides the Hogwarts Express, climbing aboard at King's Cross Station platform nine and three-quarters, to the Hogwarts School of Witchcraft and Wizardry and a new life in J. K. Rowling's *Harry Potter and the Sorcerer's Sone* (1997); and a boy rides a train to the North Pole, where he meets Santa Claus, in Chris Van Allsburg's *The Polar Express* (1985), to name just three examples from a long list. Perhaps no title sums up the way this image works better than Sherri Duskey Rinker's 2013 picture book *Steam Train, Dream Train.*

This idea feels fresh and new every time we encounter it again in a beautifully illustrated picture book or fantasy novel, but it goes back almost as far as train travel itself. Consider what it would have been like to be alive in the 1830s or 1840s and to see a steam locomotive for the first time, especially if you had never seen a car or a factory or any big metal machine—or even a picture of one. It is no wonder that trains were compared to dragons and monsters or that people met them with equal parts wonder and fear. Like anything new, the much-talked-about railroads became the subject of conversation, art, music, and writing. Poets, in particular, were attracted to trains.

Three important writers who published train poems in the nineteenth century were Henry David Thoreau ("What's the Railroad to Me?" from 1850), Walt Whitman ("To a Locomotive in Winter," 1881–1882), and Robert Louis Stevenson ("From a Railway Carriage," 1885). These poems, and countless others by less

WHAT DO I READ NEXT?

- Like Dickinson's poem, Walt Whitman's "To a Locomotive in Winter" (1881–1882) uses vivid imagery to describe a steam train powering through the landscape. Whitman's poem was originally published as poem 260 in his collection *Leaves of Grass* and is easily available now in various editions.

- Dickinson wrote other poems in riddle form, including "A narrow fellow in the grass." This poem has been widely anthologized; it appears, for example, in a collection of Dickinson's poems edited especially for young readers, *I'm Nobody! Who Are You?* (2002). To make the poems more accessible, the editor of this collection, Edric S. Mesmer, has standardized Dickinson's spelling and punctuation.

- Dickinson's poetry is in the public domain, which means that it can be published in books and on websites without permission or fees. There are literally thousands of books, magazines, posters, postcards, T-shirts, and websites using Dickinson's poetry. The generally accepted best editions of the poems, however, are those edited by R. W. Franklin (1999) or Thomas H. Johnson (1955).

- *From Totems to Hip-Hop: A Multicultural Anthology of Poetry across the Americas, 1900–2002* (2002), edited by the noted writer and publisher Ishmael Reed, showcases the diversity and the unity of American poetic voices. The collection includes poems by T. S. Eliot, Gertrude Stein, Ana Castillo, Tupac Shakur, and many others, grouped by theme so that the poets' commonalities become more important than their differences.

- The main character in Jenny Hubbard's award-winning young-adult novel *And We Stay* (2014) is Emily Beam, a teenaged girl who has been sent to a boarding school in Amherst, Massachusetts, after a traumatic event. Emily is a poet, like Dickinson, and she draws on her namesake as a guiding spirit, using her own writing to deal with complicated secrets.

- *Miss Emily: A Novel* (2015), by Irish writer Nuala O'Connor, fictionalizes Dickinson's private life through a story of friendship between the poet and her uneducated Irish maid, Ada Concannon. The two women narrate alternating chapters in the first person, highlighting their different temperaments and beliefs. This novel was written for general, adult readers.

- The mystery surrounding the reclusive Dickinson is so popular that it has even been developed in picture books for children. A beautiful example is the well-researched *Emily* (1992), by Michael Bedard. It tells the story of a young girl who pays a visit to her across-the-street neighbors, Dickinson and her sister, Lavinia. The illustrations, by Caldecott Medal–winning Barbara Cooney, are based on Dickinson's actual home in Amherst, Massachusetts.

- Poet Kenneth Rosen responded to Dickinson's poem with one of his own, titled "I Like to See It Lap the Miles." Rosen's poem, published in the Spring 2000 issue of the *Massachusetts Review*, raises questions about Dickinson and what she intended for readers to understand from the imagery in her description of the train.

well-known poets, were written during the same time that Dickinson was writing poetry; her "I like to see it lap the Miles" was written in 1862 and first published in 1892. The poems by Thoreau, Stevenson, and Whitman, like many other poems of the time, focus on the power of the locomotives in vivid but not romantic language. Dickinson, at the same time as admiring the power of the strange new engines, also looks forward to the dreamlike qualities of more recent evocations of trains. In "I like to see it lap the Miles," Dickinson presents the railway train as a passage to the world of imagination.

It begins with the first word of the poem. By introducing a first-person narrator, even one who is never seen clearly, the poem invites readers to see not just the train but also the person looking at the train. It would have been easy to keep the narrator offstage; all the poet would have had to do is recast the first line without that "I" and focus on the mysterious moving thing itself. To begin with the narrator is a deliberate and important choice. There are no other people in the poem—no one driving the whatever-it-is and no one riding it—so every image is filtered solely and emphatically through the consciousness of the speaker.

At first, as generations of readers have discovered, it is not clear what "it" is. By the fourth stanza, when the narrator uses the unambiguous *neighs*, it seems clear that the creature being described is a horse, but seconds later most readers will realize that it is actually a train engine being described in language that mimics the language used for a horse. The poem is a riddle. Question: What runs up mountains and through valleys, drinks from a tank, and neighs when it gets home? Answer: A steam locomotive, an "iron horse."

It works, and it does not. On the second and third reading, it makes sense to go back through the images and match them to a train, and this is what most readers do. But the initial match of images to a horse is fanciful at best. In the first lines of the poem, the thing the speaker describes appears to be a huge living creature of some kind, perhaps a dragon or a godlike being. What kind of earthly animal eats up the landscape as it passes over or through it? What being has tanks of water or food standing by in case it decides on its own to stop and eat? To whom are words like *prodigious* (great, unnatural) and *supercilious* (haughty, superior) applied? If this is a horse, it is no ordinary horse. It is a godlike horse. A horse of dreams.

Whether the "it" being described is a horse or a train, giving it emotions like self-satisfaction and pride casts it into an unearthly realm. The horse/train is grand and proud. It seems to have no master. Yet in the third stanza, when it is squeezing or slicing its way through a narrow passageway or tunnel, it struggles and makes a

lot of noise, and the narrator reports that it is annoyed or rebellious about this part of the trip. This raises a new question: If the horse/train is in control of its own destiny, as the first eight or nine lines suggest, why does it choose to go through this passageway that is difficult and uncomfortable? If it is being driven by a more powerful force, who or what is that force? Really, these images do not fit a literal horse, and they do not fit a literal train. This has become a riddle that works only if one does not think too much about it. To put it another way, this horse/train is not of this world. The speaker who observes all this is enjoying a spectacle that cannot be real.

In the final stanza, when the being returns home and the images click into place to give shape to a horse and/or to a locomotive, the different levels of duality are also revealed and enumerated. The creature is a machine and a living being; it is a train and a horse. It is, as the speaker says, controlled by a superior force and also beyond control. The imagery in the first three stanzas has been colorful and active but grounded. Here, in the final stanza, the imagery flies away from the world we know: there is a reference to the words of the Christian God from the Bible and a comparison to a *Star*, a celestial formation of burning gases. (This will lead knowing readers to think of Nathaniel Hawthorne's 1843 short story "The Celestial Railroad," which Dickinson surely had read.)

In short, if this is a train, it is no ordinary train. It carries readers into a world of imagination, and it carries them with the force of its own will (until it becomes subservient to a stronger will). The speaker introduced in the first line has already been There and Back Again; she has watched the shape-shifting horse/train, and she has enjoyed it. Although it goes against the rules of understanding a speaker or narrator, let us for a moment think of the speaker of "I like to see it lap the Miles" as Dickinson herself. What could she be saying?

If the speaker and the poet are one, Dickinson is saying that what she likes is the power of dreams and imagination. What she likes is the trick of mind that can say that "horse plus train equals two and one at the same time." This places her in the camp of J. K. Rowling, Susan Cooper, and Chris Van Allsburg, for whom a train trip is a trip into another world. If the train is a metaphor for the creative poetic process (one hesitates to cite the expression *train of thought*),

The last stanza gives the name Boanerges, *which is Greek for* son of thunder. *(© mariait / Shutterstock.com)*

the contradictory images make some sense. Writers often speak of creativity as something powerful that they struggle to control. Writing poetry is at times all-consuming, as is the being in stanzas 1 and 2, but the process leads to fretting and moaning when it entails struggling to make things fit. In the end, though, the creative process is both powerful and submissive; the brains of poets like Dickinson run wild, but they produce ordered poems with rhyme, meter—even, as line 12 suggests—stanzas.

It is ironic—or is it?—that Dickinson was the daughter of the director of the Belchertown and Amherst Railroad, the man who brought the railroad to Amherst, the Dickinson family's hometown. By the time the railroad came to Amherst, the poet had begun to withdraw from the world of cities and crowds and railroads into the world of her house and her writing and her imagination. Although there were large community celebrations when the railroad company announced that it had enough money to begin construction and again when the first train arrived, and although her own father was a prominent figure in these events, Dickinson did not attend. Once Amherst had train service, she often saw her father off on the train to Boston and welcomed friends who rode it to Amherst, but it is not clear that Dickinson ever rode a train herself. A train does not represent freedom and travel for Dickinson. For her, as it is for Harry Potter and Miss Pym's students, a train trip is a metaphorical journey to another world: the world of imagination and dreams. It is the magic carpet that poets ride to the world of poetry.

Source: Cynthia A. Bily, Critical Essay on "I like to see it lap the Miles," in *Poetry for Students*, Gale, Cengage Learning, 2016.

SOURCES

Aldrich, Thomas Bailey, "*In Re* Emily Dickinson," in *Critical Essays on Emily Dickinson*, edited by Paul J. Ferlazzo, G. K. Hall, 1984, pp. 37–39; originally published in *Atlantic Monthly*, No. 69, January 1892.

Anderson, Charles R., *Emily Dickinson's Poetry: Stairway of Surprise*, Holt, Rinehart and Winston, 1960, pp. 15–16.

Buckingham, Willis J., *Emily Dickinson's Reception in the 1890s: A Documentary History*, University of Pittsburgh Press, 1989.

Dickinson, Emily, "I like to see it lap the Miles," in *The Poems of Emily Dickinson*, edited by R. W. Franklin, Harvard University Press, 1999, p. 176.

———, "The Railway Train," in *Poems by Emily Dickinson, Second Series*, edited by T. W. Higginson and Mabel Loomis Todd, Roberts Brothers, 1891, p. 39.

Douglas, George H., "The Coming of the Iron Horse" and "The Spreading Railroad Fever," in *All Aboard! The Railroad in American Life*, Paragon House, 1992, pp. 13–49.

Ferlazzo, Paul J., "Chronology" and "Chapter One: Legend and Life," in *Emily Dickinson*, Twayne's United States Authors Series No. 280, Twayne Publishers, 1976, pp. 11–12, 13–28.

Habegger, Alfred, *My Wars Are Laid Away in Books: The Life of Emily Dickinson*, Modern Library, 2002, pp. 290, 292.

Johnson, Thomas, ed., *The Poems of Emily Dickinson*, 3 vols., Harvard University Press, 1951.

Martin, Wendy, "Chapter One: Life" and "Chapter Four: Reception," in *The Cambridge Introduction to Emily Dickinson*, Cambridge University Press, 2007, pp. 1–23, 110–31.

Mitchell, Domhnall, "The Train, the Father, His Daughter, and Her Poem: A Reading of Emily Dickinson's 'I like to see it lap the Miles,'" in *Emily Dickinson Journal*, Vol. 7, No. 1, Spring 1998, pp. 1–26.

O'Connell, Patrick F., "Emily Dickinson's Train: Iron Horse or 'Rough Beast'?," in *American Literature*, Vol. 52, No. 3, November 1980, pp. 440, 474.

Pickard, John B., *Emily Dickinson: An Introduction and Interpretation*, Holt, Rinehart and Winston, 1967, p. 76.

Winters, Yvor, "Emily Dickinson and the Limits of Judgment," in *Emily Dickinson: A Collection of Critical Essays*, edited by Richard B. Sewall, Prentice-Hall, 1963, pp. 28–29; originally published in *In Defense of Reason*, Swallow Press, 1938.

FURTHER READING

Bloom, Harold, ed., *Emily Dickinson*, Bloom's Modern Critical Views, Chelsea House Publishers, 1985.

> Although none of the nine critics writing in this collection mentions "I like to see it lap the Miles" specifically, this is an excellent introduction to the kinds of critical questions scholars have asked about Dickinson's work. Like all the volumes in the Bloom's Modern Critical Views series, the book gathers previously published articles that are relatively jargon-free and accessible for general readers and also includes a chronology of the poet's life and a list of books and articles (now somewhat out of date) for further reading.

Dickinson, Emily, *The Gorgeous Nothings: Emily Dickinson's Envelope Poems*, edited by Jen Bervin and Marta Werner, New Directions, 2013.

> This impressive full-color book reproduces fifty-two poems in Dickinson's own handwriting—full-sized, as she wrote them on scraps of envelopes. Werner, a Dickinson scholar, provides helpful commentary and help with deciphering the poet's handwriting; Bervin, an artist, has arranged the reproductions and texts beautifully on the page. This book brings readers closer to Dickinson's process and makes clear some of the challenges Dickinson scholars have faced in producing faithful transcripts of her work.

———, *The Poems of Emily Dickinson: Reading Edition*, edited by R. W. Franklin, Belknap Press, 2005.

> This volume of 1,789 poems was prepared from Franklin's longer three-volume edition, which is generally accepted as the most accurate and complete collection of Dickinson's poetry. The capitalization, spelling, and typography have been closely matched to those in Dickinson's manuscripts, so the poems appear as she wrote them, stripped of the many "corrections" supplied by other well-intended editors.

Grant, H. Roger, *Railroads and the American People*, Indiana University Press, 2012.

> With more than one hundred black-and-white illustrations and clear, readable text, this book traces the development of American railroads over the hundred-year period beginning around 1830. Grant, the author of more than

thirty books about railroads, shows how important they were to the economy, to community building, and to people's imaginations.

Martin, Wendy, ed., *All Things Dickinson: An Encyclopedia of Emily Dickinson's World*, 2 vols., ABC-CLIO/ Greenwood, 2014.
    A two-volume reference work, this encyclopedia has a timeline and more than two hundred articles about what was happening in the world during the poet's lifetime. The articles and illustrations cover history, science, art, literature, and important social movements that Dickinson was—or may have been—aware of as she wrote.

————, ed., *The Cambridge Companion to Emily Dickinson*, Cambridge University Press, 2002.
    This collection of eleven original essays is divided into broad themes: "Biography and Publication History," "Poetic Strategies and Themes," and "Cultural Contexts." The essays, geared for college-level students, are more difficult to comprehend than those in Harold Bloom's Modern Critical Views, but they reflect newer lenses for looking at literature, including feminism, gender studies, and postmodernism.

Wolff, Cynthia Griffin, *Emily Dickinson*, Knopf, 1988.
    This highly respected biography was the first serious scholarly biography to illuminate the connections between Dickinson's life and her poetry. Many of the earlier biographies focused on trying to unlock titillating secrets about the reclusive poet. In contrast, Wolff aims to be thorough in her narration of Dickinson's life but always in the service of revealing the sources and meanings of the poetry.

SUGGESTED SEARCH TERMS

Emily Dickinson

I like to see it lap the Miles

American women poets

Dickinson AND Amherst

Dickinson AND poetry

Dickinson AND The Railway Train

Dickinson AND manuscripts

Dickinson AND meter

I'm Alive, I Believe in Everything

LESLEY CHOYCE

1998

Lesley Choyce's poem "I'm Alive, I Believe in Everything," first published in his 1998 collection *Beautiful Sadness*, is a celebration of life in all its variety and potential. Simply to be alive, the poem's speaker implies through the ecstatic mood of the poem, is a gift of immeasurable value. From the cosmic grandeur of the night sky to the comfortable familiarity of a vinyl record, Choyce includes the wealth of human experience in his catalog: negative and positive, banal and extraordinary, abstract and concrete. This powerful poem that worships the individual as well as the universe inspired a later collection by Choyce, *I'm Alive, I Believe in Everything*, published in 2013, which won the Atlantic Poetry Prize.

AUTHOR BIOGRAPHY

Choyce was born in Riverside, New Jersey, on March 21, 1951. He attended Rutgers University, earning his bachelor's degree in 1972. He went on to earn a master's degree in American literature from Montclair State University in 1974 and a second master's in English literature from the City University of New York in 1983. At the age of twenty-seven, Choyce expatriated from the United States, becoming a citizen of Canada. In 1979, he founded Pottersfield Press, a publishing house specializing in Canadian

Lesley Choyce (© Getty Images)

literature as well as North Atlantic literature and funded in part by the Canada Book Fund and the Canada Council for the Arts.

Choyce teaches at Dalhousie University, in Halifax, Nova Scotia, in the English department and hosts a nationally syndicated TV talk show called *Off the Page with Lesley Choyce*. A prolific writer, he has written over eighty works of literature, including nonfiction, fiction, poetry collections, children's books, and young-adult novels. His band, Lesley Choyce and the Surf Poets, have released two albums: *Long Lost Planet* in 1996 and *Sea Level* in 1998. On their albums, the Surf Poets perform several poems from Choyce's 1998 collection *Beautiful Sadness*, in which "I'm Alive, I Believe in Everything" was first published. In his personal essay "Writing Philosophy" in *Canadian Poetry Online*, Choyce describes his decision to pursue a career in writing with characteristic lightheartedness: "I decided to be a writer with high hopes that it would allow me to avoid work. When writing turned out to be work as well as fun, I stuck with it anyway."

Choyce lives in Lawrencetown Beach in Nova Scotia with his wife. An avid North Atlantic surfer, he won the Canadian Surfing Championships in 1995. His awards as an author include the Landmark East Literacy Award (2000), *Coast Magazine*'s Best Writer of Halifax 2001–2005, the Anne Connor Brimer Award for Children's Literature in 1994 and 2003, the Order of St. John Award of Merit, poet laureate of the Peter Gzowski Invitational Golf Tournament (2000), Pierian Spring Editor's Award for poetry, and the Dartmouth Book Award in 1990 and 1995. In 2013, *I'm Alive, I Believe in Everything*, Choyce's collection of new poetry inspired by the poem of the same name, was awarded the Atlantic Poetry Prize. Choyce has appeared in *Canada's Who's Who*, published by the University of Toronto Press, every year since 1985.

POEM SUMMARY

The text used for this summary is from *Beautiful Sadness*, Ekstasis Editions, 1998, p. 81. A version of the poem can be found on the following web page: http://canpoetry.library.utoronto.ca/choyce/poem2.htm.

"I'm Alive, I Believe in Everything" begins with a list: self, brotherhood, God, Zeus, communism, capitalism, Buddha, records, baseball, ink, trees, cures for illness, saltwater, literature, walking, waking up, disagreements, and decisions. The speaker then lists many oppositional concepts in which he believes: ambiguity, absolutes, presence, absence, positive, negative, empathy, apathy, sympathy, entropy. The speaker states that he finds both nouns and verbs necessary as well as empty skies, dark nights, visions, revisions, and innocence. The speaker has seen every empty space still unfilled and every sound that will gather at the world's end, as well as the silence that will follow.

The speaker is alive and believes in everything. He believes in it all. He believes in waves, sunsets, old men dancing in public, paradoxes, possibilities, sense, sensibility, unfeeling logic, half truths, finishing touches, first impressions, fools, intellect, mayhem, clear futures, abstract ideas, certainty, and optimism triumphing over difficulties. The speaker is alive and believes in everything. He believes in it all.

MEDIA ADAPTATIONS

- Choyce maintains a YouTube channel at www.youtube.com/LesleyChoyce.

- Choyce's reading of "I'm Alive, I Believe in Everything" is available online at https://www.youtube.com/watch?v=IhqAvxueYYU.

- Several of Choyce's poems have been adapted into song by his band, Lesley Choyce and the Surf Poets, and can be found at http://www.lesleychoyce.com/#!video-reel/c1cu4.

THEMES

Consciousness

"I'm Alive, I Believe in Everything" is a meditation on the speaker's consciousness of the world around him. He first takes an active inventory of his life and lists what he observes, and then he makes the conscious decision to accept it all with open arms. He accepts the destructive and chaotic parts of life alongside the constructive and ordered, because he considers both good and bad experiences to be necessary. This is conscientious decision making, as there is no place for irrational ideals in his philosophy; for example, he does not irrationally expect a life of pure happiness, in which all of his experiences will be positive. He acknowledges suffering as well as pleasure and feels uplifted by the prospect of being alive to experience both. He is conscious of the value of life and appreciative of the miraculous sensation of existing. Rather than being bogged down by monotony or anxious for the future, the poem's speaker is conscious of the present moment. In the here and now, fears, responsibilities, regrets, hopes, memories, and dreams fade away as awareness refocuses on the present, the senses, the body, the act of breathing—life. It is this consciousness of the present that allows the speaker to accept whatever will come his way with a spirit of egalitarian openness. In such a state he is immune to pettiness, greed, and self-doubt as he allows life in all

its possibilities to flow through him. He has achieved a transcendental consciousness in which, through honest appreciation of life, he has tapped into the creative, exuberant joy of the universe itself.

Life

The speaker's philosophy of life is fundamentally to believe, as summarized by the poem's title. Because he is alive, the speaker has the ability to believe. He could choose to disbelieve, but the speaker is too conscious of the value of life to squander his life through negative thinking. Because he is alive and has chosen to believe, the speaker has the opportunity to choose what he will believe. Characteristic of the life-affirming, positive-thinking speaker, he chooses to believe in everything. Rather than nothing, something, or just one thing, *everything* encompasses the whole of human experience. The whole of human experience can also be described as life. Thus, the poem's title, "I'm Alive, I Believe in Everything," also means "I'm Alive, I Believe in Life."

For the speaker, appreciating the gift of his own existence is the least he can do in gratitude for receiving it. He believes in life in its entirety and loves to see others doing the same, like the old men he watches as they dance in the street or the celebration of color on the horizon at sunset. These are forms of the same life-loving spirit that flows through the speaker even as he considers everyday items like ink, records, and trees. As a believer in life, he sees the magnificent in the mundane. Each item in his catalog is an expression of life, so that, through watching a game of baseball or pondering a paradox, the speaker is reaffirming his love and belief in the joy of life.

Universality

The speaker of the poem applies his belief to "everything." This is an example of universality, the concept of something being everywhere at once and thus universal. In "I'm Alive, I Believe in Everything," the universality of the speaker's belief includes sports, politics, religion, economics, music, nature, literature, medicine, human relationships, philosophy, astronomy, and much more. His catalog is spatially condensed over the poem's four stanzas but exhaustive in its inclusiveness of the wealth of human experience. Everything truly means everything in the speaker's life, even fools, entropy, and negativity itself. Significantly, the universality of the speaker's belief is expressed in the form of a catalog

TOPICS FOR FURTHER STUDY

- Create a blog in which you write one post for each item listed in the poem's first nine lines. Each post should contain a relevant picture, an original poem inspired by that word, a definition, or a few sentences on that subject, for a total of thirty-three very short posts. Free blog space is available at blogger.com.

- Read *Jeremy Stone* (2013), Choyce's young-adult novel written in free verse. How would you describe the mood of the novel? How does Choyce create this emotional atmosphere? How does the mood of *Jeremy Stone* compare with the mood of "I'm Alive, I Believe in Everything"? How does an author's use of mood differ in a novel versus a poem? Summarize your thoughts in an essay.

- Working in pairs, record a performance of one of Choyce's poems from *Beautiful Sadness*. Using Choyce's YouTube channel as inspiration, incorporate music into your reading, whether through your own instruments and vocals or through background music

added postproduction. Be as creative as possible. Free video editing tools are available at EDPuzzle.com.

- Research catalog poems online in search of another example of the form by an established poet. Print the poem you find and write a brief summary of the poem: What is cataloged and for what purpose? When you are finished, compose a catalog poem of your own, using "I'm Alive, I Believe in Everything" and the poem that you found online as your inspiration.

- Choose another poem in *Beautiful Sadness* to read and explicate. Along with your explication, include a comparison of the poem to "I'm Alive, I Believe in Everything." Do they have similar structures, themes, moods, or syntax? From what you have observed of the two poems, how would you summarize Choyce's writing style? Organize your thoughts in an essay.

---

poem: an egalitarian list in which each item is of equal importance to the others. The speaker includes the entirety of human experience, and he does so without assigning rank or showing preference to one aspect of life over another. This is because each of the items listed is symbolic of life, so that entropy is representative of life as much as baseball, a tree as much as a first impression, chaos as much as brotherhood, and so on. Just as the title can be read as "I'm Alive, I Believe in Life," so can the list that makes up the poem's text be refigured as a repetition of the word *life*, replacing each of the items with its symbolic meaning. Life is the universe, the speaker is alive, the speaker is the universe, and the universe is life according to this deceptively simple poem. The speaker's belief in everything is the key to unlocking the remarkable universality of the poem.

STYLE

Catalog

"I'm Alive, I Believe in Everything" is a catalog poem, meaning that the poem is made up of a list of items. The first and third stanzas combined list approximately fifty items, ranging from tangible objects (for example, ink) to intangible, abstract concepts (for example, sensibility). These seemingly unrelated items are brought together in the poem through the speaker's expression of joy at being alive and capable of knowing and believing in each of the items listed, which explore the range of human experience. Thus the catalog mimics life itself in its unexpected combinations of the good, bad, extreme, and everyday. Rather than finding this cornucopia of experience overwhelming or unpleasant, the speaker finds it thrilling, choosing to believe

Choyce includes joyful images, including the elderly dancing in the streets. (© Madrugada Verde | Shutterstock.com)

in the importance of each item equally, as exemplified by the unrestricted, unordered list that flits effortlessly from baseball to chaos and includes everything between.

Mood

The mood of a poem refers to the emotional effect of the text on the reader. The mood is separate from the tone, which refers to the author's attitude toward the work. Another way to think of mood is as the atmosphere of the poem: it can feel tense, angry, happy, calm, and so forth. The mood is created through word choice, imagery, rhyme scheme (if any), tone, and even the poem's structure. The mood of "I'm Alive, I Believe in Everything" is exuberant and joyful. Though many generally negative aspects of life are mentioned in the poem, such as apathy and arguments, they are not only balanced by their more constructive alternatives (sympathy and decisions) but also thoroughly outnumbered by goodness and positivity. The second and third stanzas, which repeat the speaker's assertion of life and his choice to believe in the items he has cataloged, serve to solidify the

happy, empowering mood of the poem, as the speaker accepts and celebrates the miracle of existence in all its forms.

Motif

A motif in a work of literature is a recurring theme, character, image, or idea that serves to unify the work. Among the speaker's beliefs, there is a motif of images from nature. The speaker mentions trees, saltwater, the sound of waves, the shore, the horizon line, and the sky in the daylight, at night, and during sunset. Notably, this list is exclusively made up of large natural phenomena, rather than smaller aspects of nature (for example ants, pebbles, and leaves). The expansive size of the natural elements in the catalog matches the expansive tone taken by Choyce. The motif of the big natural world complements the list of similarly large concepts (paradox, certainty, chaos) and complex human emotions (empathy, brotherhood, optimism). Nothing is small or unimportant in a poem devoted to everything. The motif of the big natural world adds strength to the universal theme of the poem through portraying vast natural spaces that can be shared by countless onlookers at once: the sky, the shore, and the ocean. The image patterns provided by a motif help to solidify a work of literature by uniting disparate parts through the repetition of a literary element. In "I'm Alive, I Believe in Everything," the image motif of the enormity of nature appears throughout the poem's text, unifying the catalog's other weighty concepts.

Zeitgeist

Zeitgeist refers to the spirit of an era as observed through the culture and beliefs of the people of a specific time and place. For example, F. Scott Fitzgerald's *The Great Gatsby* depicts the zeitgeist of the Roaring Twenties in New York City. "I'm Alive, I Believe in Everything" expresses the zeitgeist of the 1990s in North America: optimistic, eager, entrepreneurial, and self-confident. Newly freed from the Cold War, the population had fewer worries, and confidence was high as society approached the new millennium. The speaker's enthusiasm mimics that of the relatively peaceful and progressive world where he lives, and his sweeping, ecstatic belief in everything is made possible by the bright horizon of a stable, progressive continent.

HISTORICAL CONTEXT

The 1990s

The final decade of the twentieth century was a time of peace and prosperity for North America. Before the new millennium dawned, bringing with it the 9/11 terrorist attacks and the resulting "war on terror," economic recession, and the proliferation of domestic surveillance, the 1990s saw lower unemployment, higher household incomes, a drop in crime rates, and social progress.

In "The Best Decade Ever? The 1990s, Obviously," in the *New York Times*, Kurt Andersen writes: "The decade had begun with a fantastically joyful and previously unimaginable development: The Soviet empire collapsed [and] global nuclear Armageddon ceased to be a thing that worried anyone very much." Choyce references this historic event obliquely in "I'm Alive, I Believe in Everything," listing both communism and capitalism in the speaker's catalog of his beliefs. No longer frightened that the Cold War would turn hot, North Americans reveled in the new technological developments of the

decade. Most significantly, the Internet and personal cell phones became available to the public, changing the very nature of communication. By the end of the 1990s, the Information Age had dawned, and the first generation of digital natives, the millennials, was born into the online world.

Abroad, many countries experienced a similarly positive decade: Israel and Palestine met in peace talks that would generate the Oslo Accords, China emerged as an industrialized power, South Africa ended apartheid, Iraqi leader Saddam Hussein's invasion of Kuwait was stopped in its tracks by a successful American military intervention, and Mexican poet Octavio Paz became the first in his country to win the Nobel Prize in Literature. Andersen writes: "A tide of progress and good sense seemed to be sweeping the whole world." This is not to say that there were not atrocities, tragedies, and disasters in the world during the decade, only that there was a significant amount of good news to balance the bad. "I'm Alive, I Believe in Everything" reflects the euphoric zeitgeist of the 1990s as the speaker celebrates life with a noteworthy absence of cynicism or irony. He is happy with the world at a time when the world was particularly full of happy people.

The New Age Movement

The New Age movement is an unorganized form of spirituality that became popular in the 1970s in North America. New Age beliefs freely combine aspects of established religions, ancient mythologies, and mysticism, as believers are encouraged to follow the spiritual path through which they feel the most empowered. Portions of Hinduism, Gnosticism, paganism, neo-paganism, and Buddhism, among other world religions, are borrowed in New Age spirituality, combined with a high regard for the natural world and mother earth. Though participation in any of the myriad practices associated with New Age is entirely optional, some commonalities of its adherents can include belief in the healing power of crystals and the predictive power of Tarot cards, faith in astrology, and the practice of yoga and meditation.

The New Age movement came under attack in the 1980s and 1990s from all sides. Scientific studies disproving the alleged power of crystals and other New Age healing techniques were published. Christian campaigns against the pseudo-religion portrayed it as a stepping-stone to hedonistic Satanism. Nonetheless, New Age

COMPARE
&
CONTRAST

- **1998:** Owing to recognition with such major awards as the Booker Prize, first won by a Canadian in 1992 (Michael Ondaatje for *The English Patient*); the Orange Prize; and the Pulitzer Prize, Canadian literature ceases to be considered a regional literature and grows in esteem in the literary world.

  Today: In 2013, the Nobel Prize committee awards Canadian author Alice Munro the Nobel Prize in Literature for her mastery of the short-story form. The first Canadian to win the Nobel Prize in Literature, Munro increases the visibility of Canadian culture, authors, and poets around the world.

- **1998:** The advent of personal cell phones and the availability of the Internet to the public increase feelings of connectivity in society, as far-flung friends and family can communicate with ease and a plethora of information becomes available online.

  Today: Smartphones combine the two great personal technological developments of the 1990s, making the Internet available in handheld form. Society is hyperconnected through social media, and information travels through the population nearly instantaneously. As a result, social awareness of other cultures and points of view is sometimes higher.

- **1998:** The New Age movement fades from the public eye, though many of its tenets, including meditation and self-empowerment, remain a part of popular culture. While it is no longer widely discussed, the movement nevertheless attracts over three million believers, though the true number of adherents is difficult to place owing to the movement's unorganized nature.

  Today: Opponents of the New Age movement take their disapproval to the Internet, defaming and debunking the still-popular movement in a massive effort to end its popularity. Searching for information about the New Age movement online yields innumerable websites featuring arguments against New Age beliefs and practices.

---

beliefs remain highly visible in today's culture, from horoscopes to holistic medicine to Western conceptions of karma and reincarnation.

Though he is not necessarily a devotee of New Age spirituality, Choyce incorporates many of its most important tenets into his writing as well as his life. He writes of his life as a young writer, "I fought the construction of street lights in the wilderness, the tedium of organizations and the relentless, good-intentioned blundering of government and science." In "I'm Alive, I Believe in Everything," his speaker professes belief in God, Zeus, and Buddha—three religious figures from three distinct religions: Christianity, Greek mythology, and Buddhism. This is suggestive of *pantheism*, a belief in all deities, and it is an important aspect of New Age beliefs, especially when paired with the concept of universality: the many gods of pantheism as representative of one life-giving entity. Additionally, the poem dwells on the natural world; the importance of a positive, self-affirming attitude; erasing difference in favor of unity, connectivity, curing illness, and the pleasure of pure sensory experience—all integral beliefs in the New Age movement. Thus, the poem's celebration of life resembles the New Age movement's focus on self-improvement through mindfulness and respect for the environment.

CRITICAL OVERVIEW

Choyce is a prominent member of the literary community of Nova Scotia and a notable Canadian poet. Just as he has adopted Canada as his

In the first stanza, the speaker considers everything from ink and record albums to the dark night sky.
(© Anemone | Shutterstock.com)

home after leaving the United States, the Canadian press has embraced him as an important voice in North Atlantic literature. George Elliot Clarke discusses Choyce's American heritage in "No Finer Choyce," his review of the 2013 collection *I'm Alive, I Believe in Everything* for the *Chronicle Herald*: like American poets William Carlos Williams and Allen Ginsberg, Clarke notes, "what distinguishes Choyce is his American openness—a capacious generosity... Choyce's American qualities are vital to English-Canadian poetry."

In her review of Choyce's nonfiction survey of his home province, *Nova Scotia: Shaped by the Sea*, for *Quill & Quire*, Kathleen Hickey describes Choyce's legacy and prowess: "Choyce, with 40 books under his belt, is an award-winning storyteller and a high-profile member of the local literary scene.... When Choyce's surfer-poet persona shines through... *Nova Scotia* is most satisfying and original."

Kelly Toughill praises Choyce's surfer persona in "Ice-Breakers," for the *Toronto Star*,

calling Choyce a "well-known local writer, publisher and surfer.... His most recent book, a memoir titled *Driving Minnie's Piano* includes several evocative descriptions of winter surfing in Nova Scotia."

As the founder of a small publishing house, Pottersfield Press, Choyce is beloved by the members of his community for supporting new and local writers as well as providing a platform for the dissemination of fiction, poetry, and nonfiction representative of the Canadian North Atlantic. Tiffany Thornton writes in "Pottersfield Press Keeps History Alive," in the *Chronicle Herald*: "With an abundance of local stories to tell, and writers who want to share them, [the] small publishing company is holding its own in a world of publishing conglomerates and e-books."

Known best for his young-adult fiction and poetry, Choyce received positive reviews for the depth and range of *Beautiful Sadness*. Anne F. Walker writes in her review of the collection for *Canadian Literature* how, with "dark humor... [and] in concert with more philosophic considerations of nothingness, *Beautiful Sadness* . . . explores the cultural emptiness of modern corporate North American life."

On Choyce's philosophy of a joyful life, observed easily in his celebratory poem "I'm Alive, I Believe in Everything" as well as in his fiction and nonfiction work, Candace Fertile writes in her review of Choyce's memoir *Seven Ravens: Two Summers in a Life by the Sea*: "Choyce's writing reveals an engagement with both the physical world and the literary one. It is a privilege to be invited on a journey with such an inquisitive and sensitive mind."

CRITICISM

Amy L. Miller

Miller is a graduate of the University of Cincinnati, and she currently resides in New Orleans, Louisiana. In the following essay, she discusses how the meaning of Choyce's "I'm Alive, I Believe in Everything" is buried within the poem's catalog of seemingly unrelated items.

The structure of Choyce's "I'm Alive, I Believe in Everything" seems relatively easy to grasp. The first stanza comprises a list. The second stanza—only two lines long—is a repetition of the poem's title and a reiteration that the speaker truly believes in everything he has listed thus far. The third stanza comprises a second list. The fourth stanza is a repetition of the second stanza. The poem is a free-verse catalog, in which the speaker provides little annotation to clarify his choices apart from the repetition of the poem's title. The end result of the combination of these poetic attributes—a four-stanza catalog poem with little narrative accompaniment—is that reading the poem without grasping its depth or meaning is easy if the reader puts no effort into unpacking the significance in the items of the list in favor of quickly scanning over the short, simple lines.

A catalog poem resembles a grocery list, in that each item of the list is there for a reason: cereal for breakfast, steaks for dinner, ice cream for a birthday party, paper towels because you ran out, and so on. Rather than write out the reason behind each item's inclusion on the list, your grocery list for these items would read: cereal, steaks, ice cream, paper towels. In a catalog poem such as "I'm Alive, I Believe in Everything," the reader is handed the list of items and must work backward to discover the reason for

> THE SPEAKER OF 'I'M ALIVE, I BELIEVE IN EVERYTHING' IS NOT AFRAID TO WALK THE BORDER BETWEEN THE KNOWN AND UNKNOWN WORLDS. HE IS A CONFIDENT EXPLORER OF LIFE'S PHILOSOPHICAL EDGES."

their inclusion. To extend the grocery-store metaphor: we see "cereal" and think "that must be for breakfast;" we see "tomato sauce" and "pasta" and assume these are ingredients for an Italian dinner. In the poem, the reader is given nearly fifty items in a list with the explanation that these items are the ingredients for "everything" and "everything" is what the speaker believes in because he is alive.

In an essay on his writing philosophy, Choyce notes: "Sometimes facts are not enough. There are times to make the leap, to get metaphysical, and suppose that we all live larger lives than appearances would suggest." Faced with the inscrutable catalog of "I'm Alive, I Believe in Everything," it is the duty of a reader and student of poetry to make that metaphysical leap into the unknown. With all the ingredients in our cart, we are ready to take a guess at the nature of the recipe. The best method through which to approach this is to first find items that are similar, then consider the purpose of that category of item against the stated purpose of the list (in this case, to believe in everything). One such category is natural imagery, which appears in a motif across the entirety of the poem. These images, of large-scale natural events like sunsets, waves, and clear skies as well as generally enormous parts of nature like trees, shorelines, the horizon, and the ocean, help create a sense of expansiveness that we will find echoed in the heightened consciousness of the speaker. A speaker who believes in everything would certainly be drawn to such grandiose imagery that is typical of what Clarke praises as Choyce's "nature-informed poetry with zest and Zen-singing soul." The natural imagery is large but serene. There are no volcanic eruptions or lightning strikes in the poem, only the soothing lap of waves and the harmless fire of the sunset. This suggests that the speaker, though he is in an excited, elevated mood,

WHAT DO I READ NEXT?

- Choyce's young-adult novel *Off the Grid* (2015) follows the struggles of Cody, a sixteen-year-old who spent his childhood deep in the wilderness living "off the grid" with his family, as he navigates life in the city, his first year in high school, and his father's failing health.

- Conrad Black's *Rise to Greatness: The History of Canada from the Vikings to the Present* (2014) tells the story of Canadian history from 874 to the present, including the explorations of the vast country, its colonial past under British and French rule, the rise of its major cities, and the growth and influence of Canadian culture.

- *The Lava of This Land: South African Poetry, 1960–1996* (1997), edited by Denis Hirson, collects the work of over fifty South African poets writing in the midst of a rapidly changing political and cultural landscape.

- *Coastlines: The Poetry of Atlantic Canada* (2002), edited by Anne Compton, Laurence Hutchman, Ross Leckie, and Robin McGrath, collects the work of Canadian poets who live and love life on the North Atlantic coast, including Elizabeth Bishop, Kay Smith, George Elliott Clarke, Michael Crummey, and Geoff Cook.

- Allen Ginsberg's *Howl and Other Poems* (1956) not only established Ginsberg as the counterculture voice of the Beat generation of American poets but also led to a protracted and bitter trial in which the collection's publisher, Lawrence Ferlinghetti, and the manager of the bookstore where the collection was released, Shigeyoshi Murao, were arrested and tried for obscenity.

- Choyce's eighth collection of poetry, *Caution to the Wind* (2000), supplements the alternately ecstatic and pensive mood of

Beautiful Sadness with further meditations on music, beauty, surfing, life on the beach, and the miracle of waking every day to new and exciting opportunities.

- *William Carlos Williams: Selected Poems* (1985) gathers the work of a legendary American poet who never lost his sense of playfulness and rebellion. Like Choyce, Williams finds poetry in everyday life. He balanced his career as a small-town doctor with his notoriety as a friend of Ezra Pound and the modernist poets of New York and Europe, paying tribute in his poetry to the little moments of joy that make life worth living.

- Sylvia Legris's third collection, *Nerve Squall* (2005), won the Pat Lowther Award and the Griffin Poetry Prize. Ghosts, brain disorders, and the weather are the three tangled subjects of this guide to the end of the world. A two-time Pushcart Prize nominee, Legris is one of Canada's most fascinating contemporary poets.

- Margaret Atwood's poetry collection *Morning in the Burned House* (1995) exemplifies her sharp and beautiful voice as a beloved writer of both poetry and prose. One of Canada's most famous authors, Atwood brings her eye for the peculiarities of the individual's role within society to her poetic work as she explores the self, the home, and the world.

- In Alice Munro's short-story collection *Runaway* (2005), women and men must decide whether to leave their broken relationships behind in favor of the open road or attempt to work the emotional knots of love and marriage just loose enough so that they may breathe easier. Munro became the first Canadian recipient of the Nobel Prize in Literature in 2013, and her works depict Canadian life at its most ordinary and remarkable.

---

is not out of control. He feels a peaceful unity with nature's grand vistas. The nature motif grounds the catalog to tangible reality, allowing the

speaker to venture into the unknown wilds of his imagination with the knowledge that he can always return to the comfort of the trees or the empty sky. Nature will always be a presence in his life, and so he freely believes in it.

A second category embedded in the poem's list is that of everyday objects and activities. This category includes records, baseball, ink, walking, literature, and the simple act of waking up. Though it is humble when compared with the poem's more lofty abstractions, this category of everyday life is critical to a sophisticated understanding of the text. Fertile writes: "Choyce embarks on a journey of self-understanding by looking carefully at what's around him." Life is defined less by its extremes and more by its constants: waking up, walking, work (for a writer: ink, revisions, and literature), and hobbies (baseball and records). The speaker recognizes not only the role of natural spectacle but also the trappings of his daily existence as integral to his life-affirming belief in everything.

The speaker includes references to empty skies, empty spaces, vacuums, absence, and entropy in a category showing an appreciation for negative space. Somewhat paradoxically, through these images the speaker includes nothingness in his list of "everything." Walker writes: "Spaces and emptiness are important in the largely narrative poetry of Lesley Choyce's *Beautiful Sadness*. These voids are locations of ironic comprehension or ominous preparedness rather than places of despair." Indeed, despair has no place in the speaker's catalog, even as he looks directly into the void. The buoyant mood of the poem is protected by the proliferation of positive items as well as by the absence of such black-hole imagery in all but the first stanza— the only category of items to appear in only one of the poem's two lists. Negative spaces, along with uncertainty, ambiguity, and vagueness, are included in the catalog, but, significantly, fear is left out. The speaker of "I'm Alive, I Believe in Everything" is not afraid to walk the border between the known and unknown worlds. He is a confident explorer of life's philosophical edges.

The largest category of items is the conceptual category, containing a series of binary (or opposite) word pairs; for example, positive and negative, or chaos and an unbroken horizon (which would appear as a perfectly straight line). While typically the use of a binary pair is indicative of black-and-white, either/or perception of the world, the speaker has established that he believes in everything; thus the listing of binaries in his catalog effectively includes not

only positive and negative but also the charged area between and the neutral ground outside. The space between two fixed states is known as liminal space: a transitive, unstable space of unpredictability and change. For example, between absolute black and absolute white is a liminal gradient of gray. The speaker claims this space, the empty spaces of the first stanza, as well as the opposed positions occupied by the binaries. Once again, as in the nature motif, the speaker has incorporated a massive space in his list of beliefs using an economy of words.

Other humans are included in the poem in the form of dancing old men, fools, refined intellects, and brotherhood. The speaker frustrates the binary opposition between intelligence and stupidity by claiming kinship with each. He provides an example of the marriage of these seemingly opposite states through the old men dancing in the streets. Old men are traditionally wise men, yet dancing in the streets is an exuberant act of foolishness. As the only other characters specifically described apart from the speaker, these silly old men share the speaker's freewheeling spirit and indomitable joy of life. The deities, however, are listed alongside economic ideologies: Zeus of ancient Greek myth, God of Christianity, and Buddha of Buddhism appear beside dollar-worshipping capitalism and, at the time of the poem's composition in the 1990s, the recently failed idealism of communism. These five systems of belief are treated within the speaker's personal system of belief as interchangeable—a show of might on the part of the speaker as he sweeps the vast differences separating these ideologies en masse into the catalog of his own, more inclusive life philosophy.

To the speaker, the differences between the individual items or their categories do not matter as much as existence itself. Through life, any and all can be experienced. Without life, in a state of nonexistence, the nothingness of experience cannot even be perceived without senses to feel it or a mind to ponder it. Life allows for belief, and the speaker chooses to believe in everything life has to offer without judgment, anger, or fear. Because of this, he is rewarded with a deep appreciation of the world around him, from the beauty and grand scale of nature, to the everyday routines that see him through each day, to the depths of the unknown, to the abstract and inscrutable, and finally to his recognition of other happy souls like himself. Clarke writes that Choyce's poetry

The image of the waves on the coast communicates the constant and eternal nature of the speaker's belief. *(© Pavelk | Shutterstock.com)*

"is sumptuously crafted—of feeling and philosophy, of whimsy and warmth. He makes us care for what he cares about—the exemplary liberty of wind, water, and light; the godly love for life itself." Choyce hands us the catalog of everything with all the confidence of his speaker, happily trusting the reader to discover the secrets to life hidden in the empty spaces between the words of his master list.

Source: Amy L. Miller, Critical Essay on "I'm Alive, I Believe in Everything," in *Poetry for Students*, Gale, Cengage Learning, 2016.

Suzanne James

In the following review, James praises the "fast-moving plots" and "catchy narrative twists" in Choyce's novel Living Outside the Lines.

Teenagers often feel frustrated by their limited control over day-to-day life and the future, and thwarted by controlling parents and situations. Reflecting these concerns, young adult novels frequently present empowered protagonists who succeed in controlling—rather than being controlled by—their environments. In Lesley Choyce's *Living Outside the Lines*, control takes the form of inspiring the creation of a future society drastically different than our own, visualized in a novel-within-a-novel composed by the book's sixteen-year-old protagonist, Nigel. Less

dramatically, but more convincingly, the teenage narrator of Susin Nielsen's *Dear George Clooney: Please Marry My Mom* succeeds in gaining control over her environment by changing herself and her interactions with others.

The first-person narrative of *Living Outside the Lines* opens with the rather clichéd device of the inspiring creative writing instructor prodding his students to write a novel "so powerful, inventive, enthralling, and revolutionary that readers take the message to heart and do something to make this a better world to live in." While most of the students remain indifferent, Nigel is inspired to "live outside the lines" and so sets out to complete a novel over the course of the term (each of his four previous attempts having stalled at page 176). Writing a novel proves surprisingly straightforward: after little creative anguish, and even less editing, Nigel's partially complete draft earns him a lucrative book contract. Far more intriguing is Nigel's relationship with Michelle, a mysterious classmate who—as we realize long before he does—has travelled back through time to meet our narrator. As the novel shifts from contemporary realism to science fiction, characters debate the ethics of time-travel and its potential to change future events, though the nature of the futuristic world inspired by the novel-within-the-novel proves far more interesting.

Nigel's creative work, sections of which are included in the text, posits a country in which discovery, endeavour, and governance are handled by young adults aged fifteen to twenty-two; mature "adults" step aside to pursue hobbies and play no more than an advisory role in the real work of society. This novel, we discover, provides the blueprint for the future to which Nigel travels in the closing section of Choyce's text. Although not a perfect Utopia, the world managed by young adults is peaceful, egalitarian, innovative, and—most importantly—takes advantage of the potential of its young citizens. As Choyce argues in an interview, "Adults have not been that good at solving some of the world's greatest problems . . . why not let young people with possibly some radical new improved ideas take over?"

. . . *Living Outside the Lines* and *Dear George Clooney: Please Marry My Mom* are well-crafted novels targeting a young adult audience. Working within generic conventions, the authors succeed in balancing accessibility, relatively fast-moving plots, and catchy narrative twists with, in Nielsen's novel, a subtlety of characterization, and in Choyce's work, an exploration of the sociopolitical issue of teenage autonomy and potential.

Source: Suzanne James, "Taking Control," in *Canadian Literature*, No. 213, Summer 2012, p. 162.

Michael Steeleworthy and Lesley Choyce

In the following interview, Choyce talks about some of his opinions on young-adult and Canadian literature.

1. What is Canadian Literature? How do you define it?

Canadian literature is a very broad area. In general, I define anything written by a Canadian as Canadian literature.

2. You have been writing novels for young adults for almost two decades. In this time, what developments and changes have you seen?

When I first started writing books for young adults many of the subjects that I wanted to write about were considered taboo. Today, my most recent novels deal with gritty subjects like death, murder, rape and young offenders. Fifteen years ago I would not have been able to get these books published.

3. Where does your writing fit within the context of Canadian Literature?

Though Canadian literature has moved away from its focus on Canadian history and landscape, books written by Canadian authors do not lose their appeal just because they are set in Canada. As long as the story is universal, it will get the attention of young people. There is no such thing as Canadian literature anymore, only literature written by Canadians.

4. Do you have a favourite Canadian YA author? If yes, why are they your favourite?

I like Farley Mowat because he understands the value of telling a good story. He is a strongly opinionated writer and is unabashedly who he is. I admire these qualities in an author. As for contemporary Canadian YA authors, I would have to say that I don't read many of them. I don't want to be influenced by other writers. I want my stories and writing to be my own.

5. Your novels for young adults tackle all sorts of subjects that range from music to the environment. How do you ensure that your subjects will appeal to a younger audience?

I write characters that are interesting to me. Some are abnormally smart, like Martin in my book *Shoulder the Sky*, while others are quirky, or funny, or incredibly complex. I do research and talk to teens to make sure my characters are believable.

6. Were you an avid reader during your teenage years? If so, did you read books by Canadian authors?

I read a lot when I was a teenager. I read science fiction and fantasy novels, which is interesting because I don't often write in these genres. My next novel, *Living Outside the Lines*, is going to be the closest I have come to writing a science fiction book. When I was younger, I did not choose to read books by Canadian authors.

7. It is often difficult to get young adults to read books by Canadian authors. They think they are boring. Can you think of a way that Canadian literature can shake this stigma?

It is important that young people are exposed to the full depth and breadth of Canadian writing for young adults. Often they are only given a limited selection by their English teacher in school. Canadian literature in high school should still be mandated as part of the curriculum, but teenagers should get to choose the books that they want to read.

8. Tell me what role, if any, you think that the public library can play in developing young people's interest in Canadian YA authors?

The public library has always been a lifeline for me. It is a very valuable institution for promoting books. There is no better way to promote a book than to have it on display at the public library. It is a way to expose young people to books that they would not otherwise pick up. Books in libraries can go really far afield, which provides a network for authors and their ideas to travel all over the world. One great way for libraries to promote Canadian authors is to invite local talent to come and speak about their books....

9. What do you see in the future for Canadian writing for Young Adults?

We are currently in a golden age of literature for young adults, but my concern is over the longevity of this age. Literature often goes through cycles and it is possible that we will see the downside of the current cycle we are in. It is important to take advantage of the time that we are in now to continue to write excellent novels for young adults.

It is the writers' job to maintain young people's interest in YA written by Canadians.

10. You have published four books in the last year: Hell's Hotel, Skate Freak, The Book of Michael, *and* Running the Risk. *Are any of these books a favorite of yours? Or are you most fond of something written earlier?*

My two favorite books are *Shoulder the Sky* and *The End of the World as We Know It.* Both these books have great characters and excellent story lines that deal with a great range of issues that are relevant for young adults.

Source: Michael Steeleworthy and Lesley Choyce, "Canadian Authors Corner: An Interview with Author Lesley Choyce," in *YA Hotline,* 2011, pp. 11–12.

Susie DeCoste

In the following excerpt, DeCoste praises Choyce's Seven Ravens: Two Summers in a Life by the Sea.

... As a memoir written in episodic journal entries over two subsequent summers, Lesley Choyce's memoir *Seven Ravens: Two Summers in a Life by the Sea* surely stands out here in genre and form. Choyce meanders through the memoir attendant to various spiritual and religious traditions including Shamanism, Buddhism, and new age thought. Some entries read as compendiums of quotable sentiment from thinkers and spiritual gurus, all with the intent of helping the narrator come to terms with life. In one memorable section, Choyce's dog becomes deathly ill, and he is afraid she will not make it through the night. Desperate for comfort, he places a picture of the Pope in front of her, feeling silly enough about the gesture to precede it with "I should not tell you this ..." But I can think of many other controversial details he should not have told readers that take precedence over the use of a Catholic figure's picture for comfort— that he doesn't believe in teaching the history of World War I is a prime example. Choyce's voice is thus quite brave; and the text is genuinely spontaneous, studious, and honest about the trials of being in the world, which makes for a satisfying reading experience.

Source: Susie DeCoste, Review of *Seven Ravens: Two Summers in a Life by the Sea,* in *Canadian Literature,* No. 208, Spring 2011, p. 182.

Martin Ware

In the following review, Ware gives a positive evaluation of Choyce's Sea of Tranquility.

The title of Lesley Choyce's new novel *Sea of Tranquility* suggests many things: a crater of the moon, an isolated island, a calm stretch of ocean, or the serene outlook of the novel's principal character. In reading it, one is reminded that its author is a rare bird in the literary landscape, an unrepentant and optimistic romantic who challenges those who would make literature into the dismal art, an unremitting record of broken relationships, unhappiness, treachery, inaccessible meanings, the cruelty of nature, aborted hopes, bitter survival struggles, premature death, and the conniving manipulations of the powerful.

It is true that our author deals with the last five of these in this new novel, which centres on the survival struggles of a Nova Scotian offshore island community. But he distances his more painful accounts of the death of a sealer, a seaman, an odd job man, and a slightly mad professor by presenting them from the perspective of a remarkable 50-year-old woman, Sylvie Young, who has developed such a strong bond with her island, the ocean, and the ocean creatures that she is able to face the painful facts of her four husbands' deaths—and, through memory, to take into herself the strength which they once shared with her in life.

Choyce very effectively intertwines the story of the old woman and her men and the story of the Ragged Island community's struggle against the conniving stratagems of politicians and bureaucrats to resettle it. Choyce's long experience as a writer of children's books contributes to his capacity to create suspense and hold our attention. The book's essence, however, is contained in the poetic evocations of island and ocean and of the strange vagaries of "the drifting men" who each in their peculiar ways endear themselves to the novel's principal character.

Source: Martin Ware, Review of *Sea of Tranquility,* in *Canadian Literature,* No. 187, Winter 2005, p. 179.

Terry McDonald

In the following review, McDonald faults Choyce's The Coasts of Canada: A History *as "dumbed down" history.*

The idea behind this book is simple and appealing. It is to recount the history of Canada by looking at its three [sic] coastlines and the peoples who dwelt along them. It naturally begins with the first Aboriginal peoples and works its way from the earliest European arrivals through to Canada's participation in the Second

World War. A few postwar occurrences are mentioned, and there is a gentle nod towards the creation of Nunavut. So far, so good, but what purports to be a work of history is really Choyce, writing in a peculiarly "street-wise" style, revealing his seeming inability to separate truth from legend and also, it must be said, revealing his prejudices. Early chapters introduce figures such as St Brendan, along with the early Norse explorers ("brave and proud but obsessively violent") and the Basque whalers and fishermen who "travelled to the Grand Banks and the coast of Newfoundland as early as 1199." No sources are given to substantiate these statements, despite the author's claim that he used a team of researchers. A noticeable feature of the text is its frequent use of phrases such as "it is believed," "there's a good chance that" and "may have visited" when discussing the period before Columbus and Cabot. There is even a suggestion that the Holy Grail "may remain" in Nova Scotia after being taken there by a member of the Knights Templar a hundred years before Columbus. Umberto Eco would have liked that one. As the book progresses, the coming of the loyalists to the Maritimes, the growth of British Columbia, and the Arctic explorations are all described.

However this is not an academic or scholarly work. There are no references or citations, although there is a three-page "select bibliography." The best adjective for this book is "simplistic" and its most curious feature is an all-pervasive anti-English (sometimes anti-British) tone which, on occasion, arguably verges on racism. Choyce is scathing throughout about the early British explorers (or "pirates" as he calls them), the merchants ("rapacious"), and the politicians ("incompetent") who helped create and shape modern Canada. This is not to blindly defend British Imperial policies or to take a jingoistic stance. None of the Europeans who came and occupied the Americas have an unblemished record, but the French, Spanish and Portuguese are, in Choyce's work, treated far more leniently than the British. The overall impression is that this is "dumbed down" history, carelessly written, making frequent use of slang terms and lacking objectivity. However, the illustrations are well chosen.

Source: Terry McDonald, Review of *The Coasts of Canada: A History*, in *British Journal of Canadian Studies*, Vol. 17, No. 1, May 2004, p. 138.

SOURCES

Andersen, Kurt, "The Best Decade Ever? The 1990s, Obviously," in *New York Times*, February 6, 2015, http://www.nytimes.com/2015/02/08/opinion/sunday/the-best-decade-ever-the-1990s-obviously.html?_r=0 (accessed August 16, 2015).

"Bio," Lesley Choyce website, https://lesleychoyce.word press.com/bio (accessed August 15, 2105).

"Breton Books Author Wins 2013 Atlantic Poetry Prize," goCapeBreton.com, http://www.whatsgoinon.ca/breton-books-author-wins-2013-atlantic-poetry-prize/#.VsTP-uaWSiM (accessed August 15, 2015).

Choyce, Lesley, "I'm Alive, I Believe in Everything," in *Beautiful Sadness*, Ekstasis Editions, 1998, p. 81.

———, "Writing Philosophy," in *Canadian Poetry Online*, University of Toronto website, 2000, http://canpoetry.library.utoronto.ca/choyce/write.htm (accessed August 15, 2015).

Clarke, George Elliot, "No Finer Choyce," in *Chronicle Herald*, October 19, 2013, http://thechronicleherald.ca/books/1161121-no-finer-choyce (accessed August 16, 2015).

Fertile, Candace, Review of *Seven Ravens: Two Summers in a Life by the Sea*, in *Quill & Quire*, October 2009, http://www.quillandquire.com/review/seven-ravens-two-summers-in-a-life-by-the-sea/ (accessed August 15, 2015).

Hickey, Kathleen, "*Nova Scotia: Shaped by the Sea—From the Beginning of Time*," in *Quill & Quire*, September 1996, http://www.quillandquire.com/review/nova-scotia-shaped-by-the-sea-from-the-beginning-of-time/ (accessed August 15, 2015).

"Lesley Choyce: Biography," in *Canadian Poetry Online*, University of Toronto website, 2000, http://canpoetry.library.utoronto.ca/choyce/index.htm (accessed August 15, 2015).

Robinson, B. A., "New Age Spirituality," ReligiousTolerance.org, April 13, 2015, http://www.religioustolerance.org/the-new-age-movement-part-2.htm (accessed August 16, 2015).

Thornton, Tiffany, "Pottersfield Press Keeps History Alive," in *Chronicle Herald*, http://thechronicleherald.ca/community/dartmouth/1171466-pottersfield-press-keeps-history-alive (accessed August 16, 2015).

Toughill, Kelly, "Ice-Breakers," in *Toronto Star*, January 20, 2007, http://www.thestar.com/life/travel/2007/01/20/icebreakers.html (accessed August 16, 2015).

Walker, Anne F., "The Void Looks Back," in *Canadian Literature*, No. 223, Winter 2014, http://canlit.ca/reviews/the_void_looks_back (accessed August 15, 2015).

FURTHER READING

Choyce, Lesley, *Revenge of the Optimist*, Ekstasis Editions, 2003.

> Choyce's 2003 collection of free-verse poetry continues his exploration of the beauty of the inner self and its reflection in the outside world as he remains among Canada's most prominent and prolific poets.

McGoogan, Ken, *50 Canadians Who Changed the World*, Phyllis Bruce Books, 2013.

> McGoogan follows the lives of Canada's greatest inventors, artists, philanthropists, activists, politicians, and entrepreneurs in this catalog of the country's best and brightest. Canadians profiled include Margaret Atwood, Leonard Cohen, Pierre Trudeau, Oscar Peterson, and Naomi Klein.

Starnino, Carmine, *The New Canon: An Anthology of Canadian Poetry*, Véhicule Press, 2006.

> This anthology collects two hundred poems by fifty modern Canadian poets, showcasing the talent range and style of the country's young artists as they redefine the world and themselves in the new millennium.

Trehearne, Brian, *Canadian Poetry 1920 to 1960*, New Canadian Library, 2010.

> Predating Choyce's entry into the field of Canadian literature, Trehearne's anthology traces the roots of today's Canadian poetry in the work of early twentieth-century poets, mapping a changing Canada as well as a changing world.

SUGGESTED SEARCH TERMS

Lesley Choyce

Choyce AND Beautiful Sadness

Choyce AND I'm Alive, I Believe in Everything

I'm Alive, I Believe in Everything AND Canadian poetry

I'm Alive, I Believe in Everything AND catalog poem

New Age movement and poetry

Canadian poetry AND Lesley Choyce

Lesley Choyce AND Surf Poets

Off the Page with Lesley Choyce

Love's Growth

JOHN DONNE

1633

John Donne is one of the best-known poets of the early seventeenth century. His poem "Love's Growth" (probably written within a few years of 1615, but not published until 1633, after his death) is a praise of love—and indirectly of his lover—as an infinite power that can nevertheless increase. In his quest to find a metaphysical conceit to describe this seeming paradox, Donne looks to the cutting-edge science of his day in the fields of medicine, alchemy, and especially astronomy. Although modern audiences are used to reading of the scientific revolution, which was then at its height, as a story of rapid and inexorable progress from superstition to science, Donne resists, rejecting and even ridiculing the new astronomy of Galileo and Kepler. He expressed fears that can still be found in the modern world that scientific progress would undermine religion and thereby dissolve the human bonds that tie society together.

AUTHOR BIOGRAPHY

John Donne was born in 1572, but the precise day is unknown. Donne's family was Catholic, and the repressive policies of the British government against Catholicism prevented the keeping of baptism registries. The English oppression of Catholicism would shape much of Donne's life. Donne's father, also named John, was a middle-class merchant in London. He died in 1576 when Donne

John Donne *(© Getty Images)*

was four years old. Donne's mother, without any possibility of supporting the family herself, contracted another middle-class marriage within a few months.

Donne was tutored at home and at age eleven was sent to Oxford (not an unusual age at the time). He eventually studied at Cambridge as well. However, no English university could grant a degree to a Catholic. Nevertheless, Donne in 1591 began to study law and in 1592 was admitted to Lincoln's Inn, effectively meaning he could practice law. In that same year, the Tudor state criminalized failure to attend Church of England services. The next year, Donne's brother Henry, still a student, fell afoul of this law, and under torture confessed that he was hiding the Catholic priest William Harrington. The priest was tortured and executed by drawing and quartering, and Donne's brother died of the plague in the Tower of London.

Donne spent his inheritance on travel on the Continent. While there, he made many connections with British diplomats and military figures like Sir Walter Raleigh. Donne probably fought in more than one piratical raid against the annual Spanish silver flotilla during this time. Returning to a Britain more tolerant after Queen Elizabeth's death, Donne became a secretary in a government office, working for Thomas Egerton, the Lord Keeper of the Great Seal. In fact, Donne lived in a room in Egerton's house and soon began courting his niece Anne More. Because Donne was still a Catholic, Egerton could never have approved a marriage, but the two married secretly. When this came out, Donne was thrown out of his position and had to rely on the charity of his wife's cousin, who allowed the couple to live in his country house while Donne attempted to start a private law practice. His business was never successful. Over the next sixteen years, Donne and Anne had twelve children, of whom only five lived to adulthood. Anne died as a result of her last pregnancy.

At the same time, Donne began circulating his poetry in manuscript to his friends. While it is impossible to precisely date much of Donne's writings, "Love's Growth" probably comes from this time, composed sometime between 1610 and 1620. His songs and sonnets were published only after his death; their erotic subject matter was considered too salacious to set in print during his lifetime. Donne's poetry brought him to the attention of wealthy patrons, including King James I. The king doubted that Donne's political career could be restarted and prevailed upon him to finally convert and take a position in the Church of England. Donne did so, was awarded an honorary doctorate of theology, and received a number of choice positions, culminating in the deanship of St. Paul's Cathedral in London from 1621 on.

Donne came to the attention of a wider literary public with the publication of his well-received sermons. He also published a series of spiritual meditations under the title *Devotions upon Emergent Occasions* (1624), which contains some of the most famous lines in English literature: *No man is an island* and *Ask not for whom the bell tolls, it tolls for thee*. He certainly continued to write poetry, and his *Sacred Sonnets* are usually dated to this later period. He died, probably of stomach cancer, in the deanery of St. Paul's, on March 31, 1631. His poems were collected and published posthumously over the next several years.

POEM TEXT

> I scarce believe my love to be so pure
> As I had thought it was,
> Because it doth endure
> Vicissitude, and season, as the grass;

MEDIA ADAPTATIONS

- In 1948, the American composer Ross Lee Finney set "Love's Growth" and two other poems by Donne as *Three Love Songs*. The piece has never been recorded.

Methinks I lied all winter, when I swore   5
My love was infinite, if spring make it more.
But if this medicine, love, which cures all sorrow
With more, not only be no quíntessence,
But mix'd of all stuffs paining soul, or sense,
And of the Sun his working vigour borrow,   10
Love's not so pure, and abstract, as they use
To say, which have no mistress but their muse,
But as all else, being elemented too,
Love sometimes would contémplate,
    sometimes do.

And yet no greater, but more eminent,   15
Love by the spring is grown;
As, in the firmament,
Stars by the sun are not enlarg'd, but shown.
Gentle love deeds, as blossoms on a bough,
From love's awakened root do bud out now.   20
If, as in waters stirr'd more circles be
Produc'd by one, love such additions take,
Those, like to many spheres, but one heaven
    make,
For they are all concentric unto thee:
And though each spring do add to love
    new heat,   25
As princes do in times of action get
New taxes, and remit them not in peace,
No winter shall abate the spring's increase.

POEM SUMMARY

The text used for this summary is from *The Songs and Sonnets of John Donne*, edited by Theodore Redpath, Harvard University Press, 2009, p. 214. A version of the poem can be found on the following web page: http://www.poetryfoundation.org/poem/180639.

"Love's Growth" is divided into two unnumbered stanzas of fourteen lines each; the

first stanza is punctuated as two unequal sentences, the second as three.

Stanza 1

LINES 1–6

The speaker of the poem is discussing his love affair with a mortal woman. He had wanted to believe that his love was pure. He clearly does not mean pure in the sense of unconsummated with sexual relations. Rather, he is speaking within the language of alchemy where something that is pure is perfect and therefore not subject to change. However, he observes that his love does change, in the same way that growing grass changes. Before, he said his love was infinite, but just as grass grows in the spring after the winter, he finds that his love is increasing, so he must have been mistaken.

LINES 7–14

This sentence extends the alchemical imagery. Love is indeed not pure and certainly is not the pure quintessence which, in alchemy, is purified aether or fire. Love, however, is a medicine. The poem supposes the alchemical school of medicine of Paracelsus. according to which like magically cures like. Therefore love, the medicine that cures sorrow, is itself a sorrow (a more technical term would be melancholy). Love, then, turns out to be a mixture of elements of the same kind that cause the soul and the senses to suffer. The idea that love is a kind of suffering goes back to Greek and Latin poets in antiquity who supposed that love was a kind of illness, attacking the body with a morbid fever and causing acts of insanity. Because like cures like, the poet thinks, and love is a sorrow, then love will cure other sorrows, in fact all sorrows. However, it is not pure, it is the stuff of sorrow (and melancholy was believed to be a humor, a physical substance in the body) mixed with its opposite, sunlight.

The poet turns now to the idea he has so far attacked and dismissed, namely that love is pure. This idea, he says, was held by those who did not take any human lover, but only made love to the muse, the Greek goddess of inspiration. He is referring to Platonic love, a reworking of Plato's teaching about love that came into fashion at the Jacobean court and that has persisted in the popular consciousness until today. This is switching the meaning of pure, so that it does now mean sexually chaste. Just like anything that is composed of different elements, love sometimes contemplates and sometimes acts.

Stanza 2

LINES 15–20

The poet changes his frame of reference from alchemy to astronomy. He returns to his initial problem: If love is infinite, how can it increase? He finds metaphors to explain the seeming paradox in the heavenly bodies. Stars, for instance, do not grow in physical size but do increase in brightness depending on their position relative to the sun. By stars, in this case, the speaker means planets, which were traditionally thought of merely as a kind of star: a planet is a wandering star that moves across the celestial sphere, as opposed to the fixed stars which move with the celestial sphere. When love grows in the spring like grass, it is like a planet becoming brighter rather than one becoming larger. Something that is infinite in one dimension might nevertheless increase in another. Acts of love break out like buds on a tree branch in spring.

LINES 21–28

The increase of an already infinite love is described again by the new metaphor of circles expanding on the surface (in this case *stirred* must mean "moved," and the circles are to be imagined as produced by an action like throwing a rock into a pond): new circles are constantly being created by the phenomenon, even though its dimensions have a fixed limit, which could suggest a way that infinity could increase by further and further division. The speaker further likens the arrangement of the circles on the water to the concentric heavenly spheres, which the poet takes to be concentric around the Earth, where the beloved is located. The beloved is here addressed in the second person, which is the first and only clue that the poem is being spoken to the beloved.

Love increases in the spring, as the cycle of generation is renewed by warmth from the sun. In the same way, during a war, a prince may get his legislature to vote him new taxes, but the new taxes are not repealed in time of peace and are increased still further during the next war. Love increases each spring, but it does not decrease during the winter, so it constantly grows from year to year.

THEMES

Philosophy

The second stanza of "Love's Growth" deals with astronomy, while the first deals with medicine and alchemy. Merely citing those two topics

TOPICS FOR FURTHER STUDY

- Ralph Fletcher's *Room Enough for Love* (1998) is an acclaimed collection of love poetry for young adults. Read through these poems and find examples whose themes resonate with your own experience. Use these poems as well as Donne's as inspiration to write your own poem that employs a metaphysical conceit, metaphorically describing a thing by a completely unrelated or even opposite idea.

- *The Ink Dark Moon: Love Poems*, by Onono Komachi and Izumi Shikibu (translated by Jane Hirschfield in 1990), is an anthology of love poems by two medieval Japanese courtiers. The social situation of the authors is in many respects analogous to Donne's. Write a paper identifying and analyzing common themes in this Japanese collection of verse and in Donne's poem.

- Donne's reputation as a poet first developed as a result of his circulating manuscript copies of his poems among a circle of contacts that included those in the leading circles of English intelligentsia of his day and in the quickly growing civil service. A modern parallel of this kind of informal circulation of literature is the publication of poetry on blogs and other personal websites. Use a search engine to find blogs that post the full text of Donne's "Love's Growth," and make a report to your class that focuses on an overview of how such blogs handle the poem. Do they include critical discussion? Is the poem ever used as an example of bad poetry? Do the posts generate extensive discussion?

- Donne's "Valediction: Forbidding Mourning" is similar to "Love's Growth" in its metaphysical conceits and subject matter. Write a paper that provides an analytical comparison of the two poems.

together suggest how foreign Donne's view is to the tide of scientific progress. Medicine in the seventeenth century was still largely Hippocratic,

The speaker nurses his love throughout the long winter. (© Hein Nouwens / Shutterstock.com)

based on the medicine of ancient Greece. This supposed that the body was composed of four substances or humors called blood, phlegm, yellow bile, and black bile or melancholy (although these terms are still used in medicine, it must be noted that in Hippocratic practice they had quite different meanings than they have today). These humors corresponded to the four elements from which all matter was supposedly composed: fire, air, water, and earth. Illness was cause by an imbalance of these humors, which in turn was caused by a magical sympathy that existed between the body and the universe. Sickness might be caused, then, by a change of direction of the wind, or by astrological events, a planet moving from one sign of the zodiac to another. Medical treatment meant trying to restore the balance. If for example, a patient had a fever, that was a sign of too much blood, so the condition had to be alleviated by bleeding, physically reducing the amount of the sanguinary humor.

The same physical scheme prevailed in alchemy (often at the time called philosophy, as still witnessed by the term *philosopher's stone*). Alchemists were especially concerned with a fifth

element, the quintessence that was aether and the substance from which the stars and planets were constructed. Alchemists believed that one element could be changed into another and that if they succeeded in manufacturing the quintessence, they would both be able to transmute base metals into gold and experience a profound spiritual awakening like a mystic. Alchemists also believed they could manufacture medicines by combining the various elements. "Love's Growth" describes love as such a medicinal compound rather than the pure quintessence, by way of punning on the supposed purity of Platonic love.

Platonic Love

Although the framework of Platonic love within which Donne assembled "Love's Growth" has often been denied, these objections have been answered in part by Sarah Powrie in her 2010 article "Transposing World Harmony":

> The physicality of the poem's images, describing a swelling, budding, fertile earth, has been interpreted as evidence of Donne's anti-Platonic intentions. However, Neoplatonic thought is not disparaging of naturalism to the extent that such criticism claims.

Donne's use of the Platonic tradition is anything but simple. Donne interweaves the theme of love with his criticism of medicine and astronomy in the two stanzas of "Love's Growth."

In the first stanza, love is a natural force like the growth of plants in spring. This familiar image is used by Plato in the *Symposium*. When the priestess Diotima is initiating the young Socrates into the mysteries of love, she tells him: "those whose procreancy is of the body turn to woman as the object of their love, and raise a family, in the blessed hope that by doing so they will keep their memory green." In other words, men who do not think beyond the concerns of the body desire to use love to have offspring. The passage seems echoed in Donne's verdant spring. The end of the stanza describes those for whom love is receiving inspiration from a muse, whereby Donne takes into account the other kind of love described by Diotima:

> But those whose procreancy is of the spirit rather than of the flesh—and they are not unknown, Socrates—conceive and bear the things of the spirit ... wisdom and all her sister virtues; it is the office of every poet to beget them, and of every artist whom we may call creative.

It would be a mistake to think that Donne is denying the second type of love. He merely says it is not as pure as some think, because the next passage of the *Symposium*, like the second stanza of his poem, describes the relationship between the two. Spiritual love grows out of procreative love. Love begins with physical love, which for a man is the love of a beautiful woman for the purpose of procreation; this ascends to the love of a beautiful young man, which is not to be confused with mere physical procreation, and goes higher to the love of beautiful laws, the love of the beauty of nature as revealed by science, and finally by gradual stages to the love of the gods.

Marsilio Ficino attached this ascent of love to a mystical ascent moving through the spiritual realms of the heavenly spheres up to God, as Donne alludes to in his mention of the heavenly spheres that surround the lover. Ficino, who was a Catholic priest, did, however, tend to read the physical and spiritual love as separable, suggesting that people could love each without feeling or expressing sexual desire. This idea became popular at the Jacobean court and eventually gave rise to the satirical play of William Davenant, *The Platonick Lovers* (1635), which coined the phrase "platonic love" to describe the idea.

STYLE

Metaphysical Poetry

Donne was the most eminent of the metaphysical poets, writers from the early seventeenth century including Andrew Marvell and Abraham Cowley. It is hard to establish a canon of metaphysical poets or metaphysical poetry, since, although the poets are all proximate in time, there is no correspondence between them, nor did they produce much in the way of theoretical literature. In fact, the first use of the term *metaphysical poet* occurs in the life of Cowley (1779) by the prominent critic and lexicographer Samuel Johnson, who notes, "About the beginning of the seventeenth century, appeared a race of writers that may be termed the metaphysical poets." The use of the term *metaphysical* in this case is satirical and refers to the habit of metaphorically describing a thing by a completely unrelated or even opposite idea (the *conceit*), for example describing physical love in terms of philosophical (i.e., *metaphysical*) or even scientific ideas. This metaphysical conceit may be compared to the contemporary style of mannerist painting, in which figures are twisted and distorted merely for the sake of showing off the skill necessary to arrange subject matter in an unnatural way.

In "Love's Growth" Donne uses a number of *metaphysical* conceits. The discussion of love as suffering in illness in the first stanza is traditional, but twisting this to make love a medicine is unexpected and borders on the satirical. This uncertainty is a hallmark of the metaphysical conceit, leaving the reader unsure whether he should laugh or not. In the first part of the second stanza, love's growth is likened to the propagation of ripples on a pond, and from that image Donne moves on to the crystal spheres of Ptolemaic cosmology. However, the poem ends with an even more outrageous conceit, comparing the growth of love to rising taxes. It is hard to read this without supposing that Donne must find the love in question to be burdensome, although that would seem to work against the overall thrust of the poem and of Donne's erotic poetry generally.

Prosody

Poetry, unlike prose, follows a fixed rhythmic pattern which is called *meter*. The basic unit of a line of metrical verse is called a *foot* and consists of a series of stressed and unstressed syllables. In English poetry, the basic foot is an iamb. An *iamb* consists of a stressed followed by an

COMPARE
&
CONTRAST

- **1610s:** The standard model of medicine is Hippocratic, part of a traditional system of magic and occultism.

  Today: Medicine is science based, making advances on the bases of observation, hypothesis, experiment, and theory (although vitalistic and occult forms of medicine, which believe that life consists of an immaterial vital force which cannot be detected, persist despite lack of any evidence for their efficacy).

- **1610s:** The dominant model of the universe is Ptolemaic, that is, with a stationary Earth orbited by the sun and other planets. The foundation of modern astronomical theories, including heliocentrism and the understanding that the stars are distant suns, has already

been laid by astronomers like Nicolaus Copernicus, Johannes Kepler, and Galileo Galilei, resulting in a revolution of scientific understanding.

  Today: The Earth is known to orbit the sun. After the work of scientists like Albert Einstein and Edwin Hubble, also the sun itself is known to be part of a galaxy consisting of billions of stars, which is a companion to billions of other galaxies in an apparently infinite and expanding universe.

- **1610s:** Platonic love is a fashionable idea at the Jacobean court.

  Today: Platonic love is a historical relic or curiosity.

---

unstressed syllable, which is the natural rhythm of English speech. A common meter in English poetry is based on lines of five such feet, known as iambic pentameter. Occasional substitution of other feet (such as a *trochee*, which is a stressed syllable followed by an unstressed) is allowed, either to produce some decided effect or because of the natural flow of speech. "Love's Growth" is divided into two fourteen-line stanzas. Sometimes it is printed divided into a larger number of smaller stanzas, but this is incorrect, because a *stanza* is the smallest unit of repeated rhythmic patterning used in a poem. Most of the fourteen lines are in iambic pentameter, but the second and third are in iambic trimeter (that is, they have only three as opposed to five feet).

Another common feature of traditional English poetry is rhyme, having certain lines end in the same syllable or group of syllables. Rhyming was introduced first into various French and Spanish dialects and then into European poetry generally during the Middle Ages from Arabic poetry in the cosmopolitan civilization of Spain and southern France. Poetic forms of comparable length to the stanzas of "Love's Growth," such as the sonnet,

often have complicated rhyme schemes, and Donne's poem is no different. It rhymes according to the sequence *ababccdeedffgg*. The way to read that notation is to see that the first and second line of the poem (*a*) end in the same rhyme, the second and fourth (*b*), and so on.

HISTORICAL CONTEXT

The New Astronomy

As a highly educated man of the seventeenth century who moved in the most sophisticated circles, Donne was well informed about the new astronomy, as heliocentrism and the other novel discoveries (such as the phases of Venus and the moons of Jupiter) were called. He was probably personally acquainted with Thomas Harriot, an English astronomer who began to use a telescope at about the same time as, and independently of, Galileo. Nor was Donne the only poet in this position in England. Donne's younger contemporary John Milton incorporated the new astronomy seamlessly into his epic *Paradise Lost*, which is a retelling of the

The image of flowers on trees, as well as the several mentions of spring, bring to mind the new life and growth of the season. *(© cowardlion / Shutterstock.com)*

biblical books of Genesis and Revelation. Neither Milton nor his readers had any objections to recasting the biblical myths in a heliocentric universe, nor was this the first time this kind of transformation had happened. The church fathers, highly educated sophisticated thinkers in the tradition of Augustine or Origen, naturally accepted the Ptolemaic model of the universe, reading it seamlessly into their scriptures. In *The Literal Meaning of Genesis,* Augustine points out the embarrassment that can befall the church if a less-educated believer starts defending the flat Earth and other outdated cosmic architecture described in the Bible to any non-Christian:

> Usually, even a non-Christian knows something about the earth, the heavens, and the other elements of this world, about the motion and orbit of the stars and even their size and relative positions, about the predictable eclipses of the sun and moon, the cycles of the years and the seasons...and so forth, and this knowledge he holds to as being certain from reason and experience. Now, it is a disgraceful and dangerous thing for an infidel to hear a

Christian, presumably giving the meaning of Holy Scripture, talking nonsense on these topics; and we should take all means to prevent such an embarrassing situation, in which people show up vast ignorance in a Christian and laugh it to scorn....If they find a Christian mistaken in a field which they themselves know well and hear him maintaining his foolish opinions about our books, how are they going to believe those books in matters concerning the resurrection of the dead, the hope of eternal life, and the kingdom of heaven?

A poet like Milton, like the church fathers before him, simply accepted the revolutions in astronomy because that is how, as far as anyone knew, the universe was arranged. Interestingly, the only argument against heliocentrism that Donne ever offered was that, if it were to be accepted, in a thousand years another new scientific theory might replace it in turn. This is an argument that change itself is bad, a failure to see that every new discovery is a closer and closer approximation of the truth: science never promises absolute certainty. Donne admitted that in his view, even if the new astronomy were true, it should be rejected simply because it was new. He did not seem to realize (or perhaps he did not care) that Ptolemaic geocentrism is itself a revolution compared to the cosmology of the Bible. However that may be, Donne uses "Love's Growth" as an occasion for mocking the new astronomy, which he completely rejected.

CRITICAL OVERVIEW

Donne's reputation has waxed and waned over the centuries. Highly regarded in his own day, by the time of Samuel Johnson, Donne was completely out of fashion, and Johnson (writing in his biography of Abraham Cowley) had little use for him and the other metaphysical poets except to mock them: "The metaphysical poets were men of learning, and to shew their learning was their whole endeavor; but, unluckily resolving to shew it in rhyme, instead of writing poetry they only wrote verses." Johnson was relentlessly hostile to the metaphysical poets starting with their prosody, claiming that the poetry is not heard clearly in a metaphysical poem, and one comes to realize it is verse only after laboriously scanning the lines. Johnson considered the metaphysical conceit to be empty display for its own sake, incapable of producing the true profundity of poetry: "Their thoughts are often new, but seldom natural; they are not obvious, but neither are they just; and the reader, far from wondering that he missed them, wonders more frequently by what perverseness of industry they were ever found." Johnson finally dismisses the metaphysical conceit as "a combination of dissimilar images, or discovery of occult resemblances in things apparently unlike."

The romantic poets had more appreciation for Donne, because his reconciliation of seeming opposites through his conceits appealed to their own program. However, Donne was especially taken up early in the twentieth century by T. S. Eliot. Eliot saw a kinship between the metaphysical poets and modern literature. In his view, modern life is chaotic and fragmentary; modern man "falls in love, or reads Spinoza, and these two experiences have nothing to do with each other, or with the noise of the typewriter or the smell of cooking; in the mind of the poet these experiences are always forming new wholes." For Eliot, the metaphysical conceit healed the dislocations of modernity, giving the world

meaning by turning its broken parts back into a unity. In particular, Eliot thought metaphysical poetry reconciled thought and feeling (an old hope of the romantics) in a way that was absolutely vital for the modern world: "Donne looked into a good deal more than the heart. One must look into the cerebral cortex, the nervous system, and the digestive tracts."

Today, Donne is among the most highly regarded English poets. Among more recent scholarship on "Love's Growth," Catherine Gimelli Martin, in her article "Milton's and Donne's Stargazing Lovers, Sex, and the New Astronomy," looks at the conjunction of love, sex, and the discoveries in astronomy in the two early seventeenth-century poets. She suggests that in his secular poetry, including "Love's Growth," "Donne is overtly critical of the new astronomers for casting doubt on the Christian assurances once visible in Ptolemy's and Aristotle's perfect starry spheres." Massimo Bucciantini, Michele Camerota, and Franco Giudice, as historians of the scientific revolution, are outsiders to the tradition of Donne scholarship. In their *Galileo's Telescope*, they recognize Donne as the leading intellectual critic of the new astronomy, explaining that he rejected the idea because he feared the social changes it might bring about. In his influential 1957 article "Donne the Space Man," William Empson suggests that the image of the lover at the center of a system of concentric spheres is not a reaffirmation of geocentrism, but instead indicates that she is on some new unidentified planet.

CRITICISM

Bradley A. Skeen

Skeen is a classicist. In the following essay, he examines "Love's Growth" as part of John Donne's reaction to the new astronomy.

The instinctual model of the universe adopted by ancient man was a flat Earth. Looking from horizon to horizon, the Earth appears to be a flat disk with the sky a dome above it. The flooding of the Earth in old myths required that the flat Earth and its dome float in an infinite salt sea. This is the cosmic architecture that is universal in Near Eastern mythology. The Bible embraces the same view, not only in Genesis and Proverbs and other Old Testament books, but even in the New Testament, written in an

WHAT DO I READ NEXT?

- The 2012 *Collected Poetry* of John Donne, edited by Ilona Bell, is a recent collection of all of Donne's poetical works in a single volume.

- *Partly Cloudy: Poems of Love and Longing* (2012), by Gary Soto, is a collection of love poetry written for a young-adult audience.

- *The Selected Letters of John Donne*, edited by P. M. Olivier in 2002, offers an overview of Donne's most important and interesting correspondence.

- *Love Poems from the Japanese* (2003) is a collection of Japanese love poems from the medieval to the modern periods, including contemporaries of Donne.

- *The English Mannerist Poets and the Visual Arts* (1998), by L. E. Semler, provides a context for the frankly contrived style of Donne's lyric poetry in the mannerist art of the preceding century that Donne would have viewed during his youthful tour of Italy.

- Surprisingly, Donne has not had a recent biography. The most modern treatment is *John Donne: A Life*, by R. C. Bald, published by Cambridge University Press in 1970.

- Michel de Montaigne's *An Apology for Raymond Sebond* (1580; translated in 1988 by M. A. Screech), from his *Essays*, is a literary rejection of the heliocentrism of Copernicus, influenced in this case by orthodox Catholicism.

---

environment in which Greek astronomy had already become commonplace. To describe the concept with a metaphysical conceit, the world was believed to be like a snow globe floating in a bathtub.

Greek civilization received this model from the Near East but quickly picked it apart using actual observations: If the Earth is flat, why is there a horizon at all? How do ships disappear a little at a time when they sail off to sea with the mast the last to go? Why is the Earth's shadow on the Moon a circle? Still, Greeks accepted the apparent evidence of their senses and generally concluded that the Earth was a stationary object at the center of the universe with the stars and planets orbiting around it each day. The heavenly bodies, they thought, were gods (angels in Christian and Islamic versions) attached to invisible crystal spheres that nested around the earth.

Once Greeks started trying to reduce this view to a mathematical model, the philosopher Aristarchus (third century BCE) pointed out that a model in which the Earth, with the other planets, orbits the sun (heliocentrism) is simpler. However, this did not prevail over what seemed to be obvious evidence of the senses that the earth does not move. In the second century, an astronomer named Claudius Ptolemy published the definitive mathematical description of geocentrism that endured as the standard model in the West and in the Islamic world until the sixteenth century. The most obvious difficulty with this model is that the planets do not simply move in a circular fashion across the sky. To explain observed details like retrograde motion (when a planet moves from west to east), Ptolemy had to assume that each planet was attached to its sphere by a complicated system of epicycles, little spheres that rotated at different speeds, in different directions, and on different axes. Posthumously published in 1543, Nicolaus Copernicus's *On the Revolutions of the Celestial Spheres* suggested that a heliocentric model required fewer epicycles to predict planetary motions and would thus make the casting of horoscopes (the sole purpose to which this kind of learning was so far put) much simpler.

Once telescopic astronomy began, however, around 1600, particularly in the work of one of its early pioneers, Galileo Galilei, it soon became obvious that the planets were indeed physical objects with disks that could be resolved just like those of the sun and moon and that Jupiter, at least, had moons of its own. No epicycles were in sight, however, so Galileo made the conjecture that the solar system is indeed actually heliocentric. The Catholic Church objected to this view on theological grounds. Galileo made the mistake of trying to justify his views through the interpretation of biblical texts, and church officials put him under house arrest and ordered him to quit publishing, though he continued to do so

" THE LONG TRADITION OF DENIAL AND
MINIMIZATION ABOUT DONNE AND THE NEW
ASTRONOMY SEEMS TO COME FROM A DESIRE TO
SEE AN ADMIRED POET STAND ON THE RIGHT SIDE
OF HISTORY."

through presses in the Protestant Netherlands, to which the authorities turned a blind eye. Astronomers in Protestant Europe quickly embraced heliocentrism, and by 1615, Johannes Kepler had worked out that the orbits of the planets were not circular, but elliptical, which did away once and for all with the epicycles and left no reasonable doubt about the truth of heliocentrism. The final blow against epicycles was the observation that the paths of comets (long thought to have been phenomena inside the atmosphere like lightning) actually moved through the orbits of the planets, making the idea of crystal spheres impossible.

In 1611, Donne wrote a satire against the new astronomy entitled *Ignatius His Conclave*. It is also a viciously abusive anti-Catholic work, depicting Ignatius Loyola, the founder of the Jesuit order, as a scheming monster worse than Satan who is exiled from hell to the moon in order to save the entire cosmic order. In this framework, Donne inserts his own views on the new astronomy. The text's narrative takes place in a literal special place in hell reserved for anyone who "attempted any innovation in this life that they gave an affront to all antiquity, and induced doubts and anxieties and scruples, and, after a liberty of believing what they would, at length established opinions directly contrary to all established before." Donne leaves no doubt that this means the proponents of the new astronomy, because he has Copernicus himself come and ask for admittance into this realm. Donne makes it clear that he considers Copernicus guilty of sins of cosmic proportions. Donne has the devil judge say in regard to Copernicus: "nor did he think that himself had attempted greater matters before his fall." He is equally hostile to Galileo (whose trial for heresy would not come until 1615), dismissing telescopic astronomy as having the audacity to summon holy angels to come and give an account of themselves.

Donne's rejection, and even opposition, to the new astronomy could hardly be clearer. Yet the modern scholarly reactions to Donne's views are nothing if not muddled. The highly unorthodox 1957 article of William Empson, "Donne the Space Man," which has had a major influence on much later work, simply denies that Donne did anything other than wholeheartedly accept the new astronomy. Empson also suggests that Donne accepted Giordano Bruno's doctrine of the plurality of worlds (i.e., that each star is a sun with its own planets, as is now known to be generally true, which in the seventeenth century could only be speculation) and suggested on his own that each planet would have its own intelligent race needing its own incarnation of Jesus and that physical travel to these planets was possible. It is hard to know how Empson came to read these views into Donne (in part he is confusing mystical ascent with flight in rockets), but Empson is only a more extreme example of a long tradition in Donne scholarship.

In the nineteenth century, Edmund Gosse, in his *The Life and Letters of John Donne*, was happy to ignore the scathing irony in *Ignatius His Conclave* to actually interpret the (literal) damning of Galileo as if Donne were praising him. Even a more moderate form of this tradition, as voiced by Lawrence Lipking in his 2014 *What Galileo Saw*, treats Donne as simply skeptical, as if the "skeptical" view is the one supporting an entrenched traditional orthodoxy protected by the most conservative institutions in a culture against a flood of new, verifiable, incontrovertible evidence. The first full corrective to this tradition comes only with works like Catherine Gimelli Martin's 2014 essay "Milton's and Donne's Stargazing Lovers."

The long tradition of denial and minimization about Donne and the new astronomy seems to come from a desire to see an admired poet stand on the right side of history. However, Donne is quite determined in his opposition. To Donne's mind, to the degree the new astronomy overturned the Ptolemaic system, it threatened to wipe away all religion and thereby all society. Because he believes in the biblical doctrine of the Fall (the idea that human beings are inherently evil because, at the time they did not know right from wrong, Adam and Eve allowed themselves to be deceived by the serpent in the Garden of Eden), Donne thinks it is only the fear of hell that keeps people from killing and robbing at will. In *Ignatius His*

Conclave, Donne spells out his fears for the world if the new astronomy is true when he has Loyola ask the devil, "do they, out of this motion of the earth, conclude that there is no Hell, or deny the punishment of sin?" If people ever do that, Donne thinks, the world will be doomed. In his later poem "An Anatomy of the World," Donne implies that new scientific discoveries like heliocentrism and atomism will destroy civilization. The social order will vanish and with it all ties between human beings and even between family members. If the Earth moves, Donne asks, why would a son honor his father or a slave honor his master (a reference to Malachi 1:6)? Many people react to change with this kind of fear, but so far, change has never produced this kind of result.

In "Love's Growth" Donne revisits, as he frequently does in his poetry, his denial of heliocentrism and the new astronomy. The main theme of the second stanza of "Love's Growth" is a detailed attack against several recent discoveries. He does not offer any evidence against them but simply gainsays them. In the opening lines, Donne describes the sky as a *firmament*, which is a common poetic term borrowed from the King James Bible (1604). However, given Donne's rejection of the new astronomy, it must be a reference to the solid crystalline spheres of the Ptolemaic universe (as it would certainly have been in older authors). In Genesis, the term *firmament* is a translation of the Hebrew *rakia*, which meant the solid dome that covers the flat earth, but Donne is happy with its early Christian or Ptolemaic interpretation.

Donne supposes that stars do not shine by their own light but by the reflection of sunlight. This is a direct denial of the new star observed (1604) and published on (*De Stella Nova*, 1606) by Johannes Kepler. In the Ptolemaic system, such a bright new star would be impossible, as Donne makes a point of reminding the reader in the poem. In fact, Kepler carried out the first scientific observations of a supernova, observations that were corroborated by many contemporary astronomers. The supernova remnant of the event is still visible to modern telescopes. Donne also claims that stars cannot change size any more than they can brightness. This is a direct denial of the telescopic observations that Galileo and others had been making over the previous decade which not only revealed the phases of Venus, but for the first time resolved the disks of the planets,

The final lines of the poem suggest that once love has grown strong, not even the cold of winter can cool its warmth. (© *Pixeljoy | Shutterstock.com*)

which indeed change in apparent size as they move closer or further from the earth.

A bit later (lines 23 and 24), Donne rolls out the traditional Ptolemaic description of the universe as a series of nested concentric spheres centered around the earth (or more precisely centered around his lover, who is, of course, on the earth). Donne is also careful to point out that there is only one heaven, that is, one solar system, contained within the fixed stars, which are objects suspended on the interior surface of the seventh crystal sphere, and, as he thinks, shining by reflected sunlight and certainly no larger than planets. This is a denial of the doctrine of the plurality of worlds, the possibility, still far on the fringe of the new astronomy, that each star might be a sun with its own planetary system. In "Love's Growth" Donne revisits in an offhand matter the same polemic he had made explicit in *Ignatius His Conclave*, assuming the truth of geocentrism the same way he assumes that trees bud in the spring but on considerably less evidence.

> IT REVERSES THE PATTERN OF MANY OF THE
> SO-CALLED CYNICAL POEMS, WHICH BEGIN WITH
> DECEPTIVE PRAISE OR TRUST, TO MOVE DISTURB-
> INGLY INTO REJECTION. THE FALSE START HERE
> BELONGS TO A FINE BLEND OF LEVITY AND DEEP
> GRAVITY WHICH MARKS THE WHOLE POEM."

Source: Bradley A. Skeen, Critical Essay on "Love's Growth," in *Poetry for Students*, Gale, Cengage Learning, 2016.

Barbara Hardy

In the following excerpt, Hardy explains how "Love's Growth" displays Donne's wit.

...Two quotations from Donne will be more economical than any reminders of T. S. Eliot on the united sensibility. In *The Progresse of the Soule* Donne speaks of "the tender well-arm'd feeling braine" and in "The Blossome" of "A naked thinking heart." These phrases perfectly express what we can call the "interinanimation" of passions and intellect. They draw attention, or may be used to draw attention, to the nakedness and vulnerability which we feel in some of these poems. History, psychology, and moral judgment are bypassed, we are strongly rooted in present time, the stress and rush of feeling is preserved, not lost to the "commanding judgment": accordingly, we have a special sense of the exposure of human beings in their relationships. This is a feeling which also forms part of the response to Shakespeare's sonnets, for instance, or to Lawrence's *Ship of Death* poems; and in these works is found the other quality which is central to Donne, the sense of pride, triumph, delight and power, felt by the artist but on behalf of a prowess and energy larger than the experience of art. Donne answers beautifully to Coleridge's description of Shakespearean wit as the overflow of artistic power, creativity exulting and scattering its energies, in a virtuosity which is never merely virtuosity.

"Love's Growth" shows Donne's wit, seriousness, sensuousness, profundity, and play. It is a restrained, though not narrow poem, remembered for its assertion that "Love's not so pure, and abstract, as they use / To say, which have no Mistresse but their Muse," a couplet no reader or critic of Donne can afford to forget. If we try to describe the tones of feeling we find that the beginning of the first stanza is deceptively and teasingly cynical, drily beginning, "I scarce beleeve my love to be so pure" and not revealing its certainty and praise until the end of the sixth line. It reverses the pattern of many of the so-called cynical poems, which begin with deceptive praise or trust, to move disturbingly into rejection. The false start here belongs to a fine blend of levity and deep gravity which marks the whole poem. It is a poem which seems surprised by joy, and permitted by surprise and joy to play, delightedly and exhilaratingly:

> I scarce beleeve my love to be so pure
> As I had thought it was,
> Because it doth endure
> Vicissitude, and season, as the grasse;
> Me thinkes I lyed all winter, when I swore,
> My love was infinite, if spring make'it more.

This upward lift, from play to seriousness, is something that recurs through the poem, but one of the things that Donne teaches his reader is the danger of so fixing patterns of feeling. There are the recurring upward movements, but their differences are as important as their resemblances. The poem's second movement of rising is one which depends more on a contrast of images than on a suspension of argument. And the range of feeling covered is individual; the quick, almost painful glance at love's pain is remarkable for its stabbing brevity, and is present rather in the aside or parenthesis that insists on taking in the whole truth, than in any bold antithetical relation to the health, energy, and joy in the sun's "working vigour." The first stanza continues:

> But if this medicine, love, which cures all sorrow
> With more, not onely bee no quintessence,
> But mixt of all stuffes, paining soule, or sense,
> And of the Sunne his working vigour borrow,
> Love's not so pure, and abstract, as they use
> To say, which have no Mistresse but their Muse,
> But as all else, being elemented too,
> Love sometimes would contemplate, sometimes do.

The third upward lift, in these final four lines, is again new, being altogether lighter, more amused than anything we have had up to now, and concluding in the blunt simplicity of "do" with that kind of rough "masculine" force so characteristic of the third, eighteenth and nineteenth *Elegies*. The heart of the poem seems to lie in the beginning of the second stanza, where the upward movement is most whole and most joyous:

> And yet not greater, but more eminent,
> Love by the spring is growne;
> As, in the firmament,
> Starres by the Sunne are not inlarg'd, but showne.
> Gentle love deeds, as blossomes on a bough,
> From loves awaken'd root do bud out now.

The movement here is a gentle stir, like the particular sexual movement which is being invoked. It seems to emerge from the movement from argument and scientific example, that of stars and sun, to the natural and self-evident comparison with blossom; from the tiny lift from simile (blossoms) to metaphor (root) which seems to blur the metaphorical into the literal; and from the emphasis on the gentle stirring after the vigour, working, and "doing" of the previous stanza. In the concluding lines of the poem, there is a change from sensuousness to formality; generalisation and argument. Such a change is appropriate to the enlargement of time in the look at the future of winter and other springs, and the enlargement of scale in the look at the public world. We move into a new thought, that of a continuing increase through the years, and a new claim, purchased after a harder look at the seasonal conceit and a refusal to take the calendar's analogy too literally. There is also the vigorous new spurt of wit in the ironic joke about taxes; an unflattering argument, this, but immediately followed by the serene and grave assurance of the last line:

> And though each spring doe adde to love new heate,
> As princes doe in times of action get
> New taxes, and remit them not in peace,
> No winter shall abate the springs encrease.

Each lifting motion is distinct, the whole poem consisting of a series of separated lifts, climbing like a smooth moving-stair. But we should be giving a very abstract account of the lyrical movement unless we said that there the praises, claims, and vows, are made in markedly differing moods, teasing, playful, witty, moving up to and away from the poem's heart, where the feeling is most sensuous, most gentle, most creative of beauty. The softness here seems to create a special intimacy, despite the total lack of personal address, and the intimate impression is ensured by the final movement into a larger area of wit and reference. The poem seems to achieve its unity by a final triumphant reach towards new and disparate material, ending on a flourish and a reassurance.

It is a staggering example of Donne's capacity for dropping and picking up wit and fancy, or, to put it another way, for using flights of wit and fancy audaciously, simply, and always passionately. His love-lyrics, like love, are eloquent both in extravagance and restraint. The quietest and most peaceful part of this poem depends on the surrounding vigour. It depends too on that literal invocation of the seasons with which the poem begins. The real world of nature is undescribed but taken for granted in the quiet references to "season" and "the grasse," which have not only the air of assuming what is present but also of assuming every man's common experience, every man's spring after his winter. But nature becomes more particularised in the sun's "working vigour" and the imagery of stars, blossom, bough, and root. It is not very easy to say how the particularity is created, since there is no description, and all the natural items are barely mentioned, neither elaborated or personified. Donne seems to interinanimate human nature and the larger vegetable and mineral world of the spring by blending his appreciation of both worlds. He rejoices in the sun's working vigour and the gentleness of the growth of flowers, blurring simile into metaphor by the spread of feeling for the beauty and tenderness of human sex and the beauty and tenderness of non-human fertility. The phallic feeling in "loves awakened root" is astonishingly gentle, and belongs to a quiet feeling for the body's movement which is continued in the "stir'd" of the water's ripples. The poem creates a rare impression by its very familiar seasonal image, succeeding in using the sun, flower, and water to enlarge, define and praise sexuality, but also in bestowing a sexual beauty on the non-human world. In the "working vigour" and in "loves awaken'd root" there is a phallic beauty which seems to appreciate the phenomenal world, and to convey an impression of unity and kinship. This sense of fusion is not only an imaginative achievement, in the most precise sense of the term, but a proof, palpable and splendid, of the poem's hopeful celebration of love's growth.

It is not a hopeful salute to wholeness made at the expense of dispassionate wisdom. The winter life, the public world, the future seasons, are all there too, not only because, as Empson reminds us, things suggest their opposites but because Donne's frequent achievement is to remind us of opposition. He is always aware of the rest of experience, can combine passionate with dispassionate appraisal. Such acknowledgement of the other side of celebration is there in the sidelook at love's pain, which cures sorrow "with more." It is there too in the last airy flight of wit, which creates a movement away from the intimate physical tenderness into the ordinary testing world, a flight earned and licensed by assurance and delight. On reflection, the final excursion seems also to continue the proof that love is "mixt of all stuffes." Donne's love-poetry, like love, is mixed of "all stuffes," embracing aesthetic praise, sexual energy, urgency, gentleness, rest, ease, bluntness, gravity, play. Like so much great poetry, this is a poem aware of itself; its image of the water's spreading ripples applies to the poem's own outward reach and centre, its circles being also "all concentrique." . . .

Source: Barbara Hardy, "Thinking and Feeling in the Songs and Sonnets," in *John Donne: Essays in Celebration*, edited by A. J. Smith, Methuen, 1972, pp. 74–79.

SOURCES

Augustine, *The Literal Meaning of Genesis*, translated by John Hammond Taylor, Paulist, Vol. 1, 1982, pp. 42–43.

Bucciantini, Massimo, Michele Camerota, and Franco Giudice, *Galileo's Telescope: A European Story*, translated by Catherine Bolton, Harvard University Press, 2015, pp. 129–54.

Donne, John, "Ignatius His Conclave," in *John Donne: The Major Works*, edited by John Carey, Oxford University Press, 1990. pp. 202–205.

———, "Love's Growth," in *The Songs and Sonnets of John Donne*, edited by Theodore Redpath, Harvard University Press, 2009, p. 215.

Eliot, T. S., "The Metaphysical Poets," in *Selected Prose of T. S. Eliot*, edited by Frank Kermode, Harcourt, 1975, pp. 59–67.

Empson, William, "Donne the Space Man," in *Kenyon Review*, Vol. 19, No. 3, 1957, pp. 337–39.

Gosse, Edmund, *The Life and Letters of John Donne*, Vol. 1, Dodd, Mead, 1899, pp. 257–58.

Hassel, R. Chris, "Donne's 'Ignatius His Conclave' and the New Astronomy," in *Modern Philology*, Vol. 68, No. 4, 1971, pp. 329–37.

Johnson, Samuel, *The Lives of the English Poets*, Vol. 1, J. F. Dove, 1826, pp. 17–18.

Lipking, Lawerence, *What Galileo Saw: Imagining the Scientific Revolution*, Cornell University Press, 2014, pp. 204–206.

Martin, Catherine Gimelli, "Milton's and Donne's Stargazing Lovers, Sex, and the New Astronomy," in *Studies in English Literature 1500–1900*, Vol. 54, No. 1, 2014, pp. 143–71.

Plato, *Symposium*, in *The Collected Dialogues of Plato*, edited by Edith Hamilton and Huntington Cairns, Princeton University Press, 1961, pp. 527–74.

Post, Jonathan F. S., "Donne's Life: A Sketch," in *The Cambridge Companion to John Donne*, edited by Achsah Guibbory, Cambridge University Press, 2006, pp. 1–22.

Powrie, Sarah, "Transposing World Harmony: Donne's Creation Poetics in the Context of a Medieval Tradition," in *Studies in Philology*, Vol. 107, No. 2, 2010, pp. 212–35.

Walton, Isaac, "Life of Dr. John Donne," in *Lives*, George Routledge and Sons, 1888, pp. 15–78.

FURTHER READING

Bunyan, John, *The Pilgrim's Progress*, edited by W. R. Owens, Oxford University Press, 2009.

> Originally published in 1678, *Pilgrim's Progress* is a Christian allegory of a journey finally leading to heaven. Distinct from most of Donne's work, *Pilgrim's Progress* has no Neoplatonic themes.

Donne, John, *Selections from Divine Poems, Sermons, Devotions and Prayers*, edited by John E. Booty, Paulist, 1990.

> This collection concentrates especially on the sacred prose that Donne produced in his professional capacity as the dean of St. Paul's.

Hester, M. Thomas, ed., *John Donne's "Desire of More": The Subject of Anne More Donne in His Poetry*, University of Delaware Press, 1996.

> Donne's lover in "Love's Growth," since the affair seemingly lasts for years, may reasonably be taken to be his wife, though, given her poor development, she could well be a stock character typical of Donne's early libertine poetry. In any case, light is thrown on the subject by this collection of essays that deal with Donne's wife in his poetry.

Saunders, Ben, *Desiring Donne: Poetry, Sexuality, Interpretation*, Harvard University Press, 2006.

> This recent study of Donne's poetry explores the reconciliation of opposites in Donne's metaphysical conceits as a dialectical process and situates Donne in newly popular topics of criticism such as gender studies and the history of sexuality.

SUGGESTED SEARCH TERMS

John Donne

Love's Growth AND Donne

metaphysical poets

new astronomy

platonic love

Ignatius His Conclave

Nicolaus Copernicus

Johannes Kepler

Galileo

Please Fire Me

DEBORAH GARRISON

1998

Deborah Garrison's career seems to be filled with contradiction. She worked as a senior editor for the *New Yorker* before moving on to the position of poetry editor for Knopf, a prestigious American publishing company, particularly in the genre of poetry. She takes her editing job seriously and also pursues her creative side by writing poetry, yet in 2000, Garrison told Dana Jennings of the *New York Times*: "My own poetry is irrelevant to my role as an editor. My book would never have been on the Knopf list." It seems a strange statement for an artist—to almost dismiss her own writing as something that she herself would not publish. Critical reaction to her work is also contradictory, with some well-known critics praising her work and others panning it. However, the accessibility of her style has made her popular with readers. Her first collection sold thirty thousand copies—ten times the sales of many Pulitzer Prize–winning poets.

Garrison has dedicated much of her life to her love of verse, both as an editor and as a poet. Her first collection, *A Working Girl Can't Win and Other Poems* (1998), is a wry look at the working world from a woman's point of view. However, she did not publish anything for almost ten years after its publication, and in the themes of her second collection, *The Second Child* (2008), she left the working world behind, focusing instead on themes of family. In "Please Fire Me," which is included in *A Working Girl*

Deborah Garrison *(© Getty Images)*

Can't Win, the speaker expresses her frustration about her coworkers. The arrogant men who try to dominate the office bear the brunt of her criticism, but she also touches on the flighty, fussy behavior of some of her female office mates. "Please Fire Me" ends with a touch of humor, which contributes to her accessible style.

AUTHOR BIOGRAPHY

Garrison was born Deborah Gottlieb on February 12, 1965, in Ann Arbor, Michigan, where she grew up. She was the second of three children in the family—all girls. While Garrison was in high school, she experienced several life-changing events. First, her father passed away when she was fourteen years old. Second, she met Matt Garrison, who would later become her husband. Finally, she discovered poetry.

After high-school graduation, Garrison enrolled at Brown University and earned a bachelor's degree in creative writing. While still an undergraduate, she served as an intern for the *New Yorker* and was hired for a full-time position immediately upon graduating, when she married her high-school sweetheart. In the more than ten years when she was working at the *New Yorker*, Garrison composed the poems that appear in her first collection, *A Working Girl*

Can't Win and Other Poems (1998), which includes "Please Fire Me." The book received fairly negative critical reviews but sold remarkably well.

In spite of her first book's popular success, Garrison did not write more poems for several years because she and her husband decided to start a family. In order to have a more flexible schedule, Garrison left the weekly deadlines of the *New Yorker* behind and found a position as poetry editor for Knopf, one of the most influential and respected publishers of poetry in the United States. She and her husband also moved out of Manhattan and into a house in family-friendly Montclair, New Jersey, where they still live. As of 2015, Garrison is still juggling her work—both as an editor and as a poet—and time spent with her husband and their three children: Daisy, Georgia, and Walter.

POEM SUMMARY

The text used for this summary is from *A Working Girl Can't Win and Other Poems*, Random House, 1998, pp. 37–38. Versions of the poem can be found on the following web pages: http://www.wenaus.com/poetry/please-fire-me.html and https://workinggirlsonoverload.wordpress.com/2011/11/30/a-working-girl-cant-win-a-poem-by-deborah-garrison/.

Stanza 1

The speaker compares her male coworkers with animals. Lines 1 and 2 bring to mind theories of the social structure of wolf packs in which a single male gains dominance over all of the other members of the pack because of his superior intelligence and strength. Garrison introduces a different metaphor in lines 3 and 4 with the image of an animal, such as a horse or a bull, striking its hooves on the ground in challenge and raising a cloud of dirt.

Stanza 2

The second stanza compares the speaker's female coworkers with chickens, making them somewhat ridiculous. They pace uselessly on shaking feet. All of the adjectives used to describe them contribute to a sense of flightiness and weakness, especially in comparison with the strength and determination stressed in stanza 1. The final line of stanza 2 hints that the birdlike coworkers react

MEDIA ADAPTATIONS

- Garrison read a selection of poems from *A Working Girl Can't Win and Other Poems*, including "Please Fire Me," during an interview with Bill Moyers (http://billmoyers.com/content/sounds-of-poetry-poet-deborah-garrison/).

- A video of Garrison reading several of her poems from her collection *The Second Child* is available at https://www.youtube.com/watch?v=nPM3X8f8NdY.

to the actions of others rather than taking the initiative themselves; they chatter about the disturbance caused by the "alphas."

Stanza 3

The speaker focuses on a particular type of male coworker. He is successful, but the speaker clearly disapproves of his methods of achieving that success. He makes deals while at business lunches, consuming large quantities of alcohol while charming his clients to get what he wants.

Stanza 4

The behavior of the "alpha" disgusts the speaker. She marvels that she must act agreeable and supportive to such men if she wants to keep her position, because men like him hold all of the power in the company. In stanza 4's final line, however, the speaker makes it clear that she is fed up with the situation. This final line grammatically carries over into the next line, connecting its ideas into the next stanza.

Stanza 5

The second line of stanza 5 introduces the image of a hen sitting on its nest, which reflects the speaker's feeling that staying in her job requires her to emulate the behavior of her chicken-like coworkers. She rejects the option of continuing to behave in such a manner, just as she rejects having to set aside her sense of self. Up to now,

she has kept her cool in the face of the problems and frustrations of her job and office politics by maintaining a disconnect and relaxation that she compares with the state of peace achieved through meditation in Zen Buddhism.

Stanza 6

The speaker fantasizes about leaving her job, though perhaps she is not ready to leave quite yet. Rather, she is expressing her longing for a different set of working conditions. The final line of the poem is almost a punch line; the speaker wants to leave and find a better place, and she jokes that she does not mean taking a vacation on another continent. She is hoping for a true departure—a real change in the established gender roles in office politics.

THEMES

Female-Male Relations

In "Please Fire Me," Garrison sets up a clear division between the men and women in the office setting of the poem. Men are bold but arrogant, as illustrated by the comparisons to alpha wolves and other dominant animals. The speaker's disapproval of this behavior is evident in stanza 3, and one can assume that she would conduct herself differently if she were in charge of business negotiations. However, Garrison makes it clear that the speaker in the poem feels contempt for her female coworkers as well. They are compared to chickens, submissive and inadequate, and in line 18, the speaker declares herself finished with tending the nest. She does not seem optimistic about what would happen if she were to express her disapproval of the alpha males. Indeed, she believes she must continue to sympathize with them if she wants to keep her job. Garrison sees that for real change to occur, both men and women would have to make significant changes in their behavior: the men must give up their boys'-club, wolf-pack mentality, and the women must be more assertive. Garrison relies on generalizations in setting up these gender roles. It is unlikely that every man in her office was an obnoxious alpha businessman and just as unlikely that every woman was an ineffectual, tittering hen, but by using these stereotypes, Garrison is able to communicate the speaker's impatience in relatively few words.

TOPICS FOR FURTHER STUDY

- Read Garrison's poem "The Boss," which, like "Please Fire Me," touches on her years working in a Manhattan office. Think about how the character of the boss is described compared with the "alphas" that populate "Please Fire Me." Which poem do you think is more realistic in portraying the conditions of a busy office? Which poem is better at communicating its themes? Write an essay in which you compare the two poems, analyzing these questions as well as Garrison's style in each and how she characterizes the people she mentions.

- Gather other poems about workplaces and working life. Make a website on which you post links to several of these poems along with a brief analysis of why you find each one interesting. Invite your classmates to comment on your choices and add poems of their own.

- Read *Bucking the Sarge* (2004), by Christopher Paul Curtis, which was chosen as the year's best young-adult novel by the American Library Association in 2005. The protagonist of the story is high-school student Luther, who gets his first job in the group home that his mother runs while struggling to come up with a project that will win him the school science fair for the third year in a row. As you read, think about how Luther reacts to the responsibilities and people at his workplace. Write a poem from Luther's point of view that mimics the style of "Please Fire Me" and illustrates how he feels about his job.

- Garrison has said, in an interview with Dana Jennings for the *New York Times*, that as an editor for Knopf, she feels a great responsibility to the world of poetry, hoping to encourage more people to read poetry and learn to love it. However, poetry does not make money: most publishers feel fortunate when sales of a poetry collection are enough to pay for its publication, and poets rarely earn more than a few thousand dollars for a book. Using print and online resources, research how many previously unpublished poets have their work accepted by major publishing houses. Do you think that publishers should use their profits from other publications to subsidize books like poetry collections? Do you support the use of federal funds, like grants from the National Endowment for the Arts, to support art forms that are not financially profitable? Stage a debate with a group of your classmates in which one side argues for supporting the arts for the sake of public enrichment and the other side argues that popular, profitable works stand on their own merit and more obscure works should have to do the same.

Frustration

Throughout "Please Fire Me," the speaker is clearly frustrated by the behavior of her cow-orkers. In the central image of the alpha businessman, Garrison shows a macho posturing and arrogance so extreme that it makes the speaker ill, as she explains in line 13. The question that appears in the following two lines also highlights the speaker's disgust for the alpha; the fact that it is a question reflects her disbelief that she must tolerate his behavior, or even seem to support it, if she wants to keep her job.

The speaker is also frustrated with the behavior of the women in the office. In fact, they come off worse than the men. They are compared to hens, submissive and ridiculous, whereas the animal metaphors used for the men at least reflect some strength and purpose. The speaker's frustration also comes through in stanzas 4 and 5, in which she declares she is finished with behaving like a chicken and with letting her frustration roll off her with hard-won indifference.

Unfortunately, it seems the speaker's frustration is not yet over. The final stanza hints that

Garrison presents an image of the stereotypical American business worker, a "man's man" who is charming but self-centered. (© Nejron Photo | Shutterstock.com)

she is not going to immediately quit her job. She wishes she could find a better place, but she is not leaving yet. Lines 21 and 22 seem wistful, but the sarcastic humor in the poem's final two lines suggest that the speaker is resigned to staying in her job a bit longer but frustrated that it is necessary.

STYLE

Free Verse

Free verse is poetry without a consistent arrangement of rhyme or meter (*meter* is the pattern of stressed and unstressed syllables in poetry). "Please Fire Me" is written in free verse, though at first glance it might appear to be a traditional poetic form, with its orderly, four-line stanzas. Also, the first line of the poem has a regular meter: it is made up of four iambic feet (an

iamb is a two-syllable metric foot with the first syllable unstressed and the second syllable stressed). In the second half of the poem's second line, however, the pattern of syllables becomes irregular, and the remainder of the poem has no clear rhythm.

The poem does contain some rhyming words, but often rather than placing them at the ends of lines, as with more traditional poetic forms, Garrison uses internal rhyme. For example, in stanza 4 the second line ends with *eyes*, and the rhyming word *sympathize* appears as the second word in the next line. The rhyme even jumps from stanza to stanza; *liquor* in the third line of stanza 3 rhymes with *sicker* in the first line of stanza 4.

As a poet, Garrison feels that poetry should be accessible to all readers rather than being overly formal, structured, and difficult to understand. She explained her philosophy of simplicity to the *Writer's Almanac*, asking herself, "Could I make poetry out of the materials of our everyday life and conversation?" Garrison's free-verse style contributes to the casual, almost conversational voice in her work.

Metaphor

A metaphor is the comparison of two unlike things used to create a verbal picture. Garrison uses metaphors in "Please Fire Me" to explain the behavior of the people she describes in the office setting. In the first stanza, she includes images that bring to mind dominant male animals. Line 3 of stanza 1 describes an animal *pawing* at the ground, like a stallion or a bull about to charge. In the poem's first two lines, Garrison introduces the idea of the alpha wolf, an image that is repeated in stanza 3.

Theoretically, the alpha is the wolf that leads the pack, having gained and defended his dominance over the others through his superior strength. Though recent research has called this hypothesis regarding wolf behavior into question, the metaphor is firmly ingrained in the popular imagination, and there are countless articles in newspapers and business magazines advising workers how to be successful in their careers by imitating an alpha wolf. This is a concept of central importance to the poem, and it is the stereotype of the arrogant "alpha" businessman that disgusts the speaker. Stanza 3 gives the details of the behavior of this particular type of male coworker. He is a hard-drinking, take-charge kind of guy. He can be charming, but, at least to the speaker, his charm rings false because he uses it only to achieve his goals.

In contrast to the dominant male is his female counterpart. Stanza 2 focuses on a negative female stereotype: the fussy office worker with high-heeled shoes, like the clawed toes of birds. Garrison compares these women to chickens, silly chattering creatures. They are flighty and weak in comparison with the strong, if brutal, metaphors used for the men.

With her choice of metaphors, Garrison relies, in part, on gender stereotypes: the men have the urge to dominate and throw their weight around, while the women are more reactionary, fussing at disruptions to their quiet, orderly world. However, by comparing people to animals, Garrison shows that their motives contradict the workers' civilized veneer: in the competitive business world, people act on the most basic of animal instincts.

HISTORICAL CONTEXT

Women in the Workforce

Throughout the twentieth century, women made huge strides forward in the working world. In the early part of the century, most women did not work outside the home or perhaps worked only until they were married, but by the century's close, most women worked. The 1960s, 1970s, and 1980s were, in particular, decades of great change. The number of women working outside the home increased from approximately 34 percent in the 1950s to 74 percent in 1990. The 1963 Equal Pay Act required that men and women be given equal compensation in terms of salary and other benefits (such as overtime pay, bonuses, insurance, vacation time, etc.), giving legal recourse to women being paid less for doing the same job as a man. Women's salaries today still lag behind men's, but the difference is less: in 1964 a woman earned, on average, 59 cents to a man's dollar, whereas in 2015 that figure has risen to almost 80 cents.

However, in the 1990s, when Garrison was working for the *New Yorker* and writing the poems included in *A Working Girl Can't Win and Other Poems*, the rate of progress for American women in the workforce began to slow. A study by Francine D. Blau and Lawrence M. Kahn examining the entry of women into the labor force in twenty-two developed countries showed that in the United States, 74 percent of women worked in 1990, but two decades later that number had risen only to just above 75 percent. In contrast, in other countries, the percentage of women who worked rose from approximately 67 percent to almost 80 percent—a far greater change. Blau and Kahn determined that other countries did more to help women enter the workforce than the United States, which falls behind in terms of public spending on child care, as well as the regulations governing parental leave and part-time work.

The difference between helpful legislation for working parents in the United States versus other nations highlights another issue that working women struggle with: trying to find balance between family and career. Garrison's personal choices reflect the juggling act many women face; she left her high-pressure job at the *New Yorker* to allow time in her schedule for family commitments when she started her family. Though most women today work full time, they carry more of the burden of child care and household duties than men.

COMPARE
&
CONTRAST

- **1990s:** There is a large contrast between the salaries of men and women. Women's salaries have increased in the last fifteen years from approximately 60 percent of what men earn for an equivalent job to approximately 70 percent.

  Today: There is still a difference between men's and women's salaries. Women earn slightly less than 80 percent what men earn for an equivalent job. The Institute for Women's Policy Research estimates that at the current rate of change in salaries, true salary equality will not be reached until 2058.

- **1990s:** Women make up approximately 45 percent of the workforce, but of the Fortune 500 companies (the five hundred largest US companies, as ranked by *Fortune* magazine), only one has a female chief executive officer (CEO) in 1998.

  Today: Women are still approximately 45 percent of the workforce, but the number of Fortune 500 companies with female CEOs has increased to twenty-four, which is

approximately 5 percent. The number of women on corporate boards of US companies has stayed at approximately 17 percent for the last decade.

- **1990s:** Sexual harassment in the workplace, including both unwanted sexual advances and a generally hostile environment, is increasingly punished in court and by public disapproval. In 1998, for example, the federal Equal Employment Opportunity Commission (EEOC) wins a class-action lawsuit against Mitsubishi Motor Manufacturing, resulting in millions of dollars in fines and awards to employees and substantial revisions to company policies.

  Today: Sexual harassment remains a problem in the workplace. However, awareness of legal protections is greater, and many companies have internal policies to address the issue. The EEOC receives fewer than twelve thousand charges in 2010, down from nearly sixteen thousand in 1997.

In a 2013 survey carried out by the Pew Research Center, women were approximately three times as likely as men (51 versus 16 percent) to respond that being a parent made advancing in their career more difficult. While only 28 percent of working fathers indicated that they had reduced their workload at some point in their careers to care for a family member, 42 percent of working mothers said they had done so. Working mothers were far more likely to quit their jobs for family reasons as well: 27 percent versus only 10 percent of working fathers. Unmarried mothers, who lead approximately 25 percent of households today, face additional salary disparity: according to the US Department of Labor they earn on average $575 weekly, considerably less than the average $768 earned by married mothers and the average $706 earned by women overall.

Race also plays a role in the struggles of working women. In 2004, 39 percent of white women and 44 percent of Asian women worked in professional, management, and related occupations. However, only 31 percent of African American women and 22 percent of Latinas worked in such fields. In 2005, the average hourly wage for all women was $12.50, but almost 60 percent of African American women and 67 percent of Hispanic women earned lower hourly rates. Even a decade later, women are much more likely to live in poverty than men, and minority women are even more at risk.

As of 2015, women make up almost half the workforce. They earn more college degrees than men. Of all American households, 40 percent have a woman as the sole or primary breadwinner for the family as opposed to only 11 percent

The speaker is tired of the posturing of "alpha males" in the workplace. (© Andrey_Popov | Shutterstock.com)

in 1960. These data give a clear picture of the changes over the last fifty years. However, there is still that gender disparity regarding salary. Women earn less in almost every occupation. Some experts believe that the reduction in the difference between men's and women's salaries is not due to women's salaries increasing, because recently women's wages have not been proportional to the rate of inflation. Instead, the gap has been reduced because men's average wages are falling as a result of economic recession.

CRITICAL OVERVIEW

Garrison's poetry has garnered very different reactions from readers and critics. The extraordinary sales of her first collection, *A Working Girl Can't Win and Other Poems* (1998), make her popular success clear. About thirty thousand copies of the book sold—an extraordinary number considering that many award-winning poets sell one-tenth as many copies.

However, many in the literary world blasted Garrison's work. A *Library Journal* review allows that Garrison "entertains, but shallowly" (quoted by Jennings in the *New York Times*). Michael Winerip of the *New York Times* relates how the "*Village Voice* suggested that Ms. Garrison might have produced the first volume of poetry that could be turned into a sitcom," and William Logan, a winner of the National Book Critics Circle Award in criticism, seems to agree. He writes in *New Criterion*, "Garrison understands the emotions of city life, but not that having emotions isn't the same as writing poems (most of her poems seem like ad layouts for poems)." Logan declares that although "Garrison's poems touch the surface of suffering, of lost chance and lost love," they only "gossip about it" with the "hapless phrasings of a beginner ... while adding a cheery self-hatred and self-pity of her very own."

Not all critics are so harsh. In *Poetry Nation Review*, David C. Ward writes that the poems in *The Second Child* are "deeply felt" and calls Garrison "an acute observer." Novelist, poet, and critic John Updike reviewed Garrison's first collection before it was published, and his remarks are quoted by Jennings in the *New York Times*:

> With their short lines, sneaky rhymes and casual leaps of metaphor, Garrison's poems have a Dickinsonian intensity.... Many a working girl will recognize herself in the poems' running heroine, and male readers will part with her company reluctantly.

A *Publishers Weekly* review praises Garrison's "accessible wit" and her "clear, unpretentious depictions of young Manhattanites' worries and joys." Several magazines that often feature fiction but only rarely mention poetry collections reviewed the book. It was described as "sweet and refreshing" by *Time* magazine, "a wonderful collection" by *Newsweek*, and "wry, sexy, appealing" by *Elle* (all quoted by Winerip in the *New York Times*). In the world of so-called serious poets, however, approval in the popular press and high sales are often considered indications that the verse is not sufficiently elevated.

CRITICISM

Kristen Sarlin Greenberg

Greenberg is a freelance writer and editor with a background in literature and philosophy. In the following essay, she examines how the structure and content of Deborah Garrison's poem "Please Fire Me" reflect her philosophy about the accessibility of poetry.

Deborah Garrison's 1998 collection *A Working Girl Can't Win and Other Poems* contains largely autobiographical poems about the life of a twenty-something working woman in Manhattan in the 1990s. The collection received very mixed reviews. Although popular with readers, many critics look down on Garrison's style as simplistic. Some reviewers grudgingly admit that her poems capture the emotion and tone of her working girl persona but not much else of value.

However, Garrison's straightforward style is no accident. Instead, it is a conscious choice. She is knowledgeable about poetry; she is the poetry editor for Knopf, an influential and respected publishing house, and before that she worked for *New Yorker* magazine, another leading light in the world of poetry. She writes in simple phrases not because she cannot emulate the work of poets who receive more critical praise but because she rejects the idea that poetry must be complicated, with obscure vocabulary

WHAT DO I READ NEXT?

- In *Help Wanted: Short Stories about Young People Working* (1997), editor Anita Silvey collects a dozen stories by well-known young-adult authors about teens tackling their first jobs. Works by Judith Ortiz Cofer, Ray Bradbury, Michael Dorris, Gary Soto, Norma Fox Mazer, and Vivien Alcock are included.

- Facebook chief operating officer Sheryl Sandberg examines the obstacles to women achieving leadership roles in business and proposes solutions in *Lean In: Women, Work, and the Will to Lead* (2013). Sandberg combines research, personal anecdotes, and humor to offer practical advice to empower women in the workplace.

- After focusing on her working life in *A Working Girl Can't Win and Other Poems*, Garrison centered her second collection, *The Second Child* (2007), around themes of motherhood and family.

- In *Making Waves: Writings By and About Asian American Women* (1989), more than fifty Asian American authors contribute poetry, essay, and fiction. *Publishers Weekly* describes the book as a "potent, fertile collection" that "challenges stereotypes of female docility and subservience that stigmatize those whose roots are in China, Japan, the Philippines, Vietnam, India, Korea, etc."

- Ed Park's 2008 novel *Personal Days* describes the politics and panic in a New York office when employees start getting fired without warning.

- Historian and radio personality Studs Terkel conducted dozens of interviews to compile the profiles in *Working: People Talk about What They Do All Day and How They Feel about What They Do* (1974). The book explores how work means different things to different people. Terkel discusses all sorts of professions, from athlete to office worker, barber to flight attendant, and pharmacist to grave digger.

> MORE THAN JUST A CREATIVE IMPULSE,
> THIS DETERMINATION TO WRITE ACCESSIBLE
> POEMS IS A DEFINITE PHILOSOPHICAL STANCE
> FOR GARRISON."

and allusions that alienate the average reader. Examination of a specific work, namely Garrison's poem "Please Fire Me," can reveal how it both fits in thematically in the collection *A Working Girl Can't Win* and also reflects her overriding philosophy about poetry's place in the world.

The composition of "Please Fire Me" on the page makes it appear much like a traditional poetic form. There are six stanzas containing four lines each, and most of the lines are of similar lengths. However, the farther down the eye travels through the text, the more the poem veers away from regularity, with line 19 being much longer than the others, the final stanza having all four lines much shorter, and the final line of the poem consisting of only a single word. Similarly, the poem starts with a regular meter, or pattern of stressed and unstressed syllables. The first line consists of four iambs (pairs of syllables, first unstressed and then stressed—a traditional and respected pattern), and the second line begins with a similar rhythm, but then the regular pattern breaks up. The remaining lines of the poem do not have a regular meter.

Just as Garrison's use of formal poetic devices falls apart in "Please Fire Me," so do her metaphors. The first two stanzas of the poem are chock full of figurative language. However, the metaphors are not used consistently. The term *alpha male* suggests the hierarchical structure of a wolf pack, but then Garrison uses language in line 3 that more closely describes the behavior of an animal like a bull or a horse than a canine. Stanza 2 focuses on the hen-like female office workers, but the mention of *claws* in line 7 does not seem to fit the image of a chicken; while chickens have talons of a sort, they walk on their splayed toes rather than on their claws. Perhaps the word is meant to bring high-heeled shoes to the reader's mind; perhaps Garrison wants to

add something feral to the comparison, chickens being thoroughly domesticated; or perhaps she intends to draw in images of other animals.

The metaphorical comparisons are used inconsistently, and they appear inconsistently in the poem. Stanzas 1 and 2 prepare the reader for a poem that reads like a fable or traditional legend with anthropomorphized animals, but immediately after the period that ends the second stanza, the use of metaphors falls off sharply. The alpha is the focus of stanza 3, but he is clearly human, making deals, drinking cocktails, and charming clients. The chicken metaphor is touched on briefly in line 18 but then only for the speaker to reject it outright as a model for her behavior.

Garrison begins "Please Fire Me" using many of the conventions of traditional poetry: regular stanzas and lines, traditional meter, and animal metaphors. The poem conforms to these conventions at first, reflecting the speaker's efforts to conform to the standard behavior and expectations in her office environment. However, very quickly, these traditional formal elements falter. The poem begins to sound more conversational as the speaker becomes overly frustrated and declares that she is *through* with playing the game. In the next-to-last stanza, the speaker decides she will let go of her ego, along with those of the men—as if she used to base her self-confidence on being able to stand with the alphas but has come to see that this is not what is important and fulfilling in life. Garrison rejects the restrictions of the traditional poetic form just as the speaker rejects the restrictive rules of office politics, which force her to wait on her nest and sympathize with the alpha males in her office.

The above analysis shows how the form of "Please Fire Me" is appropriate thematically for the content of the poem, but it is also interesting to consider how this particular poem reflects Garrison's broader philosophy about poetry. As Michael Winerip writes in the *New York Times*,

> "Accessible" is a word both fans and detractors use for her poetry. About this Ms. Garrison seems calm and balanced. "You take the good with the bad," she says. "If you're accessible that must mean you reached some degree of an audience. There's always that issue—is accessible a good thing or bad in poetry?"

Garrison believes that accessibility is a good thing, pointing out to Winerip that "the greatest poetry through the years that lasts is accessible." The primary criticism leveled at Garrison for her work—that her poems are accessible—is precisely the same quality that has made her popular with readers. She uses everyday words and writes in free verse. Rather than ending every line with punctuation or at a natural break in the flow of the text, Garrison makes frequent use of enjambment, letting her ideas flow from one line to the next, or in some cases from one stanza to the next. All of these elements add up to a style that readers apparently find very appealing, even if critics are skeptical.

As an editor, Garrison follows some of the rules of the literary poetry establishment. In a *New York Times* interview with Jennings, Garrison concedes that her own work would not have qualified for publication by the prestigious Knopf publishing house. However, she also commented: "My own poetry is irrelevant to my role as an editor." As a poet, she tries to break free from convention and create something new and fresh. More than just a creative impulse, this determination to write accessible poems is a definite philosophical stance for Garrison. She explains that she started considering the subject while in graduate school, working on her thesis about English novelist and poet Philip Larkin. She explained in an interview with *Writer's Almanac* that Larkin's

> plainspoken English, his basic good grammar and avoidance of obscurity, really spoke to me. I found it amazing the way he used the most apparently colloquial language, and yet his achievement was always supremely poetic. . . . I think somewhere along the way I made a conscious choice that I would avoid pretension and try to speak on the page almost in the same language we're speaking now. Could I make poetry out of the materials of our everyday life and conversation?

Garrison admits that walking the line between accessible verse and simple prose is "very tricky. The risk is you won't achieve poetry." Indeed, some critics believe she has not created poetry. For example, William Logan admits that "Garrison understands the emotions of city life" but harshly points out that she does not seem to grasp "that having emotions isn't the same as writing poems." Most likely, Garrison's editorial experiences make her a tough critic of her own work, and, again in *Writer's Almanac*, she has allowed that without some of the traditional formal elements of poetry, the poet must work harder. She comments: "You have to find sly musical resonances, half rhymes, things that make art of ordinary

language almost stealthily. I think some of my poems are successful in this; others, probably less so."

Her roles of editor and poet are not completely at odds—Garrison believes she can achieve more than one goal. Jennings writes that Garrison "doesn't want to overturn the Modernist and sometimes obscure tide of 20th-century poetry, but she does want to bring more readers to the joys of verse." "Poetry can be pretentious sometimes," Garrison commented to Jennings, "and if people feel poetry is this high citadel that you can't get into, it's bad for poetry." By adopting this as her personal philosophy when writing poetry, Garrison rejects the closed academic atmosphere of the poetry world.

On the most basic level, "Please Fire Me" is about a working woman frustrated by the office politics around her, the arrogant posturing of the alpha businessmen, and the fussing of her trite, hen-like female coworkers. The speaker feels out of place because she does not conform to the standards of behavior that go unchallenged by those around her. However, the poem also reflects the frustration of a poet who is criticized in the literary world for her simple, conversational style and for not conforming to the formal, academic, more obscure type of poetry that has come to be valued by the academic literary world. Garrison's use of traditional poetic conventions at the start of the poem indicates that she could likely compose poems to fit this mold if she so chose. Instead she breaks free of those conventions, uses a style that is uniquely hers, and ignores the critics.

Source: Kristen Sarlin Greenberg, Critical Essay on "Please Fire Me," in *Poetry for Students*, Gale, Cengage Learning, 2016.

Deborah Garrison

In the following essay, Garrison talks about poetry, including whether contests are important.

It's always nice to see poetry in the news, but I assume I'm not the only one in this tiny corner of the house of literature who's suffering from mixed feelings in the wake of recent press about us. We had David Orr's first "On Poetry" column for the *New York Times Book Review* (Apr. 24), in which he considered our "superstar" Jorie Graham and found her wanting, along with an April 21 *Times* piece about the "Foetry" scandal, in which, Edward Wyatt reports, Graham's name was dragged through the mud by a Web site watchdog who doesn't like the way she judges poetry contests.

Let me state up front that I'm not a friend of Graham's; I've met her exactly once, and we exchanged less than 10 words. (Read: this piece is not the sort of internecine poetry-world "favor" that fascinated Mr. Foetry.) Like David Orr, I sometimes have complicated feelings about poets with large reputations, including those whom I most admire; there are so many other good ones who never get their turn in the limelight. But really, is it as easy as Orr suggests for people to scale Mt. Parnassus by using their MFA connections? He paints a picture of the hapless poetry reader dozing off with Elizabeth Bishop in his lap and waking to find that the reputation of another "Major Poet" has been "consummated" as ruthlessly, he says, as Banana Republic has replaced the local post offices.

Whether you like Graham's work or not, and regardless of her privileged background (really, who cares?), her close ties to the critic Helen Vendler (not surprising, given Vendler's abiding interest in Graham's work), and her much-commented upon fabulous appearance (would anyone discuss Paul Muldoon's seat in the West Wing of poetry in the same breath with his looks?), she's clearly been doing for years what most poets, be they Major or Minor, are doing: struggling to remain true to themselves on the page, teaching younger poets, and presumably just getting on with it. Orr, whose criticism I value highly, has some points to make about Graham's poetry, but it seems a stretch—not to say unfair—to equate what he sees as a vagueness in her poetic diction with our "fractured" field, a grinding cultural mill he calls "part profession, part gaggle of coteries, part contest hustle." Can one poet's slack line really stand for all that?

If Orr feels some Majors are undeserving, I hope he'll convince the TBR, whose interest in stirring the poetry pot is all to the good, to let him review a few lesser known poets he's enthused about. Patronage may be a powerful force in poetry, but criticism is an equally powerful one. And as for that "contest hustle": okay, if you're sleeping with someone, you shouldn't hand them a prize. We've all intuited the regrettable instance of logrolling in our midst. But is our field egregious in this sense? Don't people in every field form alliances based on admiration of each other's work, and help and promote each other on that basis?

I'm aware, of course, that a contest win, however small the purse or resulting print run, can mean getting a job and a future in poetry. But why waste our valuable Elizabeth Bishop–reading time blogging and gossiping about how people "get ahead"? The only way to get anywhere you'd want to go is to write, do your best work, publish in magazines—to put yourself out there. If there's a messy multiplicity of schools of poetry all vying for our ear—call them coteries, if you prefer—it's a rich mess, one that's alive and even, I'd argue, fun. No, I don't think our field is all good will and democratic fellowship. But I don't think we're as troubled as this recent spate of press suggests. Day after day I'm moved by the honest faith with which people send out their work, in an atmosphere of such little chance of reward. I feel constantly challenged to reconsider what our poetry is. And I don't plan on Googling this discussion in the coming weeks to see just how much trouble I've got myself into. My time is better spent reading manuscripts.

Source: Deborah Garrison, "Let Us Go, Then: Stop Talking about Jorie Graham and Get On with It," in *Publishers Weekly*, Vol. 252, No. 19, May 9, 2005, p. 78.

David C. Ward

In the following review, Ward describes Garrison as "an important new writer."

When Harold Ross famously said that the *New Yorker* would not be edited for "the old lady in Dubuque" what he really meant was that it would be edited for "us," an "us" which has changed only slightly over the last half century. Since World War II, the magazine's tone, especially under omni-editor William Shawn, became perfectly attuned to the sensibility of New York City's hautebourgeois professionals especially as that class moved out into luxurious suburban enclaves called Cos Cob, Greenwich, and Rye. Anal replaced oral as the manic japery of the Algonquin Round Table gave way to golf club barbeques with gin used no less but perhaps more discreetly. Temperamentally and politically unable to celebrate American materialism openly (anyway, the ads took care of that), the magazine's writing evolved into the functional equivalent of its readers' affluence; it was a prose as seamlessly constructed as a Windsor knot, a set of Hogan irons, a Volvo station wagon. Yet it was a smoothness designed in art, as in the life depicted, to hide the fissures running beneath the sunny surfaces of immaculate pools and lawns.

Occasionally rising to genuine tragedy, the predominant tone was ironically wistful as characters discovered that becoming an adult means costs and losses. At their best, *New Yorker* stories, with gentle astringency, have subverted the American middle class's dependence on appearances. Updating Chekhov, that Volvo in the first paragraph of a *New Yorker* story will always break down by the end.

The *New Yorker*'s signature style has not so far changed much under the no longer so new broom of editor Tina Brown although the signs are that she wants it to. Brown assiduously follows the ad-man's credo of "sell the sizzle, not the steak" so in pursuit of "synergy" she has tarted-up the lay-out, given parties, and pandered (Roseanne as guest "editor"!) shamelessly. Fiction editor Bill Buford's main innovation is to allow writers to say f✱✱✱ and c✱✱✱ (taboo under Shawn) while pushing writers who share his agent. But the *New Yorker* style dies hard and it cannot be said that Richard Ford, for instance, is too distant from J.D. Salinger or early Updike. *New Yorker* editor Deborah Garrison's first book of poems, *A Working Girl Can't Win* indicates the persistence of the style by which one of America's cultural élites has defined itself. Yet it also suggests how that style is mutating as the needs of its class change and especially as younger people make more money (and as Tina Brown attempts to obtain at least some of that demographic windfall).

The life of the upper middle class of whatever age is not all that fascinating to hear about unless the writer has at least some stylistic flair and psychological acuity. Irony or cool, if overly self-reflective, can become tiresomely disengaged, risking not only self-absorption but self-pity. This is the tightrope Deborah Garrison walks. In his jacket blurb John Updike describes Garrison as having "Dickinsonian" intensity. This is so off the wall that it suggests a joke—or, damning with excessive praise, an insult. Dickinson had an entire self-invented cosmology backing up her wholly new style. Garrison writes mildly sharp interior monologues about being a thirty-something woman balancing work and private life. Garrison tries to give *A Working Girl* narrative drive by a table of contents which provides arch little summaries to each poem; for instance, "Please

Fire Me" is accompanied by "The desire for oblivion runs high at the office" But the poems themselves are self-contained, clean-lined descriptive vignettes. If anything she writes like Philip Larkin on Prozac. Like Larkin, nothing is always happening. From "3:00 A.M. Comedy": "Sometimes it's funny, this after-hour when / whatever hasn't happened between us / hasn't happened again..." "An Idle Thought" begins, "I'm never going to sleep / with Martin Amis / or anyone famous." "Fight Song" sounds exactly like one of Larkin's unpublished squibs:

> The type who gets the job done and the type who stands on principle; the down-to-earth and understated; the overhyped and underrated. . .

even down to the self-lacerating conclusion: "The beauty is / they'll soon forget you // and if they don't / they probably should." Garrison gets some snap out of giving a woman's perspective on work. "Please Fire Me" starts, "Here comes another alpha male, / and all the other alphas / are snorting and pawing / kicking up puffs of acrid dust . . ." But there's no traction or bite to Garrison's gender politics and the poem trails off in an "oh well" shrug, "I'd like to go / somewhere else entirely, / and I don't mean / Europe." Whatever.

Just as there is confirmatory journalism (I read the *Times* to tell me what I already know) Garrison's is confirmatory poetry. She articulates her class's sense of dissatisfaction (if not entitlement: having Europe as an option even though you want more) that life hasn't turned out like you thought, all in a style which congratulates the reader's self-protective taste for cool disengagement. In the old days, people would realize that their lives hadn't worked out and then something would happen: someone would get fired! Rabbit Angstrom actually had a past as a basketball hero that he could regret losing. Nowadays, Richard Ford's Frank Bascom is the archetype: a sportswriter, he is an observer observing his own life passing him by. So Garrison is observationally sharp but never cuts deep. *A Working Girl* has received a publicity buzz far exceeding any recent American book of poetry, suggesting either that Garrison is an important new writer or that appearances are deceiving. Or perhaps in the America of today, both.

Source: David C. Ward, Review of *A Working Girl Can't Win*, in *Poetry Nation Review*, Vol. 24, No. 6, 1998, p. 51.

SOURCES

Blau, Francine D., and Lawrence M. Kahn, "Female Labor Supply: Why Is the US Falling Behind?," National Bureau of Economic Research website, January 2013, http://www.nber.org/papers/w18702.pdf (accessed September 26, 2015).

Brenner, Mark, and Stephanie Luce, "Women and Class: What Has Happened in Forty Years?," in *Monthly Review*, Vol. 58, No. 3, July–August 2006, http://monthly review.org/2006/07/01/women-and-class-what-has-happened-in-forty-years/ (accessed September 26, 2015).

Cover, Bryce, "The U.S. Gets Left Behind When It Comes to Working Women," in *Forbes*, January 16, 2013, http://www.forbes.com/sites/brycecovert/2013/01/16/the-u-s-gets-left-behind-when-it-comes-to-working-women/ (accessed September 26, 2015).

"Data and Statistics: Women in the Labor Force," US Department of Labor website, http://www.dol.gov/wb/stats/stats_data.htm (accessed September 26, 2015).

"Deborah Garrison," Poetry Foundation website, http://www.poetryfoundation.org/bio/deborah-garrison (accessed September 19, 2015).

"Deborah Garrison," in *The Writer's Almanac with Garrison Keillor*, http://writersalmanac.publicradio.org/bookshelf/garrison.shtml (accessed September 20, 2015).

"Equal Pay/Compensation Discrimination," Equal Employment Opportunity Commission website, http://www.eeoc.gov/laws/types/equalcompensation.cfm (accessed September 26, 2015).

"Furthering the Protections against Workplace Discrimination and Harassment," Equal Employment Opportunity Commission website, http://www.eeoc.gov/eeoc/history/35th/1990s/furthering.html (accessed September 26, 2015).

Garrison, Deborah, "Please Fire Me," in *A Working Girl Can't Win and Other Poems*, Random House, 1998, pp. 37–38.

Groysberg, Boris, and Robin Abrahams, "Manage Your Work, Manage Your Life," in *Harvard Business Review*, March 2014, https://hbr.org/2014/03/manage-your-work-manage-your-life (accessed September 26, 2015).

Jennings, Dana, "Poet, Editor, Working Girl," in *New York Times*, April 23, 2000, http://www.nytimes.com/2000/04/23/nyregion/poet-editor-working-girl.html?page wanted=1 (accessed September 19, 2015).

Logan, William, "Sins & Sensibility," in *New Criterion*, December 1998, http://www.newcriterion.com/articles.cfm/sinsandsensibility-logan-2967 (accessed September 20, 2015).

Parker, Kim, "Despite Progress, Women Still Bear Heavier Load Than Men in Balancing Work and Family," Pew Research Center website, March 10, 2015, http://www.pewresearch.org/fact-tank/2015/03/10/women-still-bear-heavier-load-than-men-balancing-work-family/ (accessed September 26, 2015).

"Pay Equity & Discrimination," Institute for Women's Policy Research website, http://www.iwpr.org/initiatives/pay-equity-and-discrimination (accessed September 20, 2015).

Review of *The Second Child*, in *Publishers Weekly*, http://www.publishersweekly.com/978-1-4000-6359-8 (accessed September 20, 2015).

"Saturday, February 12, 2011," in *The Writer's Almanac with Garrison Keillor*, http://writersalmanac.publicradio.org/index.php?date=2011/02/12 (accessed September 19, 2015).

"Sexual Harassment," Equal Employment Opportunity Commission website, http://www.eeoc.gov/laws/types/sexual_harassment.cfm (accessed September 26, 2015).

"The Simple Truth about the Gender Pay Gap," American Association of University Women website, http://www.aauw.org/research/the-simple-truth-about-the-gender-pay-gap/ (accessed September 20, 2015).

Swanson, Ana, "The Number of Fortune 500 Companies Led by Women Is at an All-Time High: 5 Percent," in *Washington Post* online, June 4, 2015, http://www.washingtonpost.com/news/wonkblog/wp/2015/06/04/the-number-of-fortune-500-companies-led-by-women-is-at-an-all-time-high-5-percent/ (accessed September 26, 2015).

Ward, David C., "Post-Partum," in *Poetry Nation Review*, Vol. 34, No. 6, July/August 2008, pp. 71–73.

Winerip, Michael, "Poet, Mother, Editor, Wife," in *New York Times*, May 6, 2007, http://www.nytimes.com/2007/05/06/nyregion/nyregionspecial2/06Rpoet.html?page-wanted=all&_r=0 (accessed September 19, 2015).

"Women as a Growing Percentage of the Workforce, 1948–1998," in *Trends and Challenges for Work in the 21st Century*, US Department of Labor website, http://www.dol.gov/oasam/programs/history/herman/reports/futurework/report/chapter3/chart3-1_text.htm (accessed September 26, 2015).

"Women in the Labor Force in 2010," US Department of Labor website, http://www.dol.gov/wb/factsheets/Qf-laborforce-10.htm (accessed September 26, 2015).

"Working Mothers in the U.S.," US Department of Labor website, http://www.dol.gov/wb/Infographic_on_working_mothers.pdf (accessed September 26, 2015).

Yung, Katherine, and Patricia Montemurri, "Fewer Report Being Sexually Harassed," in *USA Today*, November 9, 2011, http://usatoday30.usatoday.com/money/workplace/story/2011-11-09/sex-harassment-incidents-down-still-prevalent/51144798/1 (accessed September 26, 2015).

FURTHER READING

Garrison, Deborah, "Giving Notice," in *Open City #23: Prose by Poets*, Open City Books, 2007, pp. 79–80.

   In a brief essay, Garrison explains why she writes poetry rather than prose.

Hirsch, Edward, *How to Read a Poem: And Fall in Love with Poetry*, Harcourt, 1999.

In this volume, Hirsch offers advice on learning to enjoy poetry even without formal education in the genre.

Logan, William, *Vain Empires*, David R. Godine, 1997.

Poet and critic Logan panned Garrison's work in a review of her first collection. This volume of Logan's poems, a *New York Times* notable book of the year, was released at around the same time.

Packard, Susan, *New Rules of the Game: 10 Strategies for Women in the Workplace*, Prentice Hall Press, 2015.

Packard shares her own experiences in business, as well as those of other female CEOs and company presidents, as a way to teach women about the concept of "gamesmanship." By following the rules of the game, Packard

believes, women can compete and succeed in a professional world still dominated by men.

SUGGESTED SEARCH TERMS

Deborah Garrison AND A Working Girl Can't Win

Deborah Garrison AND Please Fire Me

Deborah Garrison AND New Yorker

Deborah Garrison AND Knopf

animal metaphors in poetry

poems about work

women in the workplace

gender differences in the workplace

The Pomegranate and the Big Crowd

ALBERTO RÍOS

2005

"The Pomegranate and the Big Crowd" is a poem by Alberto Ríos about a young woman, Ventura, and a young man, Clemente, whose lives are about to intertwine because of a dare. Ríos is hailed as one of the most significant Chicano poets writing in the present day, being often considered alongside two other leading writers of his generation, Gary Soto and Lorna Dee Cervantes. As of 2015 Ríos had written ten poetry collections, three story collections, and a memoir, in much of which he pays tribute to the common Mexican American people and their traditions. *The Theater of Night*, Ríos's ninth collection, accomplishes as much in presenting a full volume of poems revolving around the love and lives of one couple and the family who would follow from their union. Placed early in the collection, as the first poem in which both Clemente and Ventura appear, "The Pomegranate and the Big Crowd" encapsulates the import of that union in the span of a mere—or rather a vast—quarter of a second. Notably, though no further explanation is given within the volume, Ríos affirms in *The Theater of Night*'s dedication, "This book is in good and personal debt to Clemente and Ventura and all the rest of my extended family, in whom so many of my words find treasure."

AUTHOR BIOGRAPHY

Alberto Álvaro Ríos was born on September 18, 1952, in Nogales, Arizona, to a Mexican justice of

The many seeds of the pomegranate reflect the infinite possibilities that follow the moment described in the poem. (© Tim UR | Shutterstock.com)

the peace and a British nurse. Around the household, Ríos's family had an abundance of animals, a veritable menagerie, including cats, dogs, rabbits, turtles, snakes, and chickens, most of which were free to wander in and out. Books were also common around the house, and Ríos found himself particularly interested in reading through entries in their *World Book Encyclopedia*. He also had a beloved book of fairy tales that he read through some fifty times; he appreciated the magical means of escape from his oft-uneventful small-town environment.

He grew up speaking primarily Spanish, but as soon as he got to elementary school, Ríos was told that speaking in Spanish would no longer be permitted, not even on the playground, and would earn corporal punishment, referred to as

"swats." Later in life, he became conscious of the fact that that system of punishment instilled in him and his fellow Chicano friends a reflexive aversion to their native language even outside of school. The idea that speaking Spanish was backward and wrong was implanted in their minds, to the extent that Ríos and his friends would be too embarrassed to pass along to their parents invitations to school events; they knew their parents would be able to hold conversations only in Spanish. By middle school, Ríos was no longer fluent in Spanish.

Ríos found himself writing here and there as early as elementary school, and by junior high he was already fully invested in the idea of gaining something from his writing; it was what he did. As cited by José David Saldívar in a *Chicano*

Writers volume, his early output included some "mildly rebellious, abstract poems." Late in high school, Ríos finally began to relearn Spanish, which he found enlightening; he in fact discovered that, much like riding a bicycle, he merely had to reacquaint himself with the balance of the language and everything he had known was still there. After high school, he went on to the University of Arizona, where he would earn two bachelor's degrees, first in English and creative writing in 1974, then in psychology in 1975. Thinking practically, he enrolled in the university's law school, but after a year he followed his heart, quitting law school and then earning admission to the creative writing program. Though some (white) instructors balked at his use of apparently unpronounceable Spanish names, Ríos left in 1979 with an MFA and high motivation to change cultural perceptions in the state.

Ríos proceeded to publish two chapbooks and earn a National Endowment for the Arts fellowship before publishing his first major collection, *Whispering to Fool the Wind*, in 1982. That year he would also begin his teaching career at Arizona State University, as an assistant professor. His first short-fiction collection, *The Iguana Killer: Twelve Stories of the Heart*, was published to favorable reviews in 1984, and he proceeded to publish a volume of poems or stories every several years or so over the ensuing decades. *The Theater of Night*, which contains "The Pomegranate and the Big Crowd," was published in 2005, earning Ríos the 2007 PEN/Beyond Margins Award.

Having remained at Arizona State into the 2010s, Ríos has become a regents' professor as well as the Katharine C. Turner Endowed Chair in English. He has won a variety of awards, served in a variety of extraliterary capacities, contributed to literally hundreds of journals and anthologies, and maintained constant pride in the quality of his teaching. In 2013, he was selected to serve a two-year term as Arizona's inaugural poet laureate.

Ríos married Maria Guadalupe Barron, or "Lupita," in 1979, and they have a son, Joaquin. As far as *The Theater of Night* and his extended family are concerned, in Ríos's poem "They Said I Was a Crying Bride," the names of the protagonists of the book are said to be Mr. and Mrs. Clemente Ríos. Introducing his collection *Pig Cookies and Other Stories*, Ríos indicates that Margarito is the name of his grandfather,

Refugio that of his grandmother, which would make Clemente and Ventura his paternal great-grandparents.

POEM SUMMARY

The text used for this summary is from *The Theater of Night*, Copper Canyon Press, 2005, pp. 10–12. A version of the poem can be found on the following web page: http://www.poetryfoundation.org/poem/177697.

Lines 1–13

"The Pomegranate and the Big Crowd" opens with the name of one of the two central characters in the poem's narrative, Ventura, a woman, who is doing something out of both hunger and curiosity—primarily curiosity. What she is doing is revealed in the second couplet, which refers to a dare: apparently Ventura, being hungry, has agreed to kiss someone in exchange for a pomegranate, which is an orange-sized, berry-flavored red fruit with many cells of juicy pulp inside. The presence of the pomegranate suggests a tropical climate, with the people's names further suggesting Mexico or perhaps more likely the American Southwest (since the poem was originally written in English).

The dare has become a sensation, with all the people, or at least all of Ventura's and the young man's friends, gathering to watch. The audience specifically includes boys and girls—Ventura's counterpart is later referred to as a *boy*, so these boys and girls may be their (probably teenage) friends or perhaps younger children—as well as chickens, pigs, and others. If the idea of a kiss for a pomegranate being the highlight of so many people's day has not already suggested an idyllic village setting, the wandering livestock certainly suggest as much.

Gravitating to the front of the crowd are the children—curiously enough, the children that Ventura and Clemente will one day have. Also present (in some sense) are the children that those children will have, meaning Ventura and Clemente's grandchildren. All these children are not just present but are making a fair amount of noise, like all the others, people and animals included. The children are specifically said to be as loud as the pigs and as fast, moving about the courtyard or road or square, as the chickens. Ventura cannot actually see all these children.

MEDIA ADAPTATIONS

- While no officially produced audio recording of "The Pomegranate and the Big Crowd" is available, the poem has been a favorite of the state and national Poetry Out Loud competitions, and videos of students' readings can be found by searching online.

Nonetheless, they are tightening the space in which she exists, pushing up closer to her, and she can even feel their breath, which has an air of anxiety about it.

Lines 14–33

The second half of the seventh couplet, line 14, begins a new grammatical sentence and returns the focus precisely to the present moment as it actually is, finally in the person of Clemente; this line is taken up entirely with the simple statement of Clemente's identity as it is already known, as the boy Ventura will kiss. She would have been willing to kiss him even in the absence of any pomegranate dare—but she would not acknowledge as much aloud, being perhaps too modest or traditionally feminine. Because of her disinclination to say anything, she appreciates the occasion of the dare, which is essentially a game of sorts. Clemente seems a fitting partner for her, Ventura thinks to herself. His face—perhaps with full cheekbones, a well-defined jawline—conveys a sense of strength. He is further said to feel what Clemente feels, which can be interpreted two ways: it may mean that his emotional state is the same as Ventura's emotional state, one of delighted anticipation, or it may mean that he is highly empathetic and can feel that Ventura is feeling delighted anticipation. The sentence effectively means both of these things at once.

Clemente, as Ventura sees, is looking around, but apparently not with the intent to communicate through eye contact or gesture with any of his friends in the crowd; a suggestion is that he is not looking *toward* something or someone else who interests him, but rather simply *away* from where his interest truly lies, in Ventura, out of his own modesty or heightened emotional state. The sentence bridging lines 19–20 might also suggest that Clemente is indeed looking toward, or for, certain persons—not any of their living friends, but rather their invisible future children, whose presence Ventura has noted. However strong Clemente's powers of empathy might be, Ventura's are strong enough to be triggered by sight alone: she can tell from looking at Clemente that he is feeling the idea, if not the presence, of their future children as a *shiver* or personal tremor through his body.

Their children, it is said, will include Margarito, a boy, and his two sisters. The girls will grow up to live as nuns, presumably in a convent, dedicated to their spirituality, although their only motivation may be to devote as much time as possible to praying for Margarito, in order to sustain him. Margarito's seriousness will make him feel unrelated and unknown when embraced by the sisters, suggesting that to his grave introversion (unable to allow release even to offer warmth in a hug) they are relatively convivial and extroverted. The parents, at least, are confirmed to represent quite the opposite of Margarito's unfamiliar gravity, to the extent that his gravity fairly balances out the parents' vivaciousness and the laughter they would experience and enjoy. Margarito is still being described in line 30, now as a boy who arouses curiosity in those who regard him, who will one day be an old man who never in his life had faith in the expertise of a medical doctor. Like Margarito, his wife, Refugio, will be a serious person. She is figured as a person who is *to come*, framing her relevance to the poem as being her entry into the greater story of Clemente and Ventura. Also coming in to the family, along with Refugio, will be her sisters, Matilde and Consuelo.

Lines 34–48

The second line of the seventeenth couplet (line 34) continues the sentence mentioning Margarito's wife and her sisters, now assembling those persons and all the others who will become part of the family brought about by the kiss into the collective whole of those in attendance at the kiss itself. They are all standing around, their arms raised (in one posture or another), their eyes regarding the main event. There is a great deal of sound occurring at this point in time, leading up to the kiss. The kiss itself seems to take place in the announcement of it in the appositive phrase describing *this moment*, in line 38—not with a full grammatical sentence, with a subject and verb of activity, but with the gerund *lending* (a gerund being a noun form)—and in the first three words of line 39. As if to emphasize the brevity of the moment (which the reader may at first interpret as yet being a description of what is to happen), already in the end of line 39 the present moment is departed from, as the sense of the kiss is equated with the sense of the kisses Ventura would give their children—who remain waiting impatiently among the youths and animals gathered around.

The sentence of lines 40–41 now refers to the kiss in the past tense, confirming both that it has happened and that it was a small thing, but also that it was fully infused with itself, which might be understood to change the impression of its size or significance. It was only a little moment, and yet it was one of *affection*, suggesting a noteworthy emotional component, which Ventura bestowed on Clemente. Specifically the moment lasted a quarter of a second, and with the colon ending line 43, that moment is returned to: everyone was standing around, waiting, with people urging the future couple to make the dared exchange, raising and testing the weight of the pomegranate as if to mark the significance of what hung in the balance of the moment. The people even pushed Ventura and Clemente toward each other physically it seems. During that fourth of a second, Clemente and Ventura lived out what their lives had to offer—and that fourth of a second continues still.

THEMES

Romantic Love

Ríos's poem sets a lovely scene for the initiation of a romance that will last a lifetime. The scene is very old-fashioned in several ways, which perhaps accounts for much of its appeal. To begin with, the poem apparently takes place long ago, prior to the sort of technological revolutions that would change the way people interact and get to know each other. The setting is a small village where there is no evidence that people have phones of any kind, or personal electronic devices, or computers—or even that the village has running water and electricity. Thus, there is

no suggestion that Clemente and Ventura have had any chance to flirt with each other via text messages, or phone calls, or social postings, or any such media. Accordingly, without their respective identities having been fragmented into disembodied words, voice with no body language, pictures selected for their flattering presentation, and so on, Clemente and Ventura seem to have a very full sense of each other in the moment.

Another somewhat old-fashioned aspect is Ventura's unwillingness to say anything with regard to her interest in Clemente. In the wake of several waves of feminism, twenty-first-century women are more likely to ignore traditional codes of behavior that entail their silencing and be open about their feelings toward those they desire. Still, many women retain the traditional ideal that the gentleman should be the one to approach the lady who has attracted him. For Ríos's poem, the old-fashioned ethic is almost necessary, since if Ventura were not so reticent, the dare that proves so fruitful might never have come about. A third old-fashioned facet of the poem is that the highly anticipated kiss turns out, quite late in the poem, in line 39, to be only a kiss on the cheek. The modern reader may well imagine, based on the buildup around the kiss, that it must be more serious than a peck on the cheek, and yet by the time the reader learns that it is only that, so to speak, the poem's potential energy has built to a crescendo that still rides high even after the revelation. It may be just a kiss on the cheek, but it is a wonderful, even magical kiss on the cheek nevertheless. With an emphasis on the *feelings* of both Ventura and Clemente, on their sense, prompted by their nearness and expectation, that a shared family is in their future, the poem enshrines their romantic love as the most honorable kind—a devotional love that can only lead to the commitment of procreation, a love of a lifetime.

Family

In the images the poem sets before the reader, the import of family is given pride of place. This is apparent foremost in the role that the idea of family plays in Clemente and Ventura's love; their envisioning a family, *their* family, is not just a component of their instinctive attraction toward each other, but the very pinnacle of it. The poem takes note of minor details from the occasion—who is watching, how Ventura feels about the dare, the importance of the pomegranate—but it is the idea of their children that sweeps the poem away into what feel like fully fleshed-out reveries

TOPICS FOR FURTHER STUDY

- Speak with the eldest members of your extended family in search of a pivotal moment in a marital relationship that brought about new generations of individuals. Using such a moment as a foundation, write a poem that includes description of the scene of the moment as well as mention of what would become of members born or brought into the couple's family later in life.

- Read the Ríos poems "What He Does to Me" and "Explaining a Husband," which are both also found in *The Theater of Night* and focus on the love between Clemente and Ventura. In an essay, analyze each of the poems independently and conclude by discussing the collective effect of these two poems and "The Pomegranate and the Big Crowd."

- Ríos's poems are often noted for their narrative qualities, while his stories are often noted for their poetic qualities. Choose one of the stories from his young-adult collection *The Iguana Killer: Twelve Stories of the Heart* and see if you can collapse the story into a poem-length work by selecting choice phrases and lines to communicate what takes place. Also write a brief prose reflection in which you discuss how you decided which details to include and which to leave out.

- Track through the forty-eight lines of "The Pomegranate and the Big Crowd" in order to rate the degree of engagement in three realms: (a) the *physical*, the outward occurrences of a moment; (b) the *emotional*, what people are feeling; and (c) the *imaginative*, what people are thinking or envisioning. Use a scale of, say, 0 to 5, such that line 1 might receive scores of 1, 5, and 2 in realms (a), (b), and (c), respectively (with Ventura's name providing a hint of her *physical* existence, with her *feeling* of hunger dominating the line, and with the two causal words also suggesting a *thought* process). Chart your results using a spreadsheet and then produce a paper in which you explain what you learned about the poem through analyzing each line for the different components as well as through the graphic representation of the information you gathered.

---

of what the future will actually hold. With Clemente the evidence only confirms that he imagines their children's existence, but Ventura feels the very living, breathing presence of not only their own children but also their children's children at the very occasion of what must be their first shared kiss. All those children are not only present but also are filled with anticipation, anxious for the momentous event to take place; their own existences, of course, cannot begin until Clemente and Ventura's relationship is consummated. One way to look at this supersensory experience or magical vision of Ventura's is as a manifestation of her instinctive urge to procreate; saying that her future children are urging her onward is much like saying her body and her natural will to reproduce are urging her onward. But the narrative stays old-fashioned: Ventura's mind—or at least her mind as revealed in the poem—has only the most innocent inclinations toward Clemente, appreciating his strong face, finding him generally agreeable, and then skipping far ahead in the potential relationship to imagine their children together. With the interwoven notions of love and family, the poem might be suggesting that romantic love is the foundation of a family, or it might be saying that the idea of a family is the foundation of romantic love, or at least of the purest, most idyllic kind of romantic love—the kind that was permitted to blossom as such in a small, happy village of the past.

Time

Throughout, Ríos's poem plays with time. The first way in which time is malleable in the poem is with the setting itself. It might take place fifty

It is clear that Ventura likes Clemente, even before the bet. (© Jenkedco | Shutterstock.com)

years ago, or a hundred, or even five hundred—the setting of the traditional village is, indeed, timeless (that is, within the bounds of humanity's existence). Except, while a few ethnic groups in South America, for example, decline contact with modern Western civilization and its technological accoutrements, it is unlikely that Ríos's poem—that is, the unmediated event of the kiss—would take place as such in twenty-first-century America. Appropriately, then, the portrayal of Margarito as an old man strongly suggests that the poem takes place in the fairly distant past. The poem give the sense that Margarito and the girls are not just *possible* or *potential* children for Clemente and Ventura, but rather are the actual children that they will have. The poem must be written, then, from a time when these details are known; if Margarito as an old man, is, say, seventy-five, that means the narrative of the pomegranate dare takes place at least three-quarters of a century back in the past, if not further—and it could be indefinitely further back.

No matter when the poem takes place, there is constant flux in the poem's sense of time, in that Ventura's mind, along with the narrative itself outside Ventura's mind, repeatedly drifts into the future—imagining her and Clemente's children either as pulled back into the past to watch their parents kiss or as living out their own lives separate from those of their parents. Even as the kiss is finally approached in the narrative, from line 34 onward, time is still played with. The curious description of everyone having their *arms up* may leave the reader wondering about the people's postures—perhaps hands on head in disbelief, or standing with hands on hips and elbows high, or calling to another friend far away to come see the spectacle. Regardless of what is imagined, the sentence grammatically suggests that everyone has their arms up, and all at the same time—but this would be an odd picture, and the reader may instead have to conclude that this is a time-independent description very concisely referring to the various ways that people would be raising their arms in the course of the unfolding event, at different intervals. In a sense, then, the narrative is further unhooked from regularly progressing time. Even when the kiss comes, the reader may not quite realize it, as the moment passes so quickly that it practically evades a present-tense description; all of a sudden it has happened. Even then, the kiss is multiplied forward in time to all the kisses that will be bestowed by Ventura on their children. The kiss takes only a quarter of a second, but in the way the poem is replete with time flux, moving forward and backward and yet remaining in the present all at once, it demonstrates the truth of its final assertion—which is less startling than it might have been in the absence of the poetic evidence: the kiss may last only a quarter of a second, but their entire lives are contained in that kiss, along with the lives of their children and their children's children, and as long as their descendants live on, the quarter of a second into which that powerful kiss was concentrated will never cease.

STYLE

Couplets

Like a majority of the poems in *The Theater of Night*, "The Pomegranate and the Big Crowd" is presented in the form of a series of unrhymed couplets. If accessed online (such as at the Poetry Foundation site), the poem may not have any stanzaic spacing at all, but to compress all the lines into a single long stanza is to do the poem injustice. To begin with, the form chosen by the poet should be preserved regardless of whether there is any perceived value in it, because the form of the poem is part of its artistic presentation. Moreover, in this case there is acknowledged significance to the presentation as a succession of couplets. Lawrence Olszewski, for one, in his review of Ríos's volume in *Library Journal*, finds that the couplets suggest the idea that "the two major characters are facing, talking to, and mirroring each other." The couplets also produce the sense of repeated starting and stopping, both of the stanzas and of the hesitant action of the scene, with Ventura and Clemente needing to be pushed together to complete the dare, and the narrative. Of course, the idea that Ventura and Clemente are *coupling* is at the heart of the poem.

Magical Storytelling

Being a writer clearly drawing from Latin American culture or tradition—at the very least in the sense of the village filled with people with Spanish names—Ríos may be too easily perceived as working in the literary tradition of magical realism, made famous by the likes of Gabriel García Márquez and Isabel Allende. Ríos's poem does lean toward a magical realist ambience, in that the children of people who have not yet borne them are imagined to be present at the progenitors' first kiss. This sets the poem a step or so outside ordinary reality. Yet the poem does not give the sense that the children are actually there; quite to the contrary, it is clearly stated that Ventura does not see them but only senses them, while Clemente, too, only feels them there in some indefinite way. Magical realism is more properly understood as a narrative style in which fantastic or magical things occur but are taken for granted as real and legitimate occurrences by the story's characters. In "The Pomegranate and the Big Crowd," it is more like Ríos brings the visions and sensations of Ventura especially, and to a lesser extent Clemente, to life; the children are, of course, not truly there, but they are *there* in a very meaningful sense to the couple who will bear them. Regarding Ríos's style, a *New Yorker* reviewer pointed out that it is "indebted to magic realism but rooted in naturalism." José David Saldívar, in an entry on Ríos for *Chicano Writers*, coins an appropriate term for this somewhat fantastic style, calling it "magical storytelling." What may be, perhaps even is, an essentially true story, a kiss over a pomegranate sparking the romance of a lifetime, is told in a way that brings out the magic of it—and indeed, there is something magical in the way entire persons can be created out of thin air, as it were, by means of love.

HISTORICAL CONTEXT

Modern Chicano Poetry

There has long been literature in the region that might well be called Mexican America—the land gained by the United States through the Treaty of Guadalupe Hidalgo in 1848, spanning Texas to California as far south as the Rio Grande. This was five hundred thousand square miles of territory, nearly twice the area of Texas alone. Earlier literature in this region was written in Spanish, but once it was assimilated into America, English-language prose and poetry began to appear. By 1900, the use of English was common. Still, the Spanish-speaking populations produced many of

A simple kiss on the cheek is the start of Clemente and Ventura's life together. *(© kurhan | Shutterstock.com)*

their own newspapers, and with printed space at a premium, poetry lent itself especially well to stirring people's minds.

The 1960s brought, somewhat in the wake of African Americans' civil rights movement, a Chicano movement aimed at addressing matters more particular to Hispanic populations, such as the need for labor laws to protect migrant workers. The political agitation came hand in hand with an intellectual flourishing, which manifested itself enough in the written word that the collective effort of the 1960s is referred to as the Chicano Renaissance. Carl R. Shirley and Paula W. Shirley, in *Understanding Chicano Literature*, identify four characteristics common to much of the poetry of this period: the use of traditional forms, partly as derived from the Spanish tradition; a "declamatory style," as in the harnessing of grand ideas; use of the imperative, in the manner of urging people to act; and a straightforwardness, for the sake of effective communication, reminiscent of

prose. In the wake of the Chicano Renaissance, with much having been accomplished in the political realm by the likes of Cesar Chavez and the United Farm Workers Union, poets moved beyond sociopolitical inspiration and came to favor more personal explorations in their verse. Also in the 1970s, the poetic voices of several women shifted the dialogue from one focused on masculine self-assertion to one including broader understanding of the experiences of all Mexican Americans. Bernice Zamora and Alma Villanueva were among these voices.

It was around this time that Ríos entered the field, making a name for himself in the 1980s. He has addressed his relation to the Chicano movement in commentaries such as a 1990 interview with *Confluencia*. At that time he affirmed that it lent him inspiration in remarking, "The loudness of the Movimiento caused me early on in my writing to deal with loud issues." As he evolved poetically over the next quarter century, Ríos came to focus more on communal issues from a quieter perspective. He told *Confluencia*,

> I write simply about moments in people's lives.... Everydayness, ordinariness, the real, the regular, the pedestrian. It is the one great lesson so many great writers have tried to teach us. I think Chicano literature is still young, and one could not expect these things to be what changes the literature. But they are coming.

A decade later, focusing on Chicanos' use of the Spanish and English languages in his essay "The Body of My Work," Ríos indicated that a priority of Chicano literature in the twenty-first century would be to move beyond a reaction to their forcible detachment from their native tongue in English-speaking America, beyond the affirmation of historical collective identity, to engage in broader recognition of the diversity among Chicanos of the present. He wrote:

> We are not abstractions, or easy political labels, and certainly not stereotypes. We have started recognizing who we are, and what. How we got here, and why. When this happened, and how. But all of this simply sets the stage for what must come next.

He concluded in a universalizing vein: "Chicano Studies, because they are about language, are people studies, and every person is different.... There may be rules for languages, but there are finally no rules for being Chicano."

CRITICAL OVERVIEW

Ríos is recognized as one of the foremost poetic Mexican American voices of the late twentieth and early twenty-first centuries. In their 1988 survey text *Understanding Chicano Literature*, published just six years after Ríos's first major collection, Shirley and Shirley state, "Alberto Ríos is one of the most outstanding Chicano poets currently writing. His work is both folkloric and sophisticated, simple yet complex." They observe that he uses "powerful images . . . to open a poetic world where image and human experience join forces." In the 1992 volume *Chicano Writers: Second Series*, Saldívar remarks, "No Chicano poet writing today is a more exquisite—a more fastidiously deliberate—technician than Ríos. His poetry is always lavishly textured."

The Theater of Night, like many of Ríos's collections, generally earned admiring reviews. In *Library Journal*, Olszewski matter-of-factly calls Ríos "a popular poet who successfully offers dramatic insights into the Mexican American experience." The *New Yorker* reviewer notes that Ríos utilizes the characters of Ventura and Clemente "deftly" in this "ambitious" volume's "rhapsodic" poems. One ambivalent reviewer was *Publishers Weekly*'s, who lamented what verges on the formulaic in the volume: "Ríos favors long lines, end-stopped and rhymeless couplets, and quiet, often reassuring asides. The results can end up repetitive, even predictable, and may not expand his already considerable following."

Reviewing the collection for *Prairie Schooner*, Stephen C. Behrendt calls *The Theater of Night* a "moving, poignant tribute" to the poet's extended family and hometown. Ríos's poems are found to "combine a musical, at times almost incantatory, handling of language and imagery with the narrative skill that is the hallmark of all his work." The poet's style is seen as "spellbinding" and marked by "authenticity." The poems "are warm, touching, and powerful in the sincerity of the voice that fills them," with the collective effect of "raising, ennobling, memorializing Clemente and Ventura, and with them the people—the culture—for whom they stand." In sum, "there is so much to admire, so much to engage, so much to fill and refresh mind and spirit alike."

Saldívar concludes that Ríos "has been assured an important position in American literature"; he is considered by some "the most articulate poetic voice of the American language in the 1980s" and "the most technically sophisticated and complex poet from the borderlands." All in all, in Saldívar's estimation, "Ríos is surely one of the major vernacular voices in the postmodernist age." Shirley and Shirley declare that even through Ríos's use of magic realist or surrealist elements, "the poems are nonetheless true for their insights into human experience."

CRITICISM

Michael Allen Holmes

Holmes is a writer with existential interests. In the following essay, he examines the combined effects of the repetition, enjambment, and subjective displacement in "The Pomegranate and the Big Crowd."

There is something uncanny about the way Ríos, in "The Pomegranate and the Big Crowd," brings to coalescence a scene from the past, as framed in present-tense terms, with a future made present. That the poem is, as Ríos's verse in general

WHAT DO I READ NEXT?

- While Ríos is hailed for his poetry, he has also received accolades for *Capirotada: A Nogales Memoir*, his personal story of life in the borderlands, which was selected for Arizona's statewide, one-book reading program in 2009.

- In naming his son Joaquín, Ríos perhaps found agreeable the resonance carried by the name as a result of its use by Rodolfo Gonzales in his 1967 epic poem *Yo soy Joaquín/I Am Joaquín*, an affirmation of identity and pride that was a seminal work in the Chicano Renaissance.

- Like Ríos, Lorna Dee Cervantes made a splash in the poetry world beginning in the early 1980s. One of her most highly regarded titles is her debut, *Emplumada* (1981), which includes perhaps her most famous poem, "Beneath the Shadow of the Freeway," which contrasts the perspectives of three generations of women in her family in a compromised urban setting.

- Gary Soto, the third in the triumvirate of Chicano writers entering their golden years in the 2010s, was born in the same year as Ríos and has written prose and poetry prolifically for adults, young adults, and children. One of his most recent young-adult poetry collections is *Partly Cloudy: Poems of Love and Longing* (2009).

- In her poetry collection *Women Are Not Roses* (1984), Ana Castillo makes a point of addressing topics about which women have traditionally been silenced, such as desire, and portraying the feminine figure as not just a muse for others but as acting of and for herself.

- Leo Romero's collection *Agua Negra* (1981) takes its name from a New Mexican village where Christ's face is believed by some to have once appeared on an adobe wall. Romero brings ghosts and legendary figures into a surreal and sometimes frightening portrayal of a village from times past.

- Saldívar equates the likely historical significance of Ríos's verse of the 1980s with that of Wallace Stevens's *Harmonium* (1923) from the 1920s. Saldívar calls the well-known American modernist Stevens "one of Ríos's masters."

---

has been termed, "spellbinding" is attested to by its popularity as a choice for recitation in the Poetry Out Loud youth competition series. Videos of recitations are abundant online, and as of 2014 the poem was removed from eligibility for competition by virtue of its common use. When a work of literature has a quality that earns descriptors like "spellbinding" or "magical," this often has to do with factors that shift what otherwise might fall flat as a narrative strategy—introduction of the impossible—into a realm where it *feels* possible. With such a poem, not only must it verbally create a world that demands the reader's full engagement, but it also must have some incantatory quality to (perhaps subconsciously) assure the reader's imaginative commitment to that world. The reader or listener is absorbed in the rhythm, whatever it may be, much like with song, except the only music is the words themselves. It may be true that the couplet as a stylized form is taken beyond the point of diminishing marginal utility in *The Theater of Night*, but there is no denying its role in bringing "The Pomegranate and the Big Crowd" to the point of perfection.

The uniqueness of the couplet as a form comes, if rhyme is not being employed, with the abundance of stanza breaks introduced. Few poems introduce stanza breaks more frequently than every two lines, and so the poet is obligated to work *with* those frequent breaks, not just around them, to amplify the meaning of the poem. Otherwise, the breaks will seem to slow the poem down

> HERE, THE POEM'S RENDERING AMBIGUOUS THE SUBJECT OF THE VERB EFFECTIVELY BLENDS THE CONSCIOUSNESSES OF THE TWO FIGURES WHOSE BLENDING OF EXISTENCES IS THE SEED OF THE POEM."

to the point of being gratuitous; once the reader has this sense, the stanza breaks are likely skipped right over without thought for their significance, defeating the point of having them in the first place.

From the first couplet here, the form has significance. The poem introduces the ideas of hunger and curiosity as the foundation for some action, without yet revealing what that action is, setting a tone of lingering and unresolved tension. Such tension is indeed at the heart of the scene in a real sense, with the prolonged anticipation leading up to the kiss representing the essential energy of the poem. On the other hand, when line 3 proceeds to immediately resolve the uncertainty over what Ventura has done (so far), reporting that she has taken a certain dare, there is a minor peak in narrative energy quickly spent—not unlike with a brief kiss. Throughout the poem, delays in full understanding of the sentences that span multiple couplets are common, playing off the scene's sense of building and soon-burst tension.

One aspect of the stanza break that Ríos takes full advantage of is its having a syntactic significance rivaling that of the period. As an example here, line 3, in the poem's second couplet, ends with a period. Thus, grammatically it is most closely connected with the phrasing that came before it, in lines 1–2. Yet stanzaically, the line is more closely connected with line 4, its couplet mate. Thus on the one hand, looking backward, the words in line 3 complete the reader's understanding of what has come of Ventura's hunger and curiosity; on the other hand, looking forward, the words set the scene for the gathering of all the friends. Line 3 thus pivots in a syntactically balanced way from the former to the latter. Line 4 itself, meanwhile, introduces a hint of circularity in beginning and ending with the same word. The enjambment after the second *Everyone*—ending the line in the middle of a grammatical phrase—

suggests an awe-inspiring quality to the gathering. The narrator is compelled to invoke the universality of the people present not once, but twice, and with the couplet as well ending after that word, the reader is left floating, in the line of blank space, in the midst of that awe-inspiring crowd of a certainly meaningful size.

Line 5 introduces the idea of words having altered grammatical significance when appearing at the beginning of a line, particularly the beginning of a couplet, as visibly detached from the preceding parts of the sentence. Here, the poem quite clearly presents, bridging the gaps between lines 4 and 5, the sentence "Everyone watched." Yet with line 5 simply beginning *Watched*, with a capital letter, it carries the sense of being its own sentence—as if reporting not that the following entities are the ones doing the watching but that they are the ones *being* watched—which they are, whether by Ventura, the narrator, or at last the reader, who envisions them as they are mentioned in turn. Thus, the action of watching is presented from two sides, in different senses, with a single use of the word.

Line 6, in turn, introduces the idea of delayed determination of identity. The reader is led to envision that children are shifting to the front of the crowd, likely imagining anonymous children from the community; with the delay of the stanza break, however, the reader only slowly realizes, in line 7, that these are the children of Clemente and Ventura and that something surreal is going on in the poem. This particular stanza break also illustrates how the enjambment midsentence often suggests a certain breathlessness—as if Ventura's suddenly envisioning the children she will have with the young man she is about to kiss brings about a gasp, an involuntary pause in her thinking. After the mention of their children, line 8 proceeds to figure the children's children, and this advances the underlying sense of a cycle, redoubling the investment in Ventura's vision of the future.

While every couplet might be analyzed with regard to the significance of enjambment, cyclical repetitions, and the divesting of objects and verbs from subjects, certain usages stand out. Line 13 consists of just three words: "Their anxious breathing." The reader knows this to be the conclusion of the grammatical sentence describing the imagined children, and the period at line's end seems to close the thought. Yet line 13 remains as closely linked with its couplet mate, line 14, and thus, especially if the poem is read aloud, the idea of anxious breathing is attributed as well to Clemente and Ventura. This juxtaposition deftly reinforces the way the frequent breaks of the couplet form suggest a recurring breathlessness.

The end of line 20 is another point where the placement of the break suggests a double meaning. Grammatically, the sentence proceeding to line 21 suggests that Ventura can see what Clemente is feeling, but where the stanza break introduces a pause not unlike that of a comma—especially if the poem is read aloud in a nuanced fashion—the *feel* of line 21 could also be attributed to Ventura. Here, the poem's rendering ambiguous the subject of the verb effectively blends the consciousnesses of the two figures whose blending of existences is the seed of the poem.

After the half dozen couplets elaborating on the identities of those who will follow in the wake of the kiss, the manner in which line 37 begins its couplet is significant for shifting the focus back to the present. This line continues a sentence technically begun in line 32, though in its construction the sentence is not grammatically coherent, owing to several comma splices where conjunctions would be needed. This effectively suggests a detachment from consciousness of verbal rules that aligns well with Ventura's focus on her emotions and the physicality of the present; at such a time, her thoughts come not in elaborate constructions but in more spontaneous waves of assorted phrases. Thus, even while the sentence in question travels all the way from the serious wife of Margarito—who has just been imagined as an old man, presumably when Ventura is dead—back to the moment of the kiss, it aptly reflects Ventura's present consciousness. Indeed, with line 37, though the sentence remains displaced from any focalizing consciousness, the mention of the loudness of the noise suggests that the poem has delved back into Ventura's mind and her immediate perceptions. This is effectively confirmed with the referent-less appearance of the word *herself*.

The poem ends with a series of repetitions, again suggesting cyclicality and thus again figuring the cyclicality of human procreation, bringing generation after generation into being. The words *children* or *child* appear seven times in the poem, most lately in lines 35 and 40. Also toward the poem's end, the word *kiss* ends lines 39 and 40, the two lines of a couplet, lending a heightened power to that word, which is indeed the one signifier in which the entire poem is contained. Notably, of the six times that *kiss* appears in the poem, four are at line's end, in lines 14, 34, 39, and 40; only twice does it appear in the middle of the line—and in both cases, in lines 3 and 15, the word at the end of that line is *pomegranate*. As the kiss hangs in the balance, then, the pomegranate for the time being actually has more significance, since without the fruit, there would be no kiss. The word *pomegranate* appears at line's end one last time in line 45, as the poem, having lapsed beyond the moment of the kiss, now returns the reader to that moment by invoking the weight of the fruit that embodies the weight of Ventura and Clemente's entire future. Three times in the course of the final six lines, the reader is told that the kiss lasted precisely a quarter of a second—like the flash of a shooting star across the sky; the third time is the charm, as by the poem's final line the reader viscerally understands how the kiss may have been perfectly finite but that quarter of a second can go on forever.

Source: Michael Allen Holmes, Critical Essay on "The Pomegranate and the Big Crowd," in *Poetry for Students*, Gale, Cengage Learning, 2016.

Rachid Filali and Alberto Ríos
In the following interview, Ríos talks about the importance of poetry in society as a whole.

Rachid Filali: Professor Alberto Rios, do you think that poetry is able to detect the essential dimension of the human person. Why did you choose to write poetry instead of the novel, don't you think that we have more room to express ourselves in prose better than poetry?

Alberto Rios: Poetry, I think, speaks to our moments as human beings, not our more overarching narratives. We live in the moment, while narrative sums us up and generalizes our days and years. To speak simply of a chance encounter, for example, with a red bird—without any other expectations or overlays beyond the simple encounter—this frees us. The moment does not require that we speak for all red birds, nor does it require that we know where that red bird is going next, or where it has been last. The moment is simply the moment: I see a red bird. It may remind me of other red things, or simply be beautiful or ugly, but in that moment I have authority to speak. Indeed, I am called on to speak. This is the call to poetry, which is all the call to be human.

From that one kiss, the poem imagines an entire family tree. *(© Olesya Feketa | Shutterstock.com)*

Rachid Filali: American society puts money at the first rank of its interests though there are millions of people who are keen in literature and poetry in particular, how do you explain that paradox?

Alberto Rios: I return to the idea of the moment. We may discuss in high-minded terms all sorts of things, but in that same moment a contiguous truth may be that, while I am speaking, I may also be looking at a bowl of apricots and deciding to eat one. While the larger discourse may interest us and be vital to our longer lives, the apricot—this is not a paradox, but a simultaneity—the apricot is directly in our hands. This is a poetic moment, but the larger literary moment may be to follow the adventure of the apricot as it weaves itself into the greater fabric of the world. Which wins, one might ask, at the end of the day: the apricot or the job one has or the ideas one espouses? Perhaps they all count. But the apricot is so often overlooked that it is the fresh factor in the equation of our lives.

Rachid Filali: You edited ten books so far, do you think that you said everything you wanted to? Is there a particular, deeper more smart and more interesting and more human topics you feel are best to write them?

Alberto Rios: Many years ago, when I was first a student, I remember hearing what seemed like a horrible observation, but one which I nevertheless understood immediately. The observation, in the form of an insight on writing, was simple, but devastating: the worst thing for a writer is to have your parents still be alive. This, of course, speaks to the idea of conscience and of a social censor. Every writer thinks, at some point, what if my mother reads this? And later in life, what if my child reads this? This sensibility affects one's writing. If I had a wish, it would be to have the space somewhere to say what I really think, with all the details that I really conjure, and with all the passion that I really feel. That said, I am not saying that I don't attempt to do this in my work—I do. But I am always in a battle with my own sensibilities, with the lines I have drawn for myself inside.

Rachid Filali: You are skillful in English language. Is that a direct reason for your choice of writing? In other words, does language mastery enables us to express all what we want at the best moment and need?

Alberto Rios: I write almost entirely in English, but Spanish was, arguably, my first language. I am able to speak as freely as I choose in English and be as eloquent as I want. However, I think there is much to be said for roughness in language, for obvious struggle. In this moment, it often feels like we are made to take better notice of the moment—precisely because it is not well-said. At its best, this roughness begins to feel like discovery.

Rachid Filali: Who is the American poet whom you admire his fame and subtlety in writing?

Alberto Rios: This is always a very interesting and very difficult question. I have come to understand that my loyalty is so often to the page and not to the author, so that there are many works I love, and many writers I admire, but everything and everyone is invariably imperfect. This keeps me searching for more all the time. That said, I have often been a fan of the Latin American writers, the writers from "el boom," which speak to me in both literary and cultural ways.

Rachid Filali: You won many major awards. Does it motivates you to present the best? Do you think that lot of awards have other aims even perspectives behind literature?

Alberto Rios: My favorite awards embrace the impact of the work on whole communities as much as literary circles. I have a big interest in public art, public literature—that is, work that is actually in public places, on walls, on windows, in surprising places. I think I have found ways to speak to both writers and non-writers, to both readers and non-readers. When I can think about my work being able to travel anywhere, then I think it has done well—and any rewards feel like a reward for this ethos of never excluding anyone. I want to write, and have some effect on, the baker as much as any fellow poet.

Rachid Filali: You are successfully intermingling Latin and Anglo-Saxon cultures. How did you come to associate them though they are quite different?

Alberto Rios: I think this is a crucial question, especially with regard to my own work. Indeed, the cultures are different, but this is also what I use to make my writing successful. Being able to see everything—everything!—in more than one way and to address it all with more than one vocabulary helps me to have perspective on the world. To simply think that a pen is a pen and not also a pluma diminishes the pen. In my work, I try to bring more to the moment and to work from choice, not habit, especially when it comes to both cultural and linguistic offerings. My greater work in that moment, of course, is to always be a good translator—never to assume someone else knows what I know, but to do the work and take the time of making sure that we both understand.

Rachid Filali: Do you have any idea about contemporary Arabic literature?

Alberto Rios: Arabic literature, sad to say, is not as widely represented here as it ought to be. One might say that about many other literatures as well—until quite recently, literature here in the United States has been quite stereotypically ethnocentric. I say "stereotypically," however, with care—indeed, we have always had an Arabic population, and an Australian population, and a Norwegian population, and so on. It is folly to think in terms of numbers only. Still, Arabic literature is something I know through my encounters with Arabic-American writers, such as Naomi Shihab Nye, more than Arabic writers themselves. I expect this will change and is changing in the greater culture, and I know for certain that I myself am changing. I read the world, and am always hungry for more.

Source: Rachid Filali and Alberto Ríos, "Alberto Ríos: An Interview," in *Knot*, Spring 2015.

Robert Murray Davis

In the following review, Davis praises Ríos's "subtle artifice."

Most of the poems in Alberto Rios's eighth collection are associated with memories of his childhood on the Arizona-Mexico border in the 1950s, which helps account for the duality of his vision, or from his awareness of the Sonoran desert in which he has lived all of his life, which may account for the miragelike shifting and blending of shapes. (The smallest muscle, by the way, is in the ear—see "Some Extensions on the Sovereignty of Science," the concluding poem.)

Some of the poems, like "My Chili," are essentially local color, celebrating the varied tastes and effects of the vegetable that bites as it is bitten. Even here, however, duality and mutability are evident—and they are more obvious in other poems, where oranges change into birds and back again; where body parts transpose to other functions; where a coyote becomes a (flying) carpet and dogs become birds; where a nipple is pushed through a button-hole; where water dripping from mesquite trees is "not water but water / Mixed with what it brings from the leaves."

Given the shifting quality of things, it is no wonder that Rios says, in the volume's final line, that "Words are our weakest hold on the world." Of course, as one of Eliot's characters said, "I gotta use words when I talk to you," and Rios delights in the paradoxes and uncertainties both of language and of what it attempts to describe. He is most successful, I think, when, on the one hand, he does not strive too hard for paradox and, on the other, when he does not take refuge in mere nostalgia, as in his poem about playing baseball with an artificial lemon, or in portentous striving after significance, as in the conclusion that "It is not this dog's ears that hear. / It is the centuries, / And they answer back." He is talking about species memory. Fair enough, but sometimes one longs for a dog to be just a dog.

Even so, the (late) Audenesque tone of the opening poem, "A Physics of Sudden Light," seems entirely successful not only in itself but as a keynote for the collection: "In this light / You are not where you were but you have not moved." And in "If I Leave You," addressed to his son, the curt, almost choppy lines reflect the speaker's paradoxical disbelief in heaven and, for his son's sake, the need for it to exist.

Most important, although the poems are grounded in the scenery and rituals of a specific region, at his best Rios shows by the subtle artifice with which he has crafted them that definitions of his work by region and ethnicity are artificial in the worst sense of the word.

Source: Robert Murray Davis, Review of *The Smallest Muscle in the Human Body*, in *World Literature Today*, Vol. 77, No. 2, July–September 2003, p. 105.

Publishers Weekly

In the following review, the anonymous reviewer predicts "strong sales" for Ríos's collection The Smallest Muscle in the Human Body.

In this latest poetry collection by Rios, a veteran poet and story writer and professor of English at Arizona State University, the speaker focuses squarely on childhood experiences and memories. In poems that are typically prosy ("I was born in Nogales, Arizona / On the border between / Mexico and the United States"), the animating thoughts often far outweigh linguistic

exploration, as in a meditation "My Chili": "When you bite chili, / You are not biting chili. / With its own teeth and its own tongue / For taste, / The chili, after all, / Is biting you." Food memories are, in keeping with the book's title, a major focus of these recollections, as in "Chinese Food in the Fifties": "There was only one place. / Kim Wah's, Nogales, Mexico. / I ate only the white rice." More compellingly, the notes to this poem describe how the restaurant had a birdcage with birds who would fly up suddenly "if you entered too quickly," which the poet remembers when hiking in the desert, where white seeds of cottonwood filled the air. The intentionally banal ("Eating Potato Chips in Middle Age") or the ouch-inducing "The Nipplebutton" ("I drew your nipple through a buttonhole, / Idly at first and then with purpose, / The intrigue of a nipplebutton / Suddenly discovered. . .") make the collection list a little, but Rios's wry twinkle keeps things in balance.

Forecast: Rios's memoir, *Capirotada*, covers some of the same ground as these poems, as do his short stories, collected in three volumes, the latest of which is *The Curtain of Trees*. Both of those volumes are from the University of New Mexico and were published in 1999. Look for strong regional sales of this title, along with some course adoption nationwide.

Source: Review of *The Smallest Muscle in the Human Body*, in *Publishers Weekly*, Vol. 249, No. 17, April 29, 2002, pp. 65–66.

SOURCES

"Alberto Ríos," in *Superstition Review*, No. 6, Fall 2010, https://superstitionreview.asu.edu/issue6/interviews/albertorios (accessed August 13, 2015).

"Alberto Ríos: Short Bio," Alberto Álvaro Ríos website, http://www.public.asu.edu/~aarios/bio/ (accessed August 13, 2015).

Behrendt, Stephen C., Review of *The Theater of Night*, in *Prairie Schooner*, Vol. 81, No. 4, Winter 2007, pp. 183–88.

Candelaria, Cordelia, *Chicano Poetry: A Critical Introduction*, Greenwood Press, 1986, pp. 179, 195.

Cárdenas, Lupe, and Justo Alarcón, "Entrevista con Alberto Ríos," in *Confluencia*, Vol. 6, No. 1, Fall 1990, pp. 119–26.

del Castillo, Richard Griswold, "Treaty of Guadalupe Hidalgo," PBS website, http://www.pbs.org/kera/usmexic

anwar/war/wars_end_guadalupe.html (accessed August 15, 2015).

"Ineligible Poems," Poetry Out Loud website, http://www.poetryoutloud.org/poems-and-performance/ineligible-poems (accessed August 15, 2015).

Lengel, Kerry, "Alberto Ríos Named Arizona's First Poet Laureate," AZCentral, http://www.azcentral.com/thingstodo/arts/articles/20130819alberto-ros-named-arizona-first-poet-laureate.html (accessed August 13, 2015).

Olszewski, Lawrence, Review of *The Theater of Night*, in *Library Journal*, Vol. 131, No. 8, May 1, 2006, p. 90.

Review of *The Theater of Night*, in *New Yorker*, Vol. 82, No. 9, April 17, 2006, p. 79.

Review of *The Theater of Night*, in *Publishers Weekly*, Vol. 253, No. 8, February 20, 2006, p. 138.

Ríos, Alberto, Author's Note to *Pig Cookies and Other Stories*, Chronicle Books, 1995, pp. xi–xiv.

———, "The Body of My Work," in *Genre*, Vol. 32, Nos. 1–2, Spring–Summer 1999, pp. 27–39.

———, Dedication and "The Pomegranate and the Big Crowd," in *The Theater of Night*, Copper Canyon Press, 2005, pp. v, 10–12.

Saldívar, José David, "Alberto (Alvaro) Ríos," in *Dictionary of Literary Biography*, Vol. 122, *Chicano Writers: Second Series*, edited by Francisco A. Lomeli and Carl R. Shirley, Gale Research, 1992.

Shirley, Carl R., and Paula W. Shirley, *Understanding Chicano Literature*, University of South Carolina Press, 1988, pp. 3–61.

FURTHER READING

Christie, John S., and José B. Gonzalez, eds., *Latino Boom: An Anthology of U.S. Latino Literature*, Pearson/Longman, 2006.

> This recent anthology, one of many compiling Chicano and other Latino works, offers over five hundred pages of Latino fiction, poetry, drama, and essays, including a couple of works by Ríos.

Kleinberg, Ann, *Pomegranates: 70 Celebratory Recipes*, Ten Speed Press, 2004.

> Drawing on recipes kept by aunts and grandmothers for decades, Kleinberg has assembled the most comprehensive collection of pomegranate recipes available, fit for celebrating any occasion with vivid color and tart sweetness. She includes several pages of introductory text headed "The Pomegranate: An Extraordinary Gift from Nature."

Niggli, Josephina, *Mexican Village*, University of North Carolina Press, 1945.

> Niggli, an Anglo-American born in Mexico in 1910, was one of the earliest authors to treat Mexican American experiences in the English language. This novel in stories, her most famous work, treats the experiences of an Anglo-American when he returns to the Mexican village in which he was born.

Taylor, Lawrence J., *Ambos Nogales: Intimate Portraits of the U.S.-Mexico Border*, photographs by Maeve Hickey, School of American Research Press, 2002.

> This volume contrasts through black-and-white photography the environs of Ríos's hometown of Nogales, Arizona, with those of Nogales, Sonora, Mexico, as connected by immigration, the drug cartels, and at least one tunnel.

SUGGESTED SEARCH TERMS

Alberto Ríos AND The Pomegranate and the Big Crowd

Alberto Ríos AND The Theater of Night

Alberto Ríos AND Clemente and Ventura

Chicano literature

Chicano poetry

Chicano OR Hispano AND culture

young adult Chicano AND fiction OR poetry

Alberto Ríos AND Lorna Dee Cervantes OR Gary Soto

"The Pomegranate and the Big Crowd" AND Poetry Out Loud

Punishment in Kindergarten

KAMALA DAS

1965

In Kamala Das's poem "Punishment in Kinder-garten," published in her first collection, *Summer in Calcutta*, in 1965, an adult speaker remembers her childhood embarrassment at the hands of a teacher unsympathetic to her withdrawn nature. Das was a powerhouse of Indian poetry written in English. Her characteristic flare for drama turns the tragedy of a moment in the speaker's vulnerable childhood into a triumph of her ability as an adult to leave the past behind. Using free verse, enjambment, and a casual tone revolution-ary for her time and place, Das overcomes her past as a colonial subject in her masterly explora-tion of a poetic voice all her own.

AUTHOR BIOGRAPHY

Das was born into a prominent Hindu family on March 31, 1934, in Punnayurkulam, Thrissur dis-trict, in Kerala, India. Her mother, who was the well-known poet Balamani Amma, and her grand-mother were major influences in her childhood. Das was mostly homeschooled, though she did attend the Saint Cecilia European Catholic School in Calcutta. Unlike many of her postindependence poet contemporaries, she did not attend college. In 1949, at fifteen years old, Das became the wife of Kalipurayath Madhava Das in an arranged mar-riage. A financial specialist at the Reserve Bank of India in Bombay (now Mumbai), Das's husband

The lovely image of the flowers is tied to the young girl's pain. (© Jolanta Wojcicka | Shutterstock.com)

was fourteen years her senior. Their relationship was deeply troubled, and Das suffered a nervous breakdown in the first years of the marriage. She eventually had three sons.

From 1949 to 1981, Das lived primarily in Bombay with interludes in Calcutta (now Kolkata) and Delhi. *Summer in Calcutta*, her first collection of poetry, was published in 1965, establishing her reputation as an important young writer of Indian English poetry. One of the poems in the collection, "Punishment in Kindergarten," recounts an incident from Das's childhood in which she was chastised for wandering the grounds of Victoria Gardens alone rather than playing with her classmates. Her second and third collections, *The Descendants* (1967) and *The Old Playhouse and Other Poems* (1973), debuted to similarly positive reviews. Das's autobiography, *My Story* (1976), written at the age of thirty-seven in her native tongue of Malayalam, was a shockingly honest confessional narrative of Das's struggles in her marriage. For some critics, such honesty from a woman was seen as offensive, but for many others, Das became a symbol of the feminist struggle.

After *My Story* propelled Das to fame and infamy, she founded an art collective called Bahutantrika at her home in Bombay, where artists, publishers, and members of the literary community gathered once a month for performances, readings, and socializing.

In 1984, Das entered the Indian parliamentary elections on a platform promoting the religion of love, but she lost by a wide margin. She won the Sahitya Akademi Award in English in 1985 for her *Collected Poems*, volume 1. She was nominated for the Nobel Prize in 1984 and won the Asian Poetry Prize in 1998 and the Asian World Prize in 2000. Writing as Kamala Das in English and Madhavikutty in Malayalam, Das penned six novels, numerous short-story and poetry collections, and three memoirs and contributed to a number of magazines and newspapers, including *Debonair*, *Imprint*, the *Illustrated Weekly of India*, *Poetry East and West*, *Love and Friendship*, and *Mathrubhumi*, growing to international renown.

Das's husband died in 1992. After a period of mourning, Das converted to Islam in 1999 and changed her name to Kamala Surayya. She died in Pune, Maharashtra, India, on May 31, 2009, and was buried with full state honors. Her funeral procession was attended by thousands and was broadcast live on television.

POEM SUMMARY

The text used for this summary is from *The Aesthetics of Sensuality: A Stylistic Study of the Poetry of Kamala Das*, Atlantic Publishers and Distributors, 2000, pp. 144–45. A version of the poem can be found on the following web page: http://www.english-for-students.com/Punishment-in-Kindergarten.html.

"Punishment in Kindergarten" begins as the speaker declares that today the world belongs to her a little more than it did before. She feels no need to reminisce about her childhood embarrassment—the pain a woman in a blue dress caused her with harsh words. Those words stole the pleasure from an otherwise idyllic day, falling like pots and pans. The woman called the speaker a strange child, scolding her for sitting alone rather than joining her classmates.

On that sunny day, the classmates sat on the lawn in small groups, drinking sugarcane juice. At the woman's words, they turned to laugh and jeer at the speaker, who cried. She hid her face in the hedge, where she could smell both the flowers and her pain. She wonders at the nature of children—how they can find joy in another's sadness.

In the present, the words are dampened, the children's laughing faces indistinct. Since that day, many years have passed, quickly, memory catching at the best moments before speeding onward, sadly. The speaker's mind is calm and mature in adulthood. The speaker does not need the memory of that painful picnic when she lay in the hedge, hidden and crying, watching the harsh sun stand in the sky, alone.

THEMES

Childhood

The speaker's childhood is marred by an incident on an otherwise beautiful day on a school trip when a woman supervising the class singles out the speaker as strange for choosing to play by herself rather than with the other children. Though the incident seems like an innocent

TOPICS FOR FURTHER STUDY

- Start a blog in which you discuss Indian independence. In a minimum of five posts, explore the history of British India, the push for independence, the local and global reaction to the creation of the Republic of India, the role of Mahatma Gandhi, and the changes that occurred in Indian culture, politics, and everyday life as a result. The site blogger.com offers free blog space.

- Read Preeti Shenoy's young-adult novel *Life Is What You Make It* (2011). What role does memory play in the story of Ankita? How would you compare Das's speaker's feelings toward her past to Ankita's? What other similarities can you find between the novel and "Punishment in Kindergarten"? Summarize your thoughts in an essay.

- Using a tool such as PowerPoint, create a presentation about an Indian poet of your choice from any time in the country's history. Include a biography, a bibliography, and an overview of the poet's style and influence in India and beyond. Be sure to include a slide in which you cite your sources.

- Using "Punishment in Kindergarten" as your inspiration, compose a poem in free verse about an important childhood memory of your own.

- Choose a single image from "Punishment in Kindergarten," for example, the sun or the laughing children, and in a brief essay explain the significance of the image to the poem as a whole, its symbolic value, if any, and its relation to the other images in the poem.

enough example of a shy child's being bullied by an insensitive adult and teased by her peers, the speaker feels the psychological trauma so keenly that she still experiences pangs of shame as an adult when she unexpectedly remembers what happened. The idyllic childhood setting includes a happy summer picnic in a garden with flowers blooming in the hedge and children sipping sugarcane juice. Only the sun hangs in the sky on this cloudless, pretty day for some time outdoors. The sun heats the ground pleasantly, and the day itself becomes honey colored. Yet into this magical, innocent atmosphere a villain arrives in the form of the adult antagonist, a woman who attacks rather than nurtures one of the children under her care.

The poem's narrative takes on qualities of a fairy tale as the evil woman terrorizes the quiet, thoughtful girl. Whether the exaggerations of childhood make the sunlight brighter and the tears hotter or if a truly perfect day is stolen does not matter. What is important is the speaker's perception of her own pain, which seems to remain so traumatic that even as an adult she struggles to forget the incident completely. This moment has perhaps shaped her development from kindergarten onward. The punishment she faced was too harsh for her crime of wandering the lawn by herself, happily absorbed in her own thoughts. As a result, a piece of childhood bliss was stolen from the speaker forever.

Memory

"Punishment in Kindergarten" moves back and forth through time as the narrator as an adult recalls a childhood memory. The memory of her humiliation at the hands of a teacher has troubled the speaker. She begins the poem by declaring herself free from the past incident and stronger for its erasure from her memory. Yet she cannot help but think of it one last time. She relives her shame and tears as the solitary focus of cruel, laughing faces and then returns to the present once more. As an adult, she claims that the faces, the laughter, and the emotional sting of the memory are no longer sharp but are distorted and weakened by time. She has no reason to revisit a shame so far removed from the present that the memory itself is fading. Even as she claims to be through with it, however, she drifts back again in memory to the moment she lies by the hedge, staring into the sky in pained disbelief at what has befallen her.

The tug of war between past and present is a battle the speaker must wage with the bitter memory over her self-worth. The world is hers if only she can overcome the reminder of her childhood shame. Though she seems willing and ready to let the trauma go, allowing it to be forgotten, she seems helpless in remembering

The poem describes the speaker's memory of a special picnic day at her childhood school.

(© Alexander Mazurkevich | Shutterstock.com)

it over and over, even while declaring herself free. The sharp detail may have faded with passing years, but even the barest memory can linger like a ghost.

Shame

The speaker's shame and embarrassment are products of her teacher's calling her strange in front of the class. The speaker, a kindergartener at the time, does not, it seems, feel lonely, strange, or embarrassed as she marvels at the beauty of the day. She does not see her solitude as negative or deserving of punishment. She is simply admiring the peaceful picnic setting when, without warning, she is found guilty of acting peculiar and is punished through public humiliation. As a result of being shamed, she feels the ache of loneliness, whereas before she felt peaceful solitude. She feels pain so acute she can actually smell it, whereas before she was wrapped in pleasure as she drifted through the honeyed, warm atmosphere on the lawn.

The speaker finds that the force of the unpleasant memory has followed her into adult life. Under other circumstances, the day would have been forgotten entirely or been simply a pleasant recollection. The speaker's shame was instilled in her through an outside force. She does not blame the children because she considers children to be naturally somewhat cruel, but the woman who cannot forgive the speaker's introversion has damaged her self-confidence even in adulthood. In the poem's present day, she struggles to make her claim on the world as a result of the painful lesson that she should feel ashamed to be different.

STYLE

Enjambment

In poetry, *enjambment* is the technique of continuing a sentence from one line to the next, thus interrupting the thought abruptly through a line break before continuing one line down. Das uses enjambment throughout her work as a signature of her informal poetic style. Enjambment occurs several times in each of the three stanzas of "Punishment in Kindergarten." Because the sentence is continued from one line to the next rather than ended at the last word of the line with punctuation, enjambment speeds the reader's eye down the page. Devindra Kohli writes in the introduction to *Kamala Das: Selected Poems*: "Run-on line is a distinctive feature of Kalama Das's poems.... Her enjambment propels the reader forward through the poem and keeps us reading." Suspense is created because the visual line ending does not coincide with the conclusion of the thought, adding importance to the last and first words of the lines in which enjambment is used. Enjambment thus can add tension, speed, and a sense of informality to a poem.

Free Verse

Free verse refers to poetry that is not structured by rhyme or meter. The poet is free to shape the poem on the page both phonetically and physically. Free verse is especially significant in the work of postindependence Indian poets like Das because it represents a blatant rejection of formal metered and rhymed poetry as taught and popularized during the British rule of India. "Punishment in Kindergarten" is free verse with no set line length, rhyme scheme, or structure. As a result, the poem sounds conversational, mimicking human speech rather than a predictable pattern of rhyme.

Narrative Poetry

A *narrative* poem is a poem that tells a story. It has a narrator, characters, and sometimes dialogue as found in prose but is written in poetic form instead. A narrative poem can be any length and can take any form—free verse, rhymed, blank verse, or a preset form such as a sonnet or sestina. "Punishment in Kindergarten" is a narrative poem told in free verse. The speaker acts as the first-person narrator, describing the traumatic event in her past. The characters include the speaker, the woman in the blue dress, and the speaker's young classmates. Das even includes a line of dialogue in which the speaker's antagonist humiliates her for being different. The story has a beginning, rising action, and conclusion as the speaker introduces her memory, relives it in detail, and then concludes that she is stronger now and no longer feels the shame of that day. The narrative aspects of the poem are aided by Das's use of free verse and enjambment, which allow the story to flow naturally as if it were spoken aloud or written in prose form.

Synesthesia

Synesthesia in poetry is an advanced form of figurative language in which two sensory images are blended together to create confusion between the senses. For example, a combination of sight and sound would be "I saw chirping," and a combination of taste and sight would be "He tasted the red." Synesthesia in poetry is based on a rare neurological disorder of the same name in which two or more of a person's senses are mixed; for example, a person may see specific colors when they hear certain sounds, feel sensations at the sight of color, or taste words when they hear them spoken aloud.

In poetry, synesthesia is often used to emphasize particularly powerful sensory moments. Das uses synesthesia in "Punishment in Kindergarten" when the speaker buries her face in the hedge and smells the flowers and pain. Smelling pain is an example of scent-touch synesthesia. The olfactory action of smelling is answered not by a matching olfactory reaction but by a kinesthetic one. The commingling of the two senses is indicative of the speaker's volatile emotional state. The presence of synesthetic imagery in a poem typically implies the experience of a particularly powerful sensation, as exemplified in "Punishment in Kindergarten."

HISTORICAL CONTEXT

Indian Independence

The Indian Independence Act of 1947 abolished the British governance of India and began a

COMPARE
&
CONTRAST

- **1965:** On January 25, a riot breaks out over the planned adoption of Hindi as India's official language. The unrest continues for two months, as non-Hindus demand that the English language remain in use. Approximately seventy people die during the riots, which are quelled when Prime Minister Lal Bahadur Shasti promises that Hindi will not be India's official language in light of the protests.

  Today: Although both Hindi and English remain in use in the Indian government, the nation is home to more than one thousand languages according to the 2001 census, with 122 of these languages spoken by more than ten thousand people. Twenty-two languages are included in India's constitution as scheduled (meaning major) languages.

- **1965:** *An Anthology of Commonwealth Verse*, edited by Margaret O'Donnell and published in 1963, collects the work of 234 poets from the British Commonwealth, including thirty Indian poets. Das is among the poets chosen to represent India's English-language poetry, bringing her fame outside of India. The anthology is among the first surveys of world literature in English and effectively legitimizes non-Western literature in Western studies, beginning the expansion of the Western canon to include authors of literature in English from non-Western countries.

  Today: Courses in Indian history and literature and classes focusing on world literature in English are available at Western colleges and universities. Works by Indian authors (both written in English and translated from their original languages) are widely available in Western bookstores.

- **1965:** With the debut of *Summer in Calcutta*, Das proves not only that quality poetry representative of the Indian experience can be written in English but also that a woman can write such self-affirming work. She becomes a feminist icon and inspiration to women writers, though she does not self-identify as feminist.

  Today: Das's literary legacy remains intact, though many of her feminist fans are dismayed by her late-in-life conversion to Islam, which they see as a betrayal of feminist values. Das is widely anthologized and remembered as a fearless pioneer of postindependence Indian English poetry and of the rejection of gender stereotypes and expectations.

---

transitional period known as the Dominion of India that lasted from the day the act became law on August 15, 1947, to the day the new constitution went into effect. On January 26, 1950, the Republic of India was formed, releasing the region from a history of British rule dating to the seventeenth century. A portion of India was partitioned to form Pakistan, an Islamic republic, and India was declared a secular democracy. Das came of age during the first years of the new republic and joined her fellow postindependence poets in creating a new style of poetry to mark the change in their country. Jawaharlal Nehru served as the country's first prime minister, from 1947 to 1964, and his party, the Indian National Congress, won control of the parliament in the first national election in 1952. The constitution established the position of president of India, an office first held by Rajendra Prasad.

The Indian independence movement had its foundation in the first rebellions against British rule in India nearly a hundred years before independence would be won, but the self-rule movement began in earnest in the 1930s, under the leadership of Mahatma Gandhi, a believer in nonviolent protest and civil disobedience. Though successful, independence for India came at a heavy cost. Because of the partition of India into

The speaker recalls the cruelty of her classmates, laughing at her tears. (© v.s.anandhakrishna | Shutterstock.com)

two states, tens of millions of people were displaced from both India and the newly created Pakistan, and hundreds of thousand were killed as a result of religious conflict.

The artists of postindependence India were left with the task of reclaiming the simultaneously ancient and fledgling country for their own. Devindra Kohli writes, "For Indian poets writing in English, the cry was for change and innovation. To them, themes and languages of the eminent pre-1947 poets . . . who were inspired and shaped by the Indian freedom movement, seemed remote." Thus the postindependence literary community embarked on a journey of experimentation and self-discovery.

Indian Poetry in English

Das wrote most of her prose in her native language of Malayalam and most of her poetry in English. Indian poetry in English was popularized by Nissim Ezekiel and perfected among his post-independence contemporaries, including Dom Moraes, A. K. Ramanujan, Keki Daruwalla, R. Parthasarathy, and Das. Their goal was to claim the English language for themselves, molding it to reflect their perspective and experience while rejecting traditional forms of English poetry, such as rhyme and meter. Embracing the language itself while stripping away the rigid structure lying beneath allowed the postindependence poets writing in English to simultaneously disinherit the colonial influence of the British while appropriating the language for their own use.

After the achievement of independence, English became India's language in much the same way it became the language of the United States: as passed on through colonialism and remaining after the ousting of imperial rule. The American dialect of English reflects the American experience, just as Das's English-language poems reflect life in India. The difference lies in the fact that Americans originally spoke English as colonizers, whereas Indians learned English in addition to their native languages as colonized peoples. For this reason, some critics have attacked writers of Indian poetry in English as betraying their country by paying homage to its conquerors. Paradoxically, Kohli writes, "Post-Independence Indian English writers have been criticized by writers in other Indian languages more than they were in pre-Independence India." Yet the simple fact is that English is a major Indian language. Though its arrival in the country was through colonialism, its perseverance past the colonial expiration date is, for Das and many others, no reason to mourn. The postindependence poets seized the colonizer's English and made it their own in an act of national and personal empowerment. They claimed the language for themselves but threw out the British rules governing its use, creating an open landscape of possibility for the future of truly Indian English.

CRITICAL OVERVIEW

Das is a giant of Indian poetry written in English, as Devika Nair describes in "Kamala Das: Many Selves, Many Tongues," in the *Hindu*: "Das's poetry in English...iconoclastic for a poet of her generation, has earned her the label of feminist writer and the epithet 'the mother of modern English Indian poetry.'"

As a prominent member of the postindependence poets, Das claimed the English language as her own to use as she wished, regardless of India's colonized history, allowing other authors to follow in her wake without fear. A. N. Dwivedi writes of her inescapable influence in *Kamala Das and Her Poetry*: "Das...looms large over the poetic horizon of today's India."

Mohammad Shaukat Ansari admires Das for her command of Indian English. In his essay for *Indian Language*, "Depiction of Women's Dilemmas in Select Poems of Kamala Das: A Review," he writes, "Das is one of the most significant voices of Indian English poetry."

Because of her capricious nature and penchant for scandal, Das attracted her share of harsh criticism during her lifetime from those who thought her behavior improper for a woman, as Shahnaz Habib recounts in her obituary of Das for the *Guardian*: "Das's spontaneity often translated into whimsicality and earned the ire of critics, but it allowed her to explore the paradoxes of life and relationships with emotional honesty."

Merrily Weisbord writes in her memoir of her friendship with Das, *The Love Queen of Malabar*, in praise of Das's "brilliant poetic sensibility, her playfulness, warmth, vulnerability, courage, and physical charisma...her mercurial nature, her need for love and assurance, her contradictions."

In his review of Das's first poetry collection, Devindra Kohli offers a glowing reminder of how Das came to be so widely known: "*Summer in Calcutta* was a landmark book. Kamala Das's homespun style...struck a refreshingly new chord in English Poetry in India."

With her finger always on the pulse of her country, Das remained relevant throughout a career that began as a teenager and stretched into the final years of her long life. N. V. Raveendran writes in *The Aesthetics of Sensuality: A Stylistic Study of the Poetry of Kamala Das*: "Kamala Das is an artist who is capable of transforming the impulses of the times into poetry. In this way her poetry shows the dialectical presence of individuality and universality."

V. C. Harris, in the introduction to Das's *The Old Playhouse and Other Poems*, summarizes Das's legacy as an important voice for change in the modern world: "Talking about Kamala Das today...means talking about not merely post-Independence Indian poetry in English but also a whole range of issues...relating to gender, violence, identity, and difference."

CRITICISM

Amy L. Miller
Miller is a graduate of the University of Cincinnati, and she currently resides in New Orleans, Louisiana. In the following essay, she uncovers the connection between Das's "Punishment in Kindergarten" and the search by postindependence India for an identity of its own.

In "Punishment in Kindergarten," the adult speaker struggles to overcome a childhood trauma. The memory of a teacher's harsh words and her schoolmates' laughter has faded over time, but she remains troubled by the incident. Though the poem begins with the speaker's brave declaration that she now lives free of the memory of her pain, the illusion of victory is short-lived as the past gradually comes to dominate the poem's narrative. The final lines of the poem take place in the speaker's miserable past as opposed to her more self-confident present. However, the poem does not overtly suggest either triumph over the memory or defeat by it. Instead, the text subtly suggests the power not of erasure of the past or surrender to the past but incorporation and acceptance as the surest path toward progress.

WHAT DO I READ NEXT?

- Tanuja Desai Hidier's young-adult novel *Born Confused* (2002) tells the story of Dimple Lala, an American girl who must balance her parents' Indian traditions with the pressures of high school as the time comes for the arrangement of her marriage to a suitable boy.

- Octavio Paz's nonfiction essay collection *In Light of India* (1998) recounts the six years Paz served as the Mexican ambassador to India in the 1960s. A Nobel Prize–winning poet, Paz turns his keen eye for beauty and turmoil toward Indian society, finding plenty of both during his exploration of the country's culture, people, and politics.

- Das's posthumous short-story collection *The Kept Woman and Other Stories* (2010) examines the complexities of relationships, especially when love mystifies and distorts human behavior beyond rationality.

- Walt Whitman's *Leaves of Grass* (1855) was an early inspiration for the young Das as she discovered the possibilities afforded by free-verse poetry. Whitman was a transcendentalist and a founding father of American poetry. *Leaves of Grass* is at once a journey to the center of the human soul and a celebration of the natural world.

- *Dom Moraes: Selected Poems* (2012) gathers the work of the postindependence poet Moraes, a contemporary of Das's and fellow author of Indian poetry in English. Like Das's, Moraes's experimentation with style and language solidified his place in history at the forefront of the poetic redefinition of India.

- Nissim Ezekiel's *Collected Poems* (1976) showcases the work of the preeminent writer of Indian poetry in English. Inspired by European modernists, Ezekiel's poetry breaks down the formal voice previously used in Indian poetry to better express life as a citizen of free India.

- *The Cilappatikaram of Ilanko Atikal: An Epic of South India* (1992), translated by the postindependence author R. Parthasarathy, stands as one of India's greatest epics. It is a Tamil love story centered on a pair of lovers and a magical anklet that is stolen with disastrous results.

- Eunice de Souza's *Purdah: An Anthology* (2004) is a collection of literature on *purdah*, the seclusion of women both at home and in public in some Eastern countries, including parts of India. From behind the veil and in front of it, perspectives of men and women across languages, countries, and genres are included.

- Keki Daruwalla's *Collected Poems, 1970–2005* (2006) assembles the work of a prominent postindependence Indian poet writing in English. With a love of subtle imagery and succinct language, Daruwalla demonstrates in a masterly way how the poets of his generation made the English language their own.

- A. K. Ramanujan's *Folktales from India* (1991) is a collection of folktales from across India translated, annotated, and introduced by Ramanujan. The 111 folktales represent a variety of cultures, religions, and traditions while familiar characters such as trickster gods, foolish kings, and clever animals remind the reader of the universal nature of stories.

A. N. Dwivedi discusses the anecdote from Das's life that inspired the poem: "'Punishment in Kindergarten' is warm and muffled, and recounts the picnic of the poetess at Victoria Gardens to which she and her classmates were taken, and the incident which followed it." The speaker's incident with her teacher is especially humiliating because the speaker does not feel she

> THE POEM FRUSTRATES THE READER'S DESIRE TO KNOW FOR CERTAIN THE SPEAKER'S FATE BY LEAVING BOTH THE SPEAKER OF THE PAST—THE LITTLE GIRL LYING LONELY UNDER THE SUN—AND THE ADULT IN THE PRESENT AT A CROSSROADS."

is in the wrong. Though extremely young, she knows in her heart that keeping to herself feels more natural to her than socializing. Yet the voice of authority in the form of her teacher announces that her nature is peculiar, and her classmates laugh at her when she cries as a result.

The teacher has an eye peeled for children who stand out from the crowd. Considering it her duty to fold such children back into the flock, she represents a systematic approach to education in which children are to be molded into the correct form, not encouraged in their eccentricities. Meanwhile, the speaker is too young to fight back against such a prominent figure of authority in her young life. She spends the rest of the picnic hiding, her self-affirming solitude transformed to weeping loneliness. She communes with the sun in the poem's final lines, a figure of equal loneliness in the clear, blue sky. N. V. Raveendran writes, "Instead of the usual way of glorification of childhood Kamala Das takes up the helplessness, dependency and lack of individuality of the child. Being an adult means possessing individuality and potential to create." One wonders, encountering the speaker as an adult, whether she has been hiding ever since that day, unable to take pride in her solitary nature as a result of the harsh lesson of her teacher.

Devindra Kohli praises the "sun-drenched abundance of *Summer in Calcutta*," describing the rebellious charm of Das's "speech rhythms, with their almost total disregard of the traditional iambic line of English verse [and] her imagery drawn from immediate contexts of experience." Almost all of Das's signature poetic techniques are in use in "Punishment in Kindergarten," including the wealth of literary devices that Das uses to create an informal, conversational tone. The poem is, like much of Das's work, narrative,

semiautobiographical, and written in English in free verse in the first person with liberal use of enjambment.

Das's style as a postindependence poet was a direct rejection of formal British literary structures and sought honest self-expression over adherence to a set of rules. Kohli writes, "Her sudden shifts in manner and voice, tone and syntax, imagery and rhythm, so characteristic of her, surprise with freshness but they also disconcert anyone expecting compliance with formalist poetics."

Das did not shy away from ambiguity in "Punishment in Kindergarten": the speaker contradicts her own vow to forget the past and move on almost as soon as she makes it. The poem frustrates the reader's desire to know for certain the speaker's fate by leaving both the speaker of the past—the little girl lying lonely under the sun—and the adult in the present at a crossroads.

The poem can be read as an allegory of postindependence India's search for an identity of its own. Hundreds of years of British rule left a deep imprint in Indian society, not least of which was the prevalence of the English language. In the years leading up to and following India's independence, heated debates and even riots broke out over the complex issue of using the English language—the language of the colonizers—in an India free of English rule. Would it be possible to erase the use of English entirely from India's borders? Did the use of English indicate a degree of sympathy or collusion with the imperialists, like a language version of Stockholm syndrome, in which the captive empathizes with the captor? Or was there a compromise available that would acknowledge the futility of attempting to forget a centuries-long colonial past while reshaping the language of the colonizers to suit the needs of an independent India? V. C. Harris writes, "The newly emerging post-Independence subject attempts to rework, redefine, and relocate the language and discourse of the colonial master." Das, with her flouting of the traditions of English poetry without giving up the language itself, believed in her right to take, change, and use English to express herself.

If "Punishment in Kindergarten" is considered through the lens of postcolonialism, then the role of England—the colonizer—is filled by the teacher while the adult speaker plays the role of India coming to terms with its colonial past. The teacher, a cold authority figure wearing blue, the dominant color of the Union Jack, attempts to correct the peculiar behavior of one of her many wards (the colonized countries of the Commonwealth) using words as her weapons (English language and culture). The young girl, India, cowed under such might, withdraws in pain and self-doubt. As an adult, years removed from the authority of that problematic teacher, the speaker (postcolonial India) feels comfortable claiming a stake in the world as a result of overcoming her memories of the oppression of her past. Yet memories remain of how the seclusion that came so naturally to her (India being naturally barricaded from the rest of the Asian continent by the Himalayas) is harshly interrupted by a corrective outside force. The adult speaker, or independent India, struggles with the best method by which to move on from her past now that she is free but finds that attempting to ignore it completely will not work—she can still hear the teacher's voice (the language of the colonizer) inside her head.

"Punishment in Kindergarten" is simultaneously a poetic retelling of a childhood event in Das's life and an allegory for the problems of identity and language that the postindependence Indian population faced. Such depth and subtlety is why Shahnaz Habib writes, "Das was at the forefront of a new movement in Indian English poetry, a shift in focus from the colonial experience to the personal." Though "Punishment in Kindergarten" can be read as a tract on postcolonial issues in India, those issues are expressed through the more immediate tale of the fragility of a young girl's self-conception and how that identity is crushed too easily by a careless adult.

Kohli writes: "Poetry channels into words a complex of emotions and ideas aroused by real and imagined events. . . . In a poem ideas are compressed so as to cohere in images and rhythm." Much is said between the lines of "Punishment in Kindergarten" through Das's use of imagery contrasting the bright, happy Indian summer day with the forcefulness of the teacher. Inherent in any of Das's free-verse narrative poetry in English, by nature of her personal style, is a declaration of her independence from British rule in her appropriation of the English language to express her Indian life. Unique to "Punishment in Kindergarten," however, is her oblique treatment of postcolonial issues of dominion, memory, and the language of the colonizers.

Just as the teacher has no sympathy for the speaker's quiet nature, so Das has no sympathy for the teacher, portraying her as a haplessly cruel

Although years have passed, the memory of being scolded by her teacher is still painful for the speaker. (© Zurijeta / Shutterstock.com)

tormentor. In her work, Das disdains the intolerant, the judgmental, and those too devoted to the rules to see the value in nonconformity. Kohli writes: "That the rejection of hate is a conscious choice is evident in Kamala Das's poetry." Das was a poet of love, not hatred, even for those who caused hurt. The speaker of "Punishment in Kindergarten" does not hate the children who laughed at her misery, and though she feels victimized by the teacher who upset her so thoroughly as a child, the speaker's only concern is with healing her own damaged ego, not with seeking revenge. "Punishment in Kindergarten" is a pensive and beautiful meditation on a wrongfully accused child who seeks closure as an adult. Das's sultry depiction of the perfect summer day and its sudden, stormy turn toward shame and tears exemplifies her creativity and control as a powerful force in the world of Indian poetry in English.

Source: Amy L. Miller, Critical Essay on "Punishment in Kindergarten," in *Poetry for Students*, Gale, Cengage Learning, 2016.

> IF DAS' POETRY OF PERSONAL CONFESSION IS
> TO BE COMPARED WITH ANY POET, IT IS TO BE
> COMPARED WITH THE INDIAN WOMEN POETS,
> INCLUDING THE BHAKTI POETS, WHO LIVED AND
> WROTE CENTURIES AGO."

Anisur Rahman

In the following excerpt, Rahman points out that Das's love poetry is not necessarily about romantic love.

. . . In contesting what is generally posited, I would like to assert that love in Kamala Das is not necessarily romantic love concerned with the male-female relationship and various manifestations of this relationship. Love acquires a broader meaning in her poetry; it is a principle of living and of divine sustenance. It goes beyond the stereotypical male-female syndrome, embraces a larger humanity, and incorporates greater human sympathies. In these poems, one finds an extension of a liberal self that is naturally drawn to the world outside where she engages with the figure of the male lover, the politically oppressed, the socially ostracized, and the ethnically marginalized. In relating with this world of myriad manifestations, she also transcends it and looks towards an adorable deity who remains unseen although he is eminently reachable as a lover. In fact, approaching a deity to seek one's resolution is the way in which Das defines love.

Love, lust, passion, and erotica have often been used in synonymous ways to discuss Das' poetry. It is important to note that she seeks her solace through love and this love is not a matter of consummation but of a desire to realize one's own self both in physical and spiritual terms. Let me suggest that the expression of sensuality/sexuality is only too natural for the human species and one may be unjustifiably blamed for sincerely expressing it. Precisely this is what has happened in the case of this poet. It is, therefore, important to say that her love poetry is not so much about the celebration of sexual love for which she has often been blamed as it is about the lack of genuine love. In fact, it is about desire and yearning.

In spite of being deeply rooted in a sacrosanct socio-cultural background and heritage, she chose to express herself boldly and uninhibitedly at a point of time when no one else had thought of doing so. This bold act of frank and free expression was quite clearly liable to be mistaken for the flaunting of her lust. Far from being the poetry of lust or erotica, Das' poetry glosses upon the pangs of love rather than the raptures of flesh. After reading the tame verse of Toru Dutt and Sarojini Naidu, approaching a poet like Das could not have been an easily acceptable experience for most readers. Das was the first Indian woman poet writing in English to have found her material and medium to express herself in these terms. Hers was an iconoclast's approach and this could not have been appreciated easily even by serious readers or academic critics brought up on Victorian and colonial parameters of assessing the female role or texts produced by women writers. Misrepresentations of Das as a poet started because her readers had yet to be initiated into a new worldview and were not still ready to appreciate the new poetics of resistance and representation. Das had offered a unique resistance by altering the stereotypical and initiating a new discourse on freedom, sexuality, and female identity. She did not allow herself to be appropriated as merely a preserve in the male domain: she wished to be taken as a participant in the act of sharing the pleasures of a life.

It is appropriate to add here that her poems may also be read as fine specimens of texts that obliterate the distinction between realism and fantasy. It would be rewarding to read many of these love poems of pain and pining as exercises in fantasy. Fantasy, her poetry testifies, sprouts from the bark and bole of reality and forms an integral part of the real. Real and imagined, thus, join together to create two desperate facets of love representing desire and disappointment. Yet another form of this fantasy can be seen in her poems where she assumes the persona of Radha and constructs the deity of her beloved Krishna to seek solace in him. The Radha-Krishna relationship is the most celebrated and the most sophisticated one that both Indian mythology and literature have developed and preserved over centuries. It is in this context that I have posited above that love in Das, apart from being a source of desired emotional strength, also emerges as a principle of divine sustenance.

In order to appreciate this aspect of Das' love for a deity called Krishna, a reference to the classical tradition of Indian poetry would be in order. It must be asserted that even though Das appeared to be initiating a new culture of bold and uninhibited expression for the first time in Indian English poetry, she was not actually heralding a new tradition: she was only extending the one that had already been laid down and established centuries before. Right from Vedic times to Buddhist nuns there have been women poets who have written of their condition as derelict and disappointed women, courtesans and nuns, mostly telling the tales of their woe, repression, resistance and rebellion. This tradition was carried further by the Bhakti poets who addressed the various moods and manners of *shringara*, or the erotic, in a frank and uninhibited manner. They took both union and separation into account and represented various manifestations of love in and outside marriage that included the fate of the woman bound in a nuptial knot (*kanta*), or the woman involved in an illicit love affair (*parakiya*), or indulging in a surreptitious rendezvous (*abhisarika*). These women poets have handed down a great tradition of Indian poetry to their latter day counterparts in how they have chosen their roles either in bowing down before a god, or negating a nuptial tie, or going against social norms, or marrying a god and living as a saintly wife.

The example of the Virsaiva woman saint, Mahadeviakka who wrote in the twelfth century in Kannada is the most prominent of them all. Other relevant examples may be found in the poetry of Antal (eighth century) who wrote in Tamil, Janabai (1298–1350) and Bahnibai (1628–1700) who wrote in Marathi, Lal Ded (fourteenth century) who wrote in Kashmiri, and Mirabai (1498–1565) who wrote in Rajasthani. All of them discovered for themselves roles to play as women and as poets and all of them imparted a philosophical-cum-spiritual halo to their poetic outpourings. It is interesting to note that this tradition was spread far and wide in the Indian subcontinent and covered the length and breadth of Indian soil. This could be understood against the background of the tradition that Hinduism recognizes the female principle in the universe as *shakti* and Hindu mythology has space for the sexual relations of gods who represent the interaction of "spirit" as male with "matter," the female. It is on the strength of this argument that I would like to stress that Das' contribution as a poet must be assessed with reference to the indigenous tradition rather than the Western tradition where love and expressions of love acquire an altogether different proportion and idiom. There is a greater reason for doing so as Mahadeviakka, Lal Ded, and Mirabai are venerated as saints in spite of their off-beat stances, while Das is criticized for expressing herself in a frank and uninhibited manner. This is not to assert that Das is a saint in their tradition but only to say that she draws upon them rather closely. Those poets merged with the divine and obliterated the distinction between the acceptable and unacceptable modes of living. It is this that Das tries to do in her own inimitable way. Das' spirit is akin to those representing the Bhakti tradition of poetry and she deserves to be given the same liberal space as those in that tradition of poetry.

This discussion on the forthright and assertive voice of Indian women poets from the remote past and its manifestation in the poetry of Kamala Das takes us naturally to think of how the expression of intimate and personal material is liable to turn into a confessional act. Broadly speaking, all literary expression is a kind of confession but what makes poetry characteristically confessional is related to the poet's approach to the material and the method the poet adopts to construct or configure that material. Our response to confessional literature, more especially poetry, has been conditioned in the recent past by the reception of American confessional poets whose poetry turned into a literary fashion during the 1960s. They believed in opening doors on their private lives and in speaking unabashedly of psychological states of being. In doing so, they wrote dramatic monologues of a very intimate kind and unfolded the levels of their psychological stress that would otherwise be kept away from public gaze. Choosing the ordinary idiom of expression, negating a mask or a persona, glossing over their experience of alienation, and throwing the poem open for incorporating any kind of experience whatsoever, these poets privileged the personal over the universal and developed their own mythopoeia.

One might argue that many of these qualities are also found in the poetry of Kamala Das but it should be kept in mind that American confessional poetry is rooted in its own socio-cultural ethos characterized by the pressures of contemporary American life. The major difference, therefore, lies in the fact that Das represents an entirely different milieu which is simply not comparable with any other milieu, especially that of the USA in the 1960s. Predicaments might, at times, strike a chord of similarity but they may not necessarily be compatible and comparable as is the case here. This is one major reason why Das should not be read along with the American confessional poets. There is yet another reason. If Das' poetry of personal confession is to be compared with any poet, it is to be compared with the Indian women poets, including the Bhakti poets, who lived and wrote centuries ago. It is in their company that the individual merit of her poetry would show up much more brilliantly than in comparison with the American or any other poet representing a different tradition and milieu. . . .

Source: Anisur Rahman, "Contextualizing Kamala Das," in *Marginalized: Indian Poetry in English*, edited by Smita Agarwal, Rodopi, 2014, pp. 188–93.

Shirley Geok-lin Lim

In the following excerpt, Lim explains that Das's work is sometimes misunderstood by Western readers.

. . . Das has had two audiences. Her own native Indian audience is mostly English-educated and middle-class. Its class mobility and its choice of the English language for expression are generally associated with a modern, westernized mentality (that is, with an unstable indigenous cultural identity related to an assimilation of sociopolitical values influenced by Anglo-American norms and cultures). Her other, more vocal and welcoming, audience is an international group of readers, chiefly from Australia. These non-Indian critics are interested in non-Western writing in English. They represent the old Commonwealth literature school of thought reincarnated as postcolonial, post-Orientalist sensitivities to new or national or world literatures in English. While the emphases are different, both audiences share common assumptions and make similar conclusions in approaching Das's writing.

Das is acknowledged by both Indian and Anglo critics as working within a "strong tradition of female writing . . . with a venerable ancestry." The consensus from both interpretive communities is that her achievement is limited to themes of female sexual and physical experience. Hostile readers, both Indian and international, debunk

> HER BEST WORK CANNOT BE READ EITHER AS A CELEBRATION OF LOVE OR AS AN ALLEGORICAL ABSTRACTION OF RADHA, THE GOPI COWMAID, WORSHIPING KRISHNA IN HIS MANY MANIFESTATIONS."

her subjects, describing them variously as "a poetry of thighs and sighs," "salacious" fantasies of sexual neuroticism, and "flamboyant," "weak," "self-indulgent" obsessiveness. Friendly critics valorize her as "a poet of feminine longings." She is praised (chiefly by male critics) for that "feminine sensibility [that is] manifested in her attitude to love, in the ecstasy she experiences in receiving love and the agony she feels when jilted in it." According to her most fervent defenders, both Indian and Western, her feminine sensibility is expressed in her total involvement with the sexual male Other.

The recent publication of a selected collection of her work by the Centre for Research in the New Literatures in English in Adelaide, Australia, accompanied by critical essays, all by white Australian critics, would seem to confirm a hardening of these interpretive lines. Many of the essays in the volume argue that the theme of Das's heterosexuality receives its highest apotheosis, its Indian rationale, in Das's identity as a devotee of Krishna. As Dorothy Jones informs us, Krishna, eighth avatar of Vishnu, is traditionally represented in Indian culture as "an important focus in Hinduism of Bhakti, the experience of intense religious adoration in which the soul [the female representation] abandons itself in ecstasy to the divine [the male representation]." Jones is only repeating a paradigm, first articulated by Das herself, whereby the "vulgar" (and arguably Westernized "confessional") topos of brutal or illicit sexuality becomes transformed into the "high" topos of licit Brahminic mysticism.

In approaching Das's evident concentration on sexual themes, however, the non-Indian reader would do well to keep in mind that erotic sexuality is strongly inscribed in Indian, specifically Hindu, culture. In using these materials, Das is able to appeal to both the Western tradition that emphasizes confessional writing and the Hindu tradition that places a high and visible valuation on male-female eroticism. By a shift in authorial (and critical) perception, the sensual complexities of a "sensational"—because exceptional—life are reduced to an abstract allegory of religious quest and devotion. (No American reader, however, would find Das's so-called confessions of extramarital affairs memorable if set among the Hollywood memoirs appearing today!)

Many critics have participated in this sanitization of the female subject Das constitutes in her autobiography and her poetry, and have acquiesced, even contributed, to obfuscating the notable "revolt" against male-dominant terms of sexuality in her themes. They have interpreted the persona in her poems and autobiography to be a "smoothly" acceptable, because traditional, worshiper of that most adulterous, most privileged male Indian god, Krishna. Mohan Lal Sharma, for example, argues that Das's career exhibits a "pilgrim's progress" toward Krishna-worship; thus, he congratulates her for her faults in poetic style, since, for him, they demonstrate her religious achievement. "'He shining everything else shines' is the ultimate Upanishadic dictum," Sharma advises us, unself-consciously reflecting his patriarchal reconstruction of Das's work in his choice of dictums. Sharma's male-centered critical orientation, moreover, is itself a reflection of the patriarchal structure of communities dominated by Krishna-worship. Adopting a similar critical approach, non-Indian critics such as Syd Harrex, Vincent O'Sullivan, and Dorothy Jones similarly turn Das's very specifically located materialist critiques of class and gender into a phantasm of Krishna-worship.

I argue that Das's writing and life display the anger, rage, and rebellion of a woman struggling in a society of male prerogatives. Her best work cannot be read either as a celebration of love or as an allegorical abstraction of Radha, the Gopi cowmaid, worshiping Krishna in his many manifestations. I find that the informing energy in the autobiography springs, like the pulsating rhythm of a popular 1960s rock 'n' roll song, from its central poetics, "I Can't Get No Satisfaction." Teresa de Lauretis, among other feminist commentators, has pointed out that "to feminism, the personal is epistemologically the political, and its epistemology is its politics." "Satisfaction," therefore, while it encompasses the notion of sexual desire, emerges in the autobiography, as it

does in Das's novel, *Alphabet for Lust*, as epistemologically the domain of female struggle in a patriarchal society. The inequalities and social oppressions suffered by Indian women are many and profound. As Marilyn French reports in a 1985 United Nations–sponsored publication, "Most Indian women are married young by their families to men they have not met before. . . . They then move to their husbands' parents' home, where they are, essentially, servants." French documents a series of social horrors: the dowry system, bride-burning, male abuse, the ban against divorce, women's isolation, job discrimination, female infanticide, poorly paid or unpaid female labor, high female illiteracy. Das's autobiography specifies the connections between personal/sexual and social/political struggles for a female protagonist in this traditional male-dominated society.

In her preface, Das locates the origin of her autobiography in the confessional impulse attending the deathbed. She indicates that the autobiography was written during her "first serious bout with heart disease," and that she "wanted to empty myself of all the secrets so that I could depart when the time came with a scrubbed-out conscience." This intention indicates a particular understanding of the autobiographical genre, one attuned to the confessional tradition of Christianity exemplified in Augustine's *Confessions*. The expressed wish for a "scrubbed-out conscience" itself prepares the reader for representations of "sinful" or immoral subjects, secrets that defile a conscience, and for some kind of remorse undertaken within a religious or spiritual frame of reference. Yet Das candidly reveals that she wrote her autobiography as a commercial publication, a series of articles for a popular magazine, because she needed money to pay off her medical bills. The spiritual impulse and the commercial intention are both evident in the dialogic, ambiguous, and contradictory features of the text.

The autobiography, republished in book form in 1976, possesses the characteristics that mark it as a book written hurriedly and structured to the formulaic requirements of serial publication. It has fifty chapters, each from two and a half to about four and a half pages in length. The organization of materials into so many short chapters is clearly governed by the necessity of chopping the life into as many marketable pieces as possible, thus revealing more about the magazine format and the attention span of its popular audience than about the writer's craft. Moreover, the serial form dictates the anecdotal, superficial essayistic structure, allowing little room for analysis of difficult issues or exploration of psychological experience.

The contradictions between the commercially dictated features of the text and the narrator's stated "spiritual" intention have led many critics to view Das as unreliable. "After reading such a confession," Vimala Rao says astringently, "it is difficult to determine where the poseur ends and the artist begins." Dwivedi describes the work as "more baffling and dazing [*sic*] than her poetry," and Jones admits that "it is hard to know how to respond to this book which, while adopting an openly confessional tone, conceals quite as much or more than it reveals." Because they cannot read her autobiography as a faithful account of her life, critics have generally preferred to treat it as an appendix to her poetry. Sharma claims that Das's autobiography "is the single best 'Reader's Guide' to the design and meaning of her work." Jones more cannily allows that "if considered as a literary rather than a factual recreation of the writer's life, it often serves as an illuminating comment on her poetry and fiction, exploring many of the same dilemmas and situations."

In fact, the obvious unreliability of the author's intention foregrounds the postmodernist qualities of Das's "autobiography." Thus, instead of approaching it as a text containing an authentic account of a life unmediated by literary conventions, I argue that our understanding of the constituted "autobiographical" female subject should be informed by features of the text. These features include ones that conform to a mass-market strategy (the simple anecdotal structure, unrelenting focus on sensational and popular themes, attention to domestic and marital relations as appealing to a female readership) and ones that derive from the self-reflexive nature of the prose. In "deconstructing" Das's autobiography, then, I want to elaborate how it achieves its impact less from its separate parts than from their sum. While each chapter offers a distinct picture or theme, together the chapters resonate in their emphasis on the domestic details of food, familial relations, marriage, childbirth, sexual liaisons, and the internal and external struggles of one woman in a sociopolitically repressive world....

Source: Shirley Geok-lin Lim, "Terms of Empowerment in Kamala Das's *My Story*," in *De/Colonizing the Subject: The Politics of Gender in Women's Autobiography*, edited by Sidonie Smith and Julia Watson, University of Minnesota Press, 1992, pp. 348–51.

SOURCES

Ansari, Mohammad Shaukat, "Depiction of Women's Dilemmas in Select Poems of Kamala Das: A Review," in *Language in India*, Vol. 12, February 2012, http://www.languageinindia.com/feb2012/shaukatkamaladasfinal.pdf (accessed August 12, 2015).

Das, Kamala, "Punishment in Kindergarten," in *The Aesthetics of Sensuality: A Stylistic Study of the Poetry of Kamala Das*, by N. V. Raveendran, Atlantic Publishers and Distributors, 2000, pp. 144–45.

Dougal, Sandeep, "Madhavikutty, Kamala Das, Surayya (1934–2009)," in *Outlook*, June 2, 2009, http://www.outlookindia.com/blogs/post/madhavikutty-kamala-das-surayya-19342009/1864/5 (accessed August 12, 2015).

Dwivedi, A. N., *Kamala Das and Her Poetry*, Atlantic Publishers & Distributors, 2000, pp. 1–81, 114–29.

Fox, Margarlit, "Kamala Das, Indian Poet and Daring Memoirist, Dies at 75," in *New York Times*, June 9, 2009, http://www.nytimes.com/2009/06/10/books/10das.html?_r=0 (accessed August 12, 2015).

"General Note," Government of India Ministry of Home Affairs, Office of the Registrar General & Census Committee website, http://www.censusindia.gov.in/Census_Data_2001/Census_Data_Online/Language/gen_note.html (accessed August 17, 2015).

Habib, Shahnaz, "Kamala Das," in *Guardian* (London, England), June 17, 2009, http://www.theguardian.com/world/2009/jun/18/obituary-kamala-das (accessed August 12, 2015).

Harris, V. C., Introduction to *The Old Playhouse and Other Poems*, by Kamala Das, Orient Blackswan, 2011, pp. ix–xxi.

Kaul, Chandrika, "From Empire to Independence: The British Raj in India 1858–1947," BBC website, March 3, 2011, http://www.bbc.co.uk/history/british/modern/independence1947_01.shtml (accessed August 16, 2015).

Kohli, Devindra, Introduction to *Kamala Das: Selected Poems*, Penguin Books, 2014, pp. xi–lxxxvii.

Mohan, Sriram, "The Memories of a Spark: Reconstructing the 1965 Riots in Madurai against the Imposition of Hindi," in *SubVersions*, Vol. 2, No. 2, 2014, http://subversions.tiss.edu/the-memories-of-a-spark-reconstructing-the-1965-riots-in-madurai-against-the-imposition-of-hindi (accessed August 17, 2015).

Nair, Devika, "Kamala Das: Many Selves, Many Tongues," in *Hindu*, April 2, 2015, http://www.thehindu.com/features/friday-review/kamala-das-many-selves-many-tongues/article7056859.ece (accessed August 12, 2015).

"Official Language," India.gov.in Archive, 2010, http://www.archive.india.gov.in/knowindia/profile.php?id = 33 (accessed August 17, 2015).

Raveendran, N. V., *The Aesthetics of Sensuality: A Stylistic Study of the Poetry of Kamala Das*, Atlantic Publishers and Distributors, 2000, pp. 144–45, 180.

"This Day in History: India and Pakistan Win Independence," History.com, 2010, http://www.history.com/this-day-in-history/india-and-pakistan-win-independence (accessed August 16, 2015).

Weisbord, Merrily, *The Love Queen of Malabar: Memoir of a Friendship with Kamala Das*, McGill-Queen's University Press, 2010.

of her coming of age as a fifteen-year-old bride in an arranged marriage and explores the rich family history that led to her literary gifts.

Forbes, Geraldine, *Women in Modern India*, Cambridge University Press, 2007.

Forbes examines the condition of Indian women beginning with the nineteenth century reform movement under which women were first given access to education. Since that time, women in India have achieved greater independence, contributing significantly to Indian culture in all fields. Forbes includes the personal accounts of Indian women throughout the nineteenth, twentieth, and twenty-first centuries, exemplifying their growing role.

FURTHER READING

Arkin, Andres, and Kamala Das, *Encountering Kamala: Selections from the Poetry of Kamala Das—India's Powerful Voice for Change*, Gorgeous Notions Press, 2007.

The first collection of Das's work published in the United States, *Encountering Kamala* is a compendium of both well-known and previously unpublished poetry along with personal anecdotes shared by Das and longtime friend Arkin.

Boehmer, Elleke, and Rosinka Chaudhuri, *The Indian Postcolonial: A Critical Reader*, Routledge, 2010.

This collection of scholarly essays explores the landscape of postcolonial India with a focus on India's relationship with the world, its cultural and artistic traditions, and its ethics as the people of the long-colonized nation struck out after achieving independence to define themselves and their country free of British rule.

Das, Kamala, *My Story*, DC Books, 1988.

In Das's explosively controversial autobiography, first published in 1973, she tells the story

SUGGESTED SEARCH TERMS

Kamala Das

Kamala Surayya

Madhavikutty AND Kamala Das

Summer in Calcutta AND Das

Summer in Calcutta AND Punishment in Kindergarten

Das AND Punishment in Kindergarten

Punishment in Kindergarten AND poetry

Summer in Calcutta AND 1965

Punishment in Kindergarten AND 1965

Punishment in Kindergarten AND memory

Punishment in Kindergarten AND shame

Punishment in Kindergarten AND Indian English poetry

Sadie and Maud

GWENDOLYN BROOKS

1945

"Sadie and Maud" was first published in 1945 in Gwendolyn Brooks's first poetry collection, *A Street in Bronzeville*. Set in the period of legal racial segregation and discrimination, the poem tells the story of two sisters, one of whom seems to get ahead by playing by the rules when she pursues an education, while the other finds herself in the shameful situation of having two children and no husband. Brooks's message is more subtle than self-satisfied moralizing, however. Because they live in a white supremacist society, neither sister ever had a chance of succeeding, and both end up in essentially the same place, trapped by poverty and discrimination. The sister who tried to play along is actually in the worse position, because she has neither husband nor children. The poem also appears in *Postmodernisms: 1950–Present*, volume 3 of *The New Anthology of American Poetry* (2012).

AUTHOR BIOGRAPHY

Gwendolyn Elizabeth Brooks was born on June 7, 1917, in Topeka, Kansas. Within a month, the family moved to Chicago to take advantage of the employment opportunities created by the growth of wartime industry. The city would be her principal residence for the rest of life. The family lived in the Bronzeville neighborhood, a district, like Harlem in New York, where blacks were allowed to live

Gwendolyn Brooks (© *Library of Congress*)

during the period of segregation. Of necessity, the neighborhood was originally composed of all classes, but it saw a steep decline in the 1950s when blacks were finally permitted to move into white neighborhoods, leaving behind only the poorest inhabitants. Nevertheless, Brooks chose to continue to live in Bronzeville, much as her mentor, Langston Hughes, continued to live in Harlem throughout his life. Brooks's mother worked as a schoolteacher and her father as a janitor, and together they provided relative economic security for the family. Her mother had wanted to attend medical school but could never have raised the tuition. The same bleak economics contributed to Brooks's choice to attend Wilson Junior College (rather than, say, the University of Chicago) and to support herself for many years as a typist.

When she was thirteen, Brooks published her first poem, "Eventide," in *American Childhood Magazine.* By the time she graduated from high school, she had a portfolio of seventy-five published poems and a weekly poetry column in the *Chicago Defender,* one of the leading black newspapers in America.

In the late 1930s white magazines began to accept Brooks's poetry, and in 1945 she published her first poetry collection, *A Street in Bronzeville* (which includes "Sadie and Maud"), with the mainstream house Harper and Row. Following this, Brooks spent two years on Guggenheim fellowships, and in 1950 her second poetry collection, *Annie Allen,* won the Pulitzer Prize for Poetry, the first work of a black author to do so. After more than a decade of intensive publishing, including her 1953 novel *Maud Martha,* Brooks began to teach creative writing as a visiting professor, generally at mainstream universities. In 1967, Brooks attended a writers' conference at historically black Fisk University and became a follower of the Black Arts movement. Founded in response to the assassination of Malcolm X in 1965, the Black Arts movement espoused the thinking that engagement with the white world on its own terms was pointless and that the black community should instead work to create its own art for itself and build up its own cultural institutions. Brooks began to publish more radical works that expressed the ideals of the movement, such as *In the Mecca* (1968) and *Riot* (1969), and switched from Harper and Row to the black-owned Broadside Press. In 1985, Brooks was appointed poet laureate of the United States. After that, Brooks semiretired. She died of cancer on December 3, 2000, in her Chicago home.

POEM TEXT

Maud went to college.
Sadie stayed at home.
Sadie scraped life
With a fine-tooth comb.

She didn't leave a tangle in.   5
Her comb found every strand.
Sadie was one of the livingest chits
In all the land.

Sadie bore two babies
Under her maiden name.   10
Maud and Ma and Papa
Nearly died of shame.
Every one but Sadie
Nearly died of shame.

When Sadie said her last so-long   15
Her girls struck out from home.
(Sadie had left as heritage
Her fine-tooth comb.)

Maud, who went to college,
Is a thin brown mouse.   20
She is living all alone
In this old house.

POEM SUMMARY

The text used for this summary is from *Postmodernisms: 1950–Present*, which is volume 3 of *The New Anthology of American Poetry*, edited by Steven Gould Axelrod, Camille Roman, and Thomas Travisano, Rutgers University Press, 2012, p. 110. A version of the poem can be found on the following web page: http://www.poetryfoundation.org/poem/172083.

Brooks's "Sadie and Maud" is generally divided into unnumbered quatrains, or stanzas of four lines, each in a variety of meters. The second and fourth line of each stanza rhyme.

Stanza 1

The first two lines of the poem are written in a lively anapestic meter that lures the reader into thinking of the poem as a song or ballad. The lines state that Sadie and Maud, two sisters, pursue different life strategies. Maud goes to college while Sadie stays home with their parents. The opposition suggests a contest as to which sister will succeed. Such contests are a traditional subject of ballads, contributing to the illusion of a traditional form. The type of college in this case is not defined but seems more likely to be a business or trade school of the kind that Brooks herself attended rather than a four-year liberal arts school or state university. For comparison, one of the borders of the Bronzeville neighborhood in 1945 was formed by the campus of Illinois Tech (today the Illinois Institute of Technology), a prestigious engineering school. A small number of blacks were enrolled at the school in the 1940s, but many failed to graduate because of lack of tuition support from the school and the comparative poverty of their background. At the nearby University of Chicago, a handful of black students (usually fewer than ten per each class of at least several hundreds) had been admitted to the school each year since its foundation in the nineteenth century, and they generally became important leaders of the black community, given the advantages that a degree from such a prestigious school conferred. In the 1940s, however, that had to be the limit of their horizons; for a black to become a leader in a discipline, business, or politics for Americans as a whole was unthinkable.

The second couplet of the stanza specifies the character of Sadie's life. Her way of encountering life is by scraping, which suggests a bare existence on the margin of viability. Moreover, the scraping is done with a fine-tooth comb, the kind of comb that is used to remove lice from hair. The persistent, endemic, ineradicable presence of parasites of this kind was perceived in the 1940s as indicative of the direst kind of poverty that existed in America. While it is possible for people from any group to be infected with lice, Brooks exploits its value as a symbol associated with poverty and oppression. When in a film one sees the inmates of a Victorian lunatic asylum or of Auschwitz with their heads shaved because of lice, one immediately recognizes they are victims. That is the kind of imagery Brooks is evoking here. Lice are never mentioned by name, and many in Brooks's middle-class audience may never have realized the true significance of the term in the poem.

Stanza 2

The first couplet of this stanza specifies still further the thoroughness of Sadie's delousing. The second couplet attests to Sadie's vivacity and her natural human impulse to seek pleasure. Qualified in this way, the search for lice becomes a metaphor for the search for satisfaction. The paradox between the two terms of the metaphor ironically suggests that the pleasure available for her to find is meager indeed.

Stanza 3

The first couplet here relates that Sadie sought the meaning of her life in giving birth to and raising two daughters. This is precisely what her parents did. It goes without saying that the instinct to have children is among the most powerful parts of the human character. Unlike her own mother, Sadie did not enter into a relationship of marriage with her children's father (or fathers). The obvious reason for this is that the father was never able to secure the kind of employment that was necessary to support a family. In the Depression era, which must be imagined as the time period of the births of Sadie's children, the general economic crisis combined with the discrimination against blacks to ensure that only a small proportion of black men were as lucky as Brooks's own father, who found lifetime employment as a janitor (and it is reasonable to imagine Sadie and Maud's father in the same sort of position), which barely enabled him to support his own family. Sadie repeats her mother's accomplishment in giving birth to two daughters but is unable to emulate her parents in establishing a stable economic framework for them.

The stanza's second couplet reports that Sadie's parents and sister were ashamed of her. The source of the shame in one sense is self-evident: she had sex outside marriage and hence is a sinner according to the Judeo-Christian tradition that would have been the shared worldview of Brooks's characters and readers. The difference between Sadie and her mother is not that Sadie had some monstrous desire to indulge in the sin of lust; it is that the economic discrimination against blacks in America made it impossible for her to find a husband with a steady job. The "shame" of religious morality is being used to demonize the victims of poverty and discrimination, as if they themselves were responsible for the economic and social restrictions imposed on them.

The stanza's unique third couplet points out that Sadie did not share her family's sense of shame over her actions, which is hardly surprising, since she would have been the most aware of her own motivations. This clearly indicates that the shame is ironic and not shared by Brooks herself. The third couplet is interesting in a number of respects. Since all the other stanzas are quatrains, the addition of two extra lines here is a jarring break with the illusion that the poem is a ballad or song. It is a break with the repeated patterning necessary to fit the individual couplets to the same tune if the poem were indeed a song. Of course, the variations in line length throughout the poem prevent such an adaptation in reality. Moreover, the third couplet was included in the original publication of the poem in 1945 in *A Street in Bronzeville* and is retained in most reprints but was removed from the text in the republication in Brooks's *Selected Poems*. Who was responsible for the excision of the lines, or for what reason, remains unknown, but the meaning of the poem is substantially different without it.

Stanza 4

Sadie dies at what the reader must presume is a relatively young age. Her daughters must approach life in the same way their mother did. Their only inheritance is their mother's nit-picking comb, in other words, her poverty and inequality. This appeal to a stereotype ironically underscores the poem's essential protest against racism and economic and social oppression.

Stanza 5

The fifth stanza finally takes up Maud's role in the competition between the two sisters. Her accomplishment is to have attended college and then returned home to live with her parents, with no husband or children of her own. She seems to inherit her parents' only real property, their house, which may well mean paying the monthly rent. The reader may at first suppose that in the contest between the sisters Maud was the winner because she avoided shame, but this is not the case. Part of Sadie's failure was her inability to establish her own household, and this fault Maud shares equally with her sister. They both spend their lives living with their parents. She also failed to find a marriageable husband just like Sadie. Maud's failure goes further, however, since she did not have children, even out of wedlock. Playing by the rules of the white supremacist system, with its exploitation and control of poor blacks, means that even the most basic goal of biological organisms, to reproduce, must be denied.

THEMES

Education

Education is usually supposed to be an unalloyed good. In the phrase *liberal arts*, the word *liberal* means "appropriate to a free man." The original idea was that education provided the necessary knowledge and perspective for a person to take charge of one's own affairs as well as to play one's part in the political life of the community, to become an informed voter or to hold public office. In antiquity, of course, the only people to receive such an education would be the wealthy and would also be male, because only they could engage in a political life. The phrase *seven liberal arts* comes from the book of Martianus Capella's titled *The Marriage of Philology and Mercury*. Capella was writing in Italy in the fifth century, during the general crisis that brought about the transition from antiquity to the medieval period, and wrote this encyclopedic compendium in an attempt to preserve at least the outline of true education at a time when the traditional system of education was breaking down. The idea of a liberal education, however, goes back to Athens in the fifth century BCE.

The year 1945 was the beginning of the era of the American dream, when it was hoped that this kind of education could be extended to every citizen. How, then, can Brooks give Maud's education such a negative charge? In the first case, truly liberal education was for the most part denied to the black community

TOPICS FOR FURTHER STUDY

- Brooks's *Bronzeville Boys and Girls* (1956) is a collection of poems for young adults that have the same setting and deal with the same subject matter as the poems in *A Street in Bronzeville*. It has been frequently reprinted, often in illustrated editions. Prepare an illustrated version of "Sadie and Maud" using pictures of the Bronzeville neighborhood and its inhabitants from the 1930s and 1940s gathered from online sources.

- Uniquely among African American poets of her generation, Brooks was interested in epic and produced a substantial mock epic in her Pulitzer Prize–winning volume *Annie Allen*. The Ramayana is an epic from ancient India whose final chapters concern female propriety and the role of shame in policing infidelity. Write a paper comparing this work and "Sadie and Maud" with respect to the themes of shame, infidelity, and family.

- Prior to the 1950s, most American cities had a particular neighborhood where blacks were forced to live—such as Bronzeville in Chicago or Harlem in New York—since there were both official and unofficial agreements that blacks would not be allowed to rent or own property elsewhere. Research the traditional black neighborhood in your own city or one in your region and make a Power-Point presentation to your class about its history, noting especially any important writers or artists the community produced.

- *A Street in Bronzeville* was published eighteen years later than Langston Hughes's collection *Fine Clothes to the Jew*. Both collections deal with the lives of poor blacks in a realistic manner. Hughes's collection was attacked for this in the black press, which wrote in the interest of middle- and upper-class blacks who would as soon not have had the grinding poverty that dominated their community put on public display. By 1945, however, attitudes had altered, and Brooks's poems were generally received as a call for change. Write a paper comparing the treatment of the shared themes of poverty and oppression in the two collections or in two poems from the collections.

---

because of the poverty that discrimination imposed on them. A very small number of blacks before the 1970s were able to attend elite schools like Harvard (for example, Countee Cullen), and somewhat more were able to attend elite segregated high schools and the segregated university system that existed in America side by side with the institutions reserved for whites. Even leading intellectuals and public leaders of the black community like Thurgood Marshall and Martin Luther King Jr. had to attend all-black universities. The achievements of these men testify to the quality of the education offered there even under the prevailing conditions. With things as they were as late as the 1960s, even that kind of education did little to abate racism and discrimination. Marshall could never have established a law practice with an integrated clientele, and King could never have hoped to become the minister of a white congregation. They were educated to be free men, but they were not allowed to be fully free. Education was merely a lengthening of the chains until men like Marshall and King broke them. Maud was educated long before those dramatic events, and in any case she is unlikely to have received a liberal arts education. When Brooks says Maud went to college, she probably means the same kind of trade school Brooks herself attended, where she was trained to work as a secretary, taught to be not free to control her own life and her own labor but free to conform to a job description. In this case, education is not a necessity for freedom but the means of indoctrination into an oppressive economic system.

The comb becomes a metaphor for living life thoroughly. (© Dmytro Zinkevych | Shutterstock.com)

Family

Sadie and Maude come from a conventional nuclear family where the father and mother were able to live together and care for their two daughters. This is the baseline of the idealized family of the American dream as well as the expectation or hope within the black community. Brooks herself came from such a family, which was maintained through her father's steady work as a janitor and her mother's as a schoolteacher. Even this minimal achievement cannot be maintained by the sisters in the poem. Sadie indeed has two daughters but is unable to find in their father(s) or in any other man a companion able to provide the income necessary to sustain a family. Maud is supposedly more respectable and seems to inherit the family's small property as well as its good name, but she is no more able to find a suitable husband and so will die childless. Family is a central value of American society and, if anything, even more so of the black community, but if Sadie had acted in the same way as Maud, their family would have been extinguished. Brooks's main point is that racial discrimination is destroying the black community at its foundations.

STYLE

Irony

Upon first reading "Sadie and Maud," the reader may see it as presenting a choice between a life of pleasure and a life of self-denial, and it may seem that Brooks decidedly favors Sadie's pleasure over Maud's self-denial. This image is ironic: it is an absurd opposite of the truth, as the ironic presentation will make the attentive reader realize. The truth, as Brooks sees it, is that no meaningful choice exists for the young black women in her poem. American society dictates that a child's goal is to exceed the life of their parents, living with greater success and prosperity. American society also then dictated that young black men would not be able to find good jobs that would let them support families, so neither Sadie nor Maud can replicate even their parents' achievement of raising a family. Sadie, the uneducated daughter, has two fatherless children, while Maud, though she is educated, is childless. The main image of the poem is the fine-tooth comb, the comb for picking lice, which symbolizes a combination of poverty and oppression that hangs over and destroys any hopes the two sisters might have. Sadie finds the little pleasure she has in life despite having to use such a grotesque instrument to search for it. Sadie's parents and sister are ashamed of her because she violates the forms of social control that they have internalized. This ironically becomes merely a channel for the expression of the shame that comes from degradation and oppression. Sadie does not feel this shame because she has decided to fight back against oppression by affirming life; still, she lives her life in poverty and dies young anyway. No individual's efforts can fight against the injustice built into the fabric of society.

Poetics

The meter and other elements of the prosody of "Sadie and Maud" are extremely problematic and ultimately as deceptive as its ironic discursive content. John Gery, in his "Subversive Parody in the Early Poems of Gwendolyn Brooks" (1999), gives the most extensive discussion of the prosody of "Sadie and Maud": "The poem relies on its *abcb* rhyme scheme, irregular trimeter lines, narrative economy, short sentences, repetition, substitution of phrases, hyphenated words, and commonplace idioms to create the tone of a popular ballad." The key point is *to create the tone of a popular ballad.* In fact, the structure of the poem is anything but a ballad. A ballad is a traditional song in which a series of stanzas can be sung to the same tune repeated over as many times as necessary. Each stanza of a ballad, therefore, must scan the same way, must have the same rhythm. The scansion of many lines of "Sadie and Maud" is highly rhythmical—in fact, many use an anapestic or marching cadence which gives a stronger impression of rhythm than a more naturalistic iambic meter—which suggests a ballad or song rhythm. In fact, the meter of the poem is highly variable, the lines varying in length, for example, between dimeter (two feet) and pentameter (five feet). So the poem could never be set as a traditional song. This deceptive use of prosody works in lockstep with the irony of the poem. The poem seems as if it is ordered and traditional, but further investigation shows that it is chaotic and imperfect, an illusion. This is in parallel with the poem's observation of the self-conception of American culture as just and democratic, a position that can be maintained only by covering over the fact that millions of Americans are disenfranchised and oppressed.

HISTORICAL CONTEXT

Racism

Africans had been used as slaves in Latin America since the discovery of the New World, and the French and British followed the example when they established their colonial empires in turn. Plantation slavery was used to cultivate sugarcane in Louisiana, and smaller establishments farmed tobacco in the southern British colonies, but slaves were used as domestic servants or even industrial workers in all of the thirteen colonies at one time or another. Once the cotton gin was invented, plantation slavery spread throughout the South, leading to a massive increase in the slave population. Communities of free blacks developed as early as colonial times in large northern cities like New York and Philadelphia. These neighborhoods were permitted only in certain sections of the city, however. Blacks were allowed to own their own homes and other property or rent living quarters in segregated areas, but not in neighborhoods where whites lived. Blacks continued to work mostly as servants in the white districts of the cities. In the South, even after the end of slavery with the Civil War, blacks continued to live for the most part on plantations, though as sharecroppers rather than slaves, leaving them economically dependent on rich white planters.

Between 1914 and 1945, the North received over a million black migrants from the South as factories required vast new pools of labor for war production, but social patterns in neither section changed. In the South in particular, the Jim Crow laws that followed Reconstruction effectively disenfranchised blacks from equal participation in civic life, and in both the North and South blacks were controlled by economic and social discrimination. Black neighborhoods like Harlem in Manhattan or Bronzeville in Chicago, where Brooks spent her whole life, were a segregated microcosm of the cities in which they were embedded. While all of the residents were black, many were well established in the working class, based on their labor as factory workers, schoolteachers, or middle-ranking civil servants or in other jobs. The larger proportion were poor, while a fraction became wealthy as entrepreneurs, professors at traditionally black colleges, physicians, or lawyers (limited to a black clientele). The social classes lived together because it was not possible even for the most successful members of black society to move

COMPARE
&
CONTRAST

- **1940s:** The United States is a heavily segregated society, and most blacks, even in the relatively open North, interact with the white economic world only as servants or underpaid factory workers.

  Today: While discriminatory social structures still exist, the most egregious forms of economic inequality and political disenfranchisement have been overcome. The first black president, Barack Obama, is elected.

- **1940s:** Bronzeville is a segregated neighborhood in which blacks of all social classes are forced to live together.

  Today: Bronzeville is split between sections that have become a post-gentrification neighborhood, where the population consists almost exclusively of wealthy whites, and pockets of poverty, where only the poorest blacks live, the middle and upper classes having long since moved out of the inner city.

- **1940s:** Economic opportunity for women, especially black women, is very limited. Work opportunities outside of small family businesses or jobs such as secretarial work, waitressing, or teaching are rare.

  Today: Following the reforms of the civil rights and feminist movements, some black women have a virtually unlimited choice of career paths, as exemplified by Oprah Winfrey and Condoleezza Rice, while others are kept in poverty by a variety of factors, such as the inadequacy of the social safety net and the fact that so many young black men who might contribute to a household income are housed in prisons rather than being given the kind of education that could lead to personal economic success.

into other neighborhoods occupied by whites. Beginning in the Great Depression, many more blacks fell into poverty because of joblessness, the same as the rest of the nation. The family in "Sadie and Maud" is in the working class in Bronzeville. The daughters suffer from the combination of race and gender discrimination. As poverty eats up the community from the bottom, the daughters fall into the poorest classes as neither is able to find a husband with an income to replace their father's.

CRITICAL OVERVIEW

B. J. Bolden, in *Urban Rage in Bronzeville* (1999), defends the most obvious reading of the poem, in which Maud is seen to fail by following the conventional wisdom of pursuing an education while Sadie at least achieves satisfaction through a life of pleasure: "Unlike Maud, who adheres to the societal norm of pursuing education to 'get ahead' and thereby derive a better life, Sadie opts to extract the very flavor of life on her own terms and according to her poetic legacy survives and has a good time." This is a remarkable and unacknowledged challenge to the consensus reading of the poem, which sees both sisters Sadie and Maud as equally doomed by the larger social forces that oppress the black community, a view expressed, for instance, by the civil rights leader Eleanor Holmes Norton in her 1970 essay on the poem:

> The difference in the lives of these two women cannot conceal the overriding problem they share—loneliness, a life lacking in the chance to develop a relationship with a man or satisfactory family relationships.... Black women ... continue to carry the entire array of utterly oppressive handicaps associated with race. Racial oppression of black people in America has done what neither class oppression nor sexual oppression, with all their perniciousness, has ever done: destroyed an entire people and their culture.

Sisters Maud and Sadie have different approaches to life. (© *Blend Images | Shutterstock.com*)

Norton contrasts the civil rights movement with second-wave feminism in the context of the poem, where both sisters have to become independent not because they are free, but because of the desperation created by the difficulty faced by black men in securing meaningful work that could support a family. Even if white women achieved full equality in short order, she insists, that would do nothing to change the position of black women. Norton suggests that the only good that might come from the economic and social segregation of blacks from American society is the possibility that the black community might develop in ways different from mainstream culture and, for example, embrace gender equality. D. H. Melhem, in *Gwendolyn Brooks: Poetry & the Heroic Voice*, sees a deep texturing of literary reference in Brooks's poem. She interprets Maud's name as a reference to the biblical character of Mary Magdalene (of which "Maud" is a diminutive) and, accepting the tradition by which the biblical Mary is equated with the woman taken in adultery, supposes Maud to be just as sexually active as her sister. Thinking further in this way, she connects the character of Maud to Alfred Tennyson's poem of the same name. John Gery, in his 1999 article "Subversive Parody in the Early Poems of Gwendolyn Brooks," notes the purposeful construction of the poem to at first suggest to the reader a conclusion about the choices made by the two sisters, before ironically indicating the reality that they simply have no good choices to make: "While at first reading Maud may appear as one who has failed to live 'naturally,' in fact neither woman succeeds by any discernible social standards to establish an acceptable identity. The poem . . . depicts the choices available to both Sadie and Maud as severely restrictive, if not fraudulent."

CRITICISM

Rita M. Brown

Brown is an English professor. In the following essay, she looks at Brooks's use of irony in "Sadie and Maud" to throw light on the institutionalized racism of American society.

WHAT DO I READ NEXT?

- *Annie Allen* (1949) is the collection of poems for which Brooks won the Pulitzer Prize, the first time that distinction was won by a black author. The poems chart the growth of a young black woman from a romantic to a realistic view of her limited world.

- The Newbery Honor Book *Inside Out and Back Again* (2013), by Thanhha Lai, is a memoir in verse telling of the author's growth from girlhood to womanhood as a Vietnamese immigrant to the United States, facing racism and sexism and a changing definition of family from her traditional culture.

- George E. Kent's *A Life of Gwendolyn Brooks* (1990) is the first full biography of Brooks and is based in part on access to her journals, which Brooks began keeping at age seven.

- *Selected Poems* (1999) is the most comprehensive anthology of Brooks's work, containing poems from all her major collections.

- *Tally's Corner: A Study of Negro Street-corner Men* (1969), by Elliot Liebow, is a groundbreaking sociological analysis of the effects of poverty and oppression on young black men, preventing them from taking up the role of fathers in new families and leading to the breakdown of social cohesion in black communities.

- *The Dream Keeper and Other Poems*, originally published in 1932 but frequently reprinted, is a book of poems for young adults by Langston Hughes, the great poet of the Harlem Renaissance and Brooks's mentor.

Brooks's "Sadie and Maud" is deeply ironic. It invites a superficial reading that praises Sadie's life of pleasure in contrast to Maud's seemingly pointless self-denial, but on closer analysis it forces on the reader a quite different reading in which both sisters are seen as the victims of institutionalized racism and white supremacy. American society pretended that the conditions of black life in the 1940s were somehow acceptable or normal. Brooks uses irony to force her readers to look again and see for themselves that there was something terribly wrong with the way America treated its black citizens.

Most of the poem is devoted to Sadie and her quest to satisfy the most fundamental human urge, to have children and to take comfort in any joy she can find in her life restricted by poverty. Brooks describes this quest through the extended metaphor of the fine-tooth comb. The matter of Sadie's fine-tooth comb is a crux in the text that has not been fully understood in the existing literature on the poem. The imagery is universally interpreted as referring, to one degree or another, to Sadie's enjoying what pleasures of life she can. B. J. Bolden, in *Urban Rage in Bronzeville*, offers a typical reading of the image:

> Sadie manages . . . not only to survive, but live life to the fullest. Metaphorically, she "scraped life / With a fine-tooth comb" without leaving "a tangle in": she scraped the bottom of life's barrel with no remorse and is profiled as "one of the livingest chits / In all the land."

The phrase *bottom of the barrel* is certainly an important qualification, indicating that whatever pleasure she has is conditioned by poverty. The phrase *bottom of the barrel* describes what the masters have left for the servants or what the rich have left for the poor. Scraping with a fine-tooth comb is also a highly idiomatic expression, and it cannot easily mean "pursuing pleasures." Surely its most general use is as a metaphor for conducting a thorough search, and it could thereby signify the extraordinary lengths to which the poor must go to find any pleasure in their lives.

The term's metaphorical usage is only an extension of its literal meaning. Scraping with a fine-tooth comb most pointedly means to methodically and carefully search the hair to find and remove lice. In modern-day America, at least, it is something that only the poorest would have to do as part of their day-to-day existence. The kind of lice outbreaks that occasionally trouble middle-class schools today are not associated with poverty, as indeed, anyone may become infested. However, Brooks makes having to constantly deal with lice a symbol of class identity, employing a stereotype that would be recognizable to her audience. Brooks's audience was largely white, middle class, and liberal. They wanted to discard false racial stereotypes,

> TO USE THE SEARCH FOR LICE AS A
> METAPHOR THAT EVEN HINTS AT THE SEARCH FOR
> HAPPINESS IS AN IRONIC SIGNAL OF THE DESPERATION
> AND HOPELESSNESS THAT SADIE AND HER
> DAUGHTERS FACE."

but in the 1940s this process still had a long way to go. Brooks wanted to communicate to her audience that blacks were victims of poverty, and lice infestation was a symbol of poverty that her audience would understand. As horrible as the image is, Brooks fearlessly plays with it.

Perhaps, the reader might think, Sadie is metaphorically searching with her comb for every scrap of pleasure, but the truth is that she really is searching for the lice that result from the poverty that racism has imposed on her. In the 1930s and 1940s, the leading scientific authority on lice, as well as the lice-born disease typhus, was Hans Zinsser, a professor in the faculty of the Harvard Medical School. Typhus, at the time, was a deadly epidemic disease that killed millions of people each year around the world. Typhus is almost unknown today because Zinsser was the first to isolate the microorganism responsible for the disease, and then to develop an effective vaccine against it. In 1935, Zinsser published a history of bubonic plague and typhus, *Rats, Lice, and History*, which, surprisingly for such an academic subject, became a popular best seller. Because of Zinsser's eminent scientific authority, as well as the influence of his popular book, his views can be taken as informing popular opinion about lice during the 1940s. Zinsser states unequivocally and in a manner that suggests that he considers his opinion entirely conventional, expecting neither his readers nor other experts to particularly disagree with him, that "the louse has been banished completely from fashionable society.... The louse is confined ... to the increasingly diminishing populations of civilized countries who live in distress and great poverty." Given this popular understanding of lice, Brooks uses the necessity of daily delousing invoked by the fine-tooth comb as a symbol for poverty that her audience would easily recognize.

Moreover, lice, marked by the practice of head shaving to prevent infestation, was frequently used to signal poverty in popular culture. This is illustrated in the newspaper comic strip *Nancy*. During the prosperous 1920s, the main character of the strip had been an addle-brained, middle-class flapper, but a new cartoonist took the strip over during the Depression and completely made over the comic in the image of the devastated national economy. One of the new iconic characters was Sluggo, a boy whose head was shaved. For the poorest, with no access to running water that could be used to regularly shower and wash clothes (Zinsser points out that lice infestation is comparatively rare among people who have access to running water), shaving was the most practical means of controlling lice. The Our Gang series of comedy shorts produced by Hal Roach underwent a similar change, and in a racially tinged fashion. The child characters of the series had always come from all social classes, but the composition of the group was also made over to reflect the realities of the Depression. Its white middle-class characters, such as Alfalfa and Darla, continued with the same hairstyles, but a new character was introduced in 1930, the poor black boy Stymie, whose head was shaved against lice. Ironically, Stymie was portrayed as the cleverest of the group of children, who often had to use his wits to get his playmates out of trouble that their white leader, Spanky, had gotten them into. Talent and effort ultimately made no difference for him. They could not overcome the social forces of white supremacy and segregation. While children of different races could play together, a social and economic gulf existed between their families. This reinforces the point of Brooks's poem. No matter the different responses of the two sisters, Sadie and Maud, they are ultimately doomed by the racist structure of American culture.

Brooks's use of the image of lice picking is deceptively complex. It certainly demonstrates the absolute and hopeless poverty that Sadie and her daughters live in. As a practical matter, they must have survived on the charity of Sadie's parents, occasional odd jobs that Sadie might have been able to get, and a minimal amount of government assistance (perhaps a free basic medical clinic, the occasional distribution of surplus cheese, and the like). There was no social safety net that would have provided comprehensive medical care, food, and a basic income even for the minor children. The girls' father or fathers would not have been in a position to help because of their own poverty created by the chronic unemployment, underemployment, and discriminatory wages enforced on the black community.

In other Bronzeville poems (e.g., "The Sundays of Satin-Legs Smith") Brooks often describes the young men whom unemployment drives to crime and who during their brief careers as gangsters become womanizers rather than husbands before white society sends them to prison. Yet Sadie and her daughters live to the fullest extent that their very limited resources allow. Being subject to parasitic infestation by lice is a symbol of their general economic and social disenfranchisement. To use the search for lice as a metaphor that even hints at the search for happiness is an ironic signal of the desperation and hopelessness that Sadie and her daughters face. Sadie dies at just the time her daughters are maturing, in her thirties or early forties. The cause of her death is never hinted at, but surely death at that age is the result of poverty. Whether it was from drug use, another childbirth, or perhaps simply an infection that could not be treated for lack of money—whatever the cause, her manner of death would likely not have been a consideration for a middle-class white woman. The irony is driven home since Brooks has described a woman who dies so young as the most living. Sadie lived to the extent allowed by her race and class, which was very little indeed. The only inheritance Sadie can pass on to her daughters is her comb, a symbol of poverty and degradation.

Another complex term that Brooks uses to produce the same kind of resonance as the fine-tooth comb reference is *chit*. The word was archaic even in the 1940s; it would read naturally in an eighteenth-century novel. Since it is an epithet that describes Sadie as the most living, one would expect it to have a positive connotation. Again, this is not exactly the case. Brooks seems to be purposefully building the false, superficial reading of the poem whereby the reader is meant to sympathize with Sadie's pursuit of pleasure. Her technique is to let ambiguity deceive the reader, forcing more careful thought and analysis to get to the truth. The word *chit* is cognate with *kitten* and in the strictest sense means any young mammal. Thus, both sisters are dehumanized and in fact presented as a cat and a mouse. The most common usage of *chit* is its application to young women who act like animals, that is, in a disrespectful way. Its semantic range generally overlaps

with the word *slut*, so it might be considered here a euphemism for that term. It is part of the general slut-shaming that Sadie suffers in the poem, from her parents and her sister. They are ashamed that Sadie pursued the little opportunity for happiness that she had, in romantic affairs and in raising children, since it violates the social norm of marriage established and enforced by many social institutions, including religion.

Of course, Sadie's actions are far from being her own fault. The poverty that is enforced on the black community made marriage impossible for her. The alternative would have been the path followed by Maud, denying the most basic biological instincts and the whole purpose of human life in perpetuating the family. Racism made the sisters choose between shame and exterminating their own family lineage. If their parents are ashamed of Sadie, is the reader meant to think that they are pleased that they will have no grandchildren through Maud? Since both choices are imposed by an oppressive system, neither can be considered good. Sadie's situation is rather like Huckleberry Finn's when he found himself in the difficult position of following either the dictates of basic human decency or the law that branded him a criminal (and in his own mind a terrible sinner) for stealing and freeing a black slave. The fact that Sadie's own parents and sisters feel ashamed of her shows that conventional social morality and the religious beliefs that impose it are used as a means of social control to keep the oppressed from rebelling against their oppressors (an idea Brooks borrows from Karl Marx).

The reader of "Sadie and Maud" is at first confronted with the seeming paradox that Sadie is happy, yet there is something deeply wrong with Sadie. At the same time, Maud did everything right (she got an education) and is the more miserable. In untangling these difficulties, the reader will be led to the true meaning of the poem that racism destroys black lives, whatever decisions are made.

Source: Rita M. Brown, Critical Essay on "Sadie and Maud," in *Poetry for Students*, Gale, Cengage Learning, 2016.

George Stavros and Gwendolyn Brooks

In the following interview excerpt, Brooks discusses some of her poems, including "Sadie and Maud," and talks about poetic forms versus free verse.

...Q. You've said that poetry is an entirely different thing now from what it was twenty years

When the unmarried Sadie has two children, her father and mother are ashamed. (© Matthias G. Ziegler / Shutterstock.com)

ago. *Do you feel, as some readers of yours have said, that your own poetry has abandoned its lyrical simplicity for an angrier, more polemical public voice?*

A. Those are the things that people say who have absolutely no understanding of what's going on and no desire to understand. No, I have not abandoned beauty, or lyricism, and I certainly don't consider myself a polemical poet. I'm just a black poet, and I write about what I see, what interests me, and I'm seeing new things. Many things that I'm seeing now I was absolutely blind to before, but I don't sit down at the table and say, "Lyricism is out." No, I just continue to write about what confronts me. . . . I get an idea or an impression or I become very excited about something and I can hardly wait till the time comes when I can get to the paper. In the meantime I take notes, little bits of the idea I put down on paper, and when I'm ready to write I write as urgently and directly as I possibly can.

And I don't go back to mythology or my little textbooks. I know about the textbooks, but I'm not concerned with them during the act of poetry-writing.

Q. In one of the "Sermons on the Warpland," you quote Ron Karenga to the effect that blackness "is our ultimate reality."

A. I firmly believe it.

Q. Then am I right in saying these "Sermons" are almost apocalyptic or prophetic? They seem rather . . .

A. They're little addresses to black people, that's all.

Q. The last poem in the group ("The time / cracks into furious flower . . .") suggests that there will be a rebirth.

A. Yes. . . . There's something I'd like to say about my intent as a poet that you touched upon a moment ago and which has some connection with that business of abandoning lyricism, et cetera. Changes in my work—there *is* something different that I want to do. I want to write poems that will be non-compromising. I don't want to stop a concern with words doing good jobs, which has always been a concern of mine, but I want to write poems that will be meaningful to those people I described a while ago, things that will touch them.

Let me tell you about an experience I had in Chicago. I went around with a few of those poets that I've just mentioned. They go to housing projects and out in the parks sometimes, and just start reading their poetry; and right around the corner—across the street from the Wall in Chicago, the Wall of Respect . . .

Q. That's the one you write about in "The Wall."

A. Yes. Well, right across the street is a tavern, and one Sunday afternoon, some of the poets decided to go in there and read poetry to just whoever was there. I went with them. One of them went to the front of the tavern and said, "Say, folks, we're going to lay some poetry on you." And there had been a couple of fights in there, people drinking, and all kinds of exciting things going on; and some of us wondered how they were going to respond to poetry. But the poets started reading their poetry, and before we knew it, people had turned around on their bar stools, with their drinks behind them, and were listening. Then they applauded. And I thought that was a wonderful thing, something new to me. I want to write poetry—and it won't be Ezra Pound poetry, as you can imagine—that will be exciting to such people. And I don't see why it can't be "good" poetry, putting quotes around "good."

Q. Are you suggesting that poetry should be restored to one of its original forms, that of the voice of the prophet, speaker to the people . . . ?

A. I don't want to be a prophet.

Q. . . . Or a social voice, a voice that can be heard. Do you think that poetry as it's now being written and heard by the people is becoming a social force?

A. Some of these people do want their poems to become "social forces"; others haven't, I believe, really thought of such a thing. And I am not writing poems with the idea that they are to become social forces. I don't feel that I care to direct myself in that way. I don't care to proceed from that intention.

Q. Let me ask you about the character portraits in your poetry and in your novel, Maud Martha. In the Mecca, *your most recent volume, portrays life in a large city apartment building.* A Street in Bronzeville *gave similar vignettes of people in the city. The same, I think, can be said for all of your work.*

A. It's a fascination of mine to write about ghetto people there.

Q. Are your characters literally true to your experience or do you set out to change experience?

A. Some of them are, are invented, some of them are very real people. The people in a little poem called "The Vacant Lot" really existed and really did those things. For example: "Mrs. Coley's three-flat brick / Isn't here any more. / All done with seeing her fat little form / Burst out of the basement door. . . ." Really happened! That lot is still vacant on the street where I was raised. (My mother still lives on the street.) "Matthew Cole" is based on a man who roomed

with my husband's aunt. And I remember him so well, I feel he really came through in the poem. "The Murder" really happened except for the fact that I said the boy's mother was gossiping down the street. She was working. (I guess I did her an injustice there.) "Obituary for a Living Lady" is based on a person I once knew very well.

Q. What about the characters in Maud Martha? *I'm thinking of Clement Lewy, a boy who comes home every day to prepare his own meal while his mother is at work. Or the character of the young truck driver who finds that he cannot any longer abide his home life and one day simply abandons his family.*

A. Again, not based on any specific persons.

Q. There is a quality of pathos about all of your characters and compassion in your treatment of them. Many of them make a pitiful attempt to be what they cannot be.

A. Some of them. Not all of them; some of them are very much interested in just the general events of their own lives.

Q. Let me suggest one of the frequently anthologized poems, "A Song in the Front Yard," about a girl who "gets sick of a rose" and decides she'd like to leave the comfort and pleasure of the front yard to see what life would be like in the back.

A. Or out in the alley, where the charity children play, based on my own resentment when I was a little girl, having to come inside the front gate after nine—oh, earlier than that in my case.

Q. Isn't there a yearning to get away in many such portraits?

A. I wouldn't attach any heavy significance to that particular poem, because that was the lightest kind of a little poem.

Q. How about a poem like "Sadie and Maud," a little lyric, I think in quatrains, contrasting Maud, who turns out to be a lonely brown "mouse," and Sadie, who "scraped life / With a fine tooth comb"?

A. Those are imaginary characters, purely imaginary.

Q. What about "The Sundays of Satin-Legs Smith," where the hero spends much of his morning in his lavender bath. . . .

A. . . . and in his closet, among his perfume bottles.

Q. And his neckties and umbrellas which are like "banners for some gathering war"?

A. Not his umbrellas; I think I called it hats "like bright umbrellas," which implies that he is protecting himself under that fancy wideness.... You probably don't remember the zoot-suiters; they were still around in the forties, in the early forties. They were not only black men but Puerto Ricans, too, who would wear these suits with the wide shoulders, and the pants did balloon out and then come down to tapering ends, and they wore chains—perhaps you've seen them in the movies every once in a while. That's the kind of person I was writing about in "The Sundays of Satin-Legs Smith."

Q. You write about young men in other poems perhaps like that. "Patent Leather" was an early poem describing a character who talks about his "cool chick down on Calumet," and he wears patent leather. Then there's "Bronzeville Man with a Belt in the Back," and more recently, "We Real Cool."

A. In "Patent Leather," a young woman is admiring a man (and that admiration is no longer popular) who slicks back his hair, so that it looks like it's smooth as patent leather, and shiny. "Bronzeville Man with a Belt in the Back"—"belt in the back" was a popular style for men some years ago; and this man feels dapper and equal to the fight that he must constantly wage, when he puts on such a suit.

Q. How about the seven pool players in the poem "We Real Cool"?

A. They have no pretensions to any glamor. They are supposedly dropouts, or at least they're in the poolroom when they should possibly be in school, since they're probably young enough, or at least those I saw were when I looked in a poolroom, and they.... First of all, let me tell you how that's supposed to be said, because there's a reason why I set it out as I did. These are people who are essentially saying, "Kilroy is here. We are." But they're a little uncertain of the strength of their identity. [Reads: "We Real Cool."]

The "We"—you're supposed to stop after the "We" and think about their validity, and of course there's no way for you to tell whether it should be said softly or not, I suppose, but I say it rather softly because I want to represent their basic uncertainty, which they don't bother to question every day, of course.

Q. Are you saying that the form of this poem, then, was determined by the colloquial rhythm you were trying to catch?

A. No, determined by my feeling about these boys, these young men.

Q. These short lines, then, are your own invention at this point? You don't have any literary model in mind; you're not thinking of Eliot or Pound or anybody in particular...?

A. My gosh, no! I don't even admire Pound, but I do like, for instance, Eliot's "Prufrock" and *The Waste Land*, "Portrait of a Lady," and some others of those earlier poems. But nothing of the sort ever entered my mind. When I start writing a poem, I don't think about models or about what anybody else in the world has done.

Q. Let me ask you about some of your poems that are in specific forms, however—sonnets....

A. I like to refer to that series of soldier sonnets.

Q. "Gay Chaps at the Bar."

A. A sonnet series in off-rhyme, because I felt it was an off-rhyme situation—I did think of that. I first wrote the one sonnet, without thinking of extensions. I wrote it because of a letter I got from a soldier who included that title in what he was telling me; and then I said, there are other things to say about what's going on at the front and all, and I'll write more poems, some of them based on the stuff of letters that I was getting from several soldiers, and I felt it would be good to have them all in the same form, because it would serve my purposes throughout.

Q. Then you find it challenging to write in a particular form, like the sonnet, when the occasion seems to lend itself?

A. I really haven't written extensively in many forms. I've written a little blank verse, and I have written many more sonnets than I'm sure I'll be writing in the future, although I still think there are things colloquial and contemporary that can be done with the sonnet form. And, let's see, free verse of course I'll be continuing to experiment with, dotting a little rhyme here and there sometimes as I did in part of *In the Mecca*. But I'm really not form-conscious. I don't worship villanelles, for instance.

Q. But then you have written formally, as you say, with sonnets, quatrains, the literary ballad, the folk ballad, "The Ballad of Rudolph Reed." Have you given up writing ballads?

A. I don't know. I might write other ballads, but they would be very different from those that I have written so far. I see myself chiefly writing free verse, experimenting with it as much as I can. The next book, I'm pretty sure, will be a book of small pieces of free verse. . . .

Source: George Stavros and Gwendolyn Brooks, "An Interview with Gwendolyn Brooks," in *Conversations with Gwendolyn Brooks*, edited by Gloria Wade Gayles, University Press of Mississippi, 2003, pp. 40–45.

SOURCES

Bolden, B. J., *Urban Rage in Bronzeville: Social Commentary in the Poetry of Gwendolyn Brooks, 1945–1950*, Third World Press, 1999, pp. 23–25.

Brooks, Gwendolyn, "Sadie and Maud," in *The New Anthology of American Poetry*, Vol. 3, *Postmodernisms: 1950–Present*, edited by Steven Gould Axelrod, Camille Roman, and Thomas Travisano, Rutgers University Press, 2012, p. 110.

Gery, John, "Subversive Parody in the Early Poems of Gwendolyn Brooks," in *South Central Review*, Vol. 16, No. 1, Spring 1999, pp. 44–56.

Melhem, D. H., *Gwendolyn Brooks: Poetry & the Heroic Voice*, University Press of Kentucky, 1987, pp. 28–29, 86.

Mootry, Maria K., and Gary Smith, eds., *A Life Distilled: Gwendolyn Brooks, Her Poetry and Fiction*, University of Illinois Press, 1987, pp. 283–84.

Norton, Eleanor Holmes, "For Sadie and Maud," in *On Gwendolyn Brooks: Reliant Contemplation*, edited by Stephen Caldwell Wright, University of Michigan Press, 1996, pp. 60–65.

Zinsser, Hans, *Rats, Lice, and History*, George Routledge & Sons, 1935, p. 187.

FURTHER READING

Brooks, Gwendolyn, *Maud Martha*, Harper & Brothers, 1953.
    Maud Martha is Brooks's only novel. It tells the story of a girl growing up in Bronzeville during the 1940s. The novel is highly experimental, resembling in many ways a corpus of poetry rather than ordinary narrative structure. It consists of disjointed episodes not presented in chronological order.

Malcolm X, with Arthur Haley, *The Autobiography of Malcolm X*, Grove, 1965.
    The Autobiography of Malcolm X, one of the greatest pieces of prose ever produced by an African American author, tells the life story of Malcom X, one of the principal leaders of the civil rights movement. His early life exemplifies the kind of hopeless poverty that is the focus of much of Brooks's poetry. He was the inspiration for the Black Arts movement that Brooks joined in her later career.

Roses, Lorraine Elena, and Ruth Elizabeth Randolph, eds., *Harlem's Glory: Black Women Writing, 1900–1950*, Harvard University Press, 1996.
    This anthology presents poems by women writers of the Harlem Renaissance, such as Zora Neale Hurston, as well as less well-known figures. They share Brooks's themes of oppression and poverty in her contemporary Bronzeville poems.

Shaw, Harry B., *Gwendolyn Brooks*, Twayne Unites States Authors Series No. 395, Twayne Publishers, 1980.
    Shaw gives an introductory overview of Brooks and her poetry.

SUGGESTED SEARCH TERMS

Gwendolyn Brooks

Sadie and Maud AND Brooks

Black Arts movement

Harlem Renaissance

Jim Crow

Bronzeville

fine-tooth comb

Great Migration

Speeches for Dr Frankenstein

MARGARET ATWOOD

1966

Margaret Atwood is one of the most important writers of the second half of the twentieth century. Her combined position as an acclaimed poet as well as a best-selling novelist is nearly unparalleled. Her poem "Speeches for Dr Frankenstein" (1966) is an amplification or interpretation of Mary Shelley's 1818 novel *Frankenstein*. The poem, an early but significant work for Atwood, was originally published as a collaboration with the artist Charles Pachter in fifteen unique hand-made chapbooks. The poem explores questions of identity according to the theories of the psychologist Jacques Lacan, which were highly topical in the 1960s. The ambitious poem also aims to expose the oppressive structures of Western culture implicated in constructs such as science, imperialism, racism, and sexism. "Speeches for Dr Frankenstein" is included in Atwood's collection *The Animals in That Country* (1968).

AUTHOR BIOGRAPHY

The Canadian poet and novelist Margaret Eleanor Atwood was born on November 18, 1939, in Ottawa, Ontario. Atwood's father was an entomologist, and his work often took the family to the remote forests of Quebec. As a result, Atwood did not attend school regularly until she was eight years old, but she was an early and eager reader. Her work has always been

Margaret Atwood (© *Marta Iwanek | Toronto Star via Getty Images*)

deeply influenced by myth in the broadest sense. She began to study literature at the University of Toronto at age sixteen in 1957, where she worked under the prominent literary critic Northrup Frye. As an undergraduate, she wrote award-winning poetry chapbooks (small runs of self-published books often used by poets to circulate their work). In 1962, she earned a master's degree from prestigious Radcliffe College. She began work on a PhD at Harvard University but did not finish it, marrying instead. She worked at various Canadian schools as an adjunct professor, and later in her career would often teach as a visiting professor.

"Speeches for Dr Frankenstein" was originally published in a set of fifteen handmade art books in 1966. The text was included in Atwood's 1968 collection *The Animals in That Country*. The work was a collaboration with the artist Charles Pachter, with whom Atwood had a very close working relationship. At the time, he referred to Atwood as his muse. In 1969, Atwood published her first novel, *The Edible Woman*. Released at a time when the women's movement was growing, the novel's feminist themes made it a critical and commercial success.

Although they never married, Atwood began to live with the novelist Graeme Gibson in 1973 on a farm in rural Ontario. Their daughter, Eleanor Atwood-Gibson, was born in 1976, and the family moved to Toronto in 1980. Atwood's 1981 novel *The Handmaid's Tale* established her as one of the major novelists of the late twentieth century. Like many of Atwood's novels, *The Handmaid's Tale* explores how society might change if one of its many oppressive agencies (in this case, a religious patriarchy) gained control.

Atwood became a perennial best-selling novelist and used her celebrity as a platform for animal rights activism. In 2000, her novel *The Blind Assassin* won the prestigious Booker Prize, and she is a leading contender for a Nobel Prize in Literature. In 2004, weary of book tours, Atwood conceived of the idea of the LongPen, a device by which a person could use a computer interface (a tablet along with some specialized equipment) to sign books over a distance. She contracted with a technology company to develop the product (to which she holds the patent), and it is now a successful commercial venture, though mostly used to sign business contracts and similar documents.

In 2005, Atwood wrote *The Penelopiad*, a retelling of *The Odyssey* from the perspective of Penelope, Odysseus's wife; it is the first volume in the Canongate Myth Series, which has commissioned novels interpreting mythological material from many of the world's leading novelists. One of Atwood's main efforts in the twenty-first century has been the MaddAddam series of novels (*Oryx and Crake* in 2003, *The Year of the Flood* in 2009, and *MaddAddam* in 2013), in which civilization is destroyed by uncontrolled scientific advancement, particularly in genetic engineering, fueled by commercial exploitation.

POEM SUMMARY

The text used for this summary is from *Selected Poems: 1965–1975*, Houghton Mifflin, 1987, pp. 64–69. A version of the poem can be found on the following web page: https://frankensteinresources. wikispaces.com/file/view/speeches + for + dr + frankenstein + by + margaret + atwood.pdf.

MEDIA ADAPTATIONS

- Part of "Speeches for Dr Frankenstein" (sections i, iv, vii, and ix) was set as a song cycle by Bruce Pennycook in 1980. The setting calls for recorded electronic sounds to be played in accompaniment to a soprano singing the text. The score (which specifies that the music is to be performed only using a CD obtained from the composer) was published in 1981, and a recording of a performance with Neva Pilgrim was released in 1983 by Smithsonian Folkway Recordings.

- In 2012, an e-book version of "Speeches for Dr Frankenstein" was published by Anansi Press. It is based on scans of a single unique copy of one of Pachter's original handmade books of the poem.

The text of "Speeches for Dr Frankenstein" is divided into ten numbered sections. The poem reinterprets episodes from Mary Shelley's 1818 novel *Frankenstein*. The speaker of the entire poem is Dr. Frankenstein.

i (lines 1–7)

Dr. Frankenstein is doing surgical work with a scalpel. Presumably he is cutting up human cadavers, parts of which will be reassembled into the monster. Frankenstein describes himself as someone carrying out a performance in an arena. *Arena*, like *theater*, is a common term for an operating room. It was not uncommon for an operating room in a teaching hospital to have banked rows of seats for students observing an operation (today, student observation is done through video screens). But those terms also have other connotations. *Arena* originally referred to a Roman arena like the Colosseum, where gladiators fought and killed each other and wild beasts as a public spectacle in the Roman Republic and Empire. Because Frankenstein is cutting up a human body (and perhaps because of Atwood's well-known opposition to hunting), this image is probably intended to evoke horror and disgust. At the same time, the term also suggests modern professional sports. American football, particularly in the 1960s, presented itself as a revival of the Roman games; football players were commonly called gladiators by sports writers and commentators. Gladiators and football players were equally elevated to the status of celebrities or stars, as Frankenstein has evidently become. Physicians also have a certain celebrity status in modern culture, partly because of their depiction in films and television shows. But the arena Frankenstein is in is empty; he hears only the cheers of a phantom crowd in his imagination. In this frame of mind, he starts to work with his scalpel.

ii (lines 8–16)

At the beginning of this section, the table is described as being empty, in a way that suggests that emptiness is a sort of freedom. However, it is clear that the table actually holds the body, which is described here using several metaphors related to eating: the cutting is like opening a jar, the surgical table becomes a plate, and the red flesh of the cadaver is described as a pomegranate, as though Atwood were suggesting devouring the corpse in an act of cannibalism. But there is life in it as well, and at the instant it is described as alive, Frankenstein claims it as his property.

iii (lines 17–31)

The living thing on the table starts to fight back. In the arena of the operating room, Frankenstein and his monster start to circle each other, the way wrestlers do before they come to grips and presumably the way gladiators did. The creature resists the shape that Frankenstein is trying to impose on it, moving and writhing the way a lump of dough would move and writhe if it were alive. It transforms before his eyes; it growls, so it has a mouth (with teeth, one imagines), and it grows claws. It leaps at Frankenstein, but the doctor cuts at it with his scalpel, subduing it. The specimens preserved in jars of formaldehyde on the shelves around the operating arena applaud him. It falls back onto the table; it seems to be dead, since it is now compared to a cat about to be dissected in an anatomy class.

In the last two lines of the section, the narrative veers in an entirely new direction. Frankenstein appears to reveal that he is in love with the monster he has just killed or subdued and wishes to possess it for that reason.

iv (lines 32–45)

Frankenstein begins to beautify the monster, asking it with what jewelry it would like to be decorated. Frankenstein is suited to this task because he is a human being, and the ability to create (for example, by weaving clothes) through the agency of humanity's unique hands is at his disposal. His mind is even more creative than his hands and can dress the monster in ideas and rhetoric. But dressing it becomes an act of bondage, and the web of cloth that he weaves becomes a spider's web trapping the monster, which Frankenstein pins down like an insect in a display case. Mathematics too becomes part of this oppression. Since Frankenstein is creating the monster, he has absolute control to shape it as he wishes.

v (lines 46–61)

Frankenstein has gone mad with pride at his own skill in perfecting the monster. However, he wonders if he would have been better off beginning from an egg and sperm, growing an embryo in the familiar way. It is difficult for Frankenstein to look upon his monster, which is again likened to food, since it is beginning to decay. He considers the monster a god, but one that has been destroyed, the parts of its body reduced to a heap of broken ruins. Frankenstein asks how he can love the monster, knowing that he created it. Fear is in the air.

vi (lines 62–73)

The monster comes to life, or comes to life again. Atwood describes it as a larva, suggesting yet another form the life cycle can take. Frankenstein runs away from the monster protected by nothing but his surgical gown. He runs outside into a rainstorm; the rain is described as a cape he wraps himself in. The monster, on the other hand, is a red (that is, bloody), inhuman thing. It is starved and ravenous, but Frankenstein has nothing to feed it. Keeping eating metaphors at the forefront, he asks himself what motive he himself had for creating the thing.

vii (lines 74–85)

Frankenstein accuses the monster of being his own reflection, of having stolen its existence from him. What the monster has taken—his joy and his suffering—he has lost. The monster has turned into Frankenstein. The monster accuses Frankenstein of murder, but Frankenstein feels he is not capable of that in his numb, hollowed-out state. It is the monster who is the murderer.

viii (lines 86–98)

This section parallels the episode from Mary Shelley's *Frankenstein* where Frankenstein chases the creature of that novel across the frozen Arctic Ocean. Atwood begins to refer to material from the novel that has not been mentioned before in the poem, such as Frankenstein's denial of any connection with the monster. Frankenstein pursues the creature across the frozen landscape, leaving messages for help written in the snow. Frankenstein feels he is being consumed by his emotional turmoil.

ix (lines 99–112)

The monster is now a star glittering in the spotlight. He dances across the ice, a performer in an electrified costume, like a neon updating of the matador's coat of lights. The monster has become another kind of performer in an arena, an ice dancer. But at the same time, his monstrosity is revealed in a description of his animalistic claws and his creating fire out of water. The monster is taking a positive delight in the chase, while Frankenstein follows grimly.

x (lines 113–30)

The monster, grown to godlike, cosmic proportions, finally speaks to Frankenstein. It points out that the doctor is now the one who needs to be healed. Frankenstein claimed he was performing an act of creation, but all he had accomplished was to cut off that part of himself that was the monster, and now he has a gaping wound in his side where the scalpel separated their flesh. Frankenstein is chasing the creature because the only way he can be healed is by rejoining with it, but the creature refuses.

THEMES

Art

The Greek work *poetes*, the origin of the English *poet*, means "maker" or "creator." It is hardly surprising then, that the poet Atwood is concerned with the theme of creation in the original *Frankenstein* and plays out the metaphorical possibilities of that creation in relation to poetic art. At the beginning of the second section of "Speeches for Dr Frankenstein," the narrator speaks of the operating table as if it were a blank page. He complains that too much freedom will fail to produce any result. The poet, in turn,

TOPICS FOR FURTHER STUDY

- Atwood's *Oryx and Crake* (2003) is the first leg of her dystopian MaddAddam trilogy. The novel revisits the author's unease with science and especially biology as expressed in "Speeches for Dr Frankenstein," but in a more concrete way. She sees genetic engineering being used to produce things like *chicki-nobs*, an amorphous mass of chicken breast that grows the chicken meat more efficiently and without the possibility of any conscious entity suffering, since it lacks a brain. A kind of human is also created that is biologically vegetarian and that feels the desire to have sex only during a brief annual mating period. The scientist responsible for all this eventually decides to exterminate the human race with a genetically engineered plague. Read *Oryx and Crake* and write an essay explaining in more detail how the central ideas of the novel are related to those of the poem.

- Many elements of "Speeches for Dr Frankenstein" are derived from or at least parallel to passages of Mary Shelley's *Frankenstein*. Use an infographic site (such as http://www.easel.ly) to directly compare these passages between the two works. Print out the result and display it as a poster in your classroom.

- Li Po (or Li Bai), who wrote in the eighth century, is one of the most important Chinese poets. A sample of his work is available in *The Selected Poems of Li Po* (translated by David Hinton, 1996), and translations of works are available on various websites. His poems alternate between themes of heroic exploits and alchemy, both of which involve journeys to the limits of the known world. These elements present some obvious thematic parallels with *Frankenstein* and, naturally, with Atwood's "Speeches for Dr Frankenstein." Write a paper exploring these similarities.

- *This Dark Endeavor: The Apprenticeship of Victor Frankenstein* (2012), by Canadian author Kenneth Oppel, is a young-adult novel that interacts with Mary Shelley's *Frankenstein*. It also incorporates elements of *St. Leon* (1799), the alchemical novel by Shelley's father, William Godwin. Oppel's novel imagines that Victor Frankenstein had, as a partner in his early occult research, a twin brother named Konrad. This introduces the gothic theme of the *doppelgänger*, or mysterious double, into the story, an element that is little more than implied by Shelley (in the case of the monster). This idea is similar to Atwood's development of the Lacanian theme of the *other* in "Speeches for Dr Frankenstein." Write a paper comparing how the two adaptations of Frankenstein deal with the idea of the doppelgänger or the *other*.

---

must be constrained by some form, if not by traditional meter and rhyme, or else her work would be no different from prose. Frankenstein worked, at least in part, by reassembling the body parts of the dead, but in the poem he has to give form to a shapeless mass, like rolling out bread dough. This too is an apt description for the work of the poet who must give poetry a definite, well-defined shape.

In section iv, Frankenstein's work of making the body appears to be over, but now he turns to ornamenting it, seemingly with painting, or tattooing, or perhaps jewelry. This passage, though meaningless in terms of Frankenstein's creation, has a clear relevance to the final polishing of a poem. The metaphor of the weaver is a familiar one for a poet. In the ninth section of the poem, the material about dancing also alludes to poetry. Poems were originally songs, and a good deal of Greek poetry in particular was meant to accompany dancing; the idea of poetic feet (used to analyze the rhythmic pattern of a poem)

Atwood's poem captures the gothic eeriness of the novel that inspired it. (© Boris Stroujko / Shutterstock.com)

relates to the steps of a dance. Dancing over the Arctic snow (and note that Atwood fabricates this snow for her own purposes; there would be none in nature—only ice), the monster will leave a record of his steps, similar to writing poetry.

Western Culture

Like a majority of poets working in English, Atwood is thoroughly involved in Western culture. She can no more fly out of its web and leave the West behind than she can fly out of the atmosphere and breathe in outer space. Just as the language she writes is English, the poetic idiom she uses is composed of the standards of Western literature—the Bible, William Shakespeare, Edgar Allan Poe, T. S. Eliot, and countless others. But at the same time, Atwood is a member of the counterculture that is in conscious, violent revolt against the West. Convinced that at its root, the West is an oppressive cultural construct, Atwood uses "Speeches for Dr Frankenstein" to expose the corrupt and controlling heart of Western culture. While disciplines like science and mathematics might be neutral or even good, she sees them put to restrictive and coercive

ends by the West, symbolized in the poem by Frankenstein.

Atwood is well known as an animal rights activist and essentially considers that animals should be treated no differently than humans (the theme of her poem "The Animals in That Country"). This leads in "Speeches for Dr Frankenstein" to objections to the use of animals in medical experiments. This is expressed in the monster's resistance to the procedures Frankenstein performs on it, as well as in the horror Atwood expects her readers to feel at her description of animal specimens preserved in jars, and finally in the reference to the once-common biology class exercise of dissecting a cat. This theme, which may be taken as one of the main points of the poem, is fully developed in the fourth section. There, both Frankenstein's desire and his ability to control are presented as absolute, determining the very form the monster takes. (The choices apparently offered to the creature at the beginning of the section may be illusory, standing for the choices apparently offered in capitalist consumer society between the products of one company and the nearly identical products of another, equally damaging to the environment and the exploited workers who produced them.) The form this control takes is an equation sealed in the monster's skull, like the mark of the beast sealed on the head of the worshippers of the Antichrist in the book of Revelation. In Western culture, Atwood is saying, even mathematics, the fundamental truth of the universe, can only be put to destructive and oppressive ends.

STYLE

Intertextuality

Literature often seems to be composed independently, with each new work coming into existence through the creative genius of its author, but most literature actually enters into a dialogue with the works that form the background of the author's own reading and experience. Reference to other works can occur at many levels, and the author is not necessarily consciously aware of all of them. An obvious instance is the entire framework of Atwood's poem, which is acknowledged to be derived from Mary Shelley's *Frankenstein*. One particular kind of reference is called intertextuality. In this case, the author writes a line that recalls a specific source without ever quoting it or mentioning it directly, but which the reader too will recognize. These links between the texts (and "texts" may mean not only written works but also film, music, and other cultural products) tie the author and reader together with the cord of their shared experience.

Line 6 of Atwood's poem is an intertextual reference to the beginning of the fifth stanza of Poe's "Ulalume." It shares the image of the empty air filled with supposedly human sounds made by its invisible, spiritual inhabitants. (In addition, Atwood makes a pun on surgical ether, an anesthetizing agent given in the form of a gas.) The central image of Atwood's fifth section, the ruined body of a fallen and destroyed god, recalls the long poem *The Wasteland*, by T. S. Eliot, where modern civilization lies prostrate and broken into tiny pieces like a broken statue. The final line of the poem, when the monster refuses to come at Frankenstein's call for his aid, recalls a scene from Shakespeare's *Henry IV, Part I*, act 3, in which the Welsh rebel Owen Glendower is trying to impress an ally

with his semidivine nature and his magical powers. Glendower claims to be able to summon the devil though ceremonial magic, but his companion treats him with a skeptical irony, suggesting that anyone can call the devil, but the trick is having him answer the summons.

Film

In her 1977 interview with Linda Sandler, when asked about "Speeches for Dr Frankenstein," Atwood dismissed the famous 1931 James Whale film as "just Hollywood hokum" and insisted, "My setting comes from the original novel." But in fact she does refer to the James Whale film as well as many others. To begin with, Atwood borrows the word *monster* from the film; the term is never used in the novel. Atwood's own watercolor illustrations of the poem (reproduced in Sharon Rose Wilson's *Margaret Atwood's Fairy-Tale Sexual Politics*) also evoke Whale's sequel, *The Bride of Frankenstein*. Much of the poem is set in a modern surgical theater, which differs from the scene of the monster's creation in both the novel and the films. However, with its ranks of student seating, Frankenstein's surgical mask and gown, the large circular light on an armature over the table, and its shelves of pickled lab specimens, the scene does not so much resemble a real operating arena as the familiar image of an operating room seen in so many old Hollywood movies. The action that actually brings the monster to life Atwood describes somewhat strangely as being akin to screwing off the top of a jar. This may be a reference to the strange shape of the head, which somewhat resembles a jar, in the two Whale films. In this case, Atwood's description would relate to the insertion of the brain. (Compare another movie inspired by Whale's films, the 1983 satire *The Man with Two Brains*, in which a surgical technique permits the rapid screwing on and off of the skull cap for brain surgery.) The beginning of the third section of Atwood's poem offers a clearer case. These lines make sense only in light of the countless film scenes in which two gladiators, or wrestlers, or boxers, face off by circling around the ring as each one looks for an advantage. The sudden transformation of the monster from an apparent lump of formless life (yeast) to a creature with a mouth and claws recalls scenes of transformations into monsters in old Hollywood horror movies like *Dr. Jekyll and Mr. Hyde* (1931) or *The Wolfman* (1940). Perhaps the most striking film reference comes in the eighth section, where Frankenstein, pursuing the monster across the Arctic ice floes,

COMPARE
&
CONTRAST

- **1960s:** Figure skating is an Olympic event in which the contestants carve various geometrical and artistic shapes into the ice with their skates.

  Today: Figure skating is joined as an Olympics sport by ice dancing, which developed in commercial entertainments such as the Ice Capades.

- **1960s:** This period is the golden age of the American counterculture movement, marked by rapid progress in the civil rights movement, second-wave feminism, and protests against the Vietnam War, along with the iconic emergence of the hippie in popular culture.

  Today: The mechanisms of oppression to which cultural protest responds have become more subtly based in consumerism and the manipulation of popular ideology, making the need for a countercultural reaction less obvious to the majority of the population.

- **1960s:** Jacques Lacan and other postmodernist theorists begin to exercise an influence on North American popular culture. Their ideas are spread through university liberal arts departments.

  Today: Lacan, like postmodernism in general, has fallen out of fashion and is almost unknown in the intellectual community, outside of English and film departments.

spells out on the barren white plains huge messages asking for help. This makes little sense in the context, but it is an immediately familiar idea from the countless Hollywood films and television shows in which the hero is cast away on a desert island and uses rocks or logs to spell out SOS on a clear beach where the message can be seen by passing aircraft. Written texts are always composed out of references at various levels to older literature, but Atwood in "Speeches for Dr Frankenstein" extends the practice to film. This is hardly unexpected, since film was a dominant art form of the twentieth century. But whereas her literary references are highly educated and obscure, she seems purposefully to appeal to only the most popular and overused images from movies.

HISTORICAL CONTEXT

The 1960s Counterculture

The Socratic foundation of Western civilization means that one of the West's unique features has been its ability to criticize itself and restructure itself based on that criticism. The greatest achievement of this self-criticism was the Enlightenment, a period in the 1700s when reason alone was used to overturn and reject corrupt, oppressive, and irrational traditions. Democracy replaced monarchy, science replaced magic, medicine replaced quackery, and rationality replaced superstition. The freedom and equality of all people, rather than the privilege of a few, became the goal. Wealth also replaced poverty as reason was turned to the reordering of the economic structure of society and the application of science to production. The change in the condition of life in Europe and the Americas between 1500 and 2000 is remarkable: the average human life span has tripled, famine has ended, epidemics have ended, and the standard of living has increased exponentially. None of these transformations has been completely or perfectly realized, though, so the self-examination of the West cannot cease.

Mary Shelley was part of the romantic movement in the early 1800s, a period in which many wondered whether the Enlightenment had gone too far, whether there was value in traditions that had been lost, and whether modern phenomena like science might not be entirely beneficial. These fears were embodied in the nineteenth century in the German *Wandervogel* movement: young people who called themselves "wandering birds"

The final section of the poem reflects Shelley's novel, with Frankenstein chasing the monster into the Arctic. (© Incredible Arctic / Shutterstock.com)

embraced a life based on the traditional appreciation of nature. (This movement was, paradoxically, the direct ancestor in America of the hippies, and in Germany of the Nazis.) Particularly after the period of intense American cultural conformity during the 1950s, such popular movements began to have an effect, while academics began to question whether social structures of power and oppression had only been transformed but not done away with by the Enlightenment. Phenomena like imperialism, racism, and sexism still seemed powerful.

These elements of the dominant culture called forth a counterculture of protest that embraced movements like the hippies—who protested the Vietnam War—the civil rights movement, and second-wave feminism. These movements were all at their height in 1966 and, dominating civil discourse in the United States, inevitably spilled over into Canada. "Speeches for Dr Frankenstein" is a product of this counterculture. It not only embraces many countercultural causes with a searching critique of the West and its civilization, but is also countercultural as a physical object. The poem was

originally written in 1966. It was published as a stand-alone art book (called a chapbook) in collaboration with the prominent Canadian artist Charles Pachter. The text was a combination of hand-set typography and calligraphy. The resulting pages of various materials and colors were not sewn together but kept in a portfolio. Each page was decorated with illuminations by Pachter. Fifteen copies were produced, each one unique. The book stood as a cry for the return to the tradition of individuality and craftsmanship, throwing itself provocatively in the face of industrial mass production of commercial products.

CRITICAL OVERVIEW

Perhaps because of its early place in Atwood's body of work, as well as the dense, challenging nature of the poem, "Speeches for Dr Frankenstein" has not received the extensive attention one might expect for what really is a major work. One of the earliest responses to "Speeches for Dr Frankenstein," T. D. MacLulich's "Atwood's Adult Fairy Tale: Levi-Strauss, Bettelheim, and *The Edible Woman*" (1978), offers a conventional Freudian reading of the poem as concerning anxieties about maturity and particularly sexual maturity. Beyond this, MacLulich also reads the physical hacking apart of the monster and Frankenstein as standing for the negotiation of sexual politics. Jean Mallinson, in her 1985 study *Margaret Atwood and Her Works*, characterizes Frankenstein's powers as destructive, like the glance of Medusa. The attempt to use it for creation inevitably ends in disaster, embodied in the monster. The aggressive public rhetoric implied by the term *speeches* in the title is set as an opposition to the secretive and destructive workings of science, which Mallinson finds as a typical theme of Atwood's work. The poem, then, is seen as an expression of Atwood's own anxieties about creation (namely, creation of poetry).

Sharon Rose Wilson, in the 1993 study *Margaret Atwood's Fairy-Tale Sexual Politics*, points out that Atwood produced two watercolor paintings illustrating "Speeches for Dr Frankenstein." Wilson reproduces both paintings, titled *Frankenstein I* and *Frankenstein II*. The first one, which appears to be based on publicity photos for the 1935 film *The Bride of Frankenstein*, shows the monster carrying Elizabeth, Dr. Frankenstein's adopted sister and later his wife. The second shows Elizabeth's body laid out for her funeral surrounded by mourners, with the monster hovering in the background. Wilson interprets the female figures in the images as the monster's "female creator" but is uncertain whether they are meant as some kind of female avatar of Frankenstein or whether they refer to Mary Shelley. She does not consider whether the creator in that case may be Atwood herself.

Yael Shapira, in her 2010 article "Hairball Speaks: Margaret Atwood and the Narrative Legacy of the Female Grotesque," calls attention to the Frankenstein theme in Atwood's 1993 short story "Hairball," in which she revisits many themes of "Speeches for Dr Frankenstein," expanding on them or perhaps reinterpreting them. At the beginning of the story, a woman named Kat has an ovarian cyst removed and insists on keeping it in a jar preserved in formaldehyde; she names it Hairball. Atwood establishes that Kat is in rebellion against traditional culture. Trained by her mother to be a submissive

wife, Kat instead seeks her own living and her own erotic satisfaction. She works as a fashion magazine editor and considers that her monthly arrangement of new ensembles is an act of creation. She thinks also of her own editor and superior, whom she taught how to dress, as her creation. When he eventually fires her, she conceptualizes it explicitly in terms of Frankenstein (quoting lines from the film rather than the novel) and feels that she has been betrayed by her own creation. The point is that while the novel *Frankenstein* was a cautionary tale against letting ambition lead to breaking through boundaries, it also praises precisely that kind of rebellion and shows it as heroic. Atwood seems to be saying that female transgression against the barriers of the patriarchy had by that time taken on the same heroic resonance, although it comes with a cost.

CRITICISM

Rita M. Brown

Brown is an English professor. In the following essay, she looks at Atwood's "Speeches for Dr Frankenstein" in the context of the influence that theorist Jacques Lacan had on the poem.

In 1992, Susan Squier, then an English professor at the State University of New York at Stony Brook, wrote a letter to the editor of the *New York Times*. She wanted to show that Mary Shelley's contribution to feminism was equal to that of her mother (Mary Wollstonecraft, author of *A Vindication of the Rights of Woman*), pointing out that *Frankenstein* cautions against the possibility of male science attempting to lay claim to the female power of procreation. To support her view, Squier points to Atwood's "Speeches for Dr Frankenstein," in which, Squier claims, the monster is reimagined as a woman talking back to her male creator. But Wilson, in *Margaret Atwood's Fairy-Tale Sexual Politics*, claims instead that it is the creator, Frankenstein, who is turned into a woman in the poem. Atwood's poem seems to be a Rorschach test that must be interpreted by the reader's imagination rather than its actual contents.

In fact, nowhere in the poem does Atwood use a gendered pronoun to refer to Frankenstein, while the monster is referred to at first by the neuter *it*, and later, once he has gained his own identity (or stolen it from Frankenstein), by the masculine *he*. This would suggest that Frankenstein must be

WHAT DO I READ NEXT?

- *The Blind Assassin* is Atwood's Booker Prize–winning novel from 2000. Setting aside the mythological and the fantastic elements that are often her subject matter, in this work Atwood explores character through a nested series of levels of text, with various fictional works being composed inside her larger narrative, and other works inside those.

- The *Tao Te Ching* is a collection of Chinese poetry dating back to the sixth century BCE. The work is attributed to Laozi (meaning "the old sage"), a name that is unlikely to convey information about its actual authors and compilers. Like the Greek pre-Socratic verse from the same time period, which was the beginning of Western philosophy, it deals in brief, deliberately cryptic descriptions of the physical and spiritual nature of existence. It is considered the foundational work of Chinese philosophy, as well as Chinese alchemy. While Western alchemy aimed to transform common metals into gold, in China, thanks to the obsessions of the first emperor Qin Shi Huang, alchemy focused on the problem of achieving human immortality. There are many translations of the *Tao Te Ching*, including the one prepared by Stephen Mitchel in 1992; others are easily found on the Internet.

- Atwood's most recent poetry collection, *The Door*, was written in 2007. It is a collection of fifty lyric poems on diverse topics.

- *Frankenstein by Mary Shelley: A Dark Graphic Novel* (2012), by Sergio A. Sierra and Meritxell Ribas, is an adaptation of the original novel for young adults. Although the art in this volume follows comic-book conventions, there is some attempt to echo nineteenth-century styles of engraving.

- Atwood carefully distinguishes what she considers speculative fiction by literary authors from genre science fiction. *In Other Worlds: SF and the Human Imagination* (2012) is a collection of essays by Atwood on speculative fiction, the first several of which deal with a general criticism of the genre before turning to a dozen or so specific authors, including George Orwell, Aldous Huxley, and Ursula K. LeGuin. The term "SF" stands for "speculative fiction" as well as "science fiction," and it was used by some writers within the science-fiction community during the 1980s to try to rename or rebrand a more literary science fiction they hoped would emerge from the genre.

- Atwood's novel *The Edible Woman* (1969) is an early feminist work. Its main character feels estranged from the consumer society in which she is expected to participate. She begins to feel separated from her own body and becomes unable to eat, repulsed by the act in the same way she would be by cannibalism.

---

masculine too, and given the fact that in Mary Shelley's *Frankenstein* both characters are male, there seems little evidence to reach any other conclusion but that Atwood is simply following Shelley: both characters in the poem are male. This brings up the idea of stolen identity, which is interesting. It is not especially evident in the novel, but it would certainly have fit into the gothic context, which was fascinated with the theme of the *doppelgänger*, or inhuman double. But the theme's

significance in the poem no doubt depends on a more modern source, and Atwood herself gives an important clue about it.

In a 1977 interview with Linda Sandler, Atwood was asked, with reference to "Speeches for Dr Frankenstein," "That's a mirror poem, isn't it?" She responded, "Yes. The monster is the narrator's other self, and the process of writing that poem involved separating the two selves." In the oral shorthand that Atwood must have

AS THE SUBJECT (THE MONSTER) GATHERS ITS
IDENTITY TO ITSELF, THE OBJECT (FRANKENSTEIN)
CEASES TO EXIST."

used as a university lecturer in English literature, she is associating her work with the critical theory of the French psychoanalyst Jacques Lacan. Together with Michel Foucault and Jacques Derrida, Lacan is one of the three French theorists—a historian, a philosopher, and a psychologist—whose work defines postmodernism. The influence of this trio, at least in North America, has been primarily exercised on the field of literary criticism, and it was rapidly ascending in the 1960s.

Lacan insisted that he was a strict Freudian, but his interpretations of Sigmund Freud's works created something entirely new, as is indicated by his eventual expulsion from all the formal national and international bodies of psychoanalysts. One of Lacan's main ideas was the mirror stage. He began with the simple observation that a baby is able to recognize its own image in the mirror as that of a living creature, an *other*, before it can recognize that image as a representation of itself. But Lacan hypothesized that what is going on is exactly the opposite of how it seems, that the infant does not come to recognize the other as a mere image of itself but rather starts to identify itself with the other and acquires an identity by copying the image. Obviously, the development does not depend on the child literally seeing a mirror image of itself. During the hundreds of thousands of years of human history, when humanity lived in a variety of environments as hunter-gatherers, a six-month-old child would have few opportunities to see its own reflection. Rather, the moment of the child recognizing itself in a mirror must be seen as a crystallizing metaphor for the infant's natural development of personality as it matures. The ego, or a person's inherent sense of one's own identity, comes into being, Lacan thought, as the result of self-perception, the infant's awareness of its own body and its interaction with other human beings, as something other than itself. This creates a tension between the whole of the child's perception

and the incompleteness and fragmentation of its limited understanding. This gives rise to an aggressive tension between the whole and the fragmented, which the infant resolves by identifying with the whole, that is, with its image. The child is rewarded with what Lacan called an experience of jubilation, derived from its illusory sense of mastery; this is supported by the infant's new ability to also identify itself with adults as other selves. The ego, then, is formed by the very relationship between the subject—the one doing the perceiving—and the object—the one that is perceived. The identification and the jubilation are based on a misunderstanding, and thus the ego cannot become an authentic self but only an illusion of the existence of a self. For Lacan, the self has no real existence, there is only an *other*. The self is a fictional construct. The everyday world of sensory experience perceived by the ego is also, for Lacan, a symbolic order that represents, but is not, the real world. The real world exists only in the perception of infants before the mirror stage, when they directly experience sensations like hunger. It can also break into consciousness in traumatic events that tear apart the symbolic order, such as the experience of a natural disaster.

Lacan's theories are not without their problems; for example, they tend to be falsified by more recent work in the emerging field of evolutionary psychology on the origin of human traits like altruism and the development of human interactions generally. Similarly, Lacan's theory of the symbolizing function of language depends on the linguistic theory of Ferdinand de Saussure, but his work has been largely falsified by newer theories developed by Noam Chomsky. Nevertheless, in the intellectual environment of the 1960s, Lacan's ideas were highly fashionable and obviously made a deep impact on Atwood. While Lacan has been influential on the psychoanalytic movement in France and in South America (where Lacanian psychoanalysis is unusually dominant within the medical community), in North America, Lacan is known mainly to literary critics and other scholars rather than professional therapists. Lacan's influence on Atwood can be seen at every structural level of her work.

Sherrill Grace, in *Violent Duality: A Study of Margaret Atwood* (1980), stresses that Atwood is pulled toward pairs of opposites: the natural and the human, the male and the female, the subject

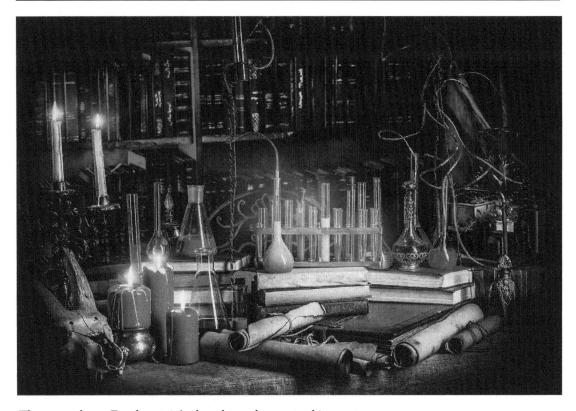

The poem shows Frankenstein's thoughts as he creates his creature. (© *Kiselev Andrey Valerevich / Shutterstock.com*)

and the object, the self and the other, art and life. Only Lacan deals with all of these dualities in a single unified theory (although Grace herself never uses Lacan's work to explain them). Looking in greater detail at "Speeches for Dr Frankenstein," it is possible to see many of Lacan's ideas put into poetic form. As Atwood explained to Sandler, the entire structure of the poem involves the splitting apart of a unified whole into two distinct selves. The monster is the undifferentiated, egoless child, who sees the image of itself in the adult, whole, and integrated Frankenstein and starts to form its own identity on the basis of that image, precisely as Lacan imagined that children do. The monster is incomplete and unformed compared with the image it perceives. This duality is suggested in this instance by the very terms *monster* (implying something unfinished or badly formed) and *doctor* (implying someone completed, mature, and whole).

The monster reacts at first with hostility, actually fighting Frankenstein, but eventually accepts identification with him. The monster's conception of himself becomes based on his perception of Frankenstein (the subject merging with the object). As the subject (the monster) gathers its identity to itself, the object (Frankenstein) ceases to exist. The reader might have expected the creator to possess the authentic identity, but in Lacan's theory, it is the newly created child who is real and who creates its own ego by embracing the unreal symbolic structure of language. Note that the monster does not acquire language until late in the poem. Frankenstein was never real to begin with, but only a fictional image created by the monster's perception, and the monster does not become real, but rather becomes the imaginary construct of the identity it creates. The original model for the new ego recedes as the perceiving subject becomes complete, turning the poem into a journey of maturation. The chase and the final statement of independence mark the emergence of an adult self.

Source: Rita M. Brown, Critical Essay on "Speeches for Dr Frankenstein," in *Poetry for Students*, Gale, Cengage Learning, 2016.

Sharon R. Wilson

In the following excerpt, Wilson examines the importance of mythology in Atwood's writing and visual art.

ATWOOD'S VISUAL ART ALSO SUGGESTS
CREATION, TRANSFORMATION, HEROIC QUEST,
AND TRICKSTER MYTHS."

From her early work, such as *Double Perse-phone*, to recent texts such as *Good Bones* and *The Robber Bride*, Margaret Atwood has used myth-ology in much the same way she has used other intertexts, or texts within texts. Folk tales, fairy tales, and legends are widely assumed to "contain an equally great concentration of mythical mean-ing" (Frye, 188; Wilson 1993, 10). Atwood inter-twines these and other cultural master narratives with radio, television, and film stories, not only to provide mythic resonance and polyphonic mel-ody, but to parody or undercut narrative author-ity in a postmodern way. Greek mythological intertexts in Atwood's visual art, poetry, and novels have frequently evoked both well-known and submerged aspects of the Great Goddess or Mother Goddess widely worshipped throughout the Neolithic and Bronze Ages around the world: Diana or Persephone, Venus or Demeter, and Hecate Crone. Whether explicitly named or sim-ply implied, Atwood's varied mythological inter-texts are central to her images, characterization, and themes. Despite hundreds of articles on Atwood published in the last few years, scholars are only beginning to recognize the variety and significance of her mythic intertexts.

Critics acknowledge that Atwood's female cre-ators tend to be engaged in artistic quests. In Cana-dian poetry, such quests often parody those of male archetypal heroes such as Perseus or Odysseus. As Annis Pratt notes in reference to the Perseus and Medusa myth, males as well as females may sym-pathize with Medusa: "The hero, or Perseus, fades into the background in Canadian poems about stones and stone/women" (93). Many of the images recognized as central in Atwood's visual art, fiction, and poetry—including the flower, circle, spiral or maze, water, mirror, reflection, moon, tree, bird, flight, wings, tower, eye, womb or cave, snake, breast, dismemberment, dance, the double or the number two, and the number three—evoke well-known Greek and Egyptian myths including the Demeter and Persephone, Isis-Osiris-Seth, Theseus

and the Minotaur, Daedalus and Icarus, Orpheus and Eurydice, and Narcissus and Echo stories. The apocalyptic, demonic, and analogical imagery of Frye's theory of myths (or parodies of this imagery) are as apparent in Atwood novels, such as *The Handmaid's Tale*, as are his mythoi of seasons (131–239; Wilson 1993, 274). Egg images in *The Edible Woman* (1969), *Bluebeard's Egg* (1983), *The Handmaid's Tale* (1985), and *The Robber Bride* (1993) suggest the cosmic eggs of numerous crea-tion myths. Atwood's widespread use of meta-phoric cannibalism and ritualistic eating in *The Edible Woman*, *Surfacing* (1972), *The Robber Bride*, and even *The CanLit Foodbook* (1987)—evident in the *Decameron*, the Grimms' "The Rob-ber Bridegroom," "The Juniper Tree," "Little Red-Cap," and "Hansel and Gretel" (Wilson 1993, 83, 86)—were prefigured in two creation stories: the Egyptian myth of Nut's swallowing the sun every night and eating her offspring every morning, and the Greek myth about Cronos eating his sons (Har-ris and Platzner, 57, 60). Similarly, major motifs about creation and the life cycle of birth–death–rebirth, including associated transformation, dis-memberment, and re-memberment, not only sug-gest fairy tales such as the Grimms' "Fitcher's Bird" and Christian myth, but Triple Goddess myths all over the world (Wilson 1993, 4–23).

Atwood's recently published visual art (Wil-son 1993, 39–79), including cover designs and illustrations for her literary works, highlights the mythological intertexts most significant for partic-ular volumes, and makes the impact of Great Goddess mythology throughout Atwood's work immediately evident. Not only the covers of her first published, rare work, *Double Persephone* (1961), but the whole series of poems, is about the Greek myth of Demeter and Persephone. Linocuts Atwood herself put into a flatbed print-ing press, the covers depict in black and white the Eve-Snake-Trees of Great Goddess, Hebrew, and Christian mythology. Departing from the Syrian sculpture of Atargatis or Dea Syria in which god-dess and tree are embraced by the serpent (Harris and Platzner, 87), the goddess's body in the cover art is simultaneously the Tree of Life and the snake symbolizing life mysteries, immortality, and healing. Atwood critics have usually associ-ated this Snake Goddess with the negative, patri-archal version of Medusa, and thus viewed Atwood's first female creator as a gorgon with freezing touch. In earlier, matriarchal stories, Medusa was part of Athena, not opposed to her, and hard to look at only because she was so beautiful. Like other Snake Goddesses such as Lamia, Kali, and Lilith, and like Atwood personae or characters based on them in "Snake Poems" (*Interlunar* 1984) and *The Robber Bride*, this Persephone, too, encompasses the life cycle, the powers of life and beauty as well as death and stasis. Although the final, title poem ends with trampling and "letters grown from branch and stem [that] / Have no green leaves enclosing them," the lost mother who appeared earlier in "Iconic Landscape" is always evident in the volume's title. In the poems as well as the covers, here, as everywhere in Atwood's texts, the double Persephone implies the entire cycle of life and creation Atwood discusses in *Survival*: Triple Goddess as Diana or crescent new moon, Venus or full moon, and Hecate Crone or old moon. "Hecate, the most forbidding of the three, is only one phase of a cycle; she is not sinister when viewed as part of a process, and she can even be a Wise Old Woman" (Wilson 1993, 59–61; *Survival*, 199). Like the brides of the "Fitcher's Bird" and "Robber Bridegroom" fairy tales, Persephone is literally married to death, but she also signifies new life. Some of Atwood's creator-goddesses are failed or parodic; all endure the female artist's double or triple bind (Wilson 1993, 16). But it is always the creator, not the White Goddess muse role, that Atwood and her characters choose.

Quite a few other Atwood covers and illustrations use mythological goddess figures or images, including parodic ones. As von Franz points out, all female deities are Great Goddess archetypes, with female demons and other "evil" mythological figures representing the shadow side (105). In Atwood's visual art the female crescent moon (*Moon* 1958), *Termite Queen* (undated), a spiral (*Circle Game* cover 1966), and several harpies—*Mother Harpy and Chics* (1974), *Male Harpy* (1970), a harpy collage (*Good Bones* 1992)—are all goddess images. Harpies or Valkyries, originally represented as beautiful, winged maidens, were children of Electra, who avenged her father's murder. As "the robbers" who carry off those who disappear without a trace, harpies suggest Atwood's many serious and parodic Robber Brides and Grooms. A number of provocative illustrations for *Good Bones and Simple Murders* (1994) also are associated with the goddess: the cover based on *Termite Queen*, a female bird, a female, a toothed stump, a female Medusa snake, a Pumpkin Woman, a trilobite and two cephalopods with female heads, a woman with a two-faced body,

an angel, a flower, and an earth goddess. In addition to goddess archetypes, several of Atwood's art works also suggest the woman as nature and the nature as monster theme in Canadian literature (Atwood, *Survival*): *Sphinx* (1970), *Angel* (undated), a Hecate Crone (*Moodie Underground* 1970), and sliced mushroom-womb (*Amanita Caesarea, Egg, Cross-Section on Cloud*, undated). The heart enclosing a running egg on the cover of *True Stories* (1981) not only implies the atrocities of human rights violations and sexual politics, but the dismemberment associated with the Isis-Osiris myth. In addition to the Demeter-Persephone duality, the cover of *Two-Headed Poems* (1978), like the poems of this volume, recalls a number of myths about two heads or faces, such as Deceit (one of the miseries released from Pandora's box), the Janus heads facing past and future, and the two-headed Sphinx as goddess of birth and death. These heads could even suggest the decapitation or splitting, also depicted in the two *Mary Queen of Scots* watercolors (1969), of Isis, Medusa, or any entity—such as Canada. As we shall see, the split into threes, as in *Mother Harpy and Chics* and the mirrored faces of the mother in *Lady Oracle* (1976), explicitly suggests the goddess trinity. The *Fitcher's Bird* watercolor (1970) is also based on the ability of Isis and other goddesses to re-member severed or dismembered pieces in the "Fitcher's Bird" fairy tale. The marriage test, forbidden or selected door, and bird and disguise motifs of this tale and of the literature to which it is connected, such as "Bluebeard's Egg" and "Hesitations Outside the Door," also appear in many other kinds of myths.

Atwood's visual art also suggests creation, transformation, heroic quest, and trickster myths. All creation myths feature gods making beings from materials at hand, such as clay or corn meal. Such creatures are often destroyed because they are flawed, like the wooden beings of *Popul Vuh*, or modified so that they won't rival the gods, like the four First Fathers of this epic (Rosenberg, 482–83). Atwood's two *Frankenstein* watercolors (1970) clearly embed mythological texts connected not only to Atwood's early poem "Speeches for Dr. Frankenstein" (published with Charles Pachter's woodcuts 1966, *The Animals in That Country* 1968), but to Mary Shelley's modern Prometheus and to all Atwood characters who feel or appear like monsters, are afraid of creating them, or project monster images onto others. Unlike the Yoruba creator Obtala, who protects creations he deforms while drinking too much palm wine ("The Creation of the Universe and Ife," Rosenberg, 406), Atwood's Dr. Frankenstein, like Shelley's, rejects his flawed creature and his monster self.

Among other watercolors, drawings, collages, and comic strips with mythological themes is *Dream: Bluejay or Archeopteryx* (1968), Atwood's visual counterpart to the poem of this name in *Procedures for Underground* (1969)—about the kind of transformation from one order of being to another that is accomplished by Proteus, Zeus, and Circe, among others. The bluejay designation suggests not only the jays the mother of *Surfacing*'s narrator seems to turn into, but the goddess association with birds evoked in *Surfacing, Bodily Harm* (1981), and *The Robber Bride*; the Bluejay tricksters of NW First Peoples; and the Toronto Bluejays team. The *Hanged God* cover (1970) Atwood designed for *Power Politics* (1971) implies not only the Tarot card but the "book of Thoth," the pack of cards believed to be an adaptation of Egyptian hieroglyphics associated with the magician-god Thoth (Leach, 1110). The two *Drowned Figures* (undated) also for *Power Politics*, the second for the volume's final poem, "He is Last Seen," suggest mythological rebirth through descent to the underworld, as in the drowning and transformation of Narcissus into a white flower. The soft, natural setting of the *Interlunar* cover (1984), which, like the title poem, doubles everything, invites mythologizing of the natural world. Even the *Undersea* (undated), *Portrait of Graeme Gibson* (1974), and *Microscope Image* (undated) watercolors, and *Tarte au Salesman Kilodny* (1987) drawing, *Murder in the Dark* (1983) and Moodie collages (1970), and *Survivalwoman* comic strip (1979) either present folklore motifs or archetypal figures and processes that parallel mythic ones....

Source: Sharon R. Wilson, "Mythological Intertexts in Margaret Atwood's Works," in *Margaret Atwood: Works and Impact*, edited by Reingard M. Nischik, Camden House, 2000, pp. 215–19.

Francis X. Gillen and Margaret Atwood

In the following interview excerpt, Atwood talks about some of her favorite authors and her writing process.

Q: Who are some of your favorite authors?

A: I was trained as a Victorianist; that was my field of study. Some of my favorite authors are the old nineteenth-century chestnuts like

> IF YOU BELIEVE THAT WRITING IS MERELY SELF-EXPRESSION, THEN YOU'LL FOREVER BE TRAPPED IN YOUR OWN PERSONA, OR A CHARACTER VERY MUCH LIKE YOURSELF."

George Eliot's midcentury Victorian novel *Middlemarch*. Dickens is one of my favorites. You're wondering about modern day? The American author who has had the most influence on Canadian writing is Faulkner. I read Faulkner at quite an early age, and I thought, "This man has a wonderful imagination; look at all the stuff he has made up." And then I met someone from Oxford, Mississippi, who told me he didn't make anything up. He just changed the names. So I was quite impressed by that. More modern writers—there are a number of women authors that I like a lot apart from the nineteenth-century ones that I was brought up with. There are a number of British ones. I don't know if you know the names: Fay Weldon, Margaret Drabble, Angela Carter. Linda Gregg from the United States is a poet whom some of the writers here may have heard of.

Q: Is there any special process you use when you write? I used to know someone who locked himself in his room with seven bottles of whiskey and wrote.

A: No, I also have a family, and if you have a family and you are involved with your family, you do not lock yourself in a room. I lock myself in my room at certain hours of the day, but I don't lock myself up for days at a time. I come out in the evenings and in the mornings. I write when my child is at school.

Q: Why do you say that writing can be political?

A: When you go to the rest of the world, nobody even thinks about this question. They assume that a writer writes about everything. In the States there is a tradition of writing that encompasses things like that: Melville, Whitman, Doctorow. Even *The Great Gatsby* is a political novel; it examines the fabric of social life. Any novelist who is not just writing total fantasy is interacting with life. It may be that you can write the life of a person in the United States who never thinks a political thought. I can hardly imagine people so isolated that they have no such thoughts. But somehow it's been decided generally that the Freudian subconscious is OK for art, but one's conscious political decisions are not. I don't know why that is. It's not universal. It's just an assumption that you often run into in the minds of people who say it's too political. What they mean is it's too political to be art. There are certain things that have been designated as OK for art, namely trees, sunsets, love, and death.

Q: Who are some Canadian authors to read?

A: Well, there are probably some that you may have read already, without knowing that they are Canadian. Robertson Davies is widely available, particularly the Deptford Trilogy. Alice Munro. You can easily get hold of Canadian writing by writing to the following address: Longhouse Book Store, 626 Yonge Street, Toronto, Ontario M4Y 12B. Alice Munro deals particularly with lives of girls and women. Try Mordecai Richler, Timothy Findley, Marian Engel.

Q: Could you talk about your work for Amnesty International?

A: Amnesty was quite small in Canada a number of years ago. It needed to raise funds, and I was involved in some of that. Amnesty is a very worthy organization. It is apolitical, it doesn't make choices of who to support or whether the country is right-wing or left-wing. It's just dealing with violations of human rights. They're also doing investigations into torture worldwide—on the increase I might add. The reason I did that: there are only a few countries left where you can. This is one of them. Canada is one, Britain is one, some of the Western European countries. In a lot of countries Amnesty is outlawed. You can be put in jail for just belonging to it.

Q: Were you a good English student?

A: One of my high-school teachers said to one of my friends who went back to school to visit, "There was nothing distinctive about her at all that I can remember." I didn't become a good English student until I was in twelfth grade. I was quite good after that. The reason was that I got a good teacher I liked, and when you have a teacher you like, you tend to put more effort into it. I started writing poetry then, and she once made a wonderful comment: "Well, I can't understand it, dear, so it must be good."

Q: Which of your own books do you like the best?

A: The next one. Otherwise why would you keep going? You never feel that anything you have ever done is perfect. If you did, you would stop.

Q: Margaret, can you tell us about the novel you're working on now?

A: That is the one question I cannot answer because I never talk about the writing I'm doing now. It's my second superstition. My first is that I don't like anyone using my typewriter. . . .

Q: Could you give an example of how art and poetry go together? Or don't?

A: There's a book you should read by Lewis Hyde, *The Gift.* It's not poetry and it's not prose fiction and it's not criticism. It's partly anthropology and partly folklore and partly sociology. Partly economics and partly political theory. Partly literary criticism. It's a study of the gift as a medium of exchange. He makes a distinction between the commodity exchange—the market economy—and the gift exchange. He puts art in the gift-transaction economy, and he examines this through primitive societies, through art, through folktales, through all kinds of things. Still, all ideologies have trouble with writers. No exceptions. Because ideologies have a "should" and writers are an eccentric bunch of people; they don't always like having their feet crammed into those particular ideological shoes, and they often refuse to put their feet *into* those shoes. That's the way it will always be unless we have some kind of dictatorship. So writing is exploration. Exploration is going into a territory without knowing what you may find. It is then recording as accurately as you can what you do find rather than what you think you should find.

Q: I was reading in the paper today how popular you are in Canada, and it struck me as very odd that a poet could be so popular because in America poets have difficulty, say, selling five thousand books. What do you perceive as the difference between Canadian people and American people that makes this possible?

A: When I was growing up, as a young writer in the 1960s in Canada, it was very hard to publish anything. The writing community was very small. What that meant in Canada at that time was that poetry became the dominant literary form for about ten years. Why? Because it was cheap to do. The number of pages in a book was smaller, and you could do it in your cellar. You could have little printing presses, and that's how most poets of my generation started. They were published by themselves in print initially in their cellars. And I did that too. In 1961 there were about four literary magazines and most of those were recent. In 1965 there began to be a cultural explosion that has not stopped, and the increase in the readership was astronomical. It was partly because the school-leaving age of Canadians was going up so they were more educated. Canadians before that read books, but not Canadian books: they had the usual colonial attitude (which corresponded with the United States' in 1820), that things in their own country were of negligible interest and that the important things were elsewhere. The audience has increased geometrically now, but the holdover from that is that poetry was considered a dominant literary form for many years and Canadians still have the highest per capita readership of poetry in the English-speaking world (compared with the U.S., Britain, Australia, and New Zealand).

But I also write novels. My highest selling book, initially, was the book of criticism (*Survival: A Thematic Guide to Canadian Literature*) that I wrote in 1972 and that sold a hundred thousand copies, which surprised me because I expected to sell five. That shows the change. Suddenly the Canadians were interested in their own literature.

Q: Do you think Canada cares more about people and America more about money?

A: Do I think Canada is more people oriented and America is more economically oriented? Canadians have the sense that things have to be spread around, that you can't let one part of the country be very, very rich and another part be very poor. They try to equalize things in that way. There are a lot of differences. It's not that Canadians aren't interested in money, but that they have other interests as well. They did a survey with Canadian college students, and the number one priority was the economy. The number two and three priorities were freedom of speech and equality for women. The big seller in Canada in the late sixties through the seventies was a man called Pierre Berton, and what he writes is popular history of Canada. He did a history of the railroads and the War of 1812. The Canadians eat these up. They don't learn a lot at school about this, not as much as should be taught. I was taught

ancient Egyptian history, Greek and Roman history, Renaissance history, European and British history, and American history, but not much Canadian history. It is still not stressed as much as it ought to be.

Q: How do you go about writing something with your own experiences?

A: That's one of the most interesting parts of writing. If you believe that writing is merely self-expression, then you'll forever be trapped in your own persona, or a character very much like yourself. But if you look at novels through the ages you'll see a great many novels that did not do that. If you hang on to the self-expression approach for two or three novels, you'll pretty much be exhausted, unless you live a wild life. I think that's what writing novels is like, that you do not impose yourself on a character all the time. To try to think the way another person would think, or feel the way you think they feel. If I'm doing a character that has a certain job that I don't have, I usually give them a job that I wish I had or would like to have. I usually write first and then research after, I have to admit, and often I find that I guess right. For instance, for the paleontologist in *Life Before Man*, I wrote a book first and then went to the museum and asked if they had a person who had this kind of job. They said yes, and lo and behold, she was a woman. I asked her if she would show me what she did. She did, and afterwards, she read my manuscript and told me, "This is how I feel!" These are the nice payoffs in what I do.

Source: Francis X. Gillen and Margaret Atwood, "A Conversation," in *Margaret Atwood: Vision and Forms*, edited by Kathryn VanSpanckeren and Jan Garden Castro, Southern Illinois University Press, 1988, pp. 233–43.

Eli Mandel

In the following excerpt, Mandel traces the themes of gothicism and fear in Atwood's work, including "Speeches for Dr Frankenstein."

... Margaret Atwood's comment, in a conversation with Graeme Gibson, that *Surfacing* "is a ghost story" provides the point of departure for more than one commentary on her work. Less often noticed is the special form of ghost story Atwood employs, the story in *Journals of Susanna Moodie*, for example. Mrs. Moodie appears to Atwood, we are told, in a dream, later manifesting herself to the poet "as a mad-looking and very elderly lady"; the poems take her "through an estranged old age, into death and beyond."

... Her earthly life, portrayed in the earlier poems, involves a pattern not unlike the heroine's journey into the backwoods in *Surfacing*: a landing on a seashore apparently occupied by dancing sandflies, a pathway into a forest, confrontation with a wolfman and other animals, men in masks, deaths of children, including a drowning, sinister plants. Gothic tale is a better name than ghost story for this form, in which the chief element is the threat to a maiden, a young girl, a woman. In a well-known passage, Leslie Fiedler, (allegorizing like mad, incidentally), comments on the chief features of the form, its motifs:

> Chief of the gothic symbols is, of course, the Maiden in flight.... Not the violation or death which sets such a flight in motion, but the flight itself figures forth the essential meaning of the anti-bourgeois gothic, for which the girl on the run and her pursuer become only alternate versions of the same plight. Neither can come to rest before the other—for each is the projection of his opposite ... actors in a drama which depends on both for its significance. Reinforcing the meaning ... is the haunted countryside, and especially the haunted castle or abbey which rises in its midst, and in whose dark passages and cavernous apartments the chase reaches its climax.

Substitute forest for haunted castle, and think of the ghosts of Mrs. Radcliffe's *The Italian*, and the ghost story or gothic form of an Atwood poem or novel begins to take shape. Obviously, it is richly suggestive of a variety of dark threats, either psychological or hidden in the social structure. Atwood's own political and social commentary on Canadian imagination employs, with superb wit and skill, a victor/victim pattern (the haunted victim, the haunted persecutor, perhaps?) to outline not only an endlessly repeated pattern, but a theory of colonialism, that is, victimization. We see the possibilities: if *Surfacing* presents itself as political and social criticism disguised as ghost story, could it be that *Survival* takes its unusual power precisely from the fact that it is a ghost story disguised as politics and criticism?

A further elaboration is suggested by Ellen Moers' comments in the chapter of *Literary Women* called "The Female Gothic": Gothic,

says Moers, is writing that "has to do with fear," writing in which "fantasy predominates over reality, the strange over the commonplace, and the supernatural over the natural, with one definite authorial intent: to scare. Not, that is, to reach down into the depths of the soul and purge it with pity and terror (as we say tragedy does), but to get to the body itself, its glands, muscles, epidermis, and circulatory system, quickly arousing and quickly allaying the physiological reactions to fear." Moers' emphasis on physiological effect seems appropriate. It points to the kind of imagination found, say, in Michael Ondaatje's work as well as in Atwood's that might appropriately be called a physiological imagination, whose purpose is evident.

Fear. But fear of what? Some say sexuality, especially taboo aspects of sexuality, incest for example: the gothic threat to a young woman carries implications of sado-masochistic fantasy, the victim/victor pattern of *Survival*. Ellen Moers suggests that in Mary Shelley's *Frankenstein*, the real taboo is birth itself: death and birth are hideously mixed in the creation of a monster out of pieces of the human body. (The image involves, as well, the hideousness of duplication and reduplication.)

... If, as he says to his monster, Dr. Frankenstein might have trusted in beginnings, in seed, the narrator of *Surfacing*, it seems, distrusts virtually all births. How much of the haunting proceeds from an abortion? We discern a pattern of mixed birth/death in the book: the baby not born, the baby aborted, the baby about to be born as a furred monster, the drowned brother who didn't drown, the baby peering out of the mother's stomach, the embryo-like frogs, the frog-like embryo, the man-frog father in the waters, hanging from the camera with which he might have photographed the gods.

Who are the ghosts of *Surfacing* then? In *Survival*, which reads like a gloss on *Surfacing*, Atwood tells us that the ghost or death goddess of *The Double Hook* represents fear, but not fear of death, fear of life. And babies? Following a rather horrendous list of miscarriages, cancers, tumours, stillbirths and worse, which she finds in Canadian novels, Atwood remarks laconically, "The Great Canadian Baby is sometimes alarmingly close to the Great Canadian Coffin." Who are the ghosts of *Surfacing*? A mother, a father, a lost child, Indians, the animals: all symbols of vitality, life, our real humanity, that has disappeared and must be brought back. "It does not approve of me or disapprove of me," the narrator says of the creature who is elemental, as she thinks her father has become: "it tells me it has nothing to tell me, only the fact of itself." And she says of her parents after her paroxysm in the woods: "they dwindle, grow, become what they were, human. Something I never gave them credit for." Ghosts: only the human body, repressed, denied; only life denied. All proceeds from the ghosts: a derealized world: victimization, sexism, deformed sexuality, sado-masochism, tearing away at nature's body, at our own bodies.

But to say this is to accept the *allegory* of gothic that Atwood allows her narrator to spell out for us (it is worth noting that in the best gothic fashion, the daylight world after the horrors of the long night reveals that the ghosts are mechanical or waxwork figures). To say this is also to explain away not only the ghosts but one of the most disturbing and most characteristic of Atwood's qualities, her sense of doubleness, of reduplication, in word and image. Even the victor/victim pattern recurs and the tale told once in *Surfacing* will be told again. At the end, nothing is resolved.

The ghosts are sexual fears, repressed contents of the imagination, social rigidity. They are also literary images, book reflections, patterns from all those readings in gothic romance, perhaps even the unwritten thesis Atwood proposed for her Ph.D., on gothic romance. Reduplication....

Source: Eli Mandel, "Atwood Gothic," in *Critical Essays on Margaret Atwood*, edited by Judith McCombs, G. K. Hall, 1988, pp. 116–20.

SOURCES

Atwood, Margaret, "Hairball," in *Wilderness Tips*, McClelland and Stewart, 1991, pp. 41–56.

———, "Speeches for Dr Frankenstein," in *Selected Poems: 1965–1975*, Houghton Mifflin, 1987, pp. 64–69.

Cooke, Nathalie, *Margaret Atwood: A Biography*, ECW, 1998, pp. 132–38.

Evans, Dylan, "From Lacan to Darwin," in *The Literary Animal: Evolution and the Nature of Narrative*, edited by Jonathan Gottschall and Davis Sloan Wilson, Northwestern University Press, 2005, pp. 38–55.

———, *An Introductory Dictionary of Lacanian Psychoanalysis*, Routledge, 1996, pp. 117–19.

Grace, Sherrill, *Violent Duality: A Study of Margaret Atwood*, Véhicule Press, 1980, p. 130.

Lacan, Jacques, "The Mirror Stage as Formative of the *I* Function as Revealed in Psychoanalytic Experience," in *Écrits: The First Complete Edition in English*, translated by Bruce Fink, W. W. Norton, 2006, pp. 75–81.

MacLulich, T. D., "Atwood's Adult Fairy Tale: Levi-Strauss, Bettelheim, and *The Edible Woman*," in *Essays on Canadian Writing*, No. 11, Summer 1978, pp. 111–29.

Mallinson, Jean, *Margaret Atwood and Her Works*, ECW, 1985, p. 23.

Pennycook, Bruce W., "Speeches for Dr Frankenstein: An Orchestral Approach to Music Synthesis," in *Canadian Music Review*, January 1, 1983, pp. 196–203.

Sandler, Linda, "A Question of Metamorphosis," in *Margaret Atwood: Conversations*, edited by Earl G. Ingersoll, Ontario Review Press, 1990, pp. 40–57.

Shapira, Yael, "Hairball Speaks: Margaret Atwood and the Narrative Legacy of the Female Grotesque," in *Narrative*, Vol. 18, No. 1, 2010, pp. 51–72.

Squier, Susan, "'Frankenstein' Has Message for Feminists," in *New York Times*, April 19, 1992, http://www.nytimes.com/1992/04/19/opinion/l-frankenstein-has-message-for-feminists-353592.html (accessed September 1, 2015).

Wilson, Sharon Rose, *Margaret Atwood's Fairy-Tale Sexual Politics*, University Press of Mississippi, 1993, pp. 48, 49, plates 6, 7.

York, Lorraine, *Margaret Atwood and the Labour of Literary Celebrity*, University of Toronto Press, 2013, pp. 153–58.

FURTHER READING

Atwood, Margaret, *The Penelopiad*, Knopf, 2005.
   The Penelopiad is a retelling of Homer's epic poem *The Odyssey*. While the original is told from the point of view of the hero Odysseus during his long voyage to return home to Ithaca after the Trojan War, *The Penelopiad* tells the story of Penelope waiting for her husband's return. The novel is feminist in perspective and relies heavily on the theories concerning myth of the mid-twentieth-century poet and novelist Robert Graves.

Hill, Philip, *Lacan for Beginners*, illustrated by David Leach, For Beginners, 2009.
   This volume combines answers to simple questions with humorous illustrations in an attempt to explain Lacan's impenetrable thought in clear and approachable terms.

Knellwold, Christa, and Jane Goodall, editors, *Frankenstein's Science*, Ashgate, 2008.

The articles in this volume contextualize the novel *Frankenstein* in terms of both Shelley's scientific (or pseudoscientific) sources and the implications of the story for the development of modern biological sciences, an interest of Atwood's. The article on galvanism is by the well-known anthropologist Jane Goodall.

Shelley, Mary, *The Annotated Frankenstein*, edited by Leonard Wolf, Clarkson N. Potter, 1977.

This volume presents a facsimile of the first edition of *Frankenstein* together with numerous illustrations and helpful explanatory notes as long as the text itself.

SUGGESTED SEARCH TERMS

Margaret Atwood

Speeches for Dr Frankenstein AND Atwood

postmodernism

Mary Shelley

Jacques Lacan

the other

doppelgänger

Ice Capades

Urban Renewal: XVIII

MAJOR JACKSON

2005

"Urban Renewal: XVIII" is one in a series of poems by Major Jackson exploring his roots and adolescent experiences in the city of Philadelphia. From a young age Jackson was familiar with the "double consciousness" posited by W. E. B. Du Bois as inherent to the social position of African Americans: being aware of derogatory perceptions of them held by others—namely, white people—while yet viewing themselves with pride and self-respect. Jackson sometimes brings issues of race to the fore in his verse and sometimes leaves them submerged, as marked by deft cultural allusions or perhaps only the faintest outward indications; he largely forsakes direct mention of race or skin color.

Poem XVIII of the "Urban Renewal" series, which spans Jackson's early collections, is set during the narrator's high-school years, when a cadre of attractive girls are seen walking down the hall with regal aplomb, as if since time immemorial. The sight is a painful one for the narrator, as he begins to explain halfway through the twenty-line poem, for reasons with which many a youth will sympathize. The poem was published first in *TriQuarterly*, No. 120, in the winter of 2005—at which time it was numbered xvii (in lowercase Roman numerals in accord with the style in Jackson's first collection)—and then in his collection *Hoops* as number XVIII in 2006.

Major Jackson (© *Stephen Shugerman / Getty Images*)

AUTHOR BIOGRAPHY

Major Jackson was born on September 9, 1968, in Philadelphia, Pennsylvania, as one of two sons of a telephone-company employee, his mother, and a psychological counselor, his father. He was raised by his maternal grandparents in North Philadelphia until age eight and would have fond memories of his grandfather's urban-space garden; his grandmother had a vast collection of reading material that Jackson enjoyed losing himself in. On the other side of his family, his paternal grandmother was a former Cotton Club dancer who once dated Cab Calloway. Later growing up also in the adjacent Germantown district, Jackson would remember such people as a kindly police-officer neighbor who greeted him by quizzing him on geography facts and the like, slipping him dollar bills for every A on his report cards. The cosmic-minded jazz musician Sun Ra lived only a few blocks away from Jackson's Germantown home. In education, his Catholic primary school sought to instill its charges with a sense of ascetic

diligence, while his secondary school, Central High, was the most highly esteemed of the city's public schools (as well as the nation's second oldest). One time, while traveling with his basketball team, a teammate swiped his journal and read his poetry aloud, to abundant laughter, which led him to stop writing for a while.

Jackson would proceed to the city's own Temple University, where he had a double-consciousness moment right off the bat: during a campus tour, as reported by Gregory Pardlo in a *Ploughshares* profile, a guide cautioned against wandering into Jackson's home neighborhoods because "out there, . . . those people are dangerous." The remark was racist, implying that all African Americans are dangerous, and yet it unfortunately reflected a degree of truth. As reported by Thabiti Lewis in introducing Jackson at a reading series in 2004, the two were once playing street basketball in North Philadelphia, when a confrontation, a threat, and one young man's departure—with a promise to return with a gun—led Jackson to tell Lewis, "Thabiti let's go. That kid is coming back." Jackson's poetry, reaching back to episodes from his youth, makes reference to time spent at a hospital while his cousin was treated for gunshot wounds and to a young barber's assistant who was killed in crossfire and deeply mourned by his onetime employer. At Temple, with an interest in literature only cemented during his senior year through a course taught by leading Black Arts figure Sonia Sanchez, Jackson majored in accounting. Soon after graduating, at age twenty-four, he parlayed his degree into a position as the finance director of the local Painted Bride Art Center, which had an annual budget of $1.8 million.

Jackson's true interest rose to prominence as he was deposed from his accounting job after only a year, to assume a part-time position as the center's poetry curator. After booking members of the Dark Room Collective, a regional association of new African American writers, Jackson joined the group himself. He was also working a Boston accounting job in 1994 when his life took a major turn, as he was awarded a Pew Fellowship in the Arts, giving him fifty thousand dollars and two years during which to mature as a professional poet. Jackson attended graduate school at the University of Oregon, earning an MFA in 1999. When a fellowship led him to the prestigious Bread Loaf Writers' Conference in Vermont, Jackson envisioned himself being at home in the highly natural and socially conscious—if mostly white—state. He was awarded a faculty position at the University of Vermont (UVM), in Burlington, in 2002. That was the year his first major collection, *Leaving Saturn*—Sun Ra used to famously report that he was from Saturn—was issued. Jackson's debut was a finalist for the National Book Critics Circle Award for poetry.

Since then Jackson has advanced his position at UVM, becoming the Richard Dennis Green and Gold Professor, while also serving as a core instructor for the low-residency Bennington Writing Seminars and in a visiting capacity at institutions such as New York University and the University of Massachusetts, Lowell, where he was the Jack Kerouac Writer-in-Residence. He has also been poetry editor for the *Harvard Review*. His second collection, *Hoops*, which includes "Urban Renewal: XVIII," was issued in 2006, and his third collection, *Holding Company*, came out in 2010. Jackson continues to be shaped by his experiences, which in 2011 included a visit to the notorious Kibera slum in Nairobi, Kenya, through the University of Iowa's International Writing Program. Jackson is married to Kristen Johanson, a psychological counselor, and has three children, Langston, Anastasia, and James.

POEM SUMMARY

The text used for this summary is from *Hoops*, W. W. Norton, 2006, p. 50. A version of the poem can be found on the following web page: http://www.poetryfoundation.org/poem/237692.

The initial phrasing of "Urban Renewal: XVIII" rhetorically indicates that something is being regarded with high interest, perhaps even awe, as in such a formulation as "How blue the sky is!" In this case, a high degree of social superiority is being attributed to a number of girls who walk confidently, arm in arm, through the hallway of Central High School; the girls are so superior that they cannot even be touched. That they are *unopposed* suggests that no one either dares or is even able to challenge their supremacy, presumably at the very top of the school's hierarchy of popularity. Curiously, the girls are said to have been walking thus for decades; this might suggest that there has been a long tradition of girls just like these—their social ancestors, one might say—monopolizing the collective gaze at the top of the adolescent

MEDIA ADAPTATIONS

Although an official reading of poem XVIII of "Urban Renewal" is not available, Jackson can be heard reading number XVII online in Poems Out Loud, at http://poemsoutloud.net/audio/archive/urban_renewal_xvii/.

popularity chain. Or perhaps they are so comfortable in their surroundings that they seem to have been there for many years.

Beginning a second sentence in the middle of line 3, the narrator, as the girls pass, puts his back to the wall to allow them as much space as possible. The girls make him uneasy, as if their effervescent spirits create a sort of aura that billows before and around them as they walk. Their collective spirit or aura is active enough to figuratively leap upon any girls of lesser confidence who happen to obstruct them. This suggests that the superior girls never need alter their stride because their presence so permeates the hall that it is hardly possible for anyone to be unaware of them and of the importance of making way. The narrator, in fact, gives the girls an electric presence, as if they use up watts like light bulbs, and provides an imagist description that conveys a sense of a lifting, glowing, sweet fluidity in their movement—specifically, it seems, the movement of their hair.

The confidence embodied in the girls' style of movement, as accentuated by blue sunglasses and jeans riding low on their hips, does not just impress the narrator but actually causes him, and others like him, pain. In some sense there are entire worlds between the girls and himself, suggesting that he does not hold nearly the same social status as they do. If the girls happen to regard him at all, in any way—even if only to suggest that they have seen him before and recognize his face—or if they happen to, say, show a glimpse of tongue while chewing their gum, the narrator is veritably intoxicated. The description of the sight of a gum-chewing mouth as *tongue-piercing* suggests three senses: literally that the girl pokes her tongue through her lips in manipulating the gum, alternatively that the girl has a pierced tongue, and figuratively that the sight produces a sort of piercing, desirous sensation in the narrator's own tongue. No matter how, the sight of the girls seems to have a chemical (indeed, a hormonal) effect on the narrator.

In line 13, continuing the sentence begun at the end of line 7, the narrator finally reveals something of his own character, succinctly describing himself as a disregarded intellectual with a penchant for the game of chess. He relates that any momentary connection with the girls would send someone like him into a tailspin of emotional difficulties, characterized by uncertainty, envisioned (and likely dismissed) possibilities, and a sustained period of low spirits, a low sense of self-worth.

After the long sentence ends in line 15, the narrator for the first (and only) time speaks directly to the reader in the second person; however, the use of *you might say* connotes more of a colloquial turn of phrase than an intent to speak directly to the reader and his or her individual sensibilities. The conclusion is certainly the narrator's own, but one that (in accord with the second person) he is ascribing to an independent observer, as if this is a conclusion that could be drawn from appearances or if one were to consider his life in an objective way. The conclusion that the narrator reaches is a somewhat ironic one: while the poem has placed the narrator in a subordinate, even an uncomfortable position, one marked by, as per line 16, *snubs and rebuffs*—rejections from the domineering girls, it would seem—he nonetheless wants to celebrate youth, even to celebrate those very rejections. The idea that his life has led up to this celebration harkens to his identity as a writer, memorializing even difficult episodes from his youth precisely through poems such as this one.

Beginning line 17 with two words that mark a return to his high-school days—confirming that the consciousness of the preceding sentence (lines 15–16) was that of the present-day poet, not the poet as school-age protagonist—the narrator describes the strategy he adopted to cope with his situation. He does not specify here what he feared and thus avoided, but one readily gathers that he is referring to the girls, their aura of popularity, and the ache it caused him. Even while avoiding interaction with them, hopeless

as it leaves him, the narrator yet cannot cease yearning for their attention. Lacking any practical means of getting it, the narrator is left to the faint hope that he might hit a game-winning basketball shot. The adjectival term *third-string* comes from the designation on a basketball team of the starting five players as the first string, the next-best five players as the second string, and the remaining, least-able players as the third string. The narrator thus might be saying that his hopes are unlikely even to get in the game, so to speak, but he is probably also acknowledging that he himself is a third-stringer on the basketball team—and so is very unlikely to even be on the court in the final seconds of a neck-and-neck game. Still, he can dream of such a moment, and as his vision plays out in the poem's closing lines, the girls would for once, upon approaching near him, slow to a halt, smiles spreading across their glossy lips, and with fairly divine benevolence share their aura of popularity, their coolness, with the narrator.

THEMES

Female-Male Relations

At the heart of poem XVIII of Jackson's "Urban Renewal" series is the relation between the narrator and a clique of popular girls at his high school—or rather, the narrator's perception of the girls, since it seems a stretch to suggest that he has any sort of relationship with them. Whether the girls who strut so certainly down the hall even know the narrator's face, never mind his name, is up in the air; they have a tangible impact on his life only to the extent that their pervading aura of coolness engulfs him in the hallway, leaving him effectively breathless. It is possible, based on the narrator's mention of rejections in line 16, that he has at least approached one of these popular girls, but it is also possible that he is referring to rejections from girls he was not so intimidated by.

What is perhaps most interesting about the narrator's description of the effect that the popular girls' passing through the hall has on him is that he declines to explicitly characterize it in terms of either love or its counterpart, lust. He does not suggest that he has fallen in love with or, say, wants to have a family with a particular girl, nor does he suggest that his interests are primarily physical. The mention of a girl's tongue is

TOPICS FOR FURTHER STUDY

- Write a lyric narrative poem revolving around a moment of social interaction, or just a brush with social interaction, characterized by distance between the narrator and the other person(s). Expand on the emotional sense that the interaction leaves the narrator with and perhaps the broader social sense of the interaction. Include text that characterizes both your short-term and long-term responses.

- Read the Maya Angelou poem "Life Doesn't Frighten Me," which can be found in the Poetry for Young People series volume *Maya Angelou* (2007), edited by Edwin Graves Wilson, and online. Then write an essay comparing and contrasting this poem with Jackson's "Urban Renewal: XVIII" with a focus on the idea of fear as well as on tone, style, and apparent authorial intents. You may wish to consult Page Richards's review of *Hoops* in *Callaloo*, Vol. 30, No. 4, 2007, which focuses on Jackson's relationship with fear.

- Peruse the rest of Jackson's "Urban Renewal" series, which begins in *Leaving Saturn* (2002) and continues in *Hoops* (2006), and choose a poem to analyze independently with regard to theme, style, and so forth. Determine what can be decisively concluded from Jackson's open-ended language, and make conjectures where the meaning of the text is uncertain. Write an essay detailing your analysis, and conclude by commenting on how the poem appears connected to number XVIII.

- Recruiting friends for actors and actresses, make a video to be played as a backdrop for a voice-over reading of "Urban Renewal: XVIII." Illustrate as much of the poem's action as well as emotion as possible and, technology allowing, be sure to include a slow-motion scene according with the poem's description. The poem's tone leaves room for humor in the presentation, but you must also be sure to honor the serious aspects and the intricacy of the poem's message.

provocative, but the narrator does not suggest that his imagination takes the image any further. The mention of the position of their jeans at the waist also represents a sensual *allusion* to their bodies, but no direct bodily image is presented there. Meanwhile, there is certainly some sort of emotional component to the pain he describes. Thus the poem, being situated somewhere between the dual motives of love and lust, aptly dramatizes that undefinable ache that can be induced by the opposite or desired sex, especially in the young, for whom direct romantic experience may yet lie in the future.

Intelligence

Through the poem's first eight lines, the narrator positions himself as subordinate to the girls who overawe him, without offering any indication as to why he should be in such a position. It may simply be a matter of age, senior girls naturally paying little to no attention to a self-effacing freshman. The narrator gradually suggests that a more substantial gulf separates them, the gulf between the cool and the not-so-cool. At least, line 9, referring to other boys similar to the narrator, indicates that he is part of a larger group well below the girls in terms of social standing, and finally he specifies in line 13 that he is not just not-so-cool but is uncool, in an intellectual way, as *geek* connotes. To be clear, that is his self-perception, as presumably founded in his peers' perceptions, however "cool" an independent observer might deem him to be. Although chess is at the top of its own hierarchy as the world's most esteemed intellectual game, it remains disregarded by those who consider it, well, geeky—precisely too intellectual. Altogether, the narrator seems to be at a social disadvantage mainly because of his intellect, which may serve to intensify his self-consciousness about his lack of social status in comparison with the girls who strut down the hall. The narrator may well be an excellent conversationalist among peers with whom he is comfortable, but these girls, with their palpable aura, take him out of his comfort zone, frazzle him, and make successful interaction with them unlikely, if not impossible.

Self-Doubt

Whether his being intimidated by the untouchable girls is warranted or not, they tend to leave the narrator in a downward spiral of self-doubt and depression, as he specifies in lines 14–15. These negative emotions, which beset him as a result of a momentary glance or even the sight of a girl

The speaker is daunted by the popular girls in school. (© *Monkey Business Images / Shutterstock.com*)

chewing gum, can last as long as a week; this is a reaction far disproportionate to the action in question, suggesting fair emotional difficulty on the narrator's part. Quite a bit of his life is compressed into the sentence contained in lines 15–16. It is "youth" that is said to snub and rebuff the narrator, but this rings as a euphemism for *girls*, as if the impact of rejection is lessened if the action is displaced from a desired girl to youth itself or to fate; perceived that way, the rejection is more impersonal and says less about the narrator's identity. Yet apparently, despite whatever coping strategies the narrator adopted, his negative experiences with the fairer sex in high school had a cumulative impact on him. However many snubs and rebuffs there were, and in whatever fashion they were communicated, they seem to have left him indeed regarding himself as a "geek" who has no choice but to embrace that identity as well as the rejections—through a poem that verily celebrates this aspect of his youth.

Youth

The drama of this poem of Jackson's is very much one of adolescence, celebrating the ache

instilled by the sight of the opposite sex and relating how a boy of lesser social standing copes with his relation to girls of social standing so high that they practically breathe different air from his. On the one hand, the admission of line 17 sounds like a defeat. Rather than conquering his uncertainties, approaching one of the popular girls, and perhaps scoring an improbable date—as a kitschy romance story would surely have it—the narrator came to simply *avoid* what he *feared*; that is, one gathers, he declined to try to interact with the popular girls at all. In the end, this may have been for the better. One thing about high school is that it functions as a cauldron of people of all kinds of qualities and interests—if the high school is big enough, practically the entire spectrum of human interests—in which, by virtue of social interactions, those qualities and interests and the people that hold them are de facto assigned varying ranks, with beautiful and athletic young women and men typically at the top. This can lead people with other qualities and interests—intellectual, theatrical, musical, vocational, existential, and so forth—to feel that they pale in comparison with the most popular people. Yet in the end this is simply a phase of youth; beyond and in contrast to high school and to a lesser extent college—where the student body is no longer contained within the physical building of a single school—populations naturally spread themselves out into communities of those with similar interests. That is to say, there is a social niche for everyone somewhere, and not under the shadow of any more "popular" group but existing in, of, and for itself. To a remarkable extent, the felt need to care about who is cool and who is not will pass with youth, and the most well-adapted—and intelligent—individuals will be able to recognize that when it comes to social status, everything is relative, and however it plays out, life is something to be celebrated.

STYLE

Free Verse

In "Urban Renewal: XVIII" Jackson presents a free-verse poem with the look of a more classical form. Its appearance is not unlike a sonnet, though it runs six lines longer than the sonnet's standard fourteen, as the lines have a length suggesting pentameter, or five feet per line. The standard sonnet meter is *iambic* pentameter, with each foot consisting of two syllables, the first unstressed, the second stressed; a poem set in such a meter but without any rhyme is termed *blank verse*. With this poem of Jackson's, however, the reader recognizes that it lacks any approximation of a standard meter. Read naturally, the poem creates its own rhythm rather than following any prescriptive one. Even so, the poem is arguably lent gravity by its semblance of the sonnet form, with the consistency of the lines suggesting a steady, levelheaded progression through the circumstances and ideas in question.

Lyric Narrative

Jackson's "Urban Renewal" series, as he has acknowledged, is founded in his own experiences as a youth in Philadelphia. This does not confirm that every episode in the series of poems is a faithful rendering of precisely what he experienced, but the sense of each poem as a personal narrative remains strong. With "Urban Renewal: XVIII" delving into not just an occasion and its offshoots but also the narrator's emotional state, it can be referred to as a *lyric* narrative.

The narrator opens the poem with a frank acknowledgment of his perception of his relation to the popular girls who stroll with great self-possession down the hall at his high school. It is at once clear that he is not posturing or dissimulating his position, such as for the sake of his ego or reputation, but intends to get at the truth of his experience. In fact, in lines 13–15 the narrator is fairly self-deprecating, casting himself as an intellectual outcast, and extends his emotional response beyond a mere momentary negative reaction into the realm of psychological difficulty, with the mention of depression. Depression can be more or less serious among those who experience it, and it is unclear how much difficulty the narrator has had in coping with it. But it is perhaps a positive sign that he declines to dwell on it. Immediately after mentioning depression, the narrator shifts to a reflection on where his life has led him, indicating that he is looking at his youth from a broader perspective, encompassing his later years—which are readily understood to include some successes, even redemption, given that his poem is being published for the public to read. That the narrator returns to his youthful self-doubt in the poem's last four lines might be thought to suggest that he has not quite moved beyond those experiences after all; still, with the direct diction and light tone, the last four lines rather suggest that he is perfectly able to look back at that time of his life, reminisce about the basketball-hero fantasy that in part sustained him, put a finger on exactly what it was that so enthralled him—being "cool"—and, as if with a wave of the hand, consider the matter closed. Not merely recording this personal narrative, then, the lyric poem serves the purpose of leading the poet precisely to that state of acceptance of his past and, by extension, his present as well.

HISTORICAL CONTEXT

Modern African American Literature

Since the turn of the twentieth century, African American literature has experienced two very prominent movements, the Harlem Renaissance in the 1920s and the Black Arts movement of the 1960s and 1970s. The Harlem Renaissance came at a time when African Americans intently sought to embody their cultural heritage in works of literature that would be universally acknowledged and

Though he plays sports as well, the mention of playing chess helps characterize the speaker as a nerd.
(© ANDROMACHI | Shutterstock.com)

recognized. As such, while black writers made a point of focusing on settings and experiences with which they were familiar, they did so with an ear to how mainstream—that is, white—audiences would respond, and necessarily so, because major publishing companies were virtually all in the hands of white interests. The Black Arts movement, coming on the heels of the civil rights movement and African Americans' finally gaining political equality, represented for many a renewed call to cultural arms, an insistence on the assertion of black identities and achievements completely independent of white approval or judgment— hence the mantra "Black Power."

As Harryette Mullen reports in her essay "'The Cracks between What We Are and What We Are Supposed to Be': Stretching the Dialogue of African-American Poetry," the Black Arts focus on affirmations of blackness entailed, to an extent, narrowing the implicit definition of blackness, as idealizing strength, activism, and even militancy. Where black interests were seen to be corrupted by white bourgeois society—such as among peaceable middle-class strivers and

homosexuals—the individuals were regarded as corrupted as well. This perspective was exemplified by Malcolm Little and LeRoi Brown, better known by the names they adopted—Malcolm X and Amiri Baraka—in gestures of radical opposition to the impact that broader white culture had had in the formation of their identities.

At the turn of the twenty-first century, some of the most noteworthy African American poets have been shifting from time-honored affirmations of blackness to open-minded interrogations of what blackness can entail—including the experiences of African Americans with diverse levels of social achievement and varying sexual orientations. In Mullen's words, this represents a new "discourse of other blackness (rather than black otherness) . . . a larger discussion of the multiplicity and dissonance—the flip side of unity or homogeneity—of African American cultures and identities."

Jackson aptly represents a facet of this movement. The very title of his twenty-poem series "Urban Renewal" speaks to the revitalization of not just urban infrastructure, such as in the housing projects to be found in North Philadelphia and elsewhere, but of cultural interests as well, moving beyond the collective urbanized identity of modern African Americans—as pop-culturally embodied especially in basketball, rap, and hip-hop music and dance—to consider matters of universal emotional and intellectual relevance. That Jackson could not necessarily live up to his era's ideal of black masculinity is made clear in "Urban Renewal: XVIII," which registers his status as a geeky chess aficionado. That Jackson did not need to live up to that ideal, however, is also made clear in the poem, in that his rejections, or more broadly his experiences with emotional challenges, paved the way for his development as a highly conscious literary artist. He can thus look back at his youth not with a sense of bitterness or resentment but in a spirit of celebration. Jackson may not have considered himself naturally blessed with the sort of coolness that the girls at Central High embodied, but the notion that the working definition of black coolness has vastly expanded since Jackson's high-school years is supported by Thabiti Lewis—who, granted, is himself an accomplished academic—in a good-humored passage from his remarks introducing Jackson:

> I realize how cool Major was back then—just as he is now. He is cooler than the brother in poet Haki Madhubuti's poem, "But He Was Cool." In a more positive way, Major is so cool that he cools other brothers' cool; now that, as Madhubuti said, is cool.

In other words, as Lewis seems to be saying, in both his person and his literary works, Jackson is legitimizing an ongoing expansion—indeed an ebbing and flowing century-long expansion—in conceptions of black identity both within and without the African American community.

CRITICAL OVERVIEW

With his first three collections of poetry and his growing collection of fellowships and honors, Jackson has quickly risen to the status of a heralded poet with the potential to achieve canonical status. Amor Kohli, in his essay "'Life Ruptured Then Looped Back': Affiliation as Process in Major Jackson's 'Urban Renewal' Series," acknowledges that "Jackson has been identified and celebrated as a poet of the city, a chronicler of black urban life," and yet he warns that "Jackson is too commonly cast as the autobiographical poet of 'the Hood,' the street, the poet of concrete." Kohli points out that such a "monological critical practice" tends to narrow the understanding of nuanced and multilayered work such as Jackson's.

Reviewing *Hoops* for *Library Journal*, Karla Huston finds that Jackson's verse "explodes over the urban landscapes" with "a mixture of elevated diction and street language." She finds that the collection as a whole reinforces the belief that in the city, as everywhere in life, "there is much to see, to remember, much to appreciate." A *New Yorker* reviewer of *Hoops*, apparently bedazzled by the accoutrements of the urban environment that Jackson celebrates, finds that the poet "seems to define himself by his eclecticism." The reviewer hails Jackson's verse as "witty, musical, and intelligent." In *Booklist*, Mark Eleveld finds that while there are "occasional weak word choices" in the collection, what the reader remembers are "the gems, the good, solid lines." A *Publishers Weekly* reviewer finds that Jackson's second collection "pays tribute to timeless and timely monuments of American culture and history" and "works to forge a large and spacious America, one capable of housing imagination."

David Wojahn, offering an ambivalent assessment of *Hoops* in the *Southern Review*, observes that Jackson has "embraced a thoroughly unfashionable style"—that is, in much of the collection, formalism over free verse—in what is "a puzzling and eccentric volume, maddening at times in its digressive self-indulgence but always brilliantly readable." The reviewer finds the collection's poems to be variously marked by "panache," "earnestness," "self-deprecating humor," and occasionally "show-stopping rhetoric." Speaking to the broadness of Jackson's aesthetic vision, Wojahn says that *Hoops* "seems less an individual collection than an ongoing installment of some larger project." Wojahn concludes that Jackson "is one of a small number of figures at work today who play for high stakes, who are immune to triviality and invite important reckonings." Writing for the *Harvard Review*, Andrew DuBois finds *Hoops* to be an "impressive, enjoyable, readable book." He remarks that "Jackson's greatest strength . . . is his ability to marry without anxiety the traditional forms of the English poetic tradition with the poetic vernacular and the human concerns of an urban, black population."

Regarding "Urban Renewal," Kohli states, "This poetic series does not create transcendence, cohesion, or an ineluctable truth, but rather showcases the continual labor and effort that is demanded of any craft in order to achieve lasting and real success." DuBois observes that some of the series' poems are written in "deft pentameter." Eleveld calls the poems in the series the book's "strongest, rendered in well-used contemporary vernacular that conveys a closeness and a familiarity in sudden flashes of emotional longing and exposes sensuality."

Pardlo, in his *Ploughshares* profile, imagines that "Jackson's sense of community is expanding and contracting in ways that can only produce a further exacting poetic vision." He declares that Jackson's third collection "is evidence of his capacity for reinvention" and his "willingness to strike out for new territory." Referring to Jackson's 176-stanza "Letter to Brooks," DuBois affirms, "It has been some time since I have read such a successful poem of our time." Wojahn states, "Jackson is clearly a significant talent, and his accomplishment may prove to be considerable." In his profile of Jackson for Vermont's *Seven Days*, David Warner cites UVM English chair Robyn Warhol as remarking, "I'm convinced that Jackson is going to be one of the voices they study when poetry of the early 21st century is written about."

CRITICISM

Michael Allen Holmes

Holmes is a writer with existential interests. In the following essay, he considers how Jackson's "Urban Renewal: XVIII" can be seen to contain a submerged discourse on race relations.

A reader's intuitive understanding of poem XVIII of Major Jackson's "Urban Renewal" series is likely to depend on the degree of one's preexisting awareness of the poet. Some will recognize Jackson's name, perhaps be able to call to mind his image, and approach the poem as written by an African American. Some will further be aware to some extent of Jackson's body of work, associating the Philadelphia-born poet with precisely the inner-city environment invoked with the first word in the title of the series. Others may not have any familiarity with Jackson but may jump to the conclusion, based on his name (Jackson being the surname of a number of famous African

> RACE IS APPARENTLY THE FURTHEST THING
>
> FROM JACKSON'S NARRATOR'S MIND."

American cultural figures—Jesse, Janet, Reggie, and others) and the city setting, that he is a black writer concerned with issues of particular relevance to the black community. Yet the unknowing, open-minded reader who proceeds through both the poet's name and the title without jumping to any conclusions will find that, within the poem itself, there is hardly a hint of race. At no point is anyone's skin color made clear, nor are there any other indisputable racial markers. The boy, his unseen caste-mates, and the girls who command his attention could all be black, white, or any shade of color in between. At least, reading the poem objectively, one fairly has to come to such an ambiguous conclusion. But few readers read anything in full objectivity, with no bias or preconceived notions, and Jackson seems to play off his poem's images to suggest a particular racial dynamic underlying the relation between the narrator and the girls.

The poem's most substantial allusion to a racial encounter comes in the very first lines. With Jackson's poetic concision, the reader may not yet understand what is going on even upon reaching the period in the middle of line 3. There are some girls, untouchable apparently out of superiority—otherwise they would be unlikely to strut—who dominate the main hall of a school called Central High; most curiously, they have been doing so for decades. There are ways to interpret this as referring to ordinary girls whose presence in high school will last only the requisite four years. Perhaps these girls are practically identical to the girls who have dominated the hall just so in years past, leaving their identities to merge into each other over time. Another way to consider this sentence, in isolation from the rest of the poem, is as referring to a photograph. This would account for the untouchability more literally than the mere sheen and aura of popularity could, and it would also explain how their action can be fixed over such a span of time—if the photograph is perhaps posted somewhere within the school, commemorating some occasion. Or

WHAT DO I READ NEXT?

- Jackson's first collection, *Leaving Saturn* (2002), includes the beginning of his "Urban Renewal" series, while his third collection, *Holding Company* (2010), delves into universal themes like art and beauty.

- Sonia Sanchez, who grew up in Harlem and was a spirited voice in the Black Arts movement, was Jackson's first significant literary mentor, at Temple University. A collection of hers issued when Jackson was in high school is *Homegirls & Handgrenades* (1984).

- Gwendolyn Brooks was a great inspiration to Jackson, not only for her verse but for her having once paid Jackson five hundred dollars to read his poetry at an event of hers that he drove her to. Jackson wrote 176 stanzas in *rime royale* under the title "Letter to Brooks," found in *Hoops*. "Urban Renewal" may have been partly inspired by Brooks's debut collection, *A Street in Bronzeville* (1945), set in urban Chicago.

- Elizabeth Alexander is a poet who has been identified as exploring "other blackness," specifically in a materially assured, socially conscious middle-class setting. Urban experiences in Harlem are among the subjects of her first two collections, *The Venus Hottentot* (1990) and *Body of Life* (1996).

- Another poet who is a representative of the Dark Room Collective, having joined while at Harvard, and who writes poetry infused with what critics recognize as musical rhythms is Kevin Young. His volume *Jelly Roll* (2003) is a collection of blues-inspired poems.

- *Words That Changed a Nation: The Most Celebrated and Influential Speeches of Barack Obama* (2009) presents public orations made by the sitting president, notably including his 2008 speech about race in America, "A More Perfect Union."

- Sharon G. Flake delves into the minds of teenage African American males, including one who takes the reader around North Philadelphia on the Fourth of July, in *You Don't Even Know Me: Stories and Poems about Boys* (2011).

- Irish poet Leanne O'Sullivan published her first book of poetry, *Waiting for My Clothes* (2004), when she was only twenty-one, with many of the poems being lyric narratives drawing on occasions and mentalities from her teenage years.

considered as a photograph, the image may be *of* the school but not *in* the school, appearing perhaps in a preserved newspaper clipping.

If the reader gets this far, the photographic image created in the mind is likely to seem somehow uncanny, as if known from somewhere else. Perhaps before long the image will indeed call to mind a certain momentous occasion in American history, one that might well have produced such an image of untouchable girls, arms locked, dominating the hall of a school—namely, the Little Rock school integration crisis of 1957. Several years had already passed since the Supreme Court's 1954 decision in *Brown v. Board of Education of Topeka* declaring that separate schooling

was not and could not be equal and that school systems nationwide needed to integrate. Throughout the South, however, state and local governments were not just dragging their feet in response to the order but were outright refusing to abide by it, repeatedly filing obstructive legal appeals and leaving African American communities stonewalled at every turn. In light of this, in Little Rock, Arkansas, the state branch of the National Association for the Advancement of Colored People (NAACP) organized a concerted effort to get nine black students—who were made well aware of the challenges they would face and ultimately volunteered on behalf of their families and community—admitted and granted access to a local, then all-white school. Jackson, in writing his poem a half century later, was surely not unaware of the fact that the school in question was named Central High School.

The drama played out over the course of several weeks in September 1957. On the first day of school, September 4, a mob of white people aware of what was being attempted literally blocked access to the school and prevented the black students from entering. Governor Orval Faubus did what he thought best to de-escalate the situation—that is, what he thought best to do so as well as ensure his reelection in 1958: though he was otherwise a moderate with regard to race relations, here he played to the white supremacists, supporting the mob and even calling in the Arkansas National Guard to bar the black students from the school. Martin Luther King Jr., among others, became involved in the effort to resolve the crisis, writing a letter to President Dwight Eisenhower, imploring him to support the rule of federal law and grant the students entry to the school. Eisenhower complied, albeit reluctantly, because the issue was an international political embarrassment. With the help of the US Army's 101st Airborne Division, the African American students entered the school through a side door on September 23—although later that day they were rushed home because of the threat of imminent violence. Federal troops as well as the state's National Guard would remain stationed at the school to protect the black students throughout the year. In response, Faubus would, in fact, close all four of the city's public high schools the following year to prevent further integration; they would be reopened only upon the Supreme Court's order in December 1959.

Returning to Jackson's poem, one recognizes that the image of girls walking together down the hall, arms not just linked but *locked*, existing on a social plane high above the narrator, is a racially loaded one. Of course, one cannot say for certain that the girls are meant to be white, but the words used in lines 6–7—*high-wattage, light, honey*—suggest the side of the spectrum opposite the dark, marked by light skin and golden, honey-colored hair. The word *honey* may be read as connoting fluidity and sweetness rather than color, and, of course, some African Americans do have honey-colored hair; given what the image of lines 1–3 is suggesting, however, the most probable reading of the poem holds that the girls who walk so domineeringly down the

hall are white. The locked arms, then, signal not only the bond between the girls but also the obstruction they represent, barring passage, or entry into the upper echelons of teenage society, to any who might oppose them—especially those with darker skin. That the girls have been doing this for decades speaks to the long period of time when African Americans were indeed barred entry to white schools, as well as to the entrenchment of racist attitudes even after schools were integrated.

Drawing such connections, one might be tempted to make the poem be about race—to suggest that underlying racial tension is the true thematic center. Yet it is difficult, if not impossible, to contend as much when Jackson so forthrightly refuses to make race an issue in the poem. The American nation certainly did not have a "postracial" consciousness at the time of his youth—and still does not—but, if the girls in the poem are white and if, like Jackson himself, the narrator is black, then he, for one, surely seems to have a postracial consciousness. The image of a young black man shrinking to the side of the high-school hall as a cadre of young white women pass by can be seen to have the most significant racial overtones, dramatizing the deference black men have been obligated to show white women in order to avoid the racist assumption that they are lusting after them—a racist assumption that led to many a tragic lynching earlier in the twentieth century. In such a reading of the poem, the worlds between the boy and the girls are *vast* above all because of their racial differences. But race is apparently the furthest thing from Jackson's narrator's mind; he, for one, is interpreting the interaction not in a racially charged way but simply in an adolescent emotional way, as something that creates a swirl of aches and uncertainties inside him—just as adolescent romance always does. His problem, as it might be called, is not his skin color but his intelligence; his coping strategy is not anger or even indignity but rather hope and, in the end, acceptance.

A last bit of potentially racial intrigue might be seen to come with the poem's last four lines. The game of basketball, first played in the 1890s, is, of course, enjoyed by people of all races, but in the present day it is stereotypically the realm of urban African Americans. Its popularity, including as a means of escape from the sort of gang violence endemic to all too many urban communities, has led to a complex social situation in which the greatest success stories—young men from the projects becoming multimillionaires in the NBA—can justify, for some, dependence on the idea of basketball as a means of salvation. For many young men and women, of whatever color, the game *can* represent salvation, if their devotion to practice and improvement might lead to consummate skills and a college scholarship; it may not be an NBA contract, but a college degree is a life-changing possession for many. Still, some have perceived that young black men are too likely to focus on playing basketball not as a means to an education, but at the expense of one. No less a figure than First Lady Michelle Obama suggested as much to an audience at Bowie State University, a historically black institution:

> Today, more than 150 years after the Emancipation Proclamation, more than 50 years after the end of "separate but equal," when it comes to getting an education, too many of our young people just can't be bothered.... Today, instead of walking miles every day to school,... instead of dreaming of being a teacher or a lawyer or a business leader, they're fantasizing about being a baller or a rapper.

An acutely politically conscious mind, not unlike Obama's, might suggest that the end of Jackson's poem is unfortunate—that it reinforces the idea that a black man should lean on the possibility of basketball greatness as a magical solution to his problems in life. But one can hardly fault Jackson for what plays out as a whimsical fantasy about success not in life, but in love, a fantasy that the narrator fully knows represents a slim hope, a third-string hope, at best. Moreover, that Jackson found a more realistic means of success in life—at least, realistic for him, given that there are far fewer successful African American poets than professional basketball players—is self-evident, given that one is reading his poem in the first place. The point is that, as Jackson may well have anticipated all along, his intelligence—a quality, like virtually all substantial human qualities, entirely independent of his race—was his salvation.

Source: Michael Allen Holmes, Critical Essay on "Urban Renewal: XVIII," in *Poetry for Students*, Gale, Cengage Learning, 2016.

Gregory Pardlo

In the following excerpt, Pardlo discusses Jackson's formation as a poet.

If, in the 1980s, you had been a resident of one of those communities associated with the

The speaker plays on the third-string team, but he hopes his basketball skills will impress the girls.
(© Monkey Business Images / Shutterstock.com)

term, "urban renewal" might occur to you as double-edged with its bureaucratic optimism, and the implied whitewashing—easy as calling a do-over—of recent history. And if parts of your community were within the expansion radius of an ambitious university, you might be ambivalent toward the opportunities offered by that advancing institution as well.

As a poet, Major Jackson was shaped by this period of his native North Philadelphia's burgeoning gentrification, when Temple University began to broaden its vision to include, along with inquiry, a spirit of acquisition. Like many from historically black urban communities, Jackson understood early on, as he writes in the poem, "Hoops," that "If the slum's our dungeon, / school's our Bethlehem." Jackson's world-view contains both the community and the institution, as he identifies with the acquired and acquiring on both sides.

❝

HIS INSTINCT IS TO SERVE AS WITNESS RATHER THAN TO JUDGE OR WAG A DISAPPROVING FINGER. THIS IS ANOTHER DISTINGUISHING CHARACTERISTIC OF HIS WORK."

School looms metaphorically in Jackson's life and work. It refers to brick and mortar, but also to a life of the mind. It refers to a life in the arts, and specifically literature. And the changing nature of that life from sequestered intellectualism to social engagement gives Jackson's poetry a sense of wistful benevolence. We find the poet balancing his esteem for tradition with the weight of his concern for the world around him.

As Jackson admits, "my path in poetry has been extremely unconventional." Indeed, there is something Hollywood about it: his good fortune in having been delivered to the right mentors at the right moments, his having the talent, temperament, and commitment to take advantage of their guidance, and his uncanny ability to navigate a welter of contradictions without any irritable reaching for resolution. His life is a screenplay waiting to be made. Let's make the opening scene a tracking shot:

At Temple University in the late 1980s, we find the future poet touring the campus with a group of fellow incoming first-year students. Picture the group's guide, shirted in the school's iconic cherry red, and walking backwards as he narrates features of the academic landscape. One of the incoming students asks the guide's advice for getting around the community at large. Jackson needs no such advice. This is where he grew up, shaped early by the studious asceticism of a Catholic primary school, and later, the pride of the Philadelphia public school system, Central High School. Given this pedigree, Jackson is used to bridging social gaps. He has developed a cosmopolitan sensibility as a result of too often being the guy with cultural knowledge others lack. He is patient with people who are unfamiliar with communities like his. He is solicitous with familiars who don't have access to the academy. All this in preparation for his mission to cut a path through the undergrowth of the American

literary mind to make way for others to share their stories.

Casting his mind's eye (in a filmic dissolve) to the surrounding neighborhood, Jackson surveys the topography of memory. These streets will be the setting for many of his poems. Amid the jagged lots' "lush epitaph of dandelions / & weed brush," he will note, "A corner lot of broken TVs empties / and spills from a suitcase of hurt." The boarded-up row houses north of the avenue named after the famed Civil Rights attorney, Cecil B. Moore, and west of arterial Broad St.—amid the real and imaginary devastation we associate with crack-ravaged urban spaces— bookend the homes and businesses of those who will soon directly and indirectly populate Jackson's poetry. The barbershop where Mr. Pate, who, by virtue of Jackson's loving artistry, will forever "cherish [the] tiny little heads" that have become casualties of street violence. There is his neighbor, a police officer, who for years greeted the young Jackson with questions, like *where is Mozambique*, in lieu of hello. *Where is Poland*, or *where is Algiers? How many boroughs in New York City?* And he would slip Jackson three dollars for every A on his report card. There is Sun Ra, the sensational and eccentric jazz musician, who lived only a few blocks away in Major's neighborhood of Germantown and held New Year's Eve concerts each year at the Painted Bride Art Center, a popular meeting place for musicians and artists. And this is the one area, as we return to the original scene, that the campus guide admonishes students to avoid at all costs. For "out there," the guide says gravely, "those people are dangerous."

Jackson cites this interaction with the campus guide as one of the more formative of many "double consciousness" moments of his life. The reference is to W. E. B. Du Bois' analysis of African American subjectivity as paradoxical, in which one is always conscious of unflattering (to say the least) cultural assumptions without, while maintaining a sense of pride and self-love within. In many ways, Jackson's evolving response to this paradox, which appears in many guises, will animate his work for years to come. The ever-changing dynamics of race and class in America, for example; and the enfolding of the mysterious and marginal "town" into the pleats of the university's corporate "gown"; the sometimes conflicting pursuit of life in the ivory tower leveraged against one's care for the roots of community.

Jackson seems little interested in choosing sides or engaging in a Pollyannaish soft-pedaling of these discrepancies. He wears them like mismatched socks (although, I must say, I've been shopping with the man and he would never wear mismatched socks). His instinct is to serve as witness rather than to judge or wag a disapproving finger. This is another distinguishing characteristic of his work. As if for Jackson, artistry were the *only* rational response one could have to the contradictions of urban life.

Major Jackson's poetry is grounded in his sense of the ethical obligation we have to the communities we claim. Noting that "our communities widen and constrict" with time and context, the tenor of his poems is as evocative of Whitman as it is of the late Black Arts milieu out of which it finds some of its most potent influences. Of note is the literary relationship he developed at Temple University with his first creative-writing professor and doyenne of the Black Arts Movement, Sonia Sanchez, whom Jackson is quick to praise as singularly responsible for his embrace of poetry. That embrace has now grown to encompass three poetry collections: *Leaving Saturn* (U. of Georgia Press, 2002), winner of the Cave Canem First Book Prize and Finalist for the National Book Critics Circle Award; *Hoops* (2007) and *Holding Company* (2012), both from W. W. Norton; and scores of awards and fellowships, including a Pew Fellowship, a Whiting Writers' Award, two nominations for the NAACP Image Award, a Witter Bynner Fellowship from the Library of Congress, and an artist fellowship from the Radcliffe Institute for Advanced Study at Harvard University.

For all the expansiveness of Jackson's poetic vision, the note he strikes most consistently is that of praise. It is "this notion of praise in poetry," he says, that affected him most deeply in the work of the earlier generation of African American poets. He points to, for example, Sanchez's invocations of the ancestors, those hypnotic roll calls that affirm our sense of belonging as much as they honor those who have come before us, and the dedication to honor our history that we find in the work of Robert Hayden. "[Jackson's] lyric tongue," Afaa Michael Weaver, another important, early mentor figure, writes in a 2002 review of *Leaving Saturn* in these pages, "rises out of the emblems of urban despair and chaos to make love his language."

I met Major in the mid '90s. Our paths first crossed sometime around 1994, when I asked the Philly poet Lamont Steptoe to organize a reading series for me at the jazz club my grandfather had opened, and which I was managing, in New Jersey, a few minutes across the river from Philadelphia. Among the poets Steptoe featured that I can easily recall were Martín Espada, the South African poet Dennis Brutus, and Major Jackson. I thought the reading series was fun. Indulgent. It certainly didn't make any money. In other words, at the time, I had no idea what a stellar lineup Steptoe had produced. But this suggests the esteem in which Major was held in the Philly literary scene very early in his writing life.

After I left the bar business, I met Major formally in a circle of metal folding chairs as we sat together beneath banks of fluorescent lights. The International Ladies' Garment Workers' Union let the *Painted Bride Quarterly* use vacant space once a week in its downtown office building to hold editorial meetings. I had been recommended to the editorial board on the basis of my enthusiasm alone, and I remember being thoroughly confused as to how this man sitting before me could refer so confidently to work by poets whose names seemed distant and mythical to me—Yusef Komunyakaa, Sharon Olds, Philip Levine, Nikki Giovanni, Gerald Stern, and even Gwendolyn Brooks—as if he had met them personally. Of course, in addition to being a hungry student of poetry, Major *had* met all of these poets, and many more. After college, where his undergraduate degree was, counterintuitively, in accounting, Major served as Curator of Literary Arts at the Painted Bride Arts Center. This was a job he cultivated out of an internship in bookkeeping at the arts center. "This was where I found myself as a writer and an artist," he says.

"What does it all come down to?" I ask him. In addition to being the Richard Dennis Green and Gold Professor at University of Vermont, a core faculty member of the Bennington Writing Seminars, a member of the Creative Writing Program faculty at New York University, and Poetry Editor of the *Harvard Review*, Jackson maintains a dizzying schedule of visiting and guest positions leading workshops on and off campuses across the country. What is the point of this peripatetic life?

"I want to be a lightning rod for someone who wants to write and sing his or her particular life," he says. That comment might send us scrambling back to the streets of North Philly in search of some Rosebud-like symbol of motivation if it weren't for Jackson's 2011 tour of the slums of Kibera, an impoverished community that borders the Royal Nairobi Golf Club in Nairobi, Kenya. This was one leg of the tour sponsored by the International Writing Program at the University of Iowa, which exposed Jackson to people bravely enduring conditions grievous far beyond any we might find in North Philly. Like North Philly, however, those conditions are, unconscionably, man-made. If neglect and indifference produced the slums of his youth, Jackson observed, here the forces are more venal. "The corruption is phenomenal," he says. But at the root of things "we find a similar class struggle."

. . . I imagine Jackson's sense of community is expanding and contracting in ways that can only produce a further exacting poetic vision. His most recent book, *Holding Company*, is evidence of his capacity for reinvention. While he explored and expanded the conventions of the lyric narrative in his first two books, *Holding Company* is more lyric, less narrative. Or rather, the narratives are more attenuated, more angular in their progress. The book hints at Jackson's willingness to strike out for new territory.

Jackson recently edited *The Collected Poems of Countee Cullen*, which will be published by the Library of Congress this year. Bringing renewed attention to this important poet of the Harlem Renaissance is a service to American letters and individual readers alike. Because of this kind of work, along with his own consistently enterprising poems, we may one day evaluate Major Jackson as an institution unto himself.

Source: Gregory Pardlo, "About Major Jackson," in *Ploughshares*, Vol. 39, No. 1, 2013, pp. 187–93.

Mark Jarman

In the following excerpt, Jarman praises Jackson's unique poetic voice.

It may be impossible to say there is an identifiable period style in contemporary American poetry. Perhaps all that can be said is that most poets in this country continue to be uncomfortable when engaging traditional English verse and prefer to disguise it, if they engage it at all. An emphasis on lyric expression at the expense of narrative is also a widely shared characteristic in the poetry of our period. But the closest anyone can come to defining our period style might be to say that it is lyric free verse, as it has been

for the past forty years or more. That really is not enough to define a period style, but it is more than one might think. When a poet like those under review here has worked to develop an individual style, there is a marked contrast between the period style and what he or she has wrought. Our period style of lyric free verse is the ground out of which the poets here have toiled to create an expression or way of expressing that will set them apart, if not from others like them, at least from each other. They have the period style in common, but the subjects of their poetry and their own genealogy as poets, along with the deliberate activity of making poems in the first place, have allowed each to speak with an identifiable voice. I used to think the term "voice" to describe a poet's unique style was too much of a contemporary buzzword, and therefore not useful or descriptive. I used to think "style" would do. But if a poet is developing at a time when a period style is so firmly established and tends to encourage an undifferentiated voice, as it will tend to do, then it is not cant to describe the unique expression of a poet, when he or she achieves that uniqueness, as being his or her voice. Once we encounter real individuality in a poet, the term becomes useful and descriptive.

In his first two collections of poetry, *Leaving Saturn* and *Hoops*, Major Jackson showed himself to be in thrall to a dense, allusive rhetoric, constantly seeking to follow a narrative thread. The result was always a rich mix of contemporary and classical reference, as you find in the poetry of Melvin Tolson, and sharp appraisal of urban life, with an eye like Gwendolyn Brooks's. And though I never thought I would say such a thing, the attachment to narrative, to telling a clear story, kept his language in check. It helped the poet toward a clarity that he would just manage to attain, but the poems were hobbled. They wanted to take flight into a more inventive realm.

With his third book, Major Jackson has slipped the surly bonds of narrative and given freedom to his lyric voice. At the same time, he has achieved a compression otherwise missing from his earlier work. He has done this in a series of ten-line poems, which resemble nothing so much as curtal sonnets. The book's epigraph from Robert Lowell's sonnet about T. S. Eliot, first published in *Notebook*, then revised ultimately for *History*, is not the only acknowledgement of Lowell's influence. Lowell, too, found in his unrhymed, quasi-blank verse sonnets a release into lyricism and pursuit of the memorable and penetrating line, while risking obscurity. The other epigraph is from Pier Paolo Pasolini's long poem "Plan of Future Works," in which the Italian poet and filmmaker seemed to embrace the ambiguity of his own life as represented in his poetry: *"neither the sign nor the existing thing matters."* That looks like permission simply to let the language have its way, to let 'er rip, clarity be damned.

> I gave the bathtub purity and honor, and the sky
> noctilucent clouds, and the kingfisher his implacable
> devotees. I gave salt & pepper the table, and the fist
> its wish for bloom, and the net, knotholes of
>   emptiness.
> I gave the loaf its slope of integrity, the countertop
> belief in the horizon, and mud its defeated boots.
> I gave morning triumphant songs which consume
>   my pen,
> and death its grief which is like a midsummer
>   thunderclap.
> But I did not give her my tomblike woe though it
>   trembled
> from my white bones and shook the walls of our
>   home.

The title of this, the second poem in the volume, is "Creationism." I can't tell you why, but I can guess that it has to do with the poet's acknowledgement of his own powers as a maker, a creator. The name "Creationism," for the pseudo-science which is meant to counter evolution, has been appropriated. It keeps its connotation—it can't lose it—but the poem gives it a new denotation. In this way, the word is yanked from its narrative, and the poet gives us something close to pure lyric expression, the kind which Hart Crane, one of Robert Lowell's own models, sought and achieved.

Hart Crane's voice, which at times in his poetry seemed almost to transcend clarity, is echoed in many of the poems in *Holding Company*. In fact, considering the literal meaning of the title, it is invested in the style Major Jackson has created for himself. And Crane is surely part of the company these poems are keeping. I hear the echo in the second half of "Narcissus":

> How many hours have I spent crushing mangrove
>   leaves,
> turning my face to the unbearable grandeur of this
>   heat-soaked
> sky? When I spun around, I felt filled with birds.
> Still, I returned, wallowing in the brothels of myself.
> I thought of my life, caressing more ruins.

There is no doubt in my mind or ear that the poetry Major Jackson offers us in *Holding*

> **AFFILIATION EXPANDS THE VISION OUTWARD, EMPHASIZING THE RENEWAL OF THOSE BONDS AS THE CONTINUITIES AND DISCONTINUITIES PLAY EQUALLY VALID ROLES. DEMOCRACY, NEIGHBORHOOD, AND FAMILY, CONCEPTS AT THE CORE OF JACKSON'S SERIES, CONTAIN REFRACTIONS OF BOTH FILIATIVE AND AFFILIATIVE IMPULSES."**

Company—unashamedly lyrical, in flight from narrative, layered with allusion and homage—sounds different from any other being written today....

Source: Mark Jarman, "The Elements of Style," in *Hudson Review*, Vol. 63, No. 4, 2011, pp. 691–93.

Amor Kohli

In the following excerpt, Kohli characterizes Jackson as part of a "new wave of black poetry."

In a special issue of *Callaloo* devoted to the new wave of black poetry, Charles H. Rowell describes its participants—part of perhaps "the largest literary group of working black writers that the US has ever known" (vii)—as a group who have "learned, and ... teach their readers to take nothing for granted" (ix). Among them, Harryette Mullen finds a number of poets whose work is situated "between declarative representations of blackness and a critical engagement with the cultural and discursive practices by which evolving identities are recognized, articulated, and defined." Their dominant ethic is suspicious of aesthetic and ideological fixity and thus, as Rowell argues, promulgates a "vision of the world [which] challenges the old verities and renders them uncertainties" (ix). While grateful beneficiaries of the black cultural tradition, poets of this cohort are nonetheless, in the best sense of the jazz tradition Rowell invokes, inspired to use all that is available to them—whatever they feel works—in their poetry. While so doing, they strive to avoid the trap the poet Thomas Sayers Ellis warns against, "that they begin to respond to the tempest (to survive and to be heard), forgetting all the time that anything they create, if they are black, is black, and is black art" (89).

Major Jackson, one of this new body of poets, writes a long epistle to Gwendolyn Brooks in his latest volume, *Hoops* (2006). Apostrophizing the now-deceased poet, Jackson recalls her influence on some of the poets of his generation (in this instance, the Cambridge-based Dark Room Collective [DRC]), styling them "the inheritors of your black pride" (*Hoops*, "Letter to Brooks: Allegheny," line 73). Not only are these poets bequeathed the elder poet's pride, but Jackson extends Brooks's legacy, suggesting that because of the ground Brooks cleared, the struggles she fought, and the model she set, these young poets were in a position to form "A cadre to unselfconsciously sound / Off Hayden, Baraka, Dove, and Wright. / To become our next black literary lights." I read Jackson's inclusion of Amiri Baraka in that list as at once inevitable and striking. Certainly Baraka must be included in any discussion of latter-day black letters as a figure whose impact needs engagement in one form or another. On the one hand, Baraka's commitment to the voices, concerns, and rhythms of black and oppressed peoples has been unyielding for more than forty years, making him for many the foremost model of the committed artist. On the other hand, his name has become poetic shorthand for an extroverted, divisive, and intransigently ideological writer, a practitioner of what Michael G. Cooke refers to as "kinship by exhortation" (131). Such criteria would appear to place him at irreconcilable odds with the more measured, introspective, lyrical poetics of Robert Hayden, Rita Dove, or Jay Wright. Could it have been possible thirty-five years ago, when many of these younger poets were just beginning to grapple with the written word and when many of these elder poets were grappling with each other, to imagine this list coming together? In effect, we might imagine the détente between Baraka and Larry Neal's *Black Fire* (1968) and Michael S. Harper and Robert B. Stepto's *Chant of Saints* (1979), the two emblematic anthologies, one nationalist, one self-consciously literary, that, although published eleven years apart, when placed adjacently appear to be at each other's throats.

In this context, the question Jackson soon follows with sounds both expansive and defiant: "Who did we not celebrate? America could / Never deal with a diverse canon of poets." On the one hand, Jackson's statement obviously announces its commitment to the issues of representation and pluralism, to "really fac[ing] a people's poetry" reflecting the multiple traditions and peoples of the United States. However, a brief return to the dissonant note that "Baraka" sounds in the midst of "Hayden…Dove, and Wright" may call our attention to fissures and discordances in literary communities. In turn, it may cause us to wonder about the kinds of diversity inadmissible in our poetic canons. For instance, how viable is what Keith D. Leonard calls Robert Hayden's "beautiful paradox," in which "his well-known resistance to political obligation in poetry, his resolute integrationism, and his even more resolute aestheticism" still function "as a model of communal ethnic self-definition and antiracist social activism" (156)? Jackson gestures toward a canon that allows for an exploration of poetic formalism that asserts rather than retreats from ethnic identity; such a canon still includes writers of varying or even competing ideologies in a broadly collaborative process.

Thus, the question "Who did we not celebrate?" signals a catholicity of tribute that in turn incites a limiting response from "America," a response both ethnocentric and ideological. Although Jackson's stanza from the "Allegheny" section of "Letter to Brooks" ends by proposing that the aim of the "DRC [was] / To test the puddles of white supremacy," Jackson does not specifically state the race of this clucking, disapproving America (90–91). White supremacy had its impact on the outlook of all the people in the United States, infecting the responses of readers, writers, and critics across the nation and creating a situation in which America as a whole was unable to frankly "deal with" a truly pluralist canon; this results in limited prescriptions of black poetic influences, themes, and approaches. To say it another way, using Ellis's words, the pressure of prescription often triggers demands that black writers expend valuable creative time and energy primarily and solely responding "to the tempest" (89).

Such prescriptions may have the insidious, albeit unintended, effect of transmuting artistry from active force into a stable, essentially formulaic set of relationships. Close attention to the way Jackson presents the inconclusiveness and ambivalence of relationships in the "Urban Renewal" poetry series initiated in *Leaving Saturn* (2002) and continued in *Hoops* (2006) challenges the presumption of an untroubled comfort in an artifactual community. Jackson's poetry resists a simplistic celebratory rhetoric of consensus in favor of the centrality of intimate relationships and the forces that challenge those bonds. Jackson's concentrations on place, broadly conceived—neighborhood, community, home, family, city—are charged with attention to the ambivalent relationships that often make up these intimate spheres. Belonging is not at question in Jackson's poetry, nor is it a process separate from persistent struggle. Singular and unbroken lines of connection are not as significant for the direction of Jackson's poetic series as are evidences of a more multidirectional associational logic. The poet attempts to incorporate instability and dissension while also realizing the humanistic intelligence that guides the text. He calls our attention to the often ignored and downplayed affiliative work that renews the bonds needed to maintain community.

Rejecting the illusory comfort of this simplistic community, however, Jackson casts the artistic process as an ideal in itself, in spite of the inexorable failures, disruptions, and instabilities of such a process, which demand a dynamic ethos. Even though Jackson chooses to participate through a more traditional formalist poetics, he critiques the idea that such a poetics is fundamentally incompatible with movement, improvisation, and vitality. In addition, such an emphasis moves us away from stubbornly dominant biographical or sociological modes of thinking about black poetry. In the "Urban Renewal" series Jackson illustrates a vision wherein domestic, social, and artistic relationships—intimate relationships of varying scales—are better understood as akin to works of art or, perhaps better, to the work *in* art, a distinction meant to highlight work as process. This poetic series does not create transcendence, cohesion, or an ineluctable truth, but rather showcases the continual labor and effort that is demanded of any craft in order to achieve lasting and real success.

Jackson's work demonstrates a vision aligned with the flexibilities of affiliation and a discomfort with the more prescriptive notes of filiation, to appropriate loosely Edward W. Said's distinction (15–20). Said's parsing of these terms is useful particularly as it distinguishes between the so-called "natural" (biological and geographic) bonds of filiation and the "transpersonal" bonds of affiliation that must be learned and continually adapted. Although Said refers to these as stages moving from one to the other, as a passage from filiation to affiliation without stressing that these

are often overlapping bonds, I envision the affiliative as a sort of palimpsest that has been written on top of and expands beyond the filiative realm. Affiliation expands the vision outward, emphasizing the renewal of those bonds as the continuities and discontinuities play equally valid roles. Democracy, neighborhood, and family, concepts at the core of Jackson's series, contain refractions of both filiative and affiliative impulses. However, affiliation foregrounds the demands for constant reorganization of bonds as a necessary complement to the filial cordoning that can often be implied in a term such as "community." Considering affiliations outside of the clan allows us to expand beyond rigid genealogical and linear patterns of influence and connectivity while also insisting we take into account failures, compulsions, and other antagonisms as part of the connective process. . . .

Source: Amor Kohli, "'Life Ruptured Then Looped Back': Affiliation as Process in Major Jackson's 'Urban Renewal' Series," in *MELUS*, Vol. 35, No. 2, Summer 2010, pp. 177–80.

SOURCES

DuBois, Andrew, Review of *Hoops*, in *Harvard Review*, No. 32, June 2007, pp. 186–88.

Eleveld, Mark, Review of *Hoops*, in *Booklist*, Vol. 102, No. 11, February 1, 2006, p. 22.

Gannon, Mary, "Exalted Utterance: An Interview with Major Jackson," in *Poets & Writers*, September/October 2010, http://www.pw.org/content/exalted_utterance_a_profile_of_major_jackson_0?cmnt_all = 1 (accessed August 9, 2015).

Huston, Karla, Review of *Hoops*, in *Library Journal*, Vol. 131, No. 8, May 1, 2006, p. 89.

Jackson, Major, "Urban Renewal: XVIII," in *Hoops*, 2006, p. 50.

Kohli, Amor, "'Life Ruptured Then Looped Back': Affiliation as Process in Major Jackson's 'Urban Renewal' Series," in *MELUS*, Vol. 35, No. 2, Summer 2010, pp. 177–98.

Lewis, Thabiti, "Introduction of Major Jackson at Willamette University Hallie Ford Chair Reading Series," October 26, 2004, http://majorjackson.com/media.html (accessed August 9, 2015).

"Little Rock School Desegregation (1957)," *King Institute Encyclopedia*, http://kingencyclopedia.stanford.edu/encyclopedia/encyclopedia/enc_little_rock_school_desegregation_1957/ (accessed August 10, 2015).

"Michelle Obama Says Too Many Black Kids Are Trying to Be 'Ballers' and Rappers," *Your Black World*, May 17, 2013, http://yourblackworld.net/2013/05/17/michelle-obama-says-too-many-black-kids-are-trying-to-be-ballers-and-rappers/ (accessed August 10, 2015).

Mullen, Harryette, "'The Cracks between What We Are and What We Are Supposed to Be': Stretching the Dialogue of African-American Poetry," in *How2*, Vol. 1, No. 5, March 2001, http://www.asu.edu/pipercwcenter/how2journal/archive/online_archive/v1_5_2001/current/in-conference/american-lit/mullen.html (accessed August 9, 2015).

Pardlo, Gregory, "About Major Jackson," in *Ploughshares*, Vol. 39, No. 1, Spring 2013, p. 187.

Pollak, Sally, "Sounds of Philadelphia," in *Burlington Free Press*, April 16, 2006, http://majorjackson.com/PDF/Burlington%20Free%20Press%20-%20Profile%20by%20Sally%20Pollak.pdf (accessed August 9, 2015).

Reed, Roy, "Orval Eugene Faubus (1910–1994)," in *The Encyclopedia of Arkansas History & Culture*, http://www.encyclopediaofarkansas.net/encyclopedia/entry-detail.aspx?entryID = 102 (accessed August 10, 2015).

Review of *Hoops*, in *New Yorker*, Vol. 82, No. 9, April 17, 2006, p. 79.

Review of *Hoops*, in *Publishers Weekly*, Vol. 253, No. 11, March 13, 2006, p. 44.

Warner, David, "Major Talent: UVM's Most Prized Poet Lines Up between Langston Hughes and Hip-Hop," in *Seven Days* (Burlington, VT), February 18, 2004, http://www.sevendaysvt.com/vermont/major-talent/Content?oid = 2129083 (accessed August 9, 2015).

Webster, Kim, and Nicole Miyashiro, "Biography of Major Jackson," Pennsylvania Center for the Book, Pennsylvania State University website, 2013, https://secureapps.libraries.psu.edu/PACFTB/bios/biography.cfm?AuthorID = 7337 (accessed August 9, 2015).

Wojahn, David, "History Shaping Selves: Four Poets," in *Southern Review*, Vol. 43, No. 1, Winter 2007, pp. 218, 222–25, 231.

FURTHER READING

Fauset, Jessie Redmon, *Plum Bun: A Novel without a Moral*, Frederick A. Stokes, 1929.

　　Fauset is a Harlem Renaissance fiction writer who, like Jackson, grew up in Philadelphia as a high academic achiever; she was regularly the only black student in her class. Her novel *Plum Bun* follows two sisters from Philadelphia in early twentieth-century America, one of whom decides to pass as white in an effort to improve her lot in life.

Greven, Alec, *How to Talk to Girls*, illustrated by Kei Acedera, Collins, 2008.

　　Ostensibly aimed primarily at elementary-age readers—Greven was nine years old when he wrote it—this volume provides spot-on advice that will enlighten many more mature readers as well—or at least lighten them up, which may be just as helpful.

Keiderling, Kyle, *Heart of a Lion: The Life, Death, and Legacy of Hank Gathers*, Morning Star Communications, 2010.

　　Gathers, a native of crime-ridden North Philadelphia for whom basketball did prove his salvation, was gaining fame as one of the nation's leading college players when he collapsed on a court in 1990 and died. The title poem of Jackson's *Hoops* is dedicated to Gathers.

Sherlock, Frank, *Space between These Lines Not Dedicated*, Ixnay Press, 2014.

　　While Sonia Sanchez served as Philadelphia's inaugural poet laureate, the mantle was assumed in 2014 by Sherlock, like Jackson a Pew fellow. Hailing from Southwest Philadelphia, Sherlock also attended Temple and writes poetry infused with the energy of the city.

SUGGESTED SEARCH TERMS

Major Jackson AND Urban Renewal

Major Jackson AND Philadelphia OR Vermont

Major Jackson AND interview

North Philadelphia AND housing projects

Philadelphia AND urban renewal

Philadelphia AND poetry

Philadelphia AND basketball

African American poetry AND twenty-first century

Central High School AND integration

Yesterday

W. S. MERWIN
1983

"Yesterday" opens with a man declaring to his friend that he was not a good son. He did not spend as much time with his parents as he felt he should have. He tells the story of the last time he saw his father alive, their time together wasted because he was more interested in finding an excuse to leave than in listening to what his father had to say. The person he tells this story to is the poem's narrator. He seems to have some bad memories of how he treated his own parents, but he is not the person talking, so that relationship is left to the reader's imagination. He agrees enthusiastically with his friend, suggesting that he knows exactly what the other man is feeling at every part of his story.

W. S. Merwin, the author of "Yesterday," has been a major force in American poetry since his first book was published in the 1950s. A two-time Pulitzer Prize winner and a former poet laureate, Merwin writes with a style all his own, one that is both intellectual and inviting. Readers may not understand the poem the first time they read it because Merwin records the discussion between the two men with no punctuation to show where quotes begin or end or to shape sentences. Still, readers who take the time to read the poem again often find that Merwin's strong rhythm makes sense of the discussion; he does not need punctuation to make the poem engaging. "Yesterday" was published in Merwin's 1983 collection *Opening the Hand*.

W. S. Merwin (© *Chris Felver | Getty Images*)

AUTHOR BIOGRAPHY

William Stanley Merwin was born in New York City on September 30, 1927. His father was a Presbyterian minister. He grew up in Union City, New Jersey, an industrial town across the Hudson River from New York, and then in Scranton, Pennsylvania. He attended Princeton University on a scholarship. It was there that he started writing poetry, studying with famed poets R. P. Blackmur and John Berryman. After graduating from Princeton in 1948, he studied languages briefly, then moved to Europe. In 1950 he accepted a position tutoring the son of poet and novelist Robert Graves. That position lasted for only a year, and then he moved to London, where he worked for the BBC translating literary works from French and Spanish. This was the beginning of a career as a translator that supported him for the decades to come.

Merwin's first poetry collection, *A Mask for Janus*, was published in 1952. It earned him the Yale Younger Poets Prize, selected that year by W. H. Auden. For the beginning of the 1950s he lived in a farmhouse in the south of France. He

returned to America in 1956, to Cambridge, Massachusetts, to accept a fellowship with the Poet's Theater. He began publishing collections of poetry regularly throughout the 1960s, developing a personal, autobiographical style. In 1970, his collection *The Carrier of Ladders* won the Pulitzer Prize.

In 1976 Merwin moved to Hawaii. Because of his dedication to nature, he bought a former banana plantation and has worked since then to revert the land to its original, uncultivated state. In Hawaii he pursued the practice of Zen Buddhism. Nature and Buddhism are constant themes in his later works. He and his third wife, Paula Dunaway, still live in Maui, forty years later.

Merwin has published over twenty books of poetry throughout his long career, including *Opening the Hand*, the 1983 collection in which "Yesterday" appeared. In 2009 Merwin won the Pulitzer Prize for Poetry for the second time, for his collection *The Shadow of Sirius*. The following year he was appointed by Congress to be the poet laureate of the United States.

POEM SUMMARY

The text used for this summary is from *Opening the Hand*, Atheneum, 1983, pp. 20–21. Versions of the poem can be found on the following web pages: https://www.poets.org/poetsorg/poem/yesterday and http://writersalmanac.publicradio.org/index.php?date=2011/06/19.

Lines 1–3

In the first stanza of the poem, Merwin sets up a dramatic situation. Two friends are having a conversation, the details of which are going to unravel throughout the rest of the poem. In this stanza, the mood of the conversation is revealed. The person to whom the narrator is talking says, with no background context, that he feels guilty about the way he has behaved toward one or both of his parents. The fact that he springs this on the narrator in the first line is an indication of how much the guilt is weighing on his conscience, struggling for release.

The poem's next two lines show the close relationship between the narrator and his friend. The friend does not ask whether or not the narrator understands what he has vaguely hinted at; he simply says that he does. He knows that what has been referred to is understood in the same

MEDIA ADAPTATIONS

- Merwin was filmed reading the poem "Yesterday" at the Geraldine R. Dodge Poetry Festival. This reading is posted at the website for the series *Poetry Everywhere* with Garrison Keillor. The series was produced by WGBH Boston and David Grubin Productions, in association with the Poetry Foundation. Merwin's reading can be found online at http://www.pbs.org/wgbh/poetryevery where/merwin.html.

way that longtime couples can leave sentences unfinished with the confidence that the other person is like-minded. The narrator confirms that this is really the way things are when he responds in the third line.

Lines 4–6

Having switched to the narrator's perspective briefly, the poem goes back to his friend's confession. To set up the story of how he has been a bad son, the friend explains an ongoing state of ignorance on his part. This is just background information. Readers will soon see his reference to both parents fade away from the poem. His plural references in these first stanzas include his mother, but the story that he feels guilty about will soon be revealed to be a specific meeting that concerns only the narrator's friend and his father. Once again, at the end of this stanza the narrator says that he understands how his friend feels. The reader gets a deeper sense of their emotional bond.

Lines 7–10

The friend explains that his relaxed attitude toward his parents took place over a long time. In that time he lived in differing degrees of proximity to his parents. Sometimes he was in the same city as they were, and, by implication, sometimes he was not. When he was in the same city, he had the opportunity to visit them more than once a month, but he did not take

advantage of that chance, which is one thing that makes him feel like a bad son.

At the end of the third stanza, the narrator does more than simply agree: he understands his friend's moral situation so well that he expresses excitement. The empathy that exists between these two friends energizes him. Whether or not they actually were bad sons, it is important for the poem to note that they do have this emotional bond.

Lines 11–12

In this brief stanza the two friends express nearly the same idea at the same time. The friend has started his story, but he has stirred an emotion in the narrator that makes the narrator want to tell his own story as well. They each want to tell the other about the last time they saw their respective fathers. Telling their stories is an effort to calm some of the guilt that these two self-admitted bad sons have stirred up.

There is one slight but significant difference between the ways each man blurts out the beginning of his story. The friend says he is starting the story of the last time he *went to see* his father, putting the emphasis on himself, while the narrator uses the less active statement that he is talking about when he *saw* his father; this puts the emphasis on the father-son interaction, not on who went to see whom. The friend's version is more aggressive about feeling guilty, and that might be why he gets to be the one to tell his story.

Lines 13–17

In line 13, the friend has adopted the narrator's language from line 11: he is not talking about whether or not he went to see his father; he is focused only on what happened when they did see each other. Although this story is told as his final memory of his father, that meeting is not related with perfect memory by the narrator's friend. He is vague about the details. He recalls the small talk that passed between his father and him, a conversation about life in general. Nothing about their talk was any more specific than just asking how things were going, as he remembers it. He does not say how long they talked or what answers he gave to his father's questions, probably because he does not know these details. He seems to not have been paying much attention, assuming that this was just another conversation that would be followed by many more like it.

The one detail that he remembers is that his father moved into the next room. He was going there to get something, though the friend does not say what that thing was, probably because he does not know. The one thing he is specific about is that it is something his father wanted to give to him.

Lines 18–20

Listening to the details about the last time his friend saw his father stirs up a memory in the narrator about the last time he saw his own father. His memory is not as involved as his friend's memory is. It is not about their last conversation. It takes place when his father was already dead and cold.

Lines 21–25

The poem returns to the friend's story after the brief diversion into the narrator's mind, picking up where it left off two stanzas earlier. The friend's father, leaving the room to get what he wanted to give his son, turned back to the son just as he was leaving. Thinking that he was walking away, the son took a glance at his watch. This concern about how much time a visit to his parents was taking is something he tried unsuccessfully to hide.

Seeing that his son was concerned about time, the father explained his position. He stated that he did like his son's company and that he would like his son to stay and talk to him. It will become clear in the following lines that he is not necessarily saying these things to make the son feel guilty about leaving, but to show how much he is willing to give up by letting his son go.

Line 26

In one line, the narrator emphasizes his enthusiastic empathy once more. He understands how his friend feels so much that he blurts out the interjection *oh*.

Lines 27–30

After the narrator's interruption, the poem returns to the friend's story. The father has expressed his desire for his son to stay and talk: now he explains why it would be all right if the son did not stay. He knows that the son is busy, and he does not want to make him feel guilty if he has to go. Although his words seem to be

giving the son a right to leave without feeling guilty, the way he organizes his words causes even more guilt: he says that his son should not feel he has to stay *just* because his father is there, which implies that there would be some other reason to go. The father is giving up his son's visit, but he is doing so by calling attention to how insignificant the son must think his own father is.

Line 31

The narrator has no response to the way the father has released his son. Maybe he is overcome with emotion, thinking about how his own father encouraged him to not spend too much time making his parents happy. Maybe he sees the father as being manipulative, stating the opposite of what he wants. Merwin is purposely vague about what the narrator thinks about this part of the conversation.

Lines 32–36

The poem returns to the last conversation the narrator's friend had with his father. The father was willing to let him go, he says, because the son might have had some important work to do or because the friend had someone important that he needed to go and see. Each point the father speculates about is prefaced with the word *maybe*: he does not want to directly ask whether either of these is the case because he is careful to not pry into the details of his son's life. In bringing up these possibilities without asking about them, the father seems to be passively fishing for information about his son's life. He is implying that his son should talk about where he has to go, but he is not taking the responsibility to request anything from him. His last statement to his son is that he does not want to *keep* him, emphasizing the sense of freedom he wants his son to have, regardless of the emotional toll on his father.

Lines 37–41

Merwin begins the stanza before the last by describing the scene for this conversation between friends and giving background information. They are talking indoors, and the narrator looks out the window, which implies that he is trying to think without the distractions he finds inside. The fact that he mentions that his friend is older could indicate two things. For one, it could be that he is looking at the friend and noticing for the first time the signs of age, such as greying hair and wrinkles: this would imply that their conversation has been so intense that he is more aware of the physical world. The second thing it might mean is that he is suddenly aware that his friend is closer to death, more familiar with it, than he is himself.

In the second half of this stanza, the friend continues his story. After his father told him that it would be all right if he left and even provided his son with an excuse to leave, the son took him up on the offer. He told his father that he did, in fact, have somewhere that he had to be, and he stood up and left.

In line 41, he draws the narrator's empathy closer to him once more. He assumes that the narrator, as his friend, understands what he was feeling at that moment. He does not ask the narrator if he knows what it was like for him; he states it as a fact.

Lines 42–43
In the poem's final lines, the narrator's friend admits that he lied in order to get out of spending any more time with his father. He did not have anywhere to go or anything that he had to do; he just said he did, taking advantage of the excuse his father offered. This lie has apparently stayed with him over the years, weighing on his conscience, until he could not keep it a secret anymore and felt that he had to confess it to his friend.

The last two lines use negative words—*nowhere* and *nothing*—to stress how insignificant anything in his life at that time must have been in comparison to spending time with his father. This was, as he explained in line 11, the last time he went to see his father, so presumably when his father died this lie was the last exchange that the two of them had.

THEMES

Parent-Child Relationships
The relationships that people have with their parents are always important ones. Freudian psychology, for example, puts the parent at the center of all of the relationships a person will have in her or his life. The relationship between parents and children is a universal pattern, known in all cultures. It is one of the few things that is common to all people. A person may have no relationship with an absent parent who has died or left, but, before modern advances in human embryo fertilization, every person has had parents.

In "Yesterday," the speaker's friend is concerned with the kind of relationship he had with his parents. He feels that there is a standard for how a child should behave toward his parents and that he has failed to meet that standard. The poem centers on how the friend and his father had a hard time interacting; in telling about that, it implies that the relationship between the narrator and his own father was not much better.

Responsibility
The two characters depicted in this poem feel some sense of responsibility toward their parents. They know that they should have visited them more often. The narrator's friend tells the story of a time when he last visited his father, making it clear that he did not want to spend time with his father as a person, that it was just out of a sense of obligation. The point of the story is that his father gave him an opportunity to escape from his responsibility, to excuse himself by claiming he had somewhere more important to be, and the narrator's friend jumped at it. He would fulfill his responsibility only if he felt that he had to, and when he was excused from it, his responsibility meant less to him than his own comfort.

The poem's last two lines drive home this sense of responsibility. Obviously, the narrator's friend was not literally going nowhere or doing nothing. He went somewhere and he did something, but he realizes now, after his father is dead, that whatever he went off to do was not as important as the time he could have had with his father.

Guilt
When people feel they have not done what they should have done or that they have done what they should not have, they experience guilt. In "Yesterday," the guilty feeling that dogs the narrator's friend is obvious. He identifies himself in the first line as not having been the son he should have been, and the rest of the poem serves as an explanation of why he should feel guilty. Some readers may feel that he mistreated his parents by not spending as much time with them as a son should, while other readers will feel that he was as dutiful as they could expect and he has nothing to feel guilty about. The important thing is how he

TOPICS FOR FURTHER STUDY

- Merwin starts this poem with his narrator's friend denying that he was a good son. Construct a survey, offering respondents six or seven possible choices of what it means to not be a good son or daughter. After giving your survey to a significant number of people either your age or over sixty-five, write a proposal for how you would spare a lot of people from later regret about how they behaved toward their parents.

- Merwin was the poet laureate of the United States from 2010 to 2011. Read the works of five poets laureate and, based on their poetry alone, write your own rules about what you think the works of a poet laureate should be like. Post it on a blog as a job description and allow your classmates to apply for the position.

- Research what gerontologists—the doctors who study the effects of aging—say about how being isolated from the world affects the mental functions of older people. Make a chart of the brain, highlighting which parts of it could be affected by being ignored, and write a report to go with your chart that explains how the physical brain cells are affected by a social-emotional situation.

- In Ravi Shankar's poem "Old Folks' Jokes" (available on the Poets.org website), he describes visiting senior citizens at a retirement community and becoming wrapped up in their humor. Determine what you like about old people, whether they are in your family or just old people you know from your community, and write a poem using Shankar's style to show yourself interacting with them and having a good time.

- Read "Warning," a poem by Jenny Joseph, a poet who writes frequently for young-adult readers. (The poem is included in her most popular collection, *Rose in the Afternoon*.) In this poem, written before she was thirty, Joseph speculated about what kind of person she would be when she was old. After reading Joseph's poem, write a letter to be hidden away for children that you might have one day, to read after your death. Include in your letter a copy of Merwin's "Yesterday" as well as an explanation of how that poem made you feel at this age, when old age is just theoretical.

- The "death poem"—a poem written on one's deathbed—is a poetic tradition in some parts of the world, particularly in Japan, where it is known as *jisei*, a farewell poem to life. Look at examples of poems written in this tradition in Yoel Hoffmann's collection *Japanese Death Poems: Written by Zen Monks and Haiku Poets on the Verge of Death*, published in 1998. Focus on the longer examples, such as works by Zen monk Seisetsu Shucho. Then, write the *jisei* that you think would have been written by the father or the mother of the narrator of "Yesterday," combining the Japanese style with the facts from Merwin's poem.

- Could this poem have been as effective if the conversation between the two friends were played out over texts or tweets? Social media have a way of stripping writing to the bare minimum and losing emotional nuances. Then again, Merwin's style is not very expressive to begin with. Write an essay explaining whether you think modern communication would help support what Merwin implies here about how people relate or would ruin his delicately balanced message.

- Both of the characters in "Yesterday" feel remorse because they did not spend enough time with their fathers. Create a visual time line of one of your days in pictures and sound clips and upload it to the media sharing site that you think is most likely to still be in existence after you are gone.

feels about it. Guilt might not be rational, but it is a powerful motivating force nonetheless.

One reason the narrator's friend feels guilty may be that his father encouraged his feeling of guilt. After seeing his son look down to check the time, the father uses language that could be considered passive-aggressive. His words may be telling his son to go ahead and leave and not feel guilty about it, but he also could be urging his son to feel that he is abandoning his own father. His statement of how little hurt he feels could be understated on purpose, to make his son build up his own sense of guilt.

Throughout the poem the narrator agrees with his friend. He seems to feel guilt about the way he treated his own parents as well, though the poem does not say why he should feel that way. Guilt is a very individualized emotion, with different causes and effects for different people.

Empathy

A central theme throughout this poem is the empathy these two friends have for each other. They understand each other's emotions. This shows itself from the very first stanza, when the narrator's friend makes a vague statement and then expects the narrator to understand what he is talking about. His expectation is well based: his friend does indeed understand him.

The empathy these two feel carries on throughout the poem. At various times, the narrator interrupts his friend's story to express his agreement, even if the point his friend is making is not one that seems to call for agreement or disagreement. To readers, the story being told is fairly straightforward, but the narrator sees more to it than is found on the surface. He knows the emotions his friend feels at various parts of his tale, and he interjects his own perspective now and then to show that their feelings are in sync.

Friendship

At the beginning of the poem the speaker refers to the person he is talking to as his friend, and the rest of the poem seems to support that. The two men have similar perspectives and like-minded outlooks, the way true friends do.

The only place this comes into doubt is in line 38. The narrator calls the man his friend again, but he also brings up a difference in their ages. Whether this is meant as a comment on his friend's closeness with his parents or not, it does significantly change the reader's understanding

The speaker admits that he did not visit his aging father often enough. (© *Anna Lurye* / *Shutterstock.com*)

of their relationship. It focuses on a way in which they are different. They are still friends, but a different kind of friends. This late piece of information defines them as friends who have one conspicuous difference, of which the narrator is very conscious.

Memory

No reason is given for the narrator's friend to tell this particular story on this particular day. Whatever triggered this memory was something that happened before the poem began. Maybe it was just a stray idea rumbling around inside of the friend's head that made him suddenly think of what a bad son he was when his parents were alive. His memory of the event he talks about here is sketchy. He does not remember how often he really went to visit his parents. He does not remember what his father was leaving the room to get for him. What he does remember are distinct sensory impressions, such as the image of his father standing in the doorway.

Readers can tell that memory is an important part of this poem by its title, "Yesterday." The narrator's friend might still be moved by the events of that final visit, regardless of how much has passed since they occurred, but he does not have a very firm grasp of the details of that day. "Yesterday" may refer to just a day ago, when the two friends had their discussion, but it evokes the way recent memories have a way of slipping away into the past.

STYLE

Absent Punctuation

Early in his career, Merwin decided to write his poems without punctuation. In an interview with the *Paris Review*, he explained this stylistic change as being in part because of the influence of French and Spanish poetry. Mostly, though, he viewed it as reflecting the strong relationship that poetry has with the spoken word, while prose relies more on punctuation because it is more closely associated with written communication.

In "Yesterday," Merwin's style is particularly noticeable because the poem has some complex linguistic moves. It presents a conversation between two people without using quotation marks to show the differences between the narrative voice and what either person says out loud. It does not even use commas to show where a quote tag, such as "he says," ends and the quote that it is introducing begins.

Once they get past this irregularity and accept the poem on its own terms, readers have little trouble following the conversation presented. One reason for this is Merwin's innate sense of rhythm: the words may not be separated by punctuation marks, but they follow patterns of natural breaks. Merwin breaks his poem into lines and stanzas, which further helps readers feel the flow of the conversation he presents in the poem. These breaks are more natural to the sound of language than punctuation marks would make them.

Passivity

Throughout "Yesterday," the one word that is used most often is *say* or its variants (*said, says,* and so on). This word performs the basic function of telling readers that some words were spoken aloud in their conversation, but it does not give readers any information about the

emotion used when spoken. *Say* has a low-key, neutral tone to it, and its constant use affects the rest of the poem, giving it a quiet, matter-of-fact feeling.

Merwin uses the passivity of his words to contrast the naturally emotional situation that he is describing in "Yesterday." The poem itself is about regrets and familial relationships and the close personal bond between friends. It could use powerful language to bring out the underlying power of these elements, but Merwin instead chose to use passive language: he trusts the situation to speak for itself, without the need for words that tell readers how they should feel about it.

Past and Present Tense

In this poem Merwin tells a story within a story: there is the conversation between the narrator and his friend and the conversation between the friend and his father. Merwin's adopted style to write without punctuation makes it difficult to untangle the two stories and tell what is happening when. He makes things somewhat easier for his readers by writing the poem in two different tenses: present tense for the current conversation and past tense for the events that are being discussed.

If the conversation between the two friends were told in the past tense, which is a technique that many writers use, then the two time frames would sound the same. As it is, however, readers can see the shift from one situation to the other, such as in a line like "he *says* and my father *turned*." The lack of quotation marks makes this shift into a direct quote unclear, but the two different tenses used in one line help readers understand the shift that is not identified by traditional punctuation methods.

HISTORICAL CONTEXT

Zen Influence

Merwin has been a practitioner of Zen Buddhism since the 1970s. Even though he is a Westerner who grew up in New York and Pennsylvania, his focus on Zen has influenced his worldview and is considered an integral part of his poetry.

Buddhism is based on the teachings of Siddhartha Gautama, who was born a nobleman in Nepal at some time in the sixth to the fourth century BCE. He led a sheltered life within a palace until he was in his late twenties. Venturing

COMPARE
&
CONTRAST

- **1983:** People visit their aged parents. Calling them on the phone is a substitute, but it often seems too impersonal.

  Today: Social media help family members keep connected and know the details of one another's lives when direct communication is difficult. Despite stereotypes about older people being befuddled by technology, many older people are comfortable with using video media such as Skype to have long-distance face-to-face conversations.

- **1983:** Generations grow and divide. People expect to move away as they develop their own lives.

  Today: Economic pressures have made a trend of more people living with their parents and grandparents. Adult children move back into their family homes for financial security, while single parents move back or never leave in order to have their children watched by family. A 2012 report by Les Christie found that 15 percent more people lived in houses with three generations of their family than had been the case just two years earlier.

- **1983:** The "glance at the wristwatch" is a well-known signal of impatience, showing that the person is concerned about how their time is being spent where they are.

  Today: Wristwatches are becoming less and less common. In modern times, most people

keep track of the time with their phones. A glance at the phone does not necessarily mean that a person is looking at the time: they might be checking messages or weather or any number of other bits of information the modern phone conveys.

- **1983:** Although poets like to remind people that the roots of poetry come from the spoken word, poetry is mostly related through print.

  Today: Competitions like the Def Poetry Jam have given poets the opportunity to perform their poems more frequently through the turn of the twenty-first century. Advances in technology make it easy to take videos and upload them to the Internet, so that spoken word poetry can be shared worldwide even more easily than printed poetry can.

- **1983:** A man who feels guilty about how he treated his parents can turn to his friends, who may or may not be receptive about the story that he tells.

  Today: Social media have given us many more ways to unburden the weight of a guilty conscience. There are chat rooms that provide anonymity, tweets that send one's message out to tens or hundreds of people, and sites where one could solicit advice from peers or professionals.

---

beyond the palace walls, he was faced with questions he had never before considered: an experience with an old man led him to think about aging, death, and suffering. After that he walked away from his kingdom to live a life of poverty. Eventually, he decided that poverty was no more real than a worldly existence. Extremism in either degree was misdirected: balance was the key. Meditating, he became the one known as Buddha ("enlightened one" or "the awakened").

In the centuries that followed the Buddha's death, his teachings spread throughout the East. The Indian monk Bodhidharma is reputed to have brought Buddhism to China in the sixth century CE, and it was introduced into Japan in the following century. It is in Japan that the word *Zen* was first used to describe the practices that Buddhists use to move toward enlightenment, including meditation and contemplation of self-contradictory questions ("koans") to

The father catches the speaker looking at his watch. (© OPOLJA | Shutterstock.com)

clear the mind of worldly distractions. For a long time after that, however, it was localized in Asia, separated from the countries of the West, which followed predominantly Christian or Jewish religions, with some familiarity with Islam, owing to the proximity of Africa to Europe.

Japanese scholar D. T. Suzuki was instrumental in bringing Zen thought to the West. Having spent time in the United States around the turn of the twentieth century, Dr. Suzuki wrote his books about Zen philosophy and practices in a way that made them accessible to Western sensibilities. After World War II introduced many Americans and Europeans to Japanese culture, Suzuki's writings became popular. The interest in Zen Buddhism that grew in the 1950s expanded even more in the 1960s with the start of the multiculturalism movement, encouraging interest in world cultures other than the ones one grew up with.

Adult Children and Parents

When this poem was written, the population of people who were at the traditional retirement age was significant, but it was nowhere near where it is today. Census Bureau statistics for 1982 maintained that in the United States, 26 million people were over the age of sixty-five, of a total population of 232 million. That is just over 11 percent. Recent projections in a 2014 report by the Census Bureau predict that the percent of the population sixty-five or older will reach 20 percent by the year 2030.

There are several reasons for the swell in the old-age population. One is the aging of the baby boom generation: families were wary of having children in the 1930s and 1940s because of the Great Depression followed immediately by World War II, but starting in the late 1940s the country saw the greatest increase in babies being born that it had ever experienced. Scientific advances, too, are instrumental in keeping older adults alive longer. This includes not only medical breakthroughs but changes in social patterns as well: the decline of tobacco usage has significantly changed life expectancy, as have greater understanding of diet (i.e., less red meat and more vegetables) and acceptance of exercise.

The problems of the aging population are more familiar for this generation than they were when Merwin wrote "Yesterday." Today, there are more books and websites about how to care for elderly parents than would ever have been imaginable at that time. A generation ago, the elderly faced being forgotten; that may be true in individual cases today, but the bulge in the population that the elderly represent assures that they have more consumer power and political attention than the senior population of thirty or forty years ago.

Although the population is living longer than in previous generations, people still die of old age. The swell in elderly population means that there has been a market for resources aimed at adult children coping with the difficulties of old age and coping with death. Blogs and websites about dementia and financial arrangements for older people abound, as do books and seminars. At the time when this poem was being written, the death of an aged parent was more of an individual matter because the lives of the elderly meant less to a population that was relatively young, but now people like the father described in the poem are increasingly becoming the social norm.

CRITICAL OVERVIEW

Merwin has been an important part of the American poetry scene since the publication of his first book in 1952, *A Mask for Janus*. In choosing that book for the Yale Younger Poets Prize, W. H. Auden identified it as the work of someone who respects poetic tradition, which set the standard for critical approaches to his work. According to Neal Bowers, writing in the *Sewanee Review* in 1990, critics tried to find a place for Merwin in the poetic tradition throughout the 1950s and 1960s. His work was considered strictly formalist, then "something resembling the confessional poetry of the 1960s—but different." He was seen as a postmodernist just as postmodernism was finished but was also resistant to the "postmodernist" tag because it held back from several key elements, such as self-obsession or self-absorbed rambling. "Small wonder he's been so hard to locate," Bowers notes, "with critics expecting to find him in the psychiatric ward or sitting like a version of the RCA dog, head cocked into the sound of his own sweet maundering." In short, Merwin distinguishes himself from postmodernism by the value his poetry puts on formal structure and from the formalists by the personal nature of the writing.

In a review of Merwin's collection *Flower & Hand: Poems, 1977–1983*, which contains *Opening the Hand*, the book in which "Yesterday" was originally published, *Publishers Weekly* steers its readers to the poet's "elegance," noting that in poems from this period in his career, "Merwin is often less concerned with the flow of a sentence than he is with the call and response of individual words that bubble through his unpunctuated lines," a recognition that by the late 1970s the poet had an individual style that he followed successfully. Edward Brunner discusses *Opening the Hand* and the poem "Yesterday" in particular in an essay from the late 1980s that examines the poet's abandonment of punctuation. Relating the style to the subject— abandonment of the father—Brunner's analysis concludes that "a poem like this, which speaks of all the barriers that exist between persons, and speaks of them in such a way that no barriers are left between the poet and his readers, is the most impressive achievement in *Opening the Hand*."

Well into the twentieth century, Merwin continues to dominate American poetry. When the Library of America published a two-volume set of *The Collected Poems of W. S. Merwin*, John Freeman noted, in the *Virginia Quarterly Review*, how the collection captures the "awesome range, intensity, and feral strangeness" of Merwin's work over his long career. He compares the changes in style throughout Merwin's career to a "radical evolution arcing through [the book's] pages, like an explosive chemical reaction that is still ongoing." Later in the review, Freeman compares the poet's lifetime of published work to a process of personal evolution: "To read *Collected Poems*," Freeman writes, "is like watching a man crawl out from the underworld and into the light. But each new summit turns out to be a false summit, a new vantage point for a reminder of the slippery shale of truth." Most critics would agree that Merwin's search for truth has made his poetry hard to characterize, and most appreciate his work at whatever phase it is encountered.

CRITICISM

David Kelly

Kelly is a college professor in creative writing and literature. In the following essay, he explores the possibility that the narrator of "Yesterday" loses interest in his friend, returning to the friend—who was disinterested in his own father—the justice he deserves.

WHAT DO I READ NEXT?

- In 1980, Merwin published *Unframed Originals: Recollections*, a collection of autobiographical sketches that start in his childhood and follow his life up through adolescence. Life in the industrial towns in Pennsylvania and New Jersey is remembered with Merwin's distinctive poetic style: far from being a comprehensive account of his life, he renders what it felt like through images and sketches.

- Merwin's 2005 book *Summer Doorways: A Memoir*, covers his young adulthood up to his twenties. The tone is what you would expect from an accomplished wordsmith like Merwin, and the settings—mostly in Europe, where he lived after graduating from Princeton—evoke the postwar period with the poet's natural grace and calm style.

- Galway Kinnell, who died in 2014, was a poet and a contemporary of Merwin's: they attended Princeton at the same time, though they were not friends then. Over the years a friendship formed, based not only on a respect for each other's writing but on a similar spiritual worldview as well. A good example of Kinnell's style is his poem "The Perch," which is available online and in his 2000 book *New Selected Poems*.

- Merwin has always been an interesting person for interviewers: his sincerity comes through in everything he says, and his way of looking at the world is uniquely his own. In his 2009 interview with Bill Moyers for the PBS show *Bill Moyers Journal*, the subject of "Yesterday" comes up: Moyers discussed how moved he was by the way the poem made him think of his father, and later in the discussion Merwin brought up that response again. A transcript of that interview is included in *Conversations with W. S.*

- *Merwin*, edited by Michael Wutz and Hal Crimmel, published in 2015.

- In 1992, two years before Merwin won it, Adrienne Rich won the prestigious Lenore Marshall Poetry Prize for her book *An Atlas of the Difficult World: Poems, 1988–1991.* The two poets' styles are considered similar in their intellectualism and political activism, and they were admirers of each other's works. The long poem that this collection is named after, "An Atlas of the Difficult World," is a good way to get to know Rich's style in comparison to Merwin's.

- Noted writer Li-Young Lee, an American poet born in Jakarta to Chinese parents, tells the story of a memorable moment with his father in his poem "The Gift." The poem centers on his father's telling him about ancient legends while removing a splinter from the young man's hand. Although Lee's Asian heritage is not the focus of the poem, it is undeniably an element of the story and the father-son relationship at the poem's center. This poem is often anthologized and was originally published in Lee's collection *Rose*, in 1986.

- In Cynthia Hand's acclaimed young-adult novel *The Last Time We Say Goodbye*, teen protagonist Lex has to come to grips with the suicide of her brother. Told in a way that makes readers think seriously about issues of life and death, the book covers the emotions that the characters in "Yesterday" must be feeling, but from the perspective of a young person who has more life ahead than they do. Published in 2015, the book has gained accolades for its deft and engaging handling of a subject that could otherwise have been morbid and depressing.

The poem "Yesterday" seems, even after multiple readings, to be a study of friendship. Two friends, grown men, discuss the way they left things with their respective fathers, both of whom are now dead. One man dominates the conversation while the other takes the supporting

> **BUT THERE HAS BEEN SOMETHING OFF ABOUT THEIR RELATIONSHIP FROM THE BEGINNING. THE WAY THE NARRATOR GIVES UP HIS TURN TO BE PART OF THE DISCUSSION IN THE FIRST STANZA DOES NOT INDICATE A HARMONIOUS BALANCE BETWEEN THESE TWO FRIENDS."**

role of agreeing to what his friend says, cheering him on, telling him that he understands how he feels because his own experiences with his father led him to similar insights. The two appear to be of one mind. This is friendship.

It is a good lesson for a poem to offer. The story the friend tells in the poem is moving, filled with life and regret. In it, the narrator's friend explains why he feels he betrayed his father by slipping out of their last visit together under false pretenses, saying he had somewhere else to be even though really he did not. The discussion between these two friends goes into the under-examined world of male bonding. It is made even more moving with the added insight it gives into male bonding. Men do not share their feelings with each other often in popular culture, not unless they are feelings of lust or revenge toward third parties. For a poem to present two men discussing grief about the loss of two other men presents a rare, honest look at how people in our culture interact, or at least how they could.

This is the poem's most obvious reading. Merwin's style is very dry, and it reflects real life in the way that he hides meanings in the shadows without comment or explanation. Other readings of the poem are possible; they are less likely, but they do work. For instance, "Yesterday" may not be about men sharing and communicating. There is good enough reason to see the poet's point as one of justice. Instead of bonding, these men may be drawing apart right before the reader's eyes, leading to the point where two men who started out as friends each wind up alone.

The story told in the poem comes from the man who is identified throughout "Yesterday" as the narrator's friend. He is the one who goes to see his father, glances at his watch, is asked if he has to be going, and answers that yes, as a matter of fact, he does. Throughout the poem the narrator eggs him on with his tale and the sorrow it has left him with, blurting out short phrases that imply enthusiasm. He seems to be agreeing. He seems to act like the choir at a revival meeting, shouting out a stray "amen" whenever the spirit moves him. Maybe he is just trying to get a word in edgewise. He may be trying to start something with each interjection—to begin his half of the conversation—only to be brushed aside each time while his more aggressive friend goes on with his own tale, paying no notice to what the narrator is trying to say.

As evidence of this reading, there is the fourth stanza. It is a two-line stanza, balanced between the two men. One line begins with "he says" and the other with "I say." Under the normal unwritten rules of conversation, the second would be a response to the first, expressing an idea that was stirred up by what the first person said. Merwin's laconic style makes this unclear, however. With "he says" and "I say" so close together, it is very possible that both men speak their lines at the very same time. In the event of a tie, who wins? In this case the winner turns out to be the more aggressive speaker. The friend of the narrator continues telling his story as if the narrator never opened his mouth, while the narrator, put in his place, goes on to think about his own traumatic moment upon the death of his father, without discussing it out loud.

His silence seems an important part of the poem. The story his friend tells of lying to get away from his father and then living to regret his lie is powerful: now that his father is dead, there will never be any way to go back and undo what has been done. The narrator, however, has an even more powerful story. Probably. He actually held his father's hand: he had the sensory impression of coldness where a human temperature ought to be. What were the circumstances? Why was he too late to grasp his father's hand while it was still alive? No one will ever know because the conversation follows his friend's story, not his.

That seems as if it could be the way the poem's narrator wants things to be. It could well be that the narrator is the shy member of the pair—one extrovert and one introvert can make a complementary team, each filling in what the other lacks. But there has been something off about their relationship from the beginning. The way the narrator gives up his turn to be part of the discussion in the first stanza does not indicate a harmonious balance between these two friends. The first time the narrator agrees with his friend, he does not do so entirely of his own accord. He does not say he agrees until after his friend has said "you understand." It is not even a question, asking whether he does understand; it is a command, telling him that he *must* understand. It is almost impossible for a reader to say definitively whether the narrator's role as a silent partner in this conversation is by choice or if it is instead a role that is forced on him.

If one reads the narrator as a voice that has been silenced, squeezed out of a two-person conversation, it becomes very easy to question whether he really is being subversive in his quiet role in the poem. He may be too calm to push back and try to take his half of the conversation by force, but if he feels he is being kept from telling his story, he does not have to accept the role he is given.

The narrator's look out of the window, late in the poem, is dripping with significance. It comes at the high point of his friend's story, at the point where the father has given his son a convenient alibi for getting up and walking out the door without causing insult to either party, but before the friend says whether he took that opportunity. The look out the window can mean anything. It may mean the narrator is embarrassed to be talking about abandoning elderly fathers and is concerned, subconsciously, that the world in general may hear their secret. It could mean that this is where the narrator stops being agreeable about his friend's behavior that night long ago, having reached a point where he can no longer keep saying "yes."

Or maybe he is bored. Having tried to enter the conversation on several occasions and been shut out each time, he may see the writing on the wall: his friend has already admitted to being a bad man, so when he gets to the point in the story where his father has opened the door to neglect, there is no doubt about what will come next. The narrator cannot participate, and the story he is hearing is not captivating, at least not as interesting as his own story about his father's cold, dead hand.

A glance out the window is like a glance at a wristwatch. It is a sign of awareness that somewhere else, at this very moment, someone might be having a good time. These are the two most clearly drawn gestures in the entire poem, and it stands to reason that they would be related to each other. If the narrator's friend did sever a bond with his father with that impatient glance at his watch, then it would be entirely just if he were judged to be uninteresting in exactly the same way.

The glance out the window is followed by the enigmatic statement that the narrator's friend is older than he. In a poem about bonding, age hardly matters. In fact, such a difference would imply that their personal understanding is strong enough to transcend minor social barriers like age. In a poem about a man's becoming bored with his friend, age takes on an ironic meaning. The fact that the narrator is suddenly thinking about their age difference at this point in the poem implies that he sees his friend in a new way. The age gap that kept this man from caring about his father has landed on him now.

When two friends talk about a subject and they agree, something magical happens. It does not matter if the thing they are agreeing about is something great or something stupid or awful; there is still the magic of human empathy. If they are agreeing about a topic that will make them better people in the future, their bond deserves being celebrated in a poem, but there is also a fine statement being made if "Yesterday" is a poem about divine, cosmic justice. The narrator's friend might talk about escaping his father because his father was old and boring, and he might look back on his behavior with regret. Still, his regret is not enough punishment for what he did. For justice, he has to be abandoned himself by a glance out a window, by wandering attention, because he is now the one who is old and boring.

Source: David Kelly, Critical Essay on "Yesterday," in *Poetry for Students*, Gale, Cengage Learning, 2016.

H. L. Hix

In the following excerpt, Hix explains that "Yesterday" and the entire first section of Opening the Hand *center around themes of family.*

... The first section of *Opening the Hand* continues the attempt, begun in *Unframed Originals*, to confront his feelings toward his parents. In the early poems in the sequence, like "The Oars" and "Sunset Water," the son's resentment of the father and his attempts at self-justification are clear. In "The Oars," the father's "passivity, his timidity in not leaving the shore, his mere waiting for the time to be up contrast sharply continents is typically by airplane, yet it is he who rocks "in smooth waves near the edge of the sea" (*OH*), not only "at home" in the water but at one with it as "one by one the red waves out of themselves reach through me."

The resentment and self-assertion soften as the sequence of poems progresses. "Strawberries" recounts two premonitory experiences, one an observation and the other a dream, related to the father's death. While the narrator is outdoors "hoeing the sand of a small vegetable plot / for my mother" (*OH*), he observes two farm wagons, one "going into the valley / carrying a casket" and the other "coming out of the valley" carrying "a high load / of two kinds of berries one of them strawberries." That night he "dreamed of things wrong in the house," including "an insect of a kind I had seen him kill / climbing around the walls of his bathroom." His mother's first words to him the next morning confirm the observation and the dream. Like the premonition in "The Waving of a Hand," the poem immediately preceding it, the premonitions in "Strawberries" are given without inflection, so they mimic the father's guardedness and also suggest that peculiar stage of grief in which the only feeling is numbness. The barely repressed anger of "The Oars," though, has disappeared.

In "The Houses" the dissonance that caused the anger is present, but the anger itself has been replaced by self-doubt. In this poem, "the son" recalls two different occasions on which he saw houses that "the father" said did not exist. In the first case, the two go to the site together, but there is no house; in the second, the disagreement ends with the father's denying the existence of the house the son believes he saw. The son "stops telling what he has seen" (*OH*), although after the father's death he returns to both sites and sees both houses again. The difference between the father's point of view and the son's is portrayed as irreconcilable, but the father's authority induces the son to experience the difference as reason for self-doubt. He can verify his own experience for himself, but not in a way that will verify it for the father.

These earlier poems all build toward "Apparitions," one of the poems that attends to "the hand" of the book's title. "The dream images of the father in 'The Oars' and 'Sunset Water,' the psychic presentiments of his death in 'The Waving of a Hand' and 'Strawberries,' the play of imagination and memory of 'Sun and Rain' and

The speaker regrets that he did not spend more time with his father. (© *MSPhotographic | Shutterstock.com*)

with the son's history, both in life and in poems, of setting out, journeying, taking risks." In contrast to Merwin himself, whose personae in the poems have undertaken Odyssean wanderings, leaving behind the strictures of custom, the father here is portrayed as paralyzed. Unlike John Otto, unlike Noah's Raven, Merwin's father "sat in a rowboat / with its end on the bank below the house / holding onto the oars while the trains roared past" (*OH*). Similarly, in "Sunset Water," although the father "seems pale and timid, and clearly out of his element, the son is at home in the water. He rides its rhythms, and accepts and values both the newness and the beauty of the scene." Water was the primary venue for travel in his father's time: cities were built and commercial transport was conducted primarily along rivers, and travel between continents was by ship. In the son's time cities have come to be built primarily along roads, trains and trucks have assumed the largest portion of commercial transport, and travel between

'The Houses' culminate in 'Apparitions.' Simply 'opening the hand' reminds the poet of the past's uncanny persistence in the present—of his bodily inheritance of a familial likeness." "Apparitions" contains all the elements that appear separately in the other poems. In dream images the poet sees his parents' hands: "I will be looking down not from a window / and once more catch a glimpse of them hovering / above a whiteness like paper and much nearer than I would have thought" (*OH*). The psychic presentiments of death are now presentiments of his own death. He remembers that he has not played the piano "for as long as their age" (*OH*) and as he "feels mistakes approach" he recognizes what the hands became. In a play of imagination and memory, he envisions precisely recollected details about the hands as if the hands were actually present. He waits "for the smell of parsley and almonds" to "float to me from the polished translucent skin" (*OH*). That play of imagination and memory culminates in the hands' absence:

> but as I recognize those hands they are gone
> and that is what they are as well as what they
>   became
> without belief I still watch them wave to no one
>   but me
> across one last room and from one receding car
> it is six years now since they touched anything
> and whatever they can be said to have held
>   at all
> spreads in widening rings over the rimless
>   surface[.]
> (OH)

His own hands "that wash my face and tie my shoestrings / and have both sides and a day around them" are the only remnants of his parents' hands. Knowing "they are nobody's children" enforces recognition that he is his family now.

That in his works having to do with family history "reticence was one of the main things I was writing about," and that his "was a very reticent family" (*RM*, 326), makes "Yesterday" an important poem. There he accepts some of the responsibility for that reticence rather than blaming it almost entirely on his parents as in the previous poems and memoirs. Itself reticent, "Yesterday" begins with "my friend" (and thereby makes use of the custom of talking about "a close friend of mine" when broaching difficult subjects) and then intentionally obscures the distinction between the friend and the "I." The first line says both that my friend blames himself for being a bad son and that my friend blames me for being a bad son,

producing an ambiguity Merwin sustains throughout the poem. The son visits the father, but their apparently long-standing reticence asserts itself. The father catches the son looking at his watch and says "maybe / you have important work you are doing / or maybe you should be seeing / somebody I don't want to keep you" (*OH*), to which the son replies that "it was so / and I got up and left him then," even though "there was nowhere I had to go / and nothing I had to do." Even if he learned it from his father, and even if it remains strong enough to necessitate only an indirect admission, the narrator clearly recognizes his own complicity in the reticence that marred his relationship with both parents. His awareness of that guilt brings about a reconciliation of sorts that leads the later family poems in *The Rain in the Trees*, *Travels*, and *The Vixen* to present more sympathetic portraits of his parents.

Source: H. L. Hix, "Family," in *Understanding W. S. Merwin*, University of South Carolina Press, 1997, pp. 119–23.

SOURCES

Bloom, Harold, "Biography of W. S. Merwin," in *W. S. Merwin*, Chelsea House, 2004, pp. 17–19.

Bowers, Neal, "W. S. Merwin and Postmodern American Poetry," in *Sewanee Review*, Vol. 98, No. 2, Spring 1990, pp. 246–59.

Brunner, Edward, "*Opening the Hand*: The Variable Caesura and the Family Poems," in *W. S. Merwin: Essays on the Poetry*, edited by Cary Nelson and Ed Folsom, University of Illinois Press, 1987, p. 294.

"Buddha," *Biography.com*, A&E Television Networks, 2015, http://www.biography.com/people/buddha-9230587#the-buddha-emerges (accessed September 15, 2015).

Christie, Les, "The New American Household: 3 Generations, 1 Roof," CNNMoney, April 3, 2012, http://money.cnn.com/2012/04/03/real_estate/multi-generation-households/ (accessed September 15, 2015).

Freeman, John, "W. S. Merwin, the Eternal Apprentice," in *Virginia Quarterly Review*, Vol. 89, No. 4, Fall 2013, pp. 239, 242.

Hirsch, Edward, "W. S. Merwin, The Art of Poetry No. 38." in *Paris Review*, No. 102, Spring 1987, http://www.theparisreview.org/interviews/2692/the-art-of-poetry-no-38-w-s-merwin (accessed September 15, 2015).

Merwin, W. S., "Yesterday," in *Opening the Hand*, Atheneum, 1983, pp. 20–21.

Morrison, Malcolm H., "The Aging of the U.S. Population: Human Resource Implications," Bureau of Labor Statistics website, May 1983, p. 14, http://www.bls.gov/

opub/mlr/1983/05/art2full.pdf (accessed September 24, 2015).

Ortman, Jennifer M., Victoria A. Velkoff, and Howard Hogan, "An Aging Nation: The Older Population in the United States," in *Current Population Reports*, U.S. Census Bureau, P25-1140, May 2014, https://www.census.gov/prod/2014pubs/p25-1140.pdf (accessed September 15, 2015).

Review of *Flower & Hand: Poems, 1977–1983*, in *Publishers Weekly*, February 24, 1997, p. 86.

"W. S. Merwin Biography," *Biography.com*, A&E Television Networks, 2015, http://www.biography.com/people/ws-merwin-38820 (accessed September 14, 2015).

"Zen," in *Encyclopædia Britannica*, 2015, http://www.britannica.com/topic/Zen (accessed September 15, 2015).

FURTHER READING

Christhilf, Mark, *W. S. Merwin, the Mythmaker*, University of Missouri Press, 1986.

This small but thorough volume follows the poet's early career up to *Opening the Hand*, the collection that "Yesterday" comes from. Christhilf examines Merwin's work in the context of mythmaking, initially in a multicultural context and later in real-world social situations.

Elliott, David L., "An Interview with W. S. Merwin," in *Conversations with W. S. Merwin*, edited by Michael Wutz and Hal Crimmel, University Press of Mississippi, 2015, pp. 91–113.

Merwin has always been generous about giving interviews. This one, conducted soon after the publication of *Opening the Hand*, focuses on the changes that his poetry had undergone up to that point in his career and the reasons he had for exploring new styles and different modes.

Even Though the Whole World Is Burning, directed by Stefan Schaefer, Passion River Films, 2015.

Merwin, his family, his friends, and his critics are interviewed in this documentary in an attempt to capture on film the personality that has made his poetry resonate throughout sixty years in the public eye.

Katchadourian, Herant, *Guilt: The Bite of Conscience*, Stanford General Books, Stanford University Press, 2010.

The whole point of Merwin's poem is the sense of underlying guilt. It is felt by the man who abandoned his aged father, but the narrator's story with his own father seems to imply an unspoken sense of guilt. In Katchadourian's book, the social, historical, and philosophical implications of guilt as a driving force of the modern world are discussed.

Kennedy, Sarah, "Millennial Merwin," in *Until Everything Is Continuous Again*, edited by Jonathan Weinert and Kevin Prufer, WordFarm, 2012, pp. 129–36.

Kennedy gives a personal response to the direction in which Merwin's work has taken him in the twenty-first century, focusing on his ability to write about dark themes without making his poetry linger in a dark mood or attitude.

Ronald, Matthew, *How to Deal with Difficult Aging Parents: A Relationship Guide for Stressed Out Adult Children*, Gipfel Publishing, 2015.

This book is a modern popular psychology approach to the ways adults interact with their aging parents. Its focus is on parents who suffer loss of mental capacity, from dementia or other causes, but Ronald's explanations of parents who are "difficult" would certainly have a familiar ring to the busy characters in "Yesterday."

SUGGESTED SEARCH TERMS

W. S. Merwin

Merwin AND Yesterday

Merwin AND Opening the Hand

Merwin AND early poetry

Merwin AND parent/child

Merwin AND punctuation

poetry AND aging parents

parents AND guilt AND poetry

W. S. Merwin AND poet laureate

Zen poetry AND W. S. Merwin

Glossary of Literary Terms

A

Abstract: Used as a noun, the term refers to a short summary or outline of a longer work. As an adjective applied to writing or literary works, abstract refers to words or phrases that name things not knowable through the five senses.

Accent: The emphasis or stress placed on a syllable in poetry. Traditional poetry commonly uses patterns of accented and unaccented syllables (known as feet) that create distinct rhythms. Much modern poetry uses less formal arrangements that create a sense of freedom and spontaneity.

Aestheticism: A literary and artistic movement of the nineteenth century. Followers of the movement believed that art should not be mixed with social, political, or moral teaching. The statement "art for art's sake" is a good summary of aestheticism. The movement had its roots in France, but it gained widespread importance in England in the last half of the nineteenth century, where it helped change the Victorian practice of including moral lessons in literature.

Affective Fallacy: An error in judging the merits or faults of a work of literature. The "error" results from stressing the importance of the work's effect upon the reader—that is, how it makes a reader "feel" emotionally, what it does as a literary work—instead of stressing its inner qualities as a created object, or what it "is."

Age of Johnson: The period in English literature between 1750 and 1798, named after the most prominent literary figure of the age, Samuel Johnson. Works written during this time are noted for their emphasis on "sensibility," or emotional quality. These works formed a transition between the rational works of the Age of Reason, or Neoclassical period, and the emphasis on individual feelings and responses of the Romantic period.

Age of Reason: See *Neoclassicism*

Age of Sensibility: See *Age of Johnson*

Agrarians: A group of Southern American writers of the 1930s and 1940s who fostered an economic and cultural program for the South based on agriculture, in opposition to the industrial society of the North. The term can refer to any group that promotes the value of farm life and agricultural society.

Alexandrine Meter: See *Meter*

Allegory: A narrative technique in which characters representing things or abstract ideas are used to convey a message or teach a lesson. Allegory is typically used to teach moral, ethical, or religious lessons but is sometimes used for satiric or political purposes.

Alliteration: A poetic device where the first consonant sounds or any vowel sounds in words or syllables are repeated.

Allusion: A reference to a familiar literary or historical person or event, used to make an idea more easily understood.

Amerind Literature: The writing and oral traditions of Native Americans. Native American literature was originally passed on by word of mouth, so it consisted largely of stories and events that were easily memorized. Amerind prose is often rhythmic like poetry because it was recited to the beat of a ceremonial drum.

Analogy: A comparison of two things made to explain something unfamiliar through its similarities to something familiar, or to prove one point based on the acceptedness of another. Similes and metaphors are types of analogies.

Anapest: See *Foot*

Angry Young Men: A group of British writers of the 1950s whose work expressed bitterness and disillusionment with society. Common to their work is an anti-hero who rebels against a corrupt social order and strives for personal integrity.

Anthropomorphism: The presentation of animals or objects in human shape or with human characteristics. The term is derived from the Greek word for "human form."

Antimasque: See *Masque*

Antithesis: The antithesis of something is its direct opposite. In literature, the use of antithesis as a figure of speech results in two statements that show a contrast through the balancing of two opposite ideas. Technically, it is the second portion of the statement that is defined as the "antithesis"; the first portion is the "thesis."

Apocrypha: Writings tentatively attributed to an author but not proven or universally accepted to be their works. The term was originally applied to certain books of the Bible that were not considered inspired and so were not included in the "sacred canon."

Apollonian and Dionysian: The two impulses believed to guide authors of dramatic tragedy. The Apollonian impulse is named after Apollo, the Greek god of light and beauty and the symbol of intellectual order.

The Dionysian impulse is named after Dionysus, the Greek god of wine and the symbol of the unrestrained forces of nature. The Apollonian impulse is to create a rational, harmonious world, while the Dionysian is to express the irrational forces of personality.

Apostrophe: A statement, question, or request addressed to an inanimate object or concept or to a nonexistent or absent person.

Archetype: The word archetype is commonly used to describe an original pattern or model from which all other things of the same kind are made. This term was introduced to literary criticism from the psychology of Carl Jung. It expresses Jung's theory that behind every person's "unconscious," or repressed memories of the past, lies the "collective unconscious" of the human race: memories of the countless typical experiences of our ancestors. These memories are said to prompt illogical associations that trigger powerful emotions in the reader. Often, the emotional process is primitive, even primordial. Archetypes are the literary images that grow out of the "collective unconscious." They appear in literature as incidents and plots that repeat basic patterns of life. They may also appear as stereotyped characters.

Argument: The argument of a work is the author's subject matter or principal idea.

Art for Art's Sake: See *Aestheticism*

Assonance: The repetition of similar vowel sounds in poetry.

Audience: The people for whom a piece of literature is written. Authors usually write with a certain audience in mind, for example, children, members of a religious or ethnic group, or colleagues in a professional field. The term "audience" also applies to the people who gather to see or hear any performance, including plays, poetry readings, speeches, and concerts.

Automatic Writing: Writing carried out without a preconceived plan in an effort to capture every random thought. Authors who engage in automatic writing typically do not revise their work, preferring instead to preserve the revealed truth and beauty of spontaneous expression.

Avant-garde: A French term meaning "vanguard." It is used in literary criticism to describe new writing that rejects traditional approaches to literature in favor of innovations in style or content.

B

Ballad: A short poem that tells a simple story and has a repeated refrain. Ballads were originally intended to be sung. Early ballads, known as folk ballads, were passed down through generations, so their authors are often unknown. Later ballads composed by known authors are called literary ballads.

Baroque: A term used in literary criticism to describe literature that is complex or ornate in style or diction. Baroque works typically express tension, anxiety, and violent emotion. The term "Baroque Age" designates a period in Western European literature beginning in the late sixteenth century and ending about one hundred years later. Works of this period often mirror the qualities of works more generally associated with the label "baroque" and sometimes feature elaborate conceits.

Baroque Age: See *Baroque*

Baroque Period: See *Baroque*

Beat Generation: See *Beat Movement*

Beat Movement: A period featuring a group of American poets and novelists of the 1950s and 1960s—including Jack Kerouac, Allen Ginsberg, Gregory Corso, William S. Burroughs, and Lawrence Ferlinghetti—who rejected established social and literary values. Using such techniques as stream of consciousness writing and jazz-influenced free verse and focusing on unusual or abnormal states of mind—generated by religious ecstasy or the use of drugs—the Beat writers aimed to create works that were unconventional in both form and subject matter.

Beat Poets: See *Beat Movement*

Beats, The: See *Beat Movement*

Belles-lettres: A French term meaning "fine letters" or "beautiful writing." It is often used as a synonym for literature, typically referring to imaginative and artistic rather than scientific or expository writing. Current usage sometimes restricts the meaning to light or humorous writing and appreciative essays about literature.

Black Aesthetic Movement: A period of artistic and literary development among African

Americans in the 1960s and early 1970s. This was the first major African-American artistic movement since the Harlem Renaissance and was closely paralleled by the civil rights and black power movements. The black aesthetic writers attempted to produce works of art that would be meaningful to the black masses. Key figures in black aesthetics included one of its founders, poet and playwright Amiri Baraka, formerly known as LeRoi Jones; poet and essayist Haki R. Madhubuti, formerly Don L. Lee; poet and playwright Sonia Sanchez; and dramatist Ed Bullins.

Black Arts Movement: See *Black Aesthetic Movement*

Black Comedy: See *Black Humor*

Black Humor: Writing that places grotesque elements side by side with humorous ones in an attempt to shock the reader, forcing him or her to laugh at the horrifying reality of a disordered world.

Black Mountain School: Black Mountain College and three of its instructors—Robert Creeley, Robert Duncan, and Charles Olson—were all influential in projective verse, so poets working in projective verse are now referred as members of the Black Mountain school.

Blank Verse: Loosely, any unrhymed poetry, but more generally, unrhymed iambic pentameter verse (composed of lines of five two-syllable feet with the first syllable accented, the second unaccented). Blank verse has been used by poets since the Renaissance for its flexibility and its graceful, dignified tone.

Bloomsbury Group: A group of English writers, artists, and intellectuals who held informal artistic and philosophical discussions in Bloomsbury, a district of London, from around 1907 to the early 1930s. The Bloomsbury Group held no uniform philosophical beliefs but did commonly express an aversion to moral prudery and a desire for greater social tolerance.

Bon Mot: A French term meaning "good word." A *bon mot* is a witty remark or clever observation.

Breath Verse: See *Projective Verse*

Burlesque: Any literary work that uses exaggeration to make its subject appear ridiculous, either by treating a trivial subject with profound seriousness or by treating a dignified subject frivolously. The word "burlesque" may also be used as an adjective, as in "burlesque show," to mean "striptease act."

C

Cadence: The natural rhythm of language caused by the alternation of accented and unaccented syllables. Much modern poetry—notably free verse—deliberately manipulates cadence to create complex rhythmic effects.

Caesura: A pause in a line of poetry, usually occurring near the middle. It typically corresponds to a break in the natural rhythm or sense of the line but is sometimes shifted to create special meanings or rhythmic effects.

Canzone: A short Italian or Provencal lyric poem, commonly about love and often set to music. The *canzone* has no set form but typically contains five or six stanzas made up of seven to twenty lines of eleven syllables each. A shorter, five- to ten-line "envoy," or concluding stanza, completes the poem.

Carpe Diem: A Latin term meaning "seize the day." This is a traditional theme of poetry, especially lyrics. A *carpe diem* poem advises the reader or the person it addresses to live for today and enjoy the pleasures of the moment.

Catharsis: The release or purging of unwanted emotions—specifically fear and pity—brought about by exposure to art. The term was first used by the Greek philosopher Aristotle in his *Poetics* to refer to the desired effect of tragedy on spectators.

Celtic Renaissance: A period of Irish literary and cultural history at the end of the nineteenth century. Followers of the movement aimed to create a romantic vision of Celtic myth and legend. The most significant works of the Celtic Renaissance typically present a dreamy, unreal world, usually in reaction against the reality of contemporary problems.

Celtic Twilight: See *Celtic Renaissance*

Character: Broadly speaking, a person in a literary work. The actions of characters are what constitute the plot of a story, novel, or poem. There are numerous types of characters, ranging from simple, stereotypical figures to intricate, multifaceted ones. In the techniques of anthropomorphism and personification, animals—and even places or things—can assume aspects of character.

"Characterization" is the process by which an author creates vivid, believable characters in a work of art. This may be done in a variety of ways, including (1) direct description of the character by the narrator; (2) the direct presentation of the speech, thoughts, or actions of the character; and (3) the responses of other characters to the character. The term "character" also refers to a form originated by the ancient Greek writer Theophrastus that later became popular in the seventeenth and eighteenth centuries. It is a short essay or sketch of a person who prominently displays a specific attribute or quality, such as miserliness or ambition.

Characterization: See *Character*

Classical: In its strictest definition in literary criticism, classicism refers to works of ancient Greek or Roman literature. The term may also be used to describe a literary work of recognized importance (a "classic") from any time period or literature that exhibits the traits of classicism.

Classicism: A term used in literary criticism to describe critical doctrines that have their roots in ancient Greek and Roman literature, philosophy, and art. Works associated with classicism typically exhibit restraint on the part of the author, unity of design and purpose, clarity, simplicity, logical organization, and respect for tradition.

Colloquialism: A word, phrase, or form of pronunciation that is acceptable in casual conversation but not in formal, written communication. It is considered more acceptable than slang.

Complaint: A lyric poem, popular in the Renaissance, in which the speaker expresses sorrow about his or her condition. Typically, the speaker's sadness is caused by an unresponsive lover, but some complaints cite other sources of unhappiness, such as poverty or fate.

Conceit: A clever and fanciful metaphor, usually expressed through elaborate and extended comparison, that presents a striking parallel between two seemingly dissimilar things—for example, elaborately comparing a beautiful woman to an object like a garden or the sun. The conceit was a popular device throughout the Elizabethan Age and Baroque Age and was the principal technique of the seventeenth-century English metaphysical poets. This usage of the word conceit is unrelated to the best-known definition of conceit as an arrogant attitude or behavior.

Concrete: Concrete is the opposite of abstract, and refers to a thing that actually exists or a description that allows the reader to experience an object or concept with the senses.

Concrete Poetry: Poetry in which visual elements play a large part in the poetic effect. Punctuation marks, letters, or words are arranged on a page to form a visual design: a cross, for example, or a bumblebee.

Confessional Poetry: A form of poetry in which the poet reveals very personal, intimate, sometimes shocking information about himself or herself.

Connotation: The impression that a word gives beyond its defined meaning. Connotations may be universally understood or may be significant only to a certain group.

Consonance: Consonance occurs in poetry when words appearing at the ends of two or more verses have similar final consonant sounds but have final vowel sounds that differ, as with "stuff" and "off."

Convention: Any widely accepted literary device, style, or form.

Corrido: A Mexican ballad.

Couplet: Two lines of poetry with the same rhyme and meter, often expressing a complete and self-contained thought.

Criticism: The systematic study and evaluation of literary works, usually based on a specific method or set of principles. An important part of literary studies since ancient times, the practice of criticism has given rise to numerous theories, methods, and "schools," sometimes producing conflicting, even contradictory, interpretations of literature in general as well as of individual works. Even such basic issues as what constitutes a poem or a novel have been the subject of much criticism over the centuries.

D

Dactyl: See *Foot*

Dadaism: A protest movement in art and literature founded by Tristan Tzara in 1916. Followers of the movement expressed their outrage at the destruction brought about by World War I by revolting against numerous forms of social convention. The Dadaists presented works marked by calculated madness and flamboyant nonsense. They stressed total freedom of expression, commonly through primitive displays of emotion and illogical, often senseless, poetry. The movement ended shortly after the war, when it was replaced by surrealism.

Decadent: See *Decadents*

Decadents: The followers of a nineteenth-century literary movement that had its beginnings in French aestheticism. Decadent literature displays a fascination with perverse and morbid states; a search for novelty and sensation—the "new thrill"; a preoccupation with mysticism; and a belief in the senselessness of human existence. The movement is closely associated with the doctrine Art for Art's Sake. The term "decadence" is sometimes used to denote a decline in the quality of art or literature following a period of greatness.

Deconstruction: A method of literary criticism developed by Jacques Derrida and characterized by multiple conflicting interpretations of a given work. Deconstructionists consider the impact of the language of a work and suggest that the true meaning of the work is not necessarily the meaning that the author intended.

Deduction: The process of reaching a conclusion through reasoning from general premises to a specific premise.

Denotation: The definition of a word, apart from the impressions or feelings it creates in the reader.

Diction: The selection and arrangement of words in a literary work. Either or both may vary depending on the desired effect. There are four general types of diction: "formal," used in scholarly or lofty writing; "informal," used in relaxed but educated conversation; "colloquial," used in everyday speech; and "slang," containing newly coined words and other terms not accepted in formal usage.

Didactic: A term used to describe works of literature that aim to teach some moral, religious, political, or practical lesson. Although didactic elements are often found in artistically pleasing works, the term "didactic" usually refers to literature in which the message is more important than the form. The term may also be used to criticize a work that the critic finds "overly didactic," that is, heavy-handed in its delivery of a lesson.

Dimeter: See *Meter*

Dionysian: See *Apollonian and Dionysian*

Discordia concours: A Latin phrase meaning "discord in harmony." The term was coined by the eighteenth-century English writer Samuel Johnson to describe "a combination of dissimilar images or discovery of occult resemblances in things apparently unlike." Johnson created the expression by reversing a phrase by the Latin poet Horace.

Dissonance: A combination of harsh or jarring sounds, especially in poetry. Although such combinations may be accidental, poets sometimes intentionally make them to achieve particular effects. Dissonance is also sometimes used to refer to close but not identical rhymes. When this is the case, the word functions as a synonym for consonance.

Double Entendre: A corruption of a French phrase meaning "double meaning." The term is used to indicate a word or phrase that is deliberately ambiguous, especially when one of the meanings is risque or improper.

Draft: Any preliminary version of a written work. An author may write dozens of drafts which are revised to form the final work, or he or she may write only one, with few or no revisions.

Dramatic Monologue: See *Monologue*

Dramatic Poetry: Any lyric work that employs elements of drama such as dialogue, conflict, or characterization, but excluding works that are intended for stage presentation.

Dream Allegory: See *Dream Vision*

Dream Vision: A literary convention, chiefly of the Middle Ages. In a dream vision a story is presented as a literal dream of the narrator. This device was commonly used to teach moral and religious lessons.

E

Eclogue: In classical literature, a poem featuring rural themes and structured as a dialogue among shepherds. Eclogues often took specific poetic forms, such as elegies or love poems. Some were written as the soliloquy of a shepherd. In later centuries, "eclogue" came to refer to any poem that was in the pastoral tradition or that had a dialogue or monologue structure.

Edwardian: Describes cultural conventions identified with the period of the reign of Edward VII of England (1901-1910). Writers of the Edwardian Age typically displayed a strong reaction against the propriety and conservatism of the Victorian Age. Their work often exhibits distrust of authority in religion, politics, and art and expresses strong doubts about the soundness of conventional values.

Edwardian Age: See *Edwardian*

Electra Complex: A daughter's amorous obsession with her father.

Elegy: A lyric poem that laments the death of a person or the eventual death of all people. In a conventional elegy, set in a classical world, the poet and subject are spoken of as shepherds. In modern criticism, the word elegy is often used to refer to a poem that is melancholy or mournfully contemplative.

Elizabethan Age: A period of great economic growth, religious controversy, and nationalism closely associated with the reign of Elizabeth I of England (1558-1603). The Elizabethan Age is considered a part of the general renaissance—that is, the flowering of arts and literature—that took place in Europe during the fourteenth through sixteenth centuries. The era is considered the golden age of English literature. The most important dramas in English and a great deal of lyric poetry were produced during this period, and modern English criticism began around this time.

Empathy: A sense of shared experience, including emotional and physical feelings, with someone or something other than oneself. Empathy is often used to describe the response of a reader to a literary character.

English Sonnet: See *Sonnet*

Enjambment: The running over of the sense and structure of a line of verse or a couplet into the following verse or couplet.

Enlightenment, The: An eighteenth-century philosophical movement. It began in France but had a wide impact throughout Europe and America. Thinkers of the Enlightenment valued reason and believed that both the individual and society could achieve a state of perfection. Corresponding to this essentially humanist vision was a resistance to religious authority.

Epic: A long narrative poem about the adventures of a hero of great historic or legendary importance. The setting is vast and the action is often given cosmic significance through the intervention of supernatural forces such as gods, angels, or demons. Epics are typically written in a classical style of grand simplicity with elaborate metaphors and allusions that enhance the symbolic importance of a hero's adventures.

Epic Simile: See *Homeric Simile*

Epigram: A saying that makes the speaker's point quickly and concisely.

Epilogue: A concluding statement or section of a literary work. In dramas, particularly those of the seventeenth and eighteenth centuries, the epilogue is a closing speech, often in verse, delivered by an actor at the end of a play and spoken directly to the audience.

Epiphany: A sudden revelation of truth inspired by a seemingly trivial incident.

Epitaph: An inscription on a tomb or tombstone, or a verse written on the occasion of a person's death. Epitaphs may be serious or humorous.

Epithalamion: A song or poem written to honor and commemorate a marriage ceremony.

Epithalamium: See *Epithalamion*

Epithet: A word or phrase, often disparaging or abusive, that expresses a character trait of someone or something.

Erziehungsroman: See *Bildungsroman*

Essay: A prose composition with a focused subject of discussion. The term was coined by Michel de Montaigne to describe his 1580 collection of brief, informal reflections on himself and on various topics relating to human nature. An essay can also be a long, systematic discourse.

Existentialism: A predominantly twentieth-century philosophy concerned with the nature and perception of human existence. There are two major strains of existentialist thought: atheistic and Christian. Followers of atheistic existentialism believe that the individual is alone in a godless universe and that the basic human condition is one of suffering and loneliness. Nevertheless, because there are no fixed values, individuals can create their own characters—indeed, they can shape themselves—through the exercise of free will. The atheistic strain culminates in and is popularly associated with the works of Jean-Paul Sartre. The Christian existentialists, on the other hand, believe that only in God may people find freedom from life's anguish. The two strains hold certain beliefs in common: that existence cannot be fully understood or described through empirical effort; that anguish is a universal element of life; that individuals must bear responsibility for their actions; and that there is no common standard of behavior or perception for religious and ethical matters.

Expatriates: See *Expatriatism*

Expatriatism: The practice of leaving one's country to live for an extended period in another country.

Exposition: Writing intended to explain the nature of an idea, thing, or theme. Expository writing is often combined with description, narration, or argument. In dramatic writing, the exposition is the introductory material which presents the characters, setting, and tone of the play.

Expressionism: An indistinct literary term, originally used to describe an early twentieth-century school of German painting. The term applies to almost any mode of unconventional, highly subjective writing that distorts reality in some way.

Extended Monologue: See *Monologue*

F

Feet: See *Foot*

Feminine Rhyme: See *Rhyme*

Fiction: Any story that is the product of imagination rather than a documentation of fact. Characters and events in such narratives may be based in real life but their ultimate form and configuration is a creation of the author.

Figurative Language: A technique in writing in which the author temporarily interrupts the order, construction, or meaning of the writing for a particular effect. This interruption takes the form of one or more figures of speech such as hyperbole, irony, or simile. Figurative language is the opposite of literal language, in which every word is truthful, accurate, and free of exaggeration or embellishment.

Figures of Speech: Writing that differs from customary conventions for construction, meaning, order, or significance for the purpose of a special meaning or effect. There are two major types of figures of speech: rhetorical figures, which do not make changes in the meaning of the words, and tropes, which do.

Fin de siecle: A French term meaning "end of the century." The term is used to denote the last decade of the nineteenth century, a transition period when writers and other artists abandoned old conventions and looked for new techniques and objectives.

First Person: See *Point of View*

Folk Ballad: See *Ballad*

Folklore: Traditions and myths preserved in a culture or group of people. Typically, these are passed on by word of mouth in various forms—such as legends, songs, and proverbs—or preserved in customs and ceremonies. This term was first used by W. J. Thoms in 1846.

Folktale: A story originating in oral tradition. Folktales fall into a variety of categories, including legends, ghost stories, fairy tales, fables, and anecdotes based on historical figures and events.

Foot: The smallest unit of rhythm in a line of poetry. In English-language poetry, a foot is typically one accented syllable combined with one or two unaccented syllables.

Form: The pattern or construction of a work which identifies its genre and distinguishes it from other genres.

Formalism: In literary criticism, the belief that literature should follow prescribed rules of construction, such as those that govern the sonnet form.

Fourteener Meter: See *Meter*

Free Verse: Poetry that lacks regular metrical and rhyme patterns but that tries to capture the cadences of everyday speech. The form allows a poet to exploit a variety of rhythmical effects within a single poem.

Futurism: A flamboyant literary and artistic movement that developed in France, Italy, and Russia from 1908 through the 1920s. Futurist theater and poetry abandoned traditional literary forms. In their place, followers of the movement attempted to achieve total freedom of expression through bizarre imagery and deformed or newly invented words. The Futurists were self-consciously modern artists who attempted to incorporate the appearances and sounds of modern life into their work.

G

Genre: A category of literary work. In critical theory, genre may refer to both the content of a given work—tragedy, comedy, pastoral—and to its form, such as poetry, novel, or drama.

Genteel Tradition: A term coined by critic George Santayana to describe the literary practice of certain late nineteenth-century American writers, especially New Englanders. Followers of the Genteel Tradition emphasized conventionality in social, religious, moral, and literary standards.

Georgian Age: See *Georgian Poets*

Georgian Period: See *Georgian Poets*

Georgian Poets: A loose grouping of English poets during the years 1912-1922. The Georgians reacted against certain literary schools and practices, especially Victorian wordiness, turn-of-the-century aestheticism, and contemporary urban realism. In their place, the Georgians embraced the nineteenth-century poetic practices of William Wordsworth and the other Lake Poets.

Georgic: A poem about farming and the farmer's way of life, named from Virgil's *Georgics*.

Gilded Age: A period in American history during the 1870s characterized by political corruption and materialism. A number of important novels of social and political criticism were written during this time.

Gothic: See *Gothicism*

Gothicism: In literary criticism, works characterized by a taste for the medieval or morbidly attractive. A gothic novel prominently features elements of horror, the supernatural, gloom, and violence: clanking chains, terror, charnel houses, ghosts, medieval castles, and mysteriously slamming doors. The term "gothic novel" is also applied to novels that lack elements of the traditional Gothic setting but that create a similar atmosphere of terror or dread.

Graveyard School: A group of eighteenth-century English poets who wrote long, picturesque meditations on death. Their works were designed to cause the reader to ponder immortality.

Great Chain of Being: The belief that all things and creatures in nature are organized in a hierarchy from inanimate objects at the bottom to God at the top. This system of belief was popular in the seventeenth and eighteenth centuries.

Grotesque: In literary criticism, the subject matter of a work or a style of expression characterized by exaggeration, deformity, freakishness, and disorder. The grotesque often includes an element of comic absurdity.

H

Haiku: The shortest form of Japanese poetry, constructed in three lines of five, seven, and five syllables respectively. The message of a *haiku* poem usually centers on some aspect of spirituality and provokes an emotional response in the reader.

Half Rhyme: See *Consonance*

Harlem Renaissance: The Harlem Renaissance of the 1920s is generally considered the first significant movement of black writers and artists in the United States. During this period, new and established black writers published more fiction and poetry than ever before, the first influential black literary journals were established, and black authors and artists received their first widespread recognition and serious critical appraisal. Among the major writers associated with this period are Claude McKay, Jean Toomer, Countee Cullen, Langston Hughes, Arna Bontemps, Nella Larsen, and Zora Neale Hurston.

Hellenism: Imitation of ancient Greek thought or styles. Also, an approach to life that focuses on the growth and development of the intellect. "Hellenism" is sometimes used to refer to the belief that reason can be applied to examine all human experience.

Heptameter: See *Meter*

Hero/Heroine: The principal sympathetic character (male or female) in a literary work. Heroes and heroines typically exhibit admirable traits: idealism, courage, and integrity, for example.

Heroic Couplet: A rhyming couplet written in iambic pentameter (a verse with five iambic feet).

Heroic Line: The meter and length of a line of verse in epic or heroic poetry. This varies by language and time period.

Heroine: See *Hero/Heroine*

Hexameter: See *Meter*

Historical Criticism: The study of a work based on its impact on the world of the time period in which it was written.

Hokku: See *Haiku*

Holocaust: See *Holocaust Literature*

Holocaust Literature: Literature influenced by or written about the Holocaust of World War II. Such literature includes true stories of survival in concentration camps, escape, and life after the war, as well as fictional works and poetry.

Homeric Simile: An elaborate, detailed comparison written as a simile many lines in length.

Horatian Satire: See *Satire*

Humanism: A philosophy that places faith in the dignity of humankind and rejects the medieval perception of the individual as a weak, fallen creature. "Humanists" typically believe in the perfectibility of human nature and view reason and education as the means to that end.

Humors: Mentions of the humors refer to the ancient Greek theory that a person's health and personality were determined by the balance of four basic fluids in the body: blood, phlegm, yellow bile, and black bile. A dominance of any fluid would cause extremes in behavior. An excess of blood created a sanguine person who was joyful, aggressive, and passionate; a phlegmatic person was shy, fearful, and sluggish; too much yellow bile led to a choleric temperament characterized by impatience, anger, bitterness, and stubbornness; and excessive black bile created melancholy, a state of laziness, gluttony, and lack of motivation.

Humours: See *Humors*

Hyperbole: In literary criticism, deliberate exaggeration used to achieve an effect.

I

Iamb: See *Foot*

Idiom: A word construction or verbal expression closely associated with a given language.

Image: A concrete representation of an object or sensory experience. Typically, such a representation helps evoke the feelings associated with the object or experience itself. Images are either "literal" or "figurative." Literal images are especially concrete and involve little or no extension of the obvious meaning of the words used to express them. Figurative images do not follow the literal meaning of the words exactly. Images in literature are usually visual, but the term "image" can also refer to the representation of any sensory experience.

Imagery: The array of images in a literary work. Also, figurative language.

Imagism: An English and American poetry movement that flourished between 1908 and 1917. The Imagists used precise, clearly presented images in their works. They also used common, everyday speech and aimed for conciseness, concrete imagery, and the creation of new rhythms.

In medias res: A Latin term meaning "in the middle of things." It refers to the technique of beginning a story at its midpoint and then using various flashback devices to reveal previous action.

Induction: The process of reaching a conclusion by reasoning from specific premises to form a general premise. Also, an introductory portion of a work of literature, especially a play.

Intentional Fallacy: The belief that judgments of a literary work based solely on an author's stated or implied intentions are false and misleading. Critics who believe in the concept of the intentional fallacy typically argue that the work itself is sufficient matter for interpretation, even though they may concede that an author's statement of purpose can be useful.

Interior Monologue: A narrative technique in which characters' thoughts are revealed in a way that appears to be uncontrolled by the author. The interior monologue typically aims to reveal the inner self of a character. It portrays emotional experiences as they occur at both a conscious and unconscious level. Images are often used to represent sensations or emotions.

Internal Rhyme: Rhyme that occurs within a single line of verse.

Irish Literary Renaissance: A late nineteenth- and early twentieth-century movement in Irish literature. Members of the movement aimed to reduce the influence of British culture in Ireland and create an Irish national literature.

Irony: In literary criticism, the effect of language in which the intended meaning is the opposite of what is stated.

Italian Sonnet: See *Sonnet*

J

Jacobean Age: The period of the reign of James I of England (1603-1625). The early literature of this period reflected the worldview of the Elizabethan Age, but a darker, more cynical attitude steadily grew in the art and literature of the Jacobean Age. This was an important time for English drama and poetry.

Jargon: Language that is used or understood only by a select group of people. Jargon may refer to terminology used in a certain profession, such as computer jargon, or it may refer to any nonsensical language that is not understood by most people.

Journalism: Writing intended for publication in a newspaper or magazine, or for broadcast on a radio or television program featuring news, sports, entertainment, or other timely material.

K

Knickerbocker Group: A somewhat indistinct group of New York writers of the first half of the nineteenth century. Members of the group were linked only by location and a common theme: New York life.

Kunstlerroman: See *Bildungsroman*

L

Lais: See *Lay*

Lake Poets: See *Lake School*

Lake School: These poets all lived in the Lake District of England at the turn of the nineteenth century. As a group, they followed no single "school" of thought or literary practice, although their works were uniformly disparaged by the *Edinburgh Review*.

Lay: A song or simple narrative poem. The form originated in medieval France. Early French *lais* were often based on the Celtic legends and other tales sung by Breton minstrels—thus the name of the "Breton lay." In fourteenth-century England, the term "lay" was used to describe short narratives written in imitation of the Breton lays.

Leitmotiv: See *Motif*

Literal Language: An author uses literal language when he or she writes without exaggerating or embellishing the subject matter and without any tools of figurative language.

Literary Ballad: See *Ballad*

Literature: Literature is broadly defined as any written or spoken material, but the term most often refers to creative works.

Lost Generation: A term first used by Gertrude Stein to describe the post-World War I generation of American writers: men and women haunted by a sense of betrayal and emptiness brought about by the destructiveness of the war.

Lyric Poetry: A poem expressing the subjective feelings and personal emotions of the poet. Such poetry is melodic, since it was originally accompanied by a lyre in recitals. Most Western poetry in the twentieth century may be classified as lyrical.

M

Mannerism: Exaggerated, artificial adherence to a literary manner or style. Also, a popular style of the visual arts of late sixteenth-century Europe that was marked by elongation of the human form and by intentional spatial distortion. Literary works that are self-consciously high-toned and artistic are often said to be "mannered."

Masculine Rhyme: See *Rhyme*

Measure: The foot, verse, or time sequence used in a literary work, especially a poem. Measure is often used somewhat incorrectly as a synonym for meter.

Metaphor: A figure of speech that expresses an idea through the image of another object. Metaphors suggest the essence of the first object by identifying it with certain qualities of the second object.

Metaphysical Conceit: See *Conceit*

Metaphysical Poetry: The body of poetry produced by a group of seventeenth-century English writers called the "Metaphysical Poets." The group includes John Donne and Andrew Marvell. The Metaphysical Poets made use of everyday speech, intellectual analysis, and unique imagery. They aimed to portray the ordinary conflicts and contradictions of life. Their poems often took the form of an argument, and many of them emphasize physical and religious love as well as the fleeting nature of life. Elaborate conceits are typical in metaphysical poetry.

Metaphysical Poets: See *Metaphysical Poetry*

Meter: In literary criticism, the repetition of sound patterns that creates a rhythm in poetry. The patterns are based on the number of syllables and the presence and absence of accents. The unit of rhythm in a line is called a foot. Types of meter are classified according to the number of feet in a line. These are the standard English lines: Monometer, one foot; Dimeter, two feet; Trimeter, three feet; Tetrameter, four feet; Pentameter, five feet; Hexameter, six feet (also called the Alexandrine); Heptameter, seven feet (also called the "Fourteener" when the feet are iambic).

Modernism: Modern literary practices. Also, the principles of a literary school that lasted from roughly the beginning of the twentieth century until the end of World War II. Modernism is defined by its rejection of the literary conventions of the nineteenth century and by its opposition to conventional morality, taste, traditions, and economic values.

Monologue: A composition, written or oral, by a single individual. More specifically, a speech given by a single individual in a drama or other public entertainment. It has no set length, although it is usually several or more lines long.

Monometer: See *Meter*

Mood: The prevailing emotions of a work or of the author in his or her creation of the work. The mood of a work is not always what might be expected based on its subject matter.

Motif: A theme, character type, image, metaphor, or other verbal element that recurs throughout a single work of literature or occurs in a number of different works over a period of time.

Motiv: See *Motif*

Muckrakers: An early twentieth-century group of American writers. Typically, their works exposed the wrongdoings of big business and government in the United States.

Muses: Nine Greek mythological goddesses, the daughters of Zeus and Mnemosyne (Memory). Each muse patronized a specific area of the liberal arts and sciences. Calliope presided over epic poetry, Clio over history, Erato over love poetry, Euterpe over music or lyric poetry, Melpomene over tragedy, Polyhymnia over hymns to the gods, Terpsichore over dance, Thalia over comedy, and Urania over astronomy. Poets and writers traditionally made appeals to the Muses for inspiration in their work.

Myth: An anonymous tale emerging from the traditional beliefs of a culture or social unit. Myths use supernatural explanations for natural phenomena. They may also explain cosmic issues like creation and death. Collections of myths, known as mythologies, are common to all cultures and nations, but the best-known myths belong to the Norse, Roman, and Greek mythologies.

N

Narration: The telling of a series of events, real or invented. A narration may be either a simple narrative, in which the events are recounted chronologically, or a narrative with a plot, in which the account is given in a style reflecting the author's artistic concept of the story. Narration is sometimes used as a synonym for "storyline."

Narrative: A verse or prose accounting of an event or sequence of events, real or invented. The term is also used as an adjective in the sense "method of narration." For example, in literary criticism, the expression "narrative technique" usually refers to the way the author structures and presents his or her story.

Narrative Poetry: A nondramatic poem in which the author tells a story. Such poems may be of any length or level of complexity.

Narrator: The teller of a story. The narrator may be the author or a character in the story through whom the author speaks.

Naturalism: A literary movement of the late nineteenth and early twentieth centuries. The movement's major theorist, French novelist Emile Zola, envisioned a type of fiction that would examine human life with the objectivity of scientific inquiry. The Naturalists typically viewed human beings as either the products of "biological determinism," ruled by hereditary instincts and engaged in an endless struggle for survival, or as the products of "socioeconomic determinism," ruled by social and economic forces beyond their control. In their works, the Naturalists generally ignored the highest levels of society and focused on degradation: poverty, alcoholism, prostitution, insanity, and disease.

Negritude: A literary movement based on the concept of a shared cultural bond on the part of black Africans, wherever they may be in the world. It traces its origins to the former French colonies of Africa and the Caribbean. Negritude poets, novelists, and essayists generally stress four points in their writings: One, black alienation from traditional African culture can lead to feelings of inferiority. Two, European colonialism and Western education should be resisted. Three, black Africans should seek to affirm and define their own identity. Four, African culture can and should be reclaimed. Many Negritude writers also claim that blacks can make unique contributions to the world, based on a heightened appreciation of nature, rhythm, and human emotions—aspects of life they say are not so highly valued in the materialistic and rationalistic West.

Negro Renaissance: See *Harlem Renaissance*

Neoclassical Period: See *Neoclassicism*

Neoclassicism: In literary criticism, this term refers to the revival of the attitudes and styles of expression of classical literature. It is generally used to describe a period in European history beginning in the late seventeenth century and lasting until about 1800. In its purest form, Neoclassicism marked a return to order, proportion, restraint, logic, accuracy, and decorum. In England, where Neoclassicism perhaps was most popular, it reflected the influence of seventeenth-century French writers, especially dramatists. Neoclassical writers typically reacted against the intensity and enthusiasm of the Renaissance period. They wrote works that appealed to the intellect, using elevated language and classical literary forms such as satire and the ode.

Neoclassical works were often governed by the classical goal of instruction.

Neoclassicists: See *Neoclassicism*

New Criticism: A movement in literary criticism, dating from the late 1920s, that stressed close textual analysis in the interpretation of works of literature. The New Critics saw little merit in historical and biographical analysis. Rather, they aimed to examine the text alone, free from the question of how external events—biographical or otherwise—may have helped shape it.

New Journalism: A type of writing in which the journalist presents factual information in a form usually used in fiction. New journalism emphasizes description, narration, and character development to bring readers closer to the human element of the story, and is often used in personality profiles and in-depth feature articles. It is not compatible with "straight" or "hard" newswriting, which is generally composed in a brief, fact-based style.

New Journalists: See *New Journalism*

New Negro Movement: See *Harlem Renaissance*

Noble Savage: The idea that primitive man is noble and good but becomes evil and corrupted as he becomes civilized. The concept of the noble savage originated in the Renaissance period but is more closely identified with such later writers as Jean-Jacques Rousseau and Aphra Behn.

O

Objective Correlative: An outward set of objects, a situation, or a chain of events corresponding to an inward experience and evoking this experience in the reader. The term frequently appears in modern criticism in discussions of authors' intended effects on the emotional responses of readers.

Objectivity: A quality in writing characterized by the absence of the author's opinion or feeling about the subject matter. Objectivity is an important factor in criticism.

Occasional Verse: Poetry written on the occasion of a significant historical or personal event. *Vers de societe* is sometimes called occasional verse although it is of a less serious nature.

Octave: A poem or stanza composed of eight lines. The term octave most often represents the first eight lines of a Petrarchan sonnet.

Ode: Name given to an extended lyric poem characterized by exalted emotion and dignified style. An ode usually concerns a single, serious theme. Most odes, but not all, are addressed to an object or individual. Odes are distinguished from other lyric poetic forms by their complex rhythmic and stanzaic patterns.

Oedipus Complex: A son's amorous obsession with his mother. The phrase is derived from the story of the ancient Theban hero Oedipus, who unknowingly killed his father and married his mother.

Omniscience: See *Point of View*

Onomatopoeia: The use of words whose sounds express or suggest their meaning. In its simplest sense, onomatopoeia may be represented by words that mimic the sounds they denote such as "hiss" or "meow." At a more subtle level, the pattern and rhythm of sounds and rhymes of a line or poem may be onomatopoeic.

Oral Tradition: See *Oral Transmission*

Oral Transmission: A process by which songs, ballads, folklore, and other material are transmitted by word of mouth. The tradition of oral transmission predates the written record systems of literate society. Oral transmission preserves material sometimes over generations, although often with variations. Memory plays a large part in the recitation and preservation of orally transmitted material.

Ottava Rima: An eight-line stanza of poetry composed in iambic pentameter (a five-foot line in which each foot consists of an unaccented syllable followed by an accented syllable), following the abababcc rhyme scheme.

Oxymoron: A phrase combining two contradictory terms. Oxymorons may be intentional or unintentional.

P

Pantheism: The idea that all things are both a manifestation or revelation of God and a part of God at the same time. Pantheism was a common attitude in the early societies of Egypt, India, and Greece—the term derives from the Greek *pan* meaning "all" and *theos* meaning "deity." It later became a significant part of the Christian faith.

Parable: A story intended to teach a moral lesson or answer an ethical question.

Paradox: A statement that appears illogical or contradictory at first, but may actually point to an underlying truth.

Parallelism: A method of comparison of two ideas in which each is developed in the same grammatical structure.

Parnassianism: A mid nineteenth-century movement in French literature. Followers of the movement stressed adherence to well-defined artistic forms as a reaction against the often chaotic expression of the artist's ego that dominated the work of the Romantics. The Parnassians also rejected the moral, ethical, and social themes exhibited in the works of French Romantics such as Victor Hugo. The aesthetic doctrines of the Parnassians strongly influenced the later symbolist and decadent movements.

Parody: In literary criticism, this term refers to an imitation of a serious literary work or the signature style of a particular author in a ridiculous manner. A typical parody adopts the style of the original and applies it to an inappropriate subject for humorous effect. Parody is a form of satire and could be considered the literary equivalent of a caricature or cartoon.

Pastoral: A term derived from the Latin word "pastor," meaning shepherd. A pastoral is a literary composition on a rural theme. The conventions of the pastoral were originated by the third-century Greek poet Theocritus, who wrote about the experiences, love affairs, and pastimes of Sicilian shepherds. In a pastoral, characters and language of a courtly nature are often placed in a simple setting. The term pastoral is also used to classify dramas, elegies, and lyrics that exhibit the use of country settings and shepherd characters.

Pathetic Fallacy: A term coined by English critic John Ruskin to identify writing that falsely endows nonhuman things with human intentions and feelings, such as "angry clouds" and "sad trees."

Pen Name: See *Pseudonym*

Pentameter: See *Meter*

Persona: A Latin term meaning "mask." *Personae* are the characters in a fictional work of literature. The *persona* generally functions as a mask through which the author tells a story in a voice other than his or her own. A *persona* is usually either a character in a story who acts as a narrator or an "implied author," a voice created by the author to act as the narrator for himself or herself.

Personae: See *Persona*

Personal Point of View: See *Point of View*

Personification: A figure of speech that gives human qualities to abstract ideas, animals, and inanimate objects.

Petrarchan Sonnet: See *Sonnet*

Phenomenology: A method of literary criticism based on the belief that things have no existence outside of human consciousness or awareness. Proponents of this theory believe that art is a process that takes place in the mind of the observer as he or she contemplates an object rather than a quality of the object itself.

Plagiarism: Claiming another person's written material as one's own. Plagiarism can take the form of direct, word-for-word copying or the theft of the substance or idea of the work.

Platonic Criticism: A form of criticism that stresses an artistic work's usefulness as an agent of social engineering rather than any quality or value of the work itself.

Platonism: The embracing of the doctrines of the philosopher Plato, popular among the poets of the Renaissance and the Romantic period. Platonism is more flexible than Aristotelian Criticism and places more emphasis on the supernatural and unknown aspects of life.

Plot: In literary criticism, this term refers to the pattern of events in a narrative or drama. In its simplest sense, the plot guides the author in composing the work and helps the reader follow the work. Typically, plots exhibit causality and unity and have a beginning, a middle, and an end. Sometimes, however, a plot may consist of a series of disconnected events, in which case it is known as an "episodic plot."

Poem: In its broadest sense, a composition utilizing rhyme, meter, concrete detail, and expressive language to create a literary experience with emotional and aesthetic appeal.

Poet: An author who writes poetry or verse. The term is also used to refer to an artist or writer who has an exceptional gift for expression, imagination, and energy in the making of art in any form.

Poete maudit: A term derived from Paul Verlaine's *Les poetes maudits* (*The Accursed Poets*), a collection of essays on the French symbolist writers Stephane Mallarme, Arthur Rimbaud, and Tristan Corbiere. In the sense intended by Verlaine, the poet is "accursed" for choosing to explore extremes of human experience outside of middle-class society.

Poetic Fallacy: See *Pathetic Fallacy*

Poetic Justice: An outcome in a literary work, not necessarily a poem, in which the good are rewarded and the evil are punished, especially in ways that particularly fit their virtues or crimes.

Poetic License: Distortions of fact and literary convention made by a writer—not always a poet—for the sake of the effect gained. Poetic license is closely related to the concept of "artistic freedom."

Poetics: This term has two closely related meanings. It denotes (1) an aesthetic theory in literary criticism about the essence of poetry or (2) rules prescribing the proper methods, content, style, or diction of poetry. The term poetics may also refer to theories about literature in general, not just poetry.

Poetry: In its broadest sense, writing that aims to present ideas and evoke an emotional experience in the reader through the use of meter, imagery, connotative and concrete words, and a carefully constructed structure based on rhythmic patterns. Poetry typically relies on words and expressions that have several layers of meaning. It also makes use of the effects of regular rhythm on the ear and may make a strong appeal to the senses through the use of imagery.

Point of View: The narrative perspective from which a literary work is presented to the reader. There are four traditional points of view. The "third person omniscient" gives the reader a "godlike" perspective, unrestricted by time or place, from which to see actions and look into the minds of characters. This allows the author to comment openly on characters and events in the work. The "third person" point of view presents the events of the story from outside of any single character's perception, much like the omniscient point of view, but the reader must understand the action as it takes place and without any special insight into characters' minds or motivations. The "first person" or "personal" point of view relates events as they are perceived by a single character. The main character "tells" the story and may offer opinions about the action and characters which differ from those of the author. Much less common than omniscient, third person, and first person is the "second person" point of view, wherein the author tells the story as if it is happening to the reader.

Polemic: A work in which the author takes a stand on a controversial subject, such as abortion or religion. Such works are often extremely argumentative or provocative.

Pornography: Writing intended to provoke feelings of lust in the reader. Such works are often condemned by critics and teachers, but those which can be shown to have literary value are viewed less harshly.

Post-Aesthetic Movement: An artistic response made by African Americans to the black aesthetic movement of the 1960s and early '70s. Writers since that time have adopted a somewhat different tone in their work, with less emphasis placed on the disparity between black and white in the United States. In the words of post-aesthetic authors such as Toni Morrison, John Edgar Wideman, and Kristin Hunter, African Americans are portrayed as looking inward for answers to their own questions, rather than always looking to the outside world.

Postmodernism: Writing from the 1960s forward characterized by experimentation and continuing to apply some of the fundamentals of modernism, which included existentialism and alienation. Postmodernists have gone a step further in the rejection of tradition begun with the modernists by also rejecting traditional forms, preferring the anti-novel over the novel and the anti-hero over the hero.

Pre-Raphaelites: A circle of writers and artists in mid nineteenth-century England. Valuing the pre-Renaissance artistic qualities of religious symbolism, lavish pictorialism, and natural sensuousness, the Pre-Raphaelites cultivated a sense of mystery and melancholy that influenced later writers associated with the Symbolist and Decadent movements.

Primitivism: The belief that primitive peoples were nobler and less flawed than civilized peoples because they had not been subjected to the tainting influence of society.

Projective Verse: A form of free verse in which the poet's breathing pattern determines the lines of the poem. Poets who advocate projective verse are against all formal structures in writing, including meter and form.

Prologue: An introductory section of a literary work. It often contains information establishing the situation of the characters or presents information about the setting, time period, or action. In drama, the prologue is spoken by a chorus or by one of the principal characters.

Prose: A literary medium that attempts to mirror the language of everyday speech. It is distinguished from poetry by its use of unmetered, unrhymed language consisting of logically related sentences. Prose is usually grouped into paragraphs that form a cohesive whole such as an essay or a novel.

Prosopopoeia: See *Personification*

Protagonist: The central character of a story who serves as a focus for its themes and incidents and as the principal rationale for its development. The protagonist is sometimes referred to in discussions of modern literature as the hero or anti-hero.

Proverb: A brief, sage saying that expresses a truth about life in a striking manner.

Pseudonym: A name assumed by a writer, most often intended to prevent his or her identification as the author of a work. Two or more authors may work together under one pseudonym, or an author may use a different name for each genre he or she publishes in. Some publishing companies maintain "house pseudonyms," under which any number of authors may write installations in a series. Some authors also choose a pseudonym over their real names the way an actor may use a stage name.

Pun: A play on words that have similar sounds but different meanings.

Pure Poetry: Poetry written without instructional intent or moral purpose that aims only to please a reader by its imagery or musical flow. The term pure poetry is used as the antonym of the term "didacticism."

Q

Quatrain: A four-line stanza of a poem or an entire poem consisting of four lines.

R

Realism: A nineteenth-century European literary movement that sought to portray familiar characters, situations, and settings in a realistic manner. This was done primarily by using an objective narrative point of view and through the buildup of accurate detail. The standard for success of any realistic work depends on how faithfully it transfers common experience into fictional forms. The realistic method may be altered or extended, as in stream of consciousness writing, to record highly subjective experience.

Refrain: A phrase repeated at intervals throughout a poem. A refrain may appear at the end of each stanza or at less regular intervals. It may be altered slightly at each appearance.

Renaissance: The period in European history that marked the end of the Middle Ages. It began in Italy in the late fourteenth century. In broad terms, it is usually seen as spanning the fourteenth, fifteenth, and sixteenth centuries, although it did not reach Great Britain, for example, until the 1480s or so. The Renaissance saw an awakening in almost every sphere of human activity, especially science, philosophy, and the arts. The period is best defined by the emergence of a general philosophy that emphasized the importance of the intellect, the individual, and world affairs. It contrasts strongly with the medieval worldview, characterized by the dominant concerns of faith, the social collective, and spiritual salvation.

Repartee: Conversation featuring snappy retorts and witticisms.

Restoration: See *Restoration Age*

Restoration Age: A period in English literature beginning with the crowning of Charles II in 1660 and running to about 1700. The era, which was characterized by a reaction against Puritanism, was the first great age of the comedy of manners. The finest literature of the era is typically witty and urbane, and often lewd.

Rhetoric: In literary criticism, this term denotes the art of ethical persuasion. In its strictest sense, rhetoric adheres to various principles developed since classical times for arranging facts and ideas in a clear, persuasive, appealing manner. The term is also used to refer to effective prose in general and theories of or methods for composing effective prose.

Rhetorical Question: A question intended to provoke thought, but not an expressed answer, in the reader. It is most commonly used in oratory and other persuasive genres.

Rhyme: When used as a noun in literary criticism, this term generally refers to a poem in which words sound identical or very similar and appear in parallel positions in two or more lines. Rhymes are classified into different types according to where they fall in a line or stanza or according to the degree of similarity they exhibit in their spellings and sounds. Some major types of rhyme are "masculine" rhyme, "feminine" rhyme, and "triple" rhyme. In a masculine rhyme, the rhyming sound falls in a single accented syllable, as with "heat" and "eat." Feminine rhyme is a rhyme of two syllables, one stressed and one unstressed, as with "merry" and "tarry." Triple rhyme matches the sound of the accented syllable and the two unaccented syllables that follow: "narrative" and "declarative."

Rhyme Royal: A stanza of seven lines composed in iambic pentameter and rhymed *ababbcc*. The name is said to be a tribute to King James I of Scotland, who made much use of the form in his poetry.

Rhyme Scheme: See *Rhyme*

Rhythm: A regular pattern of sound, time intervals, or events occurring in writing, most often and most discernably in poetry. Regular, reliable rhythm is known to be soothing to humans, while interrupted, unpredictable, or rapidly changing rhythm is disturbing. These effects are known to authors, who use them to produce a desired reaction in the reader.

Rococo: A style of European architecture that flourished in the eighteenth century, especially in France. The most notable features of *rococo* are its extensive use of ornamentation and its themes of lightness, gaiety, and intimacy. In literary criticism, the term is often used disparagingly to refer to a decadent or over-ornamental style.

Romance: A broad term, usually denoting a narrative with exotic, exaggerated, often idealized characters, scenes, and themes.

Romantic Age: See *Romanticism*

Romanticism: This term has two widely accepted meanings. In historical criticism, it refers to a European intellectual and artistic movement of the late eighteenth and early nineteenth centuries that sought greater freedom of personal expression than that allowed by the strict rules of literary form and logic of the eighteenth-century neoclassicists. The Romantics preferred emotional and imaginative expression to rational analysis. They considered the individual to be at the center of all experience and so placed him or her at the center of their art. The Romantics believed that the creative imagination reveals nobler truths—unique feelings and attitudes—than those that could be discovered by logic or by scientific examination. Both the natural world and the state of childhood were important sources for revelations of "eternal truths." "Romanticism" is also used as a general term to refer to a type of sensibility found in all periods of literary history and usually considered to be in opposition to the principles of classicism. In this sense, Romanticism signifies any work or philosophy in which the exotic or dreamlike figure strongly, or that is devoted to individualistic expression, self-analysis, or a pursuit of a higher realm of knowledge than can be discovered by human reason.

Romantics: See *Romanticism*

Russian Symbolism: A Russian poetic movement, derived from French symbolism, that flourished between 1894 and 1910. While some Russian Symbolists continued in the French tradition, stressing aestheticism and the importance of suggestion above didactic intent, others saw their craft as a form of mystical worship, and themselves as mediators between the supernatural and the mundane.

S

Satire: A work that uses ridicule, humor, and wit to criticize and provoke change in human nature and institutions. There are two major types of satire: "formal" or "direct" satire speaks directly to the reader or to a character in the work; "indirect" satire relies upon the ridiculous behavior of its characters to make its point. Formal satire is further divided into two manners: the "Horatian," which ridicules gently, and the "Juvenalian," which derides its subjects harshly and bitterly.

Scansion: The analysis or "scanning" of a poem to determine its meter and often its rhyme scheme. The most common system of scansion uses accents (slanted lines drawn above syllables) to show stressed syllables, breves (curved lines drawn above syllables) to show unstressed syllables, and vertical lines to separate each foot.

Second Person: See *Point of View*

Semiotics: The study of how literary forms and conventions affect the meaning of language.

Sestet: Any six-line poem or stanza.

Setting: The time, place, and culture in which the action of a narrative takes place. The elements of setting may include geographic location, characters' physical and mental environments, prevailing cultural attitudes, or the historical time in which the action takes place.

Shakespearean Sonnet: See *Sonnet*

Signifying Monkey: A popular trickster figure in black folklore, with hundreds of tales about this character documented since the 19th century.

Simile: A comparison, usually using "like" or "as," of two essentially dissimilar things, as in "coffee as cold as ice" or "He sounded like a broken record."

Slang: A type of informal verbal communication that is generally unacceptable for formal writing. Slang words and phrases are often colorful exaggerations used to emphasize the speaker's point; they may also be shortened versions of an often-used word or phrase.

Slant Rhyme: See *Consonance*

Slave Narrative: Autobiographical accounts of American slave life as told by escaped slaves. These works first appeared during the abolition movement of the 1830s through the 1850s.

Social Realism: See *Socialist Realism*

Socialist Realism: The Socialist Realism school of literary theory was proposed by Maxim Gorky and established as a dogma by the first Soviet Congress of Writers. It demanded adherence to a communist worldview in works of literature. Its doctrines required an objective viewpoint comprehensible to the working classes and themes of social struggle featuring strong proletarian heroes.

Soliloquy: A monologue in a drama used to give the audience information and to develop the speaker's character. It is typically a projection of the speaker's innermost thoughts. Usually delivered while the speaker is alone on stage, a soliloquy is intended to present an illusion of unspoken reflection.

Sonnet: A fourteen-line poem, usually composed in iambic pentameter, employing one of several rhyme schemes. There are three major types of sonnets, upon which all other variations of the form are based: the "Petrarchan" or "Italian" sonnet, the "Shakespearean" or "English" sonnet, and the "Spenserian" sonnet. A Petrarchan sonnet consists of an octave rhymed *abbaabba* and a "sestet" rhymed either *cdecde, cdccdc,* or *cdedce.* The octave poses a question or problem, relates a narrative, or puts forth a proposition; the sestet presents a solution to the problem, comments upon the narrative, or applies the proposition put forth in the octave. The Shakespearean sonnet is divided into three quatrains and a couplet rhymed *abab cdcd efef gg.* The couplet provides an epigrammatic comment on the narrative or problem put forth in the quatrains. The Spenserian sonnet uses three quatrains and a couplet like the Shakespearean, but links their three rhyme schemes in this way: *abab bcbc cdcd ee.* The Spenserian sonnet develops its theme in two parts like the Petrarchan, its final six lines resolving a problem, analyzing a narrative, or applying a proposition put forth in its first eight lines.

Spenserian Sonnet: See *Sonnet*

Spenserian Stanza: A nine-line stanza having eight verses in iambic pentameter, its ninth verse in iambic hexameter, and the rhyme scheme ababbcbcc.

Spondee: In poetry meter, a foot consisting of two long or stressed syllables occurring together. This form is quite rare in English verse, and is usually composed of two mono-syllabic words.

Sprung Rhythm: Versification using a specific number of accented syllables per line but disregarding the number of unaccented syllables that fall in each line, producing an irregular rhythm in the poem.

Stanza: A subdivision of a poem consisting of lines grouped together, often in recurring patterns of rhyme, line length, and meter. Stanzas may also serve as units of thought in a poem much like paragraphs in prose.

Stereotype: A stereotype was originally the name for a duplication made during the printing process; this led to its modern definition as a person or thing that is (or is assumed to be) the same as all others of its type.

Stream of Consciousness: A narrative technique for rendering the inward experience of a character. This technique is designed to give the impression of an ever-changing series of thoughts, emotions, images, and memories in the spontaneous and seemingly illogical order that they occur in life.

Structuralism: A twentieth-century movement in literary criticism that examines how literary texts arrive at their meanings, rather than the meanings themselves. There are two major types of structuralist analysis: one examines the way patterns of linguistic structures unify a specific text and emphasize certain elements of that text, and the other interprets the way literary forms and conventions affect the meaning of language itself.

Structure: The form taken by a piece of literature. The structure may be made obvious for ease of understanding, as in nonfiction works, or may obscured for artistic purposes, as in some poetry or seemingly "unstructured" prose.

Sturm und Drang: A German term meaning "storm and stress." It refers to a German literary movement of the 1770s and 1780s that reacted against the order and rationalism of the enlightenment, focusing instead on the intense experience of extraordinary individuals.

Style: A writer's distinctive manner of arranging words to suit his or her ideas and purpose in writing. The unique imprint of the author's personality upon his or her writing, style is the product of an author's way of arranging ideas and his or her use of diction, different sentence structures, rhythm, figures of speech, rhetorical principles, and other elements of composition.

Subject: The person, event, or theme at the center of a work of literature. A work may have one or more subjects of each type, with shorter works tending to have fewer and longer works tending to have more.

Subjectivity: Writing that expresses the author's personal feelings about his subject, and which may or may not include factual information about the subject.

Surrealism: A term introduced to criticism by Guillaume Apollinaire and later adopted by Andre Breton. It refers to a French literary and artistic movement founded in the 1920s. The Surrealists sought to express unconscious thoughts and feelings in their works. The best-known technique used for achieving this aim was automatic writing—transcriptions of spontaneous outpourings from the unconscious. The Surrealists proposed to unify the contrary levels of conscious and unconscious, dream and reality, objectivity and subjectivity into a new level of "super-realism."

Suspense: A literary device in which the author maintains the audience's attention through the buildup of events, the outcome of which will soon be revealed.

Syllogism: A method of presenting a logical argument. In its most basic form, the syllogism consists of a major premise, a minor premise, and a conclusion.

Symbol: Something that suggests or stands for something else without losing its original identity. In literature, symbols combine their literal meaning with the suggestion of an abstract concept. Literary symbols are of two types: those that carry complex associations of meaning no matter what their contexts, and those that derive their suggestive meaning from their functions in specific literary works.

Symbolism: This term has two widely accepted meanings. In historical criticism, it denotes an early modernist literary movement initiated in France during the nineteenth century that reacted against the prevailing standards of realism. Writers in this movement aimed to evoke, indirectly and symbolically, an order of being beyond the material world of the five senses. Poetic expression of personal emotion figured strongly in the movement, typically by means of a private set of symbols uniquely identifiable with the individual poet. The principal aim of the Symbolists was to express in words the highly complex feelings that grew out of everyday contact with the world. In a broader sense, the term "symbolism" refers to the use of one object to represent another.

Symbolist: See *Symbolism*

Symbolist Movement: See *Symbolism*

Sympathetic Fallacy: See *Affective Fallacy*

T

Tanka: A form of Japanese poetry similar to *haiku*. A *tanka* is five lines long, with the lines containing five, seven, five, seven, and seven syllables respectively.

Terza Rima: A three-line stanza form in poetry in which the rhymes are made on the last word of each line in the following manner: the first and third lines of the first stanza, then the second line of the first stanza and the first and third lines of the second stanza, and so on with the middle line of any stanza rhyming with the first and third lines of the following stanza.

Tetrameter: See *Meter*

Textual Criticism: A branch of literary criticism that seeks to establish the authoritative text of a literary work. Textual critics typically compare all known manuscripts or printings of a single work in order to assess the meanings of differences and revisions. This procedure allows them to arrive at a definitive version that (supposedly) corresponds to the author's original intention.

Theme: The main point of a work of literature. The term is used interchangeably with thesis.

Thesis: A thesis is both an essay and the point argued in the essay. Thesis novels and thesis plays share the quality of containing a thesis which is supported through the action of the story.

Third Person: See *Point of View*

Tone: The author's attitude toward his or her audience may be deduced from the tone of the work. A formal tone may create distance or convey politeness, while an informal tone may encourage a friendly, intimate, or intrusive feeling in the reader. The author's attitude toward his or her subject matter may also be deduced from the tone of the words he or she uses in discussing it.

Tragedy: A drama in prose or poetry about a noble, courageous hero of excellent character who, because of some tragic character flaw or *hamartia*, brings ruin upon him- or herself. Tragedy treats its subjects in a dignified and serious manner, using poetic language to help evoke pity and fear and bring about catharsis, a purging of these emotions. The tragic form was practiced extensively by the ancient Greeks. In the Middle Ages, when classical works were virtually unknown, tragedy came to denote any works about the fall of persons from exalted to low conditions due to any reason: fate, vice, weakness, etc. According to the classical definition of tragedy, such works present the "pathetic"—that which evokes pity—rather than the tragic. The classical form of tragedy was revived in the sixteenth century; it flourished especially on the Elizabethan stage. In modern times, dramatists have attempted to adapt the form to the needs of modern society by drawing their heroes from the ranks of ordinary men and women and defining the nobility of these heroes in terms of spirit rather than exalted social standing.

Tragic Flaw: In a tragedy, the quality within the hero or heroine which leads to his or her downfall.

Transcendentalism: An American philosophical and religious movement, based in New England from around 1835 until the Civil War. Transcendentalism was a form of American romanticism that had its roots abroad in the works of Thomas Carlyle, Samuel Coleridge, and Johann Wolfgang von Goethe. The Transcendentalists stressed the importance of intuition and subjective experience in communication with God. They rejected religious dogma and texts in favor of mysticism and scientific naturalism. They pursued truths that lie beyond the "colorless" realms perceived by reason and the senses and were active social reformers in public education, women's rights, and the abolition of slavery.

Trickster: A character or figure common in Native American and African literature who uses his ingenuity to defeat enemies and escape difficult situations. Tricksters are most often animals, such as the spider, hare, or coyote, although they may take the form of humans as well.

Trimeter: See *Meter*

Triple Rhyme: See *Rhyme*

Trochee: See *Foot*

U

Understatement: See *Irony*

Unities: Strict rules of dramatic structure, formulated by Italian and French critics of the Renaissance and based loosely on the principles of drama discussed by Aristotle in his *Poetics*. Foremost among these rules were the three unities of action, time, and place that compelled a dramatist to: (1) construct a single plot with a beginning, middle, and end that details the causal relationships of action and character; (2) restrict the action to the events of a single day; and (3) limit the scene to a single place or city. The unities were observed faithfully by continental European writers until the Romantic Age, but they were never regularly observed in English drama. Modern dramatists are typically more concerned with a unity of impression or emotional effect than with any of the classical unities.

Urban Realism: A branch of realist writing that attempts to accurately reflect the often harsh facts of modern urban existence.

Utopia: A fictional perfect place, such as "paradise" or "heaven."

Utopian: See *Utopia*

Utopianism: See *Utopia*

V

Verisimilitude: Literally, the appearance of truth. In literary criticism, the term refers to aspects of a work of literature that seem true to the reader.

Vers de societe: See *Occasional Verse*

Vers libre: See *Free Verse*

Verse: A line of metered language, a line of a poem, or any work written in verse.

Versification: The writing of verse. Versification may also refer to the meter, rhyme, and other mechanical components of a poem.

Victorian: Refers broadly to the reign of Queen Victoria of England (1837-1901) and to anything with qualities typical of that era. For example, the qualities of smug narrowmindedness, bourgeois materialism, faith in social progress, and priggish morality are often considered Victorian. This stereotype is contradicted by such dramatic intellectual developments as the theories of Charles Darwin, Karl Marx, and Sigmund Freud (which stirred strong debates in England) and the critical attitudes of serious Victorian writers like Charles Dickens and George Eliot. In literature, the Victorian Period was the great age of the English novel, and the latter part of the era saw the rise of movements such as decadence and symbolism.

Victorian Age: See *Victorian*

Victorian Period: See *Victorian*

W

Weltanschauung: A German term referring to a person's worldview or philosophy.

Weltschmerz: A German term meaning "world pain." It describes a sense of anguish about the nature of existence, usually associated with a melancholy, pessimistic attitude.

Z

Zarzuela: A type of Spanish operetta.

Zeitgeist: A German term meaning "spirit of the time." It refers to the moral and intellectual trends of a given era.

Cumulative Author/Title Index

Cumulative
Nationality/Ethnicity Index

Acoma Pueblo

Ortiz, Simon
  Hunger in New York City: V4
  My Father's Song: V16
  Speaking: V46

African American

Ai
  Reunions with a Ghost: V16
Angelou, Maya
  Africa: V47
  Alone: V53
  Harlem Hopscotch: V2
  On the Pulse of Morning: V3
  Phenomenal Woman: V42
  Still I Rise: V38
  Woman Work: V33
Baraka, Amiri
  In Memory of Radio: V9
Bontemps, Arna
  A Black Man Talks of Reaping:
    V32
Brooks, Gwendolyn
  The Bean Eaters: V2
  The Explorer: V32
  The Mother: V40
  Primer for Blacks: V46
  Sadie and Maud: V53
  The Sonnet-Ballad: V1
  Strong Men, Riding Horses: V4
  We Real Cool: V6
Clifton, Lucille
  Climbing: V14
  homage to my hips: V29
  in the inner city: V41
  Miss Rosie: V1

Cullen, Countee
  Any Human to Another: V3
  Incident: V3
  Yet Do I Marvel: V48
Dove, Rita
  Geometry: V15
  Grape Sherbet: V37
  *Hattie McDaniel Arrives at the
    Coconut Grove:* V51
  This Life: V1
Dunbar, Paul Laurence
  A Golden Day: V49
  Sympathy: V33
  We Wear the Mask: V40
Evans, Mari
  When In Rome: V36
Giovanni, Nikki
  Ego-Tripping: V28
  Knoxville, Tennessee: V17
  Winter: V35
  *The World Is Not a Pleasant Place
    to Be:* V42
Harper, Frances Ellen Watkins
  The Slave Mother: V44
Hayden, Robert
  Runagate Runagate: V31
  Those Winter Sundays: V1
  The Whipping: V45
Hughes, Langston
  Dream Variations: V15
  Dreams: V50
  Harlem: V1
  I, Too: V30
  Let America Be America Again:
    V45
  Mother to Son: V3

  The Negro Speaks of Rivers:
    V10
  Theme for English B: V6
  The Weary Blues: V38
Jackson, Major
  Urban Renewal: XVIII: V53
Johnson, James Weldon
  The Creation: V1
Knight, Etheridge
  The Idea of Ancestry: V36
Komunyakaa, Yusef
  Camouflaging the Chimera: V37
  Facing It: V5
  Ode to a Drum: V20
  Slam, Dunk, & Hook: V30
Lorde, Audre
  Hanging Fire: V32
  What My Child Learns of the Sea:
    V16
Madgett, Naomi Long
  Alabama Centennial: V10
McElroy, Colleen
  A Pièd: V3
Phillips, Carl
  All It Takes: V23
Randall, Dudley
  Ballad of Birmingham: V5
Reed, Ishmael
  Beware: Do Not Read This Poem:
    V6
Sanchez, Sonia
  An Anthem: V26
  On Passing thru Morgantown, Pa.:
    V49
Shange, Ntozake
  Bocas: A Daughter's Geography:
    V50

Subject/Theme Index

Cumulative
Index of First Lines

Y

Yes. I remember Adlestrop—
(Adlestrop) V49:3

You always read about it:
(Cinderella) V41:42

You are small and intense (To a
Child Running With

Out-stretched Arms in Canyon
de Chelly) V11:173

You can't hear? Everything here
is changing. (The River
Mumma Wants Out)
V25:191

You do not have to be good. (Wild
Geese) V15:207

You should lie down now and
remember the forest, (The
Forest) V22:36–37

You stood thigh-deep in water and
green light glanced (Lake) V23:158

You were never told, Mother, how
old Illya was drunk (The Czar's
Last Christmas Letter) V12:44

Cumulative
Index of Last Lines

For I'm sick at the heart, and I fain wad lie down." (Lord Randal) V6:105

For nothing now can ever come to any good. (Funeral Blues) V10:139

For the coming winter (Winter) V35:297

For the love of God they buried his cold corpse. (The Bronze Horseman) V28:31

For the world's more full of weeping than he can understand. (The Stolen Child) V34:217

forget me as fast as you can. (Last Request) V14:231

4:25:9 (400-Meter Freestyle) V38:3

from one kiss (A Rebirth) V21:193–194

from the face of a beautiful beloved woman. (A Jewish Cemetery in Germany) V51:147

from your arm. (Inside Out) V43:121

full moon. (New World) V41:271

G

garish for a while and burned. (One of the Smallest) V26:142

gazing at the clouds (The End and the Beginning) V41:122

going where? Where? (Childhood) V19:29

guilty about possessing appetite. (Defining the Grateful Gesture) V40:34

H

Had anything been wrong, we should certainly have heard (The Unknown Citizen) V3:303

Had somewhere to get to and sailed calmly on (Musée des Beaux Arts) V1:148

half eaten by the moon. (Dear Reader) V10:85

hand over hungry hand. (Climbing) V14:113

Happen on a red tongue (Small Town with One Road) V7:207

hard as mine with another man? (An Attempt at Jealousy) V29:24

Has no more need of, and I have (The Courage that My Mother Had) V3:80

Has set me softly down beside you. The Poem is you (Paradoxes and Oxymorons) V11:162

Hath melted like snow in the glance of the Lord! (The Destruction of Sennacherib) V1:39

Have eyes to wonder, but lack tongues to praise. (Sonnet 106) V43:251

He rose the morrow morn (The Rime of the Ancient Mariner) V4:132

He says again, "Good fences make good neighbors." (Mending Wall) V5:232

He still may leave thy garland green. (Love and Friendship) V51:182

He writes down something that he crosses out. (The Boy) V19:14

here; passion will save you. (Air for Mercury) V20:2–3

hills beckoned. (On Passing thru Morgantown, Pa.) V49:209

History theirs whose languages is the sun. (An Elementary School Classroom in a Slum) V23:88–89

home (in the inner city) V41:227

How at my sheet goes the same crooked worm (The Force That Through the Green Fuse Drives the Flower) V8:101

How can I turn from Africa and live? (A Far Cry from Africa) V6:61

How could I seek the empty world again? (Remembrance) V43:216

How sad then is even the marvelous! (An Affrician Elegy) V13:4

I

I am a true Russian! (Babii Yar) V29:38

I am black. (The Song of the Smoke) V13:197

I am going to keep things like this (Hawk Roosting) V4:55

I am not brave at all (Strong Men, Riding Horses) V4:209

I am the captain of my soul (Invictus) V43:137

I could not see to see— (I Heard a Fly Buzz—When I Died—) V5:140

I cremated Sam McGee (The Cremation of Sam McGee) V10:76

I didn't want to put them down. (And What If I Spoke of Despair) V19:2

I *guess* an' *fear*! (To a Mouse, On turning her up in her Nest, with the Plough, November, 1785) V47:262

I have been her kind. (Her Kind) V47:116–117

I have been one acquainted with the night. (Acquainted with the Night) V35:3

I have just come down from my father (The Hospital Window) V11:58

I hear it in the deep heart's core. (The Lake Isle of Innisfree) V15:121

I know why the caged bird sings! (Sympathy) V33:203

I lift my lamp beside the golden door!" (The New Colossus) V37:239

I never writ, nor no man ever loved (Sonnet 116) V3:288

I rest in the grace of the world, and am free. (The Peace of Wild Things) V30:159

I romp with joy in the bookish dark (Eating Poetry) V9:61

I see him properly buried" (Perceval, the Story of the Grail) V44:153

I see Mike's painting, called SARDINES (Why I Am Not a Painter) V8:259

I shall but love thee better after death (Sonnet 43) V2:236

I should be glad of another death (Journey of the Magi) V7:110

I stand up (Miss Rosie) V1:133

I stood there, fifteen (Fifteen) V2:78

I take it you are he? (Incident in a Rose Garden) V14:191

I the late madonna of barren lands. (Jamaica 1980) V48:131

I, too, am America. (I, Too) V30:99

I turned aside and bowed my head and wept (The Tropics in New York) V4:255

I would like to tell, but lack the words. (I Built My Hut beside a Traveled Road) V36:119

I'd understand it all— (Nebraska) V52:147–148

If Winter comes, can Spring be far behind? (Ode to the West Wind) V2:163

I'll be gone from here. (The Cobweb) V17:51

I'll dig with it (Digging) V5:71

Imagine! (Autobiographia Literaria) V34:2

In a convulsive misery (The Milkfish Gatherers) V11:112

In an empty sky (Two Bodies) V38:251

In balance with this life, this death (An Irish Airman Foresees His Death) V1:76

in earth's gasp, ocean's yawn. (Lake) V23:158

In Flanders fields (In Flanders Fields) V5:155

In ghostlier demarcations, keener sounds. (The Idea of Order at Key West) V13:164

In hearts at peace, under an English heaven (The Soldier) V7:218

In her tomb by the side of the sea (Annabel Lee) V9:14

in the family of things. (Wild Geese) V15:208

in the grit gray light of day. (Daylights) V13:102

In the rear-view mirrors of the passing cars (The War Against the Trees) V11:216

In these Chicago avenues. (A Thirst Against) V20:205

in this bastion of culture. (To an Unknown Poet) V18:221

In this old house. (Sadie and Maud) V53:195

in winter. (Ode to My Socks) V47:173–174

in your unsteady, opening hand. (What the Poets Could Have Been) V26:262

Inns are not residences. (Silence) V47:231

iness (l(a) V1:85

Into blossom (A Blessing) V7:24

Is breaking in despair. (The Slave Mother) V44:213

Is Come, my love is come to me. (A Birthday) V10:34

is love—that's all. (Two Poems for T.) V20:218

is safe is what you said. (Practice) V23:240

is going too fast; your hands sweat. (Another Feeling) V40:3

is still warm (Lament for the Dorsets) V5:191

It asked a crumb—of Me ("Hope" Is the Thing with Feathers) V3:123

It had no mirrors. I no longer needed mirrors. (I, I, I) V26:97

It hasn't let up all morning. (The Cucumber) V41:81

It is always brimming May. (A Golden Day) V49:129

It is Margaret you mourn for. (Spring and Fall: To a Young Girl) V40:236

It is our god. (Fiddler Crab) V23:111–112

it is the bell to awaken God that we've heard ringing. (The Garden Shukkei-en) V18:107

it over my face and mouth. (An Anthem) V26:34

It rains as I write this. Mad heart, be brave. (The Country Without a Post Office) V18:64

It takes life to love life. (Lucinda Matlock) V37:172

It was your resting place." (Ah, Are You Digging on My Grave?) V4:2

it's always ourselves we find in the sea (maggie & milly & molly & may) V12:150

its bright, unequivocal eye. (Having it Out with Melancholy) V17:99

It's funny how things blow loose like that. (Snapping Beans) V50:244–245

It's the fall through wind lifting white leaves. (Rapture) V21:181

its youth. The sea grows old in it. (The Fish) V14:172

J

Judge tenderly—of Me (This Is My Letter to the World) V4:233

Just imagine it (Inventors) V7:97

K

kisses you (Grandmother) V34:95

L

Laughing the stormy, husky, brawling laughter of Youth, half-naked, sweating, proud to be Hog Butcher, Tool Maker, Stacker of Wheat, Player with Railroads and Freight Handler to the Nation (Chicago) V3:61

Learn to labor and to wait (A Psalm of Life) V7:165

Leashed in my throat (Midnight) V2:131

Leaving thine outgrown shell by life's un-resting sea (The Chambered Nautilus) V24:52–53

Let my people go (Go Down, Moses) V11:43

Let the water come. (America, America) V29:4

life, our life and its forgetting. (For a New Citizen of These United States) V15:55

Life to Victory (Always) V24:15

like a bird in the sky … (Ego-Tripping) V28:113

like a shadow or a friend. *Colombia.* (Kindness) V24:84–85

like it better than being loved. (For the Young Who Want To) V40:50

Like nothing else in Tennessee. (Anecdote of the Jar) V41:3

Like Stone— (The Soul Selects Her Own Society) V1:259

like the evening prayer. (My Father in the Navy) V46:87

Little Lamb, God bless thee. (The Lamb) V12:135

Look'd up in perfect silence at the stars. (When I Heard the Learn'd Astronomer) V22:244

love (The Toni Morrison Dreams) V22:202–203

Love is best! (Love Among the Ruins) V41:248

Loved I not Honour more. (To Lucasta, Going to the Wars) V32:291

Luck was rid of its clover. (Yet we insist that life is full of happy chance) V27:292

M

'Make a wish, Tom, make a wish.' (Drifters) V10: 98

make it seem to change (The Moon Glows the Same) V7:152

May be refined, and join the angelic train. (On Being Brought from Africa to America) V29:223

may your mercy be near. (Two Eclipses) V33:221

midnight-oiled in the metric laws? (A Farewell to English) V10:126

Monkey business (Business) V16:2

More dear, both for themselves and for thy sake! (Tintern Abbey) V2:250

More simple and more full of pride. (I Am Not One of Those Who Left the Land) V36:91

must always think good thoughts. (Letter to My Wife) V38:115

My foe outstretchd beneath the tree. (A Poison Tree) V24:195–196

My love shall in my verse ever live young (Sonnet 19) V9:211

My skin alive with the pitch. (Annunciation Overheard from the Kitchen) V49:24

My soul has grown deep like the rivers. (The Negro Speaks of Rivers) V10:198

My soul I'll pour into thee. (The Night Piece: To Julia) V29:206

N

never to waken in that world again (Starlight) V8:213

newness comes into the world (Daughter-Mother-Maya-Seeta) V25:83

Nirvana is here, nine times out of ten. (Spring-Watching Pavilion) V18:198

No, she's brushing a boy's hair (Facing It) V5:110

No winter shall abate the abate the spring's increase. (Love's Growth) V53:131

no—tell them *no*— (The Hiding Place) V10:153

Noble six hundred! (The Charge of the Light Brigade) V1:3

nobody,not even the rain,has such small hands (somewhere i have never travelled,gladly beyond) V19:265

Nor swim under the terrible eyes of prison ships. (The Drunken Boat) V28:84

Not a roof but a field of stars. (Rent) V25:164

not be seeing you, for you have no insurance. (The River Mumma Wants Out) V25:191

Not even the blisters. Look. (What Belongs to Us) V15:196

Not of itself, but thee. (Song: To Celia) V23:270–271

Not to mention people. (Pride) V38:177

Nothing, and is nowhere, and is endless (High Windows) V3:108

Nothing gold can stay (Nothing Gold Can Stay) V3:203

Now! (Alabama Centennial) V10:2

nursing the tough skin of figs (This Life) V1:293

O

O Death in Life, the days that are no more! (Tears, Idle Tears) V4:220

O Lord our Lord, how excellent is thy name in all the earth! (Psalm 8) V9:182

O Roger, Mackerel, Riley, Ned, Nellie, Chester, Lady Ghost (Names of Horses) V8:142

o, walk your body down, don't let it go it alone. (Walk Your Body Down) V26:219

Of all our joys, this must be the deepest. (Drinking Alone Beneath the Moon) V20:59–60

of blackberry-eating in late September. (Blackberry Eating) V35:24

of blood and ignorance. (Art Thou the Thing I Wanted) V25:2–3

of blood on the surface of muscle. (En Route to Bangladesh, Another Crisis of Faith) V53:82

of existence (Constantly Risking Absurdity) V41:60

of gentleness (To a Sad Daughter) V8:231

of love's austere and lonely offices? (Those Winter Sundays) V1:300

Of Oxfordshire and Gloucestershire. (Adlestrop) V49:3

of peaches (The Weight of Sweetness) V11:230

of pimpled mud and your eyes (The Tall Figures of Giacometti) V50:271

Of the camellia (Falling Upon Earth) V2:64

Of the Creator. And he waits for the world to begin (Leviathan) V5:204

of our festivities (Fragment 2) V31:63

Of what is past, or passing, or to come (Sailing to Byzantium) V2:207

Of which the chronicles make no mention. (In Music) V35:105

Oh that was the garden of abundance, seeing you. (Seeing You) V24:244–245

Old Ryan, not yours (The Constellation Orion) V8:53

On rainy Monday nights of an eternal November. (Classic Ballroom Dances) V33:3

On the dark distant flurry (Angle of Geese) V2:2

on the frosty autumn air. (The Cossacks) V25:70

On the look of Death— (There's a Certain Slant of Light) V6:212

On the reef of Norman's Woe! (The Wreck of the Hesperus) V31:317

on their melting shoulders. (Snowmen) V46:175

On your head like a crown (Any Human to Another) V3:2

One could do worse that be a swinger of birches. (Birches) V13:15

"Only the Lonely," trying his best to sound like Elvis. (The Women Who Loved Elvis All Their Lives) V28:274

or a loose seed. (Freeway 280) V30:62

Or does it explode? (Harlem) V1:63

Or every man be blind— (Tell all the Truth but tell it slant) V42:240

Or hear old Triton blow his wreathed horn. (The World Is Too Much with Us) V38:301

Or help to half-a-crown." (The Man He Killed) V3:167

Or if I die. (The Fly) V34:70

Or just some human sleep. (After Apple Picking) V32:3

or last time, we look. (In Particular) V20:125

or last time, we look. (In Particular) V20:125

Or might not have lain dormant forever. (Mastectomy) V26:123

or nothing (Queen-Ann's-Lace) V6:179

Or pleasures, seldom reached, again pursued. (A Nocturnal Reverie) V30:119–120

Or the dazzling crystal. (What I Expected) V36:313–314

or the one red leaf the snow releases in March. (ThreeTimes My Life Has Opened) V16:213

Or whistling, I am not a little boy. (The Ball Poem) V47:24

ORANGE forever. (Ballad of Orange and Grape) V10:18

our every corpuscle become an elf. (Moreover, the Moon) V20:153

Our love shall live, and later life renew." (Sonnet 75) V32:215

outside. (it was New York and beautifully, snowing ... (i was sitting in mcsorley's) V13:152

owing old (old age sticks) V3:246

P

patient in mind remembers the time. (Fading Light) V21:49

Penelope, who really cried. (An Ancient Gesture) V31:3

Perhaps he will fall. (Wilderness Gothic) V12:242

Petals on a wet, black bough (In a Station of the Metro) V2:116

Plaiting a dark red love-knot into her long black hair (The Highwayman) V4:68

plunges into the heart and is gone. (The Panther) V48:147

Powerless, I drown. (Maternity) V21:142–143

Práise him. (Pied Beauty) V26:161

Pressed to the wall, dying, but fighting back! (If We Must Die) V50:145

Pro patria mori. (Dulce et Decorum Est) V10:110

Q

Quietly shining to the quiet Moon. (Frost at Midnight) V39:75

R

Rage, rage against the dying of the light (Do Not Go Gentle into that Good Night) V1:51

The hands are churches that worship the world (Daily) V47:63

The hands gripped hard on the desert (At the Bomb Testing Site) V8:3

The holy melodies of love arise. (The Arsenal at Springfield) V17:3

the knife at the throat, the death in the metronome (Music Lessons) V8:117

The Lady of Shalott." (The Lady of Shalott) V15:97

The lightning and the gale! (Old Ironsides) V9:172

The lone and level sands stretch far away. (Ozymandias) V27:173

the long, perfect loveliness of sow (Saint Francis and the Sow) V9:222

The Lord survives the rainbow of His will (The Quaker Graveyard in Nantucket) V6:159

The man I was when I was part of it (Beware of Ruins) V8:43

the quilts sing on (My Mother Pieced Quilts) V12:169

The red rose and the brier (Barbara Allan) V7:11

The sea whisper'd me. (Out of the Cradle Endlessly Rocking) V46:125

The self-same Power that brought me there brought you. (The Rhodora) V17:191

The shaft we raise to them and thee (Concord Hymn) V4:30

the skin of another, what I have made is a curse. (Curse) V26:75

The sky became a still and woven blue. (Merlin Enthralled) V16:73

The song of the Lorelei. (The Lorelei) V37:146

The spirit of this place (To a Child Running With Outstretched Arms in Canyon de Chelly) V11:173

The town again, trailing your legs and crying! (Wild Swans) V17:221

the unremitting space of your rebellion (Lost Sister) V5:217

The wide spaces between us. (Poem about People) V44:175

The woman won (Oysters) V4:91

The world should listen then—as I am listening now. (To a Sky-Lark) V32:252

their dinnerware. (Portrait of a Couple at Century's End) V24:214–215

their guts or their brains? (Southbound on the Freeway) V16:158

Then chiefly lives. (Virtue) V25:263

There are blows in life, so hard ... I just don't know! (The Black Heralds) V26:47

There in the fragrant pines and the cedars dusk and dim. (When Lilacs Last In the Dooryard Bloom'd) V51:265–269

There is the trap that catches noblest spirits, that caught— they say— God, when he walked on earth (Shine, Perishing Republic) V4:162

there was light (Vancouver Lights) V8:246

They also serve who only stand and wait." ([On His Blindness] Sonnet 16) V3:262

They also serve who only stand and wait." (When I Consider (Sonnet XIX)) V37:302

They are going to some point true and unproven. (Geometry) V15:68

They are the watchful eyes of future generations. (The Answer) V52:3

They have not sown, and feed on bitter fruit. (A Black Man Talks of Reaping) V32:21

They rise, they walk again (The Heaven of Animals) V6:76

They say a child with two mouths is no good. (Pantoun for Chinese Women) V29:242

They think I lost. I think I won (Harlem Hopscotch) V2:93

they *touch* you. They fill you like music. (What Are Friends For) V41:305

They'd eaten every one." (The Walrus and the Carpenter) V30:258–259

This bed thy centre is, these walls thy sphere. (The Sun Rising) V47:247

this is a beautiful way) (who are you,little i) V47:283

This is my page for English B (Theme for English B) V6:194

This Love (In Memory of Radio) V9:145

Tho' it were ten thousand mile! (A Red, Red Rose) V8:152

Thou mayst love on, through love's eternity. (If Thou Must Love Me) V46:72

Though I sang in my chains like the sea (Fern Hill) V3:92

Through the narrow aisles of pain. (Solitude) V49:256

Thus mayest thou ever, evermore rejoice. (Dejection: An Ode) V51:68–69)

Till human voices wake us, and we drown (The Love Song of J. Alfred Prufrock) V1:99

Till Love and Fame to nothingness do sink (When I Have Fears that I May Cease to Be) V2:295

Till the gossamer thread you fling catch somewhere, O my soul. (A Noiseless Patient Spider) V31:190–91

To an admiring Bog! (I'm Nobody! Who Are You?) V35:83

To be a queen! (Fear) V37:71

To beat real iron out, to work the bellows. (The Forge) V41:158

To every woman a happy ending (Barbie Doll) V9:33

To find they have flown away? (The Wild Swans at Coole) V42:287

To find out what it really means. (Introduction to Poetry) V50:167

to float in the space between. (The Idea of Ancestry) V36:138

to glow at midnight. (The Blue Rim of Memory) V17:39

to its owner or what horror has befallen the other shoe (A Piéd) V3:16

To live with thee and be thy love. (The Nymph's Reply to the Shepherd) V14:241

To mock the riddled corpses round Bapaume. ("Blighters") V28:3

To see the cherry hung with snow. (Loveliest of Trees, the Cherry Now) V40:160

To strengthen whilst one stands." (Goblin Market) V27:96

To strive, to seek, to find, and not to yield (Ulysses) V2:279

To the moaning and the groaning of the bells (The Bells) V3:47

To the temple, singing. (In the Suburbs) V14:201

To wound myself upon the sharp edges of the night? (The Taxi) V30:211–212

too. (Birdfoot's Grampa) V36:21

torn from a wedding brocade. (My Mother Combs My Hair) V34:133

Tread softly because you tread on my dreams. (He Wishes for the Cloths of Heaven) V51:125–126

Turned to that dirt from whence he sprung. (A Satirical Elegy on the Death of a Late Famous General) V27:216